CD-ROM
SUPERGUIDE

CD-ROM SUPERGUIDE

MIKE LANGBERG

BALLANTINE BOOKS • NEW YORK

Sale of this book without a front cover may be unauthorized. If this book is coverless, it may have been reported to the publisher as "unsold or destroyed" and neither the author nor the publisher may have received payment for it.

Copyright © 1995 by Mike Langberg

All rights reserved under International and Pan-American Copyright Conventions. Published in the United States by Ballantine Books, a division of Random House, Inc., New York, and simultaneously in Canada by Random House of Canada Limited, Toronto.

Library of Congress Catalog Card Number: 94-96244
ISBN: 0-345-39278-7

Text design by Alexander J. Klapwald

Manufactured in the United States of America

First Edition: March 1995

10 9 8 7 6 5 4 3 2 1

Contents

Introduction vii
    Welcome to the World of CD-ROM vii
    A Quick Look at CD-ROM Hardware ix
    How to Find CD-ROM Software xii
    How to Learn about New Releases xv
    How to Use This Book xvi

Author's Note xix

Chapter One: Younger Children 3
    a. Learning to Read and Count 4
    b. Stories 22
    c. Games and Activities 37

Chapter Two: Older Children 61
    a. Learning Games and Tools 62
    b. Science and Nature 89
    c. Stories 112
    d. Games and Activities 119

Chapter Three: Games for Grown-Ups 130
    a. Fantasy/Adventure 131
    b. Action and Sports 153
    c. Traditional Games 163
    d. Role-Playing, Strategy, and Simulation 171

Chapter Four: Encyclopedias and Reference 186
    a. Encyclopedias 187
    b. Dictionaries and General Reference 197
    c. Mail and Phone Directories 206
    d. Maps and Atlases 213
    e. Travel 221

Chapter Five: Art, Science, History, and Current Events 227
    a. The Arts 228
    b. Science and Nature 236
    c. U.S. and World History 255

d. Current Events and Issues 267
e. Magazines 281

Chapter Six: Movies, Television, Books, and Music 288
a. Movies 289
b. Television 302
c. Books 312
d. Music—Classical and Instruction 328
e. Music—Contemporary 347

Chapter Seven: Home, Food, Sports, and Fitness 360
a. Home Care and Design 361
b. Food and Cooking 371
c. Sports 379
d. Health and Fitness 392

Chapter Eight: Business, Career, Education, and Personal Finance 405
a. Business 406
b. College and Career Planning 413
c. Language Guides and Instruction 419
d. Personal Finance 436

Chapter Nine: Computer Applications 446
a. Applications and Utilities 447
b. Shareware 457
c. Desktop Publishing 461
d. About Computers 476

Chapter Ten: In a Class by Themselves 480
a. Special Interest 481
b. Religion 497
c. Catalog Shopping 502
d. Adults Only 509

Indexes 519
Four-Star Reviews 519
By Platform 521
By Developer 533
By Title 545

Introduction

Welcome to the World of CD-ROM

CD-ROM is your ticket to an amazing new world of information, entertainment, and education.

Once you've experienced the compelling graphics, realistic audio, and depth of content in CD-ROM software, you'll never want to go back to old-fashioned programs delivered on floppy disks. CD-ROM, an acronym for Compact Disk-Read Only Memory, is remaking personal computers. Before CD-ROM, PCs were used mostly to automate routine tasks. Word processors, for example, replaced typewriters, while personal finance packages eliminated the drudgery of balancing the family checkbook. With the addition of a CD-ROM drive, computers can suddenly play games that blow away Sega and Nintendo, deliver the entire contents of an encyclopedia, or teach you how to speak Spanish.

More and more people are discovering CD-ROM every day. But it's still pioneer territory, a wilderness with few road signs to help newcomers. That's why I've written this book. *CD-ROM Superguide* is a survey of CD-ROM software available now for IBM-compatible personal computers, which I'll abbreviate as the "PC," and Apple Computer's Macintosh. The information here is meant to help you become a more effective buyer and user of CD-ROM software.

So what qualifies me to write this book? I'm a technology reporter for the *San Jose Mercury News*, the daily newspaper of California's Silicon Valley, birthplace of much of the hardware and software inside personal computers. In July 1993, I started writing a weekly column for the *Mercury News* called "New on CD-ROM." Every Sunday since then, I've reviewed a new CD-ROM for either the PC or Mac. My column is also distributed nationally and appears occasionally in many other newspapers, including *The*

Washington Post, The Seattle Times, The Atlanta Constitution, the *Baltimore Sun, The Philadelphia Inquirer,* and the *San Diego Union Tribune.*

I decided to write this book because readers are always asking about CD-ROM software I *haven't* written about. They've just seen an interesting CD-ROM in a store, or heard about it from a friend, and want to know what I think. Or they are interested in a particular topic—anything from dinosaurs to improving their golf game—and want to know what's available. I've tried to put together *CD-ROM Superguide* in the same way I write my column, aiming at the average home computer owner who doesn't have a lot of technical expertise or money to spend. For that reader, I'd like to explain briefly how CD-ROMs work.

CD-ROMs aren't really new technology. They are physically identical to music CDs, developed in the 1970s. Indeed, most CD-ROM drives can play audio CDs, and some CD-ROMs contain audio tracks that can be heard on a regular CD player. The secret of CD-ROM is storage space. Compact disks, either CD-ROMs or music CDs, contain nothing more than 1s and 0s, the language of computers. But they contain a lot of them. A single CD-ROM holds 660 megabytes of data, equivalent to 458 regular 3.5-inch floppy diskettes. This huge amount of space opens up all kinds of possibilities.

One way to think of CD-ROM's impact is by imagining a world where printing presses could turn out only one-page documents. Printing would still be useful for creating memos and flyers, but it would be severely limited. Now, imagine printing technology suddenly changes to allow for production of 458-page books. Whole new applications would suddenly open up, everything from telephone books to romance novels.

That's what's happening with CD-ROM. Writers, artists, musicians, and software engineers are flocking to CD-ROM, eager to create new experiences that take advantage of all that storage space. Of course, change is never easy. If you're entering the world of CD-ROM, prepare for a struggle. Despite claims from hardware manufacturers that costs are falling all the time, you'll still need to spend $2,000 to $4,000 for a complete CD-ROM-equipped personal computer system.

What's more, most CD-ROM software is still too expensive, even though prices are slowly coming down. The typical CD-ROM sells for about $50, which probably doesn't seem excessive to marketing professionals in the software industry who regard anything under $100 as a bargain. But that's a big obstacle to building a library of CD-ROM titles and is significantly higher than competing media such as books, movies, and magazines.

Nor should you believe all the hype about "ease of use." Personal computers are sophisticated devices. If you've never used one, don't expect to learn everything you need to know overnight. Finally, you'll also have to be forgiving of CD-ROMs themselves. Because CD-ROM software for home computers has been a significant market for only about three years, there are still lots of bugs. Some CD-ROMs will run the first time you install them; others may never work right and will have to be returned for a refund.

Many CD-ROMs also boast that they include video. Because of the technical limits, however, you won't get an image anything like television. Most CD-ROM video runs at only ten frames per second, instead of television's thirty frames a second, causing a jerkiness similar to silent films from the 1920s. And CD-ROM video usually fills only a postage-stamp-size window on your screen.

Despite these shortcomings, CD-ROM is worth the effort. The first time your child sees a cartoon come alive on a computer screen, or you watch an animated demonstration of Thai cooking, you'll be richly rewarded for your time and money.

A Quick Look at CD-ROM Hardware

Personal computers keep getting better: New processors are more powerful, monitors offer crisper resolution, CD-ROM drives spin faster, modems send data more quickly, and printers produce sharper type. That's good, except for the depressing fact that any computer you buy today will be hopelessly obsolete in five years. CD-ROM software developers aren't helping—they love pushing the edge of the technology envelope, requiring consumers continually to upgrade their hardware to keep pace.

The result is a double whammy. You need to buy an expensive computer to enter the world of CD-ROM, and, as soon as you do, new technology starts popping up that will eventually force you to do it again.

I don't claim to be an expert on computer hardware, so I

can't offer complete advice on what to buy. But if you're looking to invest in a CD-ROM system, I can offer a few tips.

The first question is whether to buy a PC or a Macintosh. This is like arguing about politics or religion—almost everyone familiar with the subject has a strong opinion and violently disagrees with everyone else. I've always tried to stay neutral in the great PC versus Mac debate. There are pluses and minuses on both sides, and neither choice is a horrendous mistake. You should tilt toward what you know. If you use a Mac at work or school, buy a Mac. If you use a PC, buy a PC.

It's easier to select and set up a Mac. That's because the Mac is made by only one company. Apple limits your choices to the Performa line, sold in consumer electronics stores, and the Quadra and PowerPC lines, sold in computer stores. The PC, on the other hand, is generally less expensive than the Mac because many companies make PCs, and they are constantly competing with each other to cut prices. But you'll have to figure out which brand to buy among a choice of hundreds.

Most popular CD-ROM software is available for both the PC and the Mac. There are exceptions, however. Game developers have traditionally favored the PC, so if you're interested in playing the latest science-fiction adventures or storming medieval castles, you probably want a PC. If you're interested in desktop publishing and graphics, you'll find the most powerful software is written for the Mac.

Whichever you choose, don't be misled by advertising that proclaims multimedia computer packages for under $2,000. These specials are often teasers that aren't fully equipped or contain obsolete hardware—and it doesn't pay in the long run to cut corners. You're better off spending $3,000 for a state-of-the-art PC that will be useful for the next three to five years than spending $1,500 for a system that won't be able to handle next year's CD-ROM software.

Here are my recommendations for a CD-ROM system:

Processor. The processor is the brains of your computer. For PCs, the best buy is a Pentium—the most advanced chip now on the market. You can also buy a machine with the previous-generation 486 chip, but I wouldn't recommend it. If you must buy a 486, don't get anything slower than thirty-three megahertz; that leaves out the underpowered 486SX chips. For the Macintosh, make sure you get a machine containing one of the newer 68040 processors rather than the obsolete 68030 line. The best choice, though, is the new PowerPC Macintosh built around the latest-generation PowerPC chip.

Memory. Memory is where the processor stores information while work is in progress. The more Random Access Memory, or RAM, in your system, the better it performs. CD-ROM software puts heavy demands on RAM, so you'll need at least eight megabytes—not the four megabytes common in many prepackaged systems. If you can afford to spend a few hundred dollars more, go for twelve or sixteen megabytes of RAM.

Monitor. For home systems, fourteen-inch and fifteen-inch monitors are standard. Bigger monitors, such as seventeen-inch and twenty-inch models, are out of reach for most of us, typically costing $1,000 or more. The least expensive color monitors run about $250, but it's worth spending $200 more for a high-resolution monitor that displays sharper images.

CD-ROM drive. Make sure you get a "double-speed" CD-ROM drive; in techno-speak, that means a drive capable of transferring data at three hundred kilobytes per second. Quadruple-speed drives, which transfer data at six hundred kilobytes per second, are just coming onto the market at about twice the cost of double-speed drives; again, I'd recommend quad-speed if you can afford the extra money.

Soundboard. This is for PC owners only because the Macintosh includes a built-in sound system. Make sure to get a sixteen-bit soundboard, not an obsolete eight-bit board.

Options. I highly recommend including a modem in your home computer system so you can plug into the Information Superhighway. Don't buy anything slower than a 14.4-baud modem; consider the newer 28.8-baud models if cost is no object. Also, you're sure to want a printer. Unless you need to produce professional-quality documents, you'll get everything you need with inkjet printers costing $250 to $300. If you do need professional quality, laser printers start at about $600. Avoid obsolete dot-matrix printers.

If you own a PC or Mac that doesn't have a CD-ROM drive, you can consider upgrading your present system. But you'll still need a relatively new machine—don't buy a CD-ROM drive for any black-and-white Mac or older color Macs with the 68020 processor or for a PC with anything less than a 386SX processor.

Mac owners should have little trouble installing an external

CD-ROM drive. But the story is quite different for PC owners. Adding a CD-ROM drive requires a maddeningly complex reconfiguration of your computer. Unless you're a masochist or a trained computer technician, I strongly recommend having a CD-ROM drive installed by professionals.

PC owners also need to know about the "MPC" label. The Multimedia PC Marketing Council in Washington, D.C., a coalition of hardware and software manufacturers, administers a CD-ROM certification program. The council sets minimum requirements for PC hardware manufacturers who want to display the MPC logo on their products; some software developers also use the MPC logo to indicate that their CD-ROMs will run on any PC meeting MPC standards. The current MPC Level 2 specification requires a system with at least the following: a 486SX processor, four megabytes of RAM, a double-speed CD-ROM drive, and a sixteen-bit soundboard.

Not all hardware or software companies use the MPC system, however. And, of course, the MPC label doesn't apply to the Mac. So you'll still need to study carefully the specific hardware requirements for any CD-ROM software you're buying to make sure it will work on your system.

My final bit of wisdom: Don't be shy. If you're new to the technical maze of buying a computer, ask a lot of questions. Interrogate salespeople at computer stores. Visit a computer show. Track down someone at school or work who understands computers and beg for help. You'll find many computer experts love nothing more than sharing their knowledge with the uninitiated.

How to Find CD-ROM Software

Because CD-ROM is still new, individual titles can be hard to find.

If you live in a large city or nearby suburbs, you can find CD-ROMs in computer stores, bookstores, and music stores. But even the biggest CD-ROM retailers rarely carry more than one hundred or two hundred titles, so you can't be guaranteed any one store will have everything you want.

Find two or three stores in your area that have a large selection of CD-ROMs. When you want a specific title, visit all of these stores in person. That way, you'll get the best price and know for sure what's in stock. Telephone calls are usually ineffective because overworked salespeople often don't know what's on the shelf and give inaccurate information.

Don't be surprised if you see a wide range of prices for CD-ROMs. Developers and retailers are constantly juggling what they charge to keep up with the competition, so the figures given in this book should be regarded only as a general indication of actual store prices. You should also ignore any reference to "list" price, also known as "suggested retail price" or "SRP," an artificially high figure set by some CD-ROM developers so retailers can look good by appearing to offer big discounts.

A number of mail-order catalogs also sell CD-ROMs, usually for prices equivalent to the lower end of what retail stores charge. You may have to pay extra for shipping and handling, though, and you'll have to make a selection without holding the box in your hands.

To help you get started with mail-order, if that's your preference, three of the largest catalogs are listed below. An important disclaimer: I'm not endorsing the service or prices of these companies, nor am I trying to discriminate against smaller catalog merchants. You can call these companies toll-free and get price quotes on specific titles. Or you can request a copy of their free catalogs to see their full selection.

CD-ROM Warehouse
1720 Oak Street
Lakewood, NJ 08701
phone: 800-237-6623
fax: 908-370-7046

Educorp
7434 Trade Street
San Diego, CA 92121-2410
phone: 800-843-9497
fax: 619-536-2345

Tiger Software CD-ROM Software Buyer's Guide
9100 South Dadeland Blvd., Suite 1500
Miami, FL 33156
phone: 800-238-4437
fax: 305-529-2990

Even though these mail-order catalogs offer 750 to 1,000 titles each, they still don't cover the entire range of what's available. So how do you find information on truly obscure CD-ROMs?

There are two comprehensive CD-ROM directories, similar in structure and content to the familiar *Books in Print*. Each CD-ROM directory covers about six thousand titles; both publish a print edition once a year and publish CD-ROM editions every six months.

These directories aren't full-fledged guidebooks; individual entries provide little more than the CD-ROM's full name, the developer's name, the format, and a one-sentence description of the content. However, the directories are the only place you're likely to find special-interest CD-ROMs such as *Corporate Registered Bond Interest Records* from Standard & Poor's and *Pacific Ocean Temperature and Salinity Profiles* from the National Oceanographic Data Center. Because they're rather expensive, the best way to take advantage of these directories is to find one at a local library or ask the library to order a copy.

CD-ROMs in Print
Mecklermedia Corp.
20 Ketchum Street
Westport, CT 06880
phone: 800-632-5537
fax: 203-454-5840
book: $99 (includes the CD-ROM edition)
CD-ROM: $49

The CD-ROM Directory
TFPL Inc.
1301 Twentieth Street NW, #702
Washington, DC 20036
phone: 202-296-6009
fax: 202-296-6343
book: $139
CD-ROM: $149 (for the two disks prepared each year)

If you're curious about what's hot, you'll want to track the CD-ROM best-seller list. A market research firm called PC Data in Reston, Virginia, surveys retail stores and tabulates results every month. Here is PC Data's 1994 best-seller list, ranked by retail sales in units rather than dollars:

Title	Developer
1. Myst	Broderbund Software Inc.
2. Doom II: Hell on Earth	GT Interactive
3. 5-Ft. 10-Pak Volume I	Sirius Publishing Inc.
4. Rebel Assault	LucasArts Entertainment Co.
5. Microsoft Encarta	Microsoft Corporation
6. The 7th Guest	Virgin Interactive
7. Disney's Animated StoryBook: The Lion King	Disney Interactive
8. The Print Shop Deluxe CD Ensemble	Broderbund Software Inc.
9. Quicken Deluxe CD-ROM	Intuit Inc.
10. Corel Gallery	Corel Corporation
11. 5-Ft. 10-Pak Volume II	Sirius Publishing Inc.
12. Microsoft Bookshelf	Microsoft Corporation
13. Outpost	Sierra On-Line Inc.
14. Street Atlas USA	DeLorme Mapping
15. King's Quest VII	Sierra On-Line Inc.
16. Just Grandma & Me	Living Books
17. Where in the World is Carmen Sandiego? CD-ROM	Broderbund Software Inc.
18. Wing Commander III: Heart of the Tiger	Origin Systems
19. Comanche CD	NovaLogic Inc.
20. Mighty Morphin Power Rangers	Xiphias

How to Learn about New Releases

New CD-ROM software is coming out every day. If your computer has a modem, there's an easy way for you to stay on top of the news. America Online, an on-line service for both PC and Macintosh users, has established a "New on CD-ROM" area that includes my weekly newspaper column and bulletin boards devoted to discussing CD-ROM titles. The "New on CD-ROM" area is part of Mercury Center, an on-line extension of the *San Jose Mercury News*. If you're not an America Online member, call

Mercury Center at 800-818-6397 to request a free sign-up kit. If you're already subscribing to America Online, just go to keyword "MC CD-ROM." The area can also be reached through the Internet's World Wide Web. Use your Web browser to view the document "http://www.sjmercury.com/features/cdrom.htm".

How to Use This Book

There are two ways to use this book.

If you already know the name of a specific CD-ROM and want to read the review, simply turn to the title index at the back. For those CD-ROMs with complicated names, I've listed the title in more than one way. The encyclopedia *Microsoft Encarta '95*, for example, is listed under both "E" for *Encarta* and "M" for *Microsoft Encarta*. If you want to find out what CD-ROMs are available on a certain subject, look in the table of contents.

Because CD-ROM is so new, some people expect that all CD-ROMs should appeal to all computer owners. I disagree. Please keep in mind as you read these reviews that I'm evaluating each CD-ROM on how effectively it reaches the audience for which it is intended. Just because I give a favorable review to a CD-ROM on classical music doesn't mean the disk will appeal to heavy-metal rock fans. This is especially important for parents selecting CD-ROM software for their children, where it can be difficult to match the level of challenge in a program with a child's ability.

To help you easily pick out the cream of the crop, all four-star reviews appear in a shaded box.

Here is a key to what each review includes:

Rating:		
	★★★★	excellent
	★★★½	very good
	★★★	good
	★★½	acceptable
	★★	poor
	★½	very poor
	★	worthless

Developer: This is the name of the company that created the CD-ROM; a phone number is always included. Use the phone number if you have any questions, such as where to buy the title or exact hardware requirements.

Format: DOS   —for any CD-ROM-equipped IBM-compatible PC
              Windows   —for PCs running Windows
              Macintosh   —for the Macintosh
              DOS-2   —DOS title that requires a double-speed drive
              Windows-2 —Windows title that requires a double-speed drive
              Macintosh-2 —Macintosh title that requires a double-speed drive

Price: This is the *street* price, what you're likely to pay in an average retail store or through an average mail-order catalog. It's still important to shop around, however, because the actual price you pay can vary significantly from what's given here.

Author's Note

As a first-time author, I've discovered that writing a book is anything but a solitary effort. You wouldn't be reading *CD-ROM Superguide* without the help of many other people, and I want to thank some of them by name.

My wife, Debbie, gave me the confidence to tackle the biggest writing assignment of my life. Her love and encouragement as I spent many long days and nights in front of the computer kept an incredibly difficult job from becoming unbearable. No one can become a writer without first acquiring a love of reading. For giving me the gift of reading, I'll always be indebted to my mother, Meredith. No one can write a book about computer software without a certain fondness for fiddling with electronic gadgets. For inspiring me to tinker, I thank my father, Edwin.

This book grows directly from my CD-ROM column in the *San Jose Mercury News*. That column would never have happened without consistent and gracious support from Executive Business Editor Pete Hillan and Deputy Managing Editor Ann Hurst, as well as many others whom I don't have space to mention.

Mark Stevenson, Business Wire Editor at the *Mercury News*, saved me from myself as the copy editor for *CD-ROM Superguide*. His sharp eye and sure hand touched every page of this book, excising clichés and straightening out my sometimes twisted grammar. Laura Macias, the book's researcher, persevered through hundreds of phone calls to make the listings as up to date as possible.

In New York, Sherri Rifkin of Ballantine Books kept this project on track and never lost her cool even when I went through occasional moments of panic. Finally, I want to thank my agent, Marc Jaffe, for making the connection between author and publisher. Marc is everything an agent should be—he even says *ciao* at the end of phone calls.

I'm grateful to everyone I've named here. But, as with any

book, the ultimate responsibility for what's between these covers falls on the author. I've worked hard to make sure *CD-ROM Superguide* is fair and accurate, but it's impossible to write five hundred reviews without some errors.

Let me also add two footnotes here. First, you've probably heard the term "multimedia" quite a bit recently. It's a loosely defined concept referring to computers capable of combining text, graphics, audio, and video. That's what you get with a CD-ROM. But multimedia is also occasionally used to refer to other new technologies, such as interactive cable television systems. To eliminate any confusion, I've avoided the term "multimedia" in this book as much as possible.

Second, there is a spirited debate among language purists as to whether a CD-ROM should be called a "disk" or a "disc" on second reference. I've decided to use "disk," without intending any disrespect to advocates of "disc."

If you spot an error anywhere in *CD-ROM Superguide* or just want to share your opinion, drop me a line. You can send mail to Mike Langberg, *San Jose Mercury News*, 750 Ridder Park Drive, San Jose, CA 95190. You can send electronic mail through the Internet to cdrommike@aol.com, or, if you are an America Online subscriber, you can message screen name CDROM Mike. No phone calls or faxes, please.

CD-ROM
SUPERGUIDE

Chapter One:
Younger Children

No part of the burgeoning CD-ROM market is growing faster than children's software. For parents, that's good news and bad news. The good news is the large number of excellent titles available for children of all ages. The bad news is the even bigger number of second-rate programs. These first two chapters will help you sort them out.

Chapter One covers CD-ROMs for "younger children," whom I define as under age eight, while Chapter Two covers titles for "older children," whom I define as ages eight to fourteen. Although high school students might enjoy a few of the CD-ROMs in Chapter Two, most adolescents should be ready for the "grown-up" titles covered in the other eight chapters.

Parents shouldn't assume that all children's software will appeal to every child. Just like adults, a child may like certain types of games or learning activities more than others. Parents also need to match their child's abilities with the demands of the program and shouldn't automatically trust the age range listed on the box. CD-ROM developers will often tilt the age range upward to give buyers an ego boost, figuring parents will be proud to see their five-year-old mastering a program advertised for ages eight to twelve. But that is misleading for twelve-year-olds, who may find the program significantly beneath them.

a. Learning to Read and Count

ANIMALS AND HOW THEY GROW
★★★
Developer: National Geographic Society; 800-368-2728
Format: Macintosh
Price: $39

Part of the *Wonders of Learning CD-ROM Library* series from the National Geographic Society, described below. *Animals and How They Grow* presents on-screen versions of five print booklets: *Amphibians and How They Grow*, *Birds and How They Grow*, *Insects and How They Grow*, *Mammals and How They Grow*, and *Reptiles and How They Grow*.

About the *Wonders of Learning CD-ROM Library* series: Originally designed for the school market, this series of nature and science titles is intended for ages four to seven. Each CD-ROM contains the contents of four or five print booklets produced by National Geographic; copies of the booklets are also included in the box with the disk. The sixteen-page print booklets, five inches high and eight and a half inches wide, are filled with the National Geographic's deservedly famous color photographs and text simple enough for young children to read themselves. A sample, from *Insects and How They Grow*: "A ladybug, a bee and a dragonfly look very different. But they are alike in many ways. Each one is an insect. A strong shell called an exoskeleton covers an insect's body. Many insects have four wings. A dragonfly flaps its four wings to zoom through the air. It can fly faster than a person can run."

The CD-ROMs present exactly the same material on the screen, with two important enhancements. First, the text is read aloud by a narrator. Children can choose to listen to the text from beginning to end or click individual words to hear them pronounced. Second, children can click within each photograph to learn more about what they're seeing. By clicking different parts of a walrus in *Mammals and How They Grow*, children get pop-up windows naming the back flipper, front flipper, tusk, and muzzle.

The CD-ROMs also include teacher activity guides, suggesting questions for students and projects related to the booklets. Parents who want to get involved with their children's education could also use the activity guides at home. The *Wonders of Learning* series contains no multimedia bells and whistles, such as video clips or interactive games, but the high-quality photographs and kid-friendly narration combine to make a package both children and adults will find appealing. Five other titles in the series are reviewed in this section: *The Human Body, People Behind the Holidays, Our Earth, A World of Animals,* and *A World of Plants.*

BAILEY'S BOOK HOUSE
★★★½
Developer: Edmark Corp.; 800-362-2890
Format: DOS, Macintosh
Price: $35

Parents eager to help their children learn to read will get a big boost from *Bailey's Book House,* which offers five reading-related activities intended for ages two to five. The CD-ROM is part of Edmark Corporation's *Early-Learning Neighborhood* series, which also includes *Millie's Math House,* reviewed in this section, and *Sammy's Science House,* reviewed in Section c. The three titles stress parental involvement in the learning process, with a button on every screen that will instantly summon an "Adult Information Notebook" explaining the activity and suggesting related games for both home and school.

Children can go through *Bailey's Book House* in "Explore" mode, where they decide what to do next, or in "Q&A" mode, where animated characters pose questions. The CD-ROM opens in the living room of a gray cat named Bailey. Clicking on different parts of the colorful cartoon illustration launches one of the five activities. "Edmo & Houdini" is a vocabulary-building game in which children instruct a clown named Edmo or a dog named Houdini to move around a doghouse by clicking words such as "In" to move Houdini into the doghouse or "Behind" to move Edmo behind the doghouse. "Letter Machine" presents a typewriter keyboard on screen. Pressing the "F" key displays the words "foxes fiddle" as a voice pronounces the words, followed by a quick animation of two foxes fiddling away; "P" is for "penguins paint," and "V" is for "vultures vacuum." "Make-A-Story" goes through a sequence of four storybook pages in which children complete sentences by selecting an image on the screen. They can choose, for example, whether Harley the Horse should ride in a canoe, bathtub, flying carpet, or spaceship. "Read-A-Rhyme" calls for completing nursery rhymes by selecting illustrated words on the screen. Children can finish "Ding, dong, dell, Kitty's in the—" by selecting "shell," "bell," "cell," or "well" and then see an animation of their choice. "Kid Cards" lets children make greeting cards, thank-you cards, and invitations by selecting from more than a dozen messages such as "Have a Happy Valentine's Day" and several dozen decorative stamps such as a smiling sun or a birthday cake.

The "Adult Information Notebook" gives clear explanations for the various activities, as in this overview of Edmo & Houdini: "As young children develop, they ask questions about the location of objects and people. They experiment with vocabulary—in, out, over, under, on, off, behind—to ask where objects are or to indicate how to find objects. Treasure hunts with clues such as 'Look under the box' or 'Look behind the chair' can help children develop listening and comprehension skills. Children also enjoy making up the clues for others to follow." This advice is particularly useful because younger children often don't have the attention span to spend long periods in front of a computer and the activities in *Bailey's Book House* don't offer sufficient variety to be entertaining for hours on end. With the "Adult Information Notebook," Mom and Dad will have new ways to involve their children in educational play that doesn't involve CD-ROMs.

COUNTDOWN
★★

Developer: Voyager Co.; 800-446-2001
Format: Windows, Macintosh
Price: $19

CountDown will fascinate preschoolers with its three different counting games—but only for an hour or so. The games are too simple to encourage repeat play, despite colorful graphics and clever video clips.

All three games use the same set of nine objects for counting exercises. "Guesstimation" involves guessing how many items to remove from one of the nine scenes. If you enter "12" when you see the carton of eggs, the eggs disappear one by one and a chick pops out of the last one. If you enter "6" when you see the pair of gloves, six of the fingers disappear and four remain. Entering "4" causes the remaining four to disappear; then all the fingers reappear and the gloves clap together to give you a round of applause.

"Nimbles" is a two-player version of "Guesstimation," in which players take turns removing items with the goal of becoming the player to remove the last object. "Leftovers" moves into the realm of division, requiring children to remove the objects in groups. You clear one hundred pennies off a table, for example, by removing twenty groups of five coins.

It's a shame there isn't more to *CountDown*. The program is easy for children to master and offers helpful advice from a kid named Chris, whose face appears in a small window on the screen. *CountDown* can also be played in French, German, Italian, and Spanish, a good way to expose children to another language. But the three games overlap each other and quickly grow stale because they rely on such a small set of scenes.

THE HUMAN BODY
★★★
Developer: National Geographic Society; 800-368-2728
Format: Macintosh
Price: $39

Part of the *Wonders of Learning CD-ROM Library* series from the National Geographic Society, described fully in the review of *Animals and How They Grow* in this section. *The Human Body* presents on-screen versions of five print booklets: *Food for Your Body*, *The Senses*, *Your Bones and Muscles*, *Your Brain*, and *Your Teeth*. A sample of the text, from *Your Brain*: "Your brain has three main parts. Each part has special jobs to do. The cerebrum is the brain boss. It is where you think and feel. When you read, you use your cerebrum. The cerebellum helps you keep your balance. It also makes your muscles work together. Your brain stem makes you laugh when someone tickles you. It keeps you breathing day and night."

MATH RABBIT
★★★
Developer: The Learning Company; 800-852-2255
Format: Windows, Macintosh
Price: $49

A companion to the *Reader Rabbit* series, reviewed in this section, *Math Rabbit* teaches introductory arithmetic skills to children ages four though seven. The animated character Math Rabbit is the host for a visit to the Circus of Numbers, where children pick among four games, winning tickets they can redeem at the Prize Center. Colorful graphics fill half the screen, and there's lots of narration to help guide young players who aren't yet comfortable with reading. Each of the four games offers three or four difficulty levels, so the challenge can be increased as children gain skills.

The four activities are Calliope Counting Game, prompting children to count out the correct number of notes on a pipe organ; Tightrope Show, in which children must decide whether a placard in Math Rabbit's arms showing a group of squares matches a number displayed on a sign to his left; Sea Lion Show, which poses simple addition and subtraction problems; and Balloon Matching Game, in which children are presented with numbers hidden behind eight squares and must find matching pairs. After children correctly complete any of these activities, Math Rabbit rewards them with a single prize ticket. At the Prize Center, children can cash in the tickets for animated prizes such as a pair of chattering teeth, a locomotive, or a skateboarding poodle. They'll need at least three tickets for the simplest prizes and nine tickets for the most valuable. Some children, though, may be disappointed with the prizes, which perform for only a few seconds and can be enjoyed only while in the Prize Center.

Still, all the activities are easy to learn and educationally sound. I wouldn't expect children to spend hours on end with *Math Rabbit* because the four activities don't offer a lot of variety. But that's not necessarily a drawback; children will probably get the most out of *Math Rabbit* by playing the CD-ROM repeatedly in short bursts.

MILLIE'S MATH HOUSE
★★★½
Developer: Edmark Corp.; 800-362-2890
Format: Windows, Macintosh
Price: $35

Part of the excellent *Early-Learning Neighborhood* series, fully described in the review of *Bailey's Book House* in this section. *Millie's Math House*, intended for ages two to six, is hosted by a brown cow named Millie who introduces six activities. "Little, Middle & Big" asks children to select the correct size shoes for three characters named Little, Middle, and Big as a way of learning to compare object sizes. If a child puts tiny shoes on Big, for example, only his toes fit inside the footwear and he displays a sad expression. "Mouse House" teaches about geometric shapes by calling for children to identify the proper piece to follow a simple blueprint, selecting a triangle to make the roof of a house or a rectangle for the door. "Bing & Boing" teaches pattern recognition by matching simple pictures with the sounds they make. "Build-A-Bug" is counting practice, in which children select how many eyes or feet or ears to put on a brightly colored bug. "Number Machine" is a cash register with keys for zero through ten. Pushing a key produces a short narrated animation, such as one wiggling worm or two buzzing bees. "Cookie Factory" also works on counting by letting children put a specific number of jellybeans onto a cookie to feed a friendly horse.

The on-screen "Adult Information Notebook" provides helpful explanations and guidance on each activity, such as this overview of "Mouse House": "Young children will begin their attempts to follow a blueprint by trial and error. At first, they learn to identify and match triangles, circles and squares. Later, they learn other shapes and discriminate between identical shapes of different sizes. As children become more aware of how things are supposed to look, they place greater value on realism. Both realism and imagination should be encouraged."

MY FIRST INCREDIBLE, AMAZING DICTIONARY
★★½

Developer: Dorling Kindersley Publishing Inc.; 800-356-6575
Format: Windows, Macintosh
Price: $39

My First Incredible, Amazing Dictionary is the kind of CD-ROM that will appeal more to parents than to the children for whom it is supposedly intended. Full of sounds, colorful pictures, and educational merit, *My First Dictionary* offers one thousand simple definitions for youngsters just learning to read; the developer recommends it for ages three to seven. But children want to play with computers, not sit passively listening to word definitions and watching quick animations.

Children move through the dictionary by clicking a letter of the alphabet at the top of the screen, then selecting an individual word from a menu combining text and pictures, making it easy to look up a word even if they can't spell it. Each definition is presented in a full screen, with the words on the left and a picture on the right. Children who aren't yet comfortable with reading can click on the definition to hear it read aloud. Clicking the picture produces either a quick animation or five seconds of sound effects. "Jigsaw puzzle," for example, is defined as "a picture cut into pieces. You fit the pieces together to make up the picture again." Clicking on a pile of nine puzzle pieces sends them racing around the screen and ultimately snapping together into a completed picture. "Race car" is defined as "a type of car that goes very fast around a track." Clicking on the picture produces the sound of a revving engine and squealing tires.

My First Dictionary also includes three simple games. "Guess what" is a multiple-choice word-recognition quiz. In response to the question "What do airplanes have?" children can click on the word "bananas," "forks," or "wings." If they pick "forks," they see a picture of an airplane with forks in place of wings and have to try again. "Spell it" asks children to pick out the letters to spell a word they hear pronounced. "What's that noise?" is a sound-and-picture matching game; when children hear "moo," they have to click on the picture of a cow. For children who aren't interested in the games, there is a "Surprise Me" button at the bottom of the screen that calls up words at random.

Parents will undoubtedly be attracted by the educational value of *My First Dictionary*. But I'm not sure the CD-ROM contains anything to sustain a child's interest; the games quickly grow tedious, and the animations are only a momentary distraction. Nor do I foresee children running to the computer, turning it on, and loading the disk every time they wonder about the definition of a word. I think they'll just do what children always do; they'll shout across the room, "Mommmm, what does that mean?"

MY FIRST ENCYCLOPEDIA
★★★½
Developer: Knowledge Adventure Inc.; 800-542-4240
Format: Windows
Price: $35

My First Encyclopedia is a charming way for youngsters who aren't yet reading to learn about the world around them using audio and visual cues to communicate with its intended audience of children ages three to six. This isn't an encyclopedia in the classic sense, with an alphabetical collection of articles on specific topics. Instead, it's more of a place for children to explore, combining explanatory entries with games and activities.

Most of the information in *My First Encyclopedia* is delivered by a group of children, who appear to be between the ages of eight and twelve, speaking through audio and video clips. The video images, although they appear in small windows, are refreshingly sharp. The audio clips are sometimes difficult to hear over the CD-ROM's background music, but the music can be turned off by simply hitting "F2" on the keyboard. Using children as narrators is a nice touch; small children often look up to bigger kids more than adults when it comes to learning new things.

Navigating through *My First Encyclopedia* is almost completely intuitive, so preschoolers won't need more than a few minutes of parental assistance before taking control. Everything is reached from a main screen displaying "the magical tree of learning," a gateway to ten "rooms" covering various categories: astronomy, geography, arts, anatomy and medicine, buildings and towns, jobs and sports, animals, geology, transportation, and food. Children get to these rooms by clicking on pictures of children arranged in the tree branches; a young boy holding an apple, for example, is the spot to click for the food room.

Within each room, there are many activities. The geography room, for instance, displays a map of the world. Clicking on the continent of Africa, children see a map of the continent with small pictures of things related to Africa, such as a gazelle, coffee beans, and the pyramids of Egypt. By clicking on one of these objects, children hear a definition; the giraffe is identified as the tallest animal on earth, with the explanation, "An adult giraffe is taller than three tall grown-ups standing on each other's shoulders." Each room also includes a question-and-answer section in which children can listen to a dozen questions and answers. In the "Buildings" section, one of the questions is "How does a vacuum cleaner pick up dirt?" The answer: "A vacuum cleaner uses a special fan to pick up dirt. The fan doesn't push air out like most fans do. It sucks air in. The air pulls dirt along with it into a bag in the vacuum cleaner. Sometimes vacuum cleaners pick up more than dirt. Ours sucked up my sister's earring off the floor. It was lost somewhere in that big bag of dirt. Yuck!" Other activities include slider puzzles, coloring books, and matching games.

For parents, there is a convenient index to the 575 words covered in *My First Encyclopedia* that makes it easy to find a specific entry. The details of installation and instructions for all the CD-ROM's many features are clearly explained in a well-written fifty-six-page manual. My only complaint with *My First Encyclopedia* doesn't relate to the program itself; I'm bothered by the developer's decision to include a misguided marketing gimmick called *The Adventurers!*, described in the review of *JumpStart Kindergarten* in Chapter One, Section c.

OUR EARTH
★★★
Developer: National Geographic Society; 800-368-2728
Format: Windows, Macintosh
Price: $39

Part of the *Wonders of Learning CD-ROM Library* series from the National Geographic Society, described fully in the review of *Animals and How They Grow* in this section. *Our Earth* presents on-screen versions of four print booklets: *Discovering Maps*, *Our Planet Earth*, *What Air Can Do*, and *Why Does It Rain?* A sample of the text, from *Why Does It Rain?*: "When water evaporates, it changes into a gas. The gas rises high into the sky. The air in the sky is very cold. In the cold air, the gas changes into water drops. The water drops come together and make clouds. Dark clouds fill the sky. Soon rain will fall from the clouds. Over and over, water evaporates, makes clouds and falls as rain."

PEOPLE BEHIND THE HOLIDAYS
★★★
Developer: National Geographic Society; 800-368-2728
Format: Windows, Macintosh
Price: $39

Part of the *Wonders of Learning CD-ROM Library* series from the National Geographic Society, described fully in the review of *Animals and How They Grow* in this section. *People Behind the Holidays* presents on-screen versions of five print booklets: *Who Was Abraham Lincoln?*, *Who Was Christopher Columbus?*, *Who Was Martin Luther King Jr.?*, *Who Was George Washington?*, and *Who Were the Pilgrims?* A sample of the text, from *Who Was Martin Luther*

King, Jr.?: "Martin Luther King spoke out because he knew the [segregation] laws were wrong. He spoke out with a great voice that was musical and strong. He told those who came to listen, though their struggles may be great, they should not let anybody drag them so low as to hate."

THE PLAYROOM CD-ROM
★★★½

Developer: Broderbund Software Inc.; 800-521-6263
Format: Windows, Macintosh
Price: $39

The Playroom CD-ROM really is a room where children can play, full of computer-created toys that are even more fun than their real-life counterparts. Almost every activity in *The Playroom* is educational but never so heavy-handed that kids will get bored or feel inadequate if they can't get the right answer. Intended for ages three to six, *The Playroom* originated as a floppy-disk product in 1989 and has undergone several upgrades. The CD-ROM version, released in November 1994, adds a large number of animations, sound effects, and five complete songs that can also be heard on a regular audio CD player.

From the main screen of *The Playroom*, children see a room full of interesting objects rendered in colorful cartoonlike graphics. Nothing is labeled, since *The Playroom* is designed for youngsters who aren't yet reading. Children instead point and click with the mouse to discover the function of each object. Some items are just for fun; click a small purple dinosaur sleeping on the floor and it scratches itself with a hind leg. Other objects launch one of the CD-ROM's six major games.

Those six games are "The Clock," in which children learn how to tell time by moving the hour hand of a clock and watching small animations appropriate to the time of day; "The Computer," an animated spelling quiz; "The Mixed-Up Toy," which allows children to create their own creatures by mixing and matching heads, middles, and legs; "The Mousehole," a hopscotchlike counting game; "The ABC Book," which lets children call up objects by letter—such as selecting "p" for "puppy"—and then put the objects anywhere in a four-room house; and "The Spinner Toy," in which children match numbers with pictures, such as clicking the number "5" when five eggs are on the screen to produce an animation of the eggs cracking and little yellow chicks hopping out.

The Playroom is a very friendly companion; the program's animated hosts—two young mice named Pepper and Ginger—always praise correct answers. And they never criticize mistakes; they just give a hint and wait for the child to try again. As with other software designed for preschoolers, parents will have to help children at first. But *The Playroom* is so well designed that most children should be comfortable on their own within an hour or two.

DELUXE READER RABBIT 1
★★★½
Developer: The Learning Company; 800-852-2255
Format: Windows, Macintosh
Price: $49

First introduced on floppy disk in the mid-1980s, the *Reader Rabbit* series from The Learning Company has become one of the most popular programs for helping children practice reading skills. The CD-ROM version of *Reader Rabbit 1*, intended for ages three to six, is an infinitely patient playmate with lots of color, animation, and sound.

Reader Rabbit 1 offers four activities inside the Word Factory, in which the animated character Reader Rabbit—dressed in a red turtleneck sweater and blue overalls—offers guidance and encouragement. Each activity, drawing on an inventory of more than two hundred three-letter words, can be played at several difficulty levels. The challenge can be lowered for children just learning the alphabet or geared up for those beginning to master words and sentences.

"Matchup" is a matching game with ten hidden squares. At the easiest level, children look for pairs of pictures while listening to Reader Rabbit pronounce the word. At the toughest level, they match pictures with a single letter from the word, such as "- e -" with "net." As a reward for the right answer, a fish flops into the net. "Sorter" is a letter-matching game. Reader Rabbit turns a crank on the sorter machine and a word pops out. If the first letter matches the first letter of a word on the outside of the machine, children put it on the shelf. If it doesn't match, they put it in the garbage. "Labeler" is a fill-in-the-blanks exercise, in which children must select "b" when shown a picture of a paper bag and the letters "-ag." When children get the right answer, Reader Rabbit does a little dance. "Word Train" involves finding words with matching pairs of letters, such as "top" and "mop." Selecting three correct pairs in a row sends Ernest the Engine off to Wordville with his load of words.

Reader Rabbit 1 won't teach children to read, but it will help them considerably in spelling, word recognition, and learning the sounds of individual letters. Equally important, the four activities are lots of fun, so children won't require parental nagging to spend time absorbing these important lessons.

READER RABBIT 2
★★★½
Developer: The Learning Company; 800-852-2255
Format: Windows, Macintosh
Price: $49

Second in the excellent *Reader Rabbit* series from The Learning Company, moving up approximately one academic year from *Reader Rabbit 1*, reviewed in this section. Intended for ages five to eight, *Reader Rabbit 2* offers four activities for children just starting to read, using one thousand words. "Word Mine" calls for completing compound words; when "pea—" appears on the screen, children must look at six possible endings and select "nut." The animated character Reader Rabbit provides help by pronouncing the full word. "Vowel Pond" works on vowel sounds. Reader Rabbit asks children to click on fish in a pond that shows a word matching a certain vowel sound; with the short "o," for example, children must pick "hot" or "pop" but not "shell" or "give." In "Match Patch," children find either pairs of opposites or pairs of rhyming words in a vegetable patch with words hidden under twelve carrots. "Alphabet Dance" teaches the concept of alphabetization. Four animals are sitting on hay bales labeled with their names. Reader Rabbit asks children to line them up in alphabetical order; when the task is completed correctly, the characters perform a little dance. As with *Reader Rabbit 1*, each game can be played at four difficulty levels, so children can find new challenges as they master reading skills.

READER RABBIT 3
★★★½

Developer: The Learning Company; 800-852-2255
Format: Windows, Macintosh
Price: $49

Third in the excellent *Reader Rabbit* series from The Learning Company, moving up approximately one academic year from *Reader Rabbit 2*, reviewed in this section. Intended for ages six to nine, *Reader Rabbit 3* offers four activities revolving around sentence structure and developing critical thinking skills. At the beginning of the game, the animated character Reader Rabbit gets hired as a reporter for the *Daily Skywriter* in his hometown of Wordville. By helping Reader Rabbit complete the four activities, children can print out a newspaper story with their own name as the byline.

The first activity is "What's the Scoop?" Part of a sentence is displayed on the screen, and Reader Rabbit must give it to one of his four colleagues, choosing whether it is a "who/what" part of the sentence, a "did what" part, a "where" part, or a "when" part. The phrase "at five o'clock," for example, is a "when." The second activity, "Clue Hound," displays an entire sentence, and a hound asks children to click on a certain part. Asked to find the "who/what" in "Alice Armadillo flew her kite last week," children have to pick "Alice Armadillo." The third activity is "Sneak Peek," in which children must identify sentences arranged in a certain order. Asked to find the sentence in the order "who/what," "did what," and "when," the answer is "Pierre Pig stood at the plate" rather than "Pierre Pig at the plate stood." The fourth activity is "Ed Words," a short story of several sentences where children select the right type of phrase to fill in blank spaces. In the sentence "The mouse family _____ at the Vowel Pond," children have to click on the "did what" button and can then insert a phrase such as "had a picnic." After successfully completing each of these activities, children can go to the "Printing Press" and print their work.

As with the other *Reader Rabbit* titles, the difficulty of each activity can be adjusted to increase the challenge as children improve their skills. Specifically, *Reader Rabbit 3* adds the sentence parts "how" and "why" at higher levels. Whatever level they choose, children will have lots of fun with *Reader Rabbit 3* and especially enjoy the satisfaction of creating their own newspaper page.

READER RABBIT'S INTERACTIVE READING JOURNEY
★★★½
Developer: The Learning Company; 800-852-2255
Format: Windows, Macintosh
Price: $99

Reader Rabbit's Interactive Reading Journey is an ambitious—and largely successful—effort to put an entire year of classroom reading instruction onto a single CD-ROM. Part of the *Reader Rabbit* series from The Learning Company, which includes *Reader Rabbit 1*, reviewed in this section, *Interactive Reading Journey* combines forty storybooks with numerous word games that get progressively more difficult as children work through the material.

Using cartoonlike color graphics, brought to life with recorded voices and amusing sound effects, the CD-ROM opens with a tearful Sam the Lion bemoaning his lack of a kingdom. Mat the Mouse points out that reading gives everyone the key to his or her own special kingdom. Joined by Reader Rabbit, the three characters set off down the Reading Road to learn to read. There are twenty stops on the road, each offering two storybooks and a "Skill House" full of word games. In the first stop, Reader Rabbit asks children to click on objects on the screen beginning with the letter "s." After the child clicks on a saxophone, for example, the word "saxophone" is pronounced and the instrument performs a quick jazz riff. In the Skill House, there are several activities, such as word matching and combining sounds, where pushing "m" and "an" together makes the word "man."

To entice children to keep reading even when the computer is off, *Interactive Reading Journey* comes with forty story booklets reproducing the forty stories shown on screen. Parents will have to keep a sharp eye out, though, because the twenty-two-page black-and-white booklets are so small—measuring only five and a half inches by four and a quarter inches—that they are likely to quickly disappear if left in the hands of children. The stories themselves stress simple, repetitive phrases tied to line drawings that help children figure out the meaning of words. The first book starts at the most basic level: "See. I see. I see. I see Sam. Look, Sam! Look! Look at this book." By the fortieth story, the sentences and vocabulary are much further along: "Sam, Sam, I see a bee. Buzz the Bee hid in the bed. Did Sam hit him? Look! It is Buzz the Bee. Will Buzz fit in this bee net?"

Parents will appreciate a tracking feature built into *Interac-*

tive Reading Journey that monitors a child's performance, making it easy to spot any weaknesses that require extra practice or recognize when it's time to move to the next level. The Learning Company claims *Interactive Reading Journey* "does what no other software program has done before—it teaches a child to read." That's probably overselling the CD-ROM, but I'm sure the combination of on-screen instruction and print booklets will greatly accelerate any child's academic progress.

SESAME STREET: NUMBERS
★★
Developer: Electronic Arts Inc./EA Kids; 800-245-4525
Format: DOS, Macintosh
Price: $45

Sesame Street: Numbers should be one of the best CD-ROMs for children. Put together with support from the Children's Television Workshop, creators of the highly respected and long-lived "Sesame Street" show on public television, the disk features characters that children instantly recognize—Bert and Ernie, Big Bird, Elmo, and The Count. But these animated superstars can't save this flawed production; the low-quality graphics and confusing interface will quickly alienate the target audience of children ages three to six.

The DOS version of *Sesame Street: Numbers* displays colorful full-screen graphics, but the images are full of jagged lines where you expect to see curves, giving the appearance of a Sega or Nintendo video game. (I didn't get to see the Macintosh version, although I assume the graphics look the same.) What's worse, navigating through the CD-ROM is unnecessarily complicated. In the opening screen, you see Elmo standing in the middle of Sesame Street. A gold star hovers above his head. Rolling the mouse to the left or right causes the street scene to shift jerkily in that direction, a form of movement I found mildly nauseating. When the star moves over a doorway or object that does something, the object starts sparkling. But you aren't told what the object does—it might just perform a five-second animation or it might transport you to one of the CD-ROM's four games. The only way to figure out *Sesame Street: Numbers* is through a tedious process of trial and error.

The four games are also difficult to learn, despite introductory advice from the *Sesame Street* characters, and are often delayed while the characters keep repeating the same snippets of dialogue. What's more, the games are virtually identical—three of the four involve hunting for objects by moving the star around the screen. Children are likely to be more interested in the multimedia accessories included with three of the games: a television set that plays one-minute video clips taken from the TV show in a window filling a quarter of the screen, a radio that plays short selections of the TV show's songs, a telephone that plays messages from the "Sesame Street" characters and storybooks telling abbreviated versions of classic children's tales with pictures and narration. But it won't take more than an hour or two for children to go through all this content several times; then they'll have nothing left but the frustrating and dull games.

SUPER SOLVERS SPELLBOUND!
★★★
Developer: The Learning Company; 800-852-2255
Format: DOS
Price: $39

Few things in elementary school are more boring than memorizing long lists of words for a spelling test. Yet children will voluntarily spend free time playing games like "Hangman." There's an obvious message here: Learning to spell isn't such a burden when it's part of a game. *Super Solvers Spellbound!* presents one thousand words in four amusing games aimed at ages seven to twelve. As you move up through five levels of difficulty, the goal is to participate in a computer-generated version of the National Spelling Bee held every year at the White House.

"Word Search," the first game, calls for finding eight hidden words in a grid of letters with eleven rows and twelve columns. At the most difficult level, the words can run vertically, horizontally, diagonally, or in jagged steps in either direction. Even parents will have to bear down hard to find all the hidden words. "Flash Card" shows a word on the screen, that the child must reproduce, even though the word disappears from view as soon as the child starts typing. "Criss Cross" calls for fitting words into crossword puzzle squares.

After accumulating a sufficient number of points at these three games, children move on to the "Spelling Bee," in which they face two robots who occasionally make mistakes. To win, children have to spell correctly those words that tripped up the robots; they can then move to the next level. Losers at the spelling bee only need to earn half as many points to qualify for a second chance.

Children can select what type of words they'd like to spell from ten categories such as nature, people, and holidays. Players, or their parents, can also customize *Super Solvers Spellbound!* by adding up to three thousand more words of their choice. Some children, however, may be disappointed by the program's low-resolution video-game-like graphics. Originally developed for floppy disk, *Super Solvers Spellbound!* needs better artwork and more sound effects to meet the high expectations of today's elementary-school students.

WORD TALES
★★
Developer: Time Warner Interactive; 800-482-3766
Format: Windows, Macintosh
Price: $39

Word Tales is an uninspired learning game for children ages four to seven. A friendly green alien named Milo guides children through a series of spelling and word-recognition exercises that seem more like forced school drills than spontaneous fun. Each drill has two parts. Children start by supplying the missing first letter of a word depicted on the screen. Milo says, for example, "What's the first letter of monster?" as a picture of a blue monster sitting on a red motorcycle appears on the screen. Once children select the letter "m" from among three choices, they are taken to a scene filled with objects beginning with the same letter, such as a moose, mountains, and a mailbox. After the child clicks on all the "m" words, the tedious process starts over with a different letter. Milo offers a "reward" for successfully completing a word tale, a boring arcade game in which children try to control bouncing balls. With such limited action and uncompelling incentives, *Word Tales* won't hold the attention of today's young Nintendo and Sega addicts for more than a few minutes.

A WORLD OF ANIMALS
★★★
Developer: National Geographic Society; 800-368-2728
Format: Windows, Macintosh
Price: $39

Part of the *Wonders of Learning CD-ROM Library* series from the National Geographic Society, described fully in the review of *Animals and How They Grow* in this section. *A World of Animals* presents on-screen versions of five print booklets: *Butterflies*, *Dinosaurs: Giant Reptiles*, *Farm Animals*, *Spiders*, and *Whales*. A sample of the text, from *Whales*: "Whales come in different sizes. Even the smallest whales are big. A dolphin is bigger than you are. The biggest kind of whale is called a blue whale. It is bigger than any dinosaur that ever lived on earth."

A WORLD OF PLANTS
★★½
Developer: National Geographic Society; 800-368-2728
Format: Windows, Macintosh
Price: $39

Part of the *Wonders of Learning CD-ROM Library* series from the National Geographic Society, described fully in the review of *Animals and How They Grow* in this section. *A World of Plants* presents on-screen versions of four print booklets: *A Tree Through the Seasons*, *Plants Are Important*, *The Parts of a Plant*, and *What Is a Seed?* A sample of the text, from *The Parts of a Plant*: "Most plants have five parts. These parts help plants grow. Plants have roots, stems and leaves. They have flowers and seeds, too."

b. Stories

AMANDA STORIES
★★
Developer: Voyager Co.; 800-446-2001
Format: Windows, Macintosh
Price: $29

In the fast-changing field of CD-ROM, *Amanda Stories* is an almost prehistoric relic, released in 1991, at least a year before home CD-ROM systems started becoming popular. This collection of ten children's stories represented the state of the art four years ago but is now showing its age.

Children's author Amanda Goodenough provides six stories about her cat, Inigo, and four stories about a character called Your Faithful Camel. The stories unfold without narration or dialogue. Instead, children advance the action by clicking the mouse on different characters or objects shown on the screen. Not much happens, though. "Inigo Takes a Bath" shows the cat, depicted on screen as a blurry black furball, taking a bath and getting a hug from Amanda. "Inigo's Snack" has the cat raiding the refrigerator, eating a plate of cookies, and then taking a nap. Preschoolers are likely to start yawning at the lack of action.

The half-screen color illustrations in *Amanda Stories* are crude line drawings, and the sound effects, although convincing, are limited. In one scene, for instance, you click on a phone booth and hear the phone ring once. That's it. The far-superior Living Books series always gives children something more; a phone rings, then you hear someone tell a joke. Excuse me for the terrible pun, but Amanda Goodenough's CD-ROM isn't good enough anymore.

ARTHUR'S BIRTHDAY
★★★½
Developer: Living Books; 800-521-6263
Format: Windows, Macintosh
Price: $39

Birthdays are supremely important events in the lives of children, and young Arthur the aardvark is facing a dilemma: All the boys he knows are coming to his party, while all the girls are going to a birthday party on the same day for his friend Muffy. In this second

Living Book featuring the character created by children's author Marc Brown, Arthur comes up with a solution that makes everyone happy by the end of the CD-ROM's thirteen on-screen pages.

Although it's not a glaring weakness, there's no educational content in *Arthur's Birthday*, unlike the earlier *Arthur's Teacher Trouble*, which involved children in a spellathon. Both CD-ROMs are still lots of fun, and both are a compelling way to introduce children to the joys of reading. *Arthur's Birthday* also provides a whole new crop of wonderful point-and-click animations. On page six, click on the toaster and you'll discover it's actually a French toaster: Two pieces of toast pop out, a male and female wearing berets, and they dance arm in arm to "Frère Jacques." On page eight, click on a manhole cover and a marching band struts down the street. Just when you think it's over, a straggler carrying a big drum runs to catch up and falls into the manhole.

Some of these animations have a little twist intended for adults who are playing along with their children. On page twelve, click the light switch on the living room wall and a mirror ball descends from the ceiling, accompanied by 1970s disco music. In English and Spanish. For more information on features common to all the Living Books, see the review of *Just Grandma and Me* in this section.

ARTHUR'S TEACHER TROUBLE
★★★★
Developer: Living Books; 800-521-6263
Format: Windows, Macintosh
Price: $39

Arthur is an aardvark struggling to survive third grade under the watchful eye of Mr. Ratburn, the school's strictest teacher, in this adaptation by Living Books of the print book *Arthur's Teacher Trouble* by Marc Brown. Without giving away too much of the plot, Arthur decides to compete in the school spellathon and learns Mr. Ratburn isn't really such a bad guy.

The CD-ROM's twenty-four on-screen pages are full of the little surprises that make all the Living Books a delight. Click on the door of the science lab, for example, and you see a blinding flash of yellow light and hear a muffled explosion. Three of the twenty-four pages are Arthur's list of practice words for the spellathon. Children encounter forty words such as "ambulance" and "banana," each accompanied by an illustration. Clicking on the word, children hear it pronounced, hear it spelled out as each letter is highlighted, and then watch a quick, funny animation. I particularly liked the seagull, which pecks a rubber tire that deflates with an appropriate whooshing sound.

In keeping with Living Books' no-stress approach to learning, children are free to skip right past Arthur's list. There is no quiz they must complete in order to finish the story, a common tactic in other learning software that can alienate very young users who aren't ready for spelling tests. Plays in English and Spanish. For more information on features common to all the Living Books, see the review of *Just Grandma and Me* in this section.

BIG ANTHONY'S MIXED-UP MAGIC
★★★½
Developer: Putnam New Media; 800-788-6262
Format: Windows, Macintosh
Price: $29

Strega Nona, a good witch from a medieval village in the southern Italian region of Calabria, is always struggling to cope with some new disaster unleashed by her well-meaning but clumsy adolescent assistant, Big Anthony. Children's author and illustrator Tomie dePaola has written a series of books featuring Strega Nona and helped Putnam New Media bring his characters into this colorful and entertaining CD-ROM designed for children ages five to ten.

Big Anthony's Mixed-Up Magic is based on dePaola's book *Strega Nona Meets Her Match*, and a thirty-two-page paperback edition is included in the box with the CD-ROM. In the story, another good witch, named Strega Amelia, comes to visit and decides to go into the business of curing the villagers' ailments, competing with Strega Nona. "One by one the townspeople started to go to Strega Amelia," the book explains. "Everyone got *dolci*—sweets— and *cappuccino* for paying a visit, and indeed she had the latest scientific equipment—strange-looking machines that did all kinds of things. The lines of people grew longer and longer. Strega Nona had met her match." It looks like Strega Nona is out of business until Big Anthony inadvertently saves the day.

All of the illustrations and text from the book are presented on the CD-ROM, with narration by dePaola himself. But that's only the beginning of what children can do with *Big Anthony's*

Mixed-Up Magic. By entering the "Explore" mode, they are free to roam through Calabria, exploring Strega Amelia's house, the town center, and a forest grove, among other spots. Using the mouse to move a magic wand around the screen, children click on people and objects to see either amusing five-second animations or start one of nine games. Most of the games are familiar but fun—such as creating mixed-up zoo animals by selecting various heads, middles, and legs or a matching game in which children have to find pairs of objects hidden behind 16 squares. My favorite is the magic tricks game, where Big Anthony summons video clips to demonstrate how children can perform several magic tricks, including cutting a banana in slices without removing the peel and making a salt shaker disappear.

Both parents and children will appreciate how closely the full-screen illustrations match dePaola's warm artistic style. The many animations, too, mesh with the book's gentle humor—click on a bear in the woods, for example, and he plays a brief mandolin solo, or click on a steamer trunk in Strega Nona's bedroom to see her bloomers pop out and perform a little dance. Best of all, the CD-ROM's many added scenes and games will keep children amused and involved long after they've grown tired of the story itself.

SHELLEY DUVALL'S IT'S A BIRD'S LIFE
★★
Developer: Sanctuary Woods Multimedia Corp.; 800-943-3664
Format: Windows, Macintosh
Price: $39

Actress Shelley Duvall, who lives in Los Angeles with a flock of parrots, apparently harbors politically correct sentiments regarding the destruction of the Amazon rain forest and politically incorrect sentiments when it comes to keeping beautiful birds in captivity. *Shelley Duvall's It's A Bird's Life*, which Duvall wrote and narrates, tells a somewhat off-kilter story aimed at ages three and above involving Duvall's eight parrots, who become homeless after a wildfire destroys her house. The feathered group decides to move to its ancestral home in the Amazon rain forest. On reaching their destination, "they were shocked by what they saw. It appeared that the jungle was being invaded by man in every possible way. There was mining, logging and a dam being built." The disheartened parrots then return to L.A., where they are overjoyed on finding a new home built by Duvall to their exact specifications. "It was great to know they didn't have to worry anymore about food, weather, bird catchers, smog, mining or logging," the story concludes. "The aviary was like their own jungle, complete with fruit trees, palms, a stone waterfall and 'room service.' Now, this was paradise!" The birds, happily confined in their gilded cage, have done nothing to tell anyone about the dwindling rain forest—hardly an inspirational ending.

Bird's Life unfolds through sixty on-screen pages; parents will find themselves sitting through several sessions to get small children from beginning to end. Each page has color illustrations with small amounts of animation. From the pages, or from the main screen, you can access games and sing-a-longs. Even for small children, though, the five games are too simple, such as a connect-the-dots exercise that calls for nothing more than moving the mouse from one numbered dot to the next. The eleven sing-alongs are drippy and trite. I don't think children will be drawn to lyrics such as these, from the title song: "It's a bird's life, and I wouldn't change a thing/Got my very own song just in case I want to sing/From morning til night, baby, it's a bird's life." Excuse the cheap shot, but this stuff is for the birds.

THE CAT CAME BACK
★★★
Developer: Sanctuary Woods Multimedia Corp.; 800-943-3664
Format: Windows
Price: $39

Poor old Mr. Johnson just can't get rid of his nameless yellow cat. He can't give the cat to his neighbors. He sends it away on a cruise ship and a hot-air balloon, but the determined feline keeps reappearing. Even when a cyclone carries off the cat and his seven kittens, they all come back to Mr. Johnson's doorstep. This simple and familiar children's story is retold with charming illustrations in *The Cat Came Back*. Youngsters just learning to read will appreciate the simple, repetitive text. Each of the cat's adventures ends with the same refrain: "And the cat came back/the very next day./The cat came back/they thought he was a goner./The cat came back/he just wouldn't stay away."

Children can pick four ways to experience the story, presented in twenty half-screen color pages. In "listen-along" mode, the words are spoken by an adult as they scroll along the bottom of the screen. The CD-ROM is trilingual, by the way, offering audio and text in English, Spanish, and French. In "read-along" mode, children tackle reading themselves. If they need help, they can select the voice of either a young girl or a young boy to pronounce selected words. There are also a few somewhat amusing puzzles in "read-along" mode, such as identifying seven things the cat has thrown on the living room floor. In "sing-along" mode, the story is performed as a song with a soft-rock melody. Children can pick which instruments play the song or turn off the voice of the singer and sing themselves. If you've got a microphone hooked to your computer, children will be able to record their performance, although parents should be warned that these jam sessions suck up huge amounts of hard disk space. In "write-along" mode, children fill out a blank diary describing the cat's adventures, write their own captions for the story, or solve six simple missing-word puzzles.

The activities are well designed and should be easy for children to operate with a little parental assistance. But parents should take care in matching the CD-ROM to their children's skill level. I think *The Cat Came Back* is mislabeled—the box recommends it for ages seven to eleven. But all the activities are focused on early reading skills, so I'd put the age range at six to nine.

HARRY AND THE HAUNTED HOUSE
★★★½
Developer: Living Books; 800-521-6263
Format: Windows, Macintosh
Price: $39

Poking gentle fun at children's fear of the unknown, *Harry and the Haunted House* is a charming visit to a strange old home filled with more fun than fright. This installment in the *Living Books* series comes from an original story by Mark Schlichting, creator of the *Living Books* concept, with delightful surprises on each of the twelve on-screen pages.

The story opens as young Harry D. Rabbit plays baseball with his friends Stinky the skunk, Amy the cat, and Earl, also a rabbit. Harry hits Stinky's ball into the haunted house down the street, and Stinky wants it back, so all four of them head into the abandoned mansion, joined by Harry's dog, Spot. Among the point-and-click discoveries waiting inside: two dancing chairs, one that does the hula and the other a Russian Cossack kick; a girl group of tomatoes that sing, "They call us the dancing hot tomatoes, so why do they keep us on the shelf?"; and a painting of a pirate ship that fires its cannon to blow out a light fixture on a nearby wall. In a nice counterbalance to the rampant sexism in children's television and video games, Amy is the calm and collected one who shows the three boys their fears of ghosts and goblins are groundless. In English and Spanish. For more information on common features of the *Living Books*, see the review of *Just Grandma and Me* in this section.

JUST GRANDMA AND ME
★★★★
Developer: Living Books; 800-521-6263
Format: Windows, Macintosh
Price: $39

Just Grandma and Me, released in 1992, sets the standard for what a children's CD-ROM should be. This disk—the first title in the excellent Living Books series—makes a book come alive with animations, music, narration, and sound effects that easily draw young viewers into the story.

Acclaimed children's author Mercer Mayer wrote *Just Grandma and Me* as part of his "Little Critter" series for preschool children. The CD-ROM translates each of the book's twelve pages to the screen, rendered with careful detail and lots of color. At the start of *Just Grandma and Me*, you're welcomed by Little Critter himself, who appears on screen explaining how to play with a Living Book. He then breaks into a little dance, backed by a toe-tapping theme song with vaguely Caribbean influences.

Moving into the book, you hear Little Critter narrate the text on each page and see a short animated sequence that advances the story of his trip to the beach with Grandma. After the animation is completed, you can explore the on-screen page, clicking on characters and objects to see what happens. When you are ready to move on, there is a closing animation sequence to set up the next page. On page two, for example, Little Critter discovers it's too windy to set up a beach umbrella. So, on page three, he announces, "I flew my kite instead." You then watch Little Critter's independent-minded kite land on the horns of a matronly cow relaxing on a beach blanket in yellow sunglasses and a green bathing suit. Before moving to page four, Little Critter says—with a mixture of insistence and apology that only five-year-olds can carry off—"Uh, can I have my kite back?"

Exploring the pages is equally amusing. My favorite point-and-click performance is by a starfish that on page two dons a top hat, grabs a cane, and gives a five-second soft-shoe performance accompanied by a few bars of vaudeville music. Most children could probably get through *Just Grandma and Me* in an hour, but the CD-ROM is so well done that I'm convinced they'll play it again and again.

About the Living Books series: Broderbund Software, a California software company, and Random House, a large New York book publisher, have teamed up to create a string of winners based on the work of top-selling children's authors. Mindful of the needs of their young audience, the folks at Living Books have stuck to a common interface for all the titles. That means once your child has learned the few simple steps required to play a Living Book, he or she will be able to enjoy instantly any other Living Book. There is also more than one way to experience each disk. By going to an option screen, children can select to have the story read to them from beginning to end or select a "play" mode that allows exploration on each page.

And, although children will probably be having too much fun to notice, Living Books are an excellent tool for learning to read. Each CD-ROM comes with the book on which it's based so children can go back and forth between the images on screen and print on paper. Children taking their first steps beyond the ABCs can click on any word in the on-screen text and hear it pronounced, a valuable learning experience. In addition, most of the Living Books offer more than one language; *Just Grandma and Me* can be played in English, Spanish, or Japanese by clicking a button in the option screen. Parents with overcrowded computers will also be gratified to discover Living Books can be run entirely off the CD-ROM itself, without downloading any files to the hard disk.

Other Living Books: *Arthur's Birthday, Arthur's Teacher Trouble, Harry and the Haunted House, Little Monster at School, The New Kid on the Block, Ruff's Bone* and *The Tortoise and the Hare.* All are reviewed in this section.

DISNEY'S ANIMATED STORYBOOK: THE LION KING
★★★½
Developer: Walt Disney Computer Software Inc.; 800-688-1520
Format: Windows-2, Macintosh-2
Price: $39

The Lion King lives again. After the film topped the box-office charts for children's movies in 1994, *Disney's Animated Story-Book: The Lion King* on CD-ROM tells the tale in a new way. Through eighteen interactive on-screen pages, children listen to the story of how Simba the lion cub overcomes his evil uncle Scar to claim his rightful place as the Lion King. The full-screen color animations are wonderful, looking as good as the movie itself, and each page is full of hidden animations that children uncover by pointing and clicking with the mouse.

Designed for age three to nine, *The Lion King* CD-ROM gives children the choice of passively watching as the story is read to them—a process that takes about half an hour—or selecting a "Play" mode in which they can explore the pages at their own pace. At the top of each page is a sentence or two of text, read by the narrator; click on Rafiki the wise old baboon, who stands on the right side of the page, and key words in the text are highlighted. Clicking those words prompts Rafiki to give a definition. When Simba and his companion Nala visit the elephant graveyard, for example, the text says: "The elephant graveyard was full of old bones and geysers! The two cubs had a lot of fun exploring the graveyard . . . for a while." Click on the word "geyser," and Rafiki explains, "A geyser shoots hot water and steam from underground." A geyser on the screen then shoots out a blast of steam to drive home the point. Dialogue from the movie—featuring the voices of James Earl Jones, Whoopi Goldberg, Cheech Marin, and others—is borrowed for animated scenes on each page that help move the story along. After Simba's birth on the first page, for instance, Scar sticks his head into the bottom of the screen and grumbles, "Well, I was first in line until the little hairball was born."

Most of the animations are very brief and not particularly original; click on the open African plains, and a herd of giraffes trots across the screen; click on Nala, and she giggles. The CD-ROM also offers three very simple games: Bug Catching, in which children click on bugs to feed hungry Timon the meerkat; Connect the Stars, a variation on connect-the-dots; and The Pouncing Game, in which children maneuver Simba through tall grass in an effort to surprise the bird Zasu. Even three-year-olds will be able to grasp quickly the fundamentals of the games, but they are so easy that children may not want to play them for long periods.

In total, however, *The Lion King* CD-ROM is so lively and colorful that children who liked the movie will undoubtedly play with the disk again and again. But parents need to be sure the family PC is up to the task. The Windows version requires a double-speed CD-ROM drive; eight megabytes of random-access memory is "highly recommended." A Macintosh version is due in early 1995 and for it, too, eight megabytes of RAM is highly recommended. Disney ran into howls of outrage shortly after Christmas 1994 when many parents discovered their home system didn't meet the CD-ROM's high-level technical specifications—so read the label carefully before purchase.

LITTLE MONSTER AT SCHOOL
★★★★
Developer: Living Books; 800-521-6263
Format: Windows, Macintosh
Price: $39

Little Monster, a young dragon dressed like Dennis the Menace in blue overalls and a red-and-white-striped shirt, is headed off for a day of school in this CD-ROM story, the second Living Book based on the work of children's author Mercer Mayer. Before finishing a day of what appears to be either kindergarten or first grade, Little Monster befriends Yally—a problem child who doesn't enjoy any of the class activities until Little Monster praises him as the best student at drawing.

The eighteen on-screen pages of *Little Monster at School* are perfect for five-year-olds contemplating—perhaps with a little fear—their first day of class. Mr. Grithix, Little Monster's teacher, makes learning fun. All kinds of activities are covered, including storytelling, the alphabet, counting, geography, and science. Of course, no Living Book is complete without point-and-click animations. I especially liked Little Monster's lunchbox on page three. When you click on the lunchbox, you hear canned laughter and then one of the oldest jokes in the world: "What'd the apple say to the orange? Why don't you make like a banana and split?" If you're over age six, you've heard it before. If you're under age 6, you'll find it hilarious.

In English and Spanish. For more information on features common to all the Living Books, see the review of *Just Grandma and Me* in this section.

THE NEW KID ON THE BLOCK
★★★½
Developer: Living Books; 800-521-6263
Format: Windows, Macintosh
Price: $39

The New Kid on the Block is a slight departure from the Living Books format, presenting eighteen poems by children's writer Jack Prelutsky with drawings by *New Yorker* magazine cartoonist James Stevenson rather than telling a story. Also, the illustrations are predominantly black-and-white line drawings rather than the full-color cartoonlike artwork in other Living Books.

But *New Kid* is still a charmer. The poems are short and simple, featuring humor perfectly targeted to a preschool audience. Consider the two-sentence ditty "My Baby Brother:"

"My baby brother is so small, he hasn't even learned to crawl.

"He's only been around a week, and all he seems to do is bawl, and wiggle, sleep . . . and leak."

That final point is demonstrated by a yellow puddle spreading out from underneath a smiling diaper-clad baby—the kind of innocently naughty stuff that kids love.

"The Bloders Are Exploding" features chubby creatures busily chowing down on sticks of TNT. When the narrator describes Bloders "going up like rockets," you see them soar into the air. Once again, there's a hidden opportunity for children to learn. By clicking on the accompanying text, children can hear an individual word pronounced and learn its definition by watching the action on screen. Click the word "left," for example, and the leftmost of three Bloders explodes; click the word "right" and the right-most Bloder is vaporized—an ingenious way to teach the difference between left and right.

In English only. For more information on features common to all the Living Books, see the review of *Just Grandma and Me* in this section.

RUFF'S BONE
★★★
Developer:	Living Books; 800-521-6263
Format:	Windows, Macintosh
Price:	$39

Ruff is a dog with only one thing on his mind in this Living Book: finding his lost bone. He goes underground, up in the clouds, down in the ocean, and finally through space to the Bone Planet, where dogs are the predominant form of life. The point-and-click animations that make the Living Books so wonderful are slightly flat here, lacking the creativity of earlier efforts such as *Arthur's Teacher Trouble* and *Just Grandma and Me*. Maybe it's because the story for *Ruff's Bone* was created especially for Living Books, not borrowed from a successful children's book.

What's more, I discovered the only error I've ever seen in a Living Book, although I admit it's minor: Traveling through space, Ruff encounters the constellation Orion and Sirius the Dog Star, each illustrated by a point-and-click animation. But the constellation labeled the Big Dipper in the print version of *Ruff's Bone*, included with the CD-ROM, is called the Little Dipper on the disk. More significant, the twelve-page story doesn't always hang together. There's no clear explanation of how Ruff can fall out of a cave into the sky. Children, as well as adults, are likely to be puzzled.

Still, a Living Book with a few flaws is miles ahead of most children's CD-ROM software. Fans of the Living Books series won't be disappointed with *Ruff's Bone*. In English and Spanish. For more information on features common to all the Living Books, see the review of *Just Grandma and Me* in this section.

SITTING ON THE FARM
★★½
Developer:	Sanctuary Woods Multimedia Corp.; 800-943-3664
Format:	Windows, Macintosh
Price:	$39

When it comes to entertaining and instructing children, nothing makes up for the lack of a good story. That's the problem with *Sitting on the Farm*. The CD-ROM has several interesting multimedia elements, such as a "sing-along" feature in which children can record their own voice and a "write-along" feature where they can select pictures and type in words. But the story itself is unimaginative and repetitive. In fourteen on-screen pages, *Sitting on the Farm* tells of a nameless freckle-faced red-haired girl eating lunch on a farm. Larger and larger animals come sit on her knee, starting with a bug and ending with a bear. The text repeats the same refrain for each animal: "Sitting on the farm, happy as can be/I had a little bug on my knee./I said, 'Hey, bug, get off my knee!'/Well, that old bug said, 'No, siree!'" The half-screen color illustrations have only limited animations, such as the bear licking its snout, lasting just a few seconds.

Children can pick one of four ways to experience the story. In "listen-along" mode, the words of the story are spoken by an adult as they scroll along the bottom of the screen. *Sitting on the Farm* is trilingual, offering audio and text in English, Spanish, or French. In "read-along" mode, children read to themselves. If they need help, they can select the voice of either a young boy or a young girl to pronounce selected words. There are also a few mildly interesting puzzles in "read-along" mode, such as finding six items on the screen that are green. In "sing-along" mode, the story is performed as a song with a bouncy melody. Children can pick which instruments play the song and can turn off the voice of the singer. If you've got a microphone hooked to your computer, children will be able to record themselves singing along, although parents should be warned these recordings can quickly suck up huge amounts of hard disk space. In "write-along" mode, children select one of six different backgrounds such as a desert or an ocean. They can then pick individual animals to place in the picture while typing their story into a text window at the bottom of the screen.

The activities are well designed and should be easy for children to operate with a small amount of parental assistance, but young users are likely to lose interest quickly because of the boring story. I also think *Sitting on the Farm* is mislabeled. The box recommends the CD-ROM for ages seven to eleven, but all the activities are focused on early reading skills, so I'd put the age range at six to nine.

THUMBELINA: AN INTERACTIVE ADVENTURE
★★★
Developer: Time Warner Interactive; 800-482-3766
Format: Windows
Price: $29

Most children's CD-ROM software, I'm pleased to report, is gender-neutral, with as much potential appeal for girls as for boys. That's a refreshing alternative to Sega and Nintendo video games, sold almost exclusively to boys with a steady diet of games centered on kicking, punching, and shooting. *Thumbelina: An Interactive Adventure* goes to the other extreme, having been specifically designed for girls ages three to eight. Based on the animated movie *Hans Christian Andersen's Thumbelina*, with performances by Barry Manilow and Carol Channing, the CD-ROM is a narrated storybook telling the classic tale of the girl no bigger than an adult's thumb who is wooed by the equally diminutive fairy prince Cornelius. Time Warner Interactive, developer of *Thumbelina* on CD-ROM, said in a news release that it sought to create "an interactive playground full of activities for young girls to explore." Curiously, the CD-ROM's box gives no indication that it's intended for girls—other than containing a plastic charm bracelet that can be seen through a clear window.

The story of Thumbelina is told in the form of a book, with pages filling half the screen, divided into seven chapters: "A Girl No Bigger than a Thumb," "The Fairy Prince," "Singers de España," "Follow Your Heart," "The Beetle Ball," "Marry the Mole," and "A Royal Wedding." Each chapter unfolds through about a dozen on-screen pages; children can choose to read the text themselves while looking at still pictures from the movie or listen to narration from a friendly bird named Jacquimo. By clicking on the borders of some pages, children can open one of five activities: "Naming and Matching," in which children see a label on the side of the screen and must drag it to the appropriate spot in the picture; "Shapes," which calls for children to put cutout squares, stars, and triangles back into the picture; "Counting," in which children must count the number of times a certain object appears in the picture; "Painting," where children can color outlines of the characters, then watch them in a brief animation; and "Sing-Along," in which musical numbers from the movie are performed in a small on-screen window accompanied by the lyrics.

Little girls who like fairy tales will enjoy the story and artwork in *Thumbelina* and will strengthen their reading skills by listening to the narration while seeing the words. The activities will provide a brief distraction, but many children will get tired of seeing the same games over and over again. Finally, children and parents alike will appreciate the story's traditional happy ending: "You see, anything is possible if you follow your heart. And, of course, they lived happily ever after."

THE TORTOISE AND THE HARE
★★★★
Developer: Living Books; 800-521-6263
Format: Windows, Macintosh
Price: $39

We all know the story of the Tortoise and the Hare, a fable that originated with Aesop. Living Books has created its own version of the story rather than borrowing from an established work of children's literature for this CD-ROM. A friendly purple crow named Simon narrates the familiar tale of the tortoise, described by Simon as "a friendly fellow who moved at his own slow pace," challenged to a race by the hare, "a busy person who was always on the move."

High-quality animation and sound effects convey both the rabbit's sneaker-screeching speed and the turtle's glacial progress in twelve on-screen pages. The rabbit, of course, gets into trouble when he stops in a garden to gobble down carrots. But the real entertainment is the point-and-click surprises scattered throughout the book, not the predictable plot. Click on the garden's scarecrow, for example, and the straw man comes to life, shouting "Boo!" at Simon. Simon is startled at first but quickly regains his composure and says to the scarecrow, "Hey, what are you looking at?" Then Simon lifts his wings and shouts "Boo!" back at the scarecrow, who recoils in fright. All this takes place in just six seconds.

Or click on a group of four sunflowers, who whip out sunglasses to perform a finger-snapping fifteen-second jazz riff. These little flashes of wit reenergize a tired old story, making *The Tortoise and the Hare* CD-ROM an instant classic. Plays in English and Spanish. For more information on features common to all the Living Books, see the review of *Just Grandma and Me* in this section.

c. Games and Activities

THE ALADDIN ACTIVITY CENTER
★★★
Developer: Walt Disney Computer Software Inc.; 800-688-1520
Format: Windows-2, Macintosh-2
Price: $35

The Aladdin Activity Center succeeds through excess—with eleven games and projects, children are sure to find something on the CD-ROM they will enjoy. The disk presents many of the same characters as the movie on which it is based, Disney's 1992 animated hit *Aladdin*, which got an incredible manic energy from the voice of Robin Williams playing the big blue genie. Williams, unfortunately, was apparently unavailable for this assignment—the voice of the genie is supplied by an unconvincing Williams imitator. Disney, by the way, recommends *Aladdin Activity Center* for "ages 5 and up." While I agree that age five is a good starting point, I disagree with "and up" because the games and projects are much too simple for children above age twelve.

From the main screen of *Aladdin Activity Center*, children pick one of four destinations: the Agrabah Marketplace, the Cave of Wonders, the Royal Palace, or the Sultan's Theatre. I'm not sure why the developers present these four choices, however, because each destination is an identical gateway to the 11 activities. These activities are "The Art Center," where children work on four types of drawings—"watercolor" painting of coloring book pages with colors that can be mixed, "crayon" coloring in which the colors are fixed, paint-by-numbers, and connect-the-dots; "Amazing Mazes," a maze-running game; "Matching Mates," in which children look at groups of objects to find a pair with identical characteristics; "Music Mimic," challenging children to repeat a tune banged out on pots by Abu the monkey; "Picture Puzzler," in which children rearrange disorganized pieces of a picture; "Spelling Challenge," a spelling quiz; "Memory Game," in which children find pairs of objects hidden behind cards; and "Sultan's Theatre," which displays six video clips from the *Aladdin* movie, each running ninety seconds to three minutes, in a tiny four-inch diagonal window on a standard fourteen-inch monitor.

All the activities light up the screen with movie-quality animations and sound effects. Many of the games have three levels of difficulty; the number of squares in "Picture Puzzler," for example, can be increased from nine to twenty-four or sixty-four. On the downside, some of the games are very slow to respond; children may get restless waiting for Abu to strike the next note in "Music Mimic" or for the cards to flip over in "Memory Game."

THE BERENSTAIN BEARS LEARNING AT HOME VOLUME ONE
★★

Developer: Compton's NewMedia Inc.; 800-284-2045
Format: DOS
Price: $25

Released in early 1993 as an upgrade to a program previously on floppy disks, *The Berenstain Bears Learning at Home Volume One* shows its age. The graphics are low-resolution and full of the jagged lines common in the earlier era of floppy-based software, the sound effects are spread thin, and the program is too complicated for its preschool audience to navigate without parental assistance.

Learning at Home Volume One invites children to explore the treehouse of the Berenstain Bears family, familiar from a line of storybooks. Young Sister Bear is your guide through a succession of activities, such as learning to tell time, playing an "opposites" game, and brushing up on bathroom safety. Parents will like the focus on good behavior—Sister Bear conscientiously makes her bed and brushes her teeth. All this advice is delivered in rhyme, such as this tip on steering clear of the family medicine chest: "Unless given by parents, a doctor or nurse, medicine won't make you feel better, but worse!" But children exposed to more recent CD-ROMs will be disappointed with the relatively slow pace of *Learning at Home*. The program is also confusing; you navigate by clicking icons at the bottom of the screen, but it isn't always clear what each icon does or how to get from one part of the treehouse to another.

THE BERENSTAIN BEARS LEARNING AT HOME VOLUME TWO
★★

Developer: Compton's NewMedia Inc.; 800-284-2045
Format: DOS
Price: $25

More of the same from the Berenstain Bears. In *Learning at Home Volume Two*, young Sister Bear guides preschool children through a series of games and activities that are almost identical to *Volume One*, reviewed in this section. Once again, all the text is delivered in rhyme, as with this tip on fireplace safety: "Remember that when your fire needs tending, only your parents should do the mending." The games aren't especially interesting—trying to tell which color snail won a race, or throwing apples at a swarm of bees—and many of the lessons are superficial. An introduction to computers, for example, gives this nonsense couplet as a definition for the central processing unit: "The CPU is the largest part, tiny computer chips make it smart." Wrong and wrong. The CPU isn't the largest component inside a personal computer, and a CPU consists of a single chip.

WHERE IN THE WORLD IS CARMEN SANDIEGO? JUNIOR DETECTIVE EDITION
★★★

Developer: Broderbund Software Inc.; 800-521-6263
Format: Windows
Price: $39

For children just learning to read, *Where in the World is Carmen Sandiego? Junior Detective Edition* offers a passport into the popular Carmen Sandiego series, fully described in the review of *Where in the USA is Carmen Sandiego CD-ROM* in Chapter Two, Section a. The other Carmen Sandiego titles are intended for ages nine and above; the *Junior Detective Edition* is intended for ages five to eight.

Sticking with the basic Carmen Sandiego formula, the *Junior Detective Edition* substitutes audio and visual clues for text. The CD-ROM offers fifty cases in seven regions of the world and introduces children to geography by displaying maps, national flags, and pictures from many countries. Interesting facts are also delivered by "Dee Jaye," a talking radio that helps children navigate through the program. When traveling to Libya, for instance, Dee

Jaye points out that daytime temperatures in the desert can reach 160 degrees Fahrenheit.

In the box with the CD-ROM is a seventy-two-page "Junior Detective Handbook" evenly split between instructions for playing the game and a selection of noncomputer activities such as games and puzzles. The only drawback to *Junior Detective Edition* is that its educational content is delivered so gently that children won't learn nearly as much geography as with the regular Carmen series. Then again, children who play and enjoy the *Junior Detective Edition* will be eager to move up to those other Carmen titles when they're older.

COSMIC OSMO AND THE WORLDS BEYOND THE MACKEREL
★★★
Developer: Broderbund Software Inc./Cyan Inc.; 800-521-6263
Format: Macintosh
Price: $35

A CD-ROM classic, *Cosmic Osmo and the Worlds Beyond the Mackerel* was first released in 1990. It didn't sell well at the time, despite critical acclaim, and was rereleased in April 1994 after its creators—brothers Rand and Robyn Miller—hit it big with the game *Myst*, reviewed in Chapter Three, Section a.

Cosmic Osmo, like *Myst*, is full of strange adventures on unidentified planets, but *Cosmic Osmo* is aimed at children and doesn't impede users with the obscure and difficult puzzles that kept me from enjoying *Myst*. Neither game, however, gives you a clear path to follow. Instead, you just wander around until you stumble onto something interesting.

In the opening scene of *Cosmic Osmo*, a spaceship that looks something like a wingless propeller plane flies onto the screen. A door opens, and you click the mouse to go inside. Moving to the cockpit, where a pair of fuzzy dice hang in the windshield, you play with the controls for a while until you figure out how to make the ship take off. The first destination is Osmo's garage, hovering in outer space, where the doughy white creature greets you. From the garage, you can journey through a universe full of unusual encounters.

For example, I came across a mouse in dark glasses playing the piano very badly. Click on the rodent, and he declares, "What did you expect from a blind mouse playing a piano made of Swiss cheese?" Looking out another window, I saw birds flying backward as they squawked backward bird calls. There's no goal in all of this, just the joy of discovering some new bit of inspired lunacy. Illustrated with clever cartoonlike animations and accompanied by forty minutes of music and voices, *Cosmic Osmo* takes many hours to explore fully. Some children, however, may be disappointed that *Cosmic Osmo* is a black-and-white game with images filling only half the screen. That was good enough in 1990 but puts the CD-ROM way behind in today's market exploding with full-screen, full-color children's software.

CRAYOLA AMAZING ART ADVENTURE
★★★
Developer: Micrografx Inc.; 800-676-3110
Format: Windows
Price: $39

Preschool children who are getting bored with real crayons will find lots to do in *Crayola Amazing Art Adventure*, designed for ages three to six, although parents might not be quite so happy with the CD-ROM. *Art Adventure* is packed with ten coloring books, each offering eight on-screen pages that children fill in by selecting from an assortment of twelve colors. Most of these pages are interactive. In "Monster Mix-up," for example, children can cycle through a dozen choices for the head, body, and legs of the monster. "Silly Scenes" invites children to figure out what doesn't belong in the picture—a giraffe standing with cows in a barnyard, for example—and gives them a round of applause after they identify the mistake.

For the junior Picasso who feels confined by a coloring book's predrawn images, there is "Beginner Paint," which transforms the computer screen into a blank canvas. Young artists can select from a variety of tools to draw either fine lines or broad lines, play with geometric shapes, type in letters or words, add "sticker" images, or insert "moving toys," such as a frog that hops across the screen or an animated jack-in-the-box. These creations can be printed or saved in the "Art Gallery" for later viewing.

Art Adventure is complicated enough that youngsters will probably need supervision at first, but even computerphobic adults will have no trouble with the program's easy-to-understand twenty-page manual. I particularly liked the manual's useful hints on how parents and children can play with the CD-ROM together. "Help your child make a map of your neighborhood," reads one suggestion. "Use the Crazy Line tool to make streets. Use the Sticker tool to show where friends and family live. Print the map out and color it in together."

However, two aspects of *Art Adventure* that kids won't notice might annoy parents. First, installing the program requires an awesome fifteen megabytes of precious hard-disk space. *Art Adventure* can supposedly run straight off the CD-ROM without downloading any files, but I ran into several hang-ups and was forced to download. Second, the package contains almost as many commercials as a Saturday-morning cartoon. The CD-ROM includes five video clips from Crayola maker Binney & Smith, each running two to three minutes, that explain the history of crayons and how they are made. The narration, regrettably, is packed with hype for other Binney & Smith products. There's also an animated "product demonstration" that's really more of an advertisement. Inside the *Art Adventure* box, where children are sure to find them, are colorful flyers pitching *Crayola Kids Magazine* and soliciting members for an on-line service called Micrografx Kids Club.

For older children, ages six to twelve, there is a companion product called *Crayola Art Studio*. See the review in Chapter Two, Section d.

DANDY DINOSAURS
★

Developer: Multicom Publishing Inc.; 800-850-7272
Format: Windows, Macintosh
Price: $29

Dandy Dinosaurs isn't dandy and isn't really about dinosaurs. The dishonest marketing for this CD-ROM even extends to the box. Parents will be attracted by the big letters boldly proclaiming, "Exciting Stories! Stunning Games! Innovative Crafts!" Children will be lured by a six-inch plush dragon inside the box, carefully displayed behind a plastic window. But there's only one story on the disk, the games won't occupy children for more than half an hour, and the eleven craft projects appear to have been designed more to create parental panic—requiring cooking, cutting with scissors, and playing with paint—than for innovation.

Based on a series of children's activities books put out by *Bet-*

ter *Homes and Gardens* magazine, *Dandy Dinosaurs* centers not on a dinosaur but on a character named Max the Dragon, who appears to be about ten years old. In "Dandy Dragon Day," the CD-ROM's single story, Max unintentionally upsets his little sister, Marci, and organizes a surprise party to cheer her up. The story unfolds in about fifteen minutes through a dozen on-screen pages with narrated text and very limited animation; a helium balloon drifts off the page, or Max moves his mouth while the rest of his body is motionless. To navigate through the story, you have to listen from beginning to end; there's no way to jump from one place to another. Maybe that doesn't matter—the story is so lifeless that children are unlikely to sit through it more than once. The four games are even worse; each takes only a few minutes to play. "Baby Dinosaurs," for example, asks children to find five dinosaurs partially hidden behind trees and rocks. Once they've found the five, there's nothing more, not even another screen with dinosaurs hiding in different places.

The eleven craft activites require considerable parental supervision. Making dinosaur cookies, for example, calls for rounding up a long list of ingredients, mixing them together, and baking. Making "dinosaur footprints" by finger painting is a sure recipe for disaster without Mom and Dad hovering nearby. And turning plastic foam cups into fire-breathing dragon puppets involves a potentially messy combination of scissors and glue. The developers of *Dandy Dinosaurs* helpfully include brief video clips showing how to complete these projects. But they stupidly neglect to provide a way to print the instructions. As a result, any parent masochistic enough to attempt these projects will either have to write the instructions down by hand or run back and forth from the computer to the kitchen and family room.

FATTY BEAR'S BIRTHDAY SURPRISE
★★★
Developer: Humongous Entertainment Inc.; 206-485-1212
Format: Windows, Macintosh
Price: $39

A little girl named Kayla kisses her teddy bear good night and goes to sleep with a smile on her face because tomorrow is her birthday. As Kayla drifts into dreamland, all the toys in her bedroom come to life and begin planning a surprise birthday party. From this opening scene, children are transported into the entertaining world of *Fatty Bear's Birthday Surprise*, a CD-ROM that seamlessly combines games, puzzles, and exploration.

Fatty Bear, a brown bear in red overalls, wants to bake a birthday cake and help a doll named Gretchen make party decorations. Meanwhile, a mischievous puppy—one of Kayla's birthday presents—keeps running off with vital bits and pieces of Fatty Bear's projects. So Fatty Bear must wander all through the house, as well as the front yard and backyard, to retrieve the items he needs. The action unfolds through large color animations, with lots of voices and sound effects. Children will constantly stumble on interesting distractions; in the bedroom, for example, is a variation on the classic Mr. Potato Head game where kids stick various eyes, noses, mouths, and hats onto a head of lettuce.

Fatty Bear's Birthday Surprise is recommended for ages three to seven; younger players will probably need parental coaching to complete all the tasks. My only complaint is fuzziness in the audio, which makes the voices sound as if they're coming from a distant radio station. The game also plays the same background music over and over, although the developers have thankfully given parents the option of turning the music off. Along with the CD-ROM, the box for *Fatty Bear's Birthday Surprise* includes a forty-eight-page activity book with brain teasers and pictures to color. As a bonus, there's also a small Fatty Bear flying disk, a little box of crayons, a pencil, and a pencil sharpener.

FATTY BEAR'S FUN PACK
★★★
Developer: Humongous Entertainment Inc.; 206-485-1212
Format: Windows, Macintosh
Price: $19

Parents who buy *Fatty Bear's Fun Pack* for their children may find themselves more than a little embarrassed in struggling to master this selection of five games. The rules are simple enough for children to grasp, but several of the games demand considerable strategic thinking from players of any age. Although advertised for ages three to eight, most of the games are too difficult for preschoolers, who'd be happier with the companion product *Putt-Putt's Fun Pack*, reviewed in this section.

Fatty Bear's Fun Pack is hosted by the character Fatty Bear, star of *Fatty Bear's Birthday Surprise*, reviewed in this section. The most familiar and easiest game among the five is the traditional favorite *Go Fish*. Children can select regular playing cards, number cards, or cards with pictures, a nice option that opens the game to younger children who haven't yet learned numbers. As with the other games, children can also choose to play at the "easy," "medium," "hard," or "hardest" level. At the easy level, the manual explains, "Fatty Bear plays like a parent. In other words, he somewhat controls wins versus losses, so nobody gets too discouraged." At the hardest level, "Fatty Bear has a perfect memory and plays to win."

The other three strategy games are Reversi, where players try to outmaneuver each other in placing colored markers on a grid; Lines and Boxes, where the object is to draw more four-sided boxes than your opponent; and Tangrams, where you must assemble squares and triangles to make larger shapes. The fifth entry isn't really a game; "Fatty Bear's Paint Set" is an on-screen coloring book in which children mix their own colors to illustrate thirty-five different drawings. Throughout the games, presented with amusing color graphics, the voice of Fatty Bear offers children constant encouragement regardless of their performance.

FREDDI FISH AND THE CASE OF THE MISSING KELP SEEDS
★★★½
Developer: Humongous Entertainment Inc.; 206-485-1212
Format: Windows-2
Price: $39

Freddi Fish and The Case of The Missing Kelp Seeds is one of only two children's CD-ROMs I've seen that truly match the rich colors and fluid motion of a good television cartoon show; the other is *TuneLand*, reviewed in this section. Unlike *TuneLand*, in which children passively watch a performance on the computer screen, *Freddi Fish* challenges them to solve a mystery by controlling the action of various characters.

Freddi Fish, who is a girl, visits Grandma Grouper one day and discovers she is distraught over the disappearance of her kelp seeds. To keep Grandma from running out of food, Freddi vows to find the seeds and sets off with her friend Luther. Solving the mystery involves accumulating various objects from characters in the game and picking up objects scattered on the sea floor, then using them at the appropriate time. To get past Eddie the Eel, for example, Freddi must feed him the "peanut butter and jellyfish" sandwich given her by Grandma.

The many scenes in *Freddi Fish*, all accompanied by catchy musical themes, are full of animations; click on a globe, and it turns into a blue egg that hatches a turtle, or click on a coral head to see a fish pop out and swim in a loop. There's even a game called "Starfish Math" hidden in one scene that lets children pick one of five difficulty levels for a series of addition and subtraction problems. For play without a computer, the CD-ROM is packaged with a thirty-two-page activity book offering puzzles and games.

My only complaint with *Freddi Fish*, intended for ages four to nine, is that some of the puzzles may be too hard for younger children. Indeed, even adults may occasionally find themselves swimming back and forth in search of a bone to give the "junkyard dogfish" or an extra purple sea urchin needed to open a locked gate. But both children and adults will have fun searching for the answers, and children who stick with the game will get a great deal of satisfaction from solving the problems on their own.

JUMPSTART KINDERGARTEN
★★
Developer: Knowledge Adventure Inc.; 800-542-4240
Format: DOS
Price: $39

Selling children's software often comes down to manipulating parental guilt, trying to convince Mom and Dad a particular program will help their child do better in school. But most software developers wisely shy away from explicitly declaring their products will boost academic performance, probably to avoid the wrath of parents who don't see an immediate dramatic improvement in little Johnny's or Suzy's schoolwork. Knowledge Adventure Inc. has gone out on a limb, however, with its *JumpStart Kindergarten*, subtitling the program "Getting a Head Start on Kindergarten." The instruction manual touts the CD-ROM as "the first educational software program which covers the entire kindergarten curriculum." Don't believe it. While the sixteen games and activities are educational and occasionally fun, *JumpStart Kindergarten* is a pale imitation of several superior products—such as *The Playroom CD-ROM* and the *Math Rabbit* and *Reader Rabbit* series, reviewed in this chapter—that don't make such grandiose claims. What's more, *JumpStart Kindergarten* is full of minor flaws and throws in a misguided marketing gimmick called *The Adventurers!*, described below.

The main screen of *JumpStart Kindergarten* shows a kindergarten classroom, depicted in unappealing low-resolution computer graphics, in which a rabbit named Mr. Hopsalot is the teacher and guide. Children click on objects in the room to find the various games and activities, such as a coloring book, a clock that tells time, and a stack of alphabet blocks for learning the correct order of letters. The games offer less sound and animation, however, than the best children's CD-ROMs, and some of the activities are downright confusing. In a game called "Sentence Builder," for example, children have to click small pictures on a chalkboard to complete a sentence. But the images are so fuzzy it's difficult to tell what you're looking at — I had a hard time distinguishing between a dog and a sheep and didn't know hearing the word "weird" meant I should point to a drawing of a goggle-eyed man or a wild-haired boy.

JumpStart Kindergarten keeps track of a child's performance in the various games and posts the results in a "Progress Report" that can be displayed on the screen and printed. But the report is strictly statistical—a bar chart showing "attempts and successes" in each activity. I'm turned off by this by-the-numbers approach; there's much more to tracking a child's abilities than performance in computer games. Also, the "Progress Report" is accessed by clicking on a picture in the classroom, making it too easy for children to look at their own charts and possibly get discouraged by any shortcomings. I spotted one other problem: The "reference screen guide," a card included with the CD-ROM intended to show where to click in the classroom for the various activities, appears to have been printed before the design work was finished and contains several errors in pointing to the wrong spot or giving the wrong activity name.

About *The Adventurers!*: In late 1994, Knowledge Adventure began including a kind of children's magazine called *The Adventurers!* on each of its new CD-ROMs. The magazine offers essays, poems, drawings, short musical performances, and brief video clips sent in by children around the world who use Knowledge Adventure products. Kids are always fascinated by the work of other children and will probably enjoy seeing a picture of girls jumping rope drawn by seven-year-old Melissa from Iowa or watching a video clip of eight-year-old Willis from California on his in-line skates. *The Adventurers!* also makes a strong pitch for children to send in their own contribution for a future edition.

But here's the catch: Those future editions, which Knowledge Adventure plans to produce quarterly, are available only by purchasing more Knowledge Adventure products. If the company were genuinely interested in giving children a chance to share their work, *The Adventurers!* would be a stand-alone CD-ROM at a low price—perhaps selling for $5 or $10 a copy—that wouldn't force parents to keep buying one brand of software at $30 to $50 per title. When I raised this issue with representatives of the company in December 1994, they assured me *The Adventurers!* was not developed simply as a sales tactic and said they're looking at other methods of distribution—perhaps through an on-line service or as part of a mass-market CD-ROM magazine—that would resolve my concern.

KID PIX STUDIO
★★★★
Developer: Broderbund Software Inc.; 800-521-6263
Format: Windows, Macintosh
Price: $49

Ever since its introduction on floppy disk in 1990, software companies have been trying to imitate Broderbund Software Inc.'s bestselling *Kid Pix* drawing program for children. So far, none can match the real thing. *Kid Pix Studio*, the CD-ROM version of *Kid Pix*, is a powerful yet child-friendly toy box full of tools for making all kinds of pictures and animations. With dozens of features to explore, children will be hard-pressed to run out of ideas for what to do with this program.

The CD-ROM offers six "projects." Most important is the original *Kid Pix*, in which children paint on a blank screen by selecting from a variety of drawing tools. Every feature has been put together with a fine eye for detail and the needs of younger users; when selecting alphabet blocks to stamp on the screen, for example, each letter is pronounced when the child clicks on it. For children who need a creative boost, there is a "draw me" feature that throws out random ideas for pictures, such as "I'm a laughing volcano with a bright and bumpy hide and I love to dance." There is also a library of seventeen coloring book pages.

Games and Activities

> The other five projects revolve around animation. "Wacky TV" presents a library of one hundred video clips, most running only a few seconds, that can be inserted into drawings. The clips range from a group of children practicing yoga to a "video postcard" of the Big Foot monster truck with its ten-foot tires. "Moopies" lets children insert animated objects into a drawing, such as a tree waving its branches or a dog bone twirling in a circle. "Stampinator" offers a selection of animated rubber stamps so that a bird will flap its wings as it moves across the screen. "Digital Puppets" contains ten marionettelike characters that can be manipulated by tapping on the keyboard. Finally, "Slide Show" pulls it all together. Children can combine a series of illustrations, sounds, animations, and video clips to tell a story through the computer.
>
> Broderbund recommends *Kid Pix Studio* for ages three to twelve and provides a clearly written seventy-page manual documenting all the features, even though all but the youngest users should be able to figure out *Kid Pix Studio* just by experimenting. And that's the true value of *Kid Pix Studio* —by encouraging children to experiment, it helps their minds grow in ways most computer and video games can't touch.

KIDS ON SITE
★★½
Developer: Digital Pictures Inc.; 800-262-5020
Format: DOS-2, Macintosh-2
Price: $29

At age six, one of my favorite weekend activities was visiting construction sites, where I would climb on the bulldozers and steamrollers, pretending I was running these big machines. Children still dream of operating construction equipment, but today's construction sites are generally surrounded by fences and patrolled by guards to keep curious youngsters at a safe distance.

Kids On Site tries to fill the gap by offering children a chance to run four heavy machines through video clips. But the challenge is too easy—even the youngest children won't need more than an hour to see all the video and complete the game. Nor are most children likely to be interested in playing more than once because the action is the same every time. What's more, the quality of the video clips is disappointing, with a grainy look somewhat like watching television through a screen door.

The CD-ROM opens with a construction chief named Bertha introducing you to a pair of hapless workers named Dizzy and Nuts. You then choose one of four machines to operate: Eddie the Excavator, Billy the Bulldozer, Melvin the Steamroller, or Ruby the Wrecking Ball. The controls, however, are limited to just three buttons: a button to turn left, a button to turn right, and an "action" button to make the machine do its thing. With Billy the Bulldozer, for example, you turn in a circle until you locate a pile of junk, then hit the action button to push the junk into a ditch. Once you complete this task, you get a "merit badge"; collecting merit badges for all four machines qualifies you for a non-interactive reward: You click the mouse button once to watch a large building getting blown up.

There's lots of comic relief in *Kids On Site*, mostly at the expense of Nuts. You get to dump dirt on Nuts with the excavator, smash his car with the bulldozer, and knock him on the head with the wrecking ball. Children under age eight will undoubtedly enjoy this mayhem the first time through. I just wish *Kids On Site* had constructed a reason for children to visit a second time.

KID'S ZOO
★★½
Developer: Knowledge Adventure Inc.; 800-542-4240
Format: DOS
Price: $39

Kid's Zoo is something like a baby animal—cute, but not yet fully functional. This CD-ROM offers color photographs of small animals and extensive audio narration aimed at preschoolers. You're even welcomed to the program by the voice of a small child declaring, "Ready to click on someone your own size?"

Although there is a long list of games and activities in *Kid's Zoo*, the content doesn't show much creativity or storytelling ability. The "Talking Storybook," for example, opens with the fundamental question "Which came first, the chicken or the egg?" In twenty on-screen pages, the question is restated several times while children see a progression of photographs. The last page lamely declares, "It's a pretty tough question," leaving children without any kind of an answer.

The games, too, are simple and uninspired. "Who Am I?" asks children to look at a close-up picture of a small part of an animal and pick the animal from a collection of smaller pictures around the screen's edges. "Who Makes This Sound?" plays the sound of an animal and again asks the child to identify the picture—"baa baa," for instance, goes with the lamb. "Can You Find Me?" pronounces the name of an animal, leaving children to pick it out from several shown on the screen. "Where Do I Live?" displays a map of the world, challenging children to select the right continent for each animal.

The "Kid's Zoo Encyclopedia" is the central reference. Children can select which animals they want to see by type or size or lifespan, with each animal pictured in the center of the screen. Moving the mouse over the picture produces text balloons about the animal, which are then read out loud. The "Animal Dictionary" presents thumbnail photographs of all the creatures on the CD-ROM, but the photographs—surprisingly—aren't linked to the encyclopedia. Clicking on the photo of a bear cub in the dictionary should take you to the encyclopedia screen on bear cubs, but it doesn't. Within the dictionary is another matching game called "Photo Safari." Overall, younger children are likely to enjoy *Kid's Zoo* for a few hours but won't find enough to keep them coming back.

THE MANHOLE CD-ROM MASTERPIECE EDITION
★★½

Developer: Broderbund Software Inc./Cyan Inc.; 800-521-6263
Format: Macintosh
Price: $35

The Manhole CD-ROM Masterpiece Edition is beautiful to look at but doesn't go anywhere. This point-and-click exploring game for children is full of modest surprises yet never delivers enough punch to overcome youngsters' notoriously short attention span. First released on floppy disk in 1988, *The Manhole* was extensively revamped with new graphics, sound, and music for a rerelease on CD-ROM in April 1994. Fans of the best-selling game *Myst*, reviewed in Chapter Three, Section a, will recognize the high-gloss look of *The Manhole* —that's because both games were created by brothers Rand and Robyn Miller.

Strange things are always happening in *The Manhole*. At the beginning, you click on a manhole cover and watch a Jack and the Beanstalk vine quickly grow out of the hole. You can then go up the vine to visit a mysterious castle in the sky or go down to an island where the vine has its roots. Various animals materialize with offhand remarks. Deep in the castle, for example, you find Mr. Dragon, wearing granny glasses and a peace sign around his neck. "Hey, baby, welcome to my cool pad!" he booms. Click on his sneakers and they change into fuzzy-bear slippers. Click on the peace sign and he disappears.

All the backgrounds are rendered with stunning photorealistic graphics, so you'll see shimmering reflections on the surface of a pool and fine veins in marble walls. Every scene is accompanied by music and convincing sound effects, such as the trickling of a paddle dipped into water when you're riding in a canoe. The animals, in contrast, are portrayed in cartoon-style drawings, which look out of place superimposed on the highly detailed graphics. More important, the lack of structure in *The Manhole* quickly gets tiresome—you might be enjoying an exploration of Mr. Rabbit's cottage, for example, when you click on a picture of Mr. Dragon and are suddenly sent on an involuntary one-way trip back to Mr. Dragon's lair.

PUTT-PUTT GOES TO THE MOON
★★★
Developer: Humongous Entertainment Inc.; 206-485-1212
Format: Windows, Macintosh
Price: $39

Another adventure for Putt-Putt the purple convertible, following his debut in *Putt-Putt Joins the Parade*, reviewed in this section. Putt-Putt and his dog, Pep, decide to visit the Cartown fireworks factory, where an accident sends the pair shooting to the moon on top of a giant firecracker. They meet Rover, a lunar vehicle left behind by astronauts, and the three come up with a plan to get home: They'll buy an old rocket, converted to an ice-cream stand by a friendly two-headed alien, and fly it home. But first they have to collect ten "glowing moon crystals" and some rocket parts, with many fascinating puzzles standing in their way.

As with the first Putt-Putt title, *Putt-Putt Goes to the Moon* is designed for ages three to seven. Younger children are likely to need considerable parental intervention to solve some of the puzzles and keep moving through the story, but the CD-ROM is amusing enough that parents won't mind tagging along. Some of the puzzles, by the way, require persistent exploration more than skill—to trigger the fireworks accident, for example, you have to click on a butterfly floating outside the factory window. The butterfly then flutters inside, Pep jumps out of Putt-Putt's backseat to give chase, and the dog unintentionally pushes a big lever marked "Do Not Touch!" Inside the box with the CD-ROM is a forty-eight-page activity book, a Putt-Putt pen, a Putt-Putt sticker, and a washable Putt-Putt tattoo.

PUTT-PUTT JOINS THE PARADE
★★★
Developer: Humongous Entertainment Inc.; 206-485-1212
Format: DOS, Macintosh
Price: $39

A playful introduction to problem solving, *Putt-Putt Joins the Parade* is full of challenging puzzles for the preschool set. Putt-Putt is a small purple convertible with a child's voice who wants to march in the annual Cartown Pet Parade. But first he needs to acquire a balloon and a puppy. With help from friendly Smokey the Fire Engine, Putt-Putt sets out to mow lawns and deliver groceries to raise the necessary cash.

What makes the story so much fun is colorful cartoonlike illustrations and clever animations in each scene. At the story's beginning, for instance, Putt-Putt wakes up in his garage. Click on the curtains and they pull back, revealing a frog on the windowsill. Click on the frog, and its tongue shoots out to catch a fly that has been buzzing in the background. Putt-Putt then eats a breakfast of Tire-Os cereal, using his antenna to hold the spoon, while the radio plays the Tire-Os' jingle: "Tire-Os are yummy, Tire-Os are sweet. Eat them with your motor oil, but don't spill them on your feet."

As Putt-Putt goes from scene to scene, children must figure out how to overcome a variety of obstacles. When a cow blocks the road, for example, you have to honk the horn to get her to move. Designed for ages three to seven, the youngest players might need some help from parents to get through the story, but they'll still enjoy all the entertaining animations and dialogue. Included in the box with the CD-ROM is a forty-eight-page activity book with connect-the-dots, word puzzles, and other games, as well as a small Putt-Putt flying disc.

PUTT-PUTT'S FUN PACK
★★★½

Developer: Humongous Entertainment Inc.; 206-485-1212
Format: DOS, Macintosh
Price: $19

Sometimes the best games are the simplest. That's the virtue of *Putt-Putt's Fun Pack*, a reasonably priced collection of six games for young children. The colorfully illustrated and animated games are so straightforward that even preschoolers will learn each of them in only a few minutes, yet they are compelling enough to provide hours of amusement.

Your guide to the games is Putt-Putt the car, the star of two children's CD-ROMs—*Putt-Putt Joins the Parade* and *Putt-Putt Goes to the Moon*—reviewed in this section. In Checkers, children face off against Putt-Putt, pointing and clicking with the mouse to move the pieces around the board. In Cheese King, a variation on Hangman, children see a picture of an object—a mountain or a loaf of bread—and must then select the correct letters from an on-screen alphabet. In Pinball, children put bumpers on a pinball table, controlling how a ball bounces down the screen. In Puzzle Blocks, children see a scrambled picture made up of nine cubes. Each cube has six sides; by clicking on the cubes, children find the correct side to unscramble the pictures. In Remember, the goal is clicking on squares in a grid to find pairs of objects. In Tic-Tac-Toe, children again face Putt-Putt in the classic duel of Xs and Os.

Four of the games—Checkers, Cheese King, Remember, and Tic-Tac-Toe—allow children to select from one of four difficulty levels: Easy, Medium, Hard, and Hardest. It's a wonderful way to appeal to everyone in the CD-ROM's suggested age range of three to eight. Putt-Putt is also an infinitely patient and encouraging playmate. He's always congratulating children on finishing a game and never criticizes a wrong move.

RODNEY'S WONDER WINDOW
★★

Developer: Voyager Co.; 800-446-2001
Format: Windows, Macintosh
Price: $29

Rodney's Wonder Window has the awkward feel of art created by adults for other adults while deliberately imitating the style of art for children. New York artist Rodney Alan Greenblat has created twenty-three "windows," each offering a different experience in sight and sound. Some of these windows are exceedingly dull and ordinary, while a few are intriguingly off-kilter. On the dull side is the "hamster" window—you see a full-screen, full-color picture of a hamster cage. Click on the hamster, and it takes a drink of water from its bottle, eats a few food pellets, and goes for a spin on its wheel. On the off-kilter side is "Bignose." Clicking and dragging with the mouse, you stuff objects—a pepper shaker, a corn cob, a frog—into a man's large nostril while he makes appropriate snorting noises. When you've put in all ten of these objects, he sneezes them back out. It's in poor taste, so most kids will probably love it.

Few of the windows are this interesting, however. Some are passive, leaving you simply watching a short story unfold on the screen. Most children, I suspect, will get through *Rodney's Wonder Window* in an hour or two without any interest in returning. Finally, a warning to parents: The window on "tooli bugs" describes the reproductive cycle of these fictitious insects. If you aren't ready to explain the facts of life to your child, you might want to skip over this window, which shows a blue male tooli bug mounting a pink female tooli bug to create offspring called "knoblings."

SAMMY'S SCIENCE HOUSE
★★★½
Developer: Edmark Corp.; 800-362-2890
Format: DOS, Windows, Macintosh
Price: $35

Part of the excellent *Early-Learning Neighborhood* series, fully described in the review of *Bailey's Book House* in Section a. *Sammy's Science House*, intended for ages three to six, is hosted by a friendly blue snake named Sammy who introduces five activities. "Workshop" teaches pattern recognition by asking children to assemble objects such as a boat or a dinosaur skeleton from a simple group of parts. "Weather Machine" lets children select the temperature, cloud cover, and wind speed and see what kind of weather results—specifying a cold, snowy, windy day produces a ten-second cartoon animation of a blizzard. "Sorting Station" demonstrates scientific classification by challenging children to sort a group of pictures, differentiating, for example, between animals with tails and animals without tails. "Make-A-Movie" emphasizes logical thinking as children arrange three or four still pictures in proper order to make a short movie and then see the movie if they get the sequence right. "Acorn Pond" is a guide to the world of nature, showing how animals go through the four seasons around a small pond. The animals are described in an on-screen "Field Notebook" filled with interesting facts, such as "Deer lose their antlers each winter. New ones with more branches will grow."

Unlike the other Early-Learning Neighborhood titles, *Sammy's Science House* does not have an on-screen "Adult Information Notebook." But the same information and suggestions for further activities are in the print manual, including this overview of Acorn Pond: "Living things hold a special fascination for young children. Initially, children are curious about animal babies, where animals sleep, what they eat and what sounds they make. Later, they become more aware of the relationship of a specific animal to its environment. Acorn Pond helps prepare children for increasingly complex ideas about nature and the environment while encouraging children's innate interest in living things. As children observe seasonal changes of plants and animals, they develop a sense for the cyclical nature of living things."

A SILLY NOISY HOUSE
★★★½
Developer: Voyager Co.; 800-446-2001
Format: Windows, Macintosh
Price: $39

Preschool children will make themselves right at home in *A Silly Noisy House*. Populated by a family of teddy bears, the CD-ROM is described by Voyager Company as "an animated audio toybox."

Every room, depicted in color cartoons filling half the screen, is packed with activities. In the living room, for example, clicking a book on the coffee table calls up a musical matching game in which children try to link up eight pairs of sounds. In the bathroom, a scale recites the poem "One, Two, Buckle My Shoe." In the kitchen, a group of children sing "Twinkle, Twinkle, Little Star" while the pots and pans bounce along in time. In the bedroom, clicking the cradle brings a rendition of "Rock-a-bye, Baby." Clicking a spider web in the attic launches a performance of "Itsy-Bitsy Spider." Even the smallest objects on screen are linked to interesting sounds; clicking a conch shell in the bedroom summons the crash of ocean waves.

All the features in *A Silly Noisy House* require nothing more than pointing and clicking, so even three-year-olds should be able to play on their own, assuming that you're confident they won't smear peanut butter on the keyboard or stick chocolate chip cookies in the disk-drive slot.

THINKIN' THINGS COLLECTION 1
★★★

Developer: Edmark Corp.; 800-362-2890
Format: DOS, Windows, Macintosh
Price: $39

An interesting collection of six activities, intended for ages four to eight, aimed at developing important but nonquantifiable skills such as spatial reasoning and pattern recognition. The activities are fun, although they are so simple and repetitive that young minds may wander after a short session in front of the computer. Edmark Corporation, developer of *Thinkin' Things Collection 1*, helps parents prepare for just such an occasion by including suggestions for noncomputer activities in the print manual.

The six activities are "Oranga Banga," in which a big orangutan sits at a drum set. After playing a few notes, he invites children to copy his sequence on the drums, cymbal, triangle, and other instruments. "Toony Loon" is a similar game with a xylophone that can be changed from regular metal bars to a row of wineglasses, hollow logs, rubber bands, or chickens. "Blox-Flying Spheres" lets children unleash colored spheres that bounce around the screen in directions determined by dragging the mouse. "Blox-Flying Shapes" is a similar activity with triangles, squares, and rectangles instead of spheres, with the additional options of making the shapes spin and recording your own sounds for each object, provided a microphone is hooked to your computer. "Feathered Friends" helps develop logical thinking by requiring children to look for patterns in groups of cartoon birds. In a row of birds, for example, the first bird may have a dotted body, the second a striped body, and the third a dotted body. The child is asked what the fourth bird in the row should look like and must select a striped body. "Fripple Shop" also tests pattern recognition by displaying a shop wall stocked with a dozen fripples, little cartoon creatures with varied features. By clicking on the phone, a fax machine, or the shop door, children hear or see a customer place an order such as "Sell me a fripple with curly hair and small eyes but no stripes." The child must then select a fripple meeting all these conditions.

Three of the activities—"Oranga Banga," "Feathered Friends," and "Toony Loon"—have a "create" mode, in which children can simply play at picking out notes or designing birds without having to answer any questions. Four of the activities—"Oranga Banga," "Fripple Shop," "Feathered Friends," and "Toony Loon"— have "grow slides" that adjust the difficulty so children can face an increased challenge once they master the simplest level.

The manual includes a section called "Together Time" for each activity, with suggestions for parent-child games. Here's a sample of a noncomputer game from the section on Fripple Shop: "You and your child can have fun looking at family photographs while strengthening visual discrimination skills. Place three different photographs on a table. Start with simple questions such as, 'Can you find a picture with both people and animals?' or 'Where is a picture with stripes and shoes with laces?' At another time, you might make the questions more complex. 'Which one has buildings and people but no trees?' Change the selections of photographs after every three or four questions."

A companion CD-ROM called *Thinkin' Things Collection 2*, with activities aimed at ages six through twelve, is due in early 1995.

TUNELAND
★★★
Developer: 7th Level Inc.; 800-884-8863
Format: Windows
Price: $39

TuneLand is just like a Saturday-morning cartoon show. That's a compliment for the CD-ROM's sharp animations, rich musical score, and fast pace. But it's also a mild rebuke for the shallow content of *TuneLand*, a place where preschool children can experience forty-two traditional nursery rhymes such as "Twinkle, Twinkle, Little Star" and "Three Blind Mice."

The host of *TuneLand* is Lil' Howie, a cartoon bear with a voice provided by comedian Howie Mandel, electronically altered to make him sound like an eight-year-old. Lil' Howie is constantly dashing around the screen, and almost every scene is full of movement—I counted a dozen animals bobbing up and down during "Old MacDonald Had a Farm." From the opening scene of a barnyard, children click on various characters or buildings to visit one of seven locations: the farmhouse, barn, pond, Grandma's house, train station, mountain, and pasture. At each place, five or six songs await. Most objects on the screen are active—click on a chimney, and it coughs; click on a bucket, and a frog jumps out; click on a kettle, and it sings, "I'm a Little Teapot."

There are even some very old comedy routines. Lil' Howie tells knock-knock jokes, while a small turtle asks, "Why did the chicken cross the road?" and "What do you call a sleeping bull?" (Answers, for the truly joke-impaired: "To get to the other side" and "A bulldozer.") These jokes were funny the first time we heard them—and this material is likely to seem fresh for children under eight, the age range I'd pick for *TuneLand*. The CD-ROM also includes a helpful feature called "*TuneLand* Jukebox," which presents a point-and-click menu for all forty-two songs.

My only significant gripe is that *TuneLand* doesn't try to fight the short attention span of TV-addicted children. All the songs have been stripped down to less than a minute, taking some of the soul from these bedtime classics. It's disconcerting to hear "Itsy Bitsy Spider" in only fifty seconds, "Row, Row, Row Your Boat" crammed into thirty-five seconds, and "Little Bo Peep" boiled down to twenty-five seconds.

ZURK'S RAINFOREST LAB
★★★
Developer: Soleil Software Inc.; 800-697-2366
Format: Windows, Macintosh
Price: $39

A gentle and charmingly offbeat introduction to the jungle animals of South America, *Zurk's Rainforest Lab* offers an interesting mix of games and activities that both children and parents will find engaging. The CD-ROM certainly looks different from most other children's software, largely because the program displays hand-painted watercolors rather than photographs or computer-generated scenery. And, although the CD-ROM contains only a small amount of animation, the watercolor illustrations gain impact through a soundtrack that plays authentic jungle sounds.

Zurk's Rainforest Lab, which is intended for ages five to nine, contains four games. "Jungle Discovery" lets children roam up and down from the ground to the treetops, clicking on the many animals to learn about them. Picking a large green insect, for instance, summons a text window explaining: "The scarab beetle is a scavenger. It eats droppings from animals, especially cattle. People collect scarabs because they are so beautiful, but this may cause them to become extinct." In the "Egg Hunt" game, children search through another jungle scene for eleven hidden eggs. "Seek and Sort" challenges children to decide whether the animals they see are mammals, insects, reptiles, or birds. "Pattern Puzzles" is the only activity unrelated to the rain forest theme; it's a variation on the popular children's game of "tangrams," in which geometric shapes have to be moved and rotated to match a preset pattern. Children can also use the mouse to take "pictures" of the animals they encounter; those pictures are displayed in the "Photo Album," which can also display the descriptive text and lets children add their own notes or stories.

The CD-ROM is named for a rotund character in overalls named Zurk, although he makes only a few appearances. His main contribution is offering a vocabulary of fifteen words in English, French, and Spanish; by clicking on either a cowboy hat, beret, or sombrero, children can hear him say "goodbye" or "au revoir" or "hasta luego." Parents will appreciate the helpful thirty-eight-page instruction manual, full of hints on how to share in the games with children and offering suggestions for supplemental activities, along with a glossary and bibliography.

Chapter Two:
Older Children

Although there are many excellent CD-ROMs for older children in this section, the single best investment parents can make for children ages ten to sixteen is the CD-ROM encyclopedias covered in Chapter Four, Section a.

a. Learning Games and Tools

AMERICA ADVENTURE
★★★½
Developer: Knowledge Adventure Inc.; 800-542-4240
Format: DOS
Price: $35

America Adventure is an amusing and comprehensive tour that will teach elementary-school students almost everything they need to know about the United States. The CD-ROM, recommended by the developer for age six and above, contains hundreds of entries on history, people, arts, food, geography, and the presidents. You can discover, for example, that pizza came to the U.S. in 1905 when Gennaro Lombardi began serving the dish at his restaurant in New York's Little Italy. Or you can learn about the formation of the Grand Canyon and how it became a national park in 1919. The text accompanying most of these entries fills three or four paragraphs, a vast improvement over the skimpy three or four sentences in some other Knowledge Adventure titles.

Three games in *America Adventure* will lure children into effortless education. "Match the Capitals" and "Find the State" display an outline map of the U.S. Children are given quiz questions and must click on the correct state. "Where Is?" offers a multiple-choice quiz on cities—to answer the question "Where is the Liberty Bell?" children must pick Philadelphia instead of Boston or Washington, D.C.

Two other clever features are included. "America Grows Up" shows how population has increased in every decade from 1790 to 1990, coloring each state by population density. "The Presidents" is a morph of the nation's forty-two chief executives. Starting with George Washington, you see the face of each president melt and transform into his successor. The whole progession takes only a minute, but it's fascinating—and even a little scary—to see Dwight Eisenhower transformed into John F. Kennedy or Jimmy Carter rearranged to become Ronald Reagan.

The only weak spot in *America Adventure* is the collection of 15 video clips. The excerpts are too short; Martin Luther King, Jr.'s 1963 "I Have a Dream" speech is given only fifteen seconds, and the flight of a Wright Brothers airplane gets only ten seconds. For more information on common features of the Knowledge Adventure series, see the review of *3-D Dinosaur Adventure* in Section b.

MICROSOFT ANCIENT LANDS
★★★
Developer: Microsoft Corp.; 800-426-9400
Format: Windows
Price: $59

Microsoft Ancient Lands provides a fascinating, although often shallow, trip through ancient Egypt, Greece, and Rome. Microsoft has made an admirable effort to cover these empires from many angles, dividing information into three categories: "Monuments & Mysteries," covering architecture; "Work and Play," describing ordinary life; and "People & Politics," reviewing key historical events. Text and high-resolution color graphics are combined on full-screen pages, with lots of arrows pointing to related subjects. While in the screen describing the Egyptian board game Senet, for example, you can click a button transporting you to another screen describing the "Olympian" games of ancient Greece that became our modern Olympics. For children who don't want to explore alone, there are "guides"—fictional characters from each time period who talk about themselves while displaying relevant on-screen pages.

Some features of *Ancient Lands*, however, need work. Video clips and animations are displayed in a window filling half the screen. At that large size, the images often break down into ugly squares, somewhat like looking at a television through a screen door. Also, children interested in a particular topic will quickly run into blank walls. The section on mad Roman emperors, for example, covers only Nero and Caligula. The entry on Caligula is just three sentences: "Perhaps the craziest emperor was Caligula. He once led soldiers on a campaign to conquer the ocean! To prove his victory, he ordered his troops to collect seashells." We aren't told when Caligula ruled or how his bizarre behavior affected the Roman Empire. *Ancient Lands* is a valuable tool for sparking children's interest in ancient history, but parents will need to provide further resources once that spark turns into a flame.

ANNO'S LEARNING GAMES
★★★
Developer: Putnam New Media; 800-788-6262
Format: Windows, Macintosh
Price: $29

With seven activities to choose from, children are sure to find something they like in *Anno's Learning Games*, while parents will be happy the games and puzzles are designed to help strengthen math skills. The CD-ROM, intended for ages six to ten, is based on the book *Anno's Math Games* by Japanese children's author and illustrator Mitsumasa Anno.

Two animated elves named Kriss and Kross guide children through the colorfully illustrated games, which fill half the screen. "Sevens In A Row" puts the child in competition with three computer-created players to lay out playing cards in numerical order. In a nice side feature, children can create their own deck for the game by selecting different suits—so they can see a nine of penguins or a queen of carrots. "Guess My Rule" is a brain teaser in which children must deduce what groups of objects have in common; recognizing, for example, that a shovel, pot, and suitcase are all objects with handles. "Guessing Machine" tells children to think of a word, then attempt to guess the word through a series of "yes or no" questions. At first, the machine is frequently stumped. But it asks children to enter the correct answer and gradually improves its performance. "Storymaker" lets children pick among a group of characters and assign them different attributes, then hear the characters described in a five-sentence nonsense poem. A polka-dot alligator, for example, might go to the beach with a "very cool" egg wearing dark sunglasses. "Tangrams" is a puzzle in which children must move either five or seven geometric shapes across the screen to fill out a pattern. "Water Balloons" calls for children to maneuver Kross back and forth across the bottom of the screen to catch falling water balloons. The game starts out simply, but progresses through ten levels that will challenge even the most nimble player. "Weighing" requires children to match objects with their correct weight; recognizing, for example, that a tadpole weighs less than a snail.

I'd be surprised if a child liked all seven of these games; personally, I think "Guessing Machine" and "Weighing" are a bore. But I'd also be surprised if a child didn't find at least two or three of the games worthy of frequent play. Finally, I'd caution parents that, although Kriss and Kross give explanations for all the games, some are complicated enough that younger children might need some help from Mom and Dad to get started.

CAPITOL HILL
★★½
Developer: Mindscape Inc.; 800-234-3088
Format: Windows, Macintosh
Price: $35

Capitol Hill does something for our elected officials that they can't do for themselves: whitewash the soiled reputation of Congress. Apparently aimed at the junior-high age level, the CD-ROM presents an almost purely theoretical view of the House and Senate, glossing over the corrupting influence of campaign financing and highly paid lobbyists. I don't want to come across as overly cynical, but even children deserve to know the deficiencies as well as the strengths of our democracy.

Cleverly designed, *Capitol Hill* opens by asking you to enter your name and the state you live in. The program responds by displaying a newspaper headline on the screen proclaiming your election to the House of Representatives. Then you're off to Washington, going through all the steps to become a member of Congress—taking the oath of office, selecting an office, and hiring a staff. In the "orientation" section, you watch a series of narrated slide shows on the structure of the legislative branch and the process of turning a bill into law. In your office, you look through a calendar to see all the activities expected of a congressperson. The one bit of reality I spotted was an appointment to attend a colleague's fund-raiser. "Asking people to donate money to other members of Congress is part of the legislative process," the anonymous narrator explains. "Building relationships like this bears fruit when you need that one vote to move a bill out of committee." Representative Lynn Woolsey, a Democrat from California, pops up occasionally in a postage-stamp-size video window to offer superficial comments, such as how the members of Congress have undying respect for each other.

There's also a self-guided tour of the Capitol, combining still pictures with video clips, and a quiz game called "Power Play." Throughout *Capitol Hill*, you randomly receive a stream of letters and phone calls from constituents and lobbyists and are occasionally summoned to vote on a piece of legislation. I voted in favor of a bill tightening the penalties for sexual harassment, after which the program told me the bill passed by a vote of 273 to 158.

What *Capitol Hill* does, it does well. I'm more troubled by what's missing. First, the disk fails to delve into the harsh political realities of Congress. Second, the content isn't very deep—most children will experience all of *Capitol Hill* in a few hours. Third, the disk lists the members of House and Senate delegations by state, along with committee leaders, based on the Democrat-controlled Congress of 1992–1994. Much of that information became obsolete with the swearing-in of the new Republican-controlled Congress in January 1995.

WHERE IN THE USA IS CARMEN SANDIEGO? CD-ROM
★★★½
Developer: Broderbund Software Inc.; 800-521-6263
Format: Windows, Macintosh
Price: $49

Carmen Sandiego is a software phenomenon. The series of children's learning games, first released on floppy disk in 1985 by Broderbund Software Inc., is one of the all-time best-sellers in the category and went on to become the first computer game popular enough for the big leap into television. Indeed, Carmen Sandiego has inspired two television programs: a children's game show on the Public Broadcasting System and a cartoon series on the Fox network. What makes Carmen run? The series of games from Broderbund achieves that rare balance of fun that appeals to children and educational value that appeals to parents.

The Carmen games all have a similar format. Carmen Sandiego is a mysterious master criminal in a red sports car who, with a gang called V.I.L.E., steals historical objects. Children are put in the role of sleuths for the Acme detective agency who must gather clues to track down the various V.I.L.E. miscreants, with colorful names such as Armand Geddon and Dee Molish. To figure out which V.I.L.E. member to arrest, children must dig up geographical information. Young detectives have to solve a series of cases before the final confrontation with Carmen herself.

Where in the USA is Carmen Sandiego? CD-ROM presents an awesome three thousand clues so players can hunt V.I.L.E. gang members for weeks without encountering repetition. Children push on-screen buttons to summon information about their case from Acme and travel to the fifty states in search of clues. Each state, as well as the District of Columbia, is illustrated with a color photograph that fills a quarter of the screen, along with a sound clip of the state's folk music. Cartoon animations of witnesses and V.I.L.E. gang members pop up occasionally, superimposed on the photographs, to keep things lively.

The clues tell Acme detectives where to head next and provide information about the criminal. Each V.I.L.E. member is given six defining characteristics—hair color, eye color, hobby, favorite food, favorite sport, and favorite music—that are listed in the game's manual and must be entered to obtain a search warrant prior to making an arrest. Usually, children will be able to figure out the correct suspect after learning two or three of these characteristics.

Here's how one case works: The chief at Acme tells you the swallows have been stolen from Capistrano. That sends you to California, where you get a tip—"He was burnin' to see Mt. Vernon, George Washington's estate." You then go to Virginia and are told, "I knew he was a shark when he asked directions to the Baltimore National Aquarium." So you're off to Maryland, where the clue is "He bragged that the alligators in the Everglades would be more scared of him than he'd be of them. He said he loved Latin American rhythms." Only two males in V.I.L.E. like Latin American music—Hal E. Luya and Hugo Yurway—so now you've narrowed down the suspect list and head to Florida for more clues.

Children will painlessly absorb a considerable amount of knowledge while playing the game but will never feel they're being forced to learn. To help in the quest, the CD-ROM comes with *The World Almanac of the U.S.A.*, a 410-page paperback reference. Broderbund recommends the Carmen games for age nine to adult; I'd agree that nine is a good starting point, but I don't expect Carmen's lure will extend much beyond age twelve. Another title in the series, *Where in the World is Carmen Sandiego? CD-ROM*, is reviewed in this section.

WHERE IN THE WORLD IS CARMEN SANDIEGO? CD-ROM
★★★½
Developer: Broderbund Software Inc.; 800-521-6263
Format: Windows, Macintosh
Price: $49

Another burst of larceny from archcrook Carmen Sandiego matching *Where in the USA is Carmen Sandiego? CD-ROM*, reviewed in this section. *Where in the World?* takes Acme detectives to sixty countries in search of nineteen V.I.L.E. members, with a total of four thousand clues. The CD-ROM comes with *The Kingfisher Reference Atlas: An A-Z Guide to Countries of the World*, a 215-page paperback reference with extensive color maps and charts.

THE CARTOON HISTORY OF THE UNIVERSE, VOLUMES 1–7
★★★
Developer: Putnam New Media; 800-631-8571
Format: Windows, Macintosh
Price: $39

Adopting an irreverent and entertaining approach to history, *The Cartoon History of the Universe, Volumes 1–7*, is a living comic book covering everything from the Big Bang about 13 billion years ago through the conquests of Alexander the Great in 330 B.C. Intended for ages ten and above, the two-disk CD-ROM set presents almost five hours of narrated stories ranging from the first fish that crawled onto land to the pyramid builders of ancient Egypt.

A fuzzy-haired character named The Professor guides you through the seven volumes, titled *The Evolution of Everything, Sticks and Stones, River Realms, The Old Testament, Brains and Bronze, Who Are These Athenians?*, and *All About Athens*. The Professor reads the text on each comic-book-like page in a high-pitched, singsong voice that becomes grating after long stretches of listening. But the pages themselves are fascinating, full of animations that make the stories come to life. And The Professor takes a refreshingly casual approach, such as this explanation for why *Cartoon History* recounts several Greek myths: "Even if they're not true, they can tell us something about the people who made them up. So, with that pitiful excuse, here is the Greeks' own version of the collapse of Mykenae. It's not history, but it's not bad." *Cartoon History* then tells the legend of Oedipus, who killed his father and married his mother.

Along with the seven-volume history, the two CD-ROMs offer seventeen short games, such as reassembling a pyramid, stumbling through the maze of the Minotaur, and commanding an Athenian trireme warship in battle. The games are a pleasant distraction, although they aren't deep enough to occupy children for more than fifteen minutes or a half hour.

As a package, however, the stories and games in *Cartoon History* will provide many hours of educational fun for both children and adults. For adults who want to prevent their children from seeing all the details of illicit historical romances, there is a "parental guidance" option to lock out the very modest sex scenes. One final warning: *Cartoon History* wants a big chunk of your hard disk in exchange for covering such a broad span of time; the Windows version requires almost twenty megabytes and the Macintosh version ten megabytes.

CREATIVE WRITER
★½
Developer: Microsoft Corp.; 800-426-9400
Format: Windows, Macintosh
Price: $49

Creative Writer is a confusing and condescending attempt to provide children with a word processor that also helps them think of ideas for their compositions. The CD-ROM goes way over the line in trying to be cute and wacky, ignoring the values of simplicity and respect for users. Intended for ages eight and above, *Creative Writer* is full of unnecessary cartoon animations that stand in the path of young authors. A bug-eyed purple character named McZee guides children through four floors in a rickety old building: the Writing Studio, the Project Workshop, the Library, and the Idea Workshop.

The Writing Studio is the place where children actually put down their words. But this doesn't look like any conventional word processor; all the controls are replaced by icons. To figure out what to do, children must constantly click on McZee for explanations. What's worse, the program talks down to children by using silly euphemisms for terms that kids are perfectly capable of learning—instead of describing text as "bold" or "italic," for example, *Creative Writer* uses the terms "dark" and "slanty."

In the Project Workshop, children can make newspapers,

greeting cards, or banners. The Library supplies a number of prewritten stories and suggestions for stories. And the Idea Workshop offers a "magic combobulator" that generates random sentences, supposedly to help children overcome writer's block. But I don't see any particular value in looking at a sentence such as "The graceful mother got angry into the shark's jaws." The CD-ROM also supplies six hundred clip-art images and three hundred sound effects for dressing up documents.

Children deserve programs full of more than corny humor and whizzy animations. They deserve a program that takes them and their work seriously. I was particularly bothered by a story in which McZee described himself as the creative spark for great authors such as Charles Dickens and Victor Hugo, a bizarre bit of egotism that even small children will have trouble believing.

MICROSOFT EXPLORAPEDIA: THE WORLD OF NATURE
★★★
Developer: Microsoft Corp.; 800-426-9400
Format: Windows
Price: $35

Microsoft Explorapedia: The World of Nature was released in December 1994 as the first in an open-ended series of what Microsoft Corporation calls a "children's interactive encyclopedia" designed for ages six to ten. But this isn't a junior version of the excellent *Microsoft Encarta '95*, reviewed in Chapter Four, Section a. Shunning the typical encyclopedia's structure—numerous text articles arranged in alphabetical order—each title in the *Explorapedia* series will focus on a single subject area, substituting extensive audio narration, video clips, animations, songs, and games for heavy dependence on text. It's a promising concept appropriate for younger children, even though it delivers much less depth than *Encarta*.

The World of Nature covers the realm of plants and animals through four thousand on-screen pages. Each animal and plant is covered by several on-screen pages containing a color picture and just one or two sentences of text. The first page of the entry on pigs, for example, declares: "Many people mistakenly think pigs are sloppy, dirty and greedy. Pigs are actually very clean animals and do not overeat." So why do we always see pigs rolling on the ground? The answer is on the next page: "A pig's reputation as a dirty animal may come from its habit of wallowing in mud on hot days. Your body can sweat to cool off, but a pig's skin has very few sweat glands. Lying in mud or water helps pigs stay cool."

A cartoon frog named Thaddeus "Tad" Pole serves as guide throughout *The World of Nature*. His face is on every page; clicking on him produces a list of options for moving to other parts of the program. There are several ways to wander through *The World of Nature*—by visiting one of sixteen environments such as the rain forest or desert, where there are pictures of animals and plants linked to the relevant on-screen pages; picking from a list of two hundred topics also linked to on-screen pages; or using a word-search feature to find a specific entry. All of the text is narrated, a big help for younger children just learning to read. *The World of Nature* also provides thirty-eight video clips, mostly thirty-second scenes of wild animals; forty-four animations illustrating topics such as the formation of clouds; and nine original songs. A selection of games and activities is available when children get bored: "Wise Cracker" is a quiz game that sends children into *The World of Nature* to answer simple research questions; "Wise Visor" gives a list of twenty-six suggested activities such as compiling a travel story on the environment or drawing a map of the world to show where various animals live; and "InterActivities" offers twenty-four simple quiz games.

Although *The World of Nature* never goes into great detail on any subject, and many of the games aren't particularly compelling, there's so much material in the CD-ROM that children are likely to keep coming back. The next installment in the *Explorapedia* series—*The World of People*—is due in early 1995. Microsoft hasn't yet announced any additional titles but promises to release several more every year.

THE HEINEMANN CHILDREN'S MULTIMEDIA ENCYCLOPEDIA
★★
Developer: Reed Interactive; 800-308-6353
Format: Windows, Macintosh
Price: $55

Offering *The Heinemann Children's Multimedia Encyclopedia* to its intended audience of children ages six to twelve is like giving a tricycle to children who can already ride a two-wheeler — it's beneath them. The reading level required for *Heinemann* isn't significantly lower than the Big Three CD-ROM encyclopedias —

Compton's, Encarta, and *Grolier,* reviewed in Chapter Four, Section a—but *Heinemann* offers much less depth.

Heinemann contains the full text of an eleven-volume set sold primarily in Britain called *The Heinemann Children's Encyclopedia.* The CD-ROM doesn't go much beyond the print set, other than providing ninety very short video clips and animations along with narrated captions for most of the eight hundred photographs. The eleven volumes aren't alphabetical, like most encyclopedias, but instead are divided into subjects: "Arts and Entertainment," "Countries and Homes," "Earth and Beyond," "Famous Men and Women," "People, Sports and Leisure," "Technology at Work," "Travel and Communication," "Plants," "Animals," and an index. Although children can work through *Heinemann* by flipping through the on-screen pages of each volume, it's considerably easier to use the index or word-search feature.

In comparison to the Big Three, *Heinemann* comes up extremely short on content, with articles rarely exceeding three paragraphs. The entry on musician Louis Armstrong, for instance, has a brief video clip of him performing. But any educational value delivered by the video clip is canceled out by the brevity of the article: "Louis Armstrong was born in 1900 in New Orleans in the U.S. New Orleans is the birthplace of jazz music and Armstrong grew up surrounded by the new music. He left New Orleans in 1922 to join 'King' Oliver's band in Chicago. He soon became world famous for his trumpet playing. Armstrong was one of the first musicians to create a solo style in jazz. He also became famous for his rough-voiced singing and for his cheerful personality on stage. Armstrong died in 1971."

Heinemann also flunked my homegrown test drive, described in the introduction to Chapter Four, Section a. The encyclopedia had no entries on two of my three randomly chosen subjects—the Geiger counter and aviator Charles Lindbergh—and only a one-paragraph article on zebras. Everywhere else I looked, I ran into similar shortcomings. The main article on computers, for example, runs only three paragraphs and doesn't really explain how computers work; the three-paragraph article on microprocessors wasn't any better. Children who aren't ready for the Big Three encyclopedias will be much better off with other reference works, such as the excellent *My First Encyclopedia,* reviewed in Chapter One, Section a. On the other hand, children who can handle *Heinemann* should skip this CD-ROM and go straight to the Big Three.

RANDOM HOUSE KID'S ENCYCLOPEDIA
★★
Developer: Knowledge Adventure Inc.; 800-542-4240
Format: Windows
Price: $39

Random House Kid's Encyclopedia attempts to reach children ages seven to twelve by ladling a thick coat of sugar onto human knowledge. But the tactic backfires badly—the layers of cuteness will gag anyone who spends more than a few minutes with the two-disk CD-ROM set. The sugar coating also hides a surprising lack of depth; most of the two thousand articles offer only two or three paragraphs of information.

Kid's Encyclopedia is divided into three sections. "The Factory," filling one of the two disks, is the reference desk where children locate specific articles. "The Movie Theater," where children view 120 very short video clips, and "The Arcade," which offers five simple and unoriginal games, fill the other disk. Bouncy synthesizer music pours from the speakers at all times in every part of *Kid's Encyclopedia*, and, incredibly, there's no way to turn it off. The music often makes it hard to hear the extensive audio narration, forcing users to turn up the volume, a situation that's sure to drive parents crazy unless the family computer is situated far away from them.

The reference screen allows children to call up articles through an alphabetical index, a time line, a locator globe, or by category. But the articles themselves are uniformly shallow. Abraham Lincoln, for example, gets just three paragraphs. I found one obvious error in this short entry: "At the war's end, Lincoln's famous Gettysburg Address, 1863, called the people together." The Civil War, of course, didn't end until 1865. Other than a photograph of Lincoln and a bibliography listing five biographies, the only other information is a "fun fact" that appears in a pop-up window: "Abraham Lincoln, the first U.S. president to wear a beard, did so at the suggestion of an 11-year-old girl, who sent him a letter saying, 'You would look a great deal better, for your face is so thin.'"

"The Movie Theater" is the biggest disappointment in *Kid's Encyclopedia*. There are 120 video clips to view, but each one runs only ten seconds and appears in a tiny on-screen window. I don't think children will learn much about World War II by seeing 10 seconds of soldiers wading ashore on D day or gain an appreciation for arachnids by watching 10 seconds of a spider scuttling across its web. What's worse, there is no index; children instead have to flip through the clips one by one to find a particular entry.

The five games in "The Arcade" all fall flat. "Letter Rip" is a variation on Hangman, in which children get a hint and must then spell the word; "Match-O-Rama" is a concentration game challenging children to find pairs of objects hidden behind twelve squares; "Puzzle Time" is a slider puzzle, in which pieces of a jumbled picture must be moved into the correct places; "Brain Blazer" simply displays short video clips of children reciting interesting facts, such as "The average dollar bill lasts about 14 months in circulation and about 14 minutes in my pocket"; and "Zoomscape Scavenger Hunt" sends children tramping through a virtual museum looking for pictures of specific objects.

Parents also shouldn't assume *Kid's Encyclopedia* is more appropriate for seven-year-olds than the "grown-up" Big Three CD-ROM encyclopedias—*Compton's*, *Encarta*, and *Grolier*, reviewed in Chapter Four, Section a. Many of the entries in *Kid's Encyclopedia* require the same reading level as the Big Three, such as this definition that would probably baffle most children under age ten: "CD-ROM, compact disk read-only memory, is a computer storage device consisting of a metallized plastic disk. Because huge amounts of information can be stored on the disk, one CD-ROM can hold the entire contents of an encyclopedia or other lengthy text and graphics." One last gripe: Knowledge Adventure includes a misguided marketing gimmick on the disk called *The Adventurers!*, described in the review of *JumpStart Kindergarten* in Chapter One, Section c.

LENNY'S MUSICTOONS
★★½
Developer: Viacom New Media; 800-469-2539
Format: Windows, Macintosh
Price: $49

Lenny's MusicToons offers several music-related games and activities that younger children will enjoy, but parents will be disappointed with the lack of educational content and frustrated by the difficult installation process. The developers say the program is "for kids of all ages," but I didn't see anything that would appeal to adults or teenagers, so I'd recommend *Lenny's MusicToons* only for ages five to ten.

The program opens in the Manhattan penthouse pad of a cartoon character named Lenny, a large penguin wearing spectacles and a red bowtie. From Lenny's living room, children are presented with five activities. "Lenny's Theater" lets children put together a band by selecting one of fifteen "star" performers, one of fifteen backup singers, one of four bands, and one of thirty rhythms. When they've grouped together Cat-Man Cruthers, for example, backed by The Tappin' Turtles and The Fiber Tones, they push an on-screen button to hear the cartoon characters perform. However, despite the many choices, I thought the various combinations tended to sound more alike than different. "Pitch Attack" is a very confusing arcade-style game, in which children blast invading aliens by selecting the correct musical note from an on-screen keyboard. "Lenny's Puzzle Book" takes a page of music from familiar songs, such as "Mary Had A Little Lamb" and "Yankee Doodle," then chops the musical scales into jigsaw puzzle pieces that children must reassemble in the proper order. "Lenny's Matching Game" is a nonmusical concentration puzzle, in which children must find pairs of matching objects hidden behind eighteen squares. Finally, "PTV" is a variation on "Lenny's Theater." In PTV, children create music videos by selecting one of four music styles—rock and roll, hip hop, techno, and pop. There's a single tune for each style, divided into eight segments that children can arrange in any order they like. Then they select animated characters to perform on the screen. Children can also go through the balcony of Lenny's apartment for a view of Times Square. But this feature seems to be an afterthought—the only activity in Times Square is a scrolling text window with a few paragraphs describing the sights of New York City.

I found two big drawbacks to *Lenny's MusicToons*. First is the lack of educational content. Children need at least a beginner's ability to read music for the "Pitch Attack" and "Puzzle Book" games, yet the CD-ROM doesn't provide any instruction. And, while the "Lenny's Theater" and "PTV" activities are fun, they don't teach much about musical concepts. Second, the CD-ROM is burdened with a buggy and difficult installation program that requires careful reading of the manual to make sure your sound card is properly configured. During installation, for example, the program incorrectly told me I had failed to install a sound driver that was already in my system.

MARIO TEACHES TYPING ENHANCED CD-ROM
★★½
Developer: Interplay Productions Inc.; 800-969-4263
Format: DOS, Macintosh
Price: $29

Mario Teaches Typing Enhanced CD-ROM doesn't really teach typing, but it could be a useful practice program for children already studying the subject. Intended for "ages 5 to adult," the CD-ROM comes with a skimpy twenty-page instruction manual that gives no guidance for parents who want to help their children learn to type. There's also a big technical hurdle: *Mario Teaches Typing* requires expanded memory, a feature available but not activated in the typical home computer. Most users will have to create a "boot" disk, then restart the computer both before and after each *Mario* session.

The lessons themselves are fun, resembling the famous Nintendo video games featuring the Italian plumber Mario, his brother Luigi, and the eternally endangered Princess. Children pick one of the three characters to appear in the middle of the screen, running from left to right and jumping over obstacles just like in the video games. To get Mario and the others through the game requires hitting the proper keys to type words displayed on the top of the screen; Mario's gloved hands are shown at the bottom of the screen, with the correct finger highlighted in red. The first lesson, for beginners, requires typing single letters; the second lesson moves up to full words; and the third lesson presents full sentences. There's also an "expert express" screen, which presents practice letters, words, and sentences without the potentially distracting video game.

Mario Teaches Typing can keep track of individual performance for multiple students. The CD-ROM even includes a rap song called "Practice Makes Perfect" with a singer who sounds a lot like Stevie Wonder, although the song doesn't accomplish much in the way of typing instruction. Mario's animated head pops onto the screen occasionally, speaking in a high-pitched voice with an Italian accent, to offer advice and encouragement. Serious students, however, can turn off the animations and music to concentrate on the lessons.

MATH BLASTER: IN SEARCH OF SPOT
★★★
Developer: Davidson & Associates Inc.; 800-545-7677
Format: Windows, Macintosh
Price: $39

Parents will like *Math Blaster: In Search of Spot* because the CD-ROM teaches basic arithmetic skills to children ages six to twelve. Kids will like *Math Blaster* because they get to play a fun game that coincidentally happens to require a lot of addition, subtraction, multiplication, and division. The story—told through colorful graphics and amusing sound effects—isn't especially original: A green space-suited character named Blasternaut is trying to recover his pal Spot, a small purple creature that has been kidnapped by the evil, littering Trash Alien. Blasternaut must pick up the galactic litter and travel to the Trash Alien's faraway planet to rescue Spot.

The game moves through four levels. Blasternaut begins with "Trash Zapper," collecting space trash with a tractor beam controlled by children—but only after they correctly answer arithmetic questions, such as the sum of eighteen and seven. Then it's time for the "Number Recycler," in which children move columns of numbers to complete equations. The third challenge is "Cave Runner," a maze navigated by matching the number of Blasternaut's suit to the appropriate equation on the cave wall to get past the Trash Alien's defense. The final confrontation is "Math Blaster," in which children have to pick the correct answer to an equation from one of four portholes on the Trash Alien's spaceship while dodging flying bits of garbage. Children will find the video-game-like action sufficiently intriguing to put aside their normal aversion to arithmetic quiz problems. In a nice extra touch, *Math Blaster* can be set for six different levels of difficulty, so children can keep challenging themselves as their skills improve.

MATH BLASTER: EPISODE 2 — SECRET OF THE LOST CITY
★★★
Developer: Davidson & Associates Inc.; 800-545-7677
Format: Windows
Price: $39

A sequel to *Math Blaster: In Search of Spot*, reviewed in this section, that moves up roughly a year in grade level. Intended for ages eight to thirteen, *Math Blaster: Episode 2—Secret of The Lost City* follows the same format in combining education and fun. This time out, the green space-suited character Blasternaut is trying to stop the evil Dr. Minus from dominating the universe but must first work through four games in the mysterious Lost City.

"Number Hunt" calls for children to assemble correctly a simple mathematical equation after first working through a multi-chambered building to collect all the pieces. "Positron Splash" is a shooting gallery in which Blasternaut has to throw "positron pods" at little creatures called "negatrons" to make sure the right numbers drop into an equation. "Maze Craze" challenges children to perform quick calculations to determine which formulas fall within a predetermined range; for example, identifying that "4+6+5" doesn't fall in the range from sixteen to twenty. "Creature Creator" stresses logical thinking by calling on children to create funny creatures that meet certain preset design rules.

Each of the games has six levels of difficulty; three levels for the math problems and three levels for the game play. Seven subjects are covered through fifty thousand problems: addition, subtraction, multiplication, division, fractions, decimals, and percents. With all the levels and problems, children will be able to return to *Math Blaster 2* again and again without getting bored.

MATH WORKSHOP
★★½
Developer: Broderbund Software Inc.; 800-521-6263
Format: Windows, Macintosh
Price: $39

Math Workshop resembles cherry-flavored cough syrup: It's good for you and it tastes somewhat like candy, but you still know it's medicine. Ostensibly developed for ages six to twelve, *Math Workshop* seems aimed more at soothing the guilty conscience of parents worried that their children aren't learning enough arithmetic.

Broderbund Software Inc., developer of *Math Workshop*, hits the guilt angle hard in a twelve-minute "parents' video guide" included on the CD-ROM, with Broderbund chairman Doug Carlston talking about the importance of math skills for the success of the next generation and teachers stressing the necessity of parental involvement.

This hard sell would be acceptable, I suppose, if the program itself were more fun. Certainly, *Math Workshop* looks as if it should be fun, with lots of bouncy theme music and animated characters resembling Saturday morning cartoon creatures. But the seven math games in *Math Workshop* are dull and repetitive. "Bowling for Numbers," for example, is nothing more than a multiple-choice quiz asking children to solve simple arithmetic problems. After getting ten correct answers, they watch passively as Gus the Gorilla throws a bowling ball and knocks down ten pins. Three jigsaw-puzzle games—"Hidden Picture," "Puzzle Patterns," and "Super Sticklers"—simply involve moving and rotating puzzle pieces. "Rhythm Shop" is an exercise in fractions, slicing up long bars into smaller bars to play tunes and see a character named Algebird do a little dance. "Rockets" is a counting game in which children take turns launching groups of rockets with the goal of having one left over at the end. "Pattern Window" displays geometric patterns resembling stained-glass windows that children can fill in with various colors.

None of these games will hold children's attention for long, defeating the purpose of parental involvement. Also, almost all the games are too easy for twelve-year-olds; I'd put the top age for *Math Workshop* around age ten.

MAVIS BEACON TEACHES TYPING! FOR KIDS
★★
Developer: Mindscape Inc.; 800-234-3088
Format: Windows-2
Price: $35

In households with personal computers, children often learn to read from a PC rather than a book. But does that mean even preschoolers should be able to master touch typing at the same time they're grappling with the ABCs? I'm skeptical that children under age eight have the patience and motor skills to become proficient typists. That skepticism wasn't diminished by *Mavis Beacon Teaches Typing! for Kids*. A significantly modified kid-level version of the excellent *Mavis Beacon Teaches Typing!*, reviewed in Chapter Ten, Section a, *Mavis Beacon for Kids* lacks much of the depth and flexibility of its older sibling.

In the kids' version, Mavis Beacon is depicted in animated cartoons as a young girl visiting her grandparents' house. Children go to six locations: the living room, kitchen, bedroom, and bathroom in the house and the pond and forest outside the house. In each location, there is a game that requires typing the correct sequence of letters—children help Mavis clean up the bedroom, for instance, by pressing the letter "a" on the keyboard to put away an alarm clock. Every step of the games is explained through audio narration, so children who aren't yet reading will still be able to participate if they can recognize the letters of the alphabet.

Mindscape Inc., developers of the Mavis Beacon series, recommends the kids' version for ages four to eight. Children age six and under should be able to handle the CD-ROM's first two levels, where the games present individual letters and short words, but will get lost at the third level, which offers complete stories made up of long sentences. Parents, moreover, will be disappointed to find the kids' version comes with only a skimpy twenty-eight-page manual that provides no more than a few paragraphs of guidance on how to supervise their children's study; the adult version, in contrast, comes with a comprehensive eighty-four-page manual. Another drawback in the kids' version is the tiny animated keyboard tucked in the lower left corner of the screen, with a pair of disembodied hands demonstrating the correct finger movements. It's too small to see clearly. The adult version displays a large keyboard filling the bottom third of the screen, making it easy to follow the finger movements.

THE MULTIMEDIA WORKSHOP
★★½
Developer: Davidson & Associates Inc.; 800-545-7677
Format: Windows, Macintosh
Price: $49

The Multimedia Workshop is a noble effort to let children ages 10 and above control text, graphics, animation, sound, and video for school and home projects. But the result, sadly, is a jack of all trades and master of none—the individual modules aren't as good as programs dedicated to a single task.

Multimedia Workshop has three core programs: Writing Workshop, Video Workshop, and Paint Workshop. Writing Workshop is a simple desktop publishing program for creating newsletters, book reports, greeting cards, and a variety of other documents. To broaden the appeal to adults, there are templates for business cards, letterheads, and resumes. All the basic tools are available for manipulating text and importing graphics, but you'll get more features in programs such as *The Print Shop Deluxe CD-ROM Ensemble* and *Microsoft Publisher*, reviewed in Chapter Nine, Section a. Video Workshop is a tool for creating on-screen slide shows, by assembling a succession of still images that can be livened up with sound effects and video clips. Paint Workshop is a standard drawing program for creating original artwork and editing clip-art graphics.

The CD-ROM includes an impressive selection of source material: 600 clip-art images, 300 photographs, 200 sound effects, 100 video clips, 40 music clips, and 8 fonts. But there is no index or guidebook to all these extras, so you don't know what you've got unless you call up each item to take a look. In short, I think most users will have a hard time getting all the pieces of *Multimedia Workshop* to come together. The Writing and Video workshops are linked to each other, for example, but the Paint Workshop is separate—so you have to quit what you're doing in the Writing or Video Workshop to go to the Paint Workshop. The user manual is also suprisingly skimpy. I frequently complain about overly complicated and lengthy manuals, but *The Multimedia Workshop* needs more than its 84 pages.

THE MUSICAL WORLD OF PROFESSOR PICCOLO
★★★
Developer: Opcode Interactive; 800-557-2633
Format: Windows, Macintosh
Price: $49

For children eager to learn about music, *The Musical World of Professor Piccolo* is full of interesting information presented in a lively style. The CD-ROM takes you to a place called "Music Town," with a bow-tied cartoon character named Professor Piccolo providing advice in the corner of most scenes. "Think of it as a musical 'Mayberry R.F.D.,'" says a welcoming sign, although it's doubtful many of today's kids will recognize Andy Griffith's TV show from thirty-five years ago.

There are seven places to visit in "Music Town": the rock club, symphony hall, jazz club, church, music school, library, and game arcade. At the rock and jazz clubs, you can highlight each instrument playing a tune so that the bass guitar, for example, is heard clearly above the other instruments. The symphony hall displays a full orchestra in which each instrument can be sampled with the click of a mouse button. Another click brings up profiles of individual instruments, complete with a brief audio sample of the instrument being played. The electric guitar performs a Jimi Hendrix-like riff; the acoustic guitar performs a classical sonata. The accompanying text covers musical history without lapsing into dull academic prose, as in this description of the symphony: "Not one piece of music, but four separate ones; usually, it embraces a musical drama, a slow song, a lively dance and a rousing finale. A great symphony is, in effect, a trip through almost the whole range of human feeling."

The music school offers twelve text lessons on such subjects as pitch, rhythm notation, scales, and chords. Almost every on-screen page includes music clips explaining such concepts as the difference between a quarter note and a half note. The library provides a glossary of musical terms and an index to all the instruments. The arcade is the least interesting section of "Music Town," offering four unoriginal games—"Sound Off!," "Musical Pursuit," "Pitch Adventure," and "Rhythm Pursuit"—covering musical concepts and history.

Professor Piccolo is a pleasure to operate; most users won't even need to look at the manual. There is audio narration for much of the text, a big benefit for children not yet comfortable with reading longer sentences, as well as a "hint line" along the bottom of the screen that identifies the function of each icon whenever the cursor is rolled over that spot on the screen. Opcode Interactive, the CD-ROM's developer, describes *Professor Piccolo* as suitable for "ages 8 to adult," although I'd put an upper limit of age fourteen—there isn't enough depth in the lessons and explanatory text for a high school or adult audience. Even for children in the proper age range, *Professor Piccolo* doesn't give much of a reason to return after experiencing each of the seven destinations, a process I estimate would fill about three to five hours.

OPERATION NEPTUNE
★★½

Developer:	The Learning Company; 800-852-2255
Format:	DOS
Price:	$45

How to get the attention of a generation raised on Sega and Nintendo video games? One option is creating educational software that looks and sounds like a video game. *Operation Neptune* takes the "if you can't beat 'em, join 'em" approach, but there are visible suture marks where the two conflicting goals—having fun and teaching math—are stitched together.

Aimed at ages nine to fourteen, *Operation Neptune* revolves around a video-game plot. A secret space mission, carrying an elite team of astronauts and scientists, has sent an unmanned data capsule back to earth with vital information. The capsule alters its course during reentry, breaks into pieces, and crashes into the Pacific Ocean. Players take the helm of a minisubmarine called *The Neptune* to retrieve the capsule's data canisters.

Playing at either the Voyager or Expert level, children have to navigate through five undersea zones—Dragon Reef, Fossil Trench, Limestone Ridge, Sea Forest, and Hammerhead—in search of the data canisters while dodging dangerous sea creatures. In an admirable step away from the heavy dependence of video games on death rays and other weapons, the Neptune's only defense is nontoxic ink pellets that temporarily confuse predators. The action unfolds very much like a video game—the submarine moves in two dimensions through reefs, players hear chimes when they pick up a data canister, and the submarine's image flickers whenever a player collides with a deadly sea creature and loses a "life." But the pace isn't nearly as fast as a video game, something ten-year-olds will notice right away.

The math questions are delivered as an interruption to the game. Occasionally, the action stops while children are forced to answer a quiz question such as "Unidentified obstacle 14 miles ahead. Sub approaching at two miles per hour. Input hours to reach obstacle." These questions aren't relevant to *The Neptune*'s quest, although children might inadvertently improve their math skills if they're interested enough in the game to play to the end.

THE OREGON TRAIL
★★★½
Developer: MECC; 800-685-6322 x529
Format: Windows, Macintosh
Price: $45

The Oregon Trail is an absorbing simulation of a two-thousand-mile journey by covered wagon across the American West in 1848. You have to make crucial decisions—how many pounds of provisions to carry, the best way to cross deep rivers, when to stop for rest—that determine whether your wagonload of travelers makes it successfully from Independence, Missouri, to the Willamette Valley in Oregon. This game is so much fun that parents will have to pry children away from the computer, even though *The Oregon Trail* was originally developed for schools to help teach history.

At the beginning of *The Oregon Trail*, you select one of eight occupations for yourself: banker, blacksmith, carpenter, doctor, farmer, merchant, saddlemaker, or teacher. Your choice determines how much money you have to buy supplies and what skills you'll have during emergencies; it also gives children a reason to play the game more than once since the obstacles they encounter will shift with their choice of career. Next, you outfit your party at the general store, ordering oxen, clothing, bullets, food, and wagon parts.

"It was a long, difficult journey—one that often resulted in failure and death," you're warned in an introductory message. "But for those who succeeded, it led to a new and better life." The risks include thieves, drowning, disease, starvation, and getting caught on the trail in winter. But not Indians; the program explains that Indian attacks on wagon trains were rare in real life and leaves out this unnecessary bit of melodrama.

You watch the progress of your wagon in simple animations displayed at the top of the screen, as well as by tracking a line that moves slowly across a map in the middle of the screen. A text window at the bottom of the screen tells of the challenges you face—an ox dying, a wagon wheel breaking, or members of your party getting cholera. There are immediate consequences for mistakes: I overloaded my wagon, for example, causing it to suffer repeated axle breaks and then capsize during a river crossing.

There's a lot to learn on the trail. An on-screen button summons a guidebook filled with short explanations of the geography, animals, and Indian tribes of the Great Plains and Rocky Mountains. A separate on-screen user's guide, which you can access only by quitting the game, supplies more detailed information and a bibliography.

The Oregon Trail doesn't offer a lot of multimedia bells and whistles; there's a smattering of audio narration and a few synthesized renditions of folk songs from the era. But it doesn't matter because the game is much more interactive than many fancier CD-ROMs with lots of video clips that don't give children an opportunity to make life-and-death decisions. The popularity of *The Oregon Trail*, by the way, has motivated the developers to bring out a whole series of similar titles. Two others are available on CD-ROM: *The Amazon Trail*, a canoe voyage that includes a visit to the ancient Incas; and *The Yukon Trail*, which covers the Alaskan gold rush of 1897.

READING BLASTER: INVASION OF THE WORD SNATCHERS
★★★
Developer: Davidson & Associates Inc.; 800-545-7677
Format: Windows
Price: $39

Following on the success of its long-running Math Blaster series, with two titles reviewed in this section, Davidson & Associates Inc. adopted the same format for *Reading Blaster: Invasion of the Word Snatchers*, released in late 1994. Intended for ages seven to ten, *Reading Blaster* once again dispatches the animated character Blasternaut in his green spacesuit to fight the forces of intergalactic evil. The enemy this time is Illitera, who has stolen all the words from Earth.

There are five games in *Reading Blaster*, all designed to strengthen various reading skills and help children practice logical thinking. The game opens with Blasternaut flying through space, chasing Illitera and facing a game of "Word Zapper." Children must pick out the correct letter to complete a word; given the clue "comes before second" and "f—st," children have to track and target the letters "ir" among a swarm of letters leaking out of Illitera's ship. After completing six words, Blasternaut lands on the ship to tackle the other games.

"Splatter Pods" deals with antonyms. Blasternaut grabs a word such as "pretty" off a conveyor belt and must pick one of five holes labeled with the correct opposite word, in this case "ugly." In "Plate Patrol," children must move Blasternaut through a maze to put five words into correct alphabetical order. "Tank Release" is another maze; this time, children must follow written instructions on the screen to unlock doors and complete the game. "Sequence Shocker" is the final confrontation; once again, children must follow written instructions to activate a series of control rods in the proper order.

As with *Math Blaster*, these games are entertaining enough that children will gladly play them without any parental urging. All the games have three difficulty levels, so children will continue to be challenged as their skills improve. The CD-ROM also provides a brief on-screen "parent's guide" with explanations of the games and suggestions for related activities when the computer is turned off, such as this tip for a game tied to "Splatter Pods": "Around the house, on the bus or in the car, word games are a lively way to pass the time. The next time you are waiting for a bus or going for a walk or a drive with your child, play a game of 'I Spy.' Begin by saying, 'I Spy something that means the same as *automobile*. I Spy something that means the same as *hat*.' For older children, offer the challenge of calling out as many synonyms as possible for a word that you suggest."

STORYBOOK WEAVER DELUXE
★★★★
Developer: MECC; 800-685-6322 x529
Format: Windows, Macintosh
Price: $49

There's only one thing wrong with *Storybook Weaver Deluxe*: This powerful desktop publishing program is designed for children ages six to twelve. I just wish there were graphics software packages this good for adults.

With just a glance at the instruction manual, children will be able to take hold of *Storybook Weaver Deluxe* and instantly start creating their own storybooks full of colorful illustrations and amusing sounds. The CD-ROM provides an extensive library of cartoon objects and background scenes that can be effortlessly resized, edited, and moved around the screen.

Storybook Weaver is actually two programs—a simple word processor and a graphics/media editor. The word processor has all the usual features for entering, deleting, moving, and resizing text that work in either English or Spanish, as well as a spell checker and thesaurus. The graphics/media program lets you dip into a library of 1,550 images and 154 sound clips for items to put on the page.

Within five minutes of my first venture into *Storybook Weaver*, I was able to write and illustrate a simple story. I decided to invent a tale about the world's largest baby. First, I found a background showing a typical city street and put it at the top of the page. Then I located the image of a diaper-clad baby. With a few clicks of the "Bigger" button, the baby soon appeared about ten feet tall. To drive home that impression, I pulled up the image of a girl in a marching band and hit the "smaller" button so that she came up only to the big baby's waist. Then I searched through the sound files until I found an icon of a crying baby. I took the sound and "attached" it to the baby in my picture so that an infant's cry poured out of the computer's speakers whenever I clicked on the baby. Next, I summoned the "Object editor" and drew a few hairs on the head of my bald infant. Finally, I wrote a few sentences about my giant baby in the text window at the bottom of the screen, explaining how the child needed "a truck tarpulin for a diaper," then ran the spelling checker to discover that I needed to change the spelling to "tarpaulin."

With this wealth of images and editing tools, children will be able to create just about any kind of illustrated story they can imagine. It's easy to save the work to show off later, or print the stories, which will look especially good if there's a color printer available. *Storybook Weaver Deluxe*, in short, is the best kind of interactive children's software—using the computer to unleash what's inside their heads rather than forcing them to play with someone else's ideas.

STUDENT WRITING CENTER
★★★½
Developer: The Learning Company; 800-852-2255
Format: Windows
Price: $59

Today's children may never know the stomach-knotting humiliation of getting back a book report covered with the teacher's red pencil marks—at least not if they have access to *Student Writing Center*. A full-fledged word processor specifically designed for the needs of junior high and high school students, *Student Writing Center* outperforms professional software such as *WordPerfect* and *Microsoft Word* in completing class assignments.

When you enter *Student Writing Center*, you're given five options for the type of document to create: a report, a newsletter, a journal, a letter, or a sign. Young authors are then assisted by several powerful tools, including a spelling checker, a thesaurus, an automated bibliography generator, and a library of four hundred clip-art images. The clip-art isn't the silly cartoons often found in software aimed at younger children but genuinely useful drawings such as plants, animals, and outline maps of all fifty states. The library also provides borders for creating newsletters and signs.

All of the features work together flawlessly; a clip-art image of a penguin, for example, can be dropped into a science report on Antarctica and the text instantly wraps around the picture. As with any piece of powerful software, however, *Student Writing Center* requires some dedication to master fully. The program comes with a 250-page manual that is clearly written, but ten-year-olds might still need help from Mom and Dad to become proficient, assuming Mom and Dad know enough about word-processing software to render assistance.

b. Science and Nature

AMERICANS IN SPACE
★★★
Developer: Multicom Publishing Inc.; 800-850-7272
Format: Windows, Macintosh
Price: $39

Avoiding the tendency of many children's CD-ROMs to sugarcoat history, *Americans in Space* provides an accurate and honest introduction to the United States's manned space-flight program. The disk centers on a "mission control" panel, from which children summon a combination of text, narration, photos, and video clips for every U.S. spaceflight from the first suborbital *Mercury* mission in 1961 through space shuttle flights as recent as 1992, along with a prologue covering early rocket research in the United States, Germany, and Russia. *Americans in Space* is also easy to use, so easy that it comes with only a single page of instructions. Every nook and cranny of the disk can be accessed through pointing and clicking with the mouse.

I particularly liked the developer's decision not to hide the occasional mistakes that caused tragedies and near tragedies. When John Glenn became the first American to orbit the earth on February 20, 1962, ground controllers were concerned that his *Mercury* capsule had lost its heat shield, "dooming Glenn to a fiery death as the unprotected capsule faced temperatures of more than 2,900 degrees Fahrenheit" during reentry. Of course, Glenn survived, but not without some white-knuckle moments. Similarly, the *Apollo 1* fire on January 27, 1967—which killed astronauts "Gus" Grissom, Roger Chaffee, and Edward White during a ground test—is fully covered, with a photograph of the burned-out capsule and a description of subsequent design changes to prevent a recurrence. And the entry on the 1986 explosion of the space shuttle *Challenger* doesn't shy away from detailing political pressure on the National Aeronautics and Space Administration to get more flights off the ground: "NASA launched the *Challenger* despite the known O-ring defect [in the solid rocket booster motor] and several other problems, because only a stepped-up schedule could deliver the routine, low-cost access to orbit it had promised." All this information is important not because of morbid curiosity but because children need to know that remarkable human achievements such as space travel don't come without sacrifice.

Americans in Space has a few minor flaws. The video images play in a small 2.75-inch diagonal window on a standard 14-inch monitor and average only about a minute each, so the action often ends just as you start to get interested. Also, the text accompanying each mission is only a few paragraphs. Children whose minds are opened to the wonders of space flight will soon find themselves searching for more comprehensive material.

THE SAN DIEGO ZOO PRESENTS . . . THE ANIMALS!
★★★½

Developer: Mindscape Inc.; 800-234-3088
Format: Windows, Macintosh
Price: $39

The San Diego Zoo Presents . . . The Animals! is a wonderful kid-level introduction to the amazing diversity of life on earth, like a trip to the zoo without the parking hassles and sore feet from long walks. The CD-ROM is a virtual tour of the famous San Diego Zoo, with much of its text taken from the zoo's publications and video clips shot at the many zoo exhibits.

You start from the main menu screen, which displays an overhead view of the zoo. With a click of the mouse you can travel to one of ten exhibit areas representing different habitats, such as the tundra or the tropical rain forest, as well as several zoo buildings offering special programs for children. All these destinations ultimately take you to screens profiling 202 animals. Each profile screen offers several short text articles on the animal, three to six photographs, and, for most animals, either an audio or video clip. The profile of the ostrich, for example, offers four color photographs, a five-second audio clip of the bird's call, and text written at a level most appropriate for children between ages six and twelve. "Ostriches hatch from eggs that are 24 times larger than chicken eggs," *The Animals!* explains. "Their hefty legs kick hard and can move the ostrich's large body up to 30 miles per hour. Is there anything small about them? Yes. Their two-foot-long wings are tiny for their size and useless in flight."

Children aren't just left to wander aimlessly from profile to profile, however. The CD-ROM includes several video clips explaining zoo operations and a "story theater" offering fourteen narrated slide shows on topics such as "Raising Gordy Gorilla" and "Zoo Doctors." These stories are full of interesting facts; in "Feeding at the Zoo," I learned that adult elephants can eat up to three hundred pounds of food a day and that the San Diego Zoo imported special eucalyptus trees from New Zealand to feed its koala bears.

Mindscape Inc., developer of *The Animals!*, is promising an expanded "Version 2" of the CD-ROM in early 1995 with more animals and better-quality video clips. The improved video clips will be a significant plus; the eighty-two video clips in the original version, most running under a minute, are grainy and appear in a small four-inch-diagonal window on a standard fourteen-inch monitor.

ANNATOMMY
★½
Developer: IVI Publishing Inc.; 800-432-1332
Format: Windows
Price: $35

Medical schools aren't in the business of teaching computer game design. That's obvious from the incredibly clumsy *AnnaTommy*, developed with assistance from physicians at the famed Mayo Clinic. A failed experiment at grafting together video games and anatomy lessons, the CD-ROM is awkward to operate, plagiarizes game ideas, and makes it difficult to absorb the meager educational content.

The concept must have seemed promising at the start: Create a video-game-like tour through the human body for children ages 8 and above. But the developers appear to be taking a cynical view that children won't sit still long enough to learn anything unless they're twitching their thumbs to squash germs in the mouth or crush bits of food in the stomach. So the developers neglected to provide a way to view the many animations in *AnnaTommy* without playing the game, making the CD-ROM useless as a teaching or reference tool.

AnnaTommy opens with two computer-generated children named Anna and Tommy, who move like marionettes, visting a mysterious science center where they enter a spaceship, are shrunken to microscopic size, and are injected into the bloodstream of a human body. To complete the adventure, they have to play mindless games in ten body systems: the circulatory, digestive, endocrine, integumentary (skin), lymphatic, nervous, reproductive, respiratory, skeletal, and urinary. The voices of Anna and Tommy occasionally deliver a sentence or two of scientific information as they whip from one place to another, but *AnnaTommy* offers no text on human anatomy other than a brief glossary. The games have nothing to do with the subject matter; visiting the skin, for example, children find themselves stacking rows of skin cells in a way that's a blatant rip-off of the popular computer game *Tetris*.

AnnaTommy is designed to be played with a joystick or game pad, which is a huge disadvantage if you don't already own one. To my amazement, you can't use the mouse to play the games—it's one of the few Windows programs I've ever seen that totally ignores the mouse. Instead, you're stuck using the arrow keys or the keyboard to maneuver the on-screen cursor. With or without a joystick, however, *AnnaTommy* doesn't provide either education or entertainment.

AVIATION ADVENTURE
★★★½
Developer: Knowledge Adventure Inc.; 800-542-4240
Format: Windows
Price: $49

The newest and best in the Knowledge Adventure series, fully described in the review of *3-D Dinosaur Adventure* in this chapter. Released in December 1994, *Aviation Adventure* is overflowing with information and games on airplanes and the science of flight. It will take children many hours to work through all the text, photographs, video clips, animations, and flight simulators.

Aviation Adventure, designed for ages eight and above, offers nine activities. "Aviation Lab" provides close-ups of ten aircraft—from the Avro 504K biplane of World War I through the F-15E Eagle fighter and the space shuttle—with both exterior and cutaway views. "Aviation Museum," although hobbled by Knowledge Adventure's awkward "Zoomscape" feature, provides lengthy articles on topics ranging from weather research to the duties of an air traffic controller. "Aircraft Encyclopedia" provides a photo and a brief text profile for two hundred aircraft. "Aviation Reference Library" offers more text and photographs on aviation history and technology. "Aviation Theater" is a screening room for thirty-four video clips, each running from fifteen seconds to four minutes, showing everything from in-flight refueling to helicopter-launched missiles destroying a tank. "Paper Plane Factory" provides animated instructions for making twelve paper airplanes with colorful names such as "The Barnstormer" and "The Aerobat." The "Aviation Trivia Game" presents multiple-choice quiz questions based on the CD-ROM's contents. "Glider Game" is an easy-to-learn but challenging contest to fly a paper airplane across a succession of rooms, searching for air currents to provide lift while avoiding obstacles. Finally, a full-fledged flight simulator called "F4U Secret Sortie" puts you at the controls of a World War II fighter plane.

Some of the other Knowledge Adventure titles don't delve deeply enough into their chosen subject, but not this one. Children will be hard-pressed to fly through all the information in *Aviation Adventure*. The games, too, are much more compelling than in some of those in earlier Knowledge Adventure entries. One of the few sour notes is the presence of a misguided marketing gimmick called *The Adventurers!*, described in the review of *JumpStart Kindergarten* in Chapter One, Section c.

3-D BODY ADVENTURE
★★½
Developer: Knowledge Adventure Inc.; 800-542-4240
Format: DOS
Price: $49

3-D Body Adventure is a tour through the human body that never gets beneath the skin of its subject matter. A computer-generated invisible man, which can be rotated or examined layer by layer, is displayed in the main reference screen. Clicking on any body part or organ brings up a photo and article. "The heart never rests," explains the article on the heart. "During an average lifetime, the heart beats approximately 2.5 billion times. The heart is a very well-designed pump indeed. It is more reliable and energy-efficient than any pump ever created by man."

Recommended by the developer for age seven and above, *3-D Body Adventure* offers three other features. *3-D Body Theatre* is a collection of sixteen one-minute animations, mostly anatomy "fly-throughs," such as tours through the skeleton and digestive tract. The most interesting is the heart attack segment, in which you watch an artery clogging until the blood flow stops and you hear someone yell "Arggh!" A game called "Emergency" is hobbled by Knowledge Adventure's clumsy "Zoomscape" technology, which requires you to roll the mouse to move through a scene. The activity in "Emergency" is pointless; to save a young boy bitten by a rabid dog, for example, you go into the brain and zap virus cells by clicking on them—not much of a learning activity. A concentration game called "Body Recall" is too simple for older children, requiring nothing more than picking through hidden words and pictures to find matching pairs.

As with other Knowledge Adventure titles that use 3-D, the images here aren't worth the effort of donning special glasses. Children with an especially strong interest in the human body might find *3-D Body Adventure* a useful reference tool, but the CD-ROM isn't interesting enough to spur extensive exploration. For more information on common features of the Knowledge Adventure series, see the review of *3-D Dinosaur Adventure* in this section.

BUG ADVENTURE
★★★½
Developer: Knowledge Adventure Inc.; 800-542-4240
Format: DOS
Price: $35

Children love to hate insects. Bugs are everywhere, free for collecting and experimentation. Who among us can deny having conducted youthful research involving a sunny day, ants, and a magnifying glass? *Bug Adventure* is the perfect indoor companion for such explorations. Recommended by the developer for age three and above, the CD-ROM transports children into a strange world that is literally right beneath our feet. There is, for example, this fascinating self-description of a flea: "We are noted insect jumpers with a unique propulsion system that makes possible awesome leaps of 150 times our own length—vertically or horizontally. This is equivalent to a human jumping nearly a thousand feet . . . Reportedly, we can do all of the following: accelerate 50 times faster than the space shuttle; remain frozen for a year, then revive; [and] go without feeding for months and survive."

Bug Adventure starts with the classic "Flight of the Bumblebee" theme music while you watch a bug's-eye-view video clip of a bumblebee evading an angry wasp. Then comes the main menu screen, entry point to the disk's six sections. "Bug Reference" is the anchor, providing an index to reach any of the articles on individual bug species and general bug science. There are two games—"Who Am I?" in which children match pictures and "Can You Find Me?," a fact quiz—and a "Bug Storybook" in which animated pages unfold on screen while a narrator explains the action.

The contents of *Bug Adventure* can also be reached through the "Honeycomb Theater," which provides a menu to the disk's fifteen video clips, each running from ten to forty seconds and displaying such amazing sights as a large water spider catching a small fish. The weakest section is "3-D Bug Basement." Donning a pair of cardboard glasses included with *Bug Adventure*, you look through one red lens and one blue lens to get a cheesy and only partly convincing 3-D view of still photographs showing a bee, butterfly, ant, spider, beetle, and fly. Still, *Bug Adventure* is full of captivating information presented in a lively style with an interface that even small children can quickly master. For more information on common features of the Knowledge Adventure series, see the review of *3-D Dinosaur Adventure* in this section.

3-D DINOSAUR ADVENTURE
★★½
Developer: Knowledge Adventure Inc.; 800-542-4240
Format: DOS
Price: $49

"Long, long ago, animals called dinosaurs lived on the Earth. There were big ones. And small ones ... Where did they come from? From mother and father dinosaurs, of course." This opening passage from the "Dinosaur Storybook" section of *3-D Dinosaur Adventure* sums up the entire CD-ROM, which is not especially profound and is appropriate only for very small children.

Trading on the popularity of the movie *Jurassic Park*, the CD-ROM opens by taking you through the gate of a dinosaur theme park. You move through the park using Knowledge Adventure's awkward "Zoomscape" feature, bumping into dinosaurs until you enter a door to one of the nine activities in *Dinosaur Adventure*.

"Dinosaur Reference" is the anchor, providing access to all the articles on dinosaurs and dinosaur-related topics. The illustrations are colorful, but the text is often limited to two or three paragraphs. "Movies" provides twenty-five very brief video clips, mostly under thirty seconds. Many of the on-screen dinosaurs appear to be the large robotic models displayed at amusement parks. "Dinosaur Safari" is a question-and-answer game, in which children hear a quiz question and must pick the answer from one of four dinosaur pictures. A sample question: "Click on the dinosaur whose mouth was shaped like a duck's bill and lived in herds during the Cretaceous period." Answer: the Edmontosaurus.

"Who Am I?" is a game in which children must match a picture of a dinosaur body part with the correct animal, picking from eight dinosaur images on the screen. "Name-A-Saurus" pronounces the name of a dinosaur, which must be identified from a group of nine pictures. "Create-A-Saurus" lets children pick one of ten dinosaur outlines and, since no one knows what dinosaurs looked like on the outside, pick one of nine possible skins. But the choices are silly, including a rainbow, a checkerboard, and marble. "3-D Dinosaur Museum" is doubly annoying, combining the frustration of Zoomscape with muddy displays of 3-D dinosaurs. "Save the Dinosaurs" is another Zoomscape feature, a game in which children have twenty minutes to travel through the theme park searching for individual dinosaurs. Finally, there is the storybook, a series of illustrations accompanied by mindless text.

Recommended by the developer for age three and above, *3-D Dinosaur Adventure* contains so many activities that preschoolers might enjoy the CD-ROM. Older children, however, are likely to find much of the material beneath their abilities.

About the Knowledge Adventure series: Parents can easily get confused with this series of children's CD-ROM software created by Knowledge Adventure Inc. The titles have many similarities but differ in structure and focus. The recommended youngest age, for example, varies from three to eight. The quality, too, varies from dreadful to very good.

On the plus side, Knowledge Adventure titles never force children to march from a predetermined starting point to a predetermined finish. Instead, they explore on their own through a combination of pictures, short video clips, and text. Younger children will appreciate the extensive audio cues and narration, making it possible for them to enjoy the titles even if they don't know how to read, although grown-ups will get tired of the repetitive video-game-like synthesizer music that constantly plays in the background.

The common element in the Knowledge Adventure titles is the main reference screen. For each topic—such as a profile of the heart in *Body Adventure* or a description of the great white shark in *Undersea Adventure*—a photo appears in a large display window on the right side of the screen. In the lower left is a text box. In the upper left, for most titles in the series, is a globe. By clicking buttons surrounding the globe, you change the scale, zooming in to just one hundred miles or zooming out to see the entire planet Earth. All the CD-ROMs also have an index for finding specific topics.

The content in Knowledge Adventure titles is used over and over to create the maximum number of activities. Pictures of the spiders from the main reference screen in *Bug Adventure*, for example, also appear in quiz games. There's a risk in this tactic, however. Sharp-eyed children could get bored once they realize they're seeing the same image in several settings.

Knowledge Adventure is also overly fond of technical trickery. Several of the titles boast 3-D photographs and movies. Viewing these images requires a pair of cheap paper glasses, supplied with the CD-ROM, and squinting through one red plastic lens and one blue plastic lens. You'll get an occasional sensation of looking at a three-dimensional object, but it's not worth the sacrifice in image quality—all the 3-D photos and movies have a washed-out look. Another annoying feature in some of the titles is "Zoomscape," a low-level form of virtual reality developed by Knowledge Adventure. In Zoomscape sequences, you are in the middle of a fuzzily rendered open space—anything from a science museum to a dinosaur theme park—and shift your perspective by rolling the mouse to the left or right, forward or back. "This takes a little practice," admits the manual. I keep running into walls when using Zoomscape, and I don't know why Knowledge Adventure couldn't stick with the much simpler and more effective method that is a de facto standard for navigating with a mouse: Point at the spot where you want to go, and then click.

Other Knowledge Adventure titles: *America Adventure, Aviation Adventure, 3-D Body Adventure, Bug Adventure, Isaac Asimov Science Adventure II, Space Adventure II,* and *Undersea Adventure.* All are reviewed in this section, except for *America Adventure* in Section a.

MICROSOFT DINOSAURS
★★★½

Developer: Microsoft Corp.; 800-426-9400
Format: Windows, Macintosh
Price: $59

In the big, lumbering herd of dinosaur CD-ROMs for children, *Microsoft Dinosaurs* stands out as the swiftest and smartest. The disk is crammed with nine hundred windows, each describing a different species of dinosaur or exploring a related issue such as the cause of the dinosaurs' extinction. Every window offers several pointers to related subjects, effortlessly threading children from one subject to the next with a single mouse-click. Microsoft has paid attention to how children want to learn—by finding out answers to interesting questions. The window on "record breakers" for example, identifies the dumbest dinosaur: a creature called Kentrosaurus that apparently didn't need brains because it was covered with lethal spikes. The fastest dinosaur was the ostrichlike Gallimimus, certainly able to run at twenty-five miles per hour and possibly sprinting at twice that speed.

Dorling Kindersley Ltd. of London, a publisher of beautifully illustrated children's books, provides the elegant dinosaur paintings displayed on screen. "Dino" Don Lessem, founder of the Dinosaur Society in South Dartmouth, Massachusetts, provides narration for sixteen guided tours through *Microsoft Dinosaurs*, presenting lots of facts without taking himself too seriously. "If T. Rex doesn't make your palms sweat, something's wrong with you," he declares at the start of his tour of the "baddest" dinosaurs. "After all, it was as long as a school bus and might have run as fast . . . Its teeth were the size of bananas and could saw right through meat and crack bones."

There are also six "movies"—really animated cartoons with sound tracks—running from forty-five seconds to three minutes. The movies pull no punches—there are bloody fights, although they aren't sensationalized. My only complaint is that there should be more of *Microsoft Dinosaurs*. Each window contains just a few sentences of text, making it difficult to go into depth on any particular topic.

Science and Nature

EYEWITNESS ENCYCLOPEDIA OF SCIENCE
★★½
Developer: Dorling Kindersley Publishing Inc.; 800-356-6575
Format: Windows, Macintosh
Price: $49

For the same cost as *Eyewitness Encyclopedia of Science*, you could buy a full CD-ROM encyclopedia, such as those reviewed in Chapter Four, Section a, getting even more information on science, along with thousands of other topics. *Eyewitness Encyclopedia* offers a quick overview of scientific subjects with lots of pictures, animations, and audio narration but doesn't back up these bells and whistles with in-depth text.

The content is divided into four major categories—chemistry, life sciences, mathematics, and physics—and then further divided into subcategories that ultimately take children to individual screens covering single topics. From the main screen, for example, a child could click on chemistry, then go to the subtopic on elements and from there to a screen on the subject of metals. The screen displays a color picture of a heated iron bar, showing how the hottest part glows bright yellow, and six sentences of text: "Metals are a group of elements that share certain properties. They conduct heat and electricity well, which is why cooking pans and electrical wires are made of metal. They are also strong and can be shaped easily; this is why they are used to make structures such as bridges. Although there are many similarities between metals, there are also differences that determine how suitable a metal is for a particular use. Of the 109 elements known today, 87 are metals. They are rarely used in their pure state—they are usually mixed with other metals or nonmetals to form combinations known as alloys." Buttons at the bottom of the screen provide a link to other screens describing aluminum, iron, and steel, as well as a text window listing all the known metals and their key properties.

Eyewitness Encyclopedia also contains brief biographies of notable figures in science, ranging from Benjamin Franklin to Stephen Hawking. But again, the biographies are limited—just two paragraphs of text and an abbreviated "life story" time line. A game feature called "Quiz Master" is a complete flop—it simply displays a variety of questions, then invites you to push a button to jump to the appropriate encyclopedia entry for an answer. Still, most of what children will see and hear in *Eyewitness Encyclopedia* is visually appealing and informative. There just needs to be more; most of the articles and biographies stop well short of fully exploring the many intriguing facets of science.

SCHOLASTIC'S THE MAGIC SCHOOL BUS EXPLORES THE HUMAN BODY
★★★½
Developer: Microsoft Corp.; 800-426-9400
Format: Windows-2
Price: $49

The Magic School Bus first started picking up children as a series of science-education books published by Scholastic Inc. Next came a weekly animated cartoon show on the Public Broadcasting System, launched in September 1994. Then Microsoft Corporation followed with a promise to create a series of CD-ROM titles.

The first in this series, released in December 1994, is *Scholastic's The Magic School Bus Explores the Human Body*, a graphically rich, educationally sound, and consistently fun trip through the insides of a young boy named Arnold. If Scholastic and Microsoft can keep up the good work, the Magic School Bus series on CD-ROM will stay at the top of the class for its intended audience of children ages six to ten.

The Human Body opens in the classroom of Ms. Frizzle, an enthusiastic teacher prone to yelling "Wahoo!" at the slightest provocation. The classroom is full of objects that come alive with a click of the mouse, as well as a few games such as reassembling the bones of a collapsed skeleton. When children have finished exploring, they click on a yellow school bus in one corner and—through clever full-screen animation—watch the school bus magically shrink and travel into Arnold's mouth. Sitting in the driver's seat, children can explore the mouth and twelve other parts of the body: the brain, esophagus, stomach, small intestine, large intestine, kidneys, lungs, heart, nose, mouth, liver, and skin.

Arriving at the lungs, for example, children can click on a drawer above the windshield to get a string of facts on the lungs, such as "When you sneeze, air travels out of your lungs at 100 miles per hour" or "We breathe in and out around 20,000 times a day." Clicking a science-experiment monitor to the left of the steering wheel opens a window where children can adjust the mixture of oxygen, carbon dioxide, and nitrogen that Arnold is breathing—too much oxygen, and he hyperventilates; too much nitrogen and he turns blue. Clicking on the rearview mirror changes the picture to show Ms. Frizzle and a group of students in the back of the bus. Click on the students, and they hold up lined notepads displaying animations that show how the lungs function. Clicking on a hand-held video game unit starts a game called "Air Combat," in which children zap nasty viruses and particles of pollution entering the lungs. Finally, children can exit the school bus for an up-close look at the lungs.

Each of the thirteen body parts gets similiar in-depth treatment. Children will find hours and hours of fun in *The Human Body* and won't have to pester Mom and Dad for help; everything related to the program, including the forty-eight-page instruction manual, is written for children. A small green dinosaur named Liz sits in the corner of every scene, waiting to give pointers if children get stuck. Microsoft and Scholastic, by the way, haven't said how many titles they'll produce in the series, but the second CD-ROM was released in February 1995: *Scholastic's The Magic School Bus Explores the Solar System.*

OCEANS BELOW
★★
Developer: Mindscape Inc.; 800-234-3088
Format: Windows, Macintosh
Price: $35

Oceans Below is a shallow trip into the fascinating sport of scuba diving. The CD-ROM tries to take you underwater at prime dive sites but delivers so little information that you won't get deeply involved.

You enter *Oceans Below* through a world map offering dive trips in seven regions: the Caribbean, California coast, Sea of Cortez, Hawaii, Galapagos Islands, South Pacific, and Red Sea. Within each of these regions, you can select from a half-dozen specific locations. Visiting the Bahamas, for example, you see an introductory two-minute Chamber of Commerce video on the islands' tourist attractions. Then you push the dive button and see a large photograph of an underwater scene. Using the mouse to move the cursor over various sea creatures in the scene, you summon very brief narrated video clips. A ten-second clip of a nurse shark says only: "This resting nurse shark proves that not all sharks need to swim in order to move water through those gills."

We're left wondering how the nurse shark manages this trick and whether it is the only kind of shark with such a talent. On a visit to Truk lagoon in the South Pacific, where more than one hundred Japanese and U.S. ships and planes sank during a 1944 battle, the narration is similarly superficial. A sunken tank is shown in another ten-second clip, with a tacky comment that it's now "a fish tank."

Oceans Below is also hobbled by poor-quality video images. Displayed in a three-inch diagonal window on a standard fourteen-inch monitor, the images are grainy and washed out. The whole point of scuba diving—getting close to the intricate and colorful beauty of undersea life—is lost. The CD-ROM even falls short in its attempt to explain the specifics of scuba diving. All you get is a photograph of diving equipment laid out on the deck of a boat; clicking on a specific piece of equipment summons a few sentences of audio commentary telling you nothing more than that fins are used to swim faster and dive tanks hold compressed air.

PLANETARY TAXI
★★½

Developer: Voyager Co.; 800-446-2001
Format: Macintosh
Price: $29

Planetary Taxi is a game that takes children on a tour of the solar system, but it whips them through space so fast that its young audience may lose interest. To make the awesome distances of outer space comprehensible, the CD-ROM puts children at the wheel of a taxi driving down a desert highway. The sun is a yellow balloon, eight feet in diameter, at one end of the highway. Pluto, "a teeny-tiny peanut" at this scale, is 6.5 miles away. In between, the Earth is the size of a cherry tomato at a distance of nine hundred feet, while Jupiter is a pumpkin almost a mile from the sun.

The goal is earning tips from passengers with strange requests. A whiny kid climbs in the backseat, for example, and asks for a drink of water. If you take him to Earth, he presents you with a $200 tip. A man says, "Take me to the nearest star, and I don't mean Michael Jackson." Of course, he wants to go to the sun. A woman is eager to visit the planet where her pig Wilbur will gain the most weight for the county fair. She needs to reach Jupiter.

Planetary Taxi has lots of color graphics and animations. An information screen for each planet gives a complete rundown of size, orbit, and atmosphere. There is also a selection of fascinating one-minute video clips from NASA; my favorite is a simulated flight over the craggy volcanic surface of Venus. But the passenger's thinly veiled quiz questions quickly get tedious and repetitive. On my second mission, I heard a question repeated from my first mission, even though I'd picked up only five passengers the first time around. Children with a passionate interest in outer space will quickly want to flag down a different CD-ROM.

ISAAC ASIMOV SCIENCE ADVENTURE II
★½

Developer: Knowledge Adventure Inc.; 800-542-4240
Format: DOS
Price: $49

Scientists value clarity, precision, and efficiency. Judged by those standards, *Isaac Asimov Science Adventure II* is a dismal failure. The CD-ROM is crippled by Knowledge Adventure's "Zoomscape," a virtual-reality feature in which you roll the mouse to move through a room—in this case a science lab—and go up to pictures on the walls to access the program's various sections. It's a painfully inefficient way to navigate, and *Science Adventure* doesn't offer any simpler alternative such as a point-and-click menu.

The main reference screen does have an index that provides an easy route to the hundreds of short articles in *Science Adventure*, but only if you know precisely what you're looking for. A potentially useful feature called "threads of science" gives a list of subjects to explore. Selecting a subject, you get a series of articles on the topic—"engines," for instance, takes you from the steam engine through the internal combustion engine to jet aircraft. But here again, navigating is a chore. To find a thread, you start on the page listing subjects beginning with the letter "a," then click to get to the page for "b" and "c" and so on. There's no way to skip to the topics under the letter "s." Similarly, the "Science Theater" presents all of the program's one hundred animations and brief video clips without any kind of index or menu.

Another potentially intriguing idea that doesn't work is a button letting you switch between "adult-level" text and "kid-level" text for each article; surprisingly, the two levels are almost indistinguishable. Here's part of the kid-level entry on the ballpoint pen: "Hungary—In 1938, Ladislao and Georg Biro designed the first ballpoint pen. Ink from a supply inside the pen coated a tiny ball at the end of the pen. The ball then rolled and put ink on the paper." Here's the adult-level entry: "Hungary—In 1938, two Hungarian brothers, Ladislao Biro and Georg Biro, designed a ballpoint pen. Ink from an internal reservoir coated a tiny ball at the end of the pen, and the ball rolled, depositing ink on the paper."

Science Adventure, recommended by the developer for age six and above, also contains a selection of games and science activities, but it's not worth the hassle of wrestling with Zoomscape to reach them. For more information on common features in the Knowledge Adventure series, see the review of *3-D Dinosaur Adventure* in this section.

SPACE ADVENTURE II
★★
Developer: Knowledge Adventure Inc.; 800-542-4240
Format: DOS
Price: $49

Space Adventure II is rarer than a shooting star—a revised version of a successful CD-ROM that isn't as good as its predecessor. The original *Space Adventure*, released in 1992, was one of the first titles in the Knowledge Adventure series and gave an excellent introduction to space exploration and space science for ages five and above, with a simple interface perfect for children with minimal reading skills. But *Space Adventure II*, released in December 1994, dumped the previous interface for an incredibly clumsy new design. The updated version also abandoned younger children; the recommended age range is now eight and up, with articles that require a higher reading level than the orginal.

The confusion in *Space Adventure II* starts at the main screen, where children must access the CD-ROM's eight activities by rolling the mouse back and forth to turn a drum. The multisided drum displays the names of the activities; when the correct name is shown, children click the mouse to start that activity. I'm completely baffled in trying to figure out why the developers erected this obstacle course rather than simply giving us eight onscreen buttons and letting us decide which one to push.

Many of the eight activities, too, are unnecessarily difficult to operate. "Reference" is the main access for the many articles and photographs in *Space Adventure II*. But the index displays only five lines at a time, making it difficult to scroll through the contents. "Space Theatre" presents the CD-ROM's collection of thirty-six video clips, many of which are too short—a simulated flight above the surface of Mars runs just ten seconds, and astronaut Buzz Aldrin setting foot on the moon gets just seven seconds. "Simulations" offers four simple animations illustrating subjects such as the phases of the moon and continental drift. "Find the Constellations Game" is a slow and confusing quiz on spotting constellations. "Cosmic Questions" provides audio narration to answer a few common space questions, such as, "Can anything go faster than light?" The answer: Probably not. "Threads of Space" offers eighty-four topics—such as black holes and weightlessness—that children can select to call up a string of related articles. "Hyper-Gallery" uses Knowledge Adventure's awkward "Zoomscape" feature to move through a virtual room full of photographs that take you to various articles—only you don't know what article you'll see until after you click on a photograph. "SkyGlobe" is a planetarium simulator; if children can master the complex instructions, they'll be able to display a view of the stars from anywhere on earth at any time of the year and time of night.

Although the well-written articles in *Space Adventure II* are full of fascinating information, even children with an intense interest in astronomy and space flight will quickly tire of the many steps required to get from one place to another. One further drawback is the presence of a misguided marketing gimmick called *The Adventurers!*, described in the review of *JumpStart Kindergarten* in Chapter One, Section c. For more information on common features of the Knowledge Adventure series, see the review of *3-D Dinosaur Adventure* in this chapter.

SPACE SHUTTLE
★★
Developer: Mindscape Inc.; 800-234-3088
Format: Windows, Macintosh
Price: $35

Space Shuttle appears to have been stitched together from a stack of NASA handouts, without any attempt to create an interactive experience that might appeal to future astronauts. In excruciatingly excessive detail, the CD-ROM describes fifty-three shuttle flights from the first in April 1981 through January 1993. There are very short video clips, playing in a tiny on-screen window, for each launch and each landing. But with the single tragic exception of the *Challenger* disaster in January 1986, all these comings and goings look virtually identical.

The "orientation" and "training" sections offer dry tour-guide recitations of facts and figures about the shuttle program, presented as slide shows with a succession of pictures accompanied by narration. Do we really need to know that potential shuttle pilots are required to have spent one thousand hours at the controls of jet aircraft and have at least a bachelor's degree in engineering, science, or mathematics? At least *Space Shuttle* provides an answer for children's number one question about space travel: How do astronauts go to the bathroom when they're weightless? There is a quick glimpse in one video clip of the shuttle's toilet, complete with seat belt and fans for blowing waste into a storage tank.

Space Shuttle also offers a simple multiple-choice quiz game and a glossary that alternates between definitions that are too simple and too technical. "Astronaut," for example, is defined as "a person trained in space technology," while "orbit" is defined as "the path of a body as acted upon by the forces of gravity." Children will work through all this content in only an hour or two; *Space Shuttle* should offer much more. Why couldn't the developers have added simple simulators allowing children to operate the shuttle's robotic cargo-bay arm, for instance, or even take the controls during a landing?

SPEED
★★
Developer: Knowledge Adventure Inc.; 800-542-4240
Format: DOS
Price: $29

Speed is an ironically appropriate name for this CD-ROM, which appears to have been put together in a rush by Knowledge Adventure Inc. The irony continues with the choice of subject: an Imax movie also called *Speed*. Imax movies, projected on special three-story-high screens at theme parks and museums, create such a dramatic impact that many theaters have signs warning patrons to leave if they start feeling nauseated. Of course, the illusion of reality is lost when a movie like *Speed* is shrunk to fit a window filling half the screen of a computer monitor.

Speed on CD-ROM, recommended by the developer for age five and above, delivers the entire twenty-eight-minute Imax movie, which traces the human fascination with acceleration from the invention of the bicycle in 1839 through the Space Age. Narrated by British science author James Burke, best known for the "Connections" series on public television, the movie is full of race cars screeching around rain-slicked corners and jet aircraft doing barrel rolls. *Speed* slows down considerably on a PC, however, with poor image quality and occasional pauses while the next scene is downloaded from the CD-ROM.

Knowledge Adventure has added some extra material, perhaps to compensate for the lackluster showing of the movie. There are three games, two of which use Knowledge Adventure's clumsy "Zoomscape" technology, and three one-minute simulations, including a roller coaster and a man running an obstacle course. The "Extended Learning Module" is a new name for the main reference screen in the company's Knowledge Adventure series of CD-ROMs. From this screen, children can go through a succession of brief articles on speed-related topics. They'll learn, for example, the current land-speed record: 799 miles per hour, set in 1979 by a three-wheel rocket-powered car in the California desert. The module also offers four at-home projects, including how to build a small sailboat. One of the projects is potentially dangerous—learning about steam power with a boiling kettle—and children are warned they should not try it without the help of a parent or teacher.

These extras, however, won't provide most children with more than an hour or two of distraction. Although the CD-ROM isn't officially part of the Knowledge Adventure series, it shares several common features, including the main reference screen and the use of Zoomscape. For more information on the Knowledge Adventure series, see the review of *3-D Dinosaur Adventure* in this section.

UNDERSEA ADVENTURE
★★★
Developer: Knowledge Adventure Inc.; 800-542-4240
Format: DOS
Price: $49

Undersea Adventure plunges deep into the world of sea creatures and oceanography. Recommended by the developer for age three and above, most of the content is best suited for preschoolers and early elementary students. Children will find well-written text and sharp color photographs of all their favorite underwater animals—sharks, dolphins, whales, tropical fish, and more. The articles, taken in part from the *Random House Atlas of the Oceans*, are both authoritative and age-appropriate. Here's the explanation of how killer whales got their inappropriate names: "Killer whales, also called orca, have had a bad reputation ever since the great whaling days of the 1700s. Orcas were then thought of as ferocious killers . . . Today, however, we know that the killer whale is in fact a 'gentle' predator, a fierce hunter who likes human company and can often be taught to do special tricks in zoos or aquariums."

All the photos and text in *Undersea Adventure* can be easily reached through the main reference screen. The CD-ROM also includes three quiz games for older children and four storybooks—each running five pages—intended for very young children. An interesting side feature is the "Marine Animal Lab," where children can examine the individual parts of ocean creatures. Unfortunately, the lab offers only three animals—a lobster, an octopus, and a shark; I wish there were more. A less successful feature is "3-D Undersea World," hobbled by Knowledge Adventure's awkward "Zoomscape" technology. There's nothing much to do here, just roll the mouse to maneuver through rooms looking at pictures on the wall or join a not-very-interesting treasure hunt. "Undersea Movie Theatre" presents fifteen extremely brief video clips—a breaching whale gets just twenty-five seconds, while scenes of a great white shark eyeing a piece of meat hung next to a diver's cage run for only forty seconds.

Undersea Adventure has enough interesting material, however, to compensate for the weaknesses of Zoomscape and the eye-blink video clips. For more information on common features of the Knowledge Adventure series, see the review of *3-D Dinosaur Adventure* in this section.

THE WAY THINGS WORK
★★★★
Developer: Dorling Kindersley Publishing Inc.; 800-356-6575
Format: Windows, Macintosh
Price: $49

The Way Things Work is the perfect lure for children reluctant to explore science and technology. The CD-ROM presents clearly written text, beautiful illustrations, and clever animations to describe how two hundred common objects operate—everything from a grand piano to a television remote control, from a bathroom scale to a light bulb. Most of the text and drawings come from an outstanding book of the same name by David Macaulay, originally published in England and released in the United States by Houghton Mifflin in 1988. A long-running best-seller, *The Way Things Work* in print has sold 1.7 million copies in the United States alone.

The CD-ROM deserves an equally large audience. Each invention is portrayed in a single screen, with a paragraph or two of text and cartoonlike color illustrations. Supplementing these portraits are twenty-two screens on basic principles of science—such as electromagnetism, friction, and levers—as well as short biographies of well-known inventors. All the material is linked. If you're looking at the description of submarines, for example, you can click on the periscope to go to a screen that explains how a periscope works: "A periscope enables you to see around corners and over walls. It contains two flat mirrors that are set at an angle. The light rays from an object are reflected by the first to the second mirror, and from the second mirror into your eye. This double reflection produces a final image that is the right way around." To illustrate the concept, you see a large wooden tower with mirrors at the top and bottom. Click on a child holding a big red balloon with a scary face and the balloon drifts up into the periscope's field of view. A man looking through the periscope shouts in fright and falls over.

The inventor biographies, too, are a model of interesting yet economical prose, such as this four-sentence entry: "George Manby, 1765–1854—Early fire extinguishers in the 1730s were just glass balls of water that were thrown on fires. Although widely advertised, they were not much used. In 1816, an English army captain named George Manby vowed to develop a portable fire fighter after watching a fire rage on the fifth floor of a building, where hoses could not reach. He invented an extinguisher, similar to modern water models, in which compressed air forced water out of a cylinder." Jumping to a description of fire extinguishers, you then watch an animation showing exactly how the compressed air propels the water.

A friendly woolly mammoth appears on most of the screens, offering a list of related subjects. The mammoth stars in twenty "mammoth movies," one-minute animations that humorously illustrate fundamental science, such as a movie on "mammoth hygiene" showing a mammoth keeper using a lever to rouse a lazy member of the herd. *The Way Things Work* also includes a time line, running from 7000 B.C. through 1984, offering another way to explore the many inventions. Although intended for children, *The Way Things Work* is so much fun and so informative that adults, too, will find themselves eagerly traveling from one fascinating topic to another, never stopping to realize how much they're learning in the process.

WHAT'S THE SECRET?
★★
Developer: 3M Corp.; 800-219-9022
Format: Windows-2, Macintosh-2
Price: $45

A muddled attempt at making science interesting for children ages eight to twelve, *What's the Secret?* offers too many bits and pieces of information without providing an overall structure for learning. The CD-ROM is intended as the first in a series of titles from the producers of "Newton's Apple," a popular science television show that's been running on the Public Broadcasting System since 1982 in collaboration with 3M Company. The TV show does an excellent job of introducing children to science, so perhaps some significant retooling could improve the upcoming CD-ROMs, due to begin arriving in mid-1995.

What's the Secret? follows the format of "Newton's Apple": posing children's typical questions about how the world works, then providing answers that go beyond the obvious to explain fundamental scientific principles. But the television show focuses on single topics, while the CD-ROM wanders all over the map. *What's the Secret?* covers four subjects with no apparent relation to each other: sound, honeybees, the circulatory system, and the operation of roller coasters. The individual subjects are divided into a series of questions that summon text, animations, video clips from "Newton's Apple," and descriptions of simple experiments children can perform themselves.

In response to the question "What is high blood pressure?" children can watch a video clip of a doctor taking a patient's blood pressure, then click through a seven-step animation that illustrates the process while defining the terms "systolic" and "diastolic." In the section on sounds, children get this explanation for how sounds travel through the air: "A sound vibration spreads out from its source in all directions . . . Poke your finger into some water in the sink, or throw a rock in a pond, and you'll see what I mean. The water waves, like sound waves, spread in all directions on the surface." There are also instructions for an experiment in transmitting sound waves through a kite string.

Much of this material is fascinating and well crafted. But I was put off by the confusing interface surrounding the contents. The opening screen shows a mural with pictures of bees, roller coasters, people, doors, and trees. You don't know where any of these objects will take you until you click on them. Once you get to a specific question, there's no clear indication of where to go next. *What's the Secret?* desperately needs a comprehensive index so children can quickly access specific information. The other big problem—the CD-ROM's lack of focus—will apparently be fixed in future titles; according to 3M, the next releases will confine themselves to specific topics such as the brain and the physics of flight.

c. Stories

HAWAII HIGH: THE MYSTERY OF THE TIKI
★★½
Developer: Sanctuary Woods Multimedia Corp.; 800-943-3664
Format: Windows, Macintosh
Price: $39

Almost no children's software is designed specifically for girls, which may be one reason boys tend to be heavier computer users. Sanctuary Woods Multimedia Corporation tries to fill the gap with *Hawaii High: The Mystery of the Tiki*, which the company self-importantly calls "the first interactive title to specifically address the interests of young girls, 8–12, while also providing positive female role models."

Hawaii High follows a classic Nancy Drew-type formula: Jennifer, a blue-eyed, blond high school student, moves to the big island of Hawaii from New York City with her mother. Jennifer feels homesick and friendless until she meets Maleah, a native Hawaiian classmate. On a trip to the beach, Jennifer is dumped by a large wave that also washes up a stolen tiki. The girls then attempt to find the religious carving's rightful owners while being pursued by the two men who stole it.

The story progresses through a series of animated scenes that resemble low-budget Saturday morning cartoons: A scene of Jennifer and Maleah talking, for example, shows only Jennifer's fingers waving in the air. *Hawaii High* creator Trina Robbins, a San Francisco comic-book cartoonist, appears to be quite familiar with Hawaii but can occasionally lapse into political incorrectness, as when a teacher dismisses the class with the announcement "Surf's up!" an unfair slur on Hawaiians' commitment to education.

Sanctuary Woods has done a good job of adding multimedia elements to the story, with a catchy TV-sitcom-type theme song, a narrated guide to playing the game, and a selection of one-minute video clips on Hawaiian geology, animal life, and culture. There's also a helpful guidebook that can be summoned to explain Hawaiian customs and history—you can learn, for example, that "mahalo" is Hawaiian for "thank you" and "kapu" means "forbidden" or "taboo."

The story and multimedia elements together are interesting enough to attract preteen girls to play *Hawaii High* once from beginning to end. But most girls will probably get through the game in a few hours and won't be interested in playing again, making the CD-ROM a marginal investment even at its relatively low price.

THE LEGENDS OF OZ
★★
Developer: Multicom Publishing Inc.; 800-850-7272
Format: Windows, Macintosh
Price: $29

When it comes to the many interpretations of *The Wizard of Oz*, the 1939 movie starring Judy Garland gets my vote as the best way for children to experience this classic tale. Second-best is the original book, written by L. Frank Baum in 1900. *The Legends of Oz* is a distant third. The CD-ROM has five separate parts, none of which is superior to the movie or the book in print.

First, there is the book itself. *The Legends of Oz* contains all twenty-four chapters of the children's story, along with the original color illustrations by W. W. Denslow. But small children won't have the patience to read page after page of text on-screen or sit still while their parents read it to them. Books may be old-fashioned, but they're still easier to take into the nursery when reading bedtime stories. Second, in a confusing twist on the text, the story is retold through the eyes of nine individual characters, such as Dorothy, the Wizard, and the Cowardly Lion. Each character recounts a condensed version of one element in the story, with a succession of Denslow illustrations and actors playing the various voices. The characters also sing the movie's many familiar songs. Third, a dozen very short video clips from the movie—running just ten to thirty seconds each—have been tossed into the CD-ROM. The clips capture several of the movie's most famous lines, such as Dorothy saying, "Toto, I have a feeling we're not in Kansas anymore," and the Wicked Witch of the West vowing, "I'll get you, my pretty, and your little dog, too!" But watching the clips accomplished nothing more than whetting my appetite to see the entire movie.

Fourth, Baum's great-grandson, Roger S. Baum, contributes three stories about lovable creatures called Silly Ozbuls. Resembling fuzzy pink beach balls with springs connecting their heads to their bodies, Silly Ozbuls are treated like pets by the residents of Oz. The three stories are told through still pictures with occasional small bits of animation and recount unexciting adventures—such as Toto and a Silly Ozbul deciding to take a bag of cookies to the Wizard's birthday party—that notably lack the creativity and sparkle shown by Roger's great-grandfather. Fifth, the disk includes a simple and only briefly amusing matching game, in which children uncover two squares at a time to find pairs of pictures.

MIGHTY MORPHIN POWER RANGERS
★★★
Developer: Xiphias; 800-421-9194
Format: Windows, Macintosh
Price: $29

The Mighty Morphin Power Rangers are a lot like cotton candy—empty of nutritional value and highly addictive to children. The adolescent Power Rangers, stars of a megahit children's television show, engage in a silly and never-ending string of plotless battles against rubber-suited outer-space monsters unleashed by evil Queen Rita Repulsa.

But it doesn't matter what I think because I'm long past age ten—the upper limit for Power Ranger fans. Those fans will love *Mighty Morphin Power Rangers* on CD-ROM. And while the disk won't transform children into superheroes, they're sure to enjoy it and maybe even learn something in the process.

The CD-ROM is also a bargain, selling for $29 in most stores. You get five episodes of the show—*A Pressing Engagement*; *Foul Play in the Sky*; *Peace, Love and Woe*; *No Clowning Around*; and *Happy Birthday, Zack*—for less than they would cost on videotape. Each episode on the CD-ROM runs about twenty minutes, what remains after removing commercials from a half-hour children's TV show. The video appears in a window filling one eighth of the screen and has the grainy, muddy appearance of bad home movies, but that's the best performance you can get from today's personal computers. The audio quality is adequate, equivalent to what you hear through a television speaker.

The episodes are presented through the *Matrix Interface*, described in the review of *Kathy Smith's Fat Burning System* in Section d of Chapter 7, with each episode divided into eight "cells." The individual cells are accompanied by several paragraphs of text explaining some aspect of the Power Rangers story, accessed by pushing an "Info" button on the screen. You'll learn, for example, that the five Power Rangers are commanded by a mysterious leader from space named Zordan, who has reached the rather alarming conclusion that "teenage attitude is the most dangerous force in the universe." And that Kimberly, the Pink Ranger, was homecoming queen at her high school in the fictional Southern California town of Angel Grove. "Zordan saw through her helpless debutante facade and chose her for the Power Rangers because of her fearlessness and love of adventure," the CD-ROM explains. "[She can] vanquish Evil Space Aliens without ever smudging her mascara!"

Each episode ends with a brief attempt to add socially redeeming value, as the Power Rangers give children one-minute lessons on such subjects as teamwork and how to avoid schoolyard fights. When exiting the game, you see a list of eight ways to say "no" to drugs. I suspect children see right through these hollow gestures. Instead, the real educational value of the *Mighty Morphin Power Rangers* on CD-ROM is the product itself. Children who aren't otherwise motivated to learn about computers or even learn how to read might just become involved with both in the rush to spend time with their favorite superheroes.

CHUCK JONES' PETER AND THE WOLF
★★½
Developer: Time Warner Interactive; 800-482-3766
Format: Windows, Macintosh
Price: $39

Chuck Jones' Peter and the Wolf has all the right ingredients to tell a wonderful story: the music of Russian composer Sergei Prokofiev; the animation of Chuck Jones, creator of Bugs Bunny and the Road Runner; and voice performances by Kirstie Alley, best known for playing Rebecca Howe on the TV show "Cheers," actor Lloyd Bridges, and child star Ross Malinger, who played Tom Hanks's son in the movie *Sleepless in Seattle*. But the pieces don't quite fit together, leaving a CD-ROM that provides no more than an hour's entertainment.

Prokofiev's 1936 symphonic story introduces children to orchestral music by using various instruments to play the many characters—the flute is a bird, the clarinet a cat, French horns the wolf, and the string section is Peter. Alley narrates a twenty-four-minute performance of *Peter and the Wolf* for the CD-ROM, with Bridges playing the surly grandfather and Malinger the adventurous young Peter. Jones created animated characters that look like the best film animation. Unfortunately, due to the technical limitations of CD-ROM, we don't see a full-screen cartoon feature. The images fill only half the screen, with lots of still pictures and animated sequences that are confined to tiny windows. The performance would look better, and probably sell for less, if it were delivered on videotape.

Beyond the story itself, the CD-ROM has three extra sections that aren't particularly interesting. "Artist & Composer" claims to offer profiles of Jones and Prokofiev but provides only a four-minute video clip of Jones talking listlessly about the art of animation and a short text profile of Prokofiev. "Symphony Orchestra" gives a few paragraphs of text about each instrument in the orchestra, along with video clips of young music students performing. "Log Jam Game" is a dull diversion in which players help Peter cross a river by jumping from one floating log to another; children raised on lightning-fast video games will turn up their noses at the slow pace. *Chuck Jones' Peter and the Wolf* comes with a bonus audio CD containing both the narrated performance and an instrumental version of the work. The audio CD is probably the only part of the package parents and children will want to play more than once.

THE AWESOME ADVENTURES OF VICTOR VECTOR AND YONDO: THE CYBERPLASM FORMULA
★★

Developer: Sanctuary Woods Multimedia Corp.; 800-943-3664
Format: Windows, Macintosh
Price: $39

Fourth installment in the unimpressive *Victor Vector* series, described in the review of *The Awesome Adventures of Victor Vector and Yondo: The Vampire's Coffin* in this section. Time travelers Victor and Yondo visit the year 2093 to find the formula for cyberplasm, the life force of the ailing curator for the Museum of Fantastic Phenomena. They discover humans rebelling against the totalitarian rule of robots, who have taken "the necessary firm measures" to eliminate pollution, war, and famine.

THE AWESOME ADVENTURES OF VICTOR VECTOR AND YONDO: THE HYPNOTIC HARP
★★
Developer: Sanctuary Woods Multimedia Corp.; 800-943-3664
Format: Windows, Macintosh
Price: $39

Third installment in the unimpressive *Victor Vector* series, described in the review of *The Awesome Adventures of Victor Vector and Yondo: The Vampire's Coffin* in this section. Journeying back in time to Rome in 64 A.D., Victor and Yondo must snatch the harp of Emperor Nero after surviving a fight with the gladiator Spiculus.

THE AWESOME ADVENTURES OF VICTOR VECTOR AND YONDO: THE LAST DINOSAUR EGG
★★
Developer: Sanctuary Woods Multimedia Corp.; 800-943-3664
Format: Windows, Macintosh
Price: $39

Second installment in the unimpressive *Victor Vector* series, described in the review of *The Awesome Adventures of Victor Vector and Yondo: The Vampire's Coffin* in this section. This time out, Victor and Yondo are sent to retrieve a Tyrannosaurus rex egg from 70 million years ago, in the Cretaceous period. But the time machine malfunctions, depositing them 245 million years ago, in the Triassic period. Working their way to the right era, they encounter numerous dinosaurs—identified by Yondo's digital dog collar—and meet a new character, a time-traveling female scientist named Delta Mode.

THE AWESOME ADVENTURES OF VICTOR VECTOR AND YONDO: THE VAMPIRE'S COFFIN
★★
Developer: Sanctuary Woods Multimedia Corp.; 800-943-3664
Format: Windows, Macintosh
Price: $39

First installment in the unimpressive *Victor Vector* series, described below. In this episode, Victor and Yondo are assigned to recover the coffin of Count Dracula. The pair must explore Dracula's castle, using a book on vampires to learn answers to trivia questions. By answering the questions correctly and triumphing in a final battle with the evil Ram Axis, they complete their mission.

About the *Victor Vector* series: *The Awesome Adventures of Victor Vector and Yondo* is a flaccid attempt to create a series of interactive comic books for children. The plots, dialogue, artwork, and technical execution all fall short of delivering a compelling experience to the target audience of ages eight to twelve.

Victor Vector, a bland-looking superhero, and his Saint Bernard, Yondo the Digital Dog, are agents of the Museum of Fantastic Phenomena. The pair is sent traveling through time and space to recover interesting artifacts, opposed by a stock villain named Ram Axis. Most of the dialogue consists of witless repartee between the adventurous Victor and the more laid-back Yondo. Spying Dracula's castle for the first time, Victor exclaims, "Check out this pile of rocks, Yondo! You could make a major condo complex out of those things." To which Yondo replies, "Condos haven't been invented yet. Can we stick to the mission?"

Working through each episode requires solving puzzles devoid of any logical structure. In the third installment, *The Hypnotic Harp*, you can enter the temple of Zeus to get a ticket for the circus only by first purchasing a rubber chicken from a souvenir vendor to sacrifice at the altar. But the game gives no clue that you need a rubber chicken, so young players will spend hours on frustrating excursions into dead-end situations.

The comic-book-like color artwork fills only about a third of the screen with limited animations, such as a bat flapping its wings. Even worse, Victor and Yondo's lip movements are completely unsynchronized to the actual dialogue—in one sequence, Yondo's tongue just moves up and down as he speaks. The interface, too, is inconsistent. Sometimes you click on arrows outside the scene to move around; other times you have to click on the edges inside the scene. As Victor says in one of his more profound comments: "Gross me out or what."

Three other *Victor Vector* titles are reviewed in this section: *The Last Dinosaur Egg, The Hypnotic Harp,* and *The Cyberplasm Formula.*

d. Games and Activities

AMAZING ANIMATION
★★½
Developer: Claris Corp.; 800-325-2747
Format: Macintosh
Price: $39

Amazing Animation is a decent effort at providing an animation and drawing program for children, but it suffers in comparison to much superior competitors—especially *Storybook Weaver*, reviewed in this section, and *Kid Pix Studio*, reviewed in Chapter One, Section c. Designed for ages five to fourteen, *Amazing Animation* isn't as easy to learn as *Storybook Weaver* or *Kid Pix Studio* and provides significantly fewer pieces of clip art for launching children into the creative process.

Starting with a blank screen, children pull together three elements to create pictures with *Amazing Animation*. First, they select a background—a photograph of a snow-capped mountain range, for example, or a cartoonlike illustration of an underwater coral reef. Second, they select "stamps," animated cartoon images, to place in the scene. Each stamp performs a few seconds of action—a boy pedals his bicycle, and a monkey swings his arms. Dragging the stamp across the screen creates a pathway that will be repeated whenever children "play" the scene. The monkey, for example, can be made to swing from tree to tree. Third, children pick sounds to add to the scene—anything from a dog's bark to the laughter of a small child. A set of advanced tools intended for older children makes it possible to add text to the scenes as well as resize objects.

But *Amazing Animation* is woefully short on raw material. The CD-ROM offers only twelve background scenes, thirty-six stamps, and fifty-five sounds. *Kid Pix Studio* and *Storybook Weaver*, in a notable contrast, offer hundreds of picture and animation elements. Claris Corporation, distributor of *Amazing Animation*, plans to offer a series of additional stamps and scenes but will charge a steep $29 for each set. *Amazing Animation* also includes a simple drawing program, so children can create their own scenes and stamps. The on-screen controls, however, are confusing; I found it frustratingly difficult to perform simple tasks such as switching paintbrush colors.

BACKROAD RACERS
★★½
Developer: Expert Software Inc.; 800-759-2562
Format: DOS
Price: $19

Backroad Racers is really two products on one CD-ROM: a road racing game that isn't very good and a wonderful animated three-dimensional guide to assembling four model-car kits. In an upside-down marketing decision, the box for *Backroad Racers* touts the game and says nothing about the assembly instructions. The CD-ROM has one other significant drawback: a very difficult installation process, despite a dishonest label on the box declaring "easy to install."

Originally created by Revell-Monogram Inc., the world's largest manufacturer of model kits, *Backroad Racers* is now distributed by Expert Software Inc. Models are big business—Revell claims 78 percent of boys build a model kit by age fourteen. But the kits can be difficult to decipher, with dozens of tiny pieces and only a single sheet of paper giving minimal guidance on gluing the parts together. Revell hit on the bright idea of using a computer to provide animated instructions. *Backroad Racers* displays three-dimensional images of parts flying across the screen into their final assembled form. Young model builders, for instance, can watch the radiator hose and air cleaner shift into position on the engine block. These instructions can be viewed again and again, with the speed adjusted from slow to fast, until the sequence is clearly understood.

But Revell apparently didn't believe these instructions alone would entice children to buy the CD-ROM, so the company added a simple road-racing game. The game, though, isn't likely to impress the average ten-year-old; it's slower and less action-packed than most video and computer racing games.

Backroad Racers opens in a used-car lot displaying four classic "muscle" cars, all of which are available as Revell model kits: a '67 Chevelle, '71 Hemi 'Cuda, '67 Malibu SS Pro, and '70 Boss 302 Mustang. Children select one of the cars and then head to the "Garage" for model-kit assembly instructions or to the "Sales Trailer" for an introduction to the racing game. In the "Sales Trailer," children pick one of four race courses, each with an opponent who delivers taunting remarks in brief quarter-screen video clips. Billy Jean the Piston Queen awaits on the mountain race course, Lars the Cheezer [sic] in the forest, Shark on the beach, and Catfish Louie in the bayou.

The "Garage" is where modeling gets down to business. Children can summon fifteen to twenty animations for each model, showing how to fit the pieces together; view a picture gallery of tools required for assembling their model; watch three two-minute video clips on the fine points of painting, gluing, and finishing; or summon a list of "fun facts" about the car. The Mustang, for example, boasts a 302 cubic-inch 290-horsepower engine with a four-barrel carburetor capable of moving the car from zero to sixty miles per hour in just 6.9 seconds.

Selling for just under $20, *Backroad Racers* doesn't cost much more than one of the model kits—which typically run from $10 to $15—and can be as valuable a tool for young modelers as a tube of glue or a hobby knife. I'd regard the game as an optional accessory; kids should try it once and can then ignore it if they don't find the race courses entertaining. But parents and children alike should be wary of the complex installation process. *Backroad Racers* requires expanded memory, a feature that isn't used in computers running Windows. For most home computers, running *Backroads Racers* will require making a "boot" disk and restarting the PC both before and after each session. The installation program also asks questions you might not be able to easily answer, such as what type of soundboard is inside your machine and the board's internal settings. A companion program with assembly instructions for four model airplanes, *Operation AirStorm*, is reviewed in this section.

CRAYOLA ART STUDIO
★★★
Developer: Micrografx Inc.; 800-676-3110
Format: Windows
Price: $39

Many of today's children are more likely to reach for a computer mouse than a crayon when they get an urge to draw. *Crayola Art Studio*, intended for ages six through twelve, is perfect for these tiny technophiles. The best feature is "Crayola Paint," which presents a large empty window on screen surrounded by a cornucopia of drawing tools and a rainbow of twenty-four virtual crayons. Children can decide how wide a line to draw, select different geometric shapes, add "stickers," or type in text. The finished works can then be stored in the "Art Gallery," and series of pictures can be assembled into an on-screen slide show with the "Picture Show Maker."

For those who aren't feeling quite as creative, there are eight coloring books. Each contains eight interactive pages. "Fashion Designer," apparently aimed at girls, allows children to cycle through different hats, blouses, and dresses for an on-screen model. "Vehicle Designer," more for boys, provides a selection of car parts. Children who have learned to read will enjoy the four craft activities—a badge maker, certificate maker, note-paper maker and "Word Puzzler" game based on the old favorite Hangman. To play "Word Puzzler," by the way, you have to call a toll-free number and get a secret code—a headache thrown in by the CD-ROM's developer to prevent illegal copying.

Computer-literate children should have little trouble learning to use *Art Studio*. A helpful chameleon named Matisse acts as "tour dude," providing both audio and text cues for maneuvering through the program functions. The developers have also added a few nice touches on the side. Click a telephone displayed in the main screen, for example, and you'll hear a succession of corny jokes such as "Why do cows wear bells? Because their horns don't work."

Parents, however, may be annoyed by two aspects of *Art Studio* that kids aren't likely to notice. First, installing the program requires a massive sixteen megabytes of hard-disk space. *Art Studio* can supposedly run straight off the CD-ROM without downloading any files, but I ran into several hang-ups and was forced to download. Second, the package contains almost as many commercials as a Saturday-morning cartoon. The CD-ROM includes five video clips from Crayola maker Binney & Smith, each running two to three minutes, that explain the history of crayons and how they are made. The narration, regrettably, is packed with hype for other Binney & Smith products. There's also an animated "product demonstration" that's really more of an advertisement. Inside the *Art Studio* box, where children are sure to find them, are colorful flyers pitching *Crayola Kids Magazine* and soliciting members for an on-line service called "Micrografx Kids Club."

For younger children, ages three to six, there is a companion product called *Crayola Amazing Art Adventure*. See the review in Chapter One, Section c.

FIREFIGHTER!
★★★

Developer: Simon & Schuster Interactive; 800-983-5333
Format: Windows, Macintosh
Price: $29

At some point during childhood, almost all boys—and many girls—dream of becoming a firefighter. Any child at that point in life will be fascinated by *Firefighter!*, a CD-ROM intended for ages seven to twelve that gives a complete description of the job and takes you along on sixteen fire calls.

Through forty-five minutes of video clips, playing in a window filling a quarter of the screen, you become a "probie," or first-year probationary firefighter. You start by touring a firehouse, watching four two-minute videos on the operation of the dispatch room, pumper truck, ladder truck, and rescue van. Then you click on an alarm bell to go out on a fire call, watching equipment from a fire station in Cambridge, Massachusetts. During the call, the action stops periodically and you're given a multiple-choice question on what to do next. When a man is pulled out of a cold river, for example, the question is: "You see signs of hypothermia, so you get . . . (a) blankets to keep the patient warm, (b) a splint, (c) a doctor, (d) his medical history." If you select (a), the scene continues. If you select any other answer, you're sent to the "PAX 5000," an on-screen computerlike device full of information on firefighting. The PAX 5000 offers three hundred short pages, each just a paragraph or two, on firefighting technique, fire safety, and firefighting equipment. There's even a glossary, where you can pick up firefighting terminology. A "McLeod tool," for instance, is "a combination rake and hoe firefighters can use in a brush fire to scrape fire lines."

There are a few relatively minor weaknesses in *Firefighter!*—the video clips are grainy, and some of the action scenes are confined to a tiny window filling only a fourth of the bigger video window, which itself fills only a fourth of the screen. Also, *Firefighter!* lacks repeat-play value; children probably won't want to go on the fire calls more than two or three times and can read all the PAX 5000 material in under an hour.

IMAGINATION EXPRESS
★★½
Developer: Edmark Corp.; 800-362-2890
Format: Windows, Macintosh
Price: $45

Imagination Express is a noble effort to give children the tools for creating multimedia storybooks combining illustration, animation, and narration. But in putting together such a powerful program, the developers at Edmark Corporation had to sacrifice ease of use and place limits on a child's input. While some children might find *Imagination Express* fascinating, I think most will be happier making storybooks with a few blank sheets of paper and a box of crayons.

Edmark plans to develop a series of *Imagination Express* "theme packs," each a separate CD-ROM offering a different storybook environment. The original program shipped in November 1994 with a theme pack called *Destination: Neighborhood* and a bonus disk called *Destination: Castle*. The theme packs deliver page backgrounds, pictures of characters, and bits of music that can be arranged in stories. *Neighborhood*, for instance, offers fifteen backgrounds such as a kitchen, a playground, and a city street; photographic images of nine "friends" in three or four different poses; and a gallery of furniture and pets. You can select a small boy crouching, for example, and put him next to a seated dog for the opening page of a story about a lost pet. If you've got a microphone plugged into the computer, you can even add your own narration. *Castle* delivers images of a medieval castle, along with a "Fact Book" describing a castle's typical inhabitants, written at a level appropriate for early elementary school students.

To help parents and children get started, the disks include a "Dear Parents" section with video clips of an Edmark software designer explaining the educational theory behind *Imagination Express*. Another section called "Story Ideas" presents video clips of children contributing story ideas—in *Neighborhood*, for example, the ideas include writing down your dreams, imagining life as a cat, and describing a day at school. There's also a sample storybook on each disk showing what can be created with all the different features and images.

Despite this assistance, however, mastering *Imagination Express* is a daunting task. The screen is festooned with control buttons that aren't labeled, and the slender twenty-four-page instruction manual isn't much help. Children under age ten, I think, will face a considerable learning curve before becoming proficient with *Imagination Express*, so parents should expect to spend a lot of time working with younger users. I was also bothered that *Imagination Express* doesn't offer a drawing feature allowing children to make their own artwork. Even with dozens of images, it would be difficult to avoid visual repetition in telling long stories and frustrating for children who want to portray something that's not already included on the CD-ROM. Finally, be warned that *Imagination Express* requires eight megabytes of random-access memory, more RAM than many home systems contain.

KID CAD
★★½
Developer: Davidson & Associates Inc.; 800-545-7677
Format: Windows
Price: $35

Junior architects will find *Kid CAD* an inspirational, if somewhat confining, tool for creating their own three-dimensional models of buildings. Intended for ages seven and up, the program attempts to provide a scaled-down version of adult CAD—short for "computer-aided design"—software, notoriously complicated programs for designing everything from home additions to integrated circuits. *Kid CAD* succeeds in simplifying the CAD concept to the point where seven-year-olds will be able to make designs after spending only a few minutes with the easy-to-read thirty-two-page instruction manual. But there's a trade-off: *Kid CAD* lacks some important features of more sophisticated programs. Children have to work with the program's existing library of objects—offering a variety of walls, floors, windows, doors, furniture, shrubs, and stick-figure people—rather than having the freedom to create their own objects. Nor is there any way to resize an object, so children can't, for example, make a "doggy door" by shrinking a regular door.

Despite these limitations, some children will undoubtedly enjoy *Kid CAD*. The program is full of features that help the creative process. Children can select from three settings for their building—a city, a town, or a farm—and can call on a library of twenty existing structures—including an aerobics studio, treehouse, playground, baseball stadium, and several homes—if they prefer to modify someone else's design rather than starting from a blank screen. Selecting and moving objects requires nothing more than pointing and clicking with the mouse, while on-screen buttons make it easy to change a building's colors and look at the results from any angle. *Kid CAD* is smart enough to realize that knocking down model buildings is as much fun as creating them, so there are ten animated tools for destroying designs—everything from a bulldozer that grinds across the screen to a red blob that sucks up individual objects and says, "Yummy!"

KID WORKS 2
★★★½
Developer: Davidson & Associates Inc.; 800-545-7677
Format: Windows, Macintosh
Price: $39

For children just learning to read, the act of writing and the act of drawing are closely linked. *Kid Works 2* gracefully combines tools for writing and drawing so that children ages four to ten can create their own stories through words and pictures. The program is easy to learn, relying heavily on icons that younger children can memorize, rather than having to wrestle with on-screen text commands.

At the heart of *Kid Works* is "Story Writer," a very simple word processor that lets children see their work in large block letters on the lined paper commonly used in elementary schools. The text can be illustrated with "icons," postage-stamp-size illustrations that fit between words. *Kid Works* includes 250 icons showing everything from a rabbit to a volcano; children can also use the "Icon Maker" to draw their own. "Story Illustrator" is a drawing program for creating full-screen illustrations. Using "Story Player," children can combine text from the Story Writer with pictures from the Story Illustrator to make an on-screen slide show of their work. There's even a crude text-to-speech converter—click a button on the screen and a mechanical-sounding male voice reads the child's story out loud. Story pages can also be printed.

Parents will appreciate the fifty-two-page user manual that clearly explains all the features in *Kid Works*. The manual also includes three pages of tips for parents and teachers, with helpful advice on making use of the program. One teacher, quoted in the manual, sums up why programs like *Kid Works* are so effective: "Reading and writing go hand in hand. Children love to read what they have written themselves. In my classroom, the books that we write and print out are always the most popular books."

MAGIC THEATRE
★★½
Developer: Knowledge Adventure Inc.; 800-542-4240
Format: Windows
Price: $39

In the crowded field of drawing programs for children, *Magic Theatre* attempts to pull away from the pack by offering a unique twist: The CD-ROM comes with a microphone that can be plugged into the computer's sound board, so your kids can record their own voices to accompany stories they draw on the screen. It's a wonderful idea, but the overall program is too complicated for the most likely users, children ages three to seven.

Magic Theatre opens with a blank square in the middle of the screen surrounded by a proliferation of thirty buttons for controlling various drawing functions. From the scenery library, you can pick one of twenty-five backdrops, such as a castle or a city skyline. The "magic brushes" library provides fifty visual effects such as grass, fire, and clouds. The objects library holds twenty-five items, such as a birthday cake and a pitchfork. The "animation" library has fifty objects, such as a crab and a boy on a bicycle that can be made to move across the screen. The "trace" library has outline pictures that children can color, such as a frog and a house. For sound, there is a music library with twenty-five clips of a synthesizer playing such old favorites as "Row, Row, Row Your Boat" and "Yankee Doodle Dandy." There is also a full tool kit of conventional computer drawing tools, allowing children to select colors, line width, and geometric shapes.

In theory, children will use all these tools to create "movies" by drawing a series of pictures and entering them one at a time into a movie library, then adding narration with their own voice. In practice, however, I think *Magic Theatre* is too complicated for younger children to master. The buttons surrounding the main drawing screen aren't labeled, which is a considerable drawback. Pressing the right mouse button calls up an audio description of any button, but that's a time-wasting approach. Also, the library items aren't labeled, and the images are so small that it isn't always clear what you're looking at. Finally, there is no way to resize objects, a key feature in any good computer drawing program. Children attempting to conquer *Magic Theatre* might end up deeply frustrated with its complexity and run to Mom and Dad for help a lot, exhausting the precious reservoir of parental patience.

OPERATION AIRSTORM
★★½
Developer: Expert Software Inc.; 800-759-2562
Format: DOS
Price: $19

A companion to *Backroad Racers*, reviewed in this section, that is identical in structure. *Operation AirStorm* focuses on model airplanes, rather than cars, with instructions for assembling four Revell-Monogram kits: the AH-64A Apache helicopter, F-117A Stealth fighter, F-15E Strike Eagle, and F-14A Tomcat. The game, instead of road racing, is a flight simulator in which the four aircraft are dispatched on military missions. As with *Backroad Racers*, the installation process is very difficult. Most users will have to create a "boot" disk and restart their computers both before and after each session of *Operation AirStorm*.

STEPHEN BIESTY'S INCREDIBLE CROSS-SECTIONS STOWAWAY!
★★★½
Developer: Dorling Kindersley Publishing Inc.; 800-356-6575
Format: Windows, Macintosh
Price: $39

No one will ever mistake *Stephen Biesty's Incredible Cross-Sections Stowaway!* for a navy recruiting program. The CD-ROM presents a detailed and honest kid's-eye view of life aboard an eighteenth century man-of-war gunship. That life wasn't easy—the 850 crew members were crammed into damp, disease-ridden quarters. The food was poor, the medical care rudimentary, and the crew faced gruesome injury and death in battle.

Based on a popular 1993 children's book called *Stephen Biesty's Cross-Sections: Man-of-War*, published by Dorling Kindersley Ltd., the CD-ROM presents color illustrations depicting every nook and cranny of the huge ship. There are two ways to move through *Stowaway*. In "explore the ship," you see a picture of the ship on screen sliced into ten cross sections from bow to stern; you then choose one of the cross sections for further examination. Within each cross section, you move up or down through five to seven decks—in the waist cross section at the middle of the ship, for example, you can go from the hold at the bottom up through the orlop deck, lower deck, middle deck, upper deck, and quarterdeck. At each deck, there are several scenes of shipboard activity. Clicking on a scene brings up a detailed picture with a paragraph of explanatory text. The second navigation option is "meet the crew," which offers fictional autobiographies of twelve crew members from the captain down to an ordinary seaman. Here's how the seaman describes one of his lowly crew mates: "The least experienced—or stupidest—ordinary seamen serve as wasters. George Brooks is a waster who spends most of his time looking after the pigs. He also gets more than his fair share of jobs like deck swabbing, hauling back the fore and main sheets, and cleaning the ship's heads. You don't need much skill for these jobs—the officers say that if a man is not much good at anything, he's 'just a waster.'"

Children will love the animations contained in almost every scene. Click on a group of officers relaxing in the wardroom and they engage in ten seconds of fencing practice. Or, for those interested in grislier activities, click on the surgeon to watch him amputate an injured sailor's leg or click on sailors in the hold to see them clubbing rats. Each scene is accompanied by authentic sound effects of creaking timbers, crashing waves, and the roar of cannon fire. The CD-ROM gets the last word in its name from a built-in game called *Stowaway*, a nautical equivalent of the popular children's game *Where's Waldo?* A ragged young boy has sneaked onto the ship, and you have to find him. He can be anywhere, with just the top of his head peeking out of a barrel or from the side of a doorway. To help younger readers and those who haven't been to sea, many words in the text are linked to a glossary. Click any word in red—such as spitkid, capstan, or supernumerary—and a small text window pops onto the screen with a definition. The only weakness in *Stowaway* is the lack of a narrative structure; there are no heroic stories of battle or tall tales of deadly storms. But children with an interest in history will still find themselves lured into spending many hours stowed away with this fascinating CD-ROM.

Chapter Three:
Games for Grown-Ups

A really good computer game has the power to alter time itself. You'll look at the clock in stunned amazement, realizing hours have slipped by as you rearranged falling blocks in *Tetris* or explored the haunted mansion of *The 7th Guest*. But nothing is more frustrating than a poorly designed game, in which the challenges are either too easy or too difficult. What's more, the abilities and interests of game players vary greatly—so even the best games don't always have universal appeal.

Newcomers to the world of computer games face another problem. Many CD-ROM games push the limits of computer hardware in an effort to present the latest and greatest action and animation. Installing these games may require significant changes in the way your computer operates—a task inexperienced users may find overwhelming. DOS-based games, in particular, often require creation of a custom "boot" disk, a floppy disk that must be inserted in the computer at start-up. To help neophytes, I've noted in my reviews those games that present installation headaches.

Newcomers also need to know that some games are intended for experienced "gamers," hobbyists who are willing to devote large amounts of time to absorbing complex rules for simulations or mastering multifaceted controls in action games. Again, I've noted in my reviews those games that have a significant learning curve.

a. Fantasy/Adventure

BLOWN AWAY
★★★
Developer: IVI Publishing Inc.; 800-432-1332
Format: Windows
Price: $59

Blown Away the movie, released in July 1994, tried to create an atmosphere of constantly escalating tension by casting Jeff Bridges as an officer with the Boston Police Department's bomb squad in a desperate race to stop the evil bomber Gaerity, played by Tommy Lee Jones. The movie, excuse the pun, wasn't exactly a bomb but didn't get strong reviews or draw huge crowds. *Blown Away* the CD-ROM attempts to get players' adrenaline pumping by presenting twenty-four games and puzzles, mostly brain teasers that must be solved while the clock is ticking. Puzzle hounds will enjoy the CD-ROM's many challenges, while action-game fans will be disappointed with the lack of any opportunity to fire automatic weapons or punch bad guys.

The CD-ROM version of *Blown Away* also performs an impressive technical feat: Video sequences that advance the plot are displayed full-screen and look almost as good as regular television. These sequences feature fifteen unknown actors and a few clips of special effects from the movie; the big name stars are nowhere to be seen. The CD-ROM's predictable plot opens with Jimmy Dove, the character Bridges played in the movie, injured in a bomb explosion that turns out to be the handiwork of Justus, a disciple of the now deceased Gaerity. Justus has taken several of Dove's friends hostage, forcing Dove back into action.

Most of the puzzles are simple to learn, making *Blown Away* accessible for players without a lot of computer gaming experience, but they require a good deal of thought. The first puzzle, for example, calls for changing numbers in a three-by-three grid so that each row and column adds up to the same number. Another puzzle resembles the verbal section of the Scholastic Aptitude Test, calling for analysis of word relationships. A sample: Find the missing word in the sequence "pilot - (blank) - cow" based on the clues "fee - tip - end" and "first - head - foam." It took me several minutes to come up with the answer— "steer"—and I'm still not sure why it's correct.

To keep players coming back for more, specific answers to the puzzles are altered each time you play. Also, you earn more points by solving the puzzles quickly. To complete the game with a perfect score of one thousand will require multiple sessions for even the best puzzle solvers. If you're interested in *Blown Away*, make sure your computer meets the hardware requirements: The Windows version demands eight megabytes of random-access memory, a double-speed CD-ROM drive, and a 16-bit soundboard.

DRACULA UNLEASHED
★★★
Developer: Viacom New Media; 800-469-2539
Format: DOS, Macintosh
Price: $59

Dracula, the undead, first left his crypt to haunt the pages of fiction, then movies, and now CD-ROM. *Dracula Unleashed* is a credible attempt at creating an interactive horror movie, complete with blood-sucking vampires and snarling wolves.

You experience *Dracula Unleashed* through the story of Alexander Morris, a wealthy young Texan who travels to London in 1899 to investigate the mysterious death of his brother Quincey. Morris must save his virginal fiancée, Annisette, from Dracula's evil embrace while trying to solve a growing list of vampire-related murders. If you don't move fast enough, Annisette is captured by the dark side and suddenly goes for the jugular, baring newly acquired glistening white fangs to suck your blood, sending you back to the story's beginning.

The action unfolds through ninety-six minutes of video clips, each running a minute or two, that explain some aspect of the story. You navigate by clicking a series of icons. After each scene, for example, you click on the journal icon to hear Morris deliver a summary of recent events. To travel to another encounter, you click on the image of a carriage and then select your destination from an address book. You must pay careful attention to the dialogue in each scene, so you won't miss a clue to where to go next. The multistep process of summoning the carriage, selecting a destination, and then entering a new building is easy to learn but can get tedious.

The video sequences, filling a quarter of the screen, are close to television quality, and the plot is appropriately haunting without exceeding the PG-13 level for blood and gore. But the quality of writing and acting isn't up to Hollywood standards. Taped on a sound stage in Minnesota with local actors, many of the British accents are unconvincing and the script often falls into clichés, as when a friend of Morris's says, "Death is a dreadful business," or Annisette, distraught at her father's death, laments, "Why can't all the things we love stay forever?" Finally, you probably won't want to play *Dracula Unleashed* more than once. But it's exciting and fun the first time around.

HELL CAB
★★
Developer: Time Warner Interactive; 800-482-3766
Format: Macintosh
Price: $69

Hell Cab, a game in which a New York taxi ride turns into a battle for your soul, itself resembles a beat-up Checker sedan, capable of hauling you from one place to another but so hobbled with torn seats and worn shocks that you won't enjoy the ride. As the game opens, you're at John F. Kennedy International Airport with a few hours to kill between flights. A cabbie named Raul Delgado offers a tour of the Big Apple's many attractions. But you find youself $1 short when it comes to paying the fare, so Raul insists you sign a contract mortgaging your eternal soul. To get your soul back, you have to survive three historical adventures: fighting gladiators in Rome for the amusement of the emperor Nero, ducking bullets during World War I trench warfare, and dodging ravenous dinosaurs in the Jurassic period.

Hell Cab was developed by Pepe Moreno, a comic book artist best known for a 1990 "graphic novel" called *Batman: Digital Justice*, created entirely on Moreno's computer. Moreno, however, hasn't fully mastered the transition from computer graphics to interactive games. The action in *Hell Cab* is portrayed with richly detailed photorealistic graphics, accompanied by amusing sound effects such as the grinding gears of a New York cab. But these strengths come at the expense of performance. *Hell Cab* is extremely slow in transitions from one scene to the next, sometimes so slow that I inadvertently skipped past a crucial bit of the story. The dialogue, too, is out of sync with the character's lip movements. What's more, many of the challenges in *Hell Cab* are unoriginal; engaging in sword fights with gladiators, for example, is not much different from playing any number of punch-and-kick video games.

IRON HELIX
★★★
Developer: Spectrum HoloByte Inc.; 800-695-4263
Format: Windows, Macintosh
Price: $69

A refreshingly nonviolent science-fiction strategy game, *Iron Helix* will appeal to game players looking for a chance to think rather than endlessly shoot at evil aliens. The enemy, in fact, is our own future technology. *Iron Helix* opens with a training mission gone wrong: The space destroyer *SS Jeremiah Obrian* is on a training mission to test a new doomsday weapon by destroying an uninhabited planet when a mysterious virus strikes the twelve crew members. The virus alters the pattern of their DNA, marking them for death by the ship's "Defender" robot, which distinguishes friend from foe by examining DNA structures. Sure enough, the crew is wiped out, and a computer malfunction reprograms the *Obrian* to target an undefended planet full of people. You, the player, are put in the role of a rescuer. But you don't board the ship; instead, you sit at the controls of an unarmed biological probe robot sent into the *Obrian* to explore its six abandoned decks. The objective is to find scraps of the crew members' DNA, which are used to unlock the ship's computers, as you dodge the deadly Defender robot.

Iron Helix requires a lot of patience; most of the time, you're just moving the probe through long corridors in search of computer access terminals or DNA strands. You also have to put up with frustratingly small screen displays. The full probe control panel through which you play *Iron Helix* fills only half the screen; the probe's-eye-view window is a rectangle measuring just three inches by two inches on a standard fourteen-inch monitor, while the monochromatic video clips play in an even smaller square window measuring just two and a half inches diagonally. The controls, too, are often sluggish—you have to wait several seconds for a response after you instruct the probe to move. But the interesting puzzles and plot twists in *Iron Helix* will convince avid game players to ignore these limitations.

THE JOURNEYMAN PROJECT TURBO
★★½

Developer: Sanctuary Woods Multimedia Corp.; 800-943-3664
Format: Windows, Macintosh
Price: $49

A gadget-oriented science-fiction adventure game, *The Journeyman Project Turbo* will amuse only devoted computer gamers with lots of time on their hands. The CD-ROM displays beautifully rendered photorealistic images with superficial appeal, but there's very little dialogue, music, or animation to enliven the proceedings—a sure turnoff for gaming novices.

The Journeyman Project is a time-travel story, starting in the year 2318. You are put in the role of Temporal Security Agent #5, who must travel back in time to stop evil forces from altering history. You view the game through a "BioTech interface" attached to Agent #5's left eye. The interface, filling half the screen, provides information on your mission and an inventory of objects in your possession. The outside world is displayed in a rectangular window measuring only three inches by six and a half inches on a standard fourteen-inch monitor.

The challenges you face are standard computer game fare, such as disabling hostile robots and deactivating bombs. As you move through the game, you pick up important objects, such as an oxygen mask to overcome sleeping gas and a stun gun to stop the bad guys. Navigating through the virtual environments and deploying these objects require you to continually push buttons on the interface, a tiring process. And the action is not especially compelling; one of the rules of the Temporal Security service is that you can't have any contact with human beings while time traveling.

If you're interested in playing the game, make sure to buy *The Journeyman Project Turbo* released by Sanctuary Woods Multimedia Inc. in November 1994, not the much slower original version—simply called *The Journeyman Project*—released in January 1993. A sequel called *Buried in Time* is due in 1995.

KING'S QUEST VII
★★★½

Developer: Sierra On-Line Inc.; 800-757-7707
Format: Windows, Macintosh
Price: $55

Sierra On-Line calls its *King's Quest* line "the most popular series in computer gaming," with 3 million copies sold since the first floppy-disk game was released in 1984. I can't vouch for that claim, but *King's Quest* certainly deserves to wear the crown of a best-seller. The intriguing, richly illustrated adventures have the rare ability to entice both experienced gamers and novices with universally appealing tales of magic and chivalry.

King's Quest VII, released in November 1994, is the first in the series to be available only on CD-ROM. Free from the need to compress their work to fit on floppy disks, the developers have created a wondrous experience that looks and sounds like a Walt Disney cartoon, with smoothly animated artwork, the voices of professional actors, and even a few songs. Best of all, *King's Quest VII* is effortlessly easy to operate. The installation and game instructions fill just four short pages in the manual, a blessing for first-time game players who don't want to memorize complicated controls.

The story of *King's Quest VII* opens with a four-minute animation. The beautiful princess Rosella, who lives in the fictional land of Daventry, is resisting pressure from her mother, Valanice, to find a husband. Rosella notices an enchanted pond and jumps in; Valanice quickly decides to follow in pursuit of her wayward daughter.

Mother and daughter soon find themselves in the faroff kingdom of Eldritch. Here the game begins. Pointing and clicking with the mouse, you move Rosella and Valanice through hundreds of scenes, where they encounter strange characters and pick up objects that will help them later in the game. The game is divided into six chapters, half featuring Rosella and half Valanice. Players can choose to enter any of the chapters—another benefit for beginners, who don't have to complete the first chapter to go further into the game.

In the first chapter, Valanice lands in a rocky desert, where she meets a mysterious ghost and a mole that runs a curio shop, among others. In the second chapter, Rosella discovers she has been turned into a troll and is engaged to marry the ugly troll king.

Both mother and daughter must learn certain secrets and find the correct objects to escape from their respective predicaments. There's a happy ending, of course, which I won't give away.

Newcomers to the *King's Quest* series can start with this, the seventh episode, and work backward—the fifth and sixth episodes are available on CD-ROM, although they don't offer quite the same level of animation. Also, the *King's Quest Collector's Edition* offers the floppy versions of the first six episodes on a single CD-ROM.

MILLENNIUM AUCTION
★★
Developer: Eidolon Inc.; 800-245-4525
Format: Windows
Price: $55

Millennium Auction should be a great game, but it isn't. The CD-ROM is full of fresh ideas and strives to break free of the tired old spaceships-and-evil-aliens theme found in most computer games. The developers at Eidolon Inc. say their goal is to create "intellitainment," intellectually stimulating games for adults. But, sadly, *Millennium Auction* collapses under the weight of a clumsy interface, awkward animation, and an uncompelling premise.

The game is set in the year 2010. A single-world government rules amid peace and prosperity, giving the global population time to contemplate the beauty of art and the value of historical artifacts. Acquiring art and artifacts has become a public sport of the rich and famous, described by one character in the game as "the unholy marriage of art and money," conducted in the World Body Auction House. Players of *Millennium Auction* assume the identity of a bidder at the auction, picking among seven characters such as Renate Antonelli, an Italian filmmaker; Takeshi Mori, an "outrageous Japanese cyberpunk entrepreneur"; and Chanteena, a New York opera singer.

The bidders then maneuver against each other to own 140 works of art and historical relics. These items run the gamut from reality to whimsy. There is, for example, a French guillotine from 1793, purportedly employed to behead Marie Antoinette; an "astrobot" that explored the surface of Venus in 2008; and an IBM mainframe computer, with the following tongue-in-cheek explanation: "Although few would recognize the brand today, IBM was at one time quite a large company, with several hundred thousand employees ... A remnant of the company does still exist, generating mailing labels for Microsoft." The objective in *Millennium Auction* is buying low and selling high—just like real life. You search for clues by listening to the conversation of your fellow bidders and visiting the office of Zeke, the auction house janitor, to learn which items are a bargain and which items are likely to go for an inflated price.

This all sounds great in theory. But the flaws of *Millennium Auction* outweigh the potential for entertainment. The game's animated characters look like mannequins and move like marionettes, an odd contrast to the photorealistic rendition of the bidding items. The user interface is also unforgivably clunky—players move through the rooms of the auction house by clicking and dragging "open" and "close" icons into whirlpool-like vortices at the bottom of the screen. The buying and selling process quickly gets stale, especially given the constant annoyance of moving icons around the screen. Eidolon, in short, got caught in a bidding war with itself, adding more and more navigation elements to the point where I can't recommend paying the price of admission for *Millennium Auction*.

MYST
★★½
Developer: Broderbund Software Inc.; 800-521-6263
Format: Windows, Macintosh
Price: $55

Myst is a mystery to me. One of the hottest-selling games of 1994, this interactive fantasy is adored by hundreds of thousands of rabid fans and won almost universal praise from critics. But I just got frustrated with the game's unrelenting string of needlessly complex and frustrating puzzles.

Created by brothers Rand and Robyn Miller, who are reportedly working on a sequel, *Myst* is technically outstanding, with the best graphics and sound I've seen on a computer screen. The images of Myst Island, the mysterious world where the game takes place, look as if they've been lifted from a coffee-table book of classic artwork. The sound effects—from wind whispering through pine trees to the creaking gears of an old elevator—are absolutely convincing.

The plot running through *Myst* is dark and twisted. Myst Island, shrouded in perpetual fog, is apparently the creation of man named Atrus, who lived there with his wife, Catherine, and their sons, Sirrus and Achenar. Something has gone horribly wrong, however, and the island is empty as the game begins. By clicking the mouse, you move from place to place, trying to understand the purpose of numerous structures, including a rocket ship, massive gears, and a planetarium.

Beside a path, you see a scrap of paper. Click on it, and a handwritten letter appears on the screen: "Catherine: I've left for you a message of utmost importance in our forechamber beside the dock. Enter the number of Marker Switches on the island into the imager to retreive the message. Yours, Atrus." Now you have to wander across the island, counting Marker Switches—not my idea of a good time. But that's how *Myst* works. You're constantly trudging from one part of the island to another in search of some obscure piece of a puzzle. Ultimately, you have to travel back in time to four previous eras on Myst Island—The Selentic Age, The Stoneship Age, The Mechanical Age, and The Channelwood Age—to pull together the complete saga of Atrus, Catherine, Sirrus, and Achenar.

The Millers apparently didn't expect *Myst* to be easy, so they included a blank sixty-four-page notebook in the box with the CD-ROM to help players keep track of the many intricacies. If you get really stuck, you can fork over $20 for *Myst: The Official Strategy Guide*, a 160-page hint book from Prima Publishing that gives all the answers.

Even if you solve the puzzles, *Myst* is a sad and lonely pursuit. You never encounter other people or creatures while playing *Myst*, except for reading journals left on the island by Atrus. After several hours of play, I began to feel an overwhelming need for human companionship. But maybe that's just me. If you love exploring intricate fantasy worlds, you might want to join the growing ranks of "Mysties."

QUANTUM GATE: THE SAGA BEGINS
★★½
Developer: HyperBole Studios; 800-693-3253
Format: Windows-2, Macintosh-2
Price: $49

Quantum Gate: The Saga Begins, telling a strange tale where the line between reality and hallucination is rarely clear, comes across more as an interactive story than a game. And, while the story is interesting, its range is much too narrow—you "talk" to characters and even participate in a battle, but your actions don't affect how the plot unfolds. HyperBole Studios, the developer, did a better job with the sequel, *The Vortex: Quantum Gate II*, reviewed in this section.

Quantum Gate is set in the year 2057, when the Earth is dying from environmental overload and a mineral called iridium oxide is the only hope for salvation. A huge supply of iridium oxide has been discovered on a distant planet called AJ-3905, reached through a mysterious portal called the "quantum gate," airily explained as allowing "access to the parallel reality frequencies that surround our own." You, the player, are put in the role of Drew Griffin, a young medical student with a tortured past who's signed up to serve as a soldier on AJ-3905, fighting several species of huge, ferocious insects that plague the mining operations.

As Griffin, you explore the three-level mining station, portrayed in three-dimensional graphics. The story unfolds through video clips, showing the characters talking to you. Occasionally, you pick a response, such as deciding whether to answer a question "yes" or "no." You also hear Griffin's thoughts. The newly arrived private is no superhero; heading into the final battle, he thinks to himself, "I never should have come here. I'm so scared." That final battle, by the way, is a major disappointment—a video-game-like confrontation with the big bugs. You can't win this fight, but you do get a surprise ending that may or may not resolve Griffin's suspicions that everything is not what it appears to be on AJ-3905.

The interface for *Quantum Gate* is jumbled but doesn't take long to figure out. As you move the cursor around the screen, it changes shape to indicate different options—moving to another part of the building, entering a conversation, or retrieving information. Gamers will be disappointed, however, with the lack of challenge—experiencing *Quantum Gate* from beginning to end takes only a few hours. It's also too easy to cheat; the CD-ROM offers a "contents" screen from which you can jump to any one of fifteen chapters in the game, including the final scene.

An important footnote: The original Windows version of *Quantum Gate* was distributed by Media Vision Technology Inc. when it was released in December 1993. Media Vision ran into financial troubles in 1994, however, and suspended its software operations. Because a large number of copies were produced, the Media Vision package should still be available in stores and through mail-order catalogs in 1995. But HyperBole doesn't have rights to the Windows version, and it's unclear whether it will continue to be sold after the Media Vision inventory is cleared out. HyperBole does have rights to the Macintosh version, released in December 1994, which is available directly from HyperBole if you can't find it anywhere else.

RETURN TO ZORK
★★★
Developer: Activision; 800-477-3650
Format: DOS, Macintosh
Price: $49

In the prehistoric days of computer gaming, way back in 1982, one of the first hit titles was called simply *Zork*. It was a text adventure, a crude form of entertainment that has virtually disappeared from the market. The computer displayed a line of text, such as "You are standing in front of a castle. There is an ax at your feet." The player would then type "Pick up ax" to take control of the ax, followed by "Go to door and knock." This was actually considered fun in the days before most gamers even dreamed personal computers could display video images and play real music. *Zork*, one of the best text adventures, inspired a slew of sequels before disappearing in the late 1980s.

Return to Zork, released in October 1993, brought the series back to life with all the modern conveniences. In place of text, the game offers three-dimensional computer graphics, one hundred video clips of second-string Hollywood actors, and an hour of dialogue. Grizzled old gamers who loved the original will be delighted with *Return to Zork*, and even newcomers will find it easy to navigate through the game—if they have the patience to unravel its many complex puzzles.

The story is set seven hundred years after the period covered in the original *Zork* games. The Great Underground Empire of Zork, led by the evil Morphius, is once again threatening humanity. You are dispatched to the mythical Eastlands and Westlands to track down Morphius and stop his dastardly plot. Along the way, you talk to numerous characters—brought to life in video clips superimposed on the scenery—and collect important objects. At the beginning of the game, for example, you stand at the entrance to the Valley of the Vultures. A large vulture blocks your path; to get rid of it, you have to pick up a rock and throw it at the bird. You then visit such colorful locations as Snoot's Farm, Pugney's Ranch, the Dwarven Mines, and Chuckles Comedy Club.

Return to Zork is easier to master than many adventure games. You can call up your inventory of objects, including a helpful map, with a single click of the mouse button. As you move the cursor, text pops on the screen explaining what you're looking at or what actions you can take. Click on a lighthouse keeper, for example, and he'll tell you his story; or you can click a "Q&A" button to ask him a specific list of questions. Still, novices shouldn't expect to breeze through *Return to Zork*—figuring out the many puzzles may be difficult for those who don't already understand the conventions of computer adventure games. Experienced gamers, on the other hand, may already regard *Return to Zork* as over the hill. The game's low-resolution, jagged graphics, and grainy video clips already look dated compared to the latest big-budget CD-ROM titles with razor-sharp images and smooth video.

THE 7TH GUEST
★★★½

Developer: Virgin Interactive Entertainment; 800-874-4607
Format: DOS, Macintosh
Price: $59

On its release in April 1993, *The 7th Guest* became the first CD-ROM game to achieve megahit status—selling more than 1 million copies by the end of 1994. With rich three-dimensional graphics, extensive video clips of real actors, and challenging puzzles, *7th Guest* showed the world what multimedia computers could accomplish. Other games have since matched and even eclipsed the technical achievements of *7th Guest* but haven't diminished the fun of this two-disk interactive adventure.

7th Guest opens with the fascinating and chilling story of evil toymaker Henry Stauf, a murderous drifter who, in a strange dream, gained an unearthly power to make enticing dolls and puzzles. Stauf has invited seven guests to dinner at his eerie mansion on a dark night in 1931; you assume the role of the unidentified seventh guest. The game begins in the foyer of Stauf's Victorian mansion, rendered in beautifully detailed photorealistic computer graphics. A skeletal hand wags its finger in the middle of the screen; using the mouse, you move the hand to proceed through the game. The first thing you hear is the voice of your own character saying, "How did I get here? I remember nothing." Finding out why you are the seventh guest, the fate of the other six guests, and Stauf's twisted plans is your goal as you explore the mansion's twenty-two rooms.

In each room, there is a puzzle. Solving a puzzle summons a video sequence in which the other six guests—including a Broadway showgirl, a washed-up magician, and a debt-ridden businessman—provide clues to the mystery. Maneuvering through *7th Guest* is simple, with everything controlled by the mouse. The cursor changes from the skeletal hand to other shapes when you have located a "hot spot"; a throbbing skull, for instance, to show you've found a puzzle or a rotating eyeball to move puzzle pieces. But figuring out the puzzles is very difficult; you get only a sentence or two of audio instruction from Stauf before struggling to rearrange scrambled letters, run a maze, or try to memorize the notes played on a piano.

7th Guest is so elegant in presenting graphics, music, and video that it often runs very slowly; you have to wait several seconds, for example, each time you move a puzzle piece. I recommend approaching the game with a relaxed attitude—don't expect things to happen quickly, and don't expect to solve more than one or two puzzles in a single session. If you enjoy intriguing mysteries and intricate brain teasers, you'll find yourself spending many happy hours in the Stauf mansion. You'll also be able to make a second expedition—the developers are promising a sequel called *The 11th Hour* in early 1995.

SHERLOCK HOLMES, CONSULTING DETECTIVE
★★★
Developer: Viacom New Media; 800-469-2539
Format: DOS, Macintosh
Price: $59

Sherlock Holmes was always slightly ahead of his time. A century ago, the fictional London detective was solving crimes with virtuoso displays of deductive reasoning and scientific examination of evidence that didn't become standard police procedure for decades. *Sherlock Holmes, Consulting Detective* was also slightly ahead of its time. Released in February 1992, it was the first CD-ROM game to make extensive use of full-motion video and proved popular enough to spawn two sequels.

The three disks, each presenting three separate cases for the sleuth of 221B Baker Street, are faithful to the format of Holmes's creator, Arthur Conan Doyle. "London is not a beautiful city," says Holmes, clad in a dressing gown and clutching his meerschaum pipe, in the CD-ROM's introductory video clip. "Under the soot that covers its buildings is a teeming mass of four million souls trying to survive—mostly off of each other."

Each case begins with a three-minute video sequence in which some distraught soul comes to Holmes seeking the answer to a mystery. Holmes and his faithful associate, Dr. Watson, then travel around London seeking clues. You control the action through a point-and-click interface, opening an address book to select the pair's next stop and recording your progress in a notebook. A regular cast of characters, including Inspector Lestrade of Scotland Yard, help you with reports on the crime. When you feel you've accumulated enough evidence, you go before a judge to answer a series of multiple-choice questions. If you answer correctly, Holmes appears in a final video segment to explain all the details of the crime.

The *Consulting Detective* series is perfect for beginning gamers. The video clips, which appear in a window filling a quarter of the screen, keep things interesting, and the mysteries are challenging without being obscure. Take your time, and take lots of notes; you can't appear before the judge until you've examined all the clues. *Sherlock Holmes, Consulting Detective, Volume II* and *Volume III*, are reviewed briefly in this section—the interface is identical, although the video and audio images are slightly improved.

The three mysteries in the first CD-ROM are *The Mummy's Curse*, the story of a murderous rivalry about Egyptologists, *The Mystified Murderess*, about a young woman who may have been framed, and *The Tin Soldier*, about long-simmering feuds behind the death of an elderly general.

SHERLOCK HOLMES, CONSULTING DETECTIVE, VOLUME II
★★★
Developer: Viacom New Media; 800-469-2539
Format: DOS, Macintosh
Price: $59

The second installment in the *Consulting Detective* series—for a full description see the review of *Sherlock Holmes, Consulting Detective* in this section. The three mysteries in Volume II are *The Two Lions*, with Holmes and Dr. Watson looking for the connection between the killing of circus lions and the murder of a man named Lyons, *The Pilfered Paintings*, a case of two stolen masterpieces, and *The Murdered Munitions Magnate*, where infidelity, money, or politics could be the reason for a back-alley shooting.

SHERLOCK HOLMES, CONSULTING DETECTIVE, VOLUME III
★★★
Developer: Viacom New Media; 800-469-2539
Format: DOS, Macintosh
Price: $59

The third installment in the *Consulting Detective* series—for a full description, see the review of *Sherlock Holmes, Consulting Detective* in this section. The three mysteries in Volume III are *The Solicitous Solicitor*, sending Holmes and Dr. Watson searching for the killer of a young lawyer with more than one lady friend, *The Banker's Final Debt*, the case of an unassuming banker whom someone had a reason to bump off, and *The Thames Murders*, in which five bodies floating in the Thames might be the work of a serial killer.

SPACESHIP WARLOCK
★★★½

Developer: Reactor Inc.; 800-213-3673
Format: Windows, Macintosh
Price: $29

Spaceship Warlock appeared to pop out of a time warp when the CD-ROM game first arrived on the scene in mid-1991. With photographic-quality graphics filling half the screen, compelling theme music, and witty dialogue, this science-fiction adventure was at least two years ahead of its time—and it still seems fresh today, perhaps the only CD-ROM from 1991 that doesn't look seriously dated given all the technological progress of intervening years.

The story in *Spaceship Warlock* is nothing new. You are a nameless human trying to survive in the evil Kroll empire, long after the Kroll defeated earthlings—or Terrans—in a thousand-year war. The game opens on the seedy planet Stambul, and you have to find a way off the planet. You are then captured by Terran pirates, and, if you successfully complete a series of challenges, you join with the pirates to save Earth.

But the story isn't what makes *Spaceship Warlock* special. In addition to the sumptuous graphics and animations, the game is littered with little gems of cynical humor. If you get mugged and killed on Stambul, you see a medical laboratory with a green alien examining a glass jar and get the explanation: "Your brain was removed and sent to the Stambulian Medical Research Institute, where mystified scientists puzzled over its remarkably tiny size." When you succeed in getting enough money to leave Stambul, you call the spaceport and a character named "Robot Leach," imitating the twangy drawl of television host Robin Leach, describes the wonders of the *Belshazzar*, "the most luxurious ship in the galaxy," where you can hobnob with "the ridiculously wealthy."

Spaceship Warlock also dispenses with the unnecessary baggage of most computer games that intimidate novices; you just point and click with the mouse to navigate and interact with the characters. There's no need to learn complicated controls or keep a large inventory of objects. That doesn't mean *Spaceship Warlock* is easy; many situations require considerable patience and concentration to survive. But here again the developers are looking out for the interests of neophytes: The CD-ROM includes a "hints" folder. Inside the folder is a "hints and tips" file with vague suggestions on how to get out of seeming dead ends and a "final solutions" file that tells you exactly how to work through the entire game. I strongly urge you not to look at these files, however, unless you're really stuck; otherwise you'll miss too much of the fun.

UNDER A KILLING MOON
★★★
Developer: Access Software Inc.; 800-800-4880
Format: DOS
Price: $69

If big names and sheer size were the only requirements for creating a successful CD-ROM game, then *Under a Killing Moon* would be a guaranteed hit—the $2 million project features supporting performances by actors Brian Keith, Margot Kidder, and Russell Means, along with narration by James Earl Jones, and fills four disks. But while offering an enjoyable diversion, *Under a Killing Moon* treads familiar turf without contributing anything new or different.

The antihero and central character is Tex Murphy, a slovenly private investigator who makes his meager living prowling "a run-down mutant section of town" in Old San Francisco and speaks in dialogue hijacked from 1930s detective movies. The year is 2042, a decade after nuclear fallout from World War III has divided the population into mutants and "norms." "The air outside feels thick, like I'm breathing through a pair of dirty gym socks," Murphy says in the opening scene. "It's a high radiation day, so most everyone will be staying inside. But I need to hunt for work." Murphy begins investigating a small-time burglary and soon finds himself caught up in a save-the-world struggle against an evil group of norms determined to wipe out the peaceful mutants.

You look through Murphy's eyes as he wanders through numerous computer-generated three-dimensional scenes searching for clues, constantly switching between "movement" mode, which lets you walk around inside a scene, to "interactive mode," where you can examine specific objects and put them in your inventory for use later in the game. The perspective shifts during the transition from one exploration scene to the next; you see an actor playing Murphy talking with cliché-spouting characters who may or may not help him—Keith, for example, plays a crusty older detective who taught Murphy everything he knows, and Kidder is a brassy bartender. You have to select what type of conversation Murphy has with these characters and then listen as he speaks in the mood you've selected. For example, when he talks to the beautiful Chelsee Bando, owner of the local newsstand, the game asks if you want Tex's response to be "(a) subtle innuendo, (b) lovesick puppy, or (c) charmingly curious." A wrong response can deprive you of important clues or even get you killed.

Presenting all these video clips and three-dimensional scenes puts heavy demands on your hardware; a full twenty pages of the game's fifty-page instruction manual are devoted to troubleshooting and explaining the unusually frustrating installation procedure. Be warned: Although the game will run on a bare-bones 386 PC with four megabytes of random-access memory, the manual says you really need a 486 with eight megabytes of RAM for acceptable performance.

THE VORTEX: QUANTUM GATE II
★★★
Developer: HyperBole Studios; 800-693-3253
Format: Windows-2
Price: $59

A continuation of the story launched in *Quantum Gate: The Saga Begins*, reviewed in this section. If you want to experience *The Saga Begins*, you should stop reading this review now because I'm about to give away the surprise ending.

The Vortex: Quantum Gate II picks up where the previous installment concluded: medical-student-turned-soldier Drew Griffin has just been wounded in a battle with the giant insects of planet AJ-3905, then discovers the insects are actually humans. At the beginning of *The Vortex*, he learns these angelic creatures are called the Aylinde. But Griffin continues to be plagued by what might or might not be hallucinations. He must now unravel the truth about the Aylinde and why humans are invading AJ-3905.

To find the answers, you take Griffin through numerous encounters with both humans and aliens. Elegantly rendered graphics fill a third of the screen, showing AJ-3905's forests and deserts. Characters talk to you in video clips that pop up in small windows. You respond by selecting from a list of questions and statements that appear whenever a conversation is in progress. There are also "emotion icons" you select to make your tone of voice angry, sad, aggressive, or neutral. Where you go and what you say determine how long it takes to reach the ending.

The screen is filled with an odd mix of illustrations, video clips, and the numerous icons for exploring the scene in front of you. There's so much music and video, in fact, that *The Vortex* fills three CD-ROM disks. I found this interface confusing at first, then gradually adapted to it as I spent time roaming through the game. The story's depth makes *The Vortex* distinctly superior to *The Saga Begins*, but I wouldn't recommend either to anyone lacking the patience to figure out a sometimes maddeningly complex virtual world. A final note: If you're interested in entering *The Vortex*, make sure your computer is prepared—you'll need a double-speed CD-ROM drive, eight megabytes of random-access memory, and a 16-bit sound board.

VOYEUR
★★★
Developer: Interplay Productions Inc.; 800-969-4263
Format: DOS
Price: $49

Voyeur is like a trashy TV movie of the week—not especially deep or memorable but lots of fun if you're in the right mood. The game puts you in the role of a nameless voyeur, peering through a camcorder at a house across the street. That house just happens to be the mansion of morally corrupt Reed Hawke, a wealthy industrialist on the verge of announcing his intention to run for president of the United States. But first he's spending the weekend with nine members of his dysfunctional family, one of whom he will kill before Monday. You piece together clues to what's happening by peeping in different windows of the Hawke mansion, where you see nearly full-screen video clips of family members hatching plots. Robert Culp, the actor best known as Bill Cosby's partner in the classic 1960s television series "I Spy," plays Hawke; the other family members are played by lesser-known TV performers.

As the voyeur, you have three options in playing the game. You can do nothing, just watch the scenes and get a feel for the plot. You can try to save the family member in jeopardy by sending a warning; that person will then alert the press, ending Hawke's shot at the presidency. Or you can wait for the murder and then alert the police, resulting in Hawke's arrest. The victim is a different member of the family each time—it could be Hawke's grasping sister Margaret, one of his two ne'er-do-well children, or his drug-addicted niece. *Voyeur* is a race against the clock; you have only about an hour each time you play the game to examine all the clues, which include audio segments and physical evidence—such as photographs and letters—as well as video clips. There are enough clues scattered through Hawke manor that most players will have to go through *Voyeur* several times before solving the crime.

Voyeur advertises itself as a "mature" game, with a label on the box stating it is intended for "ages 17 and up." But this isn't really adult entertainment—the characters are often shown in bedrooms in the midst of teasing each other sexually, but they never move beyond PG-13 in either word or deed. Still, the developers have included a "lockout" feature so that parents can enter a secret password and keep their children from playing the game. A final caution: *Voyeur* is a DOS game that requires expanded memory, a feature not activated on most computers set up for Windows. To get *Voyeur* running, you'll need to either edit your AUTOEXEC.BAT and CONFIG.SYS files or make a "boot" disk.

WHO KILLED BRETT PENANCE?
★★★
Developer: Creative Multimedia Corp.; 800-262-7668
Format: Windows
Price: $29

Third in the *Who Killed?* series, subtitled *The Environmental Surfer*. For a full description, see the review of *Who Killed Sam Rupert?* in this section. Brett Penance, a teenage surfing champion about to leave for Stanford University on a full academic scholarship, is found dead on the beach one morning wearing only his wetsuit. In the first case, he has been shot in the chest. In the second case, he has been poisoned. In the third, he has been strangled. The nine suspects in each case include the developer of an oceanfront condominium complex that Brett had been organizing the townsfolk to oppose and an older married woman he'd been romancing. Actress Sheryl Lee, best known for playing Laura Palmer in the television series "Twin Peaks," appears in video clips as assistant detective Lucie Fairwell, offering updates on the investigation.

WHO KILLED ELSPETH HASKARD?
★★★
Developer: Creative Multimedia Corp.; 800-262-7668
Format: Windows, Macintosh
Price: $19

Second in the *Who Killed?* series, subtitled *The Magic Death*. For a full description, see the review of *Who Killed Sam Rupert?* in this section. Beautiful young Elspeth Haskard, an anthropology graduate student specializing in the study of Haitian voodoo, is found dead on the floor of her apartment. Her body is covered with a strange clay and is surrounded by remnants of a voodoo ritual. Among the twelve suspects are jilted lovers, a fellow graduate Haskard has been blackmailing, and scheming professors.

WHO KILLED SAM RUPERT?
★★½
Developer: Creative Multimedia Corp.; 800-262-7668
Format: Windows, Macintosh
Price: $15

The first, and weakest, entry in the *Who Killed?* series from Creative Multimedia Corporation. Sam Rupert is the suave owner of a fancy restaurant, with a neglected wife, jealous girlfriend, and a head chef looking to get out of his contract. One morning, Sam is found dead in the restaurant's wine cellar with only a small puncture wound in his neck. You have to find the murderer among eight suspects. Unlike the three later titles in the *Who Killed?* series, there is only one solution to *Who Killed Sam Rupert?* When you've completed the game, which requires only a few hours, there's nothing to lure you back for a repeat performance.

About the *Who Killed?* series: Police solve 90 percent of murder cases in the first six hours. That's the starting point for the *Who Killed?* series—you have six hours to solve a colorful and confusing murder case. Placed in the role of a police detective, you listen to the testimony of suspects and witnesses, presented in video clips running three to four minutes each.

The four titles in the *Who Killed* series present eight to twelve suspects for each crime, with a range of motives running from money to jealousy to fear. After interviewing the suspects and witnesses, as well as examining crime scene evidence and the autopsy report, you go to a press conference, where a horde of reporters jostle each other and throw out multiple-choice questions. You have to answer correctly seven of the ten questions, all relating to details of the case, before advancing to the next level, where you can issue an arrest warrant for the suspect you think is the murderer.

Time is relative in the *Who Killed?* series. Watching the statement of a suspect takes only three to four minutes but deducts twenty minutes from the game's six-hour clock. If you run out of time, you have to start over. Mystery buffs, though, will enjoy the challenge of deducing the real killer's identity amid numerous false leads. The series gets considerably better in the second episode, in which Creative Multimedia gives players the option of selecting from three different endings to the case. After you've solved the case once, you can play twice more, each time finding a different killer. Also, the series is strictly for adults. Although there is no graphic violence or sex, the games strive to present authentic crimes, with realistic photographs of murder scenes, descriptions of illicit love affairs, and autopsy reports covering all parts of the anatomy.

WHO KILLED TAYLOR FRENCH?
★★★
Developer: Creative Multimedia Corp.; 800-262-7668
Format: Windows
Price: $29

Fourth in the *Who Killed?* series, subtitled *The Case of the Undressed Reporter*. For a full description, see the review of *Who Killed Sam Rupert?* in this section. Taylor French, a newspaper reporter known for exposing the rich and powerful, is found dead in the town park wearing jogging clothes. In the first case, she has been killed by a blow to the head. In the second case, she has succumbed to a drug overdose. In the third, she is the victim of a hit-and-run driver. The eight suspects in each case include a former boyfriend, the subjects of an upcoming exposé, and a strange girlfriend who lives next door. Actress Sheryl Lee, best known for playing Laura Palmer in the television series "Twin Peaks," appears in video clips as assistant detective Lucie Fairwell, offering updates on the investigation.

b. Action and Sports

DRAGON'S LAIR
★★
Developer: ReadySoft Inc.; 905-475-4801
Format: DOS, Macintosh
Price: $59

A delightful action game set in a medieval castle, *Dragon's Lair* is held prisoner by its inadequate installation instructions and the omission of a crucial design feature. The CD-ROM tarnishes the sterling reputation of the original *Dragon's Lair*, a smash-hit video arcade game introduced in 1983—the first to use a laser disk to achieve the look and feel of an animated cartoon.

Dragon's Lair was created by animator Don Bluth, who went on to Hollywood fame and fortune with the movies *All Dogs Go to Heaven*, *Land Before Time*, and *An American Tail*. The story is trite—a hapless knight named Dirk the Daring must wend his way through a haunted castle to rescue the Fair Princess Daphne. But Bluth's artwork and sound effects make the story come alive. Dirk confronts a colorful collection of snakes, goons, goblins, and green ooze monsters, which dispatch him in various amusing ways as players learn the ropes. Although Dirk is constantly hacking at these apparitions with his sword, controlled by the player, the battles are comical enough to allay parental concerns with on-screen violence.

ReadySoft Inc., a software developer with rights to sell *Dragon's Lair* for home video and computer systems, did a respectable job of putting the game itself onto CD-ROM. But installing the program will stump most beginning gamers. *Dragon's Lair* requires expanded memory, a feature not in use on most PCs. Enabling expanded memory means altering the AUTOEXEC.BAT and CONFIG.SYS file or creating a "boot" disk—both unpleasant tasks for novice PC owners. If you don't already have expanded memory running on your PC, *Dragon's Lair* puts an incorrect message on your screen describing what to do. The correct answer is contained in a "readme" file on the CD-ROM, but the file doesn't clearly explain how to implement the changes.

These problems back *Dragon's Lair* into a corner. Experienced computer gamers, on the one hand, can easily handle such alterations. But they're less likely to enjoy *Dragon's Lair* because the game was created more than a decade ago and doesn't offer the high degree of challenge dedicated gamers demand. Gaming novices, on the other hand, would enjoy the game but are likely to be turned off by the installation headaches. There's one other big problem: For some strange reason, ReadySoft left out the crucial "save game" command, forcing players to go back to the beginning every time they restart the game.

FIFA INTERNATIONAL SOCCER
★★★
Developer: Electronic Arts Inc./EA Sports; 800-245-4525
Format: DOS-2
Price: $45

FIFA International Soccer looks like a video game. That's no accident; this CD-ROM is adapted from a Sega Genesis video game with the same name. Playing *FIFA International Soccer* on a computer offers several important advantages, however, including better graphics, more realistic sound effects, and the ability to save games. Soccer fans will also enjoy the extensive list of options provided by the CD-ROM, which allows an almost infinite range of matchups.

The game was developed under license from the Federation Internationale de Football Association, or FIFA, the global organization that supervises soccer's World Cup competition. You pick one of forty-eight national teams—including the United States, England, France, Germany, Hong Kong, Iraq, Nigeria, Russia, and Cameroon—for which you become both coach and star player. Unless you opt for the default setting, you then make a number of decisions to customize the game, such as picking the opposing team, the offensive and defensive strategy for your team, the weather conditions, and even whether team members will grow tired as the game progresses. Once the game begins, you control kicking and passing with either the keyboard or a joystick.

FIFA International Soccer displays animated players in full-screen action, with the view moving up and down the field just like a real game on television. A commentator with a British accent delivers a running description of the game, accompanied by appropriate sound effects from the crowd. In keeping with the international spirit of soccer, you can choose to have the on-screen instructions presented in French, German, Italian, or Spanish as well as English, although the in-game commentary is available in English only. There is just one limitation: This is a single-player game, where you face off against computer-controlled opponents, unlike video games, which typically allow two people to play each other.

MICROSOFT GOLF
★★★½
Developer: Microsoft Corp.; 800-426-9400
Format: Windows
Price: $49

Personal computers, according to some economists, have done nothing to improve business productivity. For all the time we save using PCs to track finances and generate mailing lists, the researchers say, we're wasting an equal amount of time creating unnecessary reports and presentations. There's one other productivity killer that's rarely mentioned: games. *Microsoft Golf* is one of the worst offenders; originally released on floppy disk, the golf game is especially popular in offices and no doubt accounts for hundreds of thousands of hours of lost work time.

Microsoft Golf on CD-ROM is so good that it should be banned outright from every workplace. Up to eight players can go for eighteen holes at the famed Torrey Pines Municipal Golf Course, spread along cliffs above the Pacific Ocean in San Diego. In a window filling about an eighth of the screen, you control the swing of a lifelike male or female golfer. Clicking on the "swing gauge" with your mouse, you've got to hit the ball just right to make par. All the obstacles of a real golf course confront you—sand traps, wind, and trees—depicted in photo-realistic images. Players can select from three ability levels—beginner, amateur, or professional—and can even call on a "Caddie Wizard" to select the best club for each shot.

With the CD-ROM's extra storage space, you get a narrated slide show describing Torrey Pines, a "fly by" showing the lay of the course, and thirty-second video clips of golf pros giving you tips for each hole. The toughest at Torrey Pines, by the way, is number twelve, where you're going uphill and into the wind. Complete newcomers to the world of golf might have some trouble with *Microsoft Golf*—the program doesn't explain how the game works, although there is a helpful glossary. But experienced golfers will experience all the game's joys and frustrations without paying greens fees.

After you've mastered Torrey Pines, Microsoft sells several additional golf courses as floppy-disk add-ons, including Mauna Kea in Hawaii and Banff Springs in Canada. One additional course is also available on CD-ROM; see the review of *Microsoft Golf Championship Course Pinehurst* in this section.

MICROSOFT GOLF CHAMPIONSHIP COURSE PINEHURST
★★★½
Developer: Microsoft Corp.; 800-426-9400
Format: Windows
Price: $25

For golf enthusiasts who already own *Microsoft Golf*, reviewed in this section, *Pinehurst* lets you play the famous Pinehurst number two course in the North Carolina woods. The virtual Pinehurst on CD-ROM includes "fly by" tours of the course and brief video clips of golf pros giving you tips for each hole. Watch out for holes ten and fifteen—each has a dogleg to the left and lots of bunkers.

THE HORDE
★★
Developer: Crystal Dynamics Inc.; 415-473-3434
Format: DOS
Price: $49

Back in the Middle Ages, alchemists were always falsely claiming they could turn lead into gold. *The Horde*, an action game with a medieval theme, is a modern-day piece of false alchemy. TV star Kirk Cameron, best known for his role on the series "Growing Pains," is pictured on the game's box holding a very big sword. Next to him is a breathless announcement, "35 minutes of video on CD-ROM!" This is a less-than-honest attempt to pitch *The Horde* as some sort of cutting-edge interactive movie in which players are involved in the video action. While there are thirty-five minutes of flawlessly produced video clips in *The Horde*, with Cameron in many of the scenes, the material is chopped into brief vignettes—running fifteen seconds to three minutes—that serve only as introductions to the various levels of the actual game.

The game itself is a clumsy attempt to blend a strategy program like *Sim City* with the bloody mayhem of video games such as *Mortal Kombat* and *Street Fighter II*. In the opening video sequence, which fills a quarter of the screen, good King Winthrop is feasting with his retinue when serving boy Chauncey—played by Cameron—saves him from choking. The grateful king rewards Chauncey with the royal sword, Grimthwacker, and a parcel of land in the Shimto Plains. Chauncey's quest is to build a thriving village by planting trees, growing corn, and raising cows. That's the *Sim City* part; depicted in simple computer-generated animations. But he must also defend the village against the ravenous Horde, devilish creatures that eat everything in their path. Eliminating the "hordlings" requires swinging Grimthwacker, resulting in an explosion of blood and a gooey pile of red hordling innards. That's the *Street Fighter* part.

If you succeed in building the village and repelling the Horde, you progress from the Shimto Plains to the Tree Realms of Alburga, the Fetid Swamps of Buuzal, the Kar-Nyar Desert, and finally the Frozen Wastes of Vesh. Along the way, you must learn how to destroy a variety of hordlings by acquiring an arsenal of magic weapons. Although *The Horde* offers better sound and graphics than a typical video game, it still depends on mindless eye-hand coordination to slay hordlings. Players who appreciate such "twitch" games will enjoy the carnage but probably won't want to bother with the intricacies of building a village. Fans of strategy games, on the other hand, will get frustrated or bored with the constant swordplay. Installing the game is also a big headache; most users will have to create a "boot" disk to reconfigure their system's memory managers.

JUMP RAVEN
★★★
Developer: Viacom New Media/Cyberflix Inc.; 800-469-2539
Format: Windows, Macintosh
Price: $69

A shoot-'em-up game with attitude, *Jump Raven* provides a constant stream of wiseguy humor as you blow away a colorful parade of mutants and misfits. The story is set in a dark near future where global warming has flooded much of the planet. Earth's best hope for survival is a collection of genetic samples from recently extinct species. An evil gang of New York City skinheads has stolen the samples, and you, in the role of mercenary hovercraft pilot Jump Raven, must recover them. To complete the mission, you must survive thirty firefights against the skinheads, a vicious group of Chinese smugglers called the Da Kuan, and a gang of mutants called the Cyberpunks.

Before venturing into combat, you go through an introductory sequence explaining the game and letting you configure the mission. You start by picking one of six computer-generated copilots, picking from characters such as Thrash, a former skateboarder, and Chablis, a Southern California mall rat. The copilots all have their strengths and weaknesses, which affect your combat performance. Next, you get $1,000 to spend at the "Arms Mart," where you shop for lasers, shells, rockets, missiles, bombs, and defensive systems. Finally, you choose one of four hard-edged soundtracks: grunge, hip-hop, rave, or heavy metal.

Jump Raven displays the firefights in a window filling a quarter of the screen, surrounded by your hovercraft's control panel. The copilot and your opponents occasionally appear in a smaller window to deliver advice or taunts. As you zoom around the streets of New York, you encounter video billboards delivering cynical advertising of the future. "When you can't take the heat, pack some of your own" is the slogan for one advertiser named "Bazooka Hut." The firefights are rendered in three-dimensional graphics that, while far from lifelike, are superior to most CD-ROM action games. The animated characters, such as the copilots, are less convincing; only the eyes and lips of their cartoon faces move when they're talking. Action-game fans, however, won't be bothered by these minor shortcomings; they'll be too busy enjoying all the flying and shooting. Two important footnotes: Both the Windows and Macintosh versions of *Jump Raven* require eight megabytes of random-access memory. Also, a sequel called *Jump Raven II* is due in late 1995.

MEGA RACE
★★½
Developer: Mindscape Inc.; 800-234-3088
Format: DOS
Price: $45

MegaRace should really be called *MediocreRace*. This road-race shoot-'em-up is standard stuff in the world of Sega and Nintendo video games—there's nothing here that video gamers haven't seen before. Indeed, *MegaRace* has also been released for the Sega CD and 3DO game systems.

The game's introduction uses every cliché in the book: You are "the Enforcer" in a futuristic virtual reality TV show called "MegaRace." The goal is wiping out five "speed gangs" with names like The Vultures and The Scabs. You pick from a selection of armored, missile-firing cars and then whip around fourteen different racetracks through cities, deserts, deserted factories, and even under the ocean. An oily TV host named Lance Boyle appears in an introductory video clip explaining how to play the game and pops up throughout the game to deliver either congratulations or condemnation, depending on your performance. While racing, you have to keep your eye on the surface of the road for special symbols. Driving your car over the symbols can give you extra weapons, a speed boost, or a temporary shield against your opponents' weapons.

Although the race cars can be controlled with either the keyboard or a mouse, *MegaRace* was clearly designed to be played with a joystick. If you don't already have a joystick, I'd recommend getting one before buying the game.

NHL HOCKEY '95
★★★
Developer: Electronic Arts Inc./EA Sports; 800-245-4525
Format: DOS
Price: $45

NHL Hockey '95 nearly conveys the full experience of professional ice hockey; the only thing missing is stick fights. Based on a popular video game for the Super Nintendo Entertainment System and Sega Genesis, *NHL Hockey '95* lets you serve as both general manager and player for the National Hockey League team of your choice. Graduating from a video-game cartridge to a CD-ROM offers two big benefits: better sound effects and the ability to save games. The developers didn't do much to improve the graphics, however; the CD-ROM game displays the same tiny, fuzzy hockey players as the video game version.

Hockey fans willing to overlook the poor graphics will be delighted with the wide range of choices they have in *NHL Hockey '95*. They can play against the computer or against another human, trade players from one team to another, organize a full season culminating in the Stanley Cup play-offs, and consult a complete database of statistics from the real NHL 1993-94 season. Using either the keyboard, mouse, or a joystick, players also take charge of the action on the ice—battling for control of the puck during face-offs, passing to teammates, and taking slap shots at the goal. What you see on the computer screen resembles a television broadcast, with the camera moving up and down the ice while the crowd roars. A final note: If you're interested in *NHL Hockey '95*, make sure you've got enough room on your hard disk—the program demands space for eighteen megabytes of files.

PGA TOUR GOLF 486
★★★½
Developer: Electronic Arts Inc./EA Sports; 800-245-4525
Format: DOS
Price: $45

PGA Tour Golf 486 is as close as you can come to playing the game without getting grass stains on your favorite putter. A complete simulation best suited for experienced golfers, the CD-ROM lets players face off against computer-generated replicas of nine top-ranked professionals: Brad Faxon, Lee Janzen, Tom Kite, Bruce Lietzke, Davis Love III, Mark O'Meara, Jeff Sluman, Craig Stadler, and Fuzzy Zoeller. You can also choose from three different courses: River Highlands in Hartford, Connecticut; Sawgrass in Ponte Vedra, Florida; and Summerlin in Las Vegas.

Almost every aspect of the game can be altered to suit your whim. You can add draw, fade, or backspin to maneuver out of tight situations; adjust the wind level to breezy, windy, or calm; and even adjust the fairway conditions to slow, fast, or normal. When you select a target for your ball, *PGA Tour Golf* displays a "target arc," a yellow line showing the path the ball will follow—if you make the swing exactly right. As with other golf games, you swing by clicking the mouse three times—first to start the backswing, second to stop the backswing, and third to strike the ball. Unless the second click is perfectly timed, your shot will be either underpowered or overpowered. Muff the third click, and the ball will hook or slice.

PGA Tour Golf displays digitized photographic images of the three courses and digitized video clips of the nine PGA players, so you actually see Tom Kite or Craig Stadler take his swing. A selection of sound effects completes the illusion, with chirping birds and the "thwack" of a club hitting a ball. You can compete alone against the computer or against as many as three of your friends; you can also select the scoring format for stroke play, match play, and skins play. *PGA Tour Golf* requires almost as much patience to master as the real game, but the realistic on-screen images keep the action interesting, making it a perfect indoor distraction for dedicated duffers.

REBEL ASSAULT
★★★½
Developer: LucasArts Entertainment Co.; 800-782-7927
Format: DOS, Macintosh
Price: $49

"The Force," that mysterious supernatural power in the *Star Wars* movies, was definitely on the side of LucasArts Entertainment Company when the company released *Rebel Assault* in November 1993. The title quickly shot to the top of the best-seller lists and stayed there through most of 1994, with 1 million copies sold by year-end. *Rebel Assault* captured the hearts and minds of computer gamers by delivering a nonstop spaceflight simulator thrill ride with panoramic full-screen, three-dimensional action.

As a pilot named Rookie One, you take the helm of four vehicles from the *Star Wars* movie trilogy—an X-wing fighter, an A-wing fighter, a T-16 Skyhopper, and a Snowspeeder—to fight evil Imperial storm troopers and, ultimately, confront the dreaded Death Star. All the battles are accompanied by stirring *Star Wars* theme music; in between the action sequences, you're treated to movielike scenes that advance the plot as you try to rescue the rebel alliance from the dark legions controlled by Darth Vader.

Players advance through three levels, from easy to normal to hard. That makes it easy for gaming novices to get a feel for the flight controls but provides enough challenge to keep experienced gamers busy as they seek to master every aspect of *Rebel Assault*. And, in a nod to the relatively small number of women who play action games, the face and voice of Rookie One can be changed from male to female.

There are two minor flaws in *Rebel Assault*. First, the response to the flight controls can be slow at times. The best fix for the problem is buying a joystick, which can be adjusted more easily than the keyboard or mouse. Second, the DOS version can be difficult to install; most users will have to create a "boot" disk and may have to make other changes. Installation of the Macintosh version, of course, is a cinch—you just stick the disk into the computer and double-click on the *Rebel Assault* icon.

c. Traditional Games

BATTLE CHESS ENHANCED CD-ROM
★★
Developer: Interplay Productions Inc.; 800-969-4263
Format: Windows, Macintosh
Price: $39

Chess is the ultimate game of human intellect; the shape of the pieces and the size of the board have almost nothing to do with the excitement and challenge of outwitting your opponent. But *Battle Chess Enhanced CD-ROM* focuses almost entirely on the empty externals of chess—offering pretty animations and amusing sound effects—while ignoring the game's fundamentals.

Battle Chess displays a three-dimensional chessboard populated by animated medieval characters. There is a small white-haired man in regal robes for the king, a hip-wiggling woman in a clingy dress for the queen, an armored warrior for the knight, and so on. When you move the pieces, by pointing and clicking the mouse, they actually walk across the chessboard and you hear their heels clicking on the wooden surface. When one piece takes another, a little drama plays out—the queen unleashes a green lightning bolt to take a pawn, while the king smites the queen with his scepter.

The computer can be set to play at ten levels of difficulty, from novice to expert. *Battle Chess* also offers instruction on the rules of chess in a thirty-four-page manual and in a twenty-five-minute animated tutorial that lets the pieces explain themselves. The animated tutorial appears aimed at children, however, with lowbrow attempts at humor. At the end of the tutorial, for example, the king says he wants to give one last piece of advice: "Avoid losing; that way you'll always win."

Watching the chess pieces slowly cross the board and repeat the same actions when capturing each other quickly grows tiresome. The pieces also block the view, sometimes making it difficult to determine which piece is standing on which square. After about fifteen minutes, I expect most players will switch to the "Quickplay" mode, which dispenses with the animations, or go to the two-dimensional view that shows regular chess pieces. Of course, that cancels out the reason for getting *Battle Chess* in the first place. A much better alternative is *The Chessmaster 3000*, reviewed in this section, which skips the tedious animations and not-so-clever humor in favor of a well-designed but serious approach to playing a serious game.

BICYCLE LIMITED EDITION CD-ROM
★★★
Developer: Swfte International Ltd.; 302-234-1740
Format: Windows
Price: $35

For card players, *Bicycle Limited Edition CD-ROM* covers all the action: bridge, cribbage, poker, and solitaire. As long as you have a computer and this CD-ROM, you'll never be without an eager partner. There's nothing fancy here—the CD-ROM, capable of holding 660 megabytes of data, contains only 3.5 megabytes. But the on-screen images of the playing cards are sharp, and there's an occasional sound effect such as the shuffling of a deck or the stacking of poker chips. Each game also comes with an on-screen guidebook explaining the rules. The CD-ROM gets its unusual name, by the way, from the popular Bicycle brand name of playing cards.

The four games on *Bicycle Limited Edition* offer a range of options to keep things interesting. There are forty-nine variations on Solitaire, for example, grouped in four categories: easy, medium, hard, and kids. Poker players can pick from five-card draw or five-card, six-card, or seven-card stud against three to seven opponents. Cribbage can be played as a regular, duplicate, or "losing" game. The bridge game is standard contract bridge, with a practice mode for those who are just learning.

THE CHESSMASTER 3000
★★★½
Developer: Mindscape Inc.; 800-234-3088
Format: Windows
Price: $39

The Chessmaster 3000 is the best computer chess program I've seen, capable of both explaining the game to beginners and challenging expert players to rigorous tournaments. The program is also incredibly flexible—almost any feature can be adjusted to suit the player's whim.

Perhaps the single most important feature in *Chessmaster* is the ability to customize the computer's performance as an opponent. You can create and save multiple "personalities" for your computer opponent, altering the value each personality attaches to the various chess pieces, the priority of attack versus defense, and how far ahead the computer looks in evaluating moves and countermoves. For chess novices, this means you can occasionally win a game. For experts, this means you can keep surprising yourself by giving the *Chessmaster* new talents.

All the physical aspects of the game are also easy to customize. You can switch from a three-dimensional side view of the chess board to an overhead two-dimensional view, select one of four chess sets, or display timers on the screen. *Chessmaster* has an excellent memory and will instantly produce a list of all captured pieces or every move from the beginning of the game. And there are numerous instructional features, including an on-screen rule book, automated analysis of game strategy, and a library of 150 classic games played by grandmasters. Beginners will especially appreciate a feature called "natural language" advice: A reassuring male voice recommends your next move and gives a brief explanation of the strategy. At the beginning of a game, for example, *Chessmaster* suggests the traditional advancing of the king's pawn and says, "The king's pawn opening move is both popular and logical. It controls the center, opens lines for both the queen and the bishop, and usually leads to an open game in which tactics rather than slow maneuvering predominates."

Mindscape Inc., developer of the Chessmaster series, first introduced *The Chessmaster 2000* on floppy disk in 1986, then followed with *The Chessmaster 3000* on floppy disk in 1991. The CD-ROM version came out in 1992. Mindscape released *The Chessmaster 4000* on floppy disk in 1993, offering expanded tutorials, more computer "personalities," and support for playing other humans through a modem or local-area network. A CD-ROM version of *The Chessmaster 4000* is due in early 1995.

COWBOY CASINO
★★
Developer: Intellimedia Sports Inc.; 800-269-2101
Format: Windows, Macintosh
Price: $49

If you're looking for a friendly, supportive place to learn the intricacies of poker, don't linger in *Cowboy Casino*. The CD-ROM takes you to a Wild West saloon to face five ornery opponents who rarely have anything nice to say to you or each other. What's more, there's only limited assistance for newcomers to the game.

Cowboy Casino lets you play four types of poker: Five-Card Draw, Five-Card Stud, Seven-Card Stud, and Texas Hold 'Em. You can adjust the house rules to control the minimum and maximum bet, the ante, and the limit on raises. You can also choose to receive advice on each hand, but all you get is one-word instructions on whether to fold, call, or raise. On the screen, you see cartoonlike illustrations of your five opponents—identified only as the Dude, Miner, Cowboy, Bandito, and Gambler—seated around a poker table. Chips and cards fly across the screen as the game moves forward, and you're presented with on-screen buttons to push indicating how you want to bet.

Video clips, playing in a four and a half inch diagonal window on a standard fourteen-inch monitor, pop up randomly during the game, allowing your five opponents to make insulting remarks. When you lose a hand, for example, the Gambler might say: "That's why I like playing cards with strangers. They're too smart to cheat and too dumb to win." The Bandito, a tasteless portrayal of a Hispanic character, declares: "You play cards the way I like, gringo—stupido!" Nor are the video clips perfectly matched to the action; the gambler told me he'd won a hand by bluffing, even though he had two pairs and I had only one pair.

Other than the video clips, *Cowboy Casino* lacks any significant amount of audio or movement. An annoying repetitive loop of honky-tonk piano music plays in the background, although it can be turned off. But other than the movement of cards and chips, the poker games are static and dull. You'll probably learn more from a pocket-sized sixty-four-page book called *The Basics of Winning Poker*, included in the box with the CD-ROM, than from playing *Cowboy Casino*.

STAR WARS CHESS
★½

Developer: Mindscape Inc.; 800-234-3088
Format: Windows
Price: $49

Star Wars Chess is a gimmick that quickly grows tiresome. The CD-ROM offers a conventional computer chess game, except the pieces are replaced by animated figures from the *Star Wars* movies. The white king is Luke Skywalker, while the black king is the evil emperor. The all-powerful queens are played by Princess Leia and Darth Vader. Chewbacca is a knight, Yoda a rook, and the white pawns are played by R2-D2 facing black pawns who are Imperial Stormtroopers. Whenever you make a move, there is a stirring bit of Star Wars theme music and the characters stride purposefully in the direction you've sent them. When one piece takes another, you're treated to a colorful animated battle. Princess Leia and Darth Vader, for example, shoot each other with hand blasters. An Imperial Stormtrooper uses a large rifle to dispatch R2-D2, who explodes with a high-pitched squeal. Then a giant pipe descends from the ceiling and vacuums up the small robot's charred bits and pieces.

All this dramatic activity is amusing for about five minutes. Then it becomes nothing more than a repetitive obstacle to actually playing a game of chess. Moving a piece takes thirty seconds for the music and walking. Moving and capturing another piece takes almost a minute. It's also difficult to keep track of which character represents which piece—you'll have to think twice to remember that C-3PO is a bishop and the enemy rooks are Imperial Walkers. Nor do you have the option of switching to regular chess pieces. At least you can speed things up by turning off the music, walking, and battles, but then you've eliminated the only reason for buying *Star Wars Chess* in the first place. What's more, the CD-ROM greedily demands eight megabytes of hard-disk space.

TETRIS GOLD
★★★

Developer: Spectrum HoloByte Inc.; 800-695-4263
Format: DOS, Windows, Macintosh
Price: $45

I spent about two years of my life addicted to the computer game *Welltris*, a variation on the incredibly popular *Tetris*. Created by Russian computer programmer Alexey Pajitnov in the mid-1980s in what was then the Soviet Union, *Tetris* was the first Soviet computer game to find a market in the West. Pajitnov's simple yet bewitching game displays geometric shapes made of four squares that fall slowly down the screen like snowflakes. You maneuver the shapes in an effort to form neat rows when they touch bottom. If you complete a row, it disappears from the screen to make room for more squares. Learning the rules for *Tetris* takes less than five minutes, but the task is so compelling that you can spend hours and hours playing the game without getting bored. *Tetris* is one of the few computer games with universal appeal—women like it as much as men, children as much as senior citizens. It even made the leap into the world of video games, becoming one of the most popular titles for Nintendo's hand-held Game Boy.

Pajitnov and his associates went on to create five sequels to *Tetris*, all revolving around the same idea of rearranging geometric shapes. Spectrum HoloByte Inc., the primary U.S. company to license Pajitnov's work, has put all six of these games onto *Tetris Gold*. In addition to the original *Tetris*, which runs in DOS or on the Macintosh, there is *Welltris*, with shapes dropping down a four-sided well, also for DOS and Macintosh; *Faces . . . Tris III*, in which the shapes are parts of faces, for DOS and Mac; *Wordtris*, a Scrabble-like variation where the blocks are letters that must be formed into words, for DOS and the Mac; *Tetris Classic*, a reissue of the original with improved graphics and sound, for DOS and Windows; and *Super Tetris*, an expanded version with bonuses such as falling bombs that blast away excess pieces, for DOS, Windows, and Mac.

The manuals for each game are included on the CD-ROM and can be printed. Spectrum HoloByte also threw in two interesting extras: the original crude DOS prototype for *Tetris* and a ten-minute video clip of an interview with Pajitnov. As a package, *Tetris Gold* is a wonderful way for first-timers to discover the allure of *Tetris* and a chance for recovering addicts like me to revisit the entire enchanting series.

TRIVIAL PURSUIT
★★

Developer: Virgin Interactive Entertainment; 800-874-4607
Format: DOS, Macintosh
Price: $39

Trivial Pursuit is one of my favorite board games. What makes it so much fun is the social interaction—a group of four or six people laughing or groaning as they correctly or incorrectly answer trivia questions. This friendly banter is one thing a computer can't deliver, making *Trivial Pursuit* on CD-ROM a hollow imitation of the real thing. The CD-ROM lets you play *Trivial Pursuit* by yourself, but without a circle of friends the game is nothing more than a string of quiz questions. Up to six players can face each other with the CD-ROM, but trying to cluster a group of people around a computer keyboard and monitor isn't my idea of a good time—I think most players would quickly shift back to the original board game.

The CD-ROM version of *Trivial Pursuit* faithfully re-creates the original's structure, with four thousand new questions in six categories: "Arts & Entertainment," "History," "People & Places," "Science & Nature," "Sports & Leisure" and "Wild Card." Players move pieces around a circular board on the screen, "rolling" a computer-generated die. The questions are displayed as text along with a photograph or, occasionally, a video clip. Players are supposed to say the answer out loud, then click the "Answer" button on the screen to see if they were correct. There's also a "Fast" mode, which dispenses with the game board; the computer selects categories at random and keeps score.

The questions will sound familiar to *Trivial Pursuit* fans. Among them: "What character did this actor portray in *Trading Places*?" with a picture of Dan Aykroyd. The answer: Louis Winthorpe III. And "What fly's appearance in 1975 threatened California's $6 billion agriculture industry?" with a picture of a pile of tomatoes. The answer: the Mediterranean fruit fly.

Putting aside the lack of social interaction, the CD-ROM has two annoying features that, mercifully, can be turned off: syrupy New Age background music and silly animations of cartoon characters performing tricks whenever you win a "wedge." If you want to pursue *Trivial Pursuit*, skip this trivialized CD-ROM and stay with the classic board game.

VIDEO CUBE: SPACE
★½

Developer: SoftKey International Inc.; 800-227-5609
Format: Windows
Price: $19

A totally unappealing game, *Video Cube: Space* is the CD-ROM equivalent of a Rubik's Cube. The object of the game is to assemble fragmented pictures, and the reward is viewing a brief, muddy, space-related video clip such as a close-up of Jupiter or a rocket launch. Each of the video cube's six sides is divided into a grid of sixteen squares. Each of these squares is actually a smaller cube; clicking on the cube reveals its six sides. The game consists of clicking on the small cubes to assemble each side into a complete picture. When you've solved all six sides of the bigger cube, you go to the next and more difficult level—through eighteen levels of tedium. At the time of its release in October 1993, *Video Cube: Space* was advertised as the first in a series offering the same game with different videos. Subsequent titles were due by the end of that year. None of these games ever emerged, no doubt because the original is so unworthy of duplication.

d. Role-Playing, Strategy, and Simulation

AEGIS: GUARDIAN OF THE FLEET
★★★
Developer: Time Warner Interactive; 800-482-3766
Format: DOS
Price: $49

Hard-core naval officer wanna-bes will love *Aegis: Guardian of the Fleet*. This extraordinarily detailed simulation game puts you at the controls of a U.S. Navy *Ticonderoga*-class cruiser equipped with the ultrasophisticated *Aegis* computer-controlled combat system. "The simulation is built around the premise that defines modern-day warfare: The winner of an engagement is the side that can detect an opponent first and then be the 'firstest with the mostest' in terms of weapons delivery," the *Aegis* manual explains. Through various control screens, you monitor enemy movements with radar and sonar, then respond with an array of armaments that includes missiles, torpedoes, and deck guns.

The game is fully explained in a ninety-four-page manual that even includes a glossary of navy terms so that you can distinguish between such acronyms as SLAM (Standoff Land Attack Missile) and SLAR (Side-Looking Airborne Radar). First-time skippers can start with eighteen training missions before shipping out for combat encounters in the Falkland Islands, the Persian Gulf, and off the coast of Libya. The simulation is helped by suitably blaring orchestral music, brief video clips of *Aegis* systems in action, and on-screen access to detailed navy technical manuals. But *Aegis* the CD-ROM, like the real-life combat system, is complicated enough that I'd recommend it only to serious game players. Novices should also be warned that *Aegis* demands twenty megabytes of hard-disk space and, for some users, may require creation of a boot disk to operate properly.

BETRAYAL AT KRONDOR
★★½
Developer: Sierra On-Line Inc./Dynamix Inc.; 800-757-7707
Format: DOS
Price: $55

Betrayal at Krondor is an intensely complicated role-playing game that will appeal only to fantasy hobbyists willing to spend many hours learning the customs of a strange world and solving numerous puzzles. Also, the CD-ROM is hampered by low-resolution graphics, betraying the game's origin on floppy disks, which have far less capacity for artwork and animation. In moving to CD-ROM, the developers added a sound track but didn't upgrade what you see on the screen.

Set in the mythical kingdom of Midkemia, *Betrayal at Krondor* spins a tale of brave knights, evil elflike creatures called Moredhels, and powerful magicians. The top half of the screen displays your location in Midkemia, depicted in blocky graphics that resemble a video game. The bottom half of the screen contains numerous buttons for the complex interface to move through the landscape, interact with characters, and retrieve objects you've collected on your journey. To complete the game, you must engage in swordfights, work through mazes, and cast magic spells.

The CD-ROM also provides two bonus features. There is a five-minute video clip of an interview with Raymond E. Feist, author of a series of fantasy novels that inspired *Betrayal at Krondor*, and an on-screen "hint book" that describes how to play the game and gives solutions for the puzzles. You'll learn, for example, that it's important to buy a lute in the village of Tyr-sog and practice with the instrument. "When minstrel skill is high enough, you can earn money barding at inns," the book explains.

But newcomers to computer gaming may think they've fallen under an evil spell in trying to install *Betrayal at Krondor*. Getting the game to run requires making a "boot" disk that, on most computers, will make it impossible to run Windows without restarting the machine. Yet the hint book runs only under Windows, so moving from the game to the book and back is very frustrating.

CASTLES II: SIEGE & CONQUEST ENHANCED CD-ROM
★★★
Developer: Interplay Productions Inc.; 800-969-4263
Format: DOS
Price: $49

A complicated and fascinating simulation game, *Castles II: Siege & Conquest Enhanced CD-ROM* puts you in the position of a feudal lord who must build castles, recruit an army, maintain diplomatic relations with rivals, and care for the populace. The game is set in

France and opens in the year 1312, during the Hundred Years War. The king has just died without leaving an heir, and you assume the role of one of five scheming nobles determined to outmaneuver your rivals for the throne.

Castles requires considerable strategic thinking. The main game screen displays a map of France, showing your territory and the land controlled by your rivals. Working with a complex system of points, you attempt to build up resources while subduing opponents through either alliances or war. The primary goal is building new castles, which you must design to withstand attack successfully. A twenty-minute narrated tutorial is a big help in getting started, as is the fifty-six-page instruction manual.

The CD-ROM also has two nice bonus features. There are twenty-eight minutes of video clips on the history of castles taken from a documentary produced by the British Broadcasting Corporation. The clips, which fill the entire screen with slightly washed out images, are full of fascinating details: The first castles, for instance, were made of wood, but the builders quickly switched to stone after discovering how easily attackers could put a torch to timber. There is also a guide to ten real-life castles, with color photographs and narration, including Windsor Castle and the Tower of London.

If you've never played a simulation game before, be warned that *Castles* demands a good deal of time and effort to master. Expect to spend several hours learning the ropes before claiming any battlefield victories. Also, the CD-ROM requires expanded memory, a feature available but not activated on the typical home computer. Most users will need to make a "boot" disk, then restart their computers before and after each session of *Castles*.

COMANCHE CD
★★½
Developer: NovaLogic Inc.; 818-880-1997
Format: DOS
Price: $49

Even real pilots may never get any closer to flying the hot new Boeing-Sikorsky RAH-66 reconnaissance/attack helicopter than *Comanche CD* because defense budget cuts could shoot down the aircraft before it enters production. The RAH-66, nicknamed the Comanche, would be a powerful fighting machine, carrying Hell-fire anti-tank missiles, Stinger antiaircraft missiles, and a cannon capable of firing 1,500 rounds per minute.

Comanche CD provides a technically accurate simulation of the helicopter's cockpit controls and an impressively sweeping view through the windshield that fills half the screen. You can even go on night missions, where the landscape is depicted in shades of green as seen through night-vision goggles. But the sound and graphics in *Comanche CD*, a game first released on floppy disk in 1992, show their age—there are only a few limited sound effects for such events as the launching of missiles and explosions of military hardware on the ground, and the graphics often break into unrecognizable jagged shapes when you make quick turns.

The CD-ROM brings together three related floppy-disk titles: *Comanche Maximum Overkill*, the original simulator with fifty combat missions; *Comanche Mission Disk 1*, an add-on module with thirty new missions; and *Comanche Over the Edge*, an add-on with forty missions. The missions involve fictitious military confrontations in 1999 with Russians, Cubans, and drug smugglers; each mission has a colorful name such as "Valley of Instant Death," "Let's Get Dangerous," "Into the Fire," and "Hell From Above."

Getting *Comanche CD* into the air can be a project in itself. The game requires making a "boot" disk and restarting your computer both before and after each game. A twelve-page installation booklet does a very poor job of explaining the process, although the eighty-page user manual gives a clear explanation of how to run the simulation once you've overcome the installation hurdle.

FALCON GOLD
★★★
Developer: Spectrum HoloByte Inc.; 800-695-4263
Format: DOS
Price: $69

Before you take the controls of an F-16 fighter and zoom away to combat missions around the world, *Falcon Gold* forces you through the most rugged ground school I've ever seen in a computer game. The ground school, in this case, has nothing to do with flying. Instead, you have to earn your wings as a computer jock in making this extremely demanding flight simulator work on your computer. Specifically, the program requires 604 kilobytes of free conventional memory and the use of expanded memory; meeting these parameters will almost certainly require creating a "boot" disk that significantly reconfigures your computer's memory structure. "*Falcon* stretches memory to its limit," the installation guide explains, then drives home the point a few paragraphs later by saying: "Due to the complexities and intense realism of this simulation, *Falcon* requires a vast amount of free memory to operate." Some users may even need to change parts of their computer's operating system software to open up enough memory.

If you complete this preflight checklist, *Falcon Gold* delivers a supersonic thrill ride for would-be pilots. The CD-ROM, released in summer 1994, is a collection of four related air combat simulators from Spectrum HoloByte Inc. previously published on floppy disk. *Falcon 3.0*, the core program, puts you in the cockpit of a U.S. Air Force F-16. Through the canopy, you see simple but adequate representations of the earth and sky as well as enemy fighters. Using either the keyboard or a joystick, you work the flight controls, weapons, navigation equipment, and radar screen. After completing a series of training missions, *Falcon 3.0* sends you on combat missions to Kuwait, Israel, and Panama.

Also included on the CD-ROM are *MiG-29*, a simulator of the newest fighter from the former Soviet Union; *Hornet: Naval Strike Fighter*, a simulator for the U.S. Navy's F/A-18 fighter; and *Operation: Fighting Tiger*, an extension to *Falcon 3.0* with combat missions in Korea, Japan, and the disputed Kashmir region between Pakistan and India. As a bonus, the CD-ROM delivers a 165-page book and one-hour video called *The Art of the Kill*, describing real-life tactics for aerial combat. To help you follow the complex examples, which cover such technical concepts as "positional geometry" and "weapons envelope," the CD-ROM provides eighteen *Falcon 3.0* training missions tied to lessons in *The Art of the Kill*.

Indeed, perfecting your flying skills will require considerable study, not just an itchy trigger finger. The CD-ROM comes with an awesome eight hundred pages of manuals and handbooks, not including *The Art of the Kill*. If you're not intimidated by all this paperwork and the agonizing installation process, I wish you good luck and good hunting.

GETTYSBURG
★★½

Developer: Turner Home Entertainment; 800-294-0022
Format: Windows
Price: $69

Could the Civil War battle of Gettysburg in 1863 have turned out differently, with a victory for the Confederate forces led by General Robert E. Lee? Or could the Union forces commanded by Brigadier General John Buford have ended the battle in less than three days, with fewer than the 51,000 casualties on both sides? Here's your chance to rewrite history. *Gettysburg* is a battlefield simulation in which you command the troops on either side, or even both sides simultaneously, and watch the results unfold on maps of the Pennsylvania countryside.

In a potentially misleading marketing maneuver, however, the CD-ROM is advertised as a companion to a movie of the same name, produced by media mogul Ted Turner and released to movie theaters in 1993. The film, starring Tom Berenger, Jeff Daniels, Sam Elliott, and Martin Sheen, got tepid reviews and subsequently appeared on Turner's TNT cable television network in June 1994. The CD-ROM came out in April 1994, with a box resembling the movie poster. The box also boasted of "featuring scenes" from the movie and offering "special narration by Civil War authority Shelby Foote."

Don't be fooled. *Gettysburg* on CD-ROM is just a game with a very small amount of background material. It's not a historical reference on the battle, and it won't provide more than a half-hour of involvement for anyone who isn't interested in playing a complex battle simulation. The only nongame content is a "history" section within the game with eight one-minute "documentaries" narrated by Foote, best known for his appearance in the Civil War series on the Public Broadcasting System, that give quick overviews of the battle's origins, weaponry, and day-to-day action. There is also an audio recitation of Abraham Lincoln's Gettysburg Address and Lee's address when the Confederacy surrendered in 1865.

The game is an interesting simulation, although not particularly innovative or action-packed. You control the speed of battle and the direction of troop movements, then check to see what casualty levels your troops have sustained. Clicking the right mouse button on the icon for any unit produces an information screen listing a few key facts about the unit, as well as a ten-second clip from the movie showing the unit in action. Newcomers to simulation games should expect to spend several hours learning the ropes, however, before moving onto the battlefield.

OUTPOST
★★★½
Developer: Sierra On-Line Inc.; 800-757-7707
Format: Windows
Price: $55

Outpost is more than just a game—it's almost a college-level course in space science. An incredibly elaborate simulation adventure in which you struggle to build self-sustaining colonies on distant planets, *Outpost* is an awesome intellectual challenge requiring careful thought on such dilemmas as balancing the need to grow food against the demand for housing. The CD-ROM is so intricate that I'd recommend it only to fans of simulation games with lots of free time on their hands, but people in that category will quickly get caught up in managing their own artificial world.

The setup for *Outpost* is basic: Fifty years in the future, Earth is about to be destroyed by an asteroid. You are the commander of a spaceship departing on a one-way trip to colonize the planet of your choice in another solar system. "The colony must be managed as though it were any other city on Earth: Short-term goals include continuing the building program, keeping the rabble employed and happy, exploiting planetary resources, recycling waste and dealing with random events such as meteorite strikes," the eighty-eight-page manual explains. "Eventually, you may want to pursue long-term goals such as advancing the civilization, researching new technologies, establishing terraforming operations and establishing trade between colonies."

Outpost creator Bruce Balfour, a computer-game designer and science-fiction writer who started his career as a NASA researcher, is rigorous in his devotion to scientific and psychological accuracy. The manual even includes a four-page bibliography citing everything from NASA research papers to *The Prince* by Niccolo Machiavelli. The graphics in *Outpost* are rendered with lifelike detail, providing lots of visual information as you watch your colony's buildings, tunnels, and robotic construction units. Animated sequences give an eerie feeling of traveling through space.

But the game isn't all dry science. "When you land, a certain element of the population feels that your leadership is lacking, and they abscond with up to half of your colonists and resources to start a rebel colony," the manual declares. "You'd like to deal with it, but you're too busy trying to survive . . . When you screw up, morale goes down. When morale goes down enough, colonists begin leaving for the rebel colony. So don't screw up."

Screwing up is all you'll do, however, for at least the first several hours playing *Outpost*. Balfour apparently recognized how complicated a game he had created and provides lots of help. In addition to the manual, there are lengthy "readme," hint, and tutorial files on the CD-ROM. The game can also be played at four levels—beginner, easy, medium, or hard—so first-timers can learn the rules without too many three-hundred-mile-per-hour windstorms or rebel attacks. If that isn't enough, Balfour has written a four-hundred-page book called *Outpost: The Official Strategy Guide*, available from Prima Publishing.

RETURN TO RINGWORLD
★★½
Developer: Time Warner Interactive/Tsunami Media Inc.; 800-482-3766
Format: DOS
Price: $45

Return to Ringworld is a conventional role-playing game, the kind most commonly found on floppy disks, that takes little advantage of CD-ROM technology—the only improvement is the addition of audio narration and dialogue. Indeed, the game is the sequel to a floppy-disk adventure called *Ringworld: Revenge of the Patriarch*. Both titles are based on the novels of science-fiction author Larry Niven but substitute trite computer-game situations for Niven's subtle plots.

The setup for *Return to Ringworld* is a complicated dispute between humans and a catlike race called the Kzin, inflamed by the meddling of another race called the Puppeteers and the vigilante tactics of the United Nations' Amalgamated Regional Militia. You play one of three characters—Quinn McQuarry, a male human; Miranda Rees, a female human; or Seeker of Vengeance, a male Kzin—who blew up a Kzinti spaceship and are now trying to escape death at the hands (or is it paws?) of Kzinti leaders. The three must travel to the planet Ringworld to search for "a dramatic technology that may lay waste to all of known space."

Proceeding through this adventure requires exploration of alien environments, piloting various space vehicles, and finding secret objects in dark forests, common clichés of sci-fi computer games. The characters are maneuvered through an awkward process of selecting from different icons to walk, look at an object, talk to another character, or use an object. The graphics aren't up to CD-ROM standards—you see small, blocky two-dimensional characters and hear video-game-like synthesizer music. Fans of the first *Ringworld* game will appreciate the addition of voices in *Return to Ringworld*, but players more familiar with the full potential of CD-ROM games won't be impressed.

SSN-21 SEAWOLF
★★
Developer: Electronic Arts Inc.; 800-245-4525
Format: DOS
Price: $45

SSN-21 Seawolf sinks to a watery grave, torpedoed by poor graphics, limited sound effects, and almost no animation. The war-game simulator—based on the newest generation of U.S. Navy attack submarine that may never get built because of budget cuts—is only partly true-to-life. As the captain of a Seawolf, you study maps, peer through the periscope, listen to the sonar, and control the weapons. But the displays don't look like those on a real submarine. The sound effects, such as the propeller noise of surface ships, are more realistic, but there aren't many of them. The animations are the weakest element, showing missile launches and ships exploding in unconvincing blocky images that resemble video games. These limitations aren't suprising, considering that *Seawolf* was originally developed for floppy disk and the CD-ROM version adds only a musical soundtrack. The entire program can be installed on your hard disk, taking just fourteen megabytes, and run without the CD-ROM.

Seawolf takes players through thirty-three missions during a fictitious war launched by the now defunct Soviet Union. Each mission has a different objective; you start out just shadowing Soviet convoys, then move up to defending vital targets. In a mission called "Invasion Alaska," for example, you must sink a Russian task force intent on destroying the Alaskan oil pipeline. Mastering naval tactics, as explained in the game's sixty-page manual, is important. If you use active sonar—which emits a telltale "ping"—in the presence of Soviet subs, you give away your position and are immediately thrown out of the game.

Raw recruits to the world of computer gaming will also face the challenge of making a "boot" disk to reconfigure their computer because *Seawolf* insists on expanded memory—a feature available but not in use on most computers—and six hundred kilobytes of free conventional memory.

SIMCITY 2000 CD COLLECTION
★★★½
Developer: Maxis; 800-336-2947
Format: DOS, Windows, Macintosh
Price: $69

In a city I modestly named "Mikeberg," my people didn't appreciate the wisdom and kindness of their despotic ruler. So, unleashing all the awesome power of the computer game *SimCity 2000*, I ravaged the ungrateful populace with fires, earthquakes, and tornadoes. Serves 'em right.

Please excuse the delusions of power. Anyone who has played the excellent *SimCity 2000* or its predecessor, first released in 1989 and now called *SimCity Classic*, knows what I'm talking about. The *SimCity* product line gives ordinary mortals the heady experience of controlling life, although life has an irrepressible habit of refusing to follow your well-intentioned plans. Maxis, the developer of *SimCity*, is gradually moving its products from floppy disk onto CD-ROM. The company's first offering, released in December 1994, is *SimCity 2000 CD Collection*, a $69 disk containing three software packages that would cost about $95 if purchased separately on floppy disks. The CD-ROM provides the DOS version of *SimCity 2000* along with a utility program called *SimCity 2000 Urban Renewal Kit* for customizing your own cities and a collection of ten pre-programmed simulations called *SimCity 2000 Scenarios, Volume 1: Great Disasters*. As a bonus, the CD-ROM also offers a selection of cities designed by other *SimCity* users and the staff at Maxis. Windows and Macintosh versions of *SimCity 2000 CD Collection* were due in April 1995.

SimCity 2000 is the best kind of computer game: intellectually engaging, with minimal emphasis on keeping score or determining who's a winner and who's a loser. The object is simply to build a thriving city. You start with an empty landscape displayed on the computer screen, then add houses, factories, schools, office buildings, power plants, roads, bridges, and other necessities of modern life. As you work, the population of your city increases, but they'll complain through the pages of the local newspaper if services don't keep pace with growth. If conditions deteriorate sufficiently, people will start moving away. You've got to keep one eye on the dwindling city treasury and the other watching for randomly generated disasters that can wipe out your hard work. If you're feeling especially mean, you can deliberately trigger a flood, riot, or air crash.

Although it takes a little bit of practice to master *SimCity 2000*, most players won't need more than an hour or two to get comfortable with the basics. But because the game has so many variables—you can even rearrange the terrain or build fusion power plants if your city makes it to the year 2050—it's impossible to run out of new ways to make things interesting. The *Great Disasters* program also helps alleviate any possible ennui. You suddenly find yourself in charge of the *SimCity* re-creation of Davenport, Iowa, after the historic floods of 1993, or Silicon Valley, California, in the year 2010, when a misguided microwave beam zaps the populace.

SimCity has been so successful that Maxis has created an entire line of similar simulation games. Two others were available on CD-ROM in early 1995: *Unnatural Selection*, in which you create new life forms through genetic engineering, and *SimTown*, a simplified version of *SimCity* specially designed for ages eight to twelve. The *Unnatural Selection* CD-ROM is DOS only; *Sim Town* was launched for the Macintosh with a DOS version due in May 1995.

Maxis also licensed the CD-ROM rights for three of its titles to Interplay Productions Inc. *SimCity Enhanced CD-ROM* is a version of *SimCity Classic* with forty minutes of video clips in which actors pop onto the screen describing the latest municipal disaster. Interplay also planned to bring out CD-ROM versions of *SimAnt*, a virtual ant farm, and *SimEarth*, in which you design entire planets, by mid-1995. Computer neophytes should note, however, that *SimCity Enhanced CD-ROM* requires expanded memory, a feature available but not used in most personal computers. Running the game requires making a "boot" disk or reconfiguring the AUTOEXEC.BAT and CONFIG.SYS files. For more information on the Interplay titles, contact the company at 800-969-4263.

STAR TREK: 25TH ANNIVERSARY ENHANCED CD-ROM
★★★
Developer: Interplay Productions Inc.; 800-969-4263
Format: DOS
Price: $49

Computer gamers who love the original "Star Trek" television series will get a kick out of playing *Star Trek: 25th Anniversary Enhanced CD-ROM* if they're willing to overlook the game's out-of-date low-resolution graphics. The biggest treat is extensive audio narration provided by the TV show's original cast: William Shatner as Captain James T. Kirk, Leonard Nimoy as Mr. Spock, DeForest Kelley as Dr. Leonard McCoy, James Doohan as Scotty, George Takei as Sulu, Walter Koenig as Chekov, and Nichelle Nichols as Lieutenant Uhura.

There's lots to do in the game, which presents a training exercise followed by seven "missions" taking the U.S.S. *Enterprise* to different planets in defense of the United Federation of Planets. You have to fight three types of enemy spaceship—Klingon battle cruisers, Romulan warbirds, and Elasi pirates—as well as work through various puzzles and mysteries after beaming to the various planets. On the *Enterprise*, you get to plan and execute missions—summoning information from the computers, navigating the ship, and firing its phasers and photon torpedoes. On the ground, you operate more *Star Trek* hardware such as hand phasers, tricorders, medical kits, and communicators. Throughout the game, you click on the *Enterprise* crew members to hear them tell you what's happening.

Star Trek: 25th Anniversary was originally developed for floppy disk, and the compromises dictated by the limited storage space of floppies show on the CD-ROM. The scenes—such as the bridge of the *Enterprise* and the planet surfaces—are rendered in jagged, cartoonlike graphics reminiscent of a video game. The characters on the screen are "sprites," inch-high animated figures resembling tiny marionettes.

Newcomers to computer games will appreciate the extensive documentation; the CD-ROM comes with a thirty-two-page instruction manual and a ninety-six-page "cluebook." The cluebook is written like a novel, describing the situations behind each mission. At the back of the cluebook is a "walkthrough," detailing every step required to complete the game, so novices will always be able to get themselves out of situations in which they can't figure out what to do next. Novices need to be warned, however, that *Star Trek: 25th Anniversary* needs expanded memory, a feature available but not activated in the typical home computer. Most users will need to make a "boot" disk, then restart their computers both before and after each *Star Trek* session.

WING COMMANDER III: HEART OF THE TIGER
★★½
Developer: Electronic Arts Inc./Origin Systems Inc.; 800-245-4525
Format: DOS-2
Price: $69

In spending $4 million to create *Wing Commander III: Heart of the Tiger*, released in December 1994, Origin Systems Inc. set a record in the relatively young field of CD-ROM gaming. The money bought a big-name cast for the game's video sequences, including Mark Hamill, who played Luke Skywalker in *Star Wars*; Malcolm McDowell, the villain in *Star Trek: Generations*; and John Rhys-Davies, the ebullient sidekick to Indiana Jones in *Raiders of the Lost Ark*. What the money didn't buy was a spark of creativity—*Wing Commander III* flies through the very familiar territory of spaceship shoot-'em-ups with a formula almost identical to the hit game *Rebel Assault,* reviewed in this section, released a year earlier.

The cliché-ridden plot is absolutely predictable: It's the year 2654, and the human race is threatened by the evil and aggressive Kilrathi, who look somewhat like the flying monkeys from *The Wizard of Oz*. In the video sequences, ace pilot Christopher Blair—played by Hamill—works through various plot twists, including deciding between two women who are chasing him. "Pilots . . . they'd rather crash and burn than make a commitment," sighs the beautiful and frustrated mechanic Rachel in one of the game's corniest lines.

You control Blair's movements during the video sequences, which fill half the screen and can occasionally affect the outcome of a scene by selecting one of two choices for Blair—should he, for example, act suspicious or supportive when a fellow pilot mentions his mysterious past? There's a huge number of these scenes in *Wing Commander III*, so many that the game comes on four disks.

But the video is mostly a setup for the many combat missions, where you take the controls of five types of spaceship to battle the Kilrathi, who also have five types of spaceship. The full-screen combat missions offer everything gamers want: lots of choices for weapons and tactics, with battle scenes brought to life through three-dimensional computer graphics and vivid sound effects.

Experienced gamers will need at least thirty or forty hours to figure out the complex flight controls, complete all the missions, and reach the end of the story. Computer-game novices, on the other hand, probably shouldn't even attempt to get started with *Wing Commander III*. Not only is the game difficult to learn, but it has very steep hardware requirements: You'll need at least a 486 processor running at fifty megahertz, eight megabytes of random-access memory, and a double-speed CD-ROM drive. And, although you can play the game with either the keyboard or a mouse, you won't enjoy it unless you spend $20 to $30 more for a joystick game controller.

Even if your home computer system meets these lofty demands, installing *Wing Commander III* is almost as big a struggle as the game's many combat missions. When you open the box, you'll discover a twenty-four-page "Install Guide" full of jargon on such esoteric subjects as disabling disk cache programs and switching from double to triple video buffering. Also, you probably won't be able to avoid making a "boot disk" to get your PC properly configured. Experienced computer gamers know how to deal with such challenges, but many beginners don't and won't be interested in learning.

WOLFPACK
★★★

Developer: NovaLogic Inc.; 818-880-1997
Format: DOS, Macintosh
Price: $39

WolfPack is an elaborate reconstruction of the Battle of the Atlantic, the World War II confrontation between German U-boats and U.S. destroyers. If you're prepared for the rigors of a very detailed war-game simulation, *WolfPack* has all the features you'll want—you can assume the role of either a U-boat commander or destroyer captain working through thirty-six missions included on the CD-ROM or using a "construction set" to design your own missions. But *WolfPack* is definitely not for gaming novices; the fifty-eight-page instruction manual assumes you're already familiar with the intricacies of computer simulation games, and there's no on-screen help file to bail you out in the midst of battle.

Military history buffs will marvel at the careful attention to detail in *WolfPack*. Destroyers, for example, only have radar if the mission is set in 1942 or later since the U.S. fleet didn't have radar before that date. Also, the U-boat's radar detector changes in 1944 from a device called "Metox" to "Naxos." The construction set allows the user to control every aspect of the game, even selecting the "personality" of each captain from four options: "relentless," "resourceful," "cautious," and "by the book."

The missions themselves take you through all the rigors of a real military command. At the U-boat's helm, you see a control panel filling the screen with numerous buttons and dials. To stalk and sink a destroyer, you first spot the ship through the periscope—which displays a crude animated image that fills a quarter of the screen—while monitoring depth, speed, and range before firing a torpedo. The destroyers use radar and sonar to find the U-boats, which are dispatched with either deck guns or depth charges.

WolfPack offers nothing more than gazing at submarine and ship controls; there are no photographs or video clips and only limited sound effects. The graphics are low-resolution, and the animations, such as torpedoes striking a ship, are about at the level of video games. But these limitations won't bother dedicated simulation gamers, who care only about the mental challenge—and that's where *WolfPack* rises above the surface.

Chapter Four:
Encyclopedias and Reference

Exploiting the huge data storage capacity of CD-ROMs, developers have unleashed a large number of reference works. But, buyer, beware: The quality of these CD-ROMs is only as good as the information put on the disk. Many retailers sell obsolete reference works at discount prices, so make sure you're getting the most current version of any reference CD-ROM you purchase.

a. Encyclopedias

Everyone in the software industry dreams of creating the next "killer app"—short for "killer application"—a program so compelling that it single-handedly motivates people to buy personal computers. Spreadsheets, which allowed anybody to manipulate financial data easily, were the killer app of the early 1980s and sold the first generation of PCs. Word-processing software was the next killer app, virtually eliminating office typewriters.

Encyclopedias on CD-ROM are the closest thing yet to a killer app for multimedia, a single product convincing many PC owners to get a CD-ROM drive. It's not hard to figure out why: The three leading CD-ROM encyclopedias cost just $99 and deliver everything you'd get in print encyclopedias costing from $500 to $1,500. CD-ROM encyclopedias, in many ways, are also easier to use than their print predecessors. You can effortlessly jump from reading an article on Haiti, for example, to an article on the Dominican Republic, which shares the Caribbean island of Hispaniola with Haiti, without having to put down the "H" volume and get the "D" volume off the shelf. Text from CD-ROM encyclopedias can also be quickly copied into word-processing documents, greatly speeding up preparation of school reports. And the annual editions of CD-ROM encyclopedias, generally available for only $49 to registered users of the previous year's disk, give a fully updated reference work, far superior to the clunky yearbooks that are offered as updates for print sets.

Compton's Interactive Encyclopedia, 1995 Edition, Microsoft Encarta '95, and *The 1995 Grolier Multimedia Encyclopedia*—the three market leaders, which I call the Big Three—have also gone beyond merely presenting the text, photographs, charts, diagrams, and maps found in print encyclopedias. They've added a smattering of multimedia content, including video clips, audio narration, music excerpts, and animations. With only a few hundred such files on each disk, the odds of hitting one among 26,000 to 33,000 articles is minimal. Still, it's a treat to hear a coyote howl while reading an article on predators or to see a few seconds of an astronaut walking on the moon in an article on space exploration.

The Big Three CD-ROM encyclopedias are now selling several million copies a year, far outdistancing sales of print encyclopedias. In the last few years, each annual update—the 1996 editions should be out in September or October 1995—has made the CD-ROM encyclopedias even more powerful, with improved navigation features and expanded multimedia content. This success has forced the long-established *World Book* and *Encyclopaedia Britannica* to edge reluctantly toward delivering their product on disk. *World Book* and *Britannica*, however, still rely on door-to-door salespeople to market their print editions. These salespeople would walk away if the two products were widely available on CD-ROM for just $99. In an awkward compromise, *World Book* and *Britannica* on CD-ROM are sold by the two companies' direct sales force only at very high prices—$395 for *World Book* and $995 for *Britannica*.

So how do you decide whether you need a CD-ROM encyclopedia, and, if so, which one do you buy? Keep in mind that even the best encyclopedia can't provide infinite depth on all subjects. A good encyclopedia will give you a little bit of information on a lot of subjects, providing a starting point for further study. Most adults don't need an encyclopedia; the heaviest encyclopedia-using years, according to academic experts, are ages nine through fifteen, corresponding to fourth through tenth grades.

If you do want an encyclopedia, I recommend making a list of several subjects you'd be likely to research. Then look for a helpful store that will let you try your list on the various CD-ROM encyclopedias. To give you a sample of such a test drive, I've selected three topics at random that either a child or adult might look up and pulled the relevant articles from *Compton's*, *Encarta*, *Grolier*, *World Book*, and *Britannica*. Here's what I found:

Geiger counters. All five CD-ROM encyclopedias offer descriptions of the Geiger counter, a hand-held device for measuring atomic radiation, that are heavy on technical details and light on explanations suitable for nonscientists. *World Book* provides a color cutaway diagram and the easiest text to understand: "A typical Geiger counter has a fine wire stretched along the axis of a cylindrical metal tube. This central wire and the metal wall of the tube serve as electrodes. An electronic circuit keeps the wire at a positive voltage of about 1,000 volts, thus creating a strong electric field near the wire . . . Radiation that enters the tube collides with a gas atom, causing the atom to become ionized. This process occurs repeatedly, creating a large number of electrons. The electrons spread along the wire, where together they create an electric pulse.

The pulse is amplified electronically and is counted by a meter or some other type of registering device."

Compton's provides a five-sentence description as part of a long article on radioactivity, along with a diagram and a five-second sound bite reproducing the Geiger counter's well-known clicking noise. *Encarta* gives the subject four sentences, plus a color photograph of a Geiger counter and ten seconds of clicking noises, within an article on particle detectors. *Grolier* has a separate four-paragraph entry on Geiger counters, without any audio or illustration, that lapses into technical jargon: "The heart of the Geiger counter is the ionization tube, which may be metal, or glass with a metalized interior, and a central conductor maintained at a high positive potential with respect to the outer enclosure."

Britannica CD, however, takes the prize for technobabble with a lengthy description buried in a very long article on radiation measurement. You'd probably need a background in college-level physics to struggle through passages such as "Because the Geiger discharge is self-limiting, radiation that creates only a single ion pair in the gas will result in an output pulse as large as that produced by a particle that deposits a great deal of energy and creates many ion pairs. Therefore, the amplitude of the output pulse carries no energy information, and Geiger tubes are useful only in pulse-counting systems."

Charles Lindbergh. "Lucky Lindy" became a hero overnight in 1927 when he completed the first solo transatlantic flight from New York to Paris in thirty-three hours and thirty-nine minutes. The most famous aviator of his generation, he later suffered through the kidnapping and murder of his infant son—portrayed as the crime of the century long before similar claims were made for the O. J. Simpson murder case—and became a political lightning rod for his efforts to stop the United States from entering World War II.

Compton's offers the most colorful description of Lindbergh's life, describing his early days as a barnstorming pilot and noting that "twice he had to make parachute jumps to save his life." The text is accompanied by a fifteen-second video clip of the historic takeoff and a diagram of Lindbergh's plane, *The Spirit of St. Louis*. The shortest entry is in *Grolier*, just four paragraphs and a forty-five-second video clip. *Encarta* provides four longer paragraphs, along with a twenty-five-second audio clip of Lindbergh delivering a speech just a few weeks after his flight.

The *World Book* article is the longest and and the only one to describe in detail how Lindbergh became a conservationist in the years before his death in 1974, speaking out for protection of endangered whales and opposing development of supersonic transport aircraft out of concern for the upper atmosphere's ozone layer. *Britannica* gives Lindbergh only seven paragraphs, laden with details on his many honors and official duties through the years but skimming over the pre-World War II controversy.

Zebras. The five encyclopedias come roughly equal on the subject of zebras, with each offering articles filling half a page when printed. *Encarta* stands out by offering not only a color photograph of these strange-looking creatures but also a seven-second audio clip of a mountain zebra's harsh call. Answering the common childhood question "Why do zebras have stripes?" *Encarta* explains that the markings "serve as protective coloration in its natural habitat." *World Book* goes a little further, stating, "The lines blend together and may make it more difficult for an enemy to single out and attack an individual zebra."

Compton's and *Grolier* give the most interesting description of zebra behavior. "When stalked by a lion or leopard—their natural enemies—zebras can turn at speeds up to 40 miles per hour," *Grolier* states. *Compton's* adds: "Frequently, zebras form mixed herds with other animals who gain protection from predators by the zebras' keen sense of hearing." *Britannica* devotes an entire paragraph of its dull four-paragraph article to describing the various striping patterns of different zebra species.

I'm not sure these comparisons make choosing any easier since they don't reveal any clear winner or loser. But you can find out more about each CD-ROM encyclopedia in the individual reviews below. Also, I'll give two more thoughts on making a choice.

First, don't consider *World Book* or *Britannica*. Although both are very well written and researched, they aren't worth the considerable premium above the cost of the Big Three. For $300, you could buy *Compton's*, *Encarta*, and *Grolier*, providing considerably more value for less money than either *World Book* or *Britannica* alone.

Second, don't worry too much about choosing among the Big Three. There is no wrong answer. Each of the three is excellent, benefiting from considerable investments of time and talent by their publishers, and the differences between them are relatively minor.

Grolier tends toward text written at a higher level than *Compton's* or *Encarta*, especially in scientific and technical articles, giving it a slight edge for high school and adult users but making it less attractive for younger children. *Compton's* has the brightest writing but the least comprehensive articles of the Big Three, making it the best quick reference tool. *Encarta* has the most multimedia content and several kid-oriented activities that will be particularly appealing to elementary school and junior high users.

BRITANNICA CD
★★
Developer: Encyclopaedia Britannica Inc.; 800-323-1229
Format: Windows
Price: $995

Encyclopædia Britannica is heavy in every sense of the word. With 44 million words in 65,000 articles, the print set fills a bookshelf-bending thirty-two volumes. The prose, too, is written in a heavy academic style reminiscent of a college textbook. And *Britannica CD 1.0*, released in September 1994, carries a heavy $995 price tag, even though it contains only the print encyclopedia's text, omitting the pictures and illustrations.

With more than four times as many words as the Big Three CD-ROM encyclopedias reviewed in this section, *Britannica CD* unquestionably provides greater depth on the many subjects it covers. But the ponderous writing style will quickly turn off children, the primary users of encyclopedias. Consider this eye-glazing opening to the *Britannica CD* article on geography: "Geography is the study of the surface of the Earth. The word is derived from the Greek words *geo*, 'the Earth,' and *graphein*, 'to write.' The surface of the Earth is the interface of the atmosphere, lithosphere, hydrosphere and biosphere. It provides the habitat, or environment, in which humans are able to live." Fortunately, the CD-ROM includes a dictionary, so confused readers will be able to look up words like lithosphere and hydrosphere.

Britannica CD is also inexcusably difficult to operate. There are only two ways to sort through the contents, an awkward "Idea Search" feature in which you enter a few key words such as "kings of England" and get a list of articles related to the subject and an index of all the *Britannica* articles. The Big Three CD-ROM encyclopedias, in contrast, all offer some type of "topic tree," in which you can work down through a series of subject headings in search of specific information. Nor does *Britannica CD* offer outlines of long articles that make it possible to jump from section to section.

And in a gesture deliberately disrespectful of its customers, *Britannica CD* comes with a "hardware key." The key is a two-inch-long plastic plug that must be installed between your printer cable and computer, intended to prevent the disk from being used on more than one computer. A number of software developers tried to force hardware keys onto the market in the mid-1980s but quickly dropped them after customers complained about the inconvenience.

Encyclopædia Britannica Inc. needs to develop a better interface for *Britannica CD*, drop the obnoxious hardware key, and lower the price substantially. Version 2 of the CD-ROM is due in early 1995, with the addition of a limited selection of photographs and illustrations as well as built-in links to on-line research databases. If you already have a PC with a CD-ROM drive and you're absolutely determined to own *Britannica*, Version 2 might be a worthwhile investment—if nothing else, it's cheaper than the minimum $1,500 cost for the *Encyclopædia Britannica* in print. But I think most home users will be much happier with one of the Big Three CD-ROM encyclopedias for just $99.

COMPTON'S INTERACTIVE ENCYCLOPEDIA, 1995 EDITION
★★★★
Developer: Compton's NewMedia Inc.; 800-284-2045
Format: Windows, Macintosh
Price: $89

Compton's Interactive Encyclopedia, 1995 Edition is perfectly designed for exploration, full of features that make it easy to search through the CD-ROM's 33,000 articles. The best is called "Idea Search," in which you type a question in plain English for the encyclopedia to analyze and answer. If you enter "Who invented the steam engine?" you get back a long list of articles in less than a minute. First on the list is "Watt, James," the Scottish instrument maker who patented the first practical steam engine in 1769. Fifth on the list is a separate article on steam engines.

You can also search through *Compton's* by looking at an index of articles in alphabetical order, by working through a "topic tree" that groups the articles by content, by unrolling a time line, or by spinning an on-screen globe to find nations and cities. Children will be fascinated with the "editing room," which lets users select pictures, sound files, and video clips to organize into a multimedia presentation. By plugging a microphone into the computer, children can even record their own narration.

The clearly labeled and brightly colored on-screen control buttons are so simple that most users should be able to start using *Compton's* without any assistance, although the CD-ROM provides extensive guided tours and on-screen help for computer novices. Some of the instruction is provided by actor Patrick Stewart, best known for playing Captain Jean-Luc Picard on the television series "Star Trek: The Next Generation," who appears in a series of postage-stamp-size video clips. The 1995 edition, released in September 1994, has been updated to cover news events through April 1994, so you'll read about events from that month such as the death of Richard Nixon and the multiracial elections in South Africa.

Multimedia content in *Compton's* includes thirty video clips, eleven animations and forty-three narrated slide shows. There's also a helpful built-in dictionary; click on any word in the text and a dictionary definition pops onto the screen. One note of caution for those with limited space on their hard disks: *Compton's* is a hard-disk hog, demanding seventeen megabytes for a full installation in Windows, although you can opt for an eight-megabyte installation in exchange for slower performance.

MICROSOFT ENCARTA '95
★★★★
Developer: Microsoft Corp.; 800-426-9400
Format: Windows, Macintosh
Price: $99

Microsoft Encarta '95 is the closest thing yet to a true multimedia encyclopedia, in which sound, animation, and video contribute as much information as traditional text, photographs, charts, maps, and diagrams. The CD-ROM includes an awesome two thousand audio clips, offering a total of nine hours of sound; twenty-nine video clips, most under one minute; and eighty-three animated illustrations. While you won't encounter one of these multimedia elements in each of the 26,000 articles in *Encarta*, you're sure to run into at least a few of them in any research session involving multiple articles. The audio clips, particularly, cover a broad range—everything from a speech by Vladimir Lenin in 1919 to the national anthem of Liechtenstein and the haunting sound of Australian aborigines playing the didgeridoo.

Microsoft Corporation launched *Encarta* in 1993 after licensing electronic rights to the text of *Funk & Wagnalls Encyclopedia*, which is unfairly burdened with a low-rent reputation because it is most often sold one volume at a time in supermarkets. *Funk & Wagnalls* is actually a well-written encyclopedia, although its articles tend to be shorter than other mass-market encyclopedias and are more appropriate for children than adults. In its typical spare-no-expenses style, Microsoft has invested heavily in revamping and upgrading the *Funk & Wagnalls* text; the company says its staff of twenty-five *Encarta* editors has extensively rewritten 10,000 of the 26,000 articles and at least modestly expanded most of the rest. The 1995 edition, released in October 1994, also had later production deadlines that its competitors; there are references to the Shoemaker-Levy 9 comet hitting Jupiter in July 1994 and the Irish Republican Army's cease-fire in Northern Ireland that began on August 31.

All of the content in *Encarta* can be easily searched with a tool called "Pinpointer," as well as through an on-screen atlas or time line. The CD-ROM also contains two multimedia bonus features that will especially appeal to children. "InterActivities" offers six miniprograms in which children take charge, such as a simulator in which they can adjust the moon's orbit around the earth and a personal nutrition guide for planning healthy meals. "Mind Maze" is a quiz game that involves solving the mystery of a haunted castle by answering trivia questions based on material in the encyclopedia.

THE 1995 GROLIER MULTIMEDIA ENCYCLOPEDIA
★★★★

Developer: Grolier Electronic Publishing Inc.; 800-285-4534
Format: Windows, Macintosh
Price: $99

The most intellectual of the Big Three CD-ROM encyclopedias, *The 1995 Grolier Multimedia Encyclopedia* is designed more for adults than children. While *Grolier* isn't inappropriate for children, it doesn't offer as many child-oriented activities as *Compton's* or *Encarta* and includes many articles written at a level too sophisticated for students younger than high school age. That's because the text, photographs, and maps in *Grolier* come from the *Academic American Encyclopedia*, a print set intended for adult researchers; *Compton's* is based on a print set of the same name aimed more at children, and *Encarta* traces its roots to the *Funk & Wagnalls* print encyclopedia, also written primarily for children.

Grolier offers fewer multimedia bells and whistles than its two main competitors, with only fifty-five short video clips, thirty one-minute animations, and eleven animated maps. But *Grolier* compensates with two features that effortlessly guide you to some of the most interesting of the CD-ROM's 33,000 articles. "Knowledge Explorer" offers eighteen narrated tours covering topics such as architecture, the human body, and space exploration. At any point on the tour, you can stop the action to delve into a specific article. "Pathmakers" provides six essays about famous figures in history, with video-clip introductions from well-known experts including novelist Kurt Vonnegut, Jr., on American literature, paleontologist Stephen Jay Gould on great thinkers, and Olympic athlete Jackie Joyner-Kersee on sports legends.

Released in October 1994, the *Grolier* 1995 edition has been updated through July and mentions the deployment of French troops to war-torn Rwanda in late June and the peace agreement with Israel and Jordan signed at the White House on July 25. *Grolier*, like *Compton's*, wants lots of elbow room on your hard disk—a full installation of the Windows version requires seventeen megabytes, although you can select a 4.5-megabyte option if you don't mind sluggish performance.

THE WORLD BOOK NEW ILLUSTRATED INFORMATION FINDER
★★½
Developer: World Book Inc.; 800-621-8202
Format: Windows, Macintosh
Price: $395

Almost everything is right with *The World Book New Illustrated Information Finder* except the price. This CD-ROM version of the popular twenty-four-volume *World Book Encyclopedia* contains all of the print version's text, along with photos, illustrations, maps, charts, and tables. It's not a true "multimedia" encyclopedia because there aren't any sound clips, animations, or video sequences. But that isn't a big loss given the strength of the text in *World Book*, by far the single most important factor in judging any encyclopedia.

The *World Book* editors understand the needs of their audience—children from elementary grades through high school—and have mastered the art of writing simple sentences without condescending to their young readers. Consider this easily understood but eloquent first paragraph from one of the 17,000 articles in *World Book*: "The Civil War, 1861–1865, took more American lives than any other war in history. It so divided the people of the United States that in some families brother fought against brother. The Civil War was between the Southern States, trying to preserve slavery and an agricultural way of life, and the Northern States, dedicated to a more modern way of life and to ending slavery. The terrible bloodshed left a heritage of grief and bitterness that declined only slowly and, even today, has not fully disappeared."

The *World Book* CD-ROM is easy to install and use; most children familiar with computers probably won't even need to read the instruction manual. Information can be located quickly and is presented neatly, with text in a window on the right side of the screen. In the upper left is an outline of the article, making it easy to navigate through long entries; a window in the lower left offers a thumbnail preview of photos and maps. Articles can be located with several useful navigation tools, including a historical time line, point-and-click atlas, and "InfoTree" hierarchical guide on which children pull up a succession of menus to home in on a specific topic.

But there's still the problem of price. While I'm convinced *World Book* is a better choice for children than any of its Big Three competitors—*Compton's*, *Encarta*, and *Grolier*, all reviewed in this section—it's nowhere near three times better, even though it sells for four times as much. Indeed, buying any two of the Big Three for about $198 would give you more information than *World Book* alone for $395. I hope the executives at World Book Inc. get the message and stop pricing themselves out of the market; *World Book* on CD-ROM could blow away the competition if it sold for under $150.

b. Dictionaries and General Reference

AMERICAN HERITAGE ILLUSTRATED ENCYCLOPEDIC DICTIONARY
★½
Developer: Xiphias; 800-421-9194
Format: DOS
Price: $29

Despite the long name, *American Heritage Illustrated Encyclopedic Dictionary* is the skimpiest CD-ROM dictionary I've seen. The disk contains the definition for 180,000 words, and some of the definitions include photographs or illustrations. But the CD-ROM is crippled by gaping omissions. The worst is the absence of any way to print a definition or copy it to a word processor. Also, the wildcard search feature—in which you put an asterisk in place of letters you don't know—works only at the end of words. That means you can look up all the words related to "communication" by typing "communic*," but you can't find the correct spelling of "accommodate" by typing "ac*odate." I also found a small but amusing error in the entry on Abraham Lincoln: A photo of John Wilkes Booth displayed a caption identifying him as Lincoln's "assassinator" instead of his assassin.

THE AMERICAN HERITAGE TALKING DICTIONARY
★★½
Developer: SoftKey International Inc.; 800-227-5609
Format: Windows, Macintosh
Price: $39

In the crowded field of CD-ROM reference, *The American Heritage Talking Dictionary* is a good product that nonetheless comes up short. Houghton Mifflin Company, publisher of *The American Heritage Dictionary* in print, has licensed the electronic version to several companies. For only slightly more money, you can get all the contents of *The American Heritage Talking Dictionary*, plus several other comprehensive reference works, in the excellent *Microsoft Bookshelf*, reviewed in this section.

The American Heritage Talking Dictionary performs exactly as a CD-ROM dictionary should. There are definitions for 200,000 words, and 72,000 of those words are pronounced by actual human voices, not synthetically generated speech. The disk also contains an electronic version of *Roget's Thesaurus* for finding synonyms. For users who want to use the dictionary while working with another CD-ROM, the entire dictionary database can be loaded onto the hard drive, although you'll have to sacrifice fifteen megabytes on the Macintosh or sixteen megabytes in Windows.

Several clever search features, although not unique to *The American Heritage Talking Dictionary*, make the CD-ROM easy to use. If you're not sure how a word is spelled, for example, the program will display a list of similar words to help you find the right one. You can also perform "wild card" searches by using a question mark in place of a letter. Entering the word "Frankf?rt," for example, took me to the entry for "Frankfurt," a city in Germany, and "Frankfort," cities in Kentucky and Indiana. The "WordHunter" feature lets you work backward, entering a few words from a definition and then having the program search for matching entries. Scrabble players who are willing to cheat slightly will enjoy the anagram feature, in which the computer creates a list of possible words that can be formed by rearranging a given set of letters. I entered the word "anagram" and got a list of twenty-four words containing four or more letters, including "rang" and "ragman."

MICROSOFT BOOKSHELF '94
★★★½
Developer: Microsoft Corp.; 800-426-9400
Format: Windows, Macintosh
Price: $69

"Persons grouped around a fire or candle for warmth or light are less able to pursue independent thoughts, or even tasks, than people supplied with electric light. In the same way, the social and educational patterns latent in automation are those of self-employment and artistic autonomy." Futurist Marshall McLuhan wrote those prophetic words in 1964. I discovered them in *Microsoft Bookshelf '94* while self-employed, full of artistic autonomy as I wrote this book.

First released by Microsoft in 1987 and updated every year since, *Bookshelf* is a perfect example of what McLuhan is talking about: technological change leading to social change. Instead of calling the local library's overworked reference desk, I can now turn to *Bookshelf* for instant access to the full text of seven reference works: *The American Heritage Dictionary*, *The Columbia Dictionary of Quotations*, *The Concise Columbia Encyclopedia*, *The Hammond World Atlas*, *The People's Chronology*, *Roget's Thesaurus*, and *The World Almanac*.

These books contain hundreds of thousands of pieces of information that are invaluable for almost all kinds of writing—anything from school reports to corporate presentations. For adults, particularly, *Bookshelf* could be a more valuable research tool than CD-ROM encyclopedias. In a half-hour of browsing, I first uncovered McLuhan's quote and then went on to learn from the *Bookshelf* encyclopedia that all national banks must belong to the Federal Reserve System, established by the Federal Reserve Act of 1913; from the almanac that U.S. population was just 76 million in 1900; and from the thesaurus a list of synonyms for making a dramatic commitment (take the plunge, cross the Rubicon, burn one's boats, burn one's bridges, throw away the scabbard, throw down the gauntlet, and nail one's colors to the mast).

Microsoft has designed such a simple interface for *Bookshelf* that even users with minimal computer experience won't need to read the instruction manual. Small pictures of each book are lined up across the top of the screen. Just click on the book's picture—or an eighth button representing all the books—and then type in the word or phrase you wish to research. *Bookshelf* also contains a smattering of photographs and even a few video clips. But the most useful feature, other than the text itself, is a pronunciation guide; a real human voice, not a synthesizer, pronounces every word in the dictionary. If you wish, *Bookshelf* can also insert itself into other Windows programs through a feature called "QuickShelf," three buttons that appear in the top bar of every Windows screen, giving you access without leaving the application. Look for the 1995 edition of *Bookshelf* sometime in the first half of the year.

1994 GUINNESS MULTIMEDIA DISC OF RECORDS
★★
Developer: Grolier Electronic Publishing Inc.; 800-285-4534
Format: Windows, Macintosh
Price: $39

What is the record for a CD-ROM adapted from a book with the least amount of effort to add anything extra? No, it's not the *1994*

Guinness Multimedia Disc of Records. But *Guinness* certainly ranks high on the list of CD-ROMs that don't offer significantly more than their namesake books at a much higher price—in this case, the CD-ROM costs about $39, compared with just $6.99 for the paperback edition of *The Guinness Book of Records 1994.*

The book, to be sure, is full of interesting and bizarre facts. The longest head of hair, for example, belongs to a woman in Massachusetts whose tresses stretch twelve feet eight inches. The longest drive on a power lawn mower was 3,034 miles by a man who toured Great Britain in 1989. The fastest passenger elevator travels twenty-three miles per hour through an office building in Tokyo.

The CD-ROM faithfully produces all the book's text and photographs. The records can be located through an index similar to the twenty-five-page index at the back of the book or through a "topic tree" similar to the book's table of contents. The only additional features on the CD-ROM are the ability to search for a specific word anywhere in the text and the ability to randomly display interesting facts on screen. The developers have also added fifty video clips, each running about thirty seconds, showing record holders such as a cheetah, the fastest land animal at sixty-three miles per hour, and a man riding the world's tallest unicycle, reaching 101 feet 9 inches.

ILLUSTRATED FACTS: HOW THINGS WORK
★★
Developer: Xiphias; 800-421-9194
Format: Windows, Macintosh
Price: $29

Illustrated Facts: How Things Work strives so hard to be clever that it forgets to be informative. Intended as "a lighthearted look at man's endeavors" in technology, the CD-ROM instead comes across as superficial. Using the *Matrix Interface*, described in the review of *Kathy Smith's Fat Burning System* in Section d of Chapter 7, *How Things Work* presents seventy very brief video clips— each running only thirty to forty-five seconds—explaining such inventions as television, atomic clocks, and steam engines. The content is divided into six categories: communications, computation, transport, sensory extension, weapons, and time. Some of the profiles include an extra "info screen" with a short text time line.

But even if you stop to look at the info screens, you can still get through all of *How Things Work* in about an hour.

In the computation section, for example, there is an entry on the Univac computer, with a narrator talking in the slang of a fifties jazz musician. "Now let me lay this on you," he says. "The new Univac for 1959. It's solid. Solid state, dig. We've ditched those square tubes and plugged in these hip little transistors. Crazy." That's it. Anyone trying to learn about the crucial transition from vacuum tubes to integrated circuits won't gain anything from this flip commentary. The video images, which play in a four-inch diagonal window on a standard fourteen-inch monitor, are occasionally interesting—the entry on aviation, for example, includes early film footage of the Wright brothers—but the lack of substantial information reduces *How Things Work* to nothing more than a curiosity.

ILLUSTRATED FACTS: HOW THE WORLD WORKS
★★
Developer: Xiphias; 800-421-9194
Format: Windows, Macintosh
Price: $29

A companion to *Illustrated Facts: How Things Work*, reviewed in this section. In seventy one-minute video clips, *How the World Works* attempts to provide an overview of human history, with material divided into seven categories: government, justice, battles, culture, money, enterprise, and lifestyle. The ten entries in the government category run from the pharaohs of ancient Egypt through the United Nations, while the section on battles goes from Alexander the Great to Operation Desert Storm. But, like *How Things Work*, the content in *How the World Works* is superficial and unsatisfying.

The entry on McGuffey's Reader in the culture section, for example, provides only a few sentences of narration describing this nineteenth century elementary school textbook that showed millions of children how to read. "Along with literacy, the McGuffey Readers taught strong moral values based on the Ten Commandments," the narrator says. "These common values helped create Americans out of a nation of immigrants." That's a good start, but *How the World Works* doesn't provide anything more. An extra text screen displays only a time line on important events in education during the last two hundred years. The most obvious addition to strengthen the entry—a sample of the McGuffey Reader itself—is ignored.

THE 1994 INFORMATION PLEASE ALMANAC
★★
Developer: Parsons Technology Inc.; 800-223-6925
Format: DOS, Windows
Price: $29

The 1994 Information Please Almanac calls itself "the ultimate browser's reference," and the print version published by Houghton Mifflin certainly delivers an astonishing array of facts. You can find out everything from the highest and lowest temperatures ever recorded in Alaska (100 degrees Fahrenheit on June 27, 1915, in Fort Yukon, and minus 80 degrees Fahrenheit on January 23, 1971, in Prospect Creek) to the last championship team of the defunct North American Soccer League (the Chicago Sting in 1984). In addition to the standard almanac fare of statistics and historical records, there's also useful advice on everyday topics including personal finance and first aid, as well as a glossary of computer terms.

Big-time browsers will be disappointed, however, with The 1994 Information Please Almanac on CD-ROM—the disk contains nothing more than the text and photographs from the print version. Released in late 1994, the CD-ROM is also out of date, arriving on the market shortly before the new 1995 print Almanac.

At least the CD-ROM is easy to use. The main menu screen displays a table of contents divided into fifty-one main topics such as Postal Regulations, Aviation, and Environment. Clicking on a topic displays a submenu of specific articles and tables. There's also an alphabetical index and a word-search feature that allows you to look quickly at a list of every entry mentioning a specific word. Still, I'd bet most people could find the information they need more quickly—and for considerably less money—by flipping through the Almanac in print rather than on CD-ROM.

RANDOM HOUSE UNABRIDGED ELECTRONIC DICTIONARY
★★½

Developer: Random House Inc.; 800-733-3000
Format: Windows
Price: $79

If nothing else, *Random House Unabridged Electronic Dictionary* can save your bookshelf from sagging—the CD-ROM contains all of the 2,500-page print *Random House Unabridged Dictionary*, which tips the scales at thirteen pounds. But I'm not sure most people need a dictionary with 315,000 entries, especially when the excellent *Microsoft Bookshelf '94*, reviewed in this section, offers a dictionary as well as seven other reference works for roughly the same price.

Not that there's anything wrong with the Random House CD-ROM. It's easy to install and operate and performs all the special tricks unique to computer-based dictionaries, such as "wild card" searches, in which you enter an asterisk in place of a letter when you're not sure of the spelling. The dictionary even solves anagrams. I entered "peach" in the anagram window and discovered the letters could be rearranged to spell "cheap" and "chape." I clicked on the word "chape" to find out its definition: "the lowermost terminal mount of a scabbard." The CD-ROM also provides pronunciations for 115,000 words and displays 2,200 illustrations taken from the print dictionary.

The Random House dictionary was updated in 1993, so both the print and CD-ROM versions contain a long list of contemporary words. "Boy toy" is defined as both "a young man noted for his good looks and sexual prowess" and "a female sex object," while "waitron" is defined as "a person of either sex who waits on tables." The CD-ROM, by the way, was programmed by Novell Inc., developer of the WordPerfect word processor. If you use WordPerfect, the Random House CD-ROM can be accessed directly from the word processor's Tools menu.

TIME TABLE OF HISTORY: ARTS & ENTERTAINMENT
★½
Developer: Xiphias; 800-421-9194
Format: DOS
Price: $29

A slapdash and second-rate attempt to create original CD-ROM reference works, the three *Time Table* titles from Xiphias are uninformative, difficult to use, and littered with errors. The intent, apparently, was to create a kind of almanac with lots of very short articles covering the full range of human history. But the results are so muddled that it's difficult to tell exactly who Xiphias thought might be an appropriate audience for these disks.

The *Arts & Entertainment* CD-ROM contains 4,300 entries, most running for just a few sentences. The entries are called up through an awkward interface that requires pushing lots of on-screen buttons to search for information either through a time line, a keyword index, or by individual words. A smattering of entries are linked to photographs and illustrations; you can see, for example, a portrait of William Shakespeare and a picture of his birthplace. In a blatant and dishonest maneuver to advertise the CD-ROM as containing video, Xiphias also licensed thirty video clips, each running about thirty seconds, from the CBS News archives. The same thirty clips are presented on the three *Time Table* titles and are entirely unrelated to the subject matter, covering recent historical events such as the Kennedy assassination and the Iran-Contra scandal that have nothing to do with the arts.

I was also stunned by the lack of quality control. You won't use any of the three titles for more than a few minutes without running into signs of sloppy workmanship. Entering the keyword "television" on the *Arts & Entertainment* disk, for example, calls up 164 entries on the subject. But two of the articles cover the same event, the debut of "The Twilight Zone" in 1959. In the section on opera, an entry describes the opening of the first public opera hall in 1637. But the article neglects to say where the hall was located. You have to hit another on-screen button that displays a locator map to learn the site was San Cassiano, Italy. The other two *Time Table* titles, *Business, Politics & Media* and *Science & Innovation,* are equally bad and are reviewed in this section. Avoid them all.

TIME TABLE OF HISTORY: BUSINESS, POLITICS & MEDIA
★½
Developer: Xiphias; 800-421-9194
Format: DOS
Price: $29

A useless and error-filled reference work in the *Time Table* series from Xiphias. For a full description, see the review of *Time Table of History: Arts & Entertainment* in this section. *Business, Politics & Media* contains 6,400 brief entries, many filled with mistakes that are sadly amusing. An entry on longtime General Motors chairman Alfred P. Sloan describes how his management ideas took off "like a car without breaks." I'd like to give the *Time Table* series a break, but with gaffes like that I suggest you hit the brakes and send this one to the junkyard.

TIME TABLE OF HISTORY: SCIENCE & INNOVATION
★½
Developer: Xiphias; 800-421-9194
Format: DOS
Price: $29

A wasted effort, part of the *Time Table* series from Xiphias. For a full description, see the review of *Time Table of History: Arts & Entertainment* in this section. *Science & Innovation* contains 6,400 poorly organized and very brief entries. Selecting the keyword "economics," for example, summons fifty-two entries on the subject. But the last thirty years are almost completely ignored, other than a one-sentence entry noting the formation of the Organization of Petroleum Exporting Countries in 1961, a few sentences on president-elect Bill Clinton's economic summit in late 1992, and a list of Nobel Prize winners in economics from 1969 to 1992.

c. Mail and Phone Directories

Phone directories on CD-ROM are a great idea in theory—the huge storage capacity makes it possible to search through listings for the entire nation in a matter of seconds. But in practice, CD-ROM phone directories are hobbled by the computer phenomenon known as "garbage in, garbage out." Directories are only as good as the information they contain, and developers of CD-ROM phone directories face two serious problems.

First, there is the growing demand for privacy. According to Bellcore, the national telephone research center, about one third of all residential phone numbers in the United States are now unlisted. In Las Vegas, a city where many people move to get lost, a whopping 75 percent of home numbers aren't in the phone book. So even the most accurate and up-to-date CD-ROM phone directory is going to miss, on average, one in three residential listings.

Second, the phone companies won't sell their internal directory listings to outsiders, at least not at a price that's affordable for the home market. As a result, developers must buy data from companies that maintain mailing lists or hire huge numbers of data-entry clerks to retype existing phone books. Both these methods produce listings that are prone to errors and riddled with obsolete information. "Directory information is quite volatile," says Pro CD Inc., one CD-ROM phone directory developer, in a "help" file included on its disks. "It has been estimated that more than 20 percent of the published listings change from year to year."

Also, trying to keep pace can get expensive—CD-ROM phone directories are typically updated every quarter, forcing you to buy the whole product again if you want the most recent data.

I decided to test the various phone directories unscientifically by making a list of three listed businesses and three friends who I know have listed telephone numbers, spread around the nation in six different states, and then checking each CD-ROM phone directory to see if it contained the correct information. Although none of the disks passed my test with a perfect score, I'd recommend *PhoneDisc Business & Residential* and *PhoneDisc PowerFinder* as the best in a weak field.

CANADA PHONE
★★
Developer: Pro CD Inc.; 800-992-3766
Format: DOS, Windows, Macintosh
Price: $129

An awkwardly designed and sluggish directory containing 8 million Canadian residential and business listings, *Canada Phone* is identical in operation to *Direct Phone,* reviewed in this section. Unlike *Direct Phone,* however, this is a full reverse directory—the listings in *Canada Phone* can be searched by name, address, Canadian postal code, and SIC code as well as by name. You can enter "Toronto" and the SIC code for health-food restaurants to get a list of all the health-food restaurants in that city, although you'll have to wait a long time while the program searches for the information. Also, some individual listings are incomplete, lacking a postal code to go along with the street address and city.

DIRECT PHONE
★★
Developer: Pro CD Inc.; 800-992-3766
Format: DOS, Windows, Macintosh
Price: $89

Offering combined residential and business listings for the entire United States on two disks, *Direct Phone* isn't as easy to use as its most direct competitor—*PhoneDisc Business & Residential,* reviewed in this section—and didn't do as well on my performance test, described in the introduction to this section. *Direct Phone* gave an out-of-date address for one of my three residential test listings and gave the wrong first name in another, although it did provide correct answers for all three business listings. I also noticed that many of the business listings in *Direct Phone* aren't correctly indexed because the names are entered from beginning to end rather than picking last names. The law office of "Jane Doe, Esq.," for example, is listed under "J" rather than "D."

Direct Phone, which allows searches by name only, has an awkward on-screen design with lots of confusing buttons. After entering a name, you get a long list scrolling down the screen. You then have to click with the right mouse button to display an individual listing instead of the more common software design practice of using either the left mouse button or pressing "Enter" on the keyboard. *Direct Phone* includes a program called *MapLinx Lite* that will display a group of listings as colored dots on a map of the United States, making it easy to pinpoint the location of various homes and businesses.

11 MILLION BUSINESSES PHONE BOOK
★★
Developer: American Business Information Inc.; 402-593-4595
Format: Windows
Price: $29

The business directory companion to *70 Million Households Phone Book*, reviewed in this section. *11 Million Businesses Phone Book* boasts of covering "virtually every business in the U.S. and Canada on one CD-ROM." I can't vouch for that claim, but the disk did pass my homegrown test, described in the introduction to this section, producing listings for all three of my sample names.

11 Million Businesses shares two drawbacks of *70 Million Households*: a built-in meter that shuts the program down permanently after looking up five thousand listings and supplying only street names without specific address numbers. But, unlike *70 Million Households*, the business disk does not require entering a state, city, or ZIP code to start a search—you can enter just a name and get listings matching that name anywhere in the country. In short, the disk is a useful replacement for calling directory assistance but isn't suitable for heavy-duty applications such as assembling mailing lists or searching out sales prospects.

EUROPAGES
★★½
Developer: Pro CD Inc.; 800-992-3766
Format: DOS, Windows, Macintosh
Price: $49

Europages on CD-ROM is the electronic version of a print directory, also called *Europages*, with listings of 150,000 businesses in twenty-six European nations. The CD-ROM listings can be searched by type of product or service as well as by name and can be narrowed down to specific countries and regions within each country, making it easy, for example, to instantly display a list of all the producers of sparkling wine in the Champagne region of

France. Individual listings give the name of the company, address, phone and fax numbers, and type of business. On-screen help is available in five languages: English, French, German, Italian, and Spanish. *Europages* will also generate form letters requesting sales literature in any of these languages, with the company name automatically inserted.

FREE PHONE
★★½
Developer: Pro CD Inc.; 800-992-3766
Format: DOS, Windows, Macintosh
Price: $29

A CD-ROM version of AT&T's Toll-Free Directory, *Free Phone* is a nationwide guide to business "800" numbers. The database can be searched by address, telephone number, and SIC code as well as by name. These features allow quick custom searching; you can, for example, select "New Orleans" and the SIC code 7011 for hotels to get instantly a list of all the hotels and motels in New Orleans that have toll-free numbers. Each listing gives the full name and address for the business but doesn't give the local phone number.

HOME PHONE
★★
Developer: Pro CD Inc.; 800-992-3766
Format: DOS, Windows, Macintosh
Price: $49

A low-cost version of *Direct Phone*, reviewed in this section, that deletes the 8 million business listings in *Direct Phone* while retaining the 72 million residential listings. Otherwise, the two products are identical.

PHONEDISC BUSINESS & RESIDENTIAL
★★★
Developer: Digital Directory Assistance Inc.; 800-284-8353
Format: DOS, Windows, Macintosh
Price: $99

The simplest to operate and most complete of the CD-ROM phone directories, *PhoneDisc Business & Residential* still has a few weak spots. The three-disk set—two disks for residential listings and one for business—provided all three of the residential listings in my test, described in the introduction to this section, and two of three business listings. But two of the three residential listings gave an initial in place of the first name—"Smith, J." instead of "Smith, Jane"—that would make it hard to tell if I'd found the correct individual if I had been doing a real search. Also, the poorly written instruction manual covers all the PhoneDisc products, so you might get confused reading about features of the more advanced *PhoneDisc PowerFinder*, reviewed in this section, that aren't included with *PhoneDisc Business & Residential*.

The residential disks, divided into eastern and western states, provide 80 million listings in the United States. Entering a name, you see a long list on the screen that you can quickly skim through, looking for a specific individual. Each listing gives a full mailing address as well as the phone number. Business listings also include the SIC code, a standard four-digit classification system from the U.S. Commerce Deptartment; motor home manufacturers, for example, are in SIC code 3716. The 9.5 million business listings can be searched by SIC code, phone number, and address as well as name. You could, for example, find out what businesses are in a specific neighborhood by scanning through listings by street.

PHONEDISC POWERFINDER
★★★
Developer: Digital Directory Assistance Inc.; 800-284-8353
Format: DOS, Windows, Macintosh
Price: $149

A reverse directory version of *PhoneDisc Business & Residential*, reviewed in this section. *PhoneDisc PowerFinder* can search through all listings by street address, phone number, and business SIC code as well as name. To accommodate this indexing, *PowerFinder* comes on five disks: Northeast States, Southeast States, Central States, Midwest States, and Western States. All five disks are sold as a package, by the way; you can't order just one of the five. The data is almost identical to *PhoneDisc Business & Residential* but has at least minor discrepancies—*PowerFinder* provided only one of my three residential test listings, described in the introduction to this section, while *Business & Residential* produced two. Both versions gave the same two out of three business listings in my test.

The most impressive feature of *PowerFinder* is the ability to search by address. It's almost like walking down the road looking at names on mailboxes: You specify a city and then a street to get a list of businesses and residences by street number. Combining this feature with the SIC codes, it becomes easy to conduct quick market studies or generate cold-calling lists for salespeople.

SELECT PHONE
★★
Developer: Pro CD Inc.; 800-992-3766
Format: DOS, Windows, Macintosh
Price: $169

The reverse directory version of *Direct Phone*, reviewed in this section. *Select Phone* allows searching by address, phone number, and business SIC code as well as by name. Because of the extra indexing required to allow all these searches, *Select Phone* comes on five disks: Northeast, South, Central, Great Lakes, and Pacific. All five disks are sold as a package; you can't order just one.

70 MILLION HOUSEHOLDS PHONE BOOK
★★½
Developer: American Business Information Inc.; 402-593-4595
Format: DOS, Windows
Price: $35

An extensive database of residential phone numbers that's difficult to use, *70 Million Households Phone Book* produced correct listings for two of the names in my informal test, described in the introduction to this section. The box claims the two-disk set contains "virtually every listed residential phone number in the U.S." But the manual explains that not only are unlisted numbers excluded but also everyone "who has ever requested they be deleted from any consumer mailing list."

I found several obstacles in working with *70 Million Households*. First, the program has an internal meter that allows you to look up only five thousand addresses before permanently shutting down, forcing you to buy another set of disks. Second, you have to enter either a city, state, or ZIP code to start a search, so you can't check several states at once. Third, you have to exit the program and restart it to switch from the disk containing listings for the eastern United States to the disk for the western states. Fourth, the individual listings give the street where the person lives but not the street number, so you can't use the program to get a mailing address. Given all these limitations, I wouldn't recommend *70 Million Households* for those who need to make heavy use of a CD-ROM phone directory.

9-DIGIT ZIP CODE DIRECTORY
★★★
Developer: American Business Information Inc.; 402-593-4595
Format: DOS
Price: $19

A handy CD-ROM for people sending out lots of mail, *9-Digit ZIP Code Directory* is easier and quicker to use than the bulky print ZIP code directory published by the U.S. Postal Service. The simple fill-in-the-blanks interface asks you to enter a specific address, then immediately displays the appropriate ZIP code. I entered the address of the White House—1600 Pennsylvania Avenue in Washington, D.C.—and discovered letters to the President need to carry the ZIP code 20006-9900. The CD-ROM also works in reverse; you can enter a ZIP code and find out what city it covers. The only flaw in *9-Digit ZIP Code Directory* is a built-in meter than shuts down the program permanently after you've looked up five thousand entries, forcing you to buy another copy. This shouldn't be a problem for occasional users but could be a major annoyance for anyone wanting to use the directory on a daily basis.

d. Maps and Atlases

AAA TRIP PLANNER
★★★
Developer: Compton's NewMedia Inc.; 800-284-2045
Format: Windows
Price: $35

Without even requiring you to join the American Automobile Association, *AAA Trip Planner* puts the group's wealth of travel knowledge inside your computer. This easy-to-operate CD-ROM is an outstanding tool for organizing road trips, with comprehensive information on routes, lodging, restaurants, and attractions throughout the United States.

Planning a trip requires nothing more than entering a starting point, any stops you want to make en route, and the destination. Within seconds, you get complete directions, along with distances and travel times, that can be printed at the push of a button. Lodging, restaurant, and attraction information is accessed by entering a city name; you also have the option of sorting by AAA's well-known rating system, which runs from one to five diamonds.

I tested *AAA Trip Planner* by putting together a hypothetical excursion from Seattle, Washington, to Miami, Florida, with a stop along the way in New Orleans to sample that city's fine restaurants. Directions were precise, telling me to leave Seattle going east on Interstate 90 for 107.6 miles to Interstate 82, where I would turn southeast for 137.1 miles until reaching the Oregon border, and so on until I would reach Miami after traveling 3,608.6 miles. Total travel time, according to AAA, would be seventy-one hours and fifty-eight minutes, indicating I should average fifty miles an hour on the highway. (A look at my court records, sad to say, indicates I've occasionally driven faster.) I was surprised to find AAA isn't that impressed with New Orleans cuisine; the listings include only one five-star restaurant—the Grill Room at the Windsor Court Hotel—and the famous Brennan's Restaurant gets only three stars.

Although *AAA Trip Planner* is a five-diamond performer for its stated task of trip planning, don't rely on it to go any further. The disk doesn't contain significantly more information than what comes in AAA's print guides; the only audio clips, for example, are very brief three- to five-sentence introductions to each of the fifty states. The disk will work best when you already know your destination, not when you're deciding where to take a vacation. The maps included with *AAA Trip Planner* are also a disappointment, showing only major highways and not fully covering each area. The map of Lake Tahoe in California, for example, shows only the South Shore area, leaving out the North Shore towns favored by skiers. Also, the information is somewhat dated; *AAA Travel Planner* was released in August 1994 with data from August 1993.

AUTOMAP ROAD ATLAS
★★½

Developer: Automap Inc.; 800-564-6277
Format: Windows
Price: $49

Automap Road Atlas is a good trip-planning program covering the United States, Canada, and Mexico, but it lacks some features of the superior *AAA Trip Planner*, reviewed in this section. Like the *AAA Trip Planner*, the *Road Atlas* lets you enter an origin and destination city, then produces the directions—specifying how far to go on each road before making a turn—and displays a map. There's even a helpful gasoline consumption calculator. I found that I'd spend $119.17 for gas on a 2,949-mile cross-country trip, assuming gas costs $1.40 a gallon and my Honda Accord would get twenty-five miles per gallon in the city and thirty-five miles per gallon on the highway. But unlike *AAA Trip Planner*, the *Road Atlas* includes no information on hotels, restaurants, and attractions. So the *Road Atlas* helps you plan only the driving, not what to do when you're ready to turn off the road. The *Road Atlas* CD-ROM also includes two "locked" databases that can be unscrambled by calling Automap Inc. and giving a credit-card number in exchange for a special code. "Destination Europe," priced at $39.95, provides route information for both Eastern and Western Europe; "Destination Ski," priced at $19.95, covers 590 ski resorts in North America.

AUTOMAP STREETS
★½
Developer: Automap Inc.; 800-564-6277
Format: Windows
Price: $39

Automap Streets is an overpriced and underperforming competitor to the excellent *Street Atlas USA Version 2.0*, reviewed in this section. *Street Atlas* provides an incredibly detailed street map of the entire United States, including Alaska and Hawaii, on a single CD-ROM. *Automap Streets*, in contrast, requires two disks and doesn't include Alaska. But there's a much bigger drawback: *Automap Streets* divides the country into two hundred regions that are "locked," or scrambled. To access the maps, you have to call Automap Inc. and give a credit-card number. In exchange, they'll give you a code number to unlock the maps. Each of the two hundred maps is priced at $30, although you get one free map of your choice when you buy the product. In theory, unlocking the entire country would cost $5,970, although Automap Inc. offers substantial discounts for purchasing the entire set, reducing the total to well under $1,000. Still, the true cost of using *Automap Streets* is considerably higher than *Street Atlas USA*, even though the quality of the maps is roughly equal.

GLOBAL EXPLORER
★★½
Developer: DeLorme Mapping; 800-452-5931
Format: Windows
Price: $69

Global Explorer is a world atlas without a purpose. Its on-screen maps are more detailed than CD-ROM atlases oriented toward children but not detailed enough to substitute for a high-quality print atlas. Covering the entire planet with fifteen levels of magnification, *Global Explorer* will map out just about any piece of dry land with a name. But at the highest level of magnification, especially in cities, the many labels for roads, rivers, and important buildings run over each other, rendering the maps illegible. There is also a clumsy feature called "AirNet" that will plot commercial aircraft routes between pairs of cities. You have to call up maps of both your origin and destination, however; "AirNet" won't let you simply type in the city names. For one hundred cities around the world, *Global Explorer* includes a street map showing major arteries only. All the maps also show points of interest; by clicking an icon you get a sentence or two on a notable spot, such as the Ryogoku Kokugikan Arena in Tokyo: "The site of Japan's national sumo wrestling competition. This popular sport draws capacity crowds during the main draws, which are scheduled for January, May and September." Still, *Global Explorer* doesn't offer enough information to replace travel guides, so the CD-ROM is left without a niche to fill.

MAP'N'GO
★★★
Developer: DeLorme Mapping; 800-452-5931
Format: Windows
Price: $49

A powerful and sometimes complicated trip planner, *Map'n'Go* from DeLorme Mapping calculates and prints detailed route maps for travel anywhere in the United States, Canada, and Mexico. You specify origin and destination points by entering a place name, a ZIP code, or a phone number. *Map'n'Go* then displays a map on the screen, with buttons allowing you to zoom in for a close-up look or pull back for a sweeping view.

Routes can be calculated in several ways, including quickest and shortest. For a hypothetical jaunt from Chicago to New Orleans, *Map'n'Go* calculated that the quickest route would cover 924 miles in fifteen hours and twenty-three minutes—indicating an average speed of sixty miles per hour, mostly on major highways. The shortest route covered 917 miles but took nineteen hours and twenty-one minutes—indicating an average speed of forty-seven miles per hour, mostly on country roads. *Map'n'Go* also provides information on accommodations and attractions en route; I discovered the Chicago-New Orleans trip passed within five miles of Elvis Presley's Graceland mansion in Memphis.

Included in the box with *Map'n'Go* is DeLorme's *North America Atlas & Gazetteer*, an outsize 128-page book of maps. The route maps printed by the CD-ROM are indexed to the pages of the print atlas, a nice way of overcoming the inherent inability of computer printers to match the detail and color reproduction of a book. Printing out those route maps, by the way, is a slow process—on my DeskJet 500 printer, the fifteen pages of maps for the Chicago-New Orleans journey took close to half an hour to churn out. Also, the on-screen controls for *Map'n'Go* are unnecessarily complicated, requiring several superfluous steps to enter route information.

PICTURE ATLAS OF THE WORLD
★★½
Developer: National Geographic Society; 800-368-2728
Format: DOS, Macintosh
Price: $69

Although *Picture Atlas of the World* from the National Geographic Society advertises itself for ages nine through adult, I'd recommend the CD-ROM only for junior high school students who need a quick guide to the globe's many nations. That's because *Picture Atlas* delivers only thumbnail sketches, not in-depth understanding.

I decided to check the entry on Argentina. I got a full-screen map of the country, a collection of nine color photographs, and a page of vital statistics. The highest mountain in the Western Hemisphere, I learned, is Argentina's 22,834-foot Mount Aconcagua in the Andes. The nation has a total population of 33.5 million, a third of whom live in or near the capital of Buenos Aires. I watched a forty-five-second video clip of gauchos herding cattle and horses. Finally, I read a relatively short historical essay: "For all its beauty and productive land, Argentina is a country that has gone from riches to rags. In the early 1900s, to be 'rich like an Argentine' was to be superwealthy. But years of political turmoil and misrule ruined the economy." But that's all I learned.

Picture Atlas also includes a section called "Mapping Our World" with three animated and narrated slide shows describing how maps are made. The three shows are interesting but aren't worth watching more than once.

STREET ATLAS USA, VERSION 2.0
★★★★
Developer: DeLorme Mapping; 800-452-5931
Format: Windows, Macintosh
Price: $79

I have a friend who, until recently, lived on Haahaa Street in Kaaawa, Hawaii. If you don't believe there's really a street with that strange name, look it up in *Street Atlas USA, Version 2.0*, a truly remarkable CD-ROM that contains just about every highway, avenue, road, and boulevard in the nation. By clicking the mouse, an overview map of the United States can be enlarged through thirteen levels of magnification until just a few square blocks are displayed on screen. Any of these maps can be printed or easily copied into another application, such as a word-processing document. If any street on the map isn't labeled, another click of the mouse button supplies its name.

Although the printouts don't match the quality of a road atlas on paper, the results are more than adequate for navigating from Point A to Point B. And *Street Atlas USA* offers a level of detail no print atlas can match—information on 12 million street segments that, printed out at the maximum magnification, would cover ten football fields. The CD-ROM also provides powerful search features: Enter a city name, ZIP code, or phone number and the appropriate map is quickly displayed.

Given the overwhelming complexity of gathering up-to-date information on every highway, street, and alley, you shouldn't be surprised that *Street Atlas USA* contains many small errors. Some streets, for example, are chopped into many segments for no apparent reason, making it harder to identify where you want to go. Ridder Park Drive in San Jose, California, where I work every day, is a mile-long street given nine separate listings. But these minor flaws don't diminish the incredible power of *Street Atlas USA* to turn any personal computer into a small map-making factory.

TRIPMAKER
★★½
Developer: Rand McNally & Company; 800-671-5006 x108
Format: Windows
Price: $45

An excessively complicated trip-planning program from the mapmakers at Rand McNally & Company, *TripMaker* is noticeably more difficult to operate than its two main competitors, *AAA Trip Planner* and *Map'n'Go*, both reviewed in this section. *TripMaker* is also unacceptably slow unless you put the entire program on your hard drive, which requires sixteen megabytes.

I'm bothered, too, that Rand McNally is determined to steer you into buying more of their products. *TripMaker* contains a complete road atlas along with five "attraction packs" that provide additional information on what to see and do while traveling: "Discovering History," "Fun for Kids," "Urban Attractions," "Scenic Tours," and "Airports, Military Bases and Universities." The CD-ROM also holds six more attraction packs that are "locked"—you can't use them without first getting a password from Rand McNally. The company will give you one extra attraction pack free if you send in the registration card, a neat trick to get your mailing address for future pitches. The other packs can be unlocked for either $10 each or $20 for three. They are At the Beach, Outdoor Adventuring, Downhill Skiing, Playing Tennis & Golf, Trying Your Luck, and Camping, Fishing, Boating & Hiking. I'd encourage Rand McNally to drop this marketing tactic; the company should give us everything for one price, even if it's a higher price than is currently charged.

TripMaker works much like its two competitors. You enter an origin point and a destination anywhere in North America, along with any stopovers you want to make en route, and get both a listing of the directions and an on-screen map that can be printed. As part of the planning process, you select whether *TripMaker* should give you the quickest, shortest, or most scenic route. Figuring out all the features and options, however, will take a while—that's why *TripMaker* comes with a sixty-four-page instruction manual. The program also lists all the attractions along the way, although the information on individual sights is limited. If you're driving up the Pacific Coast from Los Angeles, for example, here's all that *TripMaker* says about the J. Paul Getty Museum in Malibu: "A re-created first century A.D. Roman country villa is the luxurious setting for a permanent collection of Greek and Roman antiquities, pre-twentieth century European paintings, drawings, sculpture, illuminated manuscripts, decorative arts, and American and European photographs."

U.S. ATLAS
★★½
Developer: Mindscape Inc.; 800-234-3088
Format: DOS
Price: $39

A companion to *World Atlas*, reviewed in this section, that is identical in structure and appearance. *U.S. Atlas* delivers color maps of the fifty states, with either geographic views of cities and highways or topographic views showing mountains and rivers. The maps are supplemented with pictures of the state flag and a synthesized rendition of the state anthem. You can also summon a few facts on major cities—the 1990 population of Atlanta, for example, was 394,017, while the mean temperature is 41.9 degrees Fahrenheit in January and 78.6 degrees in July. *U.S. Atlas* also contains a database of census statistics that can be used to create customized maps and charts, such as the number of acres of farmland in each Georgia county or a ranking of the Georgia counties by the dollar value of housing starts. Still, the maps would look better in a print atlas, and the statistical information could be retrieved more easily from a print almanac, which together would cost less than this CD-ROM. A final note: I looked at version 3.0 of *U.S. Atlas*; the developers are planning to release an upgraded version 5.0 in early 1995 with more city maps and video clips of famous sights around the country.

WORLD ATLAS
★★½
Developer: Mindscape Inc.; 800-234-3088
Format: DOS, Macintosh
Price: $39

If you want a world atlas on CD-ROM, then *World Atlas* will deliver exactly what you'd expect, although I'm not sure it's any better than buying a less-expensive print atlas and an almanac. You get full-screen color maps of all the nations of the world, supplemented with pictures of their flags, fact boxes, color photos, and one-minute video clips of their capital cities. In addition to looking at the map of Finland, for example, you can watch video images of Helsinki's Lutheran Cathedral, railroad station, and main park. While looking at the map of Malaysia, you can instantly summon a few facts on Kuala Lumpur—the population is 919,600, and the average temperature is 81 degrees Fahrenheit in both January and July. You can also print the maps, generating a paper copy that's comparable in quality to photocopying a print atlas. If you're interested in *World Atlas* and see it advertised for a remarkably low price, make sure it's the most current release—Version 5 was issued in July 1994—rather than an inventory clearance for earlier versions.

e. Travel

EVERYWHERE USA TRAVEL GUIDE
★★
Developer: Deep River Publishing Inc.; 800-643-5630
Format: Windows
Price: $45

Everywhere USA Travel Guide offers little more than the contents of a bad travel guide in print. The two-disk CD-ROM set—one disk for Eastern states, one for Western states—gives information on three thousand destinations in the United States but rarely provides more than two or three sentences and a photograph or two. You also get 122 worthless video clips, thirty-second snippets of promotional handouts from tourism bureaus, and theme parks.

For all the listings, *Everywhere* can be surprisingly shallow. Only twenty-three destinations are given for the entire state of Hawaii, one of the world's most popular tourist destinations. The individual listings tell you less than almost any print travel guide, such as this brief entry: "Waimea Valley, home of Waimea Falls Park, is an 1,800-acre historical nature park on Oahu's scenic North Shore. Visitors tour the renowned Waimea arboretum and Botanical Garden, interact with native Hawaiians as they recreate the daily life of the 1700s, enjoy performances showcasing the evolution of hula, see spectacular cliff diving shows and explore a tropical rain forest." Although *Everywhere* promises "statewide visitor information," it delivered only an address for Hawaii's visitors bureau and another address for national park information.

Everywhere may also contain out-of-date information; the guide was released in December 1993, and I'm not aware of any plans for an updated edition. If you really want to travel everywhere in the U.S.A., you're much better off buying several good guides in print for the same amount you'd spend on this inadequate CD-ROM set.

GREAT RESTAURANTS, WINERIES & BREWERIES
★★
Developer: Deep River Publishing Inc.; 800-643-5630
Format: Windows
Price: $29

Flatter than a day-old beer, *Great Restaurants, Wineries & Breweries* is poorly put together and absolutely clueless in some spots—the CD-ROM, for example, doesn't list a single brewery in Milwaukee, Wisconsin. Released in August 1994, *Great Restaurants* provides listings on 1,400 restaurants, wineries, and breweries around the United States, supposedly limited to only the most outstanding examples in each category. But there's no explanation of how the selections were made or by what authority.

The CD-ROM is also unnecessarily difficult to navigate. You can search the listings only geographically, by city and state, rather than by name. Nor can you search all three categories together; instead, you're forced to look separately for restaurants and then wineries and then breweries. Nor can you focus on a specific community. When you select a particular city, the CD-ROM produces a list for the entire region. When I tried to find restaurants in my hometown of Princeton, New Jersey, for example, I was presented with a huge list of names covering the entire region from New York to Philadelphia. I would have had to tediously call up each individual listing to find the few in Princeton.

The listings themselves are informative. A reproduction of the menu is presented for each restaurant, along with a few paragraphs of description and a photograph. The CD-ROM even includes two hundred recipes taken from the restaurants, although they're indexed by the name of the dish rather than by the name of the restaurant—another bad decision. The wineries and breweries also get a photograph and description. But the listings are far from comprehensive—as in the failure to include any Milwaukee breweries—and the restaurant industry's rapid turnover could quickly render some of the CD-ROM's information out of date.

LET'S GO: THE BUDGET GUIDE TO EUROPE 1994
★★½
Developer: Compton's NewMedia Inc.; 800-284-2045
Format: Windows
Price: $25

Let's Go: The Budget Guide to Europe 1994, a paperback book published by St. Martin's Press, is definitely worth stuffing in your backpack if you're departing for a low-cost trip to the Continent. But you can't take an entire computer system on the road, making the CD-ROM version something of a wasted effort. Even for pre-trip planning, *Let's Go Europe* on CD-ROM delivers little more than the book for more than double the price.

The added features of the CD-ROM aren't a complete waste, however. You can listen to native speakers pronouncing several dozen useful phrases in French, German, Italian, and Spanish. When you arrive in Europe, you'll already know how to say, "Where is the bathroom?" in German and "How much is the bill?" in French. There are also maps not found in the book, which can be printed and put in your luggage. Less useful are a collection of 112 video clips, most running less than thirty seconds in a window so small that the images are barely visible, and one hundred tourist-board photographs.

As a book, I like *Let's Go Europe*, and all of the book's text is reproduced in the CD-ROM. It's full of practical advice intended for under-thirty travelers. In the article on hitchhiking, for instance, the book strongly recommends against the dangerous practice but acknowledges the inevitable: "Consider this section as akin to handing out condoms to high school students: We don't endorse using it, but if you're going to do it anyway, we'll tell you how to make it safer and therefore more enjoyable." The descriptions of places to go are succinct without seeming incomplete, such as this entry on the Eiffel Tower in Paris: "Built in 1889 to celebrate the centennial of the storming of the Bastille, the world's largest Gallic symbol is breathtaking. Try it at night—even the most blasé will be impressed."

The CD-ROM is easy to install, although it demands anywhere from nine to nineteen megabytes of hard-disk space, and effortless to navigate. But I've got one more concern, other than the lack of portability: The CD-ROM edition came out in December 1994, well after the book. If you're planning a trip to Europe, you'll undoubtedly want the 1995 print edition of *Let's Go*, which is likely to be available long before the 1995 CD-ROM.

TAXI FOR NEW YORK, CHICAGO, LOS ANGELES, SAN FRANCISCO & WASHINGTON, D.C.
★★★
Developer: News Electronic Data Inc.; 800-439-8294
Format: Windows
Price: $59

An excellent planning tool for business travelers on an expense account, *Taxi* combines extensive listings from the well-known Zagat surveys of restaurants and hotels with mapping software that lets you easily print out street maps and calculate distances. The CD-ROM was released in November 1993 with coverage of five cities and surrounding suburbs—Chicago, Los Angeles, New York, San Francisco, and Washington. Two other CD-ROMs, reviewed in this section, cover other major U.S. cities. More cities are being added all the time, and updated editions of the three disks may be released in the future, so call News Electronic Data Inc. for the latest information before buying.

Taxi is really two programs linked together. The Zagat ratings are compiled from evaluations, not from professional reviewers but by volunteer business travelers who focus on upscale restaurants and hotels frequented by executives. You search for listings that meet your criteria for price; type of cuisine in restaurants; Zagat's own rating, on a 0 to 30 scale, for food, decor, and service in restaurants or rooms, service, and dining in hotels; and special features, such as after-midnight service and "in" places for restaurants or "downtown convenience" and in-room fireplaces for hotels.

The individual listings typically present one or two long sentences with lots of quotes from the Zagat reviewers. The Berghoff Restaurant in downtown Chicago, for example, is rated 20 for food, 19 for decor, and 19 for service, with this description: "A Loop tradition since 1898, this affordable German [restaurant] still reaps raves for its 'old-world ambiance' and food that's 'much heavier than the average daily allowance,' including 'legendary creamed spinach' and delicious rye bread; critics say beware of tourists, lines and 'bad food.'" The Chateau Marmont hotel in Los Angeles gets an 18 for rooms, 18 for service and 16 for dining, with these words: "'Kooky' and 'bohemian to the core,' with a comfortably musty and shabbily genteel lobby, this 'European-style' hotel 'just above the Sunset Strip' has long been popular with visiting rock musicians and British actors, who 'like it because nothing works'; still famed after a decade as the place where John Belushi spent 'his last night'; those in the know prefer the 'homey bungalows' adjacent to this 'possibly haunted' ersatz castle that's 'a must for movie buffs.'"

The mapping software displays road and street maps that can be resized with a click of the mouse button, from an entire metropolitan area to just a few square blocks. *Taxi* will automatically pinpoint the location of any restaurant or hotel listed on the CD-ROM and also contains a directory of landmarks such as shopping centers and airports. You can even enter any two addresses—such as a hotel where you're staying and a restaurant you want to visit—and measure the distance between the two points. Maps can be easily copied to another application, such as a word processor, or printed. If you take a laptop computer on road trips, you can download the entire file for a city, although you'll need about twenty megabytes of hard-disk space.

Taxi provides a generous amount of information: Chicago is covered with 630 restaurant reviews and 45 hotel reviews, Los Angeles with 608 restaurants and 50 hotels, New York with 1,130 restaurants and 88 hotels, San Francisco with 533 restaurants and 58 hotels, and Washington with 441 restaurants and 57 hotels. But I wouldn't recommend the CD-ROM for vacation travel; there's no information on tourist sights and little coverage of modestly priced hotels and restaurants favored by most people spending their own money on an out-of-town adventure.

TAXI FOR NEW ORLEANS, DENVER, SEATTLE, PHOENIX & ORANGE COUNTY
★★★
Developer: News Electronic Data Inc.; 800-439-8294
Format: Windows
Price: $59

A duplicate of the original *Taxi*, reviewed in this section, covering five other cities: Denver with 232 restaurant reviews and 20 hotel reviews, New Orleans with 408 restaurants and 34 hotels, Orange County in California with 160 restaurants and 23 hotels, Phoenix with 268 restaurants and 37 hotels, and Seattle with 335 restaurants and 17 hotels.

TAXI FOR PHILADELPHIA, BOSTON, ATLANTA, MIAMI & ORLANDO
★★★
Developer: News Electronic Data Inc.; 800-439-8294
Format: Windows
Price: $59

A duplicate of the original *Taxi*, reviewed in this section, covering five other cities: Atlanta with 486 restaurant reviews and 34 hotel reviews, Boston with 474 restaurants and 28 hotels, Miami with 474 restaurants and 49 hotels, Orlando with 260 restaurants and 31 hotels, and Philadelphia with 362 restaurants and 18 hotels.

Chapter Five:
Art, Science, History, and Current Events

This is the serious chapter. The arts includes painting, theater and other forms of art, except for literature, found in Chapter Six, Section c, and music, found in Chapter Six, Sections d and e. I've drawn an arbitrary dividing line to determine what falls in the category of history and what is considered current events; CD-ROMs covering events prior to 1990 are in Section c of this chapter, and CD-ROMs covering more recent news are in Section d.

a. The Arts

AMERICAN VISIONS JOURNEYS THROUGH ART: ACT ONE
★★½
Developer: Creative Labs Inc.; 800-998-5227
Format: Windows-2, Macintosh-2
Price: $39

American Visions Journeys through Art: Act One tries to present modern art in a very modern way, by throwing lots of bits and pieces onto a CD-ROM and letting you find your own path through the resulting chaos. I found this avant-garde approach more frustrating than enlightening and yearned for conventional indexes and pull-down menus.

The CD-ROM contains reproductions of 185 works by 129 artists from the Roy R. Neuberger Museum of Art in Purchase, New York, including such well-known names as Georgia O'Keeffe, Jackson Pollock, and Mark Rothko. The creator of the collection, wealthy art enthusiast Roy R. Neuberger, appears in a series of video clips telling stories of his long career supporting struggling young painters who later became world-famous.

American Visions is hobbled, however, by its unconventional interface, which presents hundreds of "thumbnails" on screen. The thumbnails can be an individual work of art, a photograph of the artist, a video clip, or a few sentences of commentary by the artist or by an art historian. These thumbnail images are arranged across the screen in four rows—artworks along the top, photographs in the second row, artist comments in the third row, and art historians in the fourth row. You pick one of three ways to display the thumbnails: alphabetically by artist, chronologically by year the works were created, or by picking one of thirty-two schools of art, such as expressionist, minimalist, or social realist.

When you find a thumbnail of interest, you click on it to get the full contents. O'Keeffe, for example, is the subject of nine thumbnails—a reproduction of her 1930 painting *Lake George by Moonrise*; a portrait of the artist by her companion, the noted photographer Alfred Stieglitz; two comments by art historians; and five comments by O'Keeffe herself. Here is O'Keeffe's reaction to critics who accused her of creating "pretty" paintings: "I'm one of the few artists, maybe the only one today, who is willing to talk about my work being pretty. I don't mind being pretty. I think it's a shame to discard this word. Maybe if we work hard enough, we can make it fashionable again."

Juggling all these thumbnails gets tiring, however. I'd much prefer an interface that didn't interfere with enjoying the artwork. Why not just present a single screen on O'Keeffe, with buttons to summon the relevant material? Because the interface is so confusing, I'd strongly recommend taking the "User's Guide" narrated tour offered in the introductory screen before attempting to make sense of *American Visions*.

MICROSOFT ART GALLERY
★★★½
Developer: Microsoft Corp.; 800-426-9400
Format: Windows, Macintosh
Price: $59

Art museums always make me cranky. No matter how beautiful the paintings, my feet get sore from standing on marble floors and I get eyestrain from staring at the tiny text explaining each work. Wouldn't it be easier to put the entire contents of a museum onto a CD-ROM? That's exactly what you get with *Microsoft Art Gallery*—all two thousand paintings from the permanent collection of the National Gallery at Trafalgar Square in London.

The National Gallery focuses almost exclusively on European artists of the fifteenth through the nineteenth centuries, especially those from the Netherlands and Italy. Hanging in the gallery are some of the most famous paintings by Rembrandt, Leonardo, and Van Gogh. Each work gets its own separate screen, displaying the picture and accompanying text. The reproductions are among the best I've ever seen on a computer, although they still don't match high-quality color printing. As a result, you'll miss fine details, such as the individual brush strokes in Van Gogh's famous 1888 stilllife "Sunflowers." But the loss of visual detail is more than balanced by the additional text, which goes far beyond the typical museum exhibit.

Rembrandt's biography in *Art Gallery*, for example, explains that after the death of his wife, Saskia, in 1642, he took a mistress named Hendrickje Stoffels. Even though a church in Amsterdam condemned Hendrickje for "living like a whore with Rembrandt," he refused to marry her because he was concerned that he would have to forfeit money left him in Saskia's will. Knowing this sad story brings a new depth of understanding when you look at Rembrandt's portrait of Hendrickje.

Four indexes—by artist's name, type of picture, historical period, and a glossary of art terms—provide guidance as you wander the virtual corridors of *Art Gallery*. Click on the word "tempera" in the glossary, for example, and you get a definition: "commonly refers to egg tempera, that is, paint made using egg yolk as a medium ... Most early Italian paintings are in this medium." The glossary screen also displays three thumbnail images of tempera paintings. Click on any one, and you go to the screen displaying the full image of the painting with its accompanying text. *Art Gallery* also offers four brief "audio tours," in which a narrator takes you through a series of screens exploring topics such as composition and how paintings are made.

I wish every art museum would create a product like *Art Gallery*, which opens a window into collections for people around the world. Future generations of computers with ultra-high-resolution monitors should overcome the single biggest drawback of *Art Gallery*, the lack of fine detail in on-screen reproductions. *Art Gallery*, by the way, became an important footnote in history on March 6, 1994, when *The New York Times* prestigious Book Review section picked the disk as the first CD-ROM to get its own review.

CINEMA VOLTA
★ ½
Developer: Voyager Co.; 800-446-2001
Format: Macintosh
Price: $39

When artists first encounter the many creative avenues opened up by CD-ROM technology, they sometimes react just like a five-year-old with a new set of crayons: Let's use everything just to see what happens! What happens, almost always, is a mess. *Cinema Volta* is a choppy, confusing and ultimately unsuccessful attempt to put a personal prose poem on CD-ROM.

San Francisco-area artist Jim Petrillo throws photographs, sound effects, drawings, one-second video clips, and multicolored text onto the screen, along with his own voice, which provides narration that explores his theme of how electricity has changed our lives. He adds a few pointless and undramatic personal reminiscences explaining the disk's subtitle: *Weird Science & Childhood Memory.*

Cinema Volta is named for another failure, a movie theater author James Joyce started in Dublin in 1909 that showed only Italian films. The CD-ROM is divided into twelve chapters, mostly named for historical figures such as Thomas Edison, Nikola Tesla, and Alessandro Volta, who invented the electric battery in 1779. Petrillo's thoughts on these characters are banal. He calls the fictional Victor Frankenstein "a sexually repressed, father-worshipping, northern-European type" who "behaved remarkably like a modern computer nerd." The personal computer, he declares, is "pure logic and plastic. It pretends to think. So do I."

After watching *Cinema Volta* from beginning to end, which takes only thirty-five minutes, you'll be in complete agreement with Petrillo—he's only pretending to think. Finally, a warning to parents: *Cinema Volta* contains brief depictions of nudity, several obscenities, and references to drug use.

THE CRUCIBLE CD-ROM
★★★½
Developer: Penguin USA; 800-526-0275
Format: Macintosh
Price: $65

At the height of Senator Joseph McCarthy's infamous "witch hunts" for supposed Communists infiltrating the government and Hollywood, playwright Arthur Miller wrote *The Crucible* as a warning of the danger McCarthy posed for democracy. But Miller didn't mount a direct assault; instead, he portrayed the original witch hunts of Salem, Massachusetts, in 1692. First produced in 1953, *The Crucible* is one of Miller's most popular works and continues to be performed regularly.

The Crucible CD-ROM is a study guide for anyone wanting to learn more about the play, about Miller, and about the witch hunts of the 1690s and the 1950s. Ironically, for a play so closely linked to U.S. history, the CD-ROM was produced at the University of East Anglia in England. The disk is intended primarily for schools and comes with a thirty-six-page "teacher's guide." But the material isn't dull or academic and will appeal to anyone interested in the play and the issues it confronts.

When you start *The Crucible CD-ROM,* you enter "The

Lobby," a representation of a theater lobby. Clicking on images in the lobby transports you to the CD-ROM's seven major sections. "The Play" presents the full text of *The Crucible*; "The 17th Century" contains essays on life in Salem at the time of the witch trials; "The 1950s" offers essays on the witch hunts of the 1950s, including the story of Miller's own confrontation with congressional investigators; "The Playwright" presents Miller himself in a series of video clips taken from an exclusive interview with the CD-ROM's producers in June 1992; "The Balcony" provides a half-dozen essays by theater critics; "The Dressing Room" offers video clips of actors participating in a British production of the play; and "The Bookstore" presents yet another set of essays by critics. An extensive set of on-screen navigation buttons and indexes makes it easy to search through all this material, as well as print or copy chunks of the text.

The interview with Miller, especially, is a treasure. Some forty years after writing the play, he is still passionate about his message: "On some level, there is a union between private sins and public consequences . . . One of the engines behind this play, and in my opinion it may well be why it is my most-produced play, and why so many people in different parts of the world identify with it, is the feeling that one's sins are not really private . . . They resonate. They shake the world. That's what guilt is. Guilt is really the fear that you are transparent . . . They [the Puritans] did feel that a private sin made God stumble for a moment."

TATE GALLERY — EXPLORING MODERN ART
★★
Developer: Attica Cybernetics Ltd.; 800-862-2206
Format: Windows
Price: $49

Tate Gallery—Exploring Modern Art is a coffee-table art book moved onto CD-ROM. Unfortunately, much is lost in translation. The images of the artwork are washed out and slightly fuzzy, and the text is difficult to read. *Exploring Modern Art* is also rather slender, offering reproductions and descriptions of just 150 works.

The CD-ROM presents a portion of the huge collection at the Tate Gallery in England, which has exhibit centers in London and two other British cities. From the main screen, you can choose to visit one of six "galleries" focused on specific subjects: "Dynamism," looking at works from the early twentieth century; "Hepworth," showing the creations of British sculptor Barbara Hepworth; "Men & Women," a collection of modern paintings; "Modern British Sculpture," a roundup of works by contemporary artists; "Pablo Picasso," showing paintings and drawings from the famous artist's multifaceted career; and "Pop Art," featuring works from the 1960s. Within each gallery, you see thumbnail images of the various works. Clicking on an image expands it to fill half the screen, while you listen to an audio narration describing the work. You can also call up a text window for further details.

The text is interesting but difficult to read because only a few lines are displayed at a time. Here's part of the description for Picasso's 1905 drawing *Girl in a Chemise*: "Between 1901 and 1904, Picasso went through the most difficult period of his career, trying to establish himself in Paris, unable to sell his work, sometimes near to starving and, the story goes, forced at one point in the winter of 1901 to burn a pile of his drawings in order to keep warm.... In 1904, Picasso finally left Barcelona and settled in Paris, moving into the ramshackle tenement building in Montmartre known to the mixture of poverty-stricken clerks, laundresses, actors, writers and artists who lived in it as the floating laundry.... He began to sell some work again, and, although he remained poor, he no longer starved. The blue of the previous years began to give way to pink, and his subject matter began to be drawn mainly from the world of the circus. An element of sadness remained, but the extreme gloom of the Blue Period was gone. *Girl in a Chemise* seems to belong to the beginning of this Pink, or Rose, Period."

Of course, this same text could be delivered in a book, along with better reproductions. I also expect a book on the Tate's collection of modern art would cover more than 150 works, which would make it a better investment than this CD-ROM.

I PHOTOGRAPH TO REMEMBER
★★★★
Developer: Voyager Co.; 800-446-2001
Format: Windows, Macintosh
Price: $29

Viewing the work of a great photographer on the wall of a gallery or in the pages of a coffee-table book is often a strangely detached experience. We don't really know what the photographer was feeling at the moment a picture was taken. *I Photograph to Remember* breaks through this barrier between the audience and the artist.

Photographer Pedro Meyer spent three years in the late 1980s capturing on film the slow decline of his parents, Ernesto and Liesel, who died in Mexico City just nine weeks apart after fifty-five years of marriage. The story is told through one hundred beautifully evocative black-and-white photographs, with Meyer providing quiet yet emotional narration describing how his parents coped with terminal illness and his own struggle to accept their imminent death. It's almost as if Meyer is sitting next to us on the sofa, flipping through an album of family snapshots and reminiscing, except these family snapsnots are the work of a gifted photographer.

The images in *I Photograph to Remember* are unforgettable. We see the pain in Ernesto's eyes when doctors first tell him he has cancer and will live only four to six weeks, although he held on for three years. We see Liesel cheerfully caring for her husband. "There was this complicity of tenderness between my mother and father," Meyer says. "Every moment became precious." There is a poignant scene of Ernesto's being propped up on his daily stroll through a park while a toddler nearby is assisted with her first steps. "You're helped into life, and you're helped out of life," Meyer observes. We see Ernesto's body waste away, then watch in shock as Liesel is suddenly stricken with a brain tumor. Ernesto "lost his will to continue" after Liesel's death, Meyer says, and passed away nine weeks after his wife.

I Photograph to Remember takes about thirty minutes to see and hear from beginning to end. I was transfixed for every one of those minutes. And I know I'll turn to the CD-ROM again because Meyer's powerful story deserves many retellings.

MACBETH
★★★
Developer: Voyager Co.; 800-446-2001
Format: Macintosh
Price: $39

"Will all great Neptune's ocean wash this blood/Clean from my hand? No: this my hand will rather/The multitudinous seas incarnadine,/Making the green one red." That agonized speech by

Macbeth, from William Shakespeare's classic play, illuminates the character's unshakable guilt for murdering good King Duncan. But modern readers might stumble on some of the seventeenth century vocabulary. *Macbeth* the CD-ROM solves that problem with the click of the mouse—put the cursor on the word "incarnadine," click once, and a small window pops up with the definition "stain red."

The CD-ROM offers several routes into the play. You can watch the text scroll along the screen while listening to a full performance by the Royal Shakespeare Company, recorded in 1976 and starring Ian McKellen as Macbeth. Or you can look at eight video clips taken from three movies of Shakespeare's dark tale—the 1948 *Macbeth* directed by and starring Orson Welles, the 1971 version directed by Roman Polanski, and *Throne of Blood*, a 1957 retelling by director Akira Kurosawa that transformed the characters into samurai warriors in medieval Japan. There's even a "*Macbeth* karaoke" feature in which you can become either Macbeth or Lady Macbeth in two scenes, while an actor or actress reads the other role.

Beyond the play itself, the disk contains a profusion of essays, commentaries, maps, illustrations, scene summaries, and indexes. "Macbeth is Shakespeare's eeriest play," writes David S. Rodes, an English professor at the University of California, Los Angeles, in the introduction. "Shakespeare dramatizes the violent intrusion of the demonic into the realm of human affairs." One thing is missing, however: The box for *Macbeth* incorrectly says the CD-ROM displays a video performance of the play rather than just an audio performance. Inside the box, Voyager Company includes a note apologizing for the error.

Students studying Shakespeare will find *Macbeth* on CD-ROM a powerful way to master the Bard's intricate plot and dialogue. But the heavy prose and extensive analysis may alienate those who want to experience *Macbeth* without the extra weight of academic baggage.

b. Science and Nature

A.D.A.M. THE INSIDE STORY
★★★
Developer: A.D.A.M. Software Inc.; 800-408-2326
Format: Windows, Macintosh
Price: $49

A.D.A.M. The Inside Story is the CD-ROM equivalent of "The Invisible Man" and "The Invisible Woman" model kits popular with children. With a click of the mouse button, you move through layers of an anatomy model, from skin down through the circulatory system, muscles, and internal organs to the skeleton. A.D.A.M. Software Inc. originally created the thousands of detailed, colorful drawings for a CD-ROM sold to medical students, so *A.D.A.M. The Inside Story* delivers a level of scientific accuracy unmatched in other anatomy software sold for the home market.

The CD-ROM makes it easy to manipulate the anatomy models. You can select whether to see illustrations of a male or female model, called Adam and Eve, whether to look from the front or the back. You can even choose the model's facial structure and skin tone—white, black, Hispanic, or Asian. Parents will also appreciate the "discretion option"; during installation, you can choose to have the genitals and female breasts covered by fig leaves and lock out the sections covering reproduction.

A.D.A.M., which stands for "Animated Dissection of Anatomy for Medicine," also provides an extensive "family scrapbook" which has animated essays describing how the body functions. A male and female narrator portray Adam and Eve in twelve chapters covering systems including the cardiovascular, digestive, muscular, and respiratory. Each chapter presents a succession of narrated on-screen pages; some of the pages offer short animations and video clips, such as an explanation of how blood clots are formed to close a wound and a demonstration of the Heimlich maneuver to help choking victims.

The scrapbook chapters don't offer much depth, however—watching all twelve won't take much more than an hour. The developers also detract from the educational process by inserting a lot of corny comments; in the introduction, for example, Adam says, "For those of you who are in the dark about your bodies, let's shed some light on the subject." Also, the video clips are hard to follow, showing grainy images in a tiny window.

If you want detailed and elegant anatomical illustrations, *A.D.A.M.* can't be beat. But I'm not sure there's a big demand for anatomy illustrations, other than in medical schools, and I'd recommend the CD-ROM only to students studying anatomy. Most families would be better served by a general medical reference such as the *Mayo Clinic Family Pharmacist*, reviewed in Chapter Seven, Section d.

BEYOND PLANET EARTH
★★½

Developer: Discovery Communications Inc.; 800-762-2189
Format: Windows
Price: $39

Beyond Planet Earth doesn't go far enough beyond its own source material: documentaries produced for The Discovery Channel. The CD-ROM contains fifty minutes of video, much of it narrated by actor Richard Kiley, that plays in a five-inch diagonal window on a standard fourteen-inch monitor. The video has been supplemented with two hundred photographs and a selection of brief articles on astronomy, but there isn't enough of this extra material to justify buying the CD-ROM instead of spending half as much for a videotape of The Discovery Channel's original programming.

The CD-ROM is divided into four sections. "Planetary Theater" presents five video clips on such topics as the formation of the solar system and the possibility that a comet wiped out the dinosaurs. "Solar Gallery" covers eight topics related to the planets, recycling some of the video clips from "Planetary Theater." "Space Experts" features video clips of four space scientists, including *Apollo* astronaut Buzz Aldrin, each answering the same set of questions. Most of these questions seem to be the type asked by gradeschool students, such as, "What is your favorite celestial body?" All four give the same answer: Mars. That's a perfect setup for the final section, "Mission to Mars," describing the hurdles if we ever decide to spend the $200 billion required to visit the Red Planet. Kiley explains that Mars "may have had rivers of water. Surface images show ancient riverbeds and plains scoured by great floods. Now, the water that once flowed across its surface is frozen in its ice caps." The presence of water has raised scientific speculation that life may once have flourished on Mars and human visitors might possibly find fossil evidence of that life.

BODYWORKS 3.0
★★½
Developer: SoftKey International Inc.; 800-227-5609
Format: Windows
Price: $49

BodyWorks 3.0 presents an easy and interesting way to learn about human anatomy, but is hampered by the poor quality of its illustrations. The CD-ROM displays low-resolution anatomy cross sections that fill only half the screen, making it difficult to pick out individual features.

You move through *BodyWorks* by choosing a part of the body to explore, such as the sensory organs. From a list of sensory organs, you select an individual organ—for example, the nose. You then see a color cross section of the nose and nasal cavity on the left side of the screen. In the upper right is a list of anatomical features. Click on a feature, such as the hard palate or olfactory bulb, and a line appears pointing to the correct spot in the illustration. In the lower right is a text window with a brief description of the sense of smell: "Smell is the most basic and most primitive of the senses. It is some 10,000 times more acute than our sense of taste. In fact, most food flavors are smelled, not tasted, as anyone with a heavy cold will verify. Nasal congestion prevents the little eddies of air, stirred up by the action of chewing and swallowing, from reaching the receptors in the roof of the nasal cavity."

For users who want a more structured approach, *BodyWorks* includes fourteen "lessons" in which you select a subject and are guided through the appropriate material. Supplementing the illustrations and text are thirty-eight movies, mostly five-second animations showing the movement of joints; a glossary of anatomical terms; a series of multiple-choice quizzes; and fourteen cartoon-like three-dimensional models of organs and skeletal structures that users can rotate to examine from any angle. *BodyWorks* goes beyond anatomy with sections called "Living" and "Health & Fitness" which briefly cover such subjects as the benefits of exercise, the causes of male pattern baldness, and the role of DNA in genetics.

A BRIEF HISTORY OF TIME
★★
Developer: Creative Labs Inc.; 800-998-5227
Format: Windows-2, Macintosh-2
Price: $35

A Brief History of Time, the best-selling book by physicist Stephen Hawking, isn't "brief" in this CD-ROM. The extra animations, visual images, and narration do nothing but slow down the process of understanding Hawking's complicated and fascinating ideas about the origins and future of the universe.

Hawking, a professor at Cambridge University in England, is now one of the world's most famous scientists. Confined to a wheelchair by amyotrophic lateral sclerosis, a degenerative condition also known as Lou Gehrig's disease, he nonetheless continues to pour out important and controversial theories, speaking through a voice synthesizer. *A Brief History of Time*, his 1988 book explaining those theories to a nonscientific audience, sold 8 million copies and spent a year on *The New York Times* best-seller list, then became the inspiration for a highly acclaimed 1992 documentary film of the same name.

I can't attempt a complete explanation of Hawking's ideas, but the core of his thinking is that the universe exists endlessly with no beginning or end. "When we combine quantum mechanics with general relativity, there seems to be a new possibility that did not arise before: that space and time together might form a finite, four-dimensional space without singularities or boundaries, like the surface of the earth but with more dimensions," Hawking writes in the book's conclusion. "It seems that this idea could explain many of the observed features of the universe . . . But if the universe is completely self-contained, with no singularities or boundaries, and completely described by a unified theory, that has profound implications for the role of God as Creator."

The CD-ROM, sadly, does nothing to help you wrestle with these provocative proposals. The entire text of the book is contained in the CD-ROM, with icons on the side of the screen to summon extra material related to what you're reading. These extras, however, are mostly a wasted effort. You can listen to the passage quoted above, for example, narrated in the slow, computerlike cadence of Hawking's synthesizer, a tedious alternative to simply reading the words on the screen. You can also summon a satiric illustration of a Godlike figure with a red slash across his face, a tasteless reference to Hawking's questions about the importance of divinity in a scientifically defined universe.

The CD-ROM is also incredibly frustrating to navigate. There is no instruction manual or on-screen help, nor is the layout intuitively obvious. When you start the disk, you see an office with Hawking sitting to one side in his wheelchair. Clicking on objects in the scene summons essays on Hawking and the history of physics, but you have no way of knowing what any of these objects does until you click on them. Hawking's ideas are difficult enough for ordinary people to absorb without the further burden of a poorly designed CD-ROM.

IN THE COMPANY OF WHALES
★★

Developer: Discovery Communications Inc.; 800-762-2189
Format: Windows
Price: $39

In 1992 The Discovery Channel cable network aired a one-hour documentary called *In the Company of Whales.* You can buy a videotape of the program for $19 from The Discovery Channel. Or you can pay twice as much for the CD-ROM version, which contains forty-five minutes of video clips taken from the documentary along with a small amount of extra text and photographs. I'd opt for buying the videotape—or maybe even renting it from a video store for $2 or $3—and spending the difference for a good book on whales.

In the Company of Whales on CD-ROM is full of interesting footage from the documentary, with narration from actor Patrick Stewart, best known for playing Captain Jean-Luc Picard on "Star Trek: The Next Generation." But the video clips play in a tiny three-inch diagonal window on a fourteen-inch monitor, so you miss much of the grandeur of breaching whales leaping through the air. And while the narration is clearly for adults, the extra text appears to be more suited for elementary school students. "Whales and fish are both vertebrates—animals with backbones—but they belong to different groups within the vertebrates," the text explains. "Whales are mammals, belonging to the same group humans do, while fish are a group of their own." An "Ask the Expert" section also appears to be aimed at kids. You select one of four scientists, appearing in video clips, to answer a selected list of softball questions such as "What do you find to be the most interesting thing about whales?" Assuming the developers are trying to appeal to children, they made one serious mistake: There is no way to print the text or copy it to a word processor, a significant shortcoming for students working on school reports.

MICROSOFT DANGEROUS CREATURES
★★½
Developer: Microsoft Corp.; 800-426-9400
Format: Windows, Macintosh
Price: $59

Microsoft Dangerous Creatures is a sheep in wolf's clothing. The box shows a large color picture of a grizzly bear baring its fangs, implying the CD-ROM is all about mayhem and blood lust in the animal kingdom. The subtitle, a more accurate description of the contents, is barely visible: "Explore the Endangered World of Wildlife." Prepared with assistance from the World Wildlife Fund, *Dangerous Creatures* is really an extended pitch for ecological awareness and the need to save vanishing species.

It's also not made clear on the box that *Dangerous Creatures* is written at a level more appropriate for junior high students than adults, with lots of interesting snippets of information and little depth. Consider this entry on the snapping turtle: "An alligator snapper's lightning-fast bite can snap a broomstick in half. It's the heaviest freshwater turtle in the world—an average adult weighs as much as a large man! Its cousin, the American snapping turtle, is less than a third its size but also has knife-sharp jaws. Still, humans injure these important scavengers far more than the other way around—in some places, snapper soup is a delicacy."

Dangerous Creatures presents text and photographs describing 250 animals; about one hundred entries include video clips, running about thirty seconds each in a four-and-a-half-inch diagonal window on a standard fourteen-inch monitor. All the content is linked through point-and-click headings. The snapping turtle article, for example, is linked to entries on the army ant and the evolution of turtles. The various animals can also be accessed through an atlas, a listing of habitats, an overview of animal weapons, a conventional index, or a series of guided tours. The photographs, in particular, are fascinating, showing everything from two lions making a meal out of a zebra to rats nibbling a garbage pile. But the constant succession of two-sentence articles leaves *Dangerous Creatures* without enough bite to appeal to an adult audience.

DISTANT SUNS 2.0
★★★½
Developer: Virtual Reality Laboratories Inc.; 800-829-8754
Format: Windows, Macintosh
Price: $69

You don't have to be an experienced astronomer to appreciate *Distant Suns 2.0*, a powerful desktop planetarium program, but you must at least be willing to learn the basics of celestial navigation. The CD-ROM comes with an excellent ninety-six-page instruction manual, however, that clearly explains such fundamental concepts as declination, right ascension, and azimuth and altitude, the equivalents of longitude and latitude in earthbound maps.

Distant Suns displays a portion of the night sky on your computer screen, which can be easily adjusted to meet your specific demands. You can view the stars and planets by themselves or add identifying tags. You can summon distant stars and celestial objects that aren't normally seen from earth. You can shift your location to any spot on Earth or even venture off the planet's surface to other locations in the solar system and look at the sky on any date ranging from 4,713 B.C. to 10,000 A.D. A handy "QuickAim" feature will automatically center the picture on the sun, moon, or any of the planets. With a mouse click, you can view statistical information on 9,100 stars—their name, magnitude, position, and other scientific details.

The CD-ROM also provides 1,500 photographic images taken from telescopes and NASA spacecraft showing stars, comets, asteroids, the planets, and the surface of the Earth as seen from orbit. In May 1994, the developers released a special edition in anticipation of the Shoemaker-Levy 9 comet's impact with Jupiter in July. The special edition provides a short computer-generated animation showing the impact, a science teacher's guide to comets written by NASA's Jet Propulsion Laboratory, and a collection of scientific papers on the cosmic event of the decade.

I'd recommend *Distant Suns* to anyone who wants to get seriously involved with astronomy. But this is definitely software for grown-ups; I wouldn't expect children under age twelve to be able to master the underlying concepts, and *Distant Suns* does not provide any games or activities—you have to come up with your own planetarium projects.

EARTHQUAKE
★★½

Developer: Sony Imagesoft; 800-922-7669
Format: Windows
Price: $59

Few acts of nature are as scary as an earthquake. The most stable thing in the world—the ground itself—is suddenly unhinged and dangerous. Having lived through the Northern California quake of 1989, I've gained a deep and abiding respect for this unpredictable and uncontrollable force of nature. *Earthquake* earnestly tackles the subject with forty minutes of video footage from ABC News, narrated by "Nightline" anchor Ted Koppel, along with five hundred photographs, maps, and hundreds of pages of text. But the overall impact is hobbled by some poor design decisions.

In-depth coverage is provided for five recent earthquakes: Tangshan, China, in 1976; Mexico City in 1985; Loma Prieta in 1989; Marathawada, India, in 1993; and Northridge (Los Angeles) in 1994. You can summon several video clips of each quake, as well as text, photos, and maps. Tangshan's quake is by far the most chilling. One-quarter of the industrial city's population—240,000 people—were killed in the early morning hours of July 28, 1976. "The losses were so huge because almost none of the structures in Tangshan were designed to resist seismic forces," the text explains. "The most common type of construction used unreinforced brick walls, which quickly fell down during the shaking. All four of the city's hospitals were destroyed, and the seriously injured had to be taken to other cities. The army built temporary shelters for medical workers and injured people. The entire city was sprayed with disinfectant from helicopters and planes to control the spread of disease. Fear of an epidemic was justified because it took a long time to remove the thousands of bodies from under the rubble."

A section on "Other Major Quakes" provides abbreviated entries on seventeen earthquakes throughout the twentieth century from the destruction of San Francisco in 1906 to the Lander, California, quake of 1992. Lengthy excerpts from the book *Terra Non Firma*, written by two Stanford University geologists, are divided in two sections called "Understanding Earthquakes" and "Preparing for Earthquakes."

The problem with *Earthquake* is the way in which all this information is presented. The video clips play in a six-inch diagonal window on a standard fourteen-inch monitor, too large to avoid choppy and grainy images. The text appears in a narrow rectangular window running down the right side of the screen, making it painful to read. There is no way to copy the text to a word processor, nor are you given any other printing option than outputting an entire selection. These flaws will limit the time you want to spend exploring *Earthquake*, despite the wealth of interesting material.

JOURNEY TO THE PLANETS
★★
Developer: Multicom Publishing Inc.; 800-850-7272
Format: Windows, Macintosh
Price: $29

Journey to the Planets resembles a trip to Jupiter: colorful but cold and lonely. The CD-ROM delivers lots and lots of statistics about the nine planets in our solar system, as well as the sun, along with color photographs and charts and diagrams. Seven of the planets—all but Mercury and Pluto—also have one-minute "fly-throughs," video simulations of a flight skimming the planet's surface. The fly-throughs, accompanied by New Age music that seems more than a little influenced by the theme from "Star Trek," are dramatic but not especially informative. The fly-through of Venus, for example, shows a craggy brown surface and a white sky, something like the Arizona desert on an overcast day. The facts and figures are thrown together without any attempt to create an overall structure, so you end up with little more than a big collection of trivia. Now I know that 92.8 percent of asteroids are made of stone and 5.7 percent are iron and nickel. And that Mercury "boasts the largest surface temperature variance in the solar system, ranging from –298 degrees Fahrenheit on the night side to 872 degrees Fahrenheit on the day side." I'm just not sure I care.

Science and Nature

LAST CHANCE TO SEE
★★½
Developer: Voyager Co.; 800-446-2001
Format: Windows, Macintosh
Price: $39

Douglas Adams, a British writer of science-fiction satire, traveled to the exotic island of Madagascar in 1985, sent by a magazine to search for a nearly extinct lemur called the aye-aye. Adams found the lemur and also found out from his guide, photographer and naturalist Mark Carwardine, how many of the world's rare animals are in danger of extinction. They decided to join forces and do something: Adams and Carwardine went around the world for several years, then documented their travels, first in a book, then in a series of BBC radio programs, and finally this CD-ROM.

The pair can be excused, I suppose, for running a bit low on energy by the time it came to assembling the CD-ROM. They've delivered nothing more than a slide show displaying color photographs by Carwardine and text by Adams, read by the author, along with a few audio clips from the radio programs.

Adams, best known for creating the hilarious *Hitchhiker's Guide to the Galaxy* novels, is a witty writer, and the subject matter is unquestionably important. *Last Chance to See* documents the endangered Komodo dragon in Australia, the kakapo parrot in New Zealand, Yangtze River dolphins in China, the Rodrigues fruit bat in Mauritius, and the northern white rhinoceros in Zaire, which is actually dark gray in color. "People therefore assume that zoologists are either perverse or colour-blind," Adams writes. "But it's not that, it's that they're illiterate. 'White' is a mistranslation of the Afrikaans word 'weit' meaning 'wide,' and it refers to the animal's mouth, which is wider than that of the black rhino."

Watching the CD-ROM from beginning to end while listening to Adams's narration would require about six hours. But even the most ardent environmentalist is likely to get twitchy after fifteen or twenty minutes of sitting motionless in front of a computer. CD-ROM just isn't the best way to see *Last Chance to See.*

MAMMALS: A MULTIMEDIA ENCYCLOPEDIA
★★
Developer: National Geographic Society; 800-368-2728
Format: DOS, Macintosh
Price: $59

Nobody does a better job of producing magazines, books, and television documentaries on nature than the National Geographic Society. But simply transferring content from books or TV to CD-ROM isn't enough to create a compelling title. That's the problem with *Mammals: A Multimedia Encyclopedia*. The CD-ROM delivers little more than the contents of National Geographic's print *Book of Mammals* at a much higher price.

Mammals profiles two hundred species, from humans to snowshoe hares, by presenting photographs and text from the book in a window filling half the screen. Advertised for ages seven to adult, the text, which runs five or six paragraphs for each species, is written at a level appropriate for elementary and junior-high students; adults with a serious interest in mammals will find the content superficial. I checked out the platypus. "When British scientists first saw a platypus almost 200 years ago, they thought it was a fake," the disk informed me. "But this strange Australian creature does exist. Its forefeet are webbed like those of a duck. Its muzzle looks like a duck's bill. Its tail resembles that of a beaver. And its fur looks like an otter's fur." This three-pound stream dweller, I also discovered, is one of two mammal species that lays eggs. And the male platypus has poisonous spurs on the heels of his hind feet to fight off attackers.

While these descriptions are fascinating, *Mammals* doesn't live up to the "multimedia" part of its name. There are only twenty-eight video clips, with no sound, that are so slow, showing only one or two frames a second, they almost resemble a rapid sequence of still pictures. Some 150 of the profiles include a brief audio clip of the animal's "vocalization," so you can hear a few seconds of a fox barking or a whale singing. *Mammals* also includes a "game" that's a thinly disguised study guide, forcing children to answer questions by looking up information on various animals.

MARS EXPLORER
★★½

Developer: Virtual Reality Laboratories Inc.; 800-829-8754
Format: DOS, Macintosh
Price: $49

Mars Explorer examines the Red Planet without ever taking you down to the ground. The CD-ROM presents overhead-view images of almost the entire surface taken by NASA's Viking orbiter. But that's all you get; there are no photos or illustrations showing you what it might be like to see the mountains and canyons of Mars from the surface. Nor is there any text telling you about the planet. So *Mars Explorer* will be useful only to professional astronomers, college-level astronomy students, or intensely dedicated amateurs. The CD-ROM contains all the features this specialized audience wants, such as the ability to display the images in the planet's natural red color, in a range of "false" colors that makes it easier to analyze the images, or in black and white. Each image can be examined at four levels, creating the impression of "zooming in" to look at small details, and can be exported from the CD-ROM to other applications such as a graphics program. There is also an on-screen "locate" button that makes it easy to find any named feature on the Martian surface, such as the giant volcano Olympus Mons or the huge winding canyon Valles Marineris.

MURMURS OF EARTH
★★

Developer: Time Warner Interactive; 800-482-3766
Format: DOS, Macintosh
Price: $45

In about 300,000 years, any intelligent creatures in the vicinity of the star Sirius will finally get to hear Chuck Berry's awesome guitar riffs in "Johnny B. Goode," courtesy of the *Voyager 2* spacecraft, launched by NASA in 1977. *Voyager 2* and its sibling, *Voyager 1*, also launched in 1977, each carry a gold-coated phonograph record containing digitized photographs and audio portraits of life on Earth. After surveying Jupiter and Saturn, *Voyager 1* left the solar system in 1980; *Voyager 2* also visited Uranus and Neptune before leaving our small corner of the galactic neighborhood in 1989. A group of astronomers led by author and TV commentator Carl Sagan created the phonograph record as a kind of greeting card to intelligent life-forms that might encounter one of the *Voyager*s. Printed on the surface of the golden platter is a crude diagram showing how to build a record player and decode the information. I suppose it's a good thing Sagan and his associates didn't try to send a CD-ROM; it would have been too hard to explain in pictures how to build a microprocessor, CD-ROM drive, and monitor.

Sagan, never one to pass up a commercial opportunity to extol the wonders of the universe, turned the *Voyager* project into a 1978 book called *Murmurs of Earth*, published by Random House. The book shows the *Voyager* record's 118 photographs, describes the audio sections, and includes a number of essays describing how the project came together.

For no apparent reason, *Murmurs of Earth* became a CD-ROM in 1992. The two-disk set presents the same 118 photographs along with the *Voyager* record's ninety minutes of audio. But the sound, ranging from greetings in fifty-five languages to excerpts of classical music, is presented in the CD audio format—it can be heard just as easily through a conventional CD player hooked to a stereo system as through a computer. Sagan's book is also included in the box with the two CD-ROM disks. This leaves me pondering a deep question about the nature of the universe: If we can see the pictures in the book and listen to the audio on a regular CD player, why should we pay big bucks for a CD-ROM when we could instead buy just the book and a companion CD? Like many mysteries of outer space, this question doesn't yet have an answer. But don't lie awake nights worrying about it; just spend your money on something else.

PREHISTORIA
★★½
Developer: Grolier Electronic Publishing Inc.; 800-285-4534
Format: Windows, Macintosh
Price: $39

Calling itself a "multimedia *Who's Who* of prehistoric life," *Prehistoria* doesn't quite manage to find its own place—the CD-ROM is too technical for children and too limited for adults. What *Prehistoria* delivers is a color illustration and a few sentences of text on five hundred species, most of them long extinct, spread across

500 million years, with 60 minutes of animations and video clips on paleontology and related subjects.

There isn't enough information in these profiles to meet the research needs of adults, while the text is written at a level beyond the grasp of most children. The oldest animal in *Prehistoria*, for example, is an early fish called *Arandaspis*, described as having a "jawless mouth . . . on the the underside of its head, suggesting that it may have fed on or near the seabed. Like other heterostracans, there were probably small, movable plates inside its mouth equipped with ridges of dentine." There's no definition of "heterostracans," which left me scratching my head. We *Homo sapiens sapiens* merit only five poorly written sentences: "Excluding the Neandertal [sic] people, the rest of the fossil and living types of human being are grouped into a second subspecies, *Homo sapiens sapiens*. This modern subspecies is well known throughout the world from about 35,000 years ago. Artifacts and cave paintings found in central France, dating from about 30,000 years ago, testify to their cultural sophistication. A variety of artifacts and cave paintings dating from about 30,000 years ago give us a clear picture of one particular group called the 'Cro-Magnon' people, who lived in France and Spain. The evidence suggests that they had a strong tribal system, made tools, gathered plant materials, hunted, fished and possibly herded animals, and built shelters and manufactured clothing that enabled them to survive the last stages of the Pleistoce [sic]."

Separate from the profiles, which include a variety of mammals, birds, dinosaurs, reptiles, and amphibians, is the "Grolier Museum," presenting video clips and animations on topics such as continental drift and the possible evolutionary link between birds and dinosaurs. Again, the material is superficial—most topics are covered with a few sentences of text and only a minute or two of video.

Prehistoria is also awkward to operate. There is no "Go back" button, for example, so that when you use the time line to look up an individual animal, you can't go back; instead, you have to return to the main screen and reenter the time line to look at other animals from the same era. Pop-up windows must be closed by clicking on tiny buttons that are difficult to hit on the first try. And the text can only be printed, not copied to a word processor. In total, these flaws and the lack of depth make *Prehistoria* more of a curiosity than a serious educational tool.

REDSHIFT MULTIMEDIA ASTRONOMY
★★
Developer: Maris Multimedia Ltd.; 800-336-0185
Format: Windows, Macintosh
Price: $69

RedShift Multimedia Astronomy isn't a very good CD-ROM, but it did succeed in teaching me the universe can be a lonely place. I wrote a strongly negative review of this planetarium-on-a-disk in March 1994, shortly after it was released, and got a flood of nasty letters from astronomy buffs. *RedShift*, developed in part by Russian space scientists formerly associated with the Soviet Union's space program, has gone on to win a slew of awards from multimedia groups and a number of favorable reviews from other critics.

Maybe those other critics and contest judges fell into the trap of thinking, "It must be good if it's good for you." Or maybe they were reluctant to criticize a product that clearly resulted from a lot of hard work by struggling Russian scientists. And maybe I'm the only person in this corner of the galaxy who doesn't like *RedShift*, but I still think the CD-ROM isn't appropriate for the mass market.

The program is perfectly described by the slogan on the back of its box: "a multimedia planetarium on your desktop." That's exactly what you get, and that's all you get. College-level astronomy students and well-educated amateur astronomers will love *RedShift*, which puts you in control of beautifully illustrated renderings of the planets and stars. But the rest of us will be left out in the cold. There is no audio narration or music, for example. Indeed, there is no sound at all. There is also no video, other than a half-dozen one-minute clips of *Apollo* astronauts on the moon that seem to have been added simply because NASA film footage can be obtained for free.

And there is no serious attempt to help novices understand the complex principles of astronomy. *RedShift* does contain a dictionary of astronomical terms, but it's written for a scientific audience. Consider this definition of Lagrangian points: "Points in the orbital plane of two massive objects circling about their common center of gravity where a particle of negligible mass can remain in equilibrium. There are five such points for two bodies in circular orbits around each other, but three are unstable to small perturbations. The other two, at points 60 degrees either side of the massive body and in the same orbit, are stable." Nor is *RedShift* easy to use. The disk comes with a densely written sixty-page manual; using the on-screen control panel requires understanding such terms as "right ascension," "declination," and "azimuth."

SHARKS!
★★★
Developer: Discovery Communications Inc.; 800-762-2189
Format: Windows, Macintosh
Price: $39

"If lions are the kings of the jungle, then sharks are masters of the sea. In their respective environments, both the lion and the shark sit at the top of the food chain, preying on weaker animals for their survival. Like all animals, the sole mission of these carnivorous predators seems to be finding their next meal."

Those opening lines from *Sharks!* put these powerful animals in the proper perspective, without relying on excessive hype about the threat of being eaten by one of these sharp-toothed creatures. This CD-ROM from The Discovery Channel presents thirty minutes of video clips from the cable network's vault of documentaries, as well as an impressive amount of extra text and two hundred photographs exploring everything from shark anatomy to the truth about shark attacks. What is the truth? An average of twelve people are attacked by sharks in the United States each year, most of whom survive. We're at greater risk of dying from a snake bite or a bee sting than from a shark.

The video, which plays in a four-inch diagonal window on a standard fourteen-inch monitor, is chopped into eight clips; the text is presented in thirty-two articles divided into four sections: "About Sharks," "The Shark Body," "A Shark's Life," and "People and Sharks." I absorbed lots of interesting information from the articles, such as "The fearsome dorsal fin, often the only part of a shark seen above the surface, is nothing more than a stabilizer to keep the creature from rolling over."

I was less impressed with two other features. "Ask the Experts" lets you watch video clips of four shark researchers responding to a list of ten canned questions such as "What's your most memorable shark encounter?" And a game called "Shark Tag" is a dull trivia quiz in which you have to identify shark body parts or pick out different types of sharks by looking at their outlines. Overall, however, anyone with a strong interest in sharks won't be disappointed with the wealth of images and information in *Sharks!*

THE ULTIMATE HUMAN BODY
★★★

Developer: Dorling Kindersley Publishing Inc.; 800-356-6575
Format: Windows, Macintosh
Price: $49

A carefully and colorfully illustrated guide to anatomy, *The Ultimate Human Body* is a fascinating overview of our complicated inner workings. This isn't a medical textbook; you're spared from scientific jargon, but you're also deprived of detailed information.

The CD-ROM contains seven hundred screens depicting various organs and physical processes, all linked through point-and-click buttons. Navigating this wealth of material is made easy through three different options: "Body Machine," "Body Organs," and "Body Systems." With "Body Machine," you are offered thirteen questions to explore, such as "What happens when you exercise?" and "Why do you blink?" These questions are answered through anatomical drawings, snippets of text, ten-second audio narrations, and five-second animations. In "How do you swallow?," for example, you see an animation of peristalsis in the throat, rhythmic muscle contractions that move food to the stomach. "Body Organs" lets you peel away the layers of a body to learn about organs of the head, chest, and abdomen. "Body Systems" covers ten systems, including the skeletal, muscular, circulatory, and digestive. *The Ultimate Human Body* is full of interesting sidebar screens, explaining everything from the aging process to the body's chemical composition—we're 65 percent oxygen, 18.5 percent carbon, and 9.5 hydrogen, with a number of other elements including trace amounts of copper, iron, silicon, and tin.

The detailed cutaway illustrations, however, often provide more information than the clearly written but superficial text. Here's the entire description of the pancreas: "Your pancreas is a large gland, six inches long, found behind your stomach. Most of the cells which make up the pancreas produce digestive substances called enzymes. These flow through the pancreatic duct into the small intestine to help break down foods. The pancreas also has groups of cells called islets, which produce two hormones, glucagon and insulin. These play an important role in regulating your blood sugar levels." I'd love to find out more—such as the exact nature of blood sugar and what happens in the pancreas to cause diabetes. Despite the lack of in-depth information, *The Ultimate Human Body* is a worthwhile introduction to anatomy and

THE VIEW FROM EARTH
★★½
Developer: Time Warner Interactive; 800-482-3766
Format: Windows, Macintosh
Price: $59

August 17, 2021, will be a big day in St. Louis. Residents will be treated to a total eclipse of the sun, as will millions of other Americans in a band stretching across the nation from Portland, Oregon, through Casper, Wyoming, to Columbia, South Carolina. That's just one of the fascinating facts strewn throughout *The View from Earth*, a CD-ROM adaptation of three books from the Time-Life series *Voyage Through the Universe*.

The View from Earth is an introduction to astronomy covering four topics: the Earth, the moon, the sun, and eclipses. Most of the information is presented through slide shows, combining colorful pictures and illustrations from the three Time-Life books—*The Third Planet, Moons and Rings,* and *The Sun*—with audio narration. You'll learn why Jupiter has sixteen moons, for example, while Mercury and Venus have none. And you'll discover that James Ussher, an Anglican archbishop in Ireland, worked backward through the Bible in 1650 to deduce that God created the Earth at 9 A.M. on October 23, 4004 B.C.

The slide shows, each running several minutes, are supplemented with extra text from the books, a glossary, and an "eclipse tracker" displaying the parts of the globe affected by every eclipse from 1940 through 2039. That's how I found the eclipse of 2021, the next total eclipse in the United States. While all this material is elegantly presented, the CD-ROM doesn't offer significantly more than the original books, other than the audio narration. The few added features, such as a presentation of the total eclipse on July 11, 1991, through a three-minute sequence of still pictures accompanied by a New Age music soundtrack, are disappointing.

A WORLD ALIVE
★★

Developer: Voyager Co.; 800-446-2001
Format: Windows, Macintosh
Price: $29

A World Alive is teeming with noble sentiments but doesn't offer enough information to come alive itself. The CD-ROM centers on a thirty-minute documentary produced in 1990 by the St. Louis Zoo, narrated by the actor James Earl Jones. The documentary, displayed in a three-and-a-half-inch diagonal window on a standard-sized fourteen-inch monitor, shows a blurry and seemingly random collection of animal footage. All manner of creatures are displayed, from Franquet's fruit bat to the black rhinoceros. The narration is riddled with platitudes, beyond the point of rescue by Jones's commanding voice, such as: "Life. What magic does it hold? The potential to grow, reproduce, adapt and evolve. In a multitude of themes and variations, this is the essence of the marvelous mosaic of life."

In addition to the film, the CD-ROM profiles 102 different animals. Each is described in a minimal on-screen fact sheet resembling a baseball card. The leopard, for example, is covered in just two sentences: "Leopards, hunting at night, typically drag their meals into nearby trees in order to dine undisturbed. Undaunted by water, they will sometimes hunt for crabs and fish as well as mammals and birds." You can also summon a few sentences on the leopard's habitat, along with a map of the world highlighting the leopard's territory in Africa and Asia, and watch a five-second video clip of a leopard carrying its dinner along a tree limb. But that's all you get—nothing more than what you'd learn from the signs at a typical zoo exhibit. Children might enjoy a multiple-choice quiz called "What Is That?," but both children and adults are likely to walk away from *A World Alive* unsatisfied.

c. U.S. and World History

AMERICA'S CIVIL WAR — A NATION DIVIDED
★
Developer: SoftKey International Inc.; 800-227-5609
Format: Windows
Price: $39

Painfully difficult to operate and completely lacking in depth, *America's Civil War—A Nation Divided* deserves a one-way trip to the dustbin of history. The CD-ROM tries to recount the Civil War through 2,300 "events," shallow one-paragraph descriptions of various occurrences from 1861 to 1865. The developers neglect to say where this poorly written material comes from, a significant disadvantage for anyone who would want to make use of *America's Civil War* for schoolwork.

The CD-ROM opens on a map of the eastern United States with a time line along the bottom of the screen. To navigate from one event to another requires puzzling out the meaning of seventy icons, and the incomprehensible instruction manual provides little help. There is no index that would make it possible to quickly find a specific piece of information. The inexcusably awkward search feature doesn't let you simply enter a keyword; instead, you can search only through predetermined topics presented through a complex list of menus.

Just about the only assistance comes from ten "scripts" that display a succession of events on specific subjects such as slavery, General Ulysses S. Grant, and Confederate President Jefferson Davis. Many of the events also display one of 1,200 photographs stored on the CD-ROM, and some entries include a snippet of audio narration. The box for *America's Civil War* also promises video clips of "famous battlegrounds [that] once again come alive as you watch and listen to realistic re-enactments." But the CD-ROM contains only eight video clips, each running just a minute or two, that all appear to have come from a single documentary on the battle of Antietam.

By far the biggest disappointment, though, is the text. Here's the entire description of the historic confrontation between the ironclad ships the *Monitor* and the *Merrimack* on March 9, 1862: "At 9 A.M., the waters near Hampton Roads rocked with the cannon fire of the world's most advanced ironclads, the *USS Monitor* and *CSS Virginia*, formerly the *USS Merrimack*. In an epic battle that would shape the course of naval warfare, both ships exchanged gunfire and subsequent ramming for four hours. Neither, however, would take the day." We're left with no explanation for why this inconclusive encounter is so important—much as the rest of this sorry CD-ROM fails to put the most important war in U.S. history into any understandable context.

THE D-DAY ENCYCLOPEDIA
★★

Developer: Context Systems Inc.; 215-675-5000
Format: Windows
Price: $45

To sell *The D-Day Encyclopedia*, a rather dry history of the famous invasion of June 6, 1944, the CD-ROM's developers have resorted to a small but ignoble bit of marketing trickery. The box containing the CD-ROM breathlessly calls the disk "A Multimedia Exploration!" implying that all kinds of interactive goodies await inside. But the instruction manual, which buyers don't see until after they take the box home, is much less enthusiastic and considerably more accurate in describing *D-Day Encyclopedia* as "principally a reference work designed for use in both home and school libraries."

The CD-ROM, released shortly before the fiftieth anniversary of D day, is designed around a book of the same name published in 1993 by Simon and Schuster. The book is a true encyclopedia rather than a historical narrative, offering 437 articles on every historic figure, military unit, and major battle involving an invasion force of 185,000 troops, 4,000 aircraft, and 5,000 ships. Although the text is well written, it provides frustratingly small glimpses of the overall action. For example, the entry on Omaha Beach, the main landing spot for the U.S. Army on June 6, 1944, fills only three pages.

All of the book's text, photographs, and maps are reproduced on the CD-ROM, along with a small amount of additional multimedia content, primarily fifty brief video clips taken from old newsreel footage and twenty audio clips from interviews with historians. There is also a detailed reproduction of the "Overlord tapestry," a 287-foot British embroidery recounting the events before, during, and after the Allied invasion of France. But there aren't enough of these multimedia elements to provide more than a half-hour's distraction. Then users are left with the text, photographs, and maps, all of which would be easier to absorb from the book rather than by staring at a computer screen.

D-Day Encyclopedia also lacks an index, which makes it difficult to find specific topics. Nor is there any overall structure to guide users through the many interlocking events of D day. For a somewhat less authoritative but much more compelling CD-ROM on D day, I'd recommend *Normandy: The Great Crusade*, reviewed in this section.

THE FIRST EMPEROR OF CHINA
★★½
Developer: Voyager Co.; 800-446-2001
Format: Windows, Macintosh
Price: $39

Qin Shi Huang Di, who unified China and became the nation's first emperor in 221 B.C., wanted to live forever and spent many years searching across his massive empire for the secret of immortality. Naturally, he didn't find it. So Qin did the next best thing—he built himself an incredible tomb filled with six thousand life-size pottery figures of soldiers and horses, an army that could serve him in the afterlife. Peasants digging a well in March 1974 stumbled across the tomb, one of this century's greatest archeological discoveries.

The First Emperor of China on CD-ROM, unfortunately, doesn't do justice to this awesome discovery. Adapted from a documentary produced in China, the disk contains lots of information but not enough structure to guide users. What's worse, much of the CD-ROM's text appears to have been written in Chinese and translated poorly. An example:

"The Qin [pottery army] had its own particular characteristics—for example, in terms of the style of the armor, the weapons used, the formations of the chariots and cavalry. But generally speaking, it represents the result of a rather long, drawn-out process of development in the military organization with its own new developments. So we cannot conclude that the situation reflected in the Qin figure pits is something created by Qin Shi Huang, but it is rather inherited from past developments with the its own special characteristics."

Huh?

The text is divided into five chapters covering Qin's era and the tomb's discovery. Each chapter includes a video clip, running three to five minutes, that supplies narration in either English or Chinese, along with scenes of the excavation and historical artifacts. The images are unacceptably muddy, however, even though they appear in a small window on screen. Students of Chinese history and culture might find *The First Emperor of China* a useful study tool. There are maps, a time line, a chronology, and a glossary, all packed with information. For anyone else interested in the subject, I'd recommend spending the same amount of money for a coffee-table book displaying sharp color photographs of the Qin tomb.

THE HALDEMAN DIARIES: INSIDE THE NIXON WHITE HOUSE, THE COMPLETE MULTIMEDIA EDITION
★★★
Developer: Sony Imagesoft; 800-922-7669
Format: Windows
Price: $49

I'm not going to pretend to be neutral on the subject of Richard Nixon. I think he represented the worst in American politics—a paranoid, cynical manipulator of the system whose years in the White House give the nation nothing more than a needless extension of the Vietnam War and the scandal of Watergate. What's more, I was appalled at the insincere tributes from journalists and politicians following Nixon's death on April 22, 1994.

Any hopes for a postmortem restoration of Nixon's deeply stained reputation should be squashed by the *The Haldeman Diaries: Inside the Nixon White House, The Complete Multimedia Edition.* The CD-ROM, released in June 1994, is a fascinating electronic extension of a book, *The Haldeman Diaries: Inside the Nixon White House,* published a month earlier by G. P. Putnam's Sons. The 698-page book is an edited transcript of a daily journal kept by H. R. Haldeman, the president's chief of staff and hatchet man, from January 1969 through April 1973. But the massive tome could accommodate less than a third of Haldeman's text. The CD-ROM fills the gap, containing all 2,200 pages. The disk also provides seven hundred photographs, compared with just seventeen in the book, along with an hour of video clips taken from home movies shot by Haldeman, audio narration for some diary entries, and a long letter Haldeman wrote in prison trying to explain his crimes. Haldeman, by the way, died of cancer on November 12, 1993, just as work on the book and CD-ROM were reaching an end.

The book produced a small shock wave on its release, recounting numerous incidents showing Nixon's vengeful and racist dark side. The CD-ROM provides even more fuel for the fire. Consider the book's entry for February 1, 1972, describing a meeting between Nixon and evangelist Billy Graham. "There was considerable discussion of the terrible problem arising from the total Jewish domination of the media and agreement that this was something that would have to be dealt with," the book states. But the disk provides one further damning sentence on the subject: "Graham has the strong feeling that the Bible says that there are satanic Jews, and that's where our problem arises."

The CD-ROM is easy to install and provides several ways to sort through the text—through a conventional table of contents, by diary entry date, or by searching for specific words. There are also indexes for the 107 video clips and 850 photographs and a helpful collection of one-sentence biographies. If you're reading about the negotiations to end the Vietnam War, for example, and don't recognize the name Jean Sainteny, you can call up a brief description: "French banker; former Indochina official; messenger for K (Henry Kissinger) to North Vietnamese."

There are also a few weaknesses. The CD-ROM has no narrative structure; it would have helped if the developers had included a subject index so browsers could quickly find all the important entries on a given topic. I also found some indexing errors that are probably unavoidable in organizing such a huge amount of text—a reference to the TV show "Rowan and Martin's Laugh-In" highlights the word "Rowan," for example, which is linked to a biographical entry on the newspaper columnist Hobart Rowan.

But these are relatively inconsequential shortcomings for those of us who either passionately love or hate Nixon and want to uncover more about his controversial presidency. I wouldn't recommend the CD-ROM, however, to the vast majority of people who don't particularly care about Nixon one way or the other—the diaries are too narrow to interest an impartial audience.

J.F.K. ASSASSINATION: A VISUAL INVESTIGATION
★★★
Developer: Medio Multimedia Inc.; 800-788-3866
Format: Windows
Price: $39

More than thirty years after the fact, thousands and thousands of people are still obsessed with the assassination of President John F. Kennedy in Dallas on November 22, 1963. Was Lee Harvey Oswald truly a lone gunman? Was there a plot either to convince Oswald to fire the fatal shots or use him as cover for other assassins? Given the long span of time, there may never be sufficiently documented answers to convince skeptics that there wasn't a conspiracy.

J.F.K. Assassination: A Visual Investigation is an interesting alternative to the many magazine articles, books, and documentaries mulling over the facts and suppositions. The CD-ROM presents the text of three books, four short home movies taken at the scene, and computer-generated 3-D re-creations of the shooting from every conceivable angle. Conspiracy theorists, as well as the incurably curious, will find more than enough loose ends to support any number of possibilities.

The contents are divided into six sections. "Introduction" presents a three-minute video, playing in a six-inch diagonal window on a standard fourteen-inch monitor, showing Kennedy's arrival in Dallas during a Texas campaign tour and his tragic fate. "Overview" offers five essays combining text and photos on assassination-related subjects. "Dealey Plaza" presents a map of the assassination site, with numbered markers showing the location of the many witnesses. "Films & Photos" gives four one-minute home movies shot on that day—the Zapruder, Hughes, Nix, and Muchmore films—as well as a gallery of photographs showing the evidence and key individuals. "Analysis" offers a series of 3-D simulations enacting several possibilities, tracing the possible trajectory of shots that might have been fired from the infamous "Grassy Knoll." Finally, "Text" presents the three books: the Warren Commission official government report, *Crossfire: The Plot That Killed Kennedy* by Jim Marrs, and *The Assassination of John F. Kennedy: A Complete Book of Facts* by James P. Duffy and Vincent L. Ricci.

Although the developers of *J.F.K. Assassination* claim to be neutral on the subject of conspiracies, much of the CD-ROM's content is clearly tilted away from accepting the Warren Commission's conclusion that Oswald acted alone. Certainly, some of the evidence is haunting. The Zapruder film, for example, clearly shows Kennedy's head snapping back when he is struck, making it appear the fatal shot came from in front of the president rather than from Oswald's location far to the rear.

LEONARDO, THE INVENTOR
★★½

Developer: Future Vision Multimedia Inc.; 800-472-8777
Format: Windows, Macintosh
Price: $39

Leonardo da Vinci was the true Renaissance man—painter, musician, civil engineer, and tireless inventor. The work of this multifaceted genius is probably more than can be captured on a single CD-ROM; at least, this CD-ROM falls short of providing a complete portrait, despite elegant illustrations and eloquent narration.

Leonardo, The Inventor is centered on descriptions of twenty-one inventions from thousands of notebook pages Leonardo left behind at his death in 1519. The inventions, many of them centuries ahead of their time, are divided into five categories: flight, water, music, civil engineering, and warfare. For each invention, you see a picture accompanied by a few sentences of narration and a quote from Leonardo, as well as video clips—running only ten to thirty seconds—showing the gadget's modern-day equivalent. While the photorealistic pictures are wonderful, you don't learn much from the narration or quote. The corkscrew-type helicopter envisioned by Leonardo, for example, is fascinating to see, but you don't learn if the design could have ever been made to fly. And the quote from Leonardo isn't much help: "I think if this screw instrument is well made . . . from linen stretched (to block its pores) and is turned rapidly, then said screw will . . . climb upwards." Nor do you learn anything more by watching a fifteen-second video clip of a modern helicopter ascending into the sky. The Leonardo quote accompanying his design for a diving suit is almost cryptic: "Describe underwater swimming, and you will have described the flight of birds." That's an interesting thought, but there's no follow-up to explain how Leonardo saw a similarity between swimming and flight.

A superficial collection of supplementary material gives only a smidgen more background on Leonardo. A biography fills just nineteen on-screen pages, with each page containing only three or four paragraphs. A bibliography lists a mere fifteen books. There's also a list of the museums holding thirty of his paintings, sketches, and notebooks. Eight of the inventions include uninteresting 3-D still images, which have to be viewed through flimsy cardboard glasses with one blue lens and one red lens. Finally, there are three extremely simple action games that neither inform nor entertain.

NORMANDY: THE GREAT CRUSADE
★★★
Developer: Discovery Communications Inc.; 800-762-2189
Format: Windows
Price: $39

Normandy: The Great Crusade takes full advantage of the potential for CD-ROM to retell history through a combinaton of text, photographs, audio, and video. Based on a documentary of the same name produced by The Discovery Channel, the CD-ROM goes beyond the cable network's footage by adding interesting articles, profiles of key political and military leaders, maps, radio broadcasts, and excerpts from letters written by ordinary people caught up in the extraordinary terror of war.

Focused on the summer of 1944, from the D-day invasion of June 6 through the liberation of Paris, *Normandy* covers the war and its impact in France, Germany, Britain, and the United States. You can hear, for example, a few minutes of a speech by Adolf Hitler, followed by his enthusiastic audience singing the Nazi anthem "Deutschland über Alles." Or read part of a letter from a terrified soldier on Omaha Beach: "There were Germans . . . not very far from us, so I jumped in a foxhole. And I nudged this fellow in there and looked over and he rolled over and he was dead—he was stiff. He had a bullet right between the eyelids. His gun had jammed, and he had a knife in his hand, but the Germans were such crack shots, they'd shoot you right in the head. They did not miss."

My biggest complaint with *Normandy* is that there isn't more. Most of the articles and profiles are only a few paragraphs, leaving me thirsting for further insight just when the subject gets interesting. Indeed, experiencing everything on the CD-ROM takes only a few hours. The other big shortcoming, which will particularly irritate history students, is the omission of any way to print the text or copy it to a word processor.

THE PRESIDENTS: A PICTURE HISTORY OF OUR NATION
★★
Developer: National Geographic Society; 800-368-2728
Format: DOS
Price: $49

The Presidents: A Picture History of Our Nation resembles an aging oil painting of a long-dead politician desperately in need of cleaning and touch-up work. Released in 1991, the CD-ROM from the National Geographic Society is sadly out of date. The text, for example, is presented in large, jagged white letters on a gray background, a design that was appropriate for an earlier generation of low-resolution monitors but quickly causes eyestrain. The CD-ROM's thirty-three video clips, each running a minute or two in a quarter-screen window, are choppy and accompanied by fuzzy audio. Finally, an updated CD-ROM could include the election of Bill Clinton in 1992; *The Presidents* ends with President George Bush winning the Persian Gulf War a year earlier.

Fixing these flaws would create a useful study tool for its intended audience: junior high and high school students. Each president is portrayed through a collection of text, photos, and video clips. The entry on Lyndon Johnson, for example, includes a two-minute excerpt from his speeches on civil rights and a quick twenty seconds of him accepting the Democratic nomination in 1964. The main essay pulls no punches in covering Johnson's White House years: "This complex, larger-than-life leader achieved many of his legislative goals, but he never understood why the country became increasingly divided in bitter debate over Vietnam or why he could not win that war in Indochina. By 1968, he had destroyed his political career."

Along with the presidential portraits, the CD-ROM includes a few skimpy supplements. A time line of U.S. history gives only a few words for each year. Here's the total coverage of 1968: "Martin Luther King Jr. assassinated. Inner-city riots. Robert F. Kennedy assassinated." A collection of short text and photo essays on political parties and presidential power are similarly disappointing. And "The Presidents Game" comes across more as a pop quiz in history class than anything children would do for fun. The game consists of nothing more than fill-in-the-blank questions such as "In 1914, President Wilson signed the _____ Antitrust Act." You then have to read the essay on Wilson to discover it was the Clayton Antitrust Act.

SEVEN DAYS IN AUGUST
★★★½
Developer: Time Warner Interactive; 800-482-3766
Format: DOS, Macintosh
Price: $45

For twenty-eight years, the Berlin Wall divided more than just a city—it represented the line between East and West, the physical manifestation of tensions that threatened to degenerate into nuclear war. *Seven Days in August* offers a unique perspective on the week in 1961 when East German police erected the wall to stop a flood of defections to the more prosperous West.

Assembled by the editors of *Time* magazine, *Seven Days in August* tells the story of the Berlin Wall from many sides: the Germans, both East and West; the administration of President John F. Kennedy; and the Kremlin leaders in Moscow. Most of the information is presented through slide shows combining still pictures from 1961 with narration and excerpts from speeches of the day. Berlin, the CD-ROM says, was "a twilight land of confrontation and compromise" in 1961, still ruled jointly by the victorious Allies of World War II but stranded 110 miles inside Soviet-controlled East Germany. Soviet leader Nikita Khrushchev wanted all of Berlin and wanted to stop a mass migration that had depleted East Germany's population by one-fourth. At 2 A.M. on Sunday, August 13, the barbed wire began unreeling. The makeshift fence was soon replaced by a concrete wall and machine-gun towers that endured until the collapse of the Soviet empire in 1989. President Kennedy, despite calls from West Berlin for dramatic intervention, essentially did nothing, a controversial decision at the time but one that appears in hindsight to have averted a possible war.

This dramatic story is told through an on-screen matrix. Each of the seven days, from August 10 through August 16, is given a row across the screen. The rows are split into six columns. Each column covers a different aspect of the crisis, such as the action in Berlin and the reactions of ordinary German citizens. *Seven Days in August* stands out for going beyond the immediate events of the Berlin Wall crisis to give a portrait of life in 1961. There is a profile of the tiny town of Berlin, Wisconsin, and a "Souvenirs of '61" section covering popular culture. You can hear sound bites from Top 10 hits of the year, including "Tossin' and Turnin'" and "The Lion Sleeps Tonight"; check out that week's television shows, among them an episode of "Rawhide" starring Clint Eastwood; and take a look at such Sunday comics as "Blondie" and "Dennis the Menace."

The *Time* editors also brought together a group of influential figures from the crisis for a round-table discussion, presented on the CD-ROM in audio with a succession of still pictures. The roster includes McGeorge Bundy, then national security adviser to President Kennedy; Valentin Berezkov, then first secretary of the Soviet Embassy in Berlin; and former CBS reporter Daniel Schorr, one of the first journalists on the scene. Only a few small pieces of *Seven Days in August* fall short. For no apparent reason, the CD-ROM includes two boring trivia games, one on baseball, the other on dresses worn by Jackie Kennedy. And although the matrix is an interesting way to present such diverse information, the contents would be easier to absorb with the addition of a more conventional structure such as a time line.

WHO BUILT AMERICA?
★★★
Developer: Voyager Co.; 800-446-2001
Format: Macintosh
Price: $39

U.S. history is too often confined to tales of presidents and wars, neglecting the lives of ordinary people. *Who Built America?* seeks to overcome that imbalance by delivering a social history of the United States from 1876, when the nation celebrated its centennial, to the outbreak of World War I in 1914. This thirty-eight-year period spans some of the nation's most rapid growth and profound change, fueled by a tidal wave of immigration.

The CD-ROM is based on a two-volume book of the same name, published in 1989 and 1992. But the disk, produced by Voyager Company, goes far beyond the book, with hundreds of extra pages of historical documents as well as photographs, charts, audio clips, and even video clips of early motion pictures. You can click through a series of pie charts, for example, showing how the

U.S. labor force changed decade by decade—a powerful way to visualize the stunning decline in farm employment from 63 percent of the workforce in 1840 to just 27 percent in 1920, while manufacturing employment almost tripled from 9 percent to 26 percent. Or you can listen to a West Virginia ballad, recorded in 1940, telling the sad story of a coal miner's death. Minority groups often left out of conventional history are included here, including gays and American Indians.

Along with this focus on untold stories, the authors of *Who Built America?* have a definite pro-labor point of view that might make some readers uncomfortable. Consider this description of "The Great Uprising," an 1877 railroad strike: "It is the first truly national strike in American history and the first in which the federal government has placed its full power—in the form of the army—on the side of business . . . The Great Uprising has demonstrated that the United States is condemned to suffer the class-based conflict that has plagued Europe since the birth of industrial capitalism." Certainly, labor and management in the U.S. have fought each other continuously and sometimes violently through the years. But I doubt all historians would agree that we've ever had anything resembling the rigid class structure of many European countries.

Who Built America? also has its lighter moments. You can learn how the teddy bear was born in 1902, inspired by a political cartoon of President Teddy Roosevelt, and then look at the original cartoon. Roosevelt himself didn't recognize the stuffed toy's potential, commenting: "I don't think my name will mean much to the bear business."

The four hundred pages of text in *Who Built America?* are well written and the supporting material has been carefully chosen. But, setting aside the authors' agenda, the CD-ROM is more of a textbook than light reading, making it best suited for serious students of U.S. history in the late nineteenth and early twentieth centuries.

d. Current Events and Issues

AMNESTY INTERACTIVE
★★★★
Developer: Voyager Co.; 800-446-2001
Format: Macintosh
Price: $10

"For years, I was held in a tiny cell. My only human contact was with my torturers... My only company were the cockroaches and mice... On Christmas Eve, the door to my cell opened, and the guard tossed in a crumpled piece of paper. It said, 'Take heart. The world knows you're alive. We're with you. Regards, Monica, Amnesty International.' That letter saved my life."

Those words from an ex-political prisoner in Paraguay dramatically illustrate the understated power of Amnesty International. This unique group, which claims 1.1 million members in 150 countries, employs nothing more than relentless persuasion to provide life-saving assistance for prisoners of conscience around the world. *Amnesty Interactive* is an emotionally riveting CD-ROM that bears witness to human rights abuses and delivers a surprisingly upbeat message: Just by writing a single letter, any one of us can become an effective force for change.

In keeping with the volunteer spirit of Amnesty International, *Amnesty Interactive* was developed at no cost, with donated labor and materials. Voyager Company of New York sells the CD-ROM for $10 to cover the expense of production and distribution. Despite the shoestring budget, *Amnesty Interactive* looks and sounds as good as CD-ROMs produced with budgets running in the hundreds of thousands of dollars. Actor and director Leonard Nimoy, best known as Mr. Spock from the "Star Trek" television show and movies, provides narration. Beautiful drawings, centered on the image of a candle encircled by barbed wire, come from Nancy Nimoy, Leonard's daughter-in-law and a talented professional illustrator.

The program is divided into five sections: "Rights" presents the thirty articles in the United Nations' Universal Declaration of Human Rights, adopted in 1948. Each of the articles—which seek to establish such basic guarantees as fair trial and freedom of expression—is accompanied by a one-minute animation showing what happens when we lose these rights. "Ideas" is a history of human rights, stretching from the Code of Hammurabi in 1750 B.C. to Guatemalan activist Rigoberta Menchu, awarded the Nobel Peace Prize in 1992. "Places" details human rights problems in one hundred nations. "Voices" presents eight video clips of Amnesty International activists. "Stories" profiles nine political prisoners from around the globe through photographs, text, and narration. A few of the stories have happy endings: Vaclav Havel went from playwright to prisoner to president of the Czech Republic in 1989.

Amnesty Interactive also provides very useful supplementary text in two information folders. "Things You Can Do" gives extensive background on Amnesty International, founded in Britain in 1961, and explains in careful detail how to write letters seeking the release of political prisoners. "Learning Resources" has a long bibliography on human rights and human rights law, a selection of historical documents such as the U.S. Bill of Rights, and a library of international agreements on human rights.

CLINTON: PORTRAIT OF VICTORY
★★★
Developer: Time Warner Interactive; 800-482-3766
Format: DOS, Macintosh
Price: $29

In 1992, *Time* magazine photographer P. F. Bentley achieved the dream of every journalist assigned to cover a political campaign: He became a fly on the wall, a presence so familiar that he was ignored and could capture truly candid images on film. Bentley traveled with Bill Clinton's presidential campaign from the New Hampshire primaries in February through election night on November 3. Bentley became, in his own words, "a walking oxymoron—trusted press." Bentley's work appeared in *Time*, then was transformed into a coffee-table book and this CD-ROM, both named *Clinton: Portrait of Victory*.

Although CD-ROMs are rarely a better way to view photographs than a book, *Portrait of Victory* is an exception. Bentley shot the Clinton campaign in black and white, partly to distinguish his work from other news photographers and partly because he could be less obtrusive without the flash equipment required for indoor color pictures. Because black-and-white images contain less data, they can be reproduced more faithfully on a computer screen, and the photos in *Portrait of Victory* are stunningly sharp.

Also, the CD-ROM contains 241 images, three times more than the book.

Many of the photographs in *Portrait of Victory* are clearly unstaged, a rarity in the tightly controlled world of presidential politics. There are shots of Clinton exploding in anger at his staff, practicing for his famous saxophone performance on "The Arsenio Hall Show," and huddling with ever-present adviser James Carville. You can look at the photographs one at a time or watch slide shows as a narrator explains various stages of the campaign. *Portrait of Victory* also contains a selection of supplementary material that's mostly uninteresting and unnecessary, including brief video clips of Clinton speeches and two long-winded essays on the campaign.

CNN NEWSROOM GLOBAL VIEW
★½

Developer: SoftKey International Inc./Compact Publishing; 800-227-5609
Format: Windows
Price: $29

An awkward attempt to combine a world atlas with clips from TV news, *CNN Newsroom Global View* is both shallow and stale. Even though a Windows version of *CNN Newsroom* was released in August 1994 to replace a DOS version introduced in mid-1993, the updated CD-ROM still fails to capture many significant news events from the first half of 1994. There is no mention of the genocide in Rwanda that began in April, for example, and no coverage of Nelson Mandela's inauguration as president of South Africa in May.

CNN Newsroom is divided into three parts that bear little relation to each other. The main "Newsroom" section presents about three dozen video clips, each running a minute or two, from CNN newscasts. On my computer, however, the playback was unwatchable—the images were jerky, almost like a succession of still pictures, and the audio kept breaking up. The "Atlas" section presents a map of the world. By zooming in on a specific country, you can summon data such as population statistics and the names of government leaders. But much of this information—drawn from public records put out by the U.S. government and the United Nations—dates back to 1991 and 1992. The "World Clock" displays a map of the world, divided by time zones, with a shadow lying across the part of the globe covered by night. Working simple controls, you can speed forward through time, watching how the change of seasons affects sunrise and sunset. I enjoyed the "World Clock," but the rest of *CNN Newsroom* is empty and useless.

CNN TIME CAPSULE 1994
★★½
Developer: Vicarious Entertainment; 800-696-0507
Format: Windows, Macintosh
Price: $29

If you're eager to relive 1994 in predigested chunks, *CNN Time Capsule 1994* is the CD-ROM equivalent of fast food—quick and not particularly nutritious. The disk presents 1994 through "100 defining moments" portrayed in sixty- to ninety-second video clips taken from Cable News Network broadcasts, each supplemented with a half-dozen relevant articles pulled from *USA Today* and *U.S. News & World Report*. Some of the entries also include political cartoons drawn by Chris Britt of the Tacoma *News-Tribune* newspaper in Washington state. The video plays in a five-inch diagonal window on a standard fourteen-inch monitor, with narration by CNN anchors Bobbie Battista and Don Harrison.

I looked at a special "Holiday Version" of *CNN Time Capsule* released in November 1994 with only fifty "defining moments" from January through August. The developers promised to give the final version with all one hundred moments to buyers of the "Holiday Version" for free, with a $4.95 shipping charge, when the final version was completed in early 1995. In the "Holiday Version," the top stories of the year as ranked by CNN were the civil war and massacre in Rwanda, followed by the elections in South Africa and the January 17 earthquake in Los Angeles.

CNN Time Capsule is easy to install and operate and reasonably priced at $29. I'm just not sure who should buy this CD-ROM. There isn't enough depth in the brief video clips and small selection of articles to give you a complete picture of each event. Nor do I see much demand, even among current events junkies, for shallow highlights of yesterday's news.

DESERT STORM: THE WAR IN THE PERSIAN GULF
★★
Developer: Time Warner Interactive; 800-482-3766
Format: Windows, Macintosh
Price: $39

Desert Storm: The War in the Persian Gulf would have made an excellent book, but it doesn't work as a CD-ROM. Released just a few months after the Gulf War ended in 1991, this compilation of articles, correspondent reports, and photographs from *Time* magazine gives a detailed history of the eight-week conflict. But, with the exception of a few audio clips of politicians and a limited amount of narration, there is no reason the content couldn't have been delivered in print. What's worse, the CD-ROM provides no way to print or copy any of the text, eliminating the single biggest advantage of packaging words on a disk.

It's a shame the *Time* editors couldn't have done more with this wealth of material. The CD-ROM contains 118 *Time* articles, unedited bureau reports from forty-three locations around the world, three hundred color photographs, *Time* profiles of nine key figures, illustrations of forty-one battlefield weapons, maps taken from the magazine's pages, the text of fourteen U.N. resolutions, and transcripts of four important speeches. *Time*'s reporting is powerful and occasionally prophetic. "For all he had wrong, [Iraq's ruler] Saddam [Hussein] had one thing right—that the Middle East was due for some major refurbishing," *Time* said at the war's end in late February 1991. "Religious hatred, excessive militarization, economic inequities and entrenched feudalism combine to make it a nasty neighborhood . . . The jolt of the Gulf War, however, may change the physics for the moment. 'Maybe the shock,' says British Foreign Secretary Douglas Hurd, 'will enable people to think afresh, more constructively.' Just as the allies seized the moment to finish off Saddam's army, so too should they seize the opportunity to make lasting changes in Middle Eastern politics." Even though Saddam remains in power, the Israeli-Palestinian peace accord in 1994 shows *Time*'s optimism may not have been entirely misplaced.

OPEN ROADS: DRIVING THE DATA HIGHWAY
★★★

Developer: Newsweek Inc.; 800-634-6848
Format: Windows, Macintosh
Price: $18

In December 1994, *Newsweek* magazine took two big steps in an effort to be the first national publication with its own lane on the information superhighway. First, the weekly newsmagazine launched an on-line service called *Newsweek Interactive* through the Prodigy on-line system. Second, *Newsweek* issued the first in what it promises will be a series of "special issue" CD-ROMs focused on a single subject. Additional titles are promised every few months, although not on any specific schedule.

Open Roads: Driving the Data Highway, the debut special issue, is a far-reaching look at the future of telecommunications, resembling a print version of *Newsweek* brought to life with audio and video clips. In the CD-ROM's introductory essay, presented through narration and a succession of full-screen color photographs, Newsweek Interactive Managing Editor Michael Rogers says the information superhighway has become "a cliché before we know what it means." He then explains how the merging of television, telephones, and computers during the next twenty years will "transform the world as thoroughly as industrial technology transformed it in the 19th and early 20th centuries."

The best parts of *Open Roads* are two sections called "Sidebars" and "Features." The "Sidebars" section presents six more slide-show essays by *Newsweek* editors on subjects including the future of computer hardware and crime on-line. I particularly liked the first-person story of editor Jennifer Tanaka's struggles in navigating the Internet. "Features" takes full advantage of CD-ROM's unique ability to mix text and video. A list of the year's ten best CD-ROMs, selected by Rogers, includes one-minute video demonstrations of each title. There are also profiles of six important people helping build the information superhighway, including Vice President Al Gore and futurist Howard Rheingold, with each speaking in five or six thirty-second video clips. And there are four video clips from *Box Conspiracy*, an experimental theater piece performed in San Francisco in 1994 that satirizes a world where everyone is plugged into everything. I was amused, and even a little scared, to hear one character describe the emergence of "digital Darwinism," where "some of us are ones, and some of us are zeroes."

I was less impressed with a "Clippings" section that contains 150 articles about the information superhighway yanked from *Newsweek* and *The Washington Post*, then dumped onto the disk. Many of the articles are out of date and aren't especially relevant to what's covered elsewhere on the CD-ROM. At the same time, I was frustrated that many of the multimedia essays were so brief—often no more than ten or fifteen paragraphs—and threw out interesting ideas without providing many details.

The folks at Newsweek Interactive also need to fix a few technical shortcomings before putting out their next CD-ROM special edition. I was stunned to discover the installation program commandeered twenty-three megabytes of hard-disk space, more than three times what most titles of this type require. Also, I couldn't find any way to print the text in *Open Roads* or copy it to a word processor. Still, there's enough enlightening material on the CD-ROM that I'd recommend it to anyone looking for a quick summary of what's happening on the information superhighway. If you want *Open Roads*, by the way, be advised that Newsweek isn't selling it in stores or through mail-order catalogs. The only way to get the CD-ROM is by calling Newsweek directly at the number listed above.

PEOPLE: 20 YEARS OF POP CULTURE
★★½
Developer: Voyager Co.; 800-446-2001
Format: Windows-2, Macintosh-2
Price: $25

I've only read a few issues of *People* magazine from cover to cover, but I've probably thumbed through hundreds of issues while standing in supermarket checkout lines. What makes *People* a perfect quick read is the numerous photographs; often you learn as much from the pictures and captions as you do from the articles. *People: 20 Years of Pop Culture* makes a serious mistake, I think, in delivering extensive amounts of text from the magazine with only a few photographs.

The CD-ROM is a compilation of the magazine's cover stories from the first issue on March 4, 1974, through the twentieth anniversary issue on March 7, 1994—with actress Mia Farrow on both covers. But all you get from each of the 1,038 issues is a color reproduction of the cover and the text of the cover story. The articles, of course, will delight connoisseurs of dishy gossip. In the September 13, 1993, cover story on the noisy divorce and custody fight between Burt Reynolds and Loni Anderson, for example, *People* says, "In celebrity custody battles, as in war, truth can be the first casualty." Without stopping to moan over the wounded, the magazine then recites at length every unsubstantiated rumor and bit of tattletale slander from both sides.

To liven up the text-only cover stories, the CD-ROM includes a section called "Diversions" with a selection of six features. "Best and Worst Dressed" presents two to ten photographs from the magazine's annual best and worst issue. "Star Map" shows tiny pictures of 160 covers with connecting lines to illustrate various celebrity relationships, such as the fact that Johnny Carson dated Sally Field in the early 1980s. "Shop Talk" presents dull interviews, shown in video clips, with the magazine's editors. "Face to Face" offers seven morphs of *People* covers on specific themes, so you can see Elizabeth Taylor growing older through the twenty years and Michael Jackson growing stranger. "Legends" presents seventeen one-paragraph profiles of departed celebrities, including Rita Hayworth and Laurence Olivier. The most interesting diversion is "Di-O-Rama," which showcases all thirty-two covers of Princess Diana—the magazine's most popular cover subject—along with a few video clips and the famous four-minute "Squidgy" tape, a phone conversation in which one of Diana's lovers whispers sweet nothings in her ear.

THE PLAYBOY INTERVIEW
★★
Developer: IBM Multimedia Publishing Studio; 800-898-8842
Format: Windows
Price: $39

Maybe in ten years, when we all have one-pound portable computers with high-resolution screens matching the quality of a printed page, a CD-ROM like *The Playboy Interview* will deserve a big audience. Until then, the concept is all wrong—oceans and oceans of text that can only be absorbed by sitting in front of a computer screen.

The Playboy Interview contains the full text of *Playboy* magazine's popular monthly in-depth interviews, starting with the first—jazz trumpeter Miles Davis in September 1962—and ending with actress Sharon Stone in December 1992. The material is fascinating but incredibly annoying to read. A typical interview fills forty to fifty on-screen pages, with lines running all the way across the screen. These long lines are difficult to track; the developers should have broken the text into two columns.

It's a shame *Playboy* didn't put all this material in a book—even though it would run at least several thousand pages—because the interviews offer powerful insight into the lives and thoughts of all sorts of interesting people. A book also would probably sell for much less than the $45 price of the CD-ROM. There's no question, however, that many of the *Playboy* interviews represent important journalism. Perhaps the single most famous, the November 1976 encounter with then presidential candidate Jimmy Carter, almost cost him the election when he was honest enough to admit: "I've looked on a lot of women with lust. I've committed adultery in my heart many times. This is something that God recognizes I will do, and God forgives me for it."

The interview roster includes Malcolm X (May 1963), Martin Luther King, Jr. (January 1965), Tennessee Williams (April 1973), Fidel Castro (January 1967 and August 1985), Lech Walesa (February 1982), and Betty Friedan (September 1992). Not all the interview subjects are world leaders and heavy thinkers—the list is full of Hollywood stars from Barbra Streisand (October 1977) to Tom Cruise (January 1990), sports legends such as O. J. Simpson (December 1976), and a few quirky choices such as singer Tiny Tim (June 1970), and failed presidential assassin Sara Jane Moore (June 1976). Along with the interview text, the CD-ROM displays the black-and-white close-up photographs illustrating each article. Also, twenty-five of the interviews come with poor-quality one-minute audio clips taken from the interviewer's tape recorder.

Playboy has thrown in a few extra features that aren't particularly compelling: a "Roundtable" section with a gallery of quotes on topics such as "the meaning of life" and "the feminine mystique"; text interviews with six veteran *Playboy* interviewers; and a pair of four-minute video clips from the magazine's self-congratulatory 1992 party to celebrate the Playboy Interview's thirtieth anniversary. Finally, I was disappointed more recent interviews aren't included on the CD-ROM, released in August 1994, depriving us of such interesting subjects as vampire novelist Anne Rice (March 1993) and billionaire Microsoft Corporation co-founder Bill Gates (July 1994).

TIME ALMANAC 1990s
★★½

Developer: SoftKey International Inc./Compact Publishing; 800-227-5609
Format: Windows
Price: $29

Throw away all the extraneous bells and whistles piled onto *Time Alamanac 1990s* and you ought to end up with something quite valuable: the full text of *Time* magazine from the issue of January 2, 1989, through the issue of May 2, 1994. Everything from the long "Man of the Year" cover stories to movie reviews is packed into this CD-ROM. But *Time Almanac* is hobbled by a weak search feature, making it difficult to explore obscure topics.

Of course, before you even think of buying the CD-ROM, you have to appreciate *Time* as a magazine. Those who aren't regular readers should be warned that *Time* has veered sharply toward feature writing and news analysis in recent years at the expense of hard-news reporting. Some of these trendy pieces, such as a February 14, 1994, cover story called "Men: Are They Really That Bad?" skirt the edge of outright silliness: "It may be time for men to hold a convention . . . to console themselves and to discuss their new identities as devils. Let all men be summoned to a gathering of the masculine tribes, like a jamboree of the Indian nations in Montana long ago—a Pandaemonium of the patriarchy, a sweat lodge of the Granphalloon, Le Tout Guyim: as if the entire male audience of the Super Bowl had been vacuumed through 100 million television tubes (thuuuuppp!) and reassembled in one vast bass- and baritone- and tenor-buzzing hive . . . Men have become the Germans of gender. Are we really as awful as they say we are?" I don't know how awful we really are, but gushy prose like that certainly doesn't help our tattered reputation.

Time Almanac is easy to install and operate. The main screen displays a *Time* cover for each year from 1989 through 1994. Clicking a cover takes you to a list of all the issues in that year. Another click gives you the table of contents for a specific issue, and a final click displays individual articles. Where *Time Almanac* falls short is the other method for finding articles—word searches. A good search function looks through an entire database of text for any occurrence of the designated word. *Time Almanac* takes a more expedient approach, however, by checking only against a fixed index. The word "CD-ROM" isn't in that index, so you can't pull up all the *Time* articles that include a reference to CD-ROM. Even when your topic is part of the index, the results are disappointing. If you want to read *Time*'s coverage of playwright David Mamet, for example, you type in the word "Mamet" and get a list of twenty-three articles. Many of these articles refer to Mamet only in passing, however. There's no way to figure out which of the twenty-three articles focus on Mamet without going through them one at a time.

For reasons I can't understand, the developers of *Time Almanac* apparently felt they needed something more than raw text to make this CD-ROM appealing. They've added a grab bag of extra content, including an uninspired current-events quiz game called "Newsquest," dry-as-dust almanac information from federal publications, two *Time* photo essays that are displayed on screen as slide shows, and a collection of jerky, grainy video clips from CNN. None of these added features is particularly interesting; I wish the developers had devoted the extra effort to developing a better search function.

TIME ALMANAC REFERENCE EDITION
★★

Developer: SoftKey International Inc./Compact Publishing; 800-227-5609
Format: Windows, Macintosh
Price: $49

For twice the price, you should get twice the value. Not with *Time Almanac Reference Edition*. This is a slightly expanded version of *Time Almanac 1990s*, reviewed in this section. The only added feature is a selection of *Time* articles and related historical video clips from the turn of the century through the 1980s. Although the collection totals two thousand articles, that's not enough to give anything more than a cursory overview of the twentieth century. Otherwise, the *Reference Edition* is almost identical to its less-expensive sibling—offering the full text of *Time* magazine from January 2, 1989, through Jan. 3, 1994 (although *Time Almanac 1990s* goes through May 2, 1994), along with a current-events quiz game called "Newsquest" and some dull almanac information.

TIME ALMANAC OF THE 20TH CENTURY
★★½
Developer: SoftKey International Inc./Compact Publishing; 800-227-5609
Format: Windows
Price: $29

A quick trip through history, *Time Almanac of the 20th Century* offers four thousand *Time* magazine articles through early 1994, supplemented with historical material covering the period from 1900 through *Time*'s founding in 1923. The content is broken down by decades, providing top news stories and the full text of the annual "Man of the Year" cover story. The CD-ROM also includes an uninspired current-events quiz game called "Newsquest."

Many of the vintage *Time* articles give a sense that things don't change as much as we think. Consider this sample from the January 3, 1983, article naming the personal computer as "The Machine of the Year" for 1982: "In all the technologists' images of the future, however, there are elements of exaggeration and wishful thinking. Though the speed of change is extraordinary, so is the vastness of the landscape to be changed. New technologies have generally taken at least twenty years to establish themselves, which implied that a computer salesman's dream of a micro on every desk will not be fulfilled in the very near future. If ever." We have to credit *Time* for its foresight on that point—despite furious growth in the PC industry, we're still a long way from having a PC on every school and office desk.

The main weakness in *Time Almanac of the 20th Century* is that it presents nothing more than snippets from the magazine's seven decades. We only get what the CD-ROM's developers feel like giving us. A reasonably priced set of CD-ROMs providing *Time*'s entire text through the years would be a much better research tool.

USA TODAY: THE '90s, VOLUME I
★★★
Developer: Context Systems Inc.; 215-675-5000
Format: Windows
Price: $39

A useful reference tool, *USA Today: The '90s, Volume I*, contains the national newspaper's full text from January 1990 through August 1992. A sequel, *USA Today: The '90s, Volume II*, reviewed in this section, extends the coverage from September 1992 through December 1993. Because *USA Today* is a daily newspaper, it provides information on a much broader range of subjects than other current-events reference works such as almanacs and encyclopedias. But *USA Today* also specializes in writing very short stories, most running only two or three paragraphs, so the CD-ROM won't provide the depth of an encyclopedia.

There are two ways to work through the CD-ROM. The opening screen presents a row of buttons matching the newspaper's four sections: "News," "Money," "Sports," and "Life." Clicking on one of these buttons brings up a list of major categories. Click one of the categories and you're presented with a list of specific topics that in turn take you to individual stories. The other method is a word search. Hitting the Search button displays a screen in which you can enter a key word or phrase; the CD-ROM will then produce a list of stories containing those words. You can also enter a date and get a list of all the stories in that day's edition of *USA Today*. Stories can be easily printed or copied to a word processor.

The word-search feature needs improvement, however. The list of stories isn't in chronological order and shows only the story's headline, not the date, making it difficult to research events taking place over a long period of time. To learn about the assassination of Indian Prime Minister Rajiv Gandhi by a terrorist bomber in May 1991, for example, I entered the word "Gandhi." I got a list of forty-six stories containing that word, including a profile of actor Warren Beatty that happened to mention the movie *Gandhi*. There was no easy way to pick out which stories dealt with the assassination.

The CD-ROM has several extra features that aren't essential but can be helpful. There is an atlas that will display crudely drawn maps of any part of the world, a time line showing major events month by month, a dictionary that will define any word in the text, and thirty-six audio clips, each running ten to thirty seconds, taken from important news events such as speeches by President George Bush during the Gulf War.

USA TODAY: THE '90s, VOLUME II
★★★
Developer: Context Systems Inc.; 215-675-5000
Format: Windows
Price: $39

A sequel to *USA Today: The '90s, Volume I*, reviewed in this section, with identical structure. *USA Today: The '90s, Volume II* provides the national newspaper's full text from September 1992 through December 1993. In place of audio clips, *Volume II* presents forty-eight one-minute video clips of major news events—such as President Bill Clinton taking the oath of office in January 1993—and commentary by *USA Today* reporters.

There are two shortcomings the developers should address before producing *Volume III*. First, the two volumes don't share the same files on your hard disk. You must install 7 megabytes of files to run *Volume I* and 7.5 megabytes to run *Volume II*. The third volume should be designed so that one set of files will run all three disks. Second, the developers need to shorten the production cycle. *Volume I* came out in October 1993, more than a year after the cutoff date for the CD-ROM's text. *Volume II* didn't do any better; it arrived in January 1995, again more than a year after the cutoff date. *Volume III* should be more timely; I'd urge the developers to get it out the door within three or four months of collecting the text.

e. Magazines

Because CD-ROMs are so inexpensive to produce, costing just $1 per disk before the cost of packaging and shipping, numerous developers have considered creating monthly or quarterly CD-ROM magazines. But production costs are the least of a magazine publisher's problems—finding interesting articles and signing up subscribers are the real obstacles. Several publishing neophytes have put out the first issue of what they claimed would be a regular CD-ROM magazine without ever managing to get a second issue out the door. In this section, I'm including only those CD-ROM magazines that have succeeded in meeting a regular production schedule by the end of 1994, although that doesn't mean all of them will survive indefinitely. I'd recommend against paying an annual subscription fee to any CD-ROM magazine that hasn't put out at least three issues on a consistent schedule. Meanwhile, you can get a low-risk taste for any of the magazines reviewed here by ordering a single issue.

COMPUSERVECD
★★
Developer: CompuServe Inc.; 800-848-8199
Format: Windows
Price: $7.95 per issue

CompuServeCD, a bimonthly magazine from the CompuServe on-line information service, is based on a great idea: Supplement the text-only resources of an on-line service with colorful graphics, audio, and video delivered on CD-ROM. But the folks at CompuServe Inc. haven't put enough effort into finding quality content for *CompuServeCD*, so it's hard to tell whether this great idea will ever amount to anything.

CompuServe launched the magazine with a pilot issue in May 1994, then followed with July/August and September/October issues. The company promises to start monthly publication in mid-1995 and make a Macintosh version available in early 1995.

In the September/October issue, I found lots of handout material from advertisers masquerading as news, including car-buying tips from Ford Motor Company, an article on home schooling that appears to have been prepared by a software company, and a supposed "behind-the-scenes" look at the Fox television network show "Last Call" that was nothing more than a promotional video.

The contents of *CompuServeCD* is divided into six sections—"Technology," "Entertainment," "Personal Enterprise," "Civilization," "Home & Leisure," and "Shopping"—with articles running from one to six on-screen pages. Many of the pages include buttons to summon audio and video clips or extra text. Several of the articles seemed out of place, however. An article on choosing the right college, for example, appeared in the "Civilization" section, while the home schooling article was in "Personal Enterprise."

"Entertainment" was the only section I liked, with its audio clips from jazz performers Vanessa Rubin, Mulgrew Miller, Danilo Perez, and Maceo Parker; a one-minute music-video clip from Peter Gabriel's album *Secret World Live*; and another video clip of Japanese taiko drummers. The most disappointing section was "Shopping," which mostly displayed static pictures of products that can be ordered through CompuServe.

CompuServe is touting links between the CD-ROM and its on-line service, which now claims to be the world's largest, with more than 2 million members. But these links consist mainly of text windows in the CD-ROM pointing to on-line "forums" in which CompuServe members discuss subjects related to the articles. Even if the CD-ROM were truly integrated with the on-line service, the shallow content of *CompuServeCD* would be a disappointment. And I don't expect the CD-ROM will get any better unless CompuServe hires enough professional writers, photographers, editors, and artists to create a product worth reading.

INTERACTIVE ENTERTAINMENT
★★★
Developer: Interactive Entertainment; 800-562-3624
Format: Windows
Price: $9.95 per issue

For hard-core computer gamers, the types who stay up all night blasting aliens and re-fighting World War II, *Interactive Entertainment* offers news, reviews, and product demonstrations that are both fun and informative. The CD-ROM magazine, launched in late 1993, appeared to be entering steady monthly production in late 1994 after a rocky start. I looked at "Episode 7"—the issues are given a number rather than a month—released in November 1994. It contained several dozen game reviews delivered through both text and audio narration, accompanied by still images and sound bites from the games themselves, in eight categories: Adventure, Arcade/Action, Role-playing, Simulation, Sports, Strategy, War, and Miscellaneous. Obviously written by dedicated gamers, the reviews were filled with passionate praise and disdainful criticism delivered in equal doses. Each game review included a "pro" comment and a "con" comment; in a generally enthusiastic review of *Doom II*, for example, the "con" comment noted the lack of improvement over the original *Doom* and remarked, "More than one new weapon would have been nice."

In addition to the reviews, *Interactive Entertainment* had a news section with more narrated slide shows covering upcoming games and important developments in the computer game industry. There was also a "Hints & Tips" section with advice on six popular games and a brief video-clip interview with Sid Meier, head game developer for the software company Microprose. The best part of *Interactive Entertainment*, which can't be matched by print computer-game magazines, is the demo section. Demonstration versions of four games—*Mindcraft's Siege Complete*, *Hammer of the Gods*, *Deathgate*, and *Metal Memories*—could be downloaded from the CD-ROM to your hard disk.

I also found a few shortcomings. There was no index to the contents of *Interactive Entertainment*, making it impossible to quickly scan the CD-ROM's entire contents or find a specific review. Also, the audio narration should be available in text form for those of us who'd rather read the reviews than hear them. Still, the reviews make good reading and the demonstrations are guaranteed to amuse and inform curious gamers.

MEDIO MAGAZINE
★★
Developer: Medio Multimedia Inc.; 800-788-3866
Format: Windows
Price: $9.95 per issue

Medio Magazine doesn't live up to its boastful slogan: "All the world on CD-ROM." The monthly magazine is a random and out-of-date collection of material; the developers apparently are throwing together anything they can get for free or next to nothing.

Medio Multimedia Inc. started the magazine in mid-1994; I looked at the fourth issue, released in December 1994.

The backbone of December's *Medio Magazine* was nearly five hundred stories from the Associated Press covering news, finance, sports and entertainment. But these articles were two months old, so I was reading about unemployment figures from September and movies being released on video in October. Medio Multimedia added some content on its own, but most of it appeared to come from government and corporate handouts—a fawning portrait of Boeing Company's new 777 jetliner, for example, and profiles of 264 countries from the *CIA World Fact Book*, a government almanac anyone can reproduce with no charge. The magazine also provided thirty-three video clips, each running less than a minute, that were again mostly dependent on handouts, such as trailers for four movies opening in December and an excerpt from the music video *Until the Cold on the Dark* by the heavy-metal band Danzig. A skimpy "advertising gallery" contained information for only four advertisers—Medio itself, two small software companies, and a multimedia newsletter publisher.

There may be hope for *Medio Magazine*, however. The magazine's interface is easy to navigate, with the contents divided into ten sections: Entertainment, Living, News, Finance, Sports, Kid Stuff, Technology, Reference, Backtalk, and The Advertising Gallery. With lots of pretty color pictures to look at and helpful narration explaining how to get from one topic to another, Medio Multimedia only needs to come up with a better editorial mission than merely recycling yesterday's news.

NAUTILUSCD
★★★

Developer: Metatec Corp.; 800-637-3472
Format: Windows, Macintosh
Price: $6.95 per issue

NautilusCD is the pioneer of CD-ROM magazines; the Macintosh version started monthly distribution in 1990, and a Windows version followed in 1991. Like many pioneering computer products, it can look dowdy next to newer, flashier competitors. But *NautilusCD* still manages to deliver a good value—every month, Metatec Corporation of Columbus, Ohio, sends out a disk full of software demos, photos, games, movie previews, music samples, and computer tips.

Each issue is divided into six sections: "Multimedia Guide," "Home & Office," "Desktop Media," "ComputerWare," "Entertainment," and "KidZone." Within each section are twenty to thirty on-screen pages displaying text and photographs; the pages are also festooned with buttons to summon audio clips, video clips, and in-depth text. Almost all the content is oriented toward computers, stressing software reviews and demonstrations.

In the November 1994 Windows edition, for example, the "Multimedia Guide" gave descriptions and demonstrations of several dozen new CD-ROMs, including *Star Trek Next Generation Interactive Technical Manual* and *The Way Things Work*. The magazine's editors also conducted telephone interviews with CD-ROM reviewers from five national publications and put the results on the disk in a series of audio clips. "Home & Office" provided more software reviews, along with excerpts from a series of self-help audiocassettes on how to do a better job of making customers happy. "Desktop Media" supplied a selection of sample music files in the MIDI format and several clip-art illustrations. "ComputerWare" offered a number of shareware programs, a library of audio and video drivers, a free antivirus program and a collection of computer industry news releases from the previous month. "Entertainment" was the only break from computer-centric coverage, with a full track from an album by pianist George Winston, a music video from singer Sarah McLachlan, and a trailer for the movie *Speechless* starring Michael Keaton and Geena Davis. Finally, "KidZone" offered its own selection of shareware—in this case, games for children.

If you're interested in discovering new things to do with your computer, you'll like *NautilusCD*. If you're not, you won't find enough noncomputer-related material to hold your attention. The Macintosh edition, by the way, is usually identical to the Windows edition, except for offering different shareware programs.

SUBSTANCE DIGIZINE
★★

Developer: Substance Interactive Media Inc.; 800-346-4080
Format: Windows-2
Price: $19.95 per issue

Members of Generation X, the discontented legions of post-adolescents struggling to find their place in the world, have been so bombarded by television commercials they may have a hard time distinguishing art from commerce. At least that's the impression I got from *Substance Digizine*, a quarterly CD-ROM magazine created by twenty-somethings for twenty-somethings.

Substance, by the way, has gotten off to a slow start. The young developers released a pilot issue in November 1993 and promised to put out their first regular quarterly issue in early 1994. But Volume One, Number One, didn't emerge until August, and the second issue wasn't expected until February 1995, at least two months behind schedule.

The first issue is full of clever animations and loud Generation X music, but the magazine's contents have the slapped-together shallowness of a term paper cranked out during an all-nighter. The highlight is an audio-only interview with Trent Reznor, leader of the band Nine Inch Nails. The interview was supposed to be presented in video, but the developers let slip the fact their camcorder broke. Reznor is treated to a string of softball questions and gets to carry on excessively about his musical ideas, although he appears honest when talking about the rigors of touring: "Without sounding jive, I will say it was kind of a jazz to tour when we did, because it always ended up being pretty sincere. You know, there's times when you go on stage when you don't want to be on stage. You're sick. You're tired. You're drunk. But it would always kick into gear somehow, where you always ended up meaning what you were saying."

Substance also profiles independent filmmaker Jim McKay, showing a few brief clips of his work in a window so tiny the images are almost impossible to recognize. And there's a video interview with authors Neil Howe and Bill Strauss, who've written about Generation X and share profound thoughts such as the angst Xers feel because they can't afford to buy a house. A section called "Headspace" provides a selection of New Age music, while another section called "Substance Abuse" is intended for letters to the editor, although I couldn't find any and instead stumbled across a few songs by an unknown group called Twisted Pear.

I was particularly disappointed to see *Substance* mix advertising and editorial content without any effort at separating journalism from puffery. A section called "Bendware," for example, claims to offer information on the emergence of low-cost morphing software for manipulating visual images. But what you get is nothing more than demonstrations of four pieces of commercial morphing software. Similarly, a "Special Secret Surprise" section delivers several product demonstrations from Sierra On-Line Inc., a developer of computer games, and an ad for *Multimedia World* magazine.

Substance also presumes its Generation X audience is already computer literate; there are no instructions for navigating, so you have to point and click with the mouse until you figure out the magazine's interface. Still, if the developers put more effort into creating unique articles and draw a sharper line between advertising and editorial, *Substance* could evolve into an interesting experience. Meanwhile, potential readers should take note of two significant hardware demands: Your computer must have a sixteen-bit sound board and twelve megabytes of free hard-disk space.

Chapter Six:
Movies, Television, Books, and Music

Moving from the arts and sciences in Chapter Five, this chapter covers the most popular forms of entertainment.

a. Movies

MICROSOFT CINEMANIA '95
★★★¹/₂
Developer: Microsoft Corp.; 800-426-9400
Format: Windows, Macintosh
Price: $59

Only two things really matter in Hollywood: money and fame. Microsoft Corporation has lots of money and has spent it freely to buy famous names for the stunning *Microsoft Cinemania '95*, by far the best entry in the crowded field of CD-ROM movie guides. *Cinemania* is centered on 20,000 one-paragraph movie reviews from *Leonard Maltin's Movie and Video Guide 1995*, with 1,700 longer reviews from *Roger Ebert's Video Companion* and 2,500 reviews from the book *5,001 Nights at the Movies* by film critic Pauline Kael. The material is current through mid-1994—with coverage of summer movies including *Four Weddings and a Funeral*, *The Lion King*, and *Speed*—and goes all the way back to 1914. Most of the movies are reviewed only by Maltin, although commentary from all three critics is available for some of the best-known movies of recent years. Supplementing the reviews are biographies of four thousand movie stars, directors, and producers, along with a selection of articles about the movie business taken from several film encyclopedias.

But *Cinemania* is more than just a dry reference work on disk. The computer screen lights up with 1,000 still photographs of movies, 2,000 portraits of the stars, 168 audio clips of movie dialogue, 139 tracks of movie music, and 21 video clips. You can watch battle scenes from films beginning with *The Birth of a Nation*, released in 1915, through *Platoon*, released in 1986, or watch the first meeting of Scarlett O'Hara and Rhett Butler in *Gone With the Wind*. Movie buffs will lose themselves for hours exploring all this material, which is tied together through numerous convenient links. If you're reading a review of the 1994 movie *Guarding Tess* starring Shirley MacLaine, for example, you can click her name to summon a biography. The biography tells you MacLaine was born on April 24, 1934, in Richmond, Virginia, and is the sister of Warren Beatty. Jumping to Beatty's biography, you learn he was born on March 30, 1937, also in Richmond. Then you can glance at a list of Beatty's movies, including the ones he'd probably rather forget—such as the politically incorrect 1966 comedy *Promise Her Anything*, in which he played a producer of off-color movies stuck taking care of a baby belonging to neighbor Leslie Caron. The screenplay was written by William Peter Blatty, who didn't hit it big until he switched to horror and wrote *The Exorcist*.

My only complaint with *Cinemania* is that there isn't more. Older or obscure movies often have nothing beyond the brief Maltin review. I'd love to see a future version of *Cinemania* with a still photograph, dialogue clip, and music clip for every movie covered. Assembling that much material is probably too big a task for even the deep pockets at Microsoft, but Hollywood is in the business of selling dreams, and that's my dream for the perfect CD-ROM movie guide.

COMIC BOOK CONFIDENTIAL
★★★½
Developer: Voyager Co.; 800-446-2001
Format: Macintosh
Price: $19

Comic books are one of childhood's great forbidden pleasures; the more your parents tell you comic books will rot your mind, the more you want to read. Filmmaker Ron Mann created *Comic Book Confidential* in 1989 as a ninety-minute documentary on the history of comic books from the early 1930s through the art-comic revival of the late 1980s. Using little more than static shots of comic book pages and talking-head interviews with comic book artists, Mann nevertheless told a fascinating story.

Voyager's *Comic Book Confidential* CD-ROM offers the entire movie, then expands on the film with a pile of interesting supplementary material. I was especially fascinated with the actual text of the 1954 Comic Book Code, a draconian piece of self-censorship the industry adopted one step ahead of threatened federal legislation. The code crippled the creativity of comic books for more than a decade, until the birth of underground comics in the late 1960s. Among the Code's more stunning restrictions: "Policeman, judges, government officials and respected institutions shall never be represented in such a way as to create disrespect of established authority." And "the treatment of love-romance stories shall emphasize the value of the home and the sanctity of marriage." I suppose William Shakespeare couldn't have written *Hamlet* as a comic book in the late 1950s.

Unlike some of Voyager's other movies on CD-ROM, you can actually watch *Comic Book Confidential* without suffering permanent eyestrain. Even though the movie only appears in a three-and-a-half-inch diagonal window on a standard-size fourteen-inch monitor, the broad brush strokes of the comic book pages are relatively easy to follow. The movie is also well indexed so that you can jump to the showing of "Captain America" or the interview with *Mad* magazine founder William Gaines. Among the supplementary material are biographies of twenty comic book artists, sample pages from sixteen comic books, a lengthy bibliography, and a video interview with director Mann.

CRITERION GOES TO THE MOVIES
★★★
Developer: Voyager Co.; 800-446-2001
Format: Windows, Macintosh
Price: $19

Voyager Company combines its two major lines of business—CD-ROMs and movies on laser disk—in one delightful package. The company's Criterion series of laser disks offers carefully restored movie classics. In *Criterion Goes to the Movies*, you get short video clips from 142 Criterion movies, along with cast photos, credits, and essays.

The clips run only twenty seconds to a minute, but they capture some of the greatest moments in movie history: Jimmy Stewart talking with his guardian angel, Clarence, in *It's a Wonderful Life* (1946), Sean Connery introducing himself as "Bond . . . James Bond" in *Doctor No* (1962), Ingrid Bergman forcing Sam the piano player to sing "As Time Goes By" in *Casablanca* (1943), Jack Nicholson's angry "chicken salad" scene in *Five Easy Pieces* (1970), Gene Kelly cavorting with his umbrella and letting loose with the title song from *Singin' in the Rain* (1952), and the Wicked Witch of the West telling a frightened Dorothy, "I'll get you, my pretty, and your little dog, too" in *The Wizard of Oz* (1939). The disk even makes room for what I regard as the single funniest scene ever put on film: the show-stopping Broadway performance of "Springtime for Hitler" from *The Producers*

(1967). I can't explain why it's so hilarious; you'll just have to see for yourself.

Criterion Goes to the Movies shouldn't be mistaken for a complete reference work, but it's a useful and reasonably priced introduction to some of the world's best cinema.

EPHEMERAL FILMS 1931–1960
★★½
Developer: Voyager Co.; 800-446-2001
Format: Windows, Macintosh
Price: $19

Film historian Rick Prelinger has viewed hundreds and hundreds of the 600,000 advertising, educational, and industrial films produced from the 1920s through the 1960s. Clips from thirty-eight of these "ephemeral" works, never intended to be preserved for future generations, are presented in *Ephemeral Films, 1931–1960*. Ranging through time from a 1931 ad for Oldsmobiles through the introduction of Ford's new models for 1960, the clips are occasionally hilarious and sometimes startling. On the lighter side is actor Dick York, who later starred as Darrin on the television sitcom "Bewitched," playing a lonely teenager in *Shy Guy*, a "social guidance" film from 1947. On the startling side is a 1957 film by Pfizer Corporation called *The Relaxed Wife* that advocates tranquilizers as the cure for everyday stress. In between is a grab bag of subjects, from color home movies of the 1939 World's Fair in New York to a trio of teenage girls in a 1952 film from Whirlpool Corporation that decides home appliances represent nothing less than "freedom from drudgery."

Prelinger provides a short text commentary with each clip, which I'd recommend ignoring. He seems to have a major political ax to grind, depicting most of the movies as part of some dark conspiracy by corporate America to keep wage slaves happy in their bondage. In the introduction, Prelinger says the post–World War II films "depict a society that appears to have turned inward, showing no interest in civil rights, urban decay, or world affairs. Its citizens seem mostly concerned with maintaining a pleasant, undisturbed life. But whether or not the characters in the films accurately represent their real-life counterparts, there are still hints of deep trouble throughout the Fabulous Fifties: widespread social and emotional anxieties, worries about fitting in, and always the fear of being an inadequate consumer." Maybe Prelinger should take a tranquilizer and relax. It hardly seems fair to judge a society's compassion by looking at its advertising; today's TV commercials hardly show a deep concern for the future of humanity, nor do I see why they should.

The thirty-eight clips in *Ephemeral Films*, each running three to ten minutes, appear in a four-inch diagonal window on a standard fourteen-inch monitor. At that size, the image quality is acceptable. There's an option to view the movies in a larger eight-inch diagonal window, but the pictures become choppy and blurry at that size. The bigger limitation, though, is that most people won't want to see any of these movies more than once; *Ephemeral Films* is itself ephemeral, more of a curiosity than a significant piece of history.

FUNNY
★★
Developer: Time Warner Interactive; 800-482-3766
Format: Windows
Price: $29

Funny is a movie that shouldn't have become a CD-ROM. The 1988 documentary presented eighty-four famous and not-so-famous people telling their favorite jokes. On CD-ROM, at least, you don't have to watch the movie from beginning to end. Instead, you can jump from joke to joke. There's even a screen saver function, so the jokes will play randomly whenever your computer isn't being used, presuming you'll bother to leave *Funny* in your CD-ROM drive. But just dumping a movie onto CD-ROM isn't worth the effort. Looking at video clips in a small window on a computer monitor is a poor alternative to renting a videotape for $2 or $3 and watching it on TV.

Not that watching *Funny* on videotape would be a total waste. Although few of the jokes are outright knee-slappers, the movie has a certain low-key charm. Henny Youngman delivers his famous "Take my wife, please" line. Comedian Alan King tells an amusing story about practical jokes on a movie set. The late musician Frank Zappa contributes: "What do you call a person from New Zealand with more than two girlfriends? A shepherd." And actress Susan Ruttan, best known for playing Roxanne on the television series "L.A. Law," delivers a well-worn classic: "This duck goes into a pharmacy and he says, 'Do you have any Chap Stick?' And the pharmacist says, 'Sure, will this be cash?' And the duck says, 'No, just put it on my bill.'"

A HARD DAY'S NIGHT
★★★½
Developer: Voyager Co.; 800-446-2001
Format: Windows, Macintosh
Price: $29

When *A Hard Day's Night* was released at the height of Beatlemania in 1964, the movie stood out as the first film to capture the true spirit of rock and roll. Appropriately, Voyager Company picked *A Hard Day's Night* to become the first commercially released movie on CD-ROM in early 1993. Both the movie and the CD-ROM have withstood the test of time.

The full eighty-five-minute black-and-white film plays in a window measuring three and a half inches diagonally on a standard-size fourteen-inch monitor. The images are somewhat jerky but are just good enough to watch without losing patience, although I prefer taking in movies while slouched on the sofa, not sitting upright in a chair looking into a computer screen. There's also an option to display the movie in a larger seven-inch diagonal window, but the images become unacceptably blurry at that size. *A Hard Day's Night* is a fantasy of one day in the life of John, Paul, George, and Ringo as they are chased through London and the surrounding countryside by hordes of screaming adolescent girls. The absurd humor and quick-cut editing give the movie a surprisingly contemporary look, almost twenty years before the creation of MTV. You'll see and hear the Beatles perform a dozen classics, including "A Hard Day's Night," "Can't Buy Me Love," "Tell Me Why," "And I Love Her," and "She Loves You."

But simply watching the film isn't what makes the CD-ROM stand out; if that's all you want, it's easier and cheaper to rent a videotape. The CD-ROM works best as an exploration into the Beatles and their era. You can view the movie while the original script scrolls along the screen, an especially useful tool for Americans trying to follow the Beatles' thick Liverpudlian accents. There are also biographies of the movie's cast and crew, including director Richard Lester and Beatles manager Brian Epstein; a gallery of twenty-five photos; video clips from an interview with Lester; an eleven-minute comedy Lester made in 1959 called *The Running, Jumping & Standing Still Film*; and a clip from Lester's first rock and roll movie, a forgotten 1961 piece called *It's Trad, Dad.*

MEGA MOVIE GUIDE VERSION 3.0
★★
Developer: InfoBusiness Inc.; 800-657-5300
Format: Windows
Price: $39

Mega Movie Guide Version 3.0 lives up to its name only in numbers—the CD-ROM contains 42,000 movie reviews, more than double any competing CD-ROM guide to films. *Mega Movie Guide* achieves that huge figure, however, by including made-for-TV movies that aren't typically covered in other guides. Indeed, the unidentified reviews in *Mega Movie Guide* appear to come from a data service that produces listings for newspaper TV pages. The content of these reviews is minimal, often no more than a sentence. Here's the full description for the 1948 Humphrey Bogart classic *The Treasure of the Sierra Madre*: "Greed, jealousy and suspicion plague three hard-bitten fortune hunters in the mountains of Mexico."

These minireviews, current through mid-1994, are supplemented with a few hundred short biographies of movie stars and forty-three video clips, each running about ninety seconds, from both classic and recent movies. Film critic Rex Reed contributes longer reviews for one thousand of the movies. All this material is harder to access than in other CD-ROM film guides, especially the excellent *Microsoft Cinemania '95* reviewed in this section. You can't just jump from one movie to another in *Mega Movie Guide*; instead, you have to launch a search that produces a list of possible films.

In addition to the one-sentence reviews, some movies also have a one-paragraph "synopsis" that appears to be a second review from a different source. Occasionally, the review and the synopsis clash—the 1981 thriller *Body Heat*, for example, gets a three-and-a-half-star review and a three-star synopsis. In short, there's no reason to consider buying *Mega Movie Guide* given the superior alternatives. But if you insist, make sure to get the current Version 3.0, released in October 1994, rather than the earlier editions, which were even more difficult to operate and had significant installation problems.

MIDNIGHT MOVIE MADNESS
★½
Developer: Medio Multimedia Inc.; 800-788-3866
Format: Windows
Price: $39

Midnight Movie Madness pretends to be a guide to Grade Z drive-in horror and science-fiction movies, but it's really a bigger phony than all those stop-action monsters in *Godzilla* and *Attack of the Giant Leeches*. The box claims the CD-ROM is a "collection of the 100 best drive-in movies," but all you get are truncated video clips—most running just thirty seconds to a minute and filling a quarter of the screen—taken from coming-attraction trailers. What's more, the box advertises the participation of comedian Gilbert Gottfried. But the annoying Gottfried, who always speaks in an exasperating whine, appears only in a three-minute introductory video clip.

The films in *Midnight Movie Madness* cover the entire drive-in era, from *Son of Kong* in 1933 to *Beyond Atlantis* in 1973. A few famous faces pop onto the screen, including Zsa Zsa Gabor from *Queen of Outer Space* in 1958, Steve McQueen from *The Blob* in 1958, and Raquel Welch in *One Million Years B.C.* from 1966. A pretend trivia quiz game has been grafted onto the video clips in a failed attempt at sustaining a mood of campy satire. The trivia questions come across as pointless rather than funny, such as this sample included with the 1958 classic *I Married A Monster from Outer Space*: "Why can't the monster from outer space leave? (a) He'll get killed. (b) He's out of gas. (c) She got custody of the space ship." The answer is (a), but the answer for *Midnight Movie Madness* itself is (b)—this CD-ROM runs out of gas long before showing us a good time at the movies.

POETRY IN MOTION
★★
Developer: Voyager Co.; 800-446-2001
Format: Windows, Macintosh
Price: $19

Poetry in Motion performs like an old car stuck up on blocks. The wheels are spinning, but you're not going anywhere. Voyager Company, which usually puts considerably more effort into its CD-ROMs, dumped a documentary film of twenty-four poets and singers performing their works onto a disk without even bothering to add short biographies identifying the various artists. The video images, displayed in a three and a half-inch diagonal window on a standard fourteen-inch monitor, are disappointingly grainy.

"Poetry is generally very dull, very pretentious," says poet Charles Bukowski during a whiny interview on the CD-ROM. "Reading the poets has been the dullest of things. All I get is a goddamn headache and boredom. Poetry itself contains as much energy as the Hollywood industry, as much energy as a stage play on Broadway. All it needs is practitioners who are alive to bring it alive." Those practitioners apparently weren't available for the producers of *Poetry in Motion*.

Instead of delivering artistry, most of the performances are bizarre and self-indulgent. A group called Four Horsemen spends three minutes screaming in unison and making animal-like grunting and shrieking noises. Beat poet Allan Ginsberg delivers a rap performance, backed by a rock band, filled with such profound thoughts as "I don't like Nationalist Supremacy White or Black, I don't like the Narcs and the Mafia marketing Smack." Other performers include Imamu Amiri Baraka, William S. Burroughs, John Cage, Ntozake Shange, and Tom Waits. They should have all stayed home.

SALT OF THE EARTH
★★★½
Developer: Voyager Co.; 800-446-2001
Format: Macintosh
Price: $39

Salt of the Earth tells two stories—one of a strike by Mexican-American zinc miners in the early 1950s, the other about a group of blacklisted Hollywood screenwriters trying to make a movie telling the miners' story.

The movie version of *Salt of the Earth* is a thinly fictionalized account of a fifteen-month strike near Silver City, New Mexico, that took an unusual twist when the miners' wives replaced their husbands on the picket line. The strike, which ended in January 1952, turned into a stalemate when miners went back to work after achieving only a few of their demands. But many of the women gained a new sense of self-respect and dignity, years before feminism became a force in American life.

Several screenwriters fighting McCarthy era blacklisting of suspected Communists decided to make a movie about the strike and traveled to Silver City in 1953. Shooting in just two months with unknown actors and a budget of only $200,000, they created a drama that is both passionate and grittily realistic. The ninety-four-minute black-and-white movie was suppressed by Hollywood, however, and was shown only briefly in California and New York after its 1954 premiere.

Voyager Company's CD-ROM presents the entire movie, along with a library of supporting material. There are photos of the filmmakers at work in Silver City, articles and news clippings about the strike, and a twelve-minute documentary about "the Hollywood Ten," a group of blacklisted writers each sentenced to a year in prison. *Salt of the Earth* on CD-ROM stands out for the depth of all this additional material. What's disappointing is the actual presentation of the movie. Limited by computer technology, viewers are given two bad choices: Watch a tiny window measuring three and a half inches diagonally on a standard-size fourteen-inch monitor, too small to absorb much of the movie's detail, or watch a seven-inch window with unacceptably choppy images. Fortunately, Voyager includes the shooting script for *Salt of the Earth* alongside the smaller window, so you can read about the action that you can't see clearly on the screen. I'd recommend viewing *Salt of the Earth* on videotape and then turning to the CD-ROM as a tool for further study and insight.

SECRETS OF STARGATE
★★½
Developer: Compton's NewMedia Inc.; 800-284-2045
Format: Windows, Macintosh
Price: $25

Who really built the pyramids of ancient Egypt? All the scientific evidence indicates the ancient Egyptians figured out the technology for pyramid building on their own. But that hasn't stopped generations of mystics and UFO enthusiasts from suggesting hyperintelligent aliens directed the construction work. That's the premise of the movie *Stargate*. Released in October 1994 to tepid reviews, *Stargate* nonetheless proved a modest box-office success. The predictable plot opens with a modern-day Egyptologist, played by James Spader, discovering the secret code to unlock the Stargate, a stone ring excavated in Egypt that acts as a link between worlds. A group of hard-as-nails soldiers, commanded by Kurt Russell, takes Spader on a trip through the Stargate. On the other side, they discover a desert planet where an evil alien has proclaimed himself Ra, the Sun god, and kidnapped thousands of human prisoners to work in quartz mines. Russell and Spader must then battle Ra to save the slaves and return to Earth. No one apparently stops to ask why an all-powerful alien, capable of commanding awesome forces of nature, needs a crew of miners working with nothing more than picks and shovels, but *Stargate* isn't the kind of movie intended to withstand close scrutiny.

Secrets of Stargate on CD-ROM is strictly for rabid fans of the movie, offering behind-the-scenes tour through interviews with the cast and crew, photographs, illustrations, and background information on ancient Egypt. Specifically, the disk includes eighteen clips from the movie, each running from thirty seconds to three minutes; seven behind-the-scenes video clips showing the filming on location in Yuma, Arizona, and Long Beach, California; thirteen clips of special effects from the movie; fourteen video-clip interviews with Russell, Spader, the director, and other cast and crew members; text biographies of the cast and crew; 721 "storyboard" illustrations, sketches made before the start of filming to lay out the camera angles; and four hundred photographs of costumes, sets, and props. The background material on ancient Egypt includes a family tree of the gods, explaining Ra's lineage, and a hieroglyphics glossary, defining such words as "khefa" for "fist" and "tep" for "head."

Getting through all the material in *Secrets of Stargate* will take at least several hours and offers a few fascinating insights on the process of moviemaking. You'll see, for example, production assistants with brooms sweeping the Arizona sand between takes to eliminate footprints and watch set construction inside a huge dome in Long Beach that once housed Howard Hughes's Spruce Goose airplane. There aren't enough of these nuggets, however, to sustain your interest if you haven't seen *Stargate* or didn't like the movie.

I'm also troubled by the movie's basic premise. It seems self-centered if not racist to diminish the incredible achievements of ancient Egyptians by suggesting they needed extraterrestrial assistance. Indeed, a quote from Egyptologist Stuart Smith contained in *Secrets of Stargate* makes just that point: "In this high-tech age of ours, we find it difficult to imagine low-tech solutions for complicated problems. Contemporary artifacts and tomb scenes, parallels from the last two centuries, as well as modern experimentation, all show that the Egyptians could move even colossal granite blocks using simple prepared roadways, sledges, lots of labor and good organization." To me, that's the real secret of *Stargate*—human beings have an awesome capacity for intellectual achievement and can accomplish great things without help from outer space.

VIDEOHOUND MULTIMEDIA
★★
Developer: Visible Ink Software; 800-735-4686
Format: Windows
Price: $49

VideoHound Multimedia is a dog, a movie guide on CD-ROM that's difficult to use and offers no advantages over its less-expensive print sibling, *VideoHound's Golden Movie Retriever*. The CD-ROM covers 56,000 video titles, but that includes only 25,000 movies. The rest are nonmovie titles such as children's and how-to videotapes. You can search through the listings by title, stars, director, genre, and *VideoHound* rating, among other criteria. What you get is a one-paragraph review for most movies, with a rating from one to four dog bones or "W-O-O-F" for truly bad films. Many of the nonmovie videos, however, aren't rated, and the descriptions appear to be taken from publicity handouts. The genre index is particularly difficult to operate—the developers have set up several hundred categories, such as "Cannibalism," "Teen Sex Comedies" and "Wildlife" but don't give the user a convenient index to look at all the possibilities. You have to guess at a category name; I entered "Aerobics" and "Fitness," for example, before discovering that workout-related videos were listed under "Exercise." I looked at the first release of *VideoHound Multimedia*, by the way, which came out in March 1994 with reviews through mid-1993. Don't even consider buying *VideoHound* unless an updated disk reaches the market in 1995.

VIDEO MOVIE GUIDE
★★★
Developer: Advanced Multimedia Solutions Inc.; 206-623-4011
Format: Windows
Price: $19

Video Movie Guide is perhaps the least-expensive compilation of movie reviews on CD-ROM, available for under $20. But in this case you get what you pay for—hardly anything beyond the print version of *Video Movie Guide* from Ballantine Books that sells for just $7.99.

The 1994 edition of *Video Movie Guide* on CD-ROM offers capsule reviews, most running just one or two sentences, for 13,800 movies. The roster includes both regular movies and television movies-of-the-week; all the listings are available on videotape, unlike some other movie guides, and includes films that haven't been transferred to video. The only added content on the CD-ROM is a collection of twenty-one video clips, mostly promotional trailers for old movies such as *The Wizard of Oz* and *Singin' in the Rain*. Also, about 1,300 of the reviews include a picture of the movie's videotape box cover to make it easier to spot the movie on the crowded shelf of a video store.

Reviews are indexed the same way they are in the book—by title, genre (such as comedy, drama, and musicals), cast members, director, and Academy Award winners. Many of the reviews are painfully short, such as this entry on *Gone With the Wind*: "The all-time movie classic with Clark Gable and Vivien Leigh as Margaret Mitchell's star-crossed lovers in the final days of the Old South. Need we say more?" Yes, I think they need to say more.

If you're interested in buying *Video Movie Guide*, look for the 1995 edition, which should be available no later than midyear and should cover movies released through mid-1994.

b. Television

MTV'S BEAVIS AND BUTT-HEAD MULTIMEDIA SCREEN SAVER
★★★
Developer: Sony Imagesoft; 800-922-7669
Format: Windows
Price: $35

If you watch the MTV cable television network and you're a high-school-age male, you probably love the gross-out humor of Beavis and Butt-head. The animated adolescents, both dateless losers, spend their time thinking of new ways to offend their classmates and neighbors before retiring to the sofa, where they offer inane remarks on music videos. Their sniggering laughter has become a kind of code word for teenagers everywhere.

MTV's Beavis and Butt-Head Multimedia Screen Saver will delight fans of the show. The CD-ROM delivers ninety-one video clips, each running from ten seconds to two minutes, taken from the MTV series, along with seventy-five sound files and thirty still images. Users can program the screen saver to show the material in any order they like or select one of ten pre-programmed presentations with names such as "Air Guitar," "Burger Tag!" and "Couch Fishing." All the classic moments are preserved, such as Beavis and Butt-head practicing mud wrestling in the backyard, cruising surburban streets on a riding lawn mower, and beating each other up in class.

The disk also delivers four complete MTV videos with Beavis and Butt-head commentary: *Lost in America* by Alice Cooper, *Snap Your Fingers, Snap Your Neck* and *Prove You Wrong* by Prong, and *Three Headed Mind Machine* by Infectious Grooves. This isn't the most practical CD-ROM ever developed—you have to leave the disk in your computer to operate the full screen saver program. But then again, Beavis and Butt-head revel in their status as totally useless human beings, so I suppose their CD-ROM shouldn't be hardworking and morally upright either.

DATING & MATING
★★
Developer: Time Warner Interactive; 800-482-3766
Format: Windows
Price: $39

More second-rate comedy from the creators of *It's All Relative*, reviewed in this section. This CD-ROM's forty-eight video clips cover the joys and heartaches of romance. Most of the comedians are unknowns, with a few recognizable names, including Ellen Cleghorne and Adam Sandler from "Saturday Night Live," along with Richard Lewis. All the material falls flat, as in this bit from Kevin Meaney describing how his girlfriend just got killed: "It's not my fault. You see, I bought her this raccoon coat, and she got hit with a car crossing the street. Apparently, she froze when she saw the headlights. My mother said, 'Why do you buy them raccoon coats? That's the third one this year that froze in the headlights.'"

DENNIS MILLER THAT'S GEEK TO ME
★★
Developer: Sanctuary Woods Multimedia Corp.; 800-943-3664
Format: Windows, Macintosh
Price: $39

In his second attempt at humor on CD-ROM, Dennis Miller still doesn't have a clue. The successor to *Dennis Miller's That's News to Me*, reviewed in this section, has the comedian offering supposedly satirical definitions for 172 computer terms in grainy video clips running about ten seconds each. After Miller's less-than-witty comments, an animated figure called Bill Geek—drawn to look like Microsoft founder Bill Gates, with unkempt brown hair, a pocket protector full of pens, and thick black glasses held together by tape—gives the actual definition.

Once again, Miller veers between listlessness and poor taste. Some examples: "Laptop: The only available seat in Bob Packwood's office. Serial port: Ted Bundy's favorite wine. Hard drive: Heading home through South Central Los Angeles." In the introduction to his first CD-ROM, Miller worries about becoming "roadkill on the information superhighway." I don't know if he's road kill, but he definitely falls flat.

DENNIS MILLER THAT'S NEWS TO ME
★★
Developer: Sanctuary Woods Multimedia Corp.; 800-943-3664
Format: Windows, Macintosh
Price: $39

Somebody out there must think Dennis Miller is funny. He managed to get himself hired as the anchor of "Weekend Update" on "Saturday Night Live" for several years, then convinced television network executives to give him a talk show, which promptly bombed. But Miller's dry humor is lost on me; I think his attempts at deadpan satire are just dead.

Even the most rabid Miller fans aren't likely to get much satisfaction from *Dennis Miller's That's News to Me*. The CD-ROM presents two hundred very brief video clips, averaging about 15 seconds each, of Miller delivering one-liners on the news events of 1993. Miller appears in a window filling only one ninth of the screen, sitting at a desk surrounded by a set he describes as resembling "a padded cell designed by Steve Jobs' interior decorator." The jokes are divided up by month and by four categories: politics, show business, sports, and world events.

Miller's commentary falls into a narrow range from dull to offensive. Here's a typical flat remark, on the November 1993 wildfires around Los Angeles: "It's hard to fight a fire in Malibu, because you need script approval before you can turn on the hose." At the offensive end of the scale is this joke from the show business section: "And it's official, this month Michael Jackson and George Hamilton have crossed lines on the pigmentation flow chart." When you exit the program, Miller drawls his famous exit line, "And I am outta here." Take my advice, stay outta *Dennis Miller's That's News to Me*.

IT'S ALL RELATIVE
★★
Developer: Time Warner Interactive; 800-482-3766
Format: Windows, Macintosh
Price: $39

It's All Relative takes a collection of stand-up comedy routines that could have become a mediocre videotape and instead transforms them into a bad CD-ROM. Media giant Time Warner grabbed fifty-two video clips of comedians performing on its Comedy Central cable TV channel and gave them to the company's multimedia division. Each bit, running thirty seconds to two minutes, appears in a three-inch window on a standard fourteen-inch monitor.

The video performances—from both unknowns and familiar names including Richard Lewis, Bill Maher, Kevin Meaney, Emo Philips, and Adam Sandler—are divided into nineteen categories tied to family relationships, such as "Aunts & Uncles," "Discipline," "Marriage," and "Shopping." There's also an index of all the comedians on the disk and a screen saver program that will randomly display comedy routines when your machine isn't in use. Neither of these features, however, outweighs the advantages of putting the same shtick on videotape. You could watch the entire hour's worth of jokes on your TV's full screen for a price that would likely be much cheaper than a CD-ROM.

What's more, the material on *It's All Relative* is second-string and often treads too close to the narrow line separating humor from tastelessness. Bruce Smirnoff, for instance, has this to say about his grandma: "My grandmother has Lou Gehrig's disease and Alzheimer's disease. She swears she hit a hundred home runs, but she doesn't remember when." I was especially put off by Japanese comedian Tamayo Otsuki's joke about the difference between America, where parents tell their children stories of walking to school through the snow, and her country: "Our parents always said, 'When I was your age, we had two nuclear bombs dropped on us.' How can you top that?" I can't top that, and I wouldn't want to try.

MONTY PYTHON'S COMPLETE WASTE OF TIME
★★★
Developer: 7th Level Inc.; 800-884-8863
Format: Windows
Price: $49

"I'm a lumberjack, and I'm okay." If those opening words from the classic Monty Python song immediately bring a smile to your face, then you'll enjoy *Monty Python's Complete Waste of Time* on CD-ROM. But the disk's appeal isn't likely to extend much beyond die-hard fans of the old "Monty Python's Flying Circus" television show, an import from Britain that was a big hit on U.S. public television in the 1970s.

Through a kaleidoscopic blend of color graphics, sound bites, and video clips, *Complete Waste of Time* presents all the best material from the BBC series, which first aired in 1969. You'll get such sketches as "Argument Clinic," "Dead Parrot," and "Nudge Nudge," as well as famous Python songs, including "The Lumberjack Song" and "Spam."

True to the British comedy troupe's spirit of constant anarchy and pointed satire, *Complete Waste of Time* is deliciously nonlinear, and things are seldom what they seem. You'll spend hours wandering from screen to screen, clicking different objects to see what happens. There is no menu for the various video clips, for instance; you just have to keep exploring until you find them all. Occasionally, a friendly voice tells you to press "F1" on your keyboard for help. When you press "F1," what you actually get are funny but unhelpful comments such as "'Help' is one of the better songs written by the Beatles." Or "Hello, this is help. But you didn't say please, so back to the game." Or "Exactly what sort of help would you expect from a computer? Are you some sort of namby-pamby who wants me to take you by the hand and explain it all?"

There's also a very complex and obscure game called "The Secret to Intergalactic Success." Completing the game's many puzzles, which you discover while moving through the CD-ROM, makes you eligible to win a Pentium personal computer, providing you mail in a diskette proving your prowess by September 30, 1995. Finally, *Complete Waste of Time* contains a big bonus: the *Desktop Pythonizer*, which allows you to convert many of the CD-ROM's sound files, graphics, and video clips into screen savers, icons, and Windows wallpaper.

Newcomers to the upside-down world of Monty Python, however, would do better to find videotapes of the old shows than buying *Complete Waste of Time*. The CD-ROM is an homage to Python; you already have to know the Python repertoire to appreciate the frequent in-jokes. The uninitiated should also be warned that Monty Python's humor, while never outrightly obscene or tasteless, pokes explicit fun at potentially offensive topics ranging from flatulence to religion and homosexuality.

SATURDAY NIGHT LIVE! THE FIRST TWENTY YEARS
★½
Developer: GameTek Inc.; 800-426-3832
Format: Windows, Macintosh
Price: $35

After twenty years on the air, "Saturday Night Live" the television show is running out of energy—the sketches are less and less funny and the guest hosts rarely interesting. *Saturday Night Live* the CD-ROM doesn't help the show's sinking reputation. The disk is merely a collection of sixty one-minute video clips from the show, with only a few paragraphs of pointless text thrown in for no good reason.

The clips span the show's entire history, from the early days with John Belushi and Chevy Chase through the recent performances of Dana Carvey and Mike Myers. You'll see many classic moments—Belushi training for the Olympics on a diet of "Little Chocolate Donuts," Chase falling down a flight of stairs, Eddie Murphy as Buckwheat and Myers hosting "Wayne's World." But the clips are so short that some of the best moments are lost. In Dan Aykroyd's classic "Bass-O-Matic" sketch, for example, you watch him put a real fish in the Bass-O-Matic blender, delivering a mile-a-minute sales pitch. But you're deprived of the show-stopping punch line: Aykroyd actually drinking the pureed bass. In a scrapbook section, a few of the sketches get a brief text supplement such as a glossary of alien words spoken by the Coneheads and a paragraph of dialogue from the Church Lady.

The producers of "Saturday Night Live" would never consider trying to sell these truncated sketches on videotape, even if the price were only $10 or $20. So why should we spend twice as much to get the same material on a CD-ROM, suffering the additional drawback of watching grainy video images in a tiny window? We shouldn't. In the words of George Bush, as played by Carvey: "Wouldn't be prudent. Not gonna do it."

SEINFELD CD-ROM SCREENSAVER & PLANNER
★½
Developer: Time Warner Interactive; 800-482-3766
Format: Windows-2
Price: $29

On the hit television show "Seinfeld," comedian Jerry Seinfeld is often trying to dodge unwanted dinner invitations from grumpy relatives, grasping ex-girlfriends, and his moronic colleagues on the stand-up comedy circuit. If you want to be just like Jerry Seinfeld, buy the *Seinfeld CD-ROM Screensaver & Planner*—you'll have your territory invaded by a program that quickly turns into a pest.

Screen saver programs are, by nature, purely for fun. After all, Windows comes with several perfectly adequate built-in screen savers. So a program like *Seinfeld Screensaver* shouldn't make heavy demands on your computer. But this CD-ROM overstays its welcome by grabbing fourteen megabytes of hard-disk space during installation. And if you want to put any of the 102 "Seinfeld" video clips—running an average of forty-five seconds—on your hard disk, you'll have to sacrifice another three to fifteen megabytes for each one.

Screen saver programs should also be easy to use, yet *Seinfeld Screensaver* neglects several obvious needs. To preview the 102 video clips, for example, you have to look at seventeen different screens, each showing six thumbnail photos of the opening scene in the clip. There is no index listing the contents of each clip or any way to tell what the clip is about before you run it.

The other features in *Seinfeld Screensaver* aren't much better. You can use your word processor to print four types of documents— a memo, fax cover sheet, greeting card, or letterhead—with pictures from the show, but the images will be unacceptably grainy unless you have a high-end laser printer. The planner consists of nothing more than a calendar that plays a "Seinfeld" video clip before showing a screen on which you can enter notes on your daily activities. There is also an "Episode Guide" giving a one-paragraph synopsis of each "Seinfeld" show from the pilot, aired in July 1989, through the end of the 1993-1994 season.

About the only positive thing I can say about the *Seinfeld Screensaver* is the video clips look good, filling almost a quarter of the screen with sharp images. But if your primary interest is watching snippets of old "Seinfeld" episodes, you'll be better off just taping the show with your VCR.

COMEDY CENTRAL'S SPORTS SHORTS
★★
Developer: Time Warner Interactive; 800-482-3766
Format: Windows, Macintosh
Price: $15

The third installment of second-rate stand-up comedy from the developers of *It's All Relative*, reviewed in this section. You get sixty minutes of video clips from the Comedy Central cable channel on the subject of sports, with shtick from fifty-four no-name comedians. The only performers I recognized were Adam Sandler and Janeane Garofalo from "Saturday Night Live" and seventies relic Jimmie Walker, famous for the expression "Dyn-o-MITE!" None of the material, which appears in a four-inch diagonal window on a standard fourteen-inch monitor, is particularly funny. Here's a sample of comedian Henry Cho on surfing: "Surfin' dudes are pretty stupid . . . I'm just learning . . . They go, 'You should start on a really big board.' So I'm surfing on my garage door right now. Then they have the nerve to go, 'What kind of board is that?' 'It's a Genie board, man. Hey, don't push that button, I'll flip over.'"

STAR TREK: THE NEXT GENERATION INTERACTIVE TECHNICAL MANUAL
★★½
Developer: Simon & Schuster Interactive; 800-983-5333
Format: Windows, Macintosh
Price: $54

As a longtime "Trekker" devoted to the various *Star Trek* television series and movies, I was ready to go into warp drive with *Star Trek: The Next Generation Interactive Technical Manual*. But the CD-ROM seems to be stuck on impulse power, delivering a surprisingly low-energy tour of the famous starship *Enterprise*. True to the *Star Trek* spirit, the *Technical Manual* employs cutting-edge computer technology through a feature called "QuickTime VR" that lets users guide themselves around thirteen sets from *Star Trek: The Next Generation*, a television series that showed its last original episode in June 1994 but will live for years in syndicated reruns. You click the mouse button and hold it down, then by moving the mouse you change your view of the scene, instantly calling up one of 15,000 color photographs capturing every possible angle of each set. Extensive narration is provided by the *Star Trek* computer, with the voice of actress Majel Barrett Roddenberry, who did the same job on the TV show and also portrayed Counselor Deanna Troi's libidinous mother. A five-minute "guided tour" through the *Technical Manual* is narrated by Jonathan Frakes, who played Commander William T. Riker. Appropriate *Star Trek* sounds, from the beeping of communicators to the whoosh of automatic doors and the throbbing of the warp engines, fill the background.

The thirteen destinations cover every part of the *Enterprise*: the ship's exterior, the bridge, the ready room, main engineering, the transporter room, sick bay, the Ten Forward cocktail bar, the observation lounge, the holodeck, the captain's quarters, Troi's cabin, Lieutenant Commander Data's quarters and Lieutenant Worf's cabin. Within each destination, the *Technical Manual* offers a combination of text, diagrams, and five-second animations to illustrate twenty-fourth-century technology. If you've ever wondered why the transporter needs a "pattern buffer," here's the answer: "This superconducting tokamak device delays transmissions of the matter stream so that Doppler compensators can correct for relative motion between the emitter array and the target." Or perhaps you're curious about the "synthehol" imbibed in Ten Forward: "A substitute for alcohol invented by the Ferengi which conveys the intoxicating effects of alcohol without the deleterious side effects."

But for a supposedly "interactive" CD-ROM, the *Technical Manual* doesn't give you much chance to get involved. On the bridge, for example, you can fire a photon torpedo, but all you do is push a button, then watch a short video clip of a Romulan ship exploding in a fireball. In the transporter room, you push another button and see a few objects materialize on the transporter pad. Navigating through the *Enterprise* is awkward; you're never sure whether clicking on an object will produce a close-up photograph or where to locate one of the short animations. The text is difficult to read, too, because only a few lines at a time are displayed. Finally, the *Technical Manual* doesn't fit well into the narrow confines of late twentieth-century computer technology. There are long, annoying pauses between scenes while more data is downloaded from the CD-ROM. The program also requires high-end hardware: a double-speed CD-ROM drive and eight megabytes of random-access memory for both the Windows and Macintosh versions. You can run the *Technical Manual* on a machine with just four megabytes of RAM, but QuickTime VR won't work—depriving you of the CD-ROM's most interesting feature. With all these drawbacks, I'd recommend the *Technical Manual* only to hardcore Trekkers who've spent big bucks on their home computers.

THE TWILIGHT ZONE SCREEN SAVER
★★½
Developer: Sound Source Interactive; 800-877-4778
Format: Windows
Price: $19

"You unlock this door with the key of imagination. Beyond it is another dimension. A dimension of sound. A dimension of sight. A dimension of mind. You're moving into a land of both shadows and substance, of things and ideas. You just crossed over into . . . The Twilight Zone."

Rod Serling's immortal opening lines from "The Twilight Zone" will probably always be a part of American culture, or at least as long as the series continues to live through endless reruns on late-night television. Now you can hear Serling's voice coming out of your computer while it displays random images from the show and plays the haunting theme music, courtesy of *The Twilight Zone Screen Saver*. When the screen saver sequence starts, "The Twilight Zone" logo appears on the monitor against the background of a star-filled sky. Next is Serling's monologue, followed by animated objects slipping across the screen—a blinking eye, a window that shatters, a Daliesque pocket watch with a swinging pendulum—or scenes from the show itself.

The screen saver is easy to install and fits completely on your hard disk, allowing you to set the CD-ROM aside. There's also a password protection feature, so you can keep anyone else from operating your computer while you're away. It's important to note, however, that *The Twilight Zone Screen Saver* does not include video clips—all you get are still photographs, some with a small amount of animation, and sound bites. Since Windows comes with a perfectly adequate screen saver, this CD-ROM is strictly an indulgence, an indulgence of shadows and substance, of things and ideas. An indulgence best enjoyed in . . . The Twilight Zone.

c. Books

AMERICAN POETRY: THE NINETEENTH CENTURY
★★★
Developer: Voyager Co.; 800-446-2001
Format: Macintosh
Price: $39

Garrison Keillor, host of the popular show "A Prairie Home Companion" on National Public Radio, calls this CD-ROM "a great big steamer trunk" of poetry as he delivers the disk's four-minute audio introduction. It's a perfect description for this collection of 1,000 poems from 150 poets, many of whom are gathering dust in the attic of our national consciousness. All the big names of the nineteenth century are here, including Emily Dickinson, Walt Whitman, and Ralph Waldo Emerson. But there are also some surprises—many nineteenth-century novelists also wrote poetry, so you can read the verse of Edith Wharton, Stephen Crane, and Nathaniel Hawthorne. Veering away from mainstream poetry, there are selections of slave spirituals and Native American poetry. A few of the works have become so popular that it's a shock to realize they're more than a hundred years old; those include *A Visit from St. Nicholas*, written by Clement Moore in 1822 and now commonly known as *'Twas the Night Before Christmas*, and *Casey at the Bat*, written by Ernest Lawrence Thayer in 1888.

American Poetry: The Nineteenth Century is based on a book of the same name published in 1993 by The Library of America, edited by Yale English professor John Hollander. The CD-ROM has been enhanced with six hours of audio recordings from a poetry reading held in New York to celebrate publication of the book. You can listen to readings of dozens of poems by Keillor, humorist Roy Blount, author Calvin Trillin and other literary notables. The poems, as well as the supporting biographic material and notes, can be printed or copied to a word processor, making the CD-ROM a wonderful research tool for students embarking on the study of poetry. Poetry browsers, however, may be deterred by the CD-ROM's unusually heavy demand for hard-disk space—a whopping ten megabytes.

BARRON'S COMPLETE BOOK NOTES
★★★
Developer: World Library Inc.; 800-443-0238
Format: DOS, Windows
Price: $39

Now that I'm twenty years past graduating from college, I'm willing to confess the awful truth: I once bought a "book note," those pocket-size cheat sheets offering plot summaries and character analysis of long, boring books that college students don't always have time to read. I suspect I'm not alone—most of us couldn't have survived high school and college without occasionally leaning on a book note from Barron's, Cliffs, or Monarch. Today's generation of students has it even easier—they can get Barron's or Monarch notes on CD-ROM and copy the text directly into their term papers, eliminating the messy intermediate step of retyping. Not that I'm recommending book notes as an alternative to reading the classics, I'm just acknowledging the inevitable.

Barron's Complete Book Notes delivers 101 book notes arranged alphabetically by author, from Edward Albee's *Who's Afraid of Virginia Woolf?* to Richard Wright's *Native Son*, with everything in between from William Golding's *Lord of the Flies* to Plato's *The Republic*. Each note offers a quick plot summary as well as a critical essay and a glossary. The hundreds and hundreds of pages in *Moby Dick*, for example, are boiled down to a plot summary of just sixteen paragraphs. In the glossary for *Portrait of the Artist as a Young Man* by James Joyce, there are helpful definitions for the dialect of Joyce's native Dublin—"cod" is "slang for a joke or prank," and "jackeen" is "a lower-class Dubliner." The CD-ROM also includes forty illustrations, mostly line drawings and plot diagrams taken from the pages of the book notes. Students looking for more help will find it in *Monarch Notes For Windows*, reviewed in this section.

CREATION STORIES
★1/2
Developer: Time Warner Interactive; 800-482-3766
Format: Windows
Price: $39

Creation Stories seems to have been created with technology from the dawn of time. Released in early 1993, the Windows version of this CD-ROM is painfully difficult to install and inexcusably clunky when running. A "readme" file included on the disk is no help, as it offers confusing and seemingly contradictory directions.

The idea behind *Creation Stories* is promising. The developers assembled ninety-three stories, drawn from many cultures, of how the world and human beings were created. Twelve of these stories are told through audio narration, while the other eighty-one are presented in text illuminated with tiny illustrations of the stories' characters. Although the art is well done, the result doesn't justify the price of a CD-ROM; the same content could have been delivered for less money by simply putting the stories in a book/audiocassette package. And the disk has one other major flaw—there is no way to print the stories or copy them to a word processor.

As a book, however, *Creation Stories* would be worth reading. Some of the stories are fascinating and very different from the Judeo-Christian view of God assembling heaven and earth in just six days. The ancient Aztecs of Mexico, for example, believed the world was created by the earth goddess Tlalecutli, "who had the form of a monster [with] snapping mouths on her limbs and . . . the body of a giant toad, [with] the teeth and claws of a jaguar." According to *Creation Stories*, this multifaceted goddess was watched by two jealous gods as she floated "on the unformed water." The two gods "turned themselves into serpents coiled around the goddess and tore her in two. One half they took back to heaven and from it made many gods. Those gods saw the other half of her mutilated body and heard her cries, and they felt sorry for her. They turned her body into the earth and ordered that living things would grow from it—fruits and plants and trees."

FIRST PERSON: DONALD A. NORMAN—DEFENDING HUMAN ATTRIBUTES IN THE AGE OF THE MACHINE
★★★
Developer: Voyager Co.; 800-446-2001
Format: Macintosh
Price: $39

In the never-ending battle between ordinary computer users and engineers who perversely insist on making hardware and software increasingly complex, Donald A. Norman is a tireless warrior for keeping things simple. "There should not be any such thing as human error," he declares in this CD-ROM. "Most so-called human error is a result of imposing inappropriate tasks upon people or ... poor design." Norman, a former academic psychologist who is now a research fellow with Apple Computer, has written a series of books and essays advocating better design as the best way to make technology accessible. *First Person: Donald A. Norman—Defending Human Attributes in the Age of the Machine* contains a huge treasure trove of his work. The disk includes the full text of three books—*The Psychology of Everyday Things*, *Things That Make Us Smart*, and *Turn Signals Are the Facial Expressions of Automobiles*—along with seven essays and a glossary, bibliography, and index.

Of course, Norman realizes it would be bad design simply to dump a lot of text onto a CD-ROM. So he appears in several video segments, explaining his theories and comparing the benefits of electronic books to books printed on paper. "I don't think we've got it quite right yet," he says of books on CD-ROM. "It may take years to get it quite right. But it's a good start." I agree. *Defending Human Attributes* is most powerful when you're seeing and hearing Norman. Reading the text is annoying; it takes a full second for the computer to go from one page to the next, while you can turn the page of a printed book in the blink of an eye. But only one feature of the CD-ROM is an outright flop: a "gallery of unfindable things" that presents photographs of deliberately outrageous design ideas with Norman's audio comments. We don't really need Norman to tell us a remote-control iron isn't practical or to ponder the benefits of an ergonomic piano with a semicircular keyboard.

FIRST PERSON: STEPHEN JAY GOULD — ON EVOLUTION
★★½
Developer: Voyager Co.; 800-446-2001
Format: Macintosh
Price: $45

What did Charles Darwin intend to say about life and morality when he published his groundbreaking *The Origin of Species* in 1859? Stephen J. Gould, a prolific author and natural scientist at Harvard University, has a provocative theory: Darwin's work has been seriously misunderstood for more than a century.

Gould explained this theory in a sixty-minute lecture delivered in Boston in April 1993. A videotape of that lecture is the centerpiece of *First Person: Stephen Jay Gould—On Evolution*, a CD-ROM full of fascinating ideas that are, unfortunately, delivered in an awkward format. Gould's head and shoulders appear in a tiny three-inch diagonal window on a standard fourteen-inch monitor, while the text of his remarks appears beneath him on the screen. Since we read faster than we speak, I quickly got tired of the delay and started flipping through the text without waiting for Gould's narration.

Gould sums up Darwin's theory of natural selection as three facts that form a conclusion. First, all organisms produce more offspring than can survive, such as a fish that lays millions of eggs. Second, all organisms vary among themselves, so some deer run faster than others when chased by a wolf. Third, at least some features are inherited, so the faster deer will have offspring that also run fast. Gould's conclusion: "If only some can survive, then on average the survivors will be—this is a statistical phenomenon, not every time, but on average—those within the spectrum of random variations that are fortuitously better adapted to changing local environments. And through that, the population changes."

This explains why, over a hundred generations, elephants in the cold northern climate of what is now Siberia grew thick coats of hair and became woolly mammoths. But Gould says Darwin's theory states only that animals adapt to change, not that animals get "better" over time. In other words, we shouldn't cite Darwin to support arguments that humans are superior to other forms of life or that "moral" behavior can be scientifically demonstrated as superior to "immoral" behavior. "What Darwin is telling us is that the answers do not come from nature," Gould declares. "Every man must strive to believe what he can from the sources of his own understanding."

Beyond the lecture, the CD-ROM is packed with a huge amount of text: Gould's book *Bully for Brontosaurus*, Darwin's *The Origin of Species* and *Voyage of the Beagle*, sixteen short Gould essays, and eleven historical documents including Darwin's letters and excerpts from his autobiography. Each on-screen page, however, displays only a few paragraphs, requiring constant flipping to get through even a small part of the total 3,645 pages. Other than students studying evolution, I'm not sure who would want this CD-ROM. It's quicker and more satisfying to read Gould's books in print, and his lecture would look and sound better viewed on a regular television set.

FROM ALICE TO OCEAN
★★★½
Developer: Claris Corp./Against All Odds Productions; 800-544-8554
Format: Windows, Macintosh
Price: $49

In 1977, a twenty-seven-year-old woman named Robyn Davidson set out alone from the town of Alice Springs in the heart of the Australian desert on a yearlong trek across the Outback with a dog named Diggity and four camels to carry her few possessions. Davidson's 1,700-mile journey through some of the harshest and most beautiful territory in the world was chronicled by Rick Smolan, a photographer for *National Geographic.* Smolan's breathtaking photographs and Davidson's recollections from the journey became a best-selling coffee-table book called *From Alice to Ocean: Alone Across the Outback*, published in 1992 by Addison-Wesley.

Smolan then created this extraordinary CD-ROM, also called *From Alice to Ocean*, that tells Davidson's story in a new way. The disk presents many of the photographs and some of the text from the book but adds a fascinating new dimension: You listen to Davidson's voice describing the trip as you see Smolan's photographs of endless desert horizons or click on "sidebar" articles that cover subjects such as the history of camels in Australia and aboriginal culture. As you sit in front of the computer, you feel you're sharing Davidson's trip in a way the book could never match.

Amateur photographers will also benefit from Smolan's extensive commentary on how he took the photographs. Many of the pictures displayed on screen have a button in the corner that summons Smolan's audio recollection of what was happening at the moment he pushed the shutter button. Smolan also provides six "photo tips," short essays on subjects such as "time exposure" and "silhouettes." On capturing spontaneous moments, for example, Smolan says: "Take the picture first ... You don't want to filter it through this little voice inside that says ... 'Let me set this up properly.'"

ISAAC ASIMOV'S THE ULTIMATE ROBOT
★★
Developer: Microsoft Corp.; 800-426-9400
Format: Windows, Macintosh
Price: $59

Isaac Asimov's The Ultimate Robot is much like a robot itself—shiny and efficient but lacking any spark of soul or creativity. Built around the work of Isaac Asimov, the groundbreaking science-fiction writer who died in 1992 after writing dozens of novels and hundreds of short stories in a fifty-three-year career, the CD-ROM is divided into eight sections covering different subjects related to robots.

In the "Asimov Speaks" section, you can watch a video clip of Asimov explaining his famous three laws of robotics to Jane Pauley on "The Today Show" in 1987: "The first law is that a robot may not harm a human being or allow a human being to come to harm through inaction. Two, a robot must obey orders given it by a human being except where that violates the first law. And third, a robot must protect its own existence except where that would violate the first or second laws." That's the high point in eleven brief video clips of Asimov.

"Asimov's Writings" contains thirty-six of the author's short stories and sixteen essays. But the text can be viewed only in a small window that makes extended reading painful; nor is there an option to move the text into a word-processing document or to print it. "The Robot Gallery" is stuffed with sixty-six photos of Asimov, mostly family-scrapbook-quality shots from science-fiction conventions, covers of Asimov's books, and "robot art" that turns out to be nothing more than the result of software glitches on the developer's Macintosh computers.

Veering sharply and inexplicably away from the sci-fi orientation of the Asimov-related sections is the "Robotics" category, which offers high-level discourse on mechanics and computer animation through articles on esoteric topics such as "inverse kinematics" and "exponential acceleration." But another section called "The Robotoids"—in which you build a robot from an inventory of heads, arms, and legs—is strictly for kids. There aren't enough parts to create a wide variety of robots, and the completed creations all go through the same limited set of animated movements.

"Cinerobots" is briefly amusing, with one-minute clips from eight science-fiction movies—including the debut of Robbie the

Robot in the 1956 classic *Forbidden Planet*. Some of the clips, though, don't really belong here, such as battle scenes from *The Empire Strikes Back*. The section also shows possible robot designs of the near future; my favorite is a suitcase-size housecleaning robot that scrubs toilets.

Ultimate Robot tries to cover every aspect of robots and robotics. Some of the nuts and bolts are attention-grabbing, but the disk as a whole is superficial. A potentially interesting entry on Jason Jr., the underwater robot that photographed the Titanic wreck in 1986, provides only three sentences on this real-life robotic hero. It seems the developers of *Ultimate Robot* couldn't decide whether to create a serious scientific treatise or light entertainment or whether they should appeal to adults or children.

LIBRARY OF THE FUTURE THIRD EDITION
★★½
Developer: World Library Inc.; 800-443-0238
Format: DOS, Windows
Price: $149

"Shovelware" is an insulting term in the CD-ROM business, referring to titles created by shoveling lots of material onto a disk with little regard for whether the result is useful or entertaining. *Library of the Future Third Edition* could be the white elephant of shovelware—an almost unbelievably huge project of questionable merit. The CD-ROM contains the full text of 1,750 literary works from 205 authors, mostly classics of the nineteenth century and earlier. From the plays of Aeschylus through the poetry of William Butler Yeats, the collection in *Library of the Future* wanders all over the literary map. There are the works of William Shakespeare, fairy tales by Hans Christian Andersen, philosophy from Immanuel Kant, and novels by Joseph Conrad.

The text of these works is displayed in hard-to-read type that isn't suitable for extended reading. But that's not really the point. *Library of the Future* has an extensive, multifeature search system for sorting through the acres and acres of text to quickly find a specific reference. Key passages can then be printed or copied to a word processor. To help navigate through the many entries, each work has a helpful two-sentence introduction. An example: "Hugo, Victor, 1802–1885—French poet, dramatist, and novelist who was a leader in the French romantic movement. Hugo was a politically active man whose humanitarianism was generally regarded as a poet's dream. *Les Misérables,* 1862—An epic novel of nineteenth century France. Jean Valjean, one of society's victims, steals a loaf of bread and is imprisoned for five years; a failed escape attempt increases his sentence to nineteen years. After his release he is relentlessly pursued by Inspector Javert."

I'm left with one big question about *Library of the Future*: What's the point? Selling for a relatively steep $149, this could be a very useful CD-ROM for libraries and schools. But I don't see why *Library of the Future* should be sold in the home market. I can't imagine anyone other than literature students would want the ability to search through hundreds and hundreds of classics. And despite its awesome size, even *Library of the Future* isn't guaranteed to have every literary work a student might want to examine.

THE MADNESS OF ROLAND
★★½
Developer: HyperBole Studios; 800-693-3253
Format: Windows-2, Macintosh-2
Price: $45

The Madness of Roland, described by its creator as "the world's first interactive multimedia novel," overflows with a jumble of artistic ideas that are only occasionally entertaining or enlightening. The CD-ROM retells the legend of Roland, a knight in the service of Charlemagne, from multiple perspectives. Charlemagne, for those rusty on medieval history, united much of Europe during the eighth century and became the first emperor of the Holy Roman Empire, fighting against Muslim invaders called Saracens. Set in Paris during the year 778, *The Madness of Roland* takes poor Roland through seven chapters of bloodshed, insanity, and betrayal.

Each chapter begins with a display of up to five tarot cards representing the characters contributing to the story. Clicking on one of the cards summons several pages of text, mostly written in the first person, accompanied by audio narration and music. You can also click on an icon of the sun to see a line of poetry or history related to the story or an icon of the moon for a thirty-second video clip. These clips are mostly heavy-handed cartoonlike animations depicting scenes from the story or self-involved images of Roland—portrayed by the CD-ROM's creator, Greg Roach—

muttering deep thoughts such as, "I wonder, sometimes, what history will think of me."

The first chapter, for example, unfolds through the eyes of five characters: Roland, Charlemagne, the beautiful Saracen princess Angelica, the Saracen nobleman Mandricardo, and Roland's sword Durendal. Roach, in a bibliography on the CD-ROM, credits a long list of authors for influencing his work, including psychologist Carl Jung, famous for finding phallic images in almost every aspect of life. Durendal is a blatantly Jungian symbol, thinking to itself of Roland: "He swings me like a lover. With him I am like a babe flung high by its father on strong arms—I have never tasted child!—and I coo to the throat rattles of his victims."

Not all of *The Madness of Roland* is so serious; Roach inexplicably veers into a few bursts of silliness. At one point, for instance, the moon icon produces a bar chart showing the morale of the Holy Roman Empire's population at various points in the story. Roach is full of creative energy and could do much better work with a little self-restraint and discipline. I hope that's what happens with a sequel called *The Madness of Roland Book II*, due in mid-1995.

THE COMPLETE MAUS
★★★★
Developer: Voyager Co.; 800-446-2001
Format: Macintosh
Price: $39

The Complete Maus tells a mesmerizing, emotionally wrenching story of the Holocaust—the Nazi genocide that swept away six million Jews during World War II—by letting readers choose their own path through text, pictures, audio, and video. An autobiographical recollection of New York graphic artist Art Spiegelman and his father, Vladek, a survivor of the Auschwitz concentration camp in Poland, *Maus* began as a two-volume work drawn in comic-book style, subtitled *And Here My Troubles Began* and *My Father Bleeds History*, published in 1986 and 1991.

In the world of *Maus*, Jews are depicted as mice, Germans as cats and Poles as pigs. Spiegelman, in an audio interview on the CD-ROM, explains why: "The entire Nazi project, the Final Solution, ended up dividing humanity into various species . . . What was involved was the extermination of the Jews. And extermination is a word reserved for vermin." The two books, awarded a special Pulitzer Prize in 1992, fill about 280 pages and are available in a paperback boxed set for about $25. The CD-ROM contains every page of both books. But the disk isn't a replacement for them; it's an extension. Indeed, I strongly recommend reading both volumes before turning to the CD-ROM.

On screen, the book pages are marked with icons. By clicking on the icons, viewers can see rough pencil sketches of artwork, hear comments by Spiegelman, listen to segments of his interviews with Vladek, or see supporting documents, including a photograph of the yellowing, water-stained Nazi arrest warrant for Vladek and Spiegelman's mother, Anja, also an Auschwitz survivor, carefully typed by some anonymous clerk determined to observe all the legal niceties in the midst of wanton slaughter.

The disk's introduction, which takes about forty-five minutes to view, allows Spiegelman to explain through audio and video clips how he interviewed his cantankerous father, traveled to Auschwitz, and then drew pictures. Supplementary material includes a 706-page transcript of Spiegelman's interviews with Vladek and a collection of Spiegelman's essays. The most moving parts of the CD-ROM are the simplest, such as listening to Vladek's heavy Eastern European accent: "We came to the town of Oświęcim. Before the war, I sold textiles here. And we came here to the concentration camp Auschwitz. And we knew that from here we will not come out anymore. We knew the stories—that they will gas us and throw us in the ovens. This was 1944, we knew everything. And here we were." With Serbs killing Muslims in Bosnia and tribal warfare in Rwanda, *The Complete Maus* isn't just a history of events from half a century ago—it is a story of inhuman cruelty that keeps repeating itself.

MONARCH NOTES FOR WINDOWS
★★★
Developer: Bureau of Electronic Publishing Inc.; 800-828-4766
Format: Windows
Price: $55

Another collection of shortcuts through great works of literature, similar to *Barron's Complete Book Notes*, reviewed in this section. *Monarch Notes For Windows* offers book notes on 226 authors, some of which cover multiple works. The list literally goes from A to Z, starting with contemporary Nigerian novelist Chinua Achebe and ending with nineteenth century French novelist Emile Zola. In between are a mix of literary figures from ancient Greek playwrights to modern poets, including Ray Bradbury, Charles Dickens, Euripides, Franz Kafka, Sylvia Plath, Alexander Solzhenitsyn, Henry David Thoreau, and Kurt Vonnegut. All the material in the notes can be easily printed or copied to a word processor.

Monarch Notes For Windows, released in 1993, also comes with a selection of audio and video clips that don't contribute much. The seventeen video clips, for example, are mostly ten-second cartoon animations of scenes from classic works of literature. The numerous audio clips, again averaging ten seconds, merely narrate a sentence or two of an author's work. More useful is a glossary of literary terms. If you're wondering what "dactylic" means, for example, you can click on the word and a definition pops onto the screen: "In meter, a strongly stressed syllable followed by two weak ones."

The notes, mostly written by professors of literature, provide background that will benefit even students dedicated enough to actually read the books in question. Consider this entry on J. D. Salinger's *The Catcher in the Rye*, explaining why the author tells the story of Holden Caulfield, the ultimate alienated teenager, from a first-person perspective: "Because he [Caulfield] is allowed to relate his own story in and on his own terms, we feel an empathy for him that could not have been otherwise achieved. The reader is granted an introspective view of the story; at the same time, because his background is not the same as Holden's, the reader retains his objectivity. Thus, he learns more about Holden than Holden himself knows."

Owners of Macintosh computers, or those few remaining PC owners who haven't upgraded from DOS to Windows, can buy an earlier version of the disk called *Monarch Notes on CD-ROM*, released in 1992, with slightly fewer book notes and no video clips.

PROJECT GUTENBERG
★★½
Developer: Walnut Creek CDROM; 800-786-9907
Format: DOS, Windows, Macintosh
Price: $19

Project Gutenberg is a weird, wonderful, and marginally useful volunteer effort by a group of computer programmers at Illinois Benedictine College in Champaign, Illinois, to create a huge collection of literature and historical documents available electronically at no charge to all takers. The volunteers have been working since 1971, typing and scanning works in the public domain—books old enough that copyrights have expired—for storage on computers. Project Gutenberg texts are available for free through the Internet or by requesting floppy disks from the volunteers. The group's ultimate goal: creating electronic versions of ten thousand texts by 2001.

Walnut Creek CDROM also supplies the Project Gutenberg collection on CD-ROM, although you'll have to pay about $19. If you're seriously interested in Project Gutenberg, it's money well spent—you won't have to wait for long downloads by modem or accumulate a big stack of diskettes. Walnut Creek puts out an updated *Project Gutenberg* CD-ROM twice a year, adding the volunteers' latest efforts.

I looked at the November 1994 edition of *Project Gutenberg* and found 143 entries spanning an amazing range of content—everything from President Franklin Roosevelt's first inaugural address in 1933 to *Around the World in 80 Days*. There's even a file containing the square root of two calculated to five million digits. In general, however, Project Gutenberg divides its collection into three categories: "light" literature, such as *Aesop's Fables* and *Peter Pan*; "heavy" literature, such as the plays of Shakespeare and *Moby Dick*; and reference works, such as the 1911 edition of *Roget's Thesaurus* and complete statistical tables from the 1990 U.S. Census.

All the entries in *Project Gutenberg* are stored as "plain vanilla" text; words that were originally in italics, underlined, or in boldface are capitalized. The CD-ROM comes with a simple viewer program that lets you quickly call up the text. You can also open the files with a word processor if you want to print, copy, or modify the text.

Although I regard Project Gutenberg as a noble effort, I'm

not sure the *Project Gutenberg* CD-ROM is particularly worthwhile—the collection is so varied that it doesn't meet any particular research need. But I hope the folks at Project Gutenberg meet their goal for 2001. If CD-ROM technology keeps improving, maybe the entire library of ten thousand works will fit on a single disk—a product that would be too good to pass up.

SHINING FLOWER
★★

Developer: Voyager Co.; 800-446-2001
Format: Macintosh
Price: $29

Gertrude Stein wouldn't like *Shining Flower*. It was the poet Stein who said, "A rose is a rose is a rose," a slap at generations of poets who insisted on burdening ordinary objects with deep symbolic meaning. Created in Japan, *Shining Flower* is advertised by Voyager Company as an "interactive haiku," in which "you accompany the Wanderer on a metaphorical journey toward the Flower, the source of power and enlightenment."

What you actually get are animated illustrations, some of them quite beautiful, of the Wanderer, a vaguely human character, carrying a flower that glows like a candle. He encounters strange creatures in several settings, such as a beach, a mountain, and a swamp. Soothing synthesizer music plays in the background, along with occasional sound effects such as the chirping of crickets. In the forest scene, for example, the Wanderer is confronted by a giant stick figure resembling a grasshopper. The giant grasshopper drops a blue leaf to the ground. Upon touching the ground, the leaf becomes a hole. The grasshopper then slips into the hole, followed by the trees and the Wanderer with his flower.

Don't ask me what all this means. Maybe I don't know enough about Japanese art and culture to appreciate *Shining Flower*, but I couldn't figure out what this scene—or any of the other scenes—was trying to communicate. And the CD-ROM itself is no help, containing no dialogue, narration, or explanatory essays. Nor is *Shining Flower* truly interactive. You have the option of watching the story run automatically from beginning to end, which takes less than an hour, or selecting your own sequence of scenes. But you can't do anything within the individual scenes other than watch them slowly unfold.

FIRST PERSON: MARVIN MINSKY—THE SOCIETY OF MIND
★★½
Developer: Voyager Co.; 800-446-2001
Format: Macintosh
Price: $39

A journey inside the mind of an Information Age philosopher that is sometimes inspiring, sometimes tedious. Marvin Minsky is a professor at the Massachusetts Institute of Technology and a pioneer in artificial intelligence, the study of machines and thought. Minsky's interests are much broader, however, than what can be soldered together with wires and integrated circuits. In 1984, he wrote a book called *The Society of Mind*, which explores how our brains work.

The CD-ROM version is built around the book's text, which fills 882 on-screen pages, not including an extensive appendix and bibliography. Minsky is a highly literate writer who steers clear of scientific jargon while quoting everyone from Sigmund Freud to Kurt Vonnegut. His *Society of Mind* theory contends our brains are really societies where groups of "agents" work together to handle even simple tasks. Drinking a cup of tea, Minsky suggests, requires a "grasping" agent to pick up the cup, a "balancing" agent to make sure the tea doesn't spill, a "thirst" agent to motivate the process, and a "moving" agent to connect the cup with the lips.

In many sections of the on-screen text, you can summon Minsky himself. He appears in the lower left corner of the screen, seeming to stand on the page, and delivers one-minute monologues on subjects related to the topic at hand. In total, the clips run slightly over an hour and a half. The text is also supplemented with fourteen related articles written by Minsky and a brief tour of his living room, where he explains his favorite objects. Among the most bizarre: a photo of Minsky partying at the home of then Vice President Dan Quayle with the cast of "Star Trek: The Next Generation" and the Mercury Seven astronauts.

The biggest drawback to *The Society of Mind* is that Minsky's thought processes are frequently too complicated to be easily grasped while flitting back and forth through a CD-ROM. In the introduction, he admits the brain is "dreadfully complicated." His video commentary is rarely any help—he appears to have sat in front of a camera for a few hours and done nothing more than toss off a series of one-liners.

TWAIN'S WORLD
★★½

Developer: Bureau of Electronic Publishing Inc.; 800-828-4766
Format: Windows
Price: $29

Twain's World is a powerful resource with appeal to a limited audience. The CD-ROM contains virtually the entire written work of author Mark Twain, who lived from 1835 to 1910 and is considered one of the greatest American authors. Computer screens, however, aren't an acceptable medium for reading long chunks of text, so *Twain's World* won't replace a shelf full of books for anyone interested in absorbing Twain's many novels, short stories, essays, letters, and speeches. Where *Twain's World* shines is as a research tool capable of instantly searching out specific words and phrases. I wondered if Twain had ever visited San Jose, California, where I work. I hit the on-screen search button in *Twain's World* and got my answer in this excerpt from a letter Twain wrote in San Francisco, dated September 25, 1864, to his mother and sister in St. Louis: "Been down to San Jose—generally pronounced *Sannozay*, emphasis on last syllable—today fifty miles from here, by railroad. Town of 6,000 inhabitants, buried in flowers and shrubbery. The climate is finer than ours here, because it is not so close to the ocean, and is protected from the winds by the coast range."

The depth of content on *Twain's World* is impressive. You get the full text of nine novels, including *The Adventures of Tom Sawyer*, *The Adventures of Huckleberry Finn*, *A Connecticut Yankee in King Arthur's Court*, and *The Prince and the Pauper*; 120 short stories, including *The Notorious Jumping Frog of Calaveras County*; eight nonfiction books, including *Life on the Mississippi* and *The Innocents Abroad*; forty-nine essays; and ninety-one speeches, as well as numerous letters and a selection of biographical essays about Twain. A small amount of multimedia content contributes little—there is a small gallery of photos; eleven video clips, including a grainy one-minute newsreel of Twain himself taken in 1909; and twenty-three brief narrations of text excerpts. Still, the huge amount of text in *Twain's World* is a treasure trove for students involved in serious academic study. But the CD-ROM doesn't offer anything for the casual reader who isn't interested in detailed analysis of Twain's work.

d. Music—Classical and Instruction

SO I'VE HEARD, VOLUME 1: BACH AND BEFORE
★★½
Developer: Voyager Co.; 800-446-2001
Format: Macintosh
Price: $19

Alan Rich, a music critic and occasional commentator on National Public Radio, has shouldered an overly ambitious task here: explaining the entire history of classical music in a series of five CD-ROMs. Voyager Company has published the first three installments so far, with the final two promised soon. But the series is far from comprehensive because there's simply too much ground to cover. Voyager has done much better with its CD Companion series, reviewed in this section, which provides an in-depth examination of a single piece of music.

So I've Heard, Volume 1 rushes from prehistory through the early eighteenth century in just 145 black-and-white on-screen pages, with each page containing only two or three paragraphs. The text is enriched with fifty audio clips, most running about a minute, illustrating everything from a Greek hymn of 130 A.D. to George Frideric Handel's *Water Music*. The audio clips are also meant to serve as a buyer's guide to music CDs, with a catalog card for each selection identifying the performers and record label.

Rich provides a cogent, if abbreviated, history. "It would be accurate to think of [Johann Sebastian] Bach as a conservative," Rich writes. "Most of the musical forms he used had been in vogue long before his time, but he filled out these forms with striking new ideas . . . Bach worked in these old forms with a broader vision, a more profound insight into the nature of musical expressivity, than all his predecessors. We can easily measure the difference if we just use our ears. Everything before Bach sounds like early music; Bach never does." There just aren't enough of these interesting ideas. Most readers will get through Volume 1 in an hour or two without gaining a true understanding of how classical music evolved.

BEETHOVEN'S 5TH
★★★
Developer: Future Vision Multimedia Inc.; 800-472-8777
Format: Windows
Price: $39

Almost identical in structure to the excellent *CD Companion* series from Voyager Company, reviewed in this section, *Beethoven's 5th* doesn't explain the great composer's music with Voyager's authority and depth. But the text commentary on the Fifth Symphony is still good enough to justify purchasing the CD-ROM.

Listening to a full performance of the Fifth Symphony by the Zagreb Philharmonic, you also see scrolling text linked to a glossary. The famous "da-da-da-dum" opening notes are identified in the text as the "fate motif." Clicking on those words produces the glossary definition "Legend has it that Beethoven, when asked by his friend Schindler for the real meaning of this rhythm, answered, 'Thus Fate knocks at the door.' There is no proof to the validity of Schindler's story, but the symphony was soon nicknamed the 'Fate Symphony,' and the persistent motif is still called the 'fate motif.'" You can also call up the symphony's score and listen as the notes are performed.

Beethoven's 5th falls short, however, in presenting supplementary material. A biography of the composer gives only highlights from his life, not a complete picture of the man or the artist. The Fifth Symphony, first performed in 1808, is covered in only six paragraphs without any explanation for what moved Beethoven to create this awesome piece of music. A selection of three games—a multiple-choice trivia quiz and two musical memory teasers—is predictable and boring. Finally, there is a reasonably good although brief guide to orchestral instruments. Many of the instrument profiles, providing several paragraphs of text and a photograph, include a thirty-second video clip of the instrument in action.

LUDWIG VAN BEETHOVEN: SYMPHONY NO. 9
★★★★
Developer: Voyager Co.; 800-446-2001
Format: Macintosh
Price: $45

First in the outstanding CD Companion series from Voyager Company, this CD-ROM is built around a sixty-eight-minute performance of Beethoven's Ninth Symphony by the Vienna Philharmonic and the Vienna State Opera Chorus.

Robert Winter, a classical pianist and music professor at the University of California–Los Angeles, provides commentary that clearly and elegantly illuminates this complex orchestral work. Winter explains the famous "Ode to Joy" in the symphony's fourth movement as "Beethoven's attempt to create a popular tune that would appeal to all of mankind" and then suggests why the composer, writing the Ninth in 1824, put the Ode in the form of a march: "In the wake of the Napoleonic Wars that plagued Austria from the 1790s until the final defeat of Napoleon at Waterloo in 1815, the military march was a form of music familiar to everyone."

A long essay on "The Art of Listening" delves into concepts such as "repetition" and "variation," as well as reviewing orchestral terminology and instruments. Another long essay on "Beethoven's World," combines a biography and bibliography. I was fascinated by a chapter offering excerpts from the composer's "conversation books." Deaf in his later years, Beethoven could still speak but demanded that visitors write down what they were saying to him. These notebooks tell of incidents both petty and sublime: "The cashier has demanded that whomever you have designated [to handle ticket sales] must be there at 8:30 A.M. tomorrow morning," wrote Beethoven's assistant before the premiere. After the opening night, the assistant wrote, "When the main level began to applaud for the fifth time, the police commissioner shouted, 'Quiet!'"

About the CD Companion series: Voyager has created a unique and powerful way to learn about classical music, fully exploiting CD-ROM's ability to combine text, graphics, and audio.

Each CD Companion lets you set the pace in exploring a work of classical music. The highlight is a feature called "a close reading." You listen to the music as commentary scrolls along the screen, giving perspective on what the composer is trying to accomplish with each shift in tempo or change of instruments. An easy-to-use control panel lets you effortlessly jump from one section of the performance to another, using extensive indexes and menus.

Beyond the performance itself, each CD Companion contains well-written essays, biographies, bibliographies, and a quiz offering either multiple-choice questions or a concentration game that requires looking through sixteen musical clips to find matching pairs. There is also a complete glossary of musical terms, linked to the text. On the CD Companion dedicated to Mozart, for example, you might not fully understand the term "dissonance." Click on the word and a window instantly opens on screen with the definition: "an interval or chord that sounds harsh or unstable. In music before 1900, dissonance generally required a 'resolution.' In Mozart's music, dissonance provides much of the expressive impetus." Resolution is defined as "the movement of a dissonant interval or chord to a consonant interval or chord. Throughout the eighteenth and nineteenth centuries, dissonance and its resolution provided the fuel that propelled phrases forward." Both definitions are accompanied by brief audio clips illustrating the two musical concepts.

Of course, great works of music deserve to be heard from beginning to end as the composer intended. But there's a tremendous sense of liberation in experiencing a CD Companion. You are no longer confined to a strict linear progression but are free to move around in any direction. That freedom lets you create a more enjoyable and memorable learning experience. The music tracks on each CD-ROM, by the way, can be heard on any regular audio CD player.

Other CD Companions for the Macintosh: *Antonin Dvořák's Symphony No. 9: "From the New World," Wolfgang Amadeus Mozart: The "Dissonant" Quartet, Franz Schubert: The "Trout" Quintet, Richard Strauss: Three Tone Poems,* and *Igor Stravinsky: The Rite of Spring.*

For Windows: Voyager licensed the CD Companion series to Microsoft Corporation for translation to the Windows format. With only minor changes, including the replacement of Voyager's half-screen black-and-white graphics with full-screen color graphics, Microsoft has released all but one of the Voyager titles under the following names: *Microsoft Multimedia Beethoven: The Ninth Symphony, Microsoft Multimedia Mozart: The "Dissonant" Quartet, Microsoft Multimedia Schubert: The "Trout" Quintet, Microsoft Multimedia Strauss: Three Tone Poems,* and *Microsoft Multimedia Stravinsky: The Rite of Spring.* All the Voyager and Microsoft titles are reviewed in this section.

SO I'VE HEARD, VOLUME 2: THE CLASSICAL IDEAL
★★½
Developer: Voyager Co.; 800-446-2001
Format: Macintosh
Price: $19

Music critic Alan Rich takes his history of classical composers to the late eighteenth century, focusing on Franz Joseph Haydn and Wolfgang Amadeus Mozart. As with *Volume 1*, reviewed in this section, the text is abbreviated to the point of superficiality, filling only 139 on-screen pages, with each page limited to a few paragraphs. A catalog of forty-four one-minute musical excerpts accompanies the text.

Rich explains how new thinking in science, philosophy, and architecture influenced a new generation of composers, who were eager to surpass their predecessors. "The musical geniuses of the time constantly sought to stretch the limitations of this [classical] style, to unsettle that sense of comfort and guide an audience toward intimidating kinds of newness." While such thoughts are intriguing, there isn't enough substance in *So I've Heard, Volume 2* to back them up.

COMPOSER QUEST
★★
Developer: Opcode Interactive; 800-557-2633
Format: Windows
Price: $49

Composer Quest is on a crusade to introduce both children and adults to the world of classical music. But the CD-ROM tries to accomplish too much with too little, mixing slender biographies, exceedingly short musical excerpts, and a boring game. The mission of *Composer Quest* is further muddied by a strange decision to include six jazz musicians along with the twenty-six composers of classical music.

There are two ways to work through *Composer Quest*. In the "learn" mode, you are presented with a time line for the classical composers divided into seven historical periods: "Early Baroque," "Middle Baroque," "Late Baroque," "Classical," "Early Romantic," "Romantic," and "Early Modern." If you click on "Classical," you are presented with a choice of biographies of four classical composers. Selecting Franz Josef Haydn, who lived from

1732 to 1809, you get a skimpy four paragraphs on the Austrian composer. "The demand for his music must have been extraordinary, because he wrote a lot of it," the biography says. "Although he didn't invent either the symphony or the string quartet, he wrote a great many of each—at least 104 symphonies—and these are among the finest works in both genres." You can then listen to three musical selections from Haydn symphonies, although each runs for less than a minute. For each of the seven historical periods, *Composer Quest* also provides a few paragraphs on the arts and political history of that era.

There is a separate time line for jazz, with just three sections: "Ragtime," "Dixieland/New Orleans," and "Early Swing." Only six jazz greats are profiled—Scott Joplin, Louis Armstrong, Jelly Roll Morton, King Oliver, Kid Ory, and Duke Ellington—and there's only one music clip, sixty seconds of Joplin's tune "The Entertainer." Going through the entire jazz section takes no more than fifteen minutes and won't give you even a superficial introduction to the subject.

The other way to explore *Composer Quest* is "play" mode. You enter a time machine and listen to one of the CD-ROM's music clips. To identify the music, you have to type in a year, go to that section of the time line, and then find the composer. If you pick the wrong composer, you get a one-sentence hint pointing you toward the true composer's identity. But working through all these steps is inexcusably awkward and time-consuming, robbing the game of any appeal.

ANTONIN DVOŘÁK'S SYMPHONY NO. 9, "FROM THE NEW WORLD"
★★★★
Developer: Voyager Co.; 800-446-2001
Format: Macintosh
Price: $45

"Few musical works from any period have suffered more from sustained listening in a cultural vacuum than the *New World* symphony. Few works from any period repay more richly a re-examination of their genesis. To confront the *New World* symphony is to confront an America struggling to come of age—a struggle for identity that, still laced with contradictions and paradoxes, continues to this day."

That's how pianist and music scholar Robert Winter describes *Antonin Dvořák's Symphony No. 9, "From the New World,"* in this selection from Voyager Company's outstanding *CD Companion* series. Winter, a prolific writer, with four *CD Companions* to his credit, proceeds to fill that vacuum with hundreds of on-screen pages describing the Czech composer and his era. Dvořák, who came to New York in 1892 and stayed in this country for several years, was himself a man of contradictions. An agoraphobic who hated to travel but was obsessed with trains, he was lured across the Atlantic by the princely sum of $15,000 a year to teach and conduct.

A full forty-three-minute performance of the *New World* by the Vienna Philharmonic is illuminated by Winter's skillfully written commentary. Beyond the symphony itself, Winter provides a lengthy biography of Dvořák and background on classical music's late romantic period. The most unusual feature is a section called "direct testimony," with two hundred documents relating to Dvořák's journey, everything from New York newspaper articles on his visit to the composer's letters to friends back home. There's even a scratchy 1919 recording of Harry T. Burleigh, an African-American musician, singing the spiritual "Go Down, Moses." Burleigh performed the song for Dvořák, inspiring the composer to include musical references to spirituals in the *New World*. For more information on common features of the *CD Companion* series, see the review of *Ludwig van Beethoven, Symphony No. 9* in this section.

A GERMAN REQUIEM
★★★½
Developer: Time Warner Interactive; 800-482-3766
Format: Macintosh
Price: $49

"Blessed are they, they that mourn, for they shall be comforted." Those solemn words begin the mightiest choral work of Johannes Brahms, a piece known as his *German Requiem*. This CD-ROM in the *Audio Notes* series presents the entire seventy-minute work, performed by the Atlanta Symphony Orchestra and Chorus, on two disks. The ability of CD-ROMs to play music and display text simultaneously is put to particularly good use here—you can click the mouse to choose between a commentary on the work, the choral lyrics in their original German, or the lyrics translated into English.

A German Requiem also presents extensive supplementary text covering the rise of romanticism in nineteenth century classical music, exemplified by Brahms, and a biography of the composer, as well as three musical quiz games. The text comes alive with numerous musical samples; you learn the difference between musical forms, for example, by hearing a few bars of "My Country 'Tis of Thee" played in the Baroque, Classical, and Romantic styles. For a description of the *Audio Notes* series, see the review of *The Orchestra* in this section.

ALL MY HUMMINGBIRDS HAVE ALIBIS
★★
Developer: Voyager Co.; 800-446-2001
Format: Macintosh
Price: $29

All My Hummingbirds Have Alibis flew right over my head. The CD-ROM presents two works by ultramodern composer Morton Subotnick, who combines musical instruments and voices with computer-generated music and sounds. Subotnick draws his inspiration, and the offbeat title, from the works of surrealist Max Ernst, who created deliberately obscure drawings in Paris during the 1930s.

The two performances—the title piece and a work called *Five Scenes from an Imaginary Ballet*—are constantly jumping from brief snatches of recognizable music to mechanical buzzing to male or female voices reciting pseudoprofound quotes, such as "My hand has touched clouds," from Ernst's writings. The title comes from this incomprehensible line: "All my hummingbirds have alibis, and a hundred profound virtues covered my body." On the screen, you see Ernst's black-and-white drawings, which have the look of nineteenth century woodcuts. If you want to try to understand what all this means, you can call up a commentary by Subotnick that accompanies the music or turn to several essays on the composer and his process for creating electronic music. But unless you're strongly attracted to avant-garde culture, I'd find an alibi to get away from this CD-ROM.

LEARN TO PLAY GUITAR
★★
Developer: Cambrix Publishing Inc.; 800-992-8781
Format: Windows
Price: $19

Angry adolescents eager to push their parents over the edge with high-volume guitar solos will be disappointed with *Learn to Play Guitar*. The CD-ROM claims to provide a complete course on playing heavy-metal electric guitar in eleven easy lessons. But while there's plenty of good introductory material on the disk, *Learn to Play Guitar* also leaves huge gaps in explaining basic concepts.

The CD-ROM was created by and stars Cristof Flandres, a twenty-something Seattle studio musician and guitar teacher who looks and talks like a grunge rocker but tosses around technical terms like a college professor. I have no idea why he's trying to tell me about the "Aeolian modal position," and I'm not convinced I should care. Flandres, who appears in video clips constantly shaking his chest-length black hair off his forehead, is not above an occasional flash of humor expressed in fractured adolescent English, such as this description of an electric guitar's on/off switch: "This switch is pretty self-explanatory. On is on, and off is off. If you run into any problems with this particular switch, chances are you're not going to do so good with the rest of this tutorial."

The lessons explain key concepts in a careful progression, starting with a diagram identifying the various parts of a guitar and a confusingly brief explanation of installing and tuning strings. The confusion gets more intense in later lessons; as a nonmusician, I was quickly lost when Flandres neglected to explain important concepts such as "sharp" and "flat." Complicated chords and key changes are introduced with little more than a thirty-second video pep talk from Flandres. "OK, well, we've made it to the 10th lesson," he says toward the end of the disk. "And in this lesson, we're going to be learning how to transpose keys. Unfortunately, many people have died trying to learn the information from this lesson, so keep a positive attitude." Too late. My attitude had already snapped like an overstretched E string.

Learn to Play Guitar needs an extensive tune-up. An improved version would offer the text of a basic guitar instruction book, along with a comprehensive glossary. Until then, *Learn to Play Guitar* might be useful as a tool for guitar students committed to the old-fashioned approach of learning from a human. There are several useful features for practicing, such as a metronome to help with pacing and on-screen diagrams of chords accompanied by audio of the appropriate notes.

WOLFGANG AMADEUS MOZART: THE "DISSONANT" QUARTET
★★★★
Developer: Voyager Co.; 800-446-2001
Format: Macintosh
Price: $39

Unlike larger orchestral works, explains commentator Robert Winter, "chamber music is a far more intimate and personal affair. Each performer shoulders the entire responsibility for her or his part of the musical conversation." Winter, a classical pianist and music professor at the University of California–Los Angeles, makes even novice listeners a part of that conversation in this selection from Voyager Company's outstanding *CD Companion* series.

Built around a twenty-eight-minute performance by the Los Angeles String Quartet of Mozart's "Dissonant" Quartet, Winter takes the listener step by step through the performance and also contributes three long essays: "The Instruments," explaining the separate roles played by the violin, viola, and cello; "Mozart's World," a biography with audio narration by the author; and "Quartet Listening," delving into the history and structure of chamber music.

For more information on common features of the *CD Companions*, see the review of *Ludwig van Beethoven: Symphony No. 9* in this section.

MICROSOFT MULTIMEDIA BEETHOVEN: THE NINTH SYMPHONY
★★★★
Developer: Microsoft Corp.; 800-426-9400
Format: Windows
Price: $59

Adaptation for Windows by Microsoft Corporation of an entry in Voyager Company's Macintosh-only *CD Companion* series. See the review of *Ludwig van Beethoven: Symphony No. 9* in this section.

MICROSOFT MULTIMEDIA MOZART: THE "DISSONANT" QUARTET
★★★★
Developer: Microsoft Corp.; 800-426-9400
Format: Windows
Price: $59

Adaptation for Windows by Microsoft Corporation of an entry in Voyager Company's Macintosh-only *CD Companion* series. See the review of *Wolfgang Amadeus Mozart: The "Dissonant" Quartet* in this section.

MICROSOFT MULTIMEDIA SCHUBERT: THE "TROUT" QUINTET
★★★★
Developer: Microsoft Corp.; 800-426-9400
Format: Windows
Price: $59

Adaptation for Windows by Microsoft Corporation of an entry in Voyager Company's Macintosh-only *CD Companion* series. See the review of *Franz Schubert: The "Trout" Quintet* in this section. A footnote: Microsoft's version does not include "The Trout Cookbook," a collection of ten recipes found on Voyager's CD-ROM.

MULTIMEDIA SONGBOOK
★½
Developer: Midisoft Corp.; 800-776-6436
Format: Windows
Price: $29

Delivering much less than it promises, *Multimedia Songbook* is a muddled hybrid of a sing-along program and music education software. You get a library of 190 songs divided into seven categories: holiday favorites, kids' songs, classical, jazz, rock and pop, around the world, and inspirational. Clicking on the name of a song from the main menu, you see the musical notes and the lyrics in side-by-side windows. There is a mixer that lets you change the volume of the various instruments playing the song and a feature called "The Noodler" that lets you add a few notes of your own by tapping on the keyboard. Midisoft Corporation has thrown in some text and a picture gallery of musical instruments, separate from the songs, from its other CD-ROM title, the equally unappealing *Music Men-*

tor Maestro Edition, reviewed in this section. I expect anyone unlucky enough to buy *Multimedia Songbook* will spend about half an hour fiddling around, listening to "Jingle Bells" without the bells or creating a bassoon-solo version of "God Save the Queen," get bored, and never play with it again.

MICROSOFT MULTIMEDIA STRAUSS: THREE TONE POEMS
★★★★
Developer: Microsoft Corp.; 800-426-9400
Format: Windows
Price: $59

Adaptation for Windows by Microsoft Corporation of an entry in Voyager Company's Macintosh-only *CD Companion* series. See the review of *Richard Strauss: Three Tone Poems* in this section.

MICROSOFT MULTIMEDIA STRAVINSKY: THE RITE OF SPRING
★★★★
Developer: Microsoft Corp.; 800-426-9400
Format: Windows
Price: $59

Adaptation for Windows by Microsoft Corporation of an entry in Voyager Company's Macintosh-only *CD Companion* series. See the review of *Igor Stravinsky: The Rite of Spring* in this section.

MICROSOFT MUSICAL INSTRUMENTS
★★$^{1}/_{2}$
Developer: Microsoft Corp.; 800-426-9400
Format: Windows, Macintosh
Price: $59

Judging by looks alone, *Microsoft Musical Instruments* should be a winner. A reference guide covering two hundred instruments, the CD-ROM displays beautifully rendered photographic images accessed through easy point-and-click navigation. The parts of each instrument are carefully labeled, and some of the instruments even have a "sound box" feature that lets you pick out a few notes.

But looks alone aren't enough—*Musical Instruments* falls short in delivering information. Most of the descriptions accompanying the pretty pictures are only two or three sentences. Here's the full entry on the French horn: "The French horn is a brass instrument built in a circle, with a large bell that is held down by the player's side. Its rich, velvety sound is heard mostly in orchestras and bands. The French horn first came into the orchestra in pairs to portray the sound of hunting horns but is now used in music of all sorts." You can listen to an excerpt of a French horn performing, but all you get is thirty seconds of music. There's also a baseball-card-like fact box, although it gives little more than the instrument's dimensions, musical range, and a one-sentence history.

Microsoft deserves credit for casting such a broad net with *Musical Instruments*; the disk contains entries from around the world, such as the kalanga double-headed drum of West Africa and the angklung sliding bamboo rattle of Indonesia. But despite the elegant graphics and nod to cultural diversity, *Musical Instruments* only skims the surface of its fascinating subject matter.

MUSICMENTOR MAESTRO EDITION
★½
Developer: Midisoft Corp.; 800-776-6436
Format: Windows
Price: $39

MusicMentor Maestro Edition is a well-intentioned mess. Midisoft Corporation, a developer of music notation software for the professional market, doesn't have a clue when it comes to creating CD-ROMs for the home market. Covering such diverse subjects as how to read musical notes and the history of classical music, *MusicMentor* tries to do everything and ends up accomplishing nothing.

The CD-ROM is divided into three almost completely unrelated segments. A section called "Basics" is a confused effort to teach musical notes and music theory with only a few hundred paragraphs of text and lots of short music clips. Music neophytes will quickly get in over their heads, as *MusicMentor* starts tossing around terms like "dodecaphonic octaves," "compound time signatures," "polyphonic texture," and "half-diminished seventh chords" with minimal explanation.

A section called "History" presents a time line that attempts to describe the changes in both music and society since the Middle Ages, as well as profiling famous composers from each era. But the text is so thin—only a few paragraphs on each subject—that you'll barely dip your toe in the ocean of musical history. The History section is also linked to a gallery giving brief descriptions of musical instruments. Here, for reasons I can't figure, *MusicMentor* shifts from a very serious tone to sophomoric humor. The description of the tenor saxophone, for example, ends with the comment: "If you are into honking, the tenor variety will suit you nicely and your neighbors poorly." The developers even invented a fictitious instrument called the "fargblat" that looks like two French horns welded together. In a transparent gesture to appeal to disaffected adolescents, there are also short biographies of twelve contemporary performers from Duke Ellington to Dr. Dre and Madonna.

A section called "Fun Stuff" presents an on-screen keyboard called "The Noodler" in which you can pick out tunes in different musical styles and a pointless feature called "Concert Hall" that plays a collection of nine prerecorded songs. There's also an annoying feature called "The Quiz Wizard" that randomly interrupts what you're doing with multiple-choice trivia questions. Fortunately, you can turn off The Quiz Wizard. Even more fortunately, you can skip *MusicMentor* altogether.

THE ORCHESTRA
★★★½

Developer: Time Warner Interactive; 800-482-3766
Format: Macintosh
Price: $59

Composer Benjamin Britten wrote a sixteen-minute piece called *The Young Person's Guide to the Orchestra* in 1945 as a learning tool, a way of putting all the instruments through their paces. But it's also a surprisingly good piece of music, full of interesting twists and turns, and deserves attention from audiences of any age.

The Orchestra on CD-ROM takes the Britten piece, conducted by the composer with the London Symphony Orchestra, as the jumping-off point for studying the history and structure of orchestral music. Part of the *Audio Notes* series described below, the CD-ROM contains two separate text commentaries that can be viewed as the music plays. In addition, *The Orchestra* includes text essays on Britten's life, conducting, the evolution of the orchestra, a guide to individual orchestral instruments, and a somewhat tongue-in-cheek history of classical music called "Europe Before the Walkman." Today, the history concludes, is "the Walkman era ... characterized by loud, raucous music listened to by one person at a time, which has led some to call this the Age of Musical Solitude." The essays are complemented by fifty-three music clips from the works of other composers. You can learn the meaning of the word "tempo," for example, by hearing the same passage of Beethoven's Symphony No. 7 performed quickly by conductor Christoph von Dohnányi or slowly by conductor Joseph Keilberth. The disk also includes three music trivia games.

About the *Audio Notes* series: Time Warner Interactive, then known as Warner New Media, released three *Audio Notes* titles in 1990 and 1991. The three are similar to the *CD Companion* series from Voyager Company, reviewed in this section, in exploring a piece of music through a running text commentary that you view while listening to the performance. Both series offer half-screen black-and-white graphics, which might disappoint some users expecting the bright colors and animations of more recent CD-ROMs. But this is such a powerful way to learn about music that it's worth tolerating out-of-date graphics. Although both series are top-notch, I give the edge to the *CD Companions* because the text is slightly more authoritative. The other two *Audio Notes* titles—*A German Requiem* and *The String Quartet*—are reviewed in this section.

FRANZ SCHUBERT: THE "TROUT" QUINTET
★★★★
Developer: Voyager Co.; 800-446-2001
Format: Macintosh
Price: $39

Back in junior high school, I vaguely recall learning that Franz Schubert died young. What my teachers neglected to tell me was that Schubert, only thirty-one at his death in 1828, suffered from a debilitating case of syphilis for the last six years of his life. This CD-ROM from Voyager Company's outstanding *CD Companion* series doesn't shy away from telling the whole story of the brilliant Viennese composer who gave the world hundreds of beautiful works in only a few years.

Perhaps the most beautiful of all, The "Trout" Quintet, is featured on this disk with commentary by Alan Rich, a classical music writer and frequent contributor to National Public Radio.

Here is a sample of Rich's enthusiastic description of the opening of The "Trout": "We hear the music as a conversation between the two parts of the theme; the one assertive, the other wavering. Hotter and hotter, higher and higher, Schubert's two-headed tune repeats yet again, with violin swooping up to squeals of pure delight, to punctuate the start of each phrase."

The thirty-eight-minute performance by the Alban Berg Quartet is flawless. The disk even contains a performance of the song "Die Forelle," German for "The Trout," written by Schubert two years before he composed the quintet in 1819. Schubert buffs can read the song's lyrics in German or English, following the story of "a happy fish" caught by a wily angler. Rich also contributes two extensive essays: "Inside Schubert," a biography, and "A Classical Background," which explores the musical history that preceded Schubert. Both essays are packed with on-screen buttons that play brief musical clips illuminating the text. Music students will appreciate the bibliography and glossary, while gourmets will enjoy "The Trout Cookbook," a collection of ten recipes that replaces the multiple-choice quiz found elsewhere in the *CD Companion* series.

For more information on common features of the *CD Companions*, see the review of *Ludwig van Beethoven: Symphony No. 9* in this section.

RICHARD STRAUSS: THREE TONE POEMS
★★★★
Developer: Voyager Co.; 800-446-2001
Format: Macintosh
Price: $39

Richard Strauss, a master of late-nineteenth-century romanticism, never received the adulation accorded Mozart, Beethoven, or Brahms. But Strauss's musical legacy touches us every day because his style survives in much of the theme music created for movies and television. Indeed, the three Strauss tone poems presented on this entry in the outstanding *CD Companion* series from Voyager Company all sound somewhat like the score of a 1940s Hollywood epic.

Russell Steinberg, himself a film-score composer and music instructor at the University of California–Los Angeles, presents a commentary exploring this unacknowledged homage: "Even if

Strauss's own music is not used, his musical influence is readily apparent in countless film and television scores. In fact, many film music giants were steeped in the works of Strauss. Their thickly doubled melodies, energetic rhythmic gestures, powerful brass writing and virtuoso string parts are clear references to Strauss. These techniques have become standard clichés in movie scores."

The three tone poems—*Don Juan, Death and Transfiguration* and *Till Eulenspiegel*—together run fifty-four minutes in a performance by the Cleveland Orchestra. Steinberg points out, by offering comparative musical clips, how ideas from these Strauss compositions, written from 1888 to 1895, evolved into the Tara theme from *Gone With the Wind* and the main theme for the *Superman* movies. Steinberg's commentary, along with four separate essays, covers Strauss's life and times as well as the structure of his music.

For more information on common features of the *CD Companions*, see the review of *Ludwig van Beethoven: Symphony No. 9* in this section.

IGOR STRAVINSKY: THE RITE OF SPRING
★★★★
Developer: Voyager Co.; 800-446-2001
Format: Macintosh
Price: $45

Even the most musically ignorant among us will instantly recognize the pounding kettledrums in Igor Stravinsky's *The Rite of Spring* as the theme music for the dinosaur sequence in Walt Disney's 1940 animated classic *Fantasia*. This CD-ROM, part of the outstanding *CD Companion* series from Voyager Company, presents Stravinsky's own view of his work, which has much more to do with Russian folklore than rampaging tyrannosaurs.

Built around a thirty-five-minute performance by the Orchestre symphonique de Montreal, the disk is anchored by the polished prose of Robert Winter, a classical pianist and music professor at the University of California–Los Angeles. Here is Winter's commentary on *The Rite of Spring*'s deceptively quiet opening: "A lone bassoon intones a plaintive melody that evokes dreamlike memories of a primordial past. [Then] the clarinet and bass clarinet offer a slithering accompaniment that glides to a pause. Stravinsky's listeners had never heard such exotic sounds in the concert hall—and few in the audience could have had an inkling of what was to come in the minutes ahead."

Winter also provides three long essays—"Stravinsky's World," a biography; "The Rite as Dance," which describes the ballet that originally accompanied the premiere performance in 1913; and "Rite Listening," which illustrates the structure of Stravinsky's music.

For more information on common features of all the *CD Companions*, see the review of *Ludwig van Beethoven: Symphony No. 9* in this section.

THE STRING QUARTET
★★★½
Developer: Time Warner Interactive; 800-482-3766
Format: Macintosh
Price: $49

Classical music often alienates first-time listeners because it appears difficult to understand, as if we somehow need training to enjoy the work of Beethoven, Mozart, or Haydn. *The String Quartet*, a title in the *Audio Notes* series, works to deflate this musical snobbery. "Ask yourself how the music is making you feel," the commentary says as you listen to a slow passage in Beethoven's String Quartet No. 14, performed by the Vermeer Quartet. "Some people find this movement wistful and sad; some think it is poignant. In any event, the question of emotion in music is completely subjective, with no 'right' answer."

The thirty-nine-minute performance of Beethoven's quartet is accompanied by two separate text commentaries, which you can easily switch between. There are also supplemental essays giving a basic overview of music, a history of chamber music, and a biography of Beethoven, along with three trivia games. For a description of the *Audio Notes* series, see the review of *The Orchestra* in this section.

THE VIKING OPERA GUIDE
★★★
Developer: Penguin USA; 800-526-0275
Format: Windows
Price: $99

From the first true opera—*Orfeo* by Claudio Monteverdi, performed in Italy in 1600—through contemporary composers including Marvin Hamlisch, famous for the Broadway show *A Chorus Line*, *The Viking Opera Guide* is a comprehensive encyclopedia with short biographies of 845 composers and descriptions of 1,500 operas. The book, published by Penguin in 1993, fills 1,300 pages. The CD-ROM, released in 1994, goes a step further by adding 134 audio clips of operatic performances. Opera buffs will delight in the broad span of history covered by the book and disk, although they may be disappointed with the CD-ROM's truncated musical excerpts—most of the clips run only a minute or two.

The CD-ROM, which contains all the book's text and photographs, adds a narrated introduction by Nicholas Kenyon, an opera commentator for the British Broadcasting Corporation and a coauthor of the book. Here is Kenyon's view on the current state of opera: "In the 1960s, Pierre Boulez thought that we should blow up our opera houses. But increasingly, opera and opera houses are now back in fashion as the place where our most adventurous musical minds do their thinking. Philip Glass brought minimalism to opera in *Einstein on the Beach* and *Akhnaten*. John Adams' *Nixon in China* gives that minimalism a human face, with expressive melodies and real characterizations. New operas large and small are now created in their hundreds, from taut little music-theater pieces by Peter Maxwell Davies to extravaganzas for the Met in New York by John Corigliano. Not all succeed, not all travel or transplant well. But they bear witness to the continual fascination of composers with this most challenging of musical media."

The Viking Opera Guide on CD-ROM is easy to navigate, with a complete index as well as a composers time line, maps showing the location of opera houses, and a search feature that will comb through the text for specific words. Newcomers to opera might be frustrated, however, that the *Guide* doesn't go further—there are no entries on famous performers, so you won't learn anything about Luciano Pavarotti or Enrico Caruso and no explanation of how operas are written and staged.

e. Music—Contemporary

THE RESIDENTS' FREAK SHOW
★★★★
Developer: Voyager Co.; 800-446-2001
Format: Macintosh
Price: $39

The Residents' Freak Show is a masterpiece, an eye-popping performance that combines music, art, and storytelling in a totally new way, defining the very best of what CD-ROM can accomplish. This mind-bending experience comes from The Residents, a San Francisco cult rock band whose members have never revealed their true identities in a twenty-two-year career. Instead, they hide behind giant eyeball masks on stage and perform haunting, mysterious music that is anything but mainstream. *Freak Show* transports you to The Residents' strange world, taking you inside a large red tent where a traveling troupe of human curiosities are about to appear.

Maneuvering with the mouse, you watch performances by Wanda, a grossly overweight woman who eats worms; Jelly Jack, a Silly Putty–like blob with eyeballs; Harry the Head, who is nothing but a head and is now dead; Bouncy Benny the Bump, who displays a strange mass of flesh dangling from his chest; Mickey the Mumbling Midget, actually a shaved baboon; and Herman the Human Mole, who lives in a trailer filled with dirt and is visible only through tiny portholes. The characters are depicted in strikingly realistic animations that blur the line between photographs and cartoons.

Tex the Barker, inexplicably speaking in a heavy German accent, introduces all the acts. At the far side of the tent is "Pickled Punks," a gallery displaying vintage black-and-white photographs of circus freaks from the early 1800s through the end of the sideshow era in the 1950s. It's more than a little politically incorrect to gawk at such long-gone real-life characters as the Flip the Frog Boy and Grace Daniels, the Mule-Faced Woman, but there's also an undeniable fascination in these strangely disfigured people.

The Residents apparently feel their obsession with freaks deserves some explanation, which they deliver in a printed booklet accompanying the CD-ROM. "These career performers took pride, and often wealth and fame, from their uniqueness," the booklet explains. "They viewed the outsider—you and me—in contempt for our naiveté and drabness. They may have been the 'freaks,' but we were the 'suckers,' and that was much worse."

Freak Show doesn't really begin until you push past the "No Admittance" sign to go backstage and explore each character's personal trailer. (A hint: Click on the sign three times, ignoring Tex's warnings.) Inside Wanda's trailer, for example, you find a box of letters telling her sad life story. Once a beautiful young nun, Wanda fell into a tragic and unconsummated love affair with a priest. You'll even learn how she became fascinated with worms. The Residents' trailer offers eight of their music videos and a selection of items from their "Buy or Die!" catalog.

Unlike several other rock music CD-ROMs, *Freak Show* doesn't force you to solve any unnecessary puzzles or waste time searching for hidden clues. You're free to wander through the tent and the trailers, finding bits and pieces of the story at your own pace. Of course, *Freak Show* isn't for everyone. The disk is absolutely not for children and may offend any number of special interest groups. But *Freak Show* will stand out as great art and great fun for those who can appreciate The Residents' dark and twisted slant on life.

THE RESIDENTS' GINGERBREAD MAN
★★★
Developer: Ion; 415-455-5939
Format: Windows-2, Macintosh-2
Price: $39

It's hard to imagine a CD-ROM weirder than *The Residents' Freak Show*, a wonderful combination of music and bizarre storytelling reviewed in this section. But the mysterious San Francisco rock group pulled it off with its second CD-ROM, *The Residents' Gingerbread Man*, released in late 1994 about ten months after *Freak Show*. There is nothing predictable and almost nothing comprehensible in *Gingerbread Man*, nor is there a clear unifying theme such as the *Freak Show* carnival acts.

Followers of The Residents will almost surely like *Gingerbread Man*, feasting on the CD-ROM's haunting music and strange artistic images. But I'd strongly recommend anyone not already familiar with The Residents start with *Freak Show* and move to *Gingerbread Man* only if the first CD-ROM strikes a chord.

Gingerbread Man doubles as an audio CD with thirty-seven minutes of The Residents' music, which can be played on a regular stereo system. The disk holds nine songs, each telling the story of a different character: "The Weaver," "The Dying Oilman," "The Confused Transsexual," "The Sold-Out Artist," "The Ascetic," "The Old Soldier," "The Aging Musician," "The Butcher," and "The Old Woman." The characters speak their inner thoughts in a seemingly random monologue during the songs; you have to listen closely, and probably more than once, to pick up the threads of a story.

Playing the disk on a computer takes *Gingerbread Man* into another dimension. The songs become animated performances. The face of each character appears on-screen as the music plays. Following a map in the instruction manual, you hit letters on the keyboard to alter the images and uncover bits of the character's story. The Weaver, for instance, is apparently trying to forget a murder she once witnessed. I'm still not sure why the Butcher is so angry. I pressed one key and heard him say, "All I saw were eels . . . Eels, squirming everywhere." I pressed another key and the words "Damn, this knife is dull!" popped out of his head onto the screen. The Aging Musician ponders suicide, saying, "Maybe if I put a bullet in my brain, I'd be remembered like Kurt Cobain."

The many elements in these scenes are shuffled around every time you enter the world of *Gingerbread Man*. You never feel completely in control or completely sure of what you're doing when you press a key or click with the mouse. *Freak Show*, in contrast, offered several havens in which things were relatively normal, such as a gallery of real-life freak-show photographs and a selection of video clips tracing The Residents' career. *Gingerbread Man* doesn't give you an easy link to reality; you have to create your own logic for this upside-down experience.

JAZZ: A MULTIMEDIA HISTORY
★★½
Developer: Compton's NewMedia Inc.; 800-284-2045
Format: Windows, Macintosh
Price: $29

A college textbook on CD-ROM is still a college textbook. *Jazz: A Multimedia History* consists mostly of the text and black-and-white photographs found in *Jazz: From the Origins to the Present,* a textbook published in 1993 by Prentice-Hall. The multimedia additions to the CD-ROM are minimal—six brief video clips of historic jazz performances and a selection of 120 one-minute synthesizer renditions of key passages from jazz classics.

The text traces the history of jazz from its coalescence in turn-of-the-century New Orleans, heavily influenced by the earlier musical styles of ragtime and the blues, through avant-garde experimentation in the 1990s. As you'd expect with a textbook, the prose is dry and academic and also presupposes a technical understanding of music. Consider this passage from the Listening to Jazz section: "Probably the single most useful skill for a jazz listener to work on is to be able to identify the underlying form of the improvisation one is hearing. Most pieces played by jazz musicians either have the form of popular songs with an easily identifiable structure or they are based on the blues. A song chorus with its chord progression most frequently occupies thirty-two measures in 4/4 meter." I've listened to—and enjoyed—jazz for years without worrying about chord progressions or 4/4 meter.

Jazz: A Multimedia History is also agonizing to read. The text is displayed in a small window on the screen, requiring constant scrolling. The music clips are one-note renditions, useful for music students but lifeless to the casual listener. While the video clips are interesting—with a 1933 performance by Louis Armstrong and a 1957 television appearance by Billie Holiday—the images are displayed in a postage-stamp-size window. Serious music students might find this CD-ROM a valuable study tool, but jazz novices should search for a more inviting doorway into the compelling world of jazz.

JUMP: THE DAVID BOWIE INTERACTIVE CD-ROM
★★½
Developer: Ion; 415-455-5939
Format: Windows, Macintosh
Price: $39

David Bowie is an artistic enigma, a man who lurks behind many masks. Since bursting on the music scene in 1970, he's gone from the androgynous glitter-rock persona Ziggy Stardust to a starring role in *The Elephant Man* on Broadway. *Jump: The David Bowie Interactive CD-ROM* doesn't really take you behind the masks because Bowie doesn't really open up in the brief interview included on the disk.

Jump at least looks good and sounds good. The graphics are elegant, with near-TV-quality video clips and music tracks almost matching the sound of an audio CD. After watching the opening credits, you enter an elevator and walk down the corridors of a gray office building matching the set for the music video *Jump They Say* from Bowie's recent album *Black Tie, White Noise*. You are then given a choice of entering three rooms: the David Bowie Suite, Room 2901, or the Video Suite.

Inside the David Bowie Suite is an office with desk, filing cabinet, and chair. By clicking a camera sitting on the desk, you hear a ten-minute audio interview with shallow off-the-cuff commentary from Bowie, illustrated with photographs from a recording session. Clicking a briefcase on the floor launches an equally unsatisfying ten-minute video interview.

Room 2901 contains a telescope. Looking through the telescope, you enter rooms in a hotel across the street to watch four music videos: *Jump They Say*; *Black Tie, White Noise*; *Miracle Goodnight*; and *You've Been Around*. Inexplicably, the hotel rooms contain little hidden surprises that seem to have wandered onto the disk from some children's game—click on a dog, for example, and it barks; click on a bowling trophy, and a bowling ball rolls across the floor.

The Video Suite puts you at the controls of a video editing machine where you create a customized version of *Jump They Say*. The creativity is strictly limited, however, to selecting which one of five video tracks to display on the main screen. You can also sit down in front of an audio mixer and experiment with the song "Black Tie, White Noise" by raising and lowering the volume of vocal and instrumental tracks. "Don't be passive; be interactive," declares the *Jump* box. "The future of music is here—and it's in your hands." Maybe, maybe not. I want to lose myself inside the music, but I'm far from convinced we're all eagerly waiting for a chance to rearrange the work of our favorite artists.

NO WORLD ORDER
★★

Developer: Electronic Arts Inc.; 800-245-4525
Format: Macintosh
Price: $45

Todd Rundgren hit the rock-and-roll charts twenty-five years ago with the single "Hello, It's Me." He then made an interesting and possibly unique career transition into computer programming, creating some of the first color graphics software for the Macintosh. Today, Rundgren is seen more frequently at technology conferences pushing the concept of "interactive music" than on the concert stage. *No World Order* is his first effort at creating interactive music, where the listener can change the sound. True to its name, the CD-ROM provides no order or structure for easily accomplishing Rundgren's ambitious goals.

According to Rundgren, *No World Order* contains one thousand "digital audio musical events"—short snippets of music—that can be arranged in almost infinite combinations. But the on-screen controls for rearranging the music are so convoluted that even Rundgren fans will quickly retreat to the old-fashioned world of prerecorded songs that don't change from beginning to end.

No World Order is controlled through "The Editor Screen," a bewildering combination of buttons that isn't clearly explained in the tiny instruction manual or by an audio help feature on the CD-ROM. The music can be altered by playing with seven buttons called "flavors." The "direction" flavor button, for instance, determines whether the songs play forward or backward, while the "tempo" button controls the number of beats per minute.

Rundgren deserves credit for pursuing such innovative ideas. Each of the ten songs in *No World Order* has been arranged by Rundgren and then rearranged by four other record producers—Don Was, Jerry Harrison, Hal Wilmer, and Bob Clearmountain. Listeners can switch from hearing how Rundgren plays his compositions to a version by any of the other four. The style, too, is adjustable, allowing a shift from "conservative" to "creative" or changing the mood from "bright" to "thoughtful." These features would be worth exploring on a different CD-ROM on which users weren't left wondering how to make everything work.

"PRINCE" INTERACTIVE
★★½
Developer: Graphix Zone; 714-833-3838
Format: Windows-2, Macintosh-2
Price: $49

In June 1993, the rock star Prince stunned the music industry by committing what appeared to be career suicide: He changed his name to an unpronounceable symbol resembling the combination of a circle, an arrow, and a trumpet. His unfortunate publicity people must now refer to him as "the artist formerly known as Prince." I'll just call him Ex-Prince. Ex-Prince's name change isn't the first big demand he has made of his fans—his immense musical talent, and even more immense ego, has been channeled into increasingly obscure, noncommercial music. His CD-ROM, which I'm going to refer to as *"Prince" Interactive*, is a perfect reflection of its self-indulgent subject, technically demanding and allowing Ex-Prince's vanity to overwhelm his artistry.

The technical demands are daunting. *"Prince" Interactive*, which runs on either a Windows-equipped PC or a Macintosh, requires a level of hardware far beyond what most of us have at home. For Windows, that includes a double-speed CD-ROM drive, fifteen megabytes of space on a hard disk, four megabytes of RAM (although eight megabytes is recommended), a sixteen-bit sound card, and a high-resolution monitor capable of supporting sixteen-bit color. For Macintosh, the specs include a double-speed CD-ROM drive, eight megabytes of RAM, ten megabytes of hard disk space, and a monitor equipped to display thousands of colors.

If you have sufficient computing horsepower, you'll be transported to a nameless structure built in the shape of Ex-Prince's new name. Your mission is to find five "jewel pieces" hidden throughout the building that together form the key to access a hidden bonus: a video of Ex-Prince singing an unreleased song called "Endorphinemachine." The interior is full of beautifully rendered photorealistic images, although the artistic effort has been wasted on tacky scenes—much of the building looks like an overdone Las Vegas hotel penthouse, with black marble columns and gold trim surrounding vaguely obscene Kama Sutra frescoes on the walls. Ex-Prince is everywhere, with photos and tour posters filling every nook and cranny. Scantily clad young women from his music videos pop up occasionally to coquettishly spout vague dialogue such as "Welcome to the dawn, playground for the power generation" and "The shortest distance between the here and the beyond is to play."

As you explore the various rooms, you stumble across audio and video clips of Ex-Prince's music. Most of them are frustratingly brief—six videos in the "Music Club" run only thirty to ninety seconds each, and the images, although very sharp, fill only a postage-stamp-size window on the screen. The audio clip of my favorite Ex-Prince song, "Little Red Corvette," is just forty-five seconds. In the "Studio," you get a chance to play with the volume on five sound tracks in one Ex-Prince song. In the "Boudoir," you can recline on Ex-Prince's circular bed and lower yourself into the "Love Pit," a private chamber with a few surprises.

But the many puzzles are annoying and pointless. What does figuring out the combination to a safe or sorting through playing cards have to do with Ex-Prince? And why should we have to solve puzzles to experience his music? The closest *"Prince" Interactive* comes to an answer is a brief video clip of Eric Clapton, who delivers a very insightful comment: "You never seem to get a middle ground with this guy. There's no one I've ever met that can say, 'He's just Okay.' You either hate him or you love him." If you love Ex-Prince's music and don't mind his growing sense of self-importance, you might enjoy *"Prince" Interactive*. But the rest of us will succeed in finding a middle ground: boredom. Finally, parents should be warned that although *"Prince" Interactive* doesn't include any nudity or obscene language, many of Ex-Prince's songs are explicitly sexual.

MEGA ROCK RAP 'N ROLL
★★½
Developer: Viacom New Media; 800-469-2539
Format: Windows, Macintosh
Price: $29

A do-it-yourself recording studio for the musically uneducated, *Mega Rock Rap 'N Roll* is lots of fun for only a little while. The CD-ROM lets you create one-minute songs in ten musical styles by controlling a prepackaged collection of audio clips. You can even plug a microphone into the computer and record your own voice, a step up from singing in the shower.

In the main menu screen of *Rock Rap 'N Roll*, you pick one of ten music styles for your composition: African, big band, blues,

Latin, rap, reggae, rock sampler, soulful sampler, street jazz, or techno-pop. Then you go to an on-screen studio. A list of ten "song loops" runs down the left side of the screen, bare-bones instrumental music clips each running five to ten seconds. Along the bottom of the screen is the "Song-A-Lizer," which allows you to arrange the song loops in any order you choose. Above the Song-A-Lizer are the "Vibe-A-Tron," "Bop-O-Rama," and "Voc-a-lizer," which add instrumental sounds and snippets of vocals every time you click the mouse. While playing a rock number, for example, you can click the Vibe-A-Tron in time with the music to add the sound of a fuzz guitar or cowbell, then hit the Voc-a-lizer buttons to hear a woman sing, "Yeah, yeah, yeah" or "C'mon, baby."

Playing around with all these musical bits and pieces is fun for about half an hour. But then *Rock Rap 'N Roll* gets stale. The CD-ROM doesn't teach you anything about music and offers no new avenues to explore once you've tried all ten musical styles.

VID GRID
★★½

Developer: Jasmine Multimedia Publishing Inc.; 800-798-7535
Format: Windows-2
Price: $29

Vid Grid is MTV with a gimmick. The CD-ROM contains nine complete music videos, divided up into jumbled squares that you must rearrange, creating something the developers call "the Rubik's Cube of rock 'n' roll." As the videos play on screen, you have to point and click with the mouse to solve the puzzle. The more time you spend playing *Vid Grid*, the more difficult the puzzles get.

If nothing else, the CD-ROM delivers a lot of music from top-name bands: "Cryin'" by Aerosmith, "Sledgehammer" by Peter Gabriel, "November Rain" by Guns N' Roses, "Are You Experienced?" by Jimi Hendrix, "Enter Sandman" by Metallica, "No More Tears" by Ozzy Osbourne, "Give It Away" by the Red Hot Chili Peppers, "Spoonman" by Soundgarden and "Right Now" by Van Halen. The images are sharp and clean, filling one fourth of the screen, and the sound quality is adequate, although it doesn't match audio CDs.

The puzzles are surprisingly difficult. You start with a three by three grid of nine pieces. But because the images in rock videos are constantly changing, it's much more difficult to figure out where to put the pieces than it is with a regular jigsaw puzzle. The grid grows to sixteen, twenty-five, and thirty-six pieces; the puzzles get even more confusing when some of the pieces are inverted, so bits of the image are right-side-up and others upside-down. If you like working jigsaw puzzles and rock music, you'll have to watch each of the videos more than once to master the game. Nongamers, though, will get bored with sliding squares around the screen and will just click the "Solve" button to watch the videos without interruption.

WOODSTOCK: THE 25TH ANNIVERSARY CD-ROM
★★★½
Developer: Time Warner Interactive; 800-482-3766
Format: Windows-2, Macintosh-2
Price: $45

"There was a time there during the festival when it seemed like music could right a lot of wrongs in the world," says rock musician Levon Helm, reminiscing a quarter century after the three-day Woodstock concert became a symbol for the 1960s. Helm's words, along with a wonderful selection of music, photographs, and video clips, are captured on *Woodstock: The 25th Anniversary CD-ROM*, released just before the twenty-fifth anniversary of the August 1969 festival.

The CD-ROM opens with the haunting song "Woodstock" from Crosby, Stills and Nash, a bittersweet ode to one bright moment that couldn't be dampened by massive thunderstorms or long toilet lines. From the main screen, you can explore five sections: "Music," "Backstage," "Time and Place," "People," and "Performers." The "Music" section contains eight full Woodstock performances—a welcome alternative to many other rock CD-ROMs that offer only excerpts—from Janis Joplin to Richie Havens and Sly Stone. You can watch a collage of photographs on screen while listening or call up each song's lyrics. Backstage provides a photo album and seven brief video clips of performers, in 1969 as well as 1994, talking about Woodstock. Time and Place presents eight video clips of the local population reacting to the sudden arrival of 400,000 rock fans and displays a selection of newspaper front pages from the weekend of Woodstock, showing the many other stories of the day—the Charles Manson murders, for example, had occurred just a week earlier. People provides another photo album and eight video clips of the Woodstock crowd. Performers profiles fourteen musicians and bands, an eclectic bunch ranging from Joan Baez to Sha Na Na, with short text biographies, photos, video clips, and a list of albums.

Almost everything on *Woodstock* the CD-ROM is first-rate—the music, of course, is the best of its generation; the mixture of black-and-white and color photos brings back the shaggy look of the sixties; and the video clips let the participants speak to us directly. Most of the CD-ROM's video, by the way, comes from *Woodstock* the movie, released in 1970 and rereleased in 1994 with additional footage. I found only two false notes in *Woodstock*. First is a satiric trivia game called "Then & Now," hosted by "Baba CD Ram Das," that isn't very much fun. Second is a very confusing "Blazing Trails" feature that supposedly allows you to draw psychedelic images on screen but lacks clear operating instructions. Then again, maybe "Blazing Trails" is a perfect representative of the era—psychedelic, confusing, and unsure of its direction.

WORLD BEAT
★★½

Developer: Medio Multimedia Inc.; 800-788-3866
Format: Windows
Price: $39

World Beat stretches itself thinner than the goatskin head of an African drum in trying to cover world music, the growing category of music from Third World countries and minority cultures in the First World. With only thirty-six video clips and fifteen audio clips, each running just a minute or two, *World Beat* skims through the many sounds of world music and never delivers full performances.

The contents of *World Beat* are divided into five sections. "Style List" is an index to all the video clips, audio clips, and articles. "Interactive Documentary" presents four-minute narrated slide shows on the music of Africa, Asia, and Latin America. "Book" presents a collection of twenty exceedingly dull articles by academics with titles such as "Symbol and Function in South American Indian Music" and "Secular Classical Music in the Arabic Near East." "Music Studio" plays ten-second samples of thirty-five musical styles, everything from Chicago blues to Hawaiian slack-key guitar, while displaying the musical notes on screen.

"Discography" is the most interesting feature, offering the "All-Music Guide" database of 19,294 compact discs. The database is an excellent source for tracking down obscure recordings, although this version is indexed only by the name of the group or individual artist, so you can't search by album name or record label.

XPLORA 1: PETER GABRIEL'S SECRET WORLD
★★★½
Developer: Interplay Productions Inc./MacPlay; 800-969-4263
Format: Windows, Macintosh
Price: $49

Xplora 1: Peter Gabriel's Secret World is one of the few music CD-ROMs in which you really go inside the artist's head. Peter Gabriel, the ethereal British rock star, opened the doors—figuratively and literally—in providing a wealth of previously private material. *Xplora*, like Gabriel's music, is hard to describe in a few sentences. Some of the features are what you'd expect: There are four music videos from Gabriel's 1992 album *Us*—*Blood of Eden*, *Digging in the Dirt*, *Kiss That Frog*, and *Steam*—and, through video clips, backstage visits to the Grammy awards and Gabriel's personal recording studio in the English town of Box. But you'll keep stumbling on numerous unexpected diversions—everything from what appear to be home movies of Gabriel as an infant to a pitch for Amnesty International, the global human-rights organization supported by Gabriel and a number of other musicians.

Gabriel has also developed a strong interest in the emerging field of world music, which is bringing artists from Africa and Asia to audiences in Europe and the United States. *Xplora* includes video clips from the WOMAD world music festival founded by Gabriel, performances by fifty world music artists, and an interactive guide to musical instruments that lets you pluck out a few notes on the ko chung, a twenty-one-string Chinese harp, and the kaliba, an African thumb piano.

In a sixty-page book that comes in the box with *Xplora*, Gabriel explains that he wants to be an "experience designer," guiding his audience on a journey to create individual artistic encounters. *Xplora* doesn't quite deliver on that grandiose promise, but there are several interesting opportunities to get involved. In the studio visit, for example, you see a mixer board and can control the volume of the bass, drums, guitar, and vocals on a performance of "Digging in the Dirt." The on-screen artwork is beautiful, and Gabriel pops up occasionally to offer advice on what to do next. But the developers fall into a few traps by trying to match Gabriel's deliberately enigmatic lyrics. *Xplora* doesn't explain itself—you have to learn how to navigate from one section to another by experimentation—and it is full of puzzles, many of which are unnecessary barriers to enjoying the CD-ROM. Before visiting the Grammy awards, for example, you must go through the annoying step of finding a hidden backstage pass. Still, there's always another interesting new avenue to explore after you hit one of these brick walls.

Chapter Seven:
Home, Food, Sports, and Fitness

This chapter brings together all the CD-ROM categories related to self-improvement and leisure activities.

a. Home Care and Design

BETTER HOMES AND GARDENS COMPLETE GUIDE TO GARDENING
★½
Developer: Multicom Publishing Inc.; 800-850-7272
Format: Windows, Macintosh
Price: $39

An insult to the intelligence of even the most amateur gardener, *Better Homes and Gardens Complete Guide to Gardening* never digs below the topsoil. Pretty color pictures of plants and flowers, accompanied by relaxing music, don't hide a surprising shortage of detailed information.

The CD-ROM is divided into three main sections: Gardening Fundamentals, Garden Types, and Gardener's Almanac. Gardening fundamentals delivers information even novice yard-warriors will find condescending. A subsection on garden tools, for instance, delivers only five paragraphs beginning with these obvious thoughts: "Choose the right tool for the job. That sage advice is as true in the garden as it is in the workshop indoors. A high-quality tool will last longer; it will also make gardening easier and more enjoyable." You're then offered a selection of ten- to twenty-second video clips describing various garden tools. "The shovel works best for lifting and moving soil and other materials," the narrator declares. Gee, now I know why I've had so much trouble using my shovel to prune bushes. Garden Types offers similarly shallow hints on setting up fourteen types of garden, such as herb, rose, and wildflower. Gardener's Almanac tosses out one-sentence tips tied to the twelve months of the year, along with a calendar of major garden shows around the country.

Inexplicably, the CD-ROM's index requires you to search for content by working through menus for the sections and subsections rather than allowing a word search to find, for example, every article mentioning the term "Japanese beetle." The index lets you access specific information on a long list of plants, although you'd learn more reading the back of seed packets. Here, for example, is all you'll get on planting marigolds: "Start seeds indoors six to eight weeks before last frost date or outdoors after frost danger. Or buy transplants." *Better Homes and Gardening Complete Guide to Gardening* is based on five print books from Better

Homes and Gardens. You'll save money and learn more by skipping the CD-ROM and buying the books instead.

COMPLETE HOUSE
★★
Developer: Deep River Publishing Inc.; 800-643-5630
Format: Windows
Price: $29

Calling itself "a multimedia exploration of American home design," *Complete House* examines residential architecture from a rather strange academic perspective. This isn't a how-to guide for remodelers—it's a philosophical treatise on the meaning of home construction. Nor does the CD-ROM offer much that you couldn't get from a book; mostly you're just looking at text, photographs, and architectural sketches displayed on the screen with an occasional bit of audio narration.

Complete House centers on a series of essays on various aspects of home design. There's a heavy and annoying dose of New Age environmentalism throughout, implying we're insensitive to the impact of four-bedroom suburban ramblers on the planet's ecology, but the disk offers only fuzzy solutions. "By various estimates, buildings in America consume between 30 and 40 percent of our national energy budget," declares one essay on the principles of design. "This sobering fact establishes a relationship between the creation of built environment and the destruction of natural environment which is far more insidious than the impact of a single building on its site . . . It is valuable to consider houses as another form of biological system—one that mediates for us humans in the world but that is clearly not human."

In addition to these wordy diatribes, *Complete House* presents descriptions of several dozen architecturally interesting homes. There are also several questionnaires to help you in the planning process, although here again there is more New Age fuzziness, such as the question, "What do you want this house to say about you?" If you're eager to delve even further into design philosophy, the CD-ROM includes a bibliography, a short glossary, and a list of companies making environmentally correct building supplies.

Complete House also includes a program for creating your own design layouts called *CAD/FP Floor Planner*. But it's difficult to use and short on features. If you want to draw your own floor plans, skip *Complete House* and get the excellent *3D Home Architect*, reviewed in this section.

THE EXOTIC GARDEN
★★
Developer: VT Productions Inc.; 408-464-1552
Format: Windows
Price: $39

The Exotic Garden should be a book, not a CD-ROM. This guide to five hundred tropical plants and flowers is full of color photographs that would look better on the printed page than on a computer screen. The only possible reason for *Exotic Garden* to come on a CD-ROM instead of a less-expensive book is a three-minute movie called *Why Plants Flower*. But the film, a time-lapse display of buds bursting into bloom and seedlings pushing through the soil, loses all its impact because the CD-ROM shows it in a tiny, grainy three-inch-diagonal window on a standard fourteen-inch monitor.

The main section of *Exotic Garden* is a series of articles describing various types of plants and how to care for them. Tiny camera icons are scattered throughout the text; clicking on one produces a relevant photograph. You can also summon a brief profile of any plant pictured on the disk that gives a few sentences on its care. The text is a mix of practical advice and dry botanical information, such as this entry on orchids: "Orchids are perhaps the most exquisite flowers in the plant kingdom. Few plant families rival the orchid or *Orchidaceae* family in terms of complexity, diversity of form, habitat and abundance of species. This perennial herb family contains over 25,000 species and even more hybrids . . . Many species and hybrids are relatively easy to grow. However, careful observation should be paid to their active growth and rest requirements, which vary greatly between species."

EXPERT CD-ROM HOME DESIGN GOLD EDITION FOR WINDOWS
★★
Developer: Expert Software Inc.; 800-759-2562
Format: Windows
Price: $29

Expert CD-ROM Home Design Gold Edition for Windows, despite its very long name, comes up short in every category when compared with the excellent *3D Home Architect*, reviewed in this section. Both programs fill the same purpose: allowing nonprofessionals to create blueprints for home construction projects. But *Home Design* only allows you to work in two dimensions, looking down from an overhead view. *3D Home Architect* will also display a three-dimensional side view from anywhere in the room, so you can see a rendering of what your design would look like in real life. *Home Design* includes 25 sample floor plans and 125 images of furniture and fixtures to insert in your designs; *3D Home Architect* provides 150 floor plans and 400 furniture images. While *Home Design* has a project costing program where you must manually enter the amount and price of materials for your design to get the total cost, *3D Home Architect* will automatically analyze your design and calculate the amount of materials required. And *3D Home Architect* offers a library of helpful magazine articles on home improvement projects and video clips with advice from the host of a television home-improvement show. *Home Design* merely provides video clips produced by furniture and appliance manufacturers that are little more than advertisements for their products. Finally, *Home Design* is more difficult to learn, requiring mastery of complex on-screen controls similar to those in professional design software programs.

HOME REPAIR ENCYCLOPEDIA
★★★
Developer: Books That Work Inc.; 800-242-4546
Format: Windows
Price: $29

Ignorance is never bliss when it comes to the many skills required for home repair. Lack of knowledge, much more than time or money, is the chief enemy of weekend do-it-yourselfers trying to fix a leaky kitchen faucet or patch a pothole in the driveway. *Home Repair Encyclopedia* is a good place to start a wide range of household projects, offering quick tips that will point you in the right direction.

The CD-ROM is divided into nineteen sections covering common repairs, how to select tools and supplies, and even guidelines for hiring a contractor. The repair categories include electrical, plumbing, heating and cooling, painting, indoor structural work, and roofs. There are several "Survival Guides" describing how to remove stains from all types of surfaces, how to select paint, and how to chose adhesives. The most unique feature is three "estimators" for paint, attic venting, and concrete. You simply enter the dimensions of a room in the paint estimator, and the program instantly calculates how many gallons are required for the job. Similarly, you can estimate how many vents are necessary to air out an attic or how many cubic feet of concrete is needed to fill a hole.

The repair instructions themselves are easy to follow, although somewhat brief, and many are illustrated with thirty-second animations that show how the job should proceed. Here are the instructions for replacing worn-out grout in a shower stall: "To regrout a section of tile, remove the old grout with a grout saw. Vacuum out any dust, then dampen with water. Press new grout into the joints with a rubber float, a squeegee or a stiff plastic spatula. Use diagonal strokes. Wipe off the excess as soon as the grout firms up, usually an hour or less. Allow the grout to cure for twenty-four hours, then wipe off the dried film with a damp sponge." If you don't know what a grout saw is, you can click on the word to get a picture and definition: "An abrasive-tipped hand tool available from tile suppliers."

Home Repair Encyclopedia also deserves credit for advising caution rather than encouraging a rush to tackle complicated jobs. "Doing-it-yourself can be risky business, especially if you're a klutz or not in good physical shape," the CD-ROM says in the "Safety" section. "Think twice about jobs that involve lifting heavy objects; operating cumbersome machinery or power tools; and climbing up on your roof. Weigh all the odds and put your health and safety as a top priority."

My only significant complaint with *Home Repair Encyclopedia* is that some of the repair descriptions are too brief and the illustrations too simple for do-it-yourself novices. I was also somewhat surprised to see "infomercial"-type ads in some sections for Benjamin Moore paints, Kohler plumbing fixtures, Black &

Decker power tools, and Pella windows. By clicking on a small picture for each of these brand names, you get pictures and text describing their products. You don't have to look at these ads, but it's strange to encounter commercial messages in the middle of a reference work.

LANDDESIGNER MULTI-MEDIA FOR GARDENS
★★
Developer: Green Thumb Software Inc.; 800-336-3127
Format: Windows
Price: $49

Most amateur gardeners enjoy the feel of dirt between their fingers and presumably would rather spend time digging in the backyard than fiddling with their computer. *LandDesigner Multi-Media for Gardens*, however, requires spending long hours indoors deciphering a complex program for laying out garden designs. Green Thumb Software primarily develops computer-aided design packages for professional landscape architects, and the company didn't do enough to make *LandDesigner* easy for nonprofessionals. The ninety-five-page instruction manual is full of terms like "auto snapping," "grid selection," and "multiple assigning" that will confuse CAD newcomers. What's more, the models you create can be viewed only from overhead in two dimensions; unlike *3D Landscape*, reviewed in this section, which will translate overhead two-dimensional images into three-dimensional models viewed from the side.

LandDesigner also includes one thousand color photographs of flowers and other plants from White Flower Farm, a mail-order plant company, along with audio pronunciations of plant names and four narrated slide shows that come across as thinly veiled advertising for the White Flower Farms catalog. The taint of commercial influence shows up in another feature that automatically translates the specifications of your garden design into a White Flower Farm order form.

3D HOME ARCHITECT
★★★½
Developer: Broderbund Software Inc.; 800-521-6263
Format: Windows
Price: $69

Home owners are always dreaming of ways to improve their houses, perhaps by adding a fireplace, a deck, or a second bathroom. But it's always been difficult to visualize what those dreams might look like, short of hiring an architect to prepare drawings. *3D Home Architect* is a wonderful alternative, capable of bringing design dreams to life on a computer screen as well as providing lots of advice on how to tackle home improvement projects.

The core program is an easy-to-use and incredibly powerful tool for creating residential floor plans. Starting from a blank screen, you put walls, doors, windows, fireplaces, stairways, and furniture into a two-dimensional overhead-view blueprint. With a click of the mouse button, you can convert the design to a three-dimensional side view—so you can see a drawing of your design from the perspective of someone standing in the room. With another click of the mouse button, you can get a list of all the required materials to build your design. You can then enter the cost of those materials, plus labor, and get the project's bottom line. If you're not comfortable starting from scratch, the disk comes with 150 sample floor plans. The odds are good one of these plans closely resembles what you have in mind, and you can alter that design to meet your needs.

The CD-ROM also includes a library of one hundred articles from *American Homestyle Magazine* with tips on remodeling and fifty one-minute video clips of Gerry Connell, host of *The Home Pro* television series shown on The Learning Channel. Connell discusses such subjects as the relative merits of gas and electric kitchen appliances, concluding that most chefs prefer gas burners and an electric oven. The magazine articles, heavy on charts and checklists, cover everything from hiring contractors to selecting cabinets. Let's say you're thinking of adding a family room. The article on estimating construction costs prepares you for the sticker shock: A typical 375-square-foot family room with patio doors, eight windows, and a hardwood floor costs a whopping $35,000.

Although I'd recommend *3D Home Architect* highly to anyone interested in using a computer for home design, I also want to issue a warning: Making architecturally sound designs isn't simple.

No computer program can prevent you from selecting the wrong size bathroom cabinet or sinking foundations for a deck in unstable soil. What's more, even though *3D Home Architect* is easier to learn than just about any design software I've seen, you shouldn't expect to master the program immediately. Plan to spend a fair amount of time practicing with the software and reading carefully through the 230-page manual.

3D LANDSCAPE
★★★
Developer: Books That Work Inc.; 800-242-4546
Format: Windows
Price: $49

Before spending hundreds, or even thousands, of dollars redecorating the grounds of your family castle, it's worth investing $49 in *3D Landscape*. The do-it-yourself CD-ROM offers two interrelated packages—a comprehensive "How-to Guide" and a powerful, although complicated, "Landscape Designer" that lets you visualize a new yard on your computer screen.

The "How-to Guide" is an excellent resource for everything from planting a shrub to re-creating the gardens of Versailles, with text divided into eight chapters covering such subjects as preparing the site, selecting plants, and buying materials. Many of the on-screen pages include helpful thirty-second animations depicting such essential tasks as measuring your yard and how to build and hang a wooden gate. The advice in *3D Landscape* is simple and practical. "Before deciding on a plant, find out how big it will grow and how fast it will reach its mature size," the guide says in the section on selecting plants. "Don't plant a tree where you only want a shrub. Think ahead. Will the tree you planted in the middle of your yard end up casting too much shade and destroying all sense of proportion? Will a shrub grow to block a view, or require hours of pruning?"

Supplementing the text is a "Survival Guide" giving names and phone numbers for dozens of suppliers and trade associations. The best added feature, however, are five "Estimators" that automate landscaping calculations. A "Screening for Privacy" estimator will tell you the minimum height for a shrub or tree to block the view of a larger object in the distance, a grading estimator figures how much dirt is needed to fill in a slope, a grass selector specifies the type of lawn grass to buy for any given climatic condition, a soil pH estimator tells the amount of sulfur or limestone needed to remedy an acidity-alkilinity imbalance, and a concrete estimator works out how many cubic feet of mix will fill a given hole.

The "Landscape Designer," on the other hand, is too much of a good thing. Selecting from an extensive menu of drawings of plants, shrubs, trees, and structures, you can build a computer-generated replica of your landscape design. This model can be examined in a two-dimensional overhead view or in a three-dimensional side view. You can then play with your design, studying shadows at different times of day or quickly aging your yard to see how it will look after twenty-five years of growth. Putting a model together, however, is quite complicated—the explanation fills two-thirds of the sixty-page manual for *3D Landscape*. Computer novices may have a tough time mastering the controls for selecting, moving, and sizing landscape elements. Even experienced computer users should expect to spend at least several hours constructing the model for a typical yard.

HOMETIME WEEKEND HOME PROJECTS
★★½
Developer: IVI Publishing Inc.; 800-432-1332
Format: DOS, Macintosh
Price: $45

Dean Johnson, host of the Public Broadcasting System series *Hometime*, is a raging optimist when facing the challenges of household repair. He seems convinced the average butterfingered homeowner will eagerly tackle difficult jobs such as putting in a toilet or setting roof trusses after watching just a minute or two of video clips on *Hometime Weekend Home Projects*. I'm more pessimistic; I think most do-it-yourselfers won't get enough guidance from this CD-ROM.

The content of *Weekend Home Projects* is divided into twelve categories: ceramic tile; hand and power tools; cabinets and counters; paints and stains; plumbing; windows, doors and trim; wallpaper; drywall; framing; wiring and lighting; flooring; and building a deck. Each section has three or four one- to two-minute video clips from the PBS show, along with helpful text sidebars offering project tips and descriptions of the materials and tools required. Johnson is full of practical advice, such as this tip on wallpapering: "Hanging even pre-pasted wall coverings is a messy job, and some adhesives are all but impossible to remove after they dry. Wash your hands often. Use clean water to sponge away paste after you put up each strip. Keep the pasting table free of adhesive. And immediately clean any smears from brush handles, knives and scissors, as well as the seam roller and handle."

Several material calculators are included, so you can enter the dimensions of a room, for example, and find out exactly how much paint or wallpaper is required for refinishing. The CD-ROM also contains an extensive product directory, listing the addresses and phone numbers of building supply manufacturers.

The main weakness in *Weekend Home Projects* is too much reliance on video clips. I wouldn't feel comfortable installing track lighting after watching a one-minute demonstration, but that's all the CD-ROM provides. The disk should include more detailed text instructions for each task, which could be printed and carried to the job site. Also, the Macintosh version of *Weekend Home Projects* requires eight megabytes of RAM, more than the minimum five megabytes found on many Macintosh computers sold for home use.

b. Food and Cooking

BETTER HOMES AND GARDENS HEALTHY COOKING CD COOKBOOK
★★★
Developer: Multicom Publishing Inc.; 800-850-7272
Format: Windows, Macintosh
Price: $39

Taking a sneak-attack approach to dieting, *Better Homes and Gardens Healthy Cooking CD Cookbook* doesn't tell you anywhere—except for one passing reference in the user's manual—that its 425 recipes come from a print book called *Better Homes and Gardens New Dieter's Cookbook*. So most buyers of the CD-ROM might not be aware they're going on a diet, even after they start whipping up what appear to be high-calorie recipes such as apricot custards (only 120 calories) and meatball sandwiches (324 calories).

The CD-ROM is full of useful features that only a cookbook on computer can offer. A feature called "What's for Dinner?" searches through the recipes to find those matching your desired ingredients and nutritional needs. If, for example, you want chicken dishes under four hundred calories with low levels of cholesterol, fat, and sodium, you get three recipes: mustard and honey chicken, poached chicken breast with apples, and lime-sauce chicken. The ingredient lists can also be resized. If you're cooking only ten stuffed mushrooms instead of the recipe's twenty, you can print a shopping list that shows all the quantities divided in half. Finally, the CD-ROM offers a selection of eighty video clips, each running an average of fifteen seconds, that quickly show common cooking procedures, such as skinning chicken, coring an apple, or poaching eggs.

CD Cookbook includes a number of helpful indexes drawn from the print book. My favorite is the index by preparation time. When you're on a tight schedule, it's nice to know sherried fillet steaks require only six minutes to prepare. You can also look at the recipes by category, such as take-along lunches or meatless main dishes, to help with menu planning. And there's an illustrated utensil guide for novice chefs. A Dutch oven, I discovered, is "a lidded metal container used for cooking large quantities on rangetops or in an oven, usually available in 4, 4-1/2, 6, 8 and 10-quart sizes."

CHINESE FAMILY COOKING
★★
Developer: SunMedia Inc.; 800-862-3766
Format: Windows
Price: $45

Lightly seasoned with only a hint of narration and video, *Chinese Family Cookbook* is essentially a print cookbook delivered on CD-ROM. What's worse, many of the two hundred recipes are much too abbreviated for cooks taking their first venture into Chinese cuisine.

Chinese Family Cookbook at least looks good—each recipe is illustrated with a mouth-watering color photograph. Health-conscious users will appreciate the nutritional chart included with each dish, listing cholesterol, carbohydrate, protein, fat, and calorie content. The disk also includes several hundred sound bites on various aspects of Chinese cooking and culture, although these ten-second comments are often superficial. Nine video clips, each running less than a minute, on subjects such as stir frying and dicing, are equally unsatisfying.

But the biggest drawback in *Chinese Family Cooking* is the short shrift given to preparation instructions. Here, for example, is the entire recipe for Drunken Chicken Casserole: "Ingredients—2 chicken drumsticks, 4 c. ice water, a little coriander, 1 T. salt, 1 c. Shaoshing wine, 1 c. chicken soup. Method—1. Steam chicken for 15 minutes. Remove. Rinse with ice water immediately. 2. Mix salt, wine and chicken soup well. Add chicken to soak for 6 hours before serving."

4 PAWS OF CRAB
★★★
Developer: Live Oak Multimedia Inc.; 800-454-7557
Format: Windows, Macintosh
Price: $35

4 Paws of Crab is a unique and quirky experience, an introduction to Thai cuisine and culture that is part cookbook, part travelogue, and part personal history. Created by a three-person company called Live Oak Multimedia, the CD-ROM has a personal charm lacking in most multimedia titles churned out by big software companies. The project grew from a 1989 trip to Bangkok by Nora Bateson, one of Live Oak's founders, where she met Bancha "Bird"

Leelaguagoon, a budding chef and restaurateur. "We always ended up in the kitchen," Bateson explains in the disk's introductory screen, "cooking and telling stories. Our stories gave us glimpses into the parallel worlds we lived in. We cooked each other's foods so that we would know where we had come from."

After the introduction, *4 Paws* divides into four sections: "Recipes," "Happy Market," "Mirrors," and "Time Romp." The recipe section presents instructions from Bird for preparing forty-five Thai dishes, everything from the relatively familiar "pad thai and chicken soup with coconut milk" to more exotic choices such as "looking glass noodle salad." There's even a recipe for "weeping tiger BBQ," with Bird's explanation of the name: "This dish comes from poor areas in the northeastern part of Thailand and is traditionally made with such low-quality meat that you can barely chew it. Hence, even tigers cry when they eat it. We've adapted it to the Western palate, so you won't weep." The recipes are easy to follow and print and are illustrated with high-resolution color photos. Some of the recipes also feature video clips of Bird that aren't as useful; the grainy clips run only thirty to ninety seconds and focus more on Bird's comments about Thailand than on actual cooking demonstrations. The name *4 Paws of Crab*, by the way, comes from Bird, who wrote out a recipe in English accidentally using the word "paws" when he meant to say "claws."

The "Happy Market" section is a perfect complement to "Recipes," with descriptions and photographs of sixty-three common ingredients in Thai cooking, accompanied by the sounds of Bangkok's main market. The CD-ROM even includes a form to print for ordering seventeen hard-to-find Thai ingredients from a company called Thai Kitchen Products in Berkeley, California. The "Mirrors" section presents text, audio narration, and photographs of Nora's visits to Thailand and a journey by Bird to San Francisco in 1993. "Time Romp" offers side-by-side capsule histories of Thailand and the United States.

There are a few small disappointments, however. The CD-ROM runs very slowly, with long pauses between scenes, and doesn't offer an index. Live Oak Multimedia also didn't pay enough attention to editing the text; some of the material contains spelling and grammatical errors.

THE FOUR SEASONS OF GOURMET FRENCH CUISINE
★★
Developer: Cambrix Publishing Inc.; 800-892-8781
Format: Windows-2, Macintosh-2
Price: $29

The Four Seasons of Gourmet French Cuisine resembles a sorry souffle that collapsed in the oven. This CD-ROM cookbook delivers only one hundred recipes for roughly double the price of a typical print cookbook that would contain three or four times as much material. The developers of *Gourmet French Cuisine* try to give their CD-ROM confection some life by adding 155 very short video clips demonstrating various cooking procedures, but these fifteen-second snippets play in a minuscule window measuring just two and a half inches diagonally on a standard fourteen-inch monitor—so small that you can't really see what's happening.

The one hundred dishes certainly look mouth-watering; each is depicted in a glamorous color photograph accompanied by a performance of Vivaldi's *The Four Seasons*. But only the most dedicated chefs will have the time and patience for these intricate recipes, taken from a French gourmet magazine called *Thuries*. Making bouillabaisse, for example, requires finding four types of seafood—scorpion fish, John Dory, conger eel, and red mullet—and spending ninety minutes in the kitchen gutting, slicing, and skinning. Nor does *Gourmet French Cuisine* spare us vivid descriptions of some recipes not often seen on this side of the Atlantic—preparation of head cheese requires obtaining "a pig's head, deboned, blanched and prepared by a butcher"; you then "use a chef's knife to cut the head . . . into large cubes." That's one dish I neither want to eat nor watch taking shape.

In keeping with the seasonal theme in its name, *Gourmet French Cuisine* divides the recipes into categories by time of year. "Sweet and Sour Scallops and Fresh Fruit" is a spring dish, for instance, while "Blanquette of Hake" is for winter. The recipes can also be arranged into twenty-five complete meals, also by season. In August, for example, the CD-ROM suggests an appetizer of "Salmon and Cucumber Quadrille" followed by "Sea Bass in Lime Marinade" as a main course and "Caramelized Peaches on a Bed of Thyme Granita" for dessert. All the recipes can be printed; you can also select whether the list of ingredients should serve four, six, eight, or twelve. But most amateur chefs will learn more and spend less by seeking out a good French cookbook in print. A companion product, *The Art of Making Great Pastries*, is reviewed in this section.

THE ART OF MAKING GREAT PASTRIES
★★
Developer: Cambrix Publishing Inc.; 800-892-8781
Format: Windows-2, Macintosh-2
Price: $29

A companion to *The Four Seasons of Gourmet French Cuisine*, reviewed in this section, that is virtually identical in structure. *The Art of Making Great Pastries* delivers 101 recipes, also drawn from the French gourmet magazine *Thuries*, along with 180 video clips that are extremely difficult to follow in the tiny on-screen window. The recipes are divided into four categories: forty-two dough desserts, thirty cake, eighteen cream, and eleven fruit. The CD-ROM also provides twenty-five lessons in fundamental techniques, such as how to make whipped cream, prepare a cake, and apply icing. But *Great Pastries*, like *Gourmet French Cuisine*, offers nothing you couldn't find in a print cookbook for half the price, other than the useless video clips.

THE LIFESTYLES OF THE RICH AND FAMOUS COOKBOOK
★★★
Developer: Compton's NewMedia Inc.; 800-284-2045
Format: Windows
Price: $25

Most of us will probably never join Ivana Trump at a charity ball or get invited to Roger Moore's place for breakfast. But now, thanks to host Robin Leach of the TV show "Lifestyles of the Rich and Famous," we can at least peek inside their recipe books to fulfill our personal "champagne wishes and caviar dreams."

This CD-ROM combines thirty minutes of video clips from the show with two hundred recipes from the exotic to the ordinary. We can go behind the scenes at Elizabeth Taylor's most recent wedding, for example, to see how the caterers prepared lobster salad on artichokes and chocolate tulips. Joan Collins contributes her personal recipe for spaghetti Bolognese. And supermodel Elle MacPherson provides instructions for making her smoked salmon bruschetta. Based on a book of the same name published in 1992 by Penguin Books USA, *The Lifestyles of the Rich and Famous Cookbook* is divided into four sections: Extravagant Affairs, with recipes from big events such as the Cannes Film Festival and a New York charity ball; Casual Entertaining, describing meals served at smaller gatherings; Relaxing at Home, emphasizing simpler fare such as Bruce Jenner's cheese bread and Eva Gabor's chicken paprika; and favorite recipes of the rich and famous, with selections such as Florence Griffith Joyner's spicy shrimp creole.

Leach provides audio narration—pronouncing CD-ROM as "see-dee-rome" in his unique nasal accent—that gushes over the beautiful people's close relationship with their food of choice. The recipes are illustrated with glamorous color photographs of the celebrities and the dishes themselves. If you want to follow in the footsteps of the rich and famous, you can print the recipes directly from the program or transfer them to a word processor for editing. Of course, this isn't a serious cookbook. But if you buy *The Lifestyles of the Rich and Famous Cookbook* in search of a good time and perhaps one or two recipes you might actually use, you won't be disappointed.

THE NEW BASICS ELECTRONIC COOKBOOK
★★★
Developer: Xiphias; 800-421-9194
Format: DOS
Price: $29

Starting with a gourmet food shop in Manhattan called The Silver Palate, Julee Rosso and Sheila Lukins combined their culinary talent and marketing savvy to create a series of cookbooks that became runaway bestsellers. *The New Basics Electronic Cookbook* is a CD-ROM version of Rosso and Lukins's biggest and best work, a weighty 850-page paperback. The disk contains everything in the print version of *The New Basics Cookbook*, along with twenty minutes of audio commentary by the authors and twenty minutes of video clips illustrating food preparation and display.

Translating the cookbook to CD-ROM allows you to jump quickly from one subject to another, a wonderful way to explore the many facets of *New Basics*. I put the CD-ROM through its paces by asking to see all the dishes containing capers, one of my favorite condiments. The program instantly responded with fifty recipes. One caught my eye: "The Pig Stands Alone Roast Pig," which calls for a fifteen-pound suckling pig and a third of a cup of capers, among other ingredients. I then jumped to the hints section and found a two-paragraph essay on capers. "Capers are the unopened bud of a shrub that grows wild all over the Mediterranean, North Africa and India," the text explained. "The green buds are picked by hand before sunrise, while they are still tightly closed, and then pickled." All these entries can be printed at the push of a button.

This ability to create your own path through the recipes is the best reason to consider switching from the print cookbook to the CD-ROM; the program is also easy to install and operate. The additional audio and video are of little benefit; the quarter-screen video images are very grainy and focus more on the appearance of finished dishes than on how to prepare them.

WINES OF THE WORLD
★★★
Developer: Multicom Publishing Inc.; 800-850-7272
Format: Windows, Macintosh
Price: $39

Next time you're in a fancy French restaurant trying to impress your dinner companions, casually ask the wine steward if the recommended cabernet sauvignon was prepared at a vineyard suitably concerned with "*ouillage.*" The term is just one small sip of knowledge from *Wines of the World*, a pert yet fruity CD-ROM that wine lovers will find a worthy addition to their cellars. ("*Ouillage,*" by the way, is defined in the CD-ROM's glossary as a "French term for topping up barrels to make up for the loss from evaporation. It is essential that barrels are kept full, for otherwise the wine will oxidize.")

Wines is easy to operate, with all the user instructions on a single sheet, and is free from the taint of wine snobbery. In reviewing how to find the right wine for a certain meal, the disk cheerily advises: "If all else fails, an eccentric match of wine and food can always be passed off as one's own personal taste." *Wines* also provides a suitably relaxed atmosphere for contemplating the merits of chardonnay and pinot noir. Beautiful photographs of vineyards and wineries are used as backdrops throughout the disk, with the soothing sounds of classical guitar solos introducing each of the four major sections.

Those sections are: Wine Quality, which explains the production process down to such esoteric details as the difference between compressed clay and alluvial soil; Wine Appreciation, covering wine tasting and collecting; Wine Regions, a guide to eighteen wine-growing areas around the world from Austria to New Zealand; and Wine Browser, a data base containing information on twenty thousand individual wines. Most of the text comes from a book called *The Companion to Wine*; the ratings of individual wines come from *The Wine Connoisseur's Companion* magazine. The CD-ROM also includes a few video clips so that you can see grapes being harvested or listen to California wine maker Tim Mondavi talk about the world-class growing conditions in the Napa Valley.

The Wine Browser is both the most impressive and weakest part of the package. Users can control any variable in scanning through the huge database, asking, for example, to see only Sonoma Valley merlots priced under $10. But the program is slow to respond, won't print the search results, and doesn't offer any way to navigate quickly when the search produces a long list.

c. Sports

THE AMERICAN GOLF GUIDE PRESENTED BY ARNOLD PALMER
★½
Developer: DataTech Software Inc.; 800-556-7526
Format: Windows
Price: $39

The American Golf Guide Presented by Arnold Palmer calls itself "a multimedia tour of America's golf courses." But that's cheating, like tossing your ball out of a sand trap. *American Golf Guide* isn't a true multimedia CD-ROM; you only get text along with occasional photographs, course layouts, and scorecards—the same things you'd get in a print guide to golf courses. Nor is Arnold Palmer anywhere to be seen on the CD-ROM, other than in a thumbnail photograph in the opening menu screen; he apparently collected his money for the use of his well-known name and then took a powder.

The CD-ROM contains information on 11,500 golf courses across the United States. The listings, however, are mostly minimal citations of the course name, address, name of the club professional, course type (public or private), architect, tee-time policy, operating hours, and operating season. Many of the listings are filled with blanks, so you may get the operating hours but not the name of the professional or tee-time policy. A small number of better-known courses are illustrated from a library of five hundred color photographs; there are also one thousand course scorecards. *American Golf Guide* promises video "fly-overs" of "some of America's greatest courses" but delivers only fifteen one-minute clips of courses in three southeastern states—Georgia, North Carolina and South Carolina—with no explanation for why the rest of the country is excluded. Finally, *American Golf Guide* makes unreasonable technical demands on your computer, insisting on sixteen megabytes of space on your hard disk—even though it performs sluggishly—and changing the AUTOEXEC.BAT file.

BASEBALL'S GREATEST HITS
★★★½
Developer: Voyager Co.; 800-446-2001
Format: Windows, Macintosh
Price: $39

For die-hard fans of the national pastime, *Baseball's Greatest Hits* will be a must-have on the strength of one item alone: actual footage of Babe Ruth's famous and still controversial "called shot" in the 1932 World Series. The Babe, taunted by Chicago Cubs fans that day at Wrigley Field, may or may not have pointed to center field to indicate where he intended to hit a home run. Whatever the meaning of Ruth's gestures, he immediately hit one out of the park, and the New York Yankees went on to win the Series. A Chicago printer named Matt Kandle was sitting in the stands with a sixteen-millimeter movie camera, and his amateur effort is the only film of the moment. The developers of *Baseball's Greatest Hits* call Kandle's footage "baseball's equivalent of Abraham Zapruder's home movie of the Kennedy assassination." And, like the Zapruder film, Kandle's grainy and poorly lighted effort won't settle the controversy. But it's fascinating to see Babe Ruth making several dramatic arm movements before taking the fateful swing. Except for one previous showing on televison, the developers claim their CD-ROM is the first time Kandle's film is available to the public.

While the rest of *Baseball's Greatest Hits* doesn't quite match the drama of Ruth's called shot, it is packed with historical highlights that will entrance aficionados. The best part of the CD-ROM is the seventy "great moments" drawn from the past six decades, such as Lou Gehrig's emotional farewell to New York Yankees fans in 1939 and Hank Aaron's record-breaking 715th home run in 1974. These moments are depicted with video clips and narration by sportscaster Mel Allen, along with supporting statistics and excerpts from the works of sportswriters such as Grantland Rice, Red Smith, and Thomas Boswell. The second-best feature is "Voices from the Hall," brief audio clips of famous players, including Jackie Robinson and Yogi Berra.

Rounding out *Baseball's Greatest Hits* are a time line running from 1845 through the 1993 World Series, brief histories of the twenty-eight major league teams, a two-player trivia game, and an index to the players mentioned in the disk. *Baseball's Greatest Hits* isn't a comprehensive history of baseball, but it's a wonderful way to experience several generations of baseball excitement.

MICROSOFT COMPLETE BASEBALL, 1994 EDITION
★★★½

Developer: Microsoft Corp.; 800-426-9400
Format: Windows
Price: $49

After suffering through the 1994 players' strike, baseball team owners might be excused a moment of nostalgia for the 1901 season, when the National League imposed a salary cap of $2,400 per player. This long-ago outburst of owner greed is recounted in *Microsoft Complete Baseball, 1994 Edition*, which delivers just about every possible statistic and trivia item about America's pastime.

Complete Baseball, current through the 1993 season, is divided into six sections: "Almanac," "Chronicle," "Players," "Records," "Teams," and "Trivia." "Almanac" presents detailed information on every major league baseball season back to 1901, when the Pittsburgh Pirates won the National League pennant with the help of shortstop Honus Wagner and the Chicago White Stockings led the new American League. "Chronicle" combines a history of baseball along with biographies from *The New York Times* of the game's one hundred all-time great players. "Players" presents an on-screen baseball card with a one-paragraph bio and lifetime stats for 2,500 major leaguers. "Records" is the gateway to a seemingly endless parade of statistics, such as the stolen-base leaders (topped by Rickey Henderson of the Oakland A's, with 1,095 stolen bases from 1979 to 1993). "Teams" provides the history of each of the twenty-eight major league clubs, along with player rosters and 1994 schedules. "Trivia" contains nine hundred questions at two levels of difficulty. A sample: Which player has made the most postseason appearances? Answer: Reggie Jackson in seventy-seven games for the Yankees, A's, and Angels.

Almost every screen is illustrated with sharp color photographs of players and games. Interesting sound effects pop up at random to keep things from getting dull, from a steel-guitar rendition of *Take Me Out to the Ball Game* to the shouts of a ballpark hot dog vendor. The disk also contains eighty-four audio clips, mostly from radio broadcasts of historic games, and twelve video clips, each running about a minute, of game highlights.

For all these hits, *Complete Baseball* commits one error—a poorly designed service called "Microsoft Baseball Daily" accessed by modem. For a fee of $1.25 ($2.25 in Canada) during the baseball season, *Complete Baseball* will dial an on-line service and fetch an extensive report covering the previous day's games. Retrieving the information at 9,600 baud takes slightly less than four minutes; I didn't try the slower 2,400 baud service, but it would probably require an unacceptably long wait of sixteen minutes. What's more, the information isn't worth the price or the wait—the report offers nothing you won't find in the sports section of your daily newspaper, at a cost of fifty cents or less. A news release from Microsoft boasts that downloaded stats can be copied "into a spreadsheet file to participate in the increasingly popular Rotisserie, or fantasy baseball leagues." But the flow of incoming data can't be customized to match a Rotisserie roster, so *Complete Baseball* doesn't replace on-line services dedicated to Rotisserie participants.

Microsoft originally promised to have *Complete Baseball* in stores by Opening Day in 1994 but whiffed on the deadline and didn't hit the shelves until mid-June. The company promises to do better with the 1995 edition.

MICROSOFT COMPLETE NBA BASKETBALL
★★★½
Developer: Microsoft Corp.; 800-426-9400
Format: Windows
Price: $49

Released in November 1994 just after the start of the National Basketball Association's '94–95 season, this CD-ROM is a carbon copy of the impressive *Microsoft Complete Baseball*, reviewed in this section. *Complete Basketball* is divided into the same six sections: "Almanac" gives a season-by-season recap of the NBA back to 1946–47, when the Philadelphia Warriors beat the Chicago Stags for the championship of what was then called the Basketball Association of America. "Chronicle" provides an overall history of the game, invented in 1891 at a YMCA in Springfield, Massachusetts. "Players" gives biographical and statistical information for all current players as well as retired stars. "Teams" provides rosters, histories, statistics, and the '94–95 schedule for all twenty-seven NBA clubs. "Records" is a massive repository of statistics, such as a list of highest career point totals, led by Kareem Abdul-Jabbar with 38,387 from '69–70 through '88–89. Finally, "Trivia" delivers almost one thousand quiz questions that thoughtfully include a two-sentence explanation after the correct answer is selected. A sample: "Which player scored 22 points in a Finals match while wearing a cast on his wrist? (A) Hakeem Olajuwon, (B) James Worthy, (C) Bill Russell, (D) George Mikan?" The answer is Mikan, and the story is: "After breaking his wrist in a Game 4 collision in the 1949 BAA Finals, Mikan returned in a cast to face the Washington Capitols in Game 5. Despite his 22 points, the Minneapolis Lakers lost the game, 74-65. However, the Lakers took the title with a 77-56 home-court victory in Game 6."

Complete Basketball is extensively illustrated with sharp color photographs and enlivened with sound effects such as sneakers squeaking on wooden floors. The CD-ROM also offers eighty-six video clips, mostly thirty-second game highlights, and fifty-two audio clips of famous players. The only weakness, as with *Complete Baseball*, is an on-line service called *Microsoft NBA Basketball Daily*. Accessed by modem, the service gives daily updates during the season for $1.25 each with scores, statistics, and standings. But this isn't anything more than most daily newspapers provide in their sports sections and has the added hassle and expense of calling up Microsoft's computer network.

ESPN BASEBALL: HITTING
★★½
Developer: Intellimedia Sports Inc.; 800-269-2101
Format: Windows, Macintosh
Price: $49

Weekend softball players eager to knock one out of the park might learn something from *ESPN Baseball: Hitting*, but this CD-ROM falls well short of a grand slam. Combining text, pictures, audio, and a smattering of video clips, *ESPN Baseball* delivers a long lecture on batting fundamentals and strategy—everything from how to stand at the plate to coping with curveballs.

The main part of the program is laid out like a book, with a table of contents running down the left side of the screen. Clicking on a section in the table summons text or a video clip into a window on the right side of the screen. The message will sound familiar to anyone who's ever been on a baseball team. "You must look at each pitch as a new challenge," the disk declares. "Confidence is essential when you're at bat." You also get slogans to memorize, such as "MVP" to remember to be "Mentally, Visually and Physically" alert before stepping into the batter's box.

Two other features complete the roster. "Ask the Coach" presents sixty one-minute audio clips of an interview with Ron Fraser, former head baseball coach at the University of Miami and for the 1992 U.S. Olympic team, on subjects such as "the difficulty of hitting" and "determining your strike zone." "What's the Call?" is an interesting game that helps you learn the rules of baseball by evaluating complicated situtations in which a player could be out or safe. An example: "A batter hits to the third baseman, who makes a bad throw to first. The ball bounces in front of the first baseman and lodges under his arm. The ball is trapped there when the batter crosses first. The first baseman takes the ball in his hand after the runner passes first. What's the call?" The answer: "The batter is safe, because the first baseman did not establish control of the ball in his hand or glove until after the runner passed first base. The ball is alive and in play."

Although *ESPN Baseball* is full of helpful information, the developers committed one huge error, crippling the CD-ROM's usefulness: There's no way to print the text or copy it to a word processor. I'd strongly advise against holding batting practice in front of your computer, so players are left without an easy method of taking their favorite tips to the ballpark.

ESPN GOLF: LOWER YOUR SCORE WITH TOM KITE — SHOT MAKING
★★
Developer: Intellimedia Sports Inc.; 800-269-2101
Format: Windows, Macintosh
Price: $45

Despite the long and impressive-sounding title, *ESPN Golf: Lower Your Score with Tom Kite—Shot Making* is a slice into the rough. The two-disk CD-ROM set delivers the equivalent of a videotape and audiocassette of tips from golfer Tom Kite, winner of the 1992 U.S. Open, and sports psychologist Bob Rotella.

The first disk, called "Shot Making," is the videotape. You see Tom Kite in thirty-five video clips, each running one or two minutes, explaining everything from chip shots to gauging the effect of a strong wind. But the video images play in a four-and-a-half-inch diagonal window on a standard four-inch monitor, making it difficult to follow all of Kite's movements. The lessons Kite is trying to teach would be much better absorbed through a real videotape playing on a large-screen color television.

The second disk, called "Ask the Pro," is the audiocassette. You sit and listen to an interview with Kite and Rotella, staring at pictures of their faces on the screen. Much of the advice is aimed at overstressed amateurs. Kite, for example, counsels weekend duffers not to expect immediate improvement after practicing: "Improvement in golf sometimes comes at sporadic levels. It doesn't always come in a nice, consistent, straight line that people expect." Rotella makes the sensible point that a relaxed attitude pays big dividends: "The first objective is to have fun ... When you have fun, you can play, and when you play, you can score low ... The beautiful thing is, even if you didn't score good on that day, you're going to at least go away with one certainty—that you had fun playing golf." But again, it would be easier to absorb these words of wisdom from an audiotape, perhaps listening on a Walkman while hitting a bucket of balls at the driving range.

ESPN LET'S PLAY SOCCER
★½
Developer: Intellimedia Sports Inc.; 800-269-2101
Format: Windows, Macintosh
Price: $29

ESPN Let's Play Soccer isn't really a CD-ROM. Sure, it comes on a shiny platter that can be played only in a computer. But all you get is a videotape dumped onto a disk rather than interactive software. There's about an hour of instruction on soccer strategy, sliced into thirty-eight clips, and nothing else—no text, no glossary of soccer terms, no database of soccer statistics, not even a soccer trivia quiz game. John Harkes and Mia Hamm, both former members of the U.S. National Team, are the teachers; their primary student is Zachery Ty Bryan, a child star on the television series "Home Improvement" and avid soccer player. Although Harkes and Hamm deliver some valuable tips on offense and defense, the video clips play in a four-and-a-half-inch diagonal window on a standard fourteen-inch monitor, a sorry alternative to watching the same material in full screen on a color television. What's worse, a videotape of the same material would undoubtedly sell for considerably less. This is one CD-ROM to kick aside.

ESPN SPORTS SHORTS
★★½

Developer: Moon Valley Software; 800-473-5509
Format: Windows
Price: $25

To enjoy *ESPN Sports Shorts*, you have to be doubly fanatic—fanatic about sports and fanatic about fiddling with your computer. The CD-ROM offers an impressive collection of 278 photos, 100 sound bites, and 266 ten-second video clips taken from sports broadcasts on the ESPN cable television network, along with a few tools for converting this material into screen savers, Windows wallpaper, or animated icons. If you're a sports nut who enjoys spending hours and hours making your PC look and sound different, you could set up your machine to emit a karate chop every time you close a window or display video clips of road racing as a screen saver. But I wouldn't recommend *ESPN Sports Shorts* to anyone else, especially computer novices. Customizing Windows is a risky undertaking for beginners, and the CD-ROM's slender instruction manual doesn't give much help. Also, *ESPN Sports Shorts* grabs eight megabytes of hard-disk space, a big chunk of real estate for a program that doesn't do anything useful.

LEGENDS AND SUPERSTARS BASEBALL
★½

Developer: Kelly Russell Studios Inc.; 800-224-4448
Format: Windows
Price: $39

Kelly Russell Studios specializes in selling what it calls sports "collectibles," high-priced paintings and coffee mugs bearing the images of sports stars sold to grown-up fans who are perhaps a little embarrassed to be seen playing with baseball cards. *Legends and Superstars Baseball* is Kelly Russell's misguided attempt to market its artwork on CD-ROM. The box touts *Legends and Superstars* as "the first interactive baseball collectible" with "highlight videos," but it's not really interactive and there's only a scant eleven minutes of video clips.

Legends and Superstars is actually a do-it-yourself screen saver program, which isn't made clear until you've bought the CD-ROM, opened the box, and taken a look at the instruction manual. The disk contains 110 reproductions of Kelly Russell artwork featuring such major-league players as Wade Boggs, Jose Canseco, Dennis Eckersley, Ken Griffey, Jr., Don Mattingly, Deion Sanders, Darryl Strawberry, and Dave Winfield. Using a confusing set of on-screen buttons and menus, you can assemble these pictures into a customized screen saver, although you have to take the impractical step of always leaving the *Legends and Superstars* disk in your CD-ROM drive for the screen saver to operate. I wasn't able to figure out how to use the video clips, which show a montage of players on the field, because the instruction manual doesn't cover the subject. *Legends and Superstars*, in short, isn't major-league software and deserves to be sent down for a long tour in the minors.

THE OFFICIAL NFL INTERACTIVE YEARBOOK '94–'95
★★★
Developer: RealTime Sports Inc.; 800-728-4000 x3136
Format: Windows-2, Macintosh-2
Price: $39

Football fans who are determined to keep track of every team, player, and statistic will love *The Official NFL Interactive Yearbook '94-95*. The CD-ROM provides reams and reams of data on the 1993 season and, through an on-line service, offers the option of downloading complete coverage of the 1994 season. Hosted by veteran broadcaster Pat Summerall, who narrates sixty minutes of video clips, the *NFL Yearbook* also gives a summary of National Football League rules, historical records such as first-round draft picks back to 1936, and a suitably brain-teasing trivia quiz game.

The yearbook's contents are divided into four major sections. "The 1993 Season" provides box-score results for every game, along with week-by-week statistics and standings. "The 1994 Season" offers the same coverage, but the disk—released in early November 1994—contains information only for the first three weeks of the season, through mid-September. Users can dial an on-line service, however, to get updates through the end of the season; the service itself is free, except for the cost of a toll call to the 212 area code. "Players" gives a roster of all the current NFL team members, with season and career statistics. You can find out at a glance, for example, that Kansas City Chiefs quarterback Joe Montana completed 61 percent of his passes in 1993, while San Francisco 49ers quarterback Steve Young completed 68 percent.

"Teams" gives the yearly win-loss records and rosters for each of the twenty-eight NFL clubs.

The long-bomb passes, bone-crunching tackles, and triumphant touchdowns of the 1993 season are preserved in the video clips, covering every team and every week of play. After a promising rookie performance, this CD-ROM deserves a long professional career, although I can't resist a little coaching: The '95-96 yearbook needs to get onto the playing field before the start of the preseason in August.

THE SPORTING NEWS 1994 MULTIMEDIA PRO FOOTBALL GUIDE
★★½
Developer: Compton's NewMedia Inc.; 800-284-2045
Format: Windows
Price: $25

Like a blocker faked off his feet by a running back, *The Sporting News 1994 Multimedia Pro Football Guide* is outmaneuvered by *The Official NFL Interactive Yearbook '94-'95*, reviewed in this section. For starters, the *NFL Yearbook* provides an update service by modem to get game results during football season—a feature *Sporting News Football* doesn't match. *NFL Yearbook* also hit store shelves in October 1994, about two months ahead of *Sporting News Football*. That delay hurt *Sporting News Football*, which included a schedule for the 1994-95 season even though the season was almost over before the CD-ROM reached any football fans.

The contents of *Sporting News Football*, however, aren't bad—an impressive array of statistics and 116 video clips, each running thirty seconds to one minute, in seven sections. "Highlights" presents box scores and a video clip for three or four games during each week of the regular season, as well as the play-offs and the Super Bowl on January 30, 1994. "NFL Teams" gives scores and statistics for all twenty-eight clubs. "Players and Coaches" provides a one-paragraph profile and career statistics for every player and coach in the game since 1970. "Statistics" delivers rankings in twelve categories such as rushing, interceptions, and kickoff returns, either by player or team. "Hall of Fame" presents a short biography and statistics for every member of the Pro Football Hall of Fame. "Week in Review" provides week-by-week box scores and standings for every team during the 1993 season. "Trivia" is a poorly designed multiple-choice quiz; the game doesn't tell you the correct answer when you make a mistake. A sample question: "In 1948, what team was the first to put emblems on its helmets? The Bears, Rams or Eagles?" Answer: The Rams.

SPORTS ILLUSTRATED MULTIMEDIA SPORTS ALMANAC, 1995 EDITION
★★½
Developer: StarPress Multimedia Inc.; 800-782-7944
Format: Windows, Macintosh
Price: $45

When your favorite team runs out of steam at the end of the season, you can always console yourself with the thought, "Wait 'til next year." That's my suggestion for *Sports Illustrated Multimedia Sports Almanac, 1995 Edition*, an imperfect compendium of articles and photographs from *Sports Illustrated* magazine supplemented with sports statistics and video clips. The 1995 edition, released in December 1994, represents a modest improvement over the poorly designed 1994 edition, released eight months earlier. If the improvement trend continues, the 1996 edition—due in December 1995—just might be worth buying.

The CD-ROM has two main parts. First, there is a year's worth of the namesake weekly magazine, from the issue of October 4, 1993, through September 26, 1994. Perhaps to test the dedication of its mostly male audience to a diet of nothing but sports, the CD-ROM includes only two photographs from the annual swimsuit edition. Second, there is the full text and statistical tables from the print *Sports Illustrated 1995 Sports Almanac*. The almanac section covers eighteen sports categories: baseball, professional football, professional basketball, hockey, college football, college basketball, tennis, golf, horse racing, boxing, auto racing, soccer, the Olympics, swimming, NCAA, track & field, figure skating, and skiing. For each sport, there is a recap of the most recent season and many pages of historical stats.

For a brief distraction, the developers added fifty video clips covering everything from Tonya Harding's broken skate lace during her performance at the Olympics to statements by owner and player representatives during the 1994 baseball strike. But the clips are so short, averaging just thirty seconds each, that they feel more like a preview of coming attractions than the real thing. The CD-ROM also includes a routine five-hundred-question sports trivia quiz. A sample: "What future Hall of Famer had a brush with the law after killing a sea gull during a pregame warmup? Andre Dawson, George Brett, Dave Winfield or Robin Yount?" After picking the correct player, you get a brief explanation of the event—Winfield accidentally knocked down the bird in August 1993 at a road game in Toronto. Charges of cruelty to animals were later dropped.

My biggest gripe with the CD-ROM is technical flaws. Both the Macintosh and Windows versions can be launched without taking up any space on your hard disk, but the program runs unacceptably slowly unless you choose the "optimum installation" option and surrender fourteen megabytes of hard-disk space. And I found the Macintosh version contained some strange bugs; the program kept crashing after displaying cryptic error messages.

StarPress Multimedia Inc., the developer, also gets five minutes in the penalty box for including a piece of software called *A Man's Guide to Buying Diamonds* on the CD-ROM. Although this program is presented as a bonus, it's actually an extended advertising pitch from the DeBeers diamond cartel. If StarPress wants to put advertising in its products, the ads should be clearly labeled.

Still, I hope StarPress doesn't give up. If the 1996 edition ditches the tacky diamond-buying guide, removes the bugs, and runs speedily with minimal use of the hard disk, the almanac would be a worthwhile addition to the growing field of sports CD-ROM titles.

SPORTZ FREAKZ
★

Developer: Great Bear Technology Inc.; 800-795-4325
Format: Windows
Price: $19

Sportz Freakz pretends to be a sports trivia game, but it's really a tasteless insult to everyone involved—the sports stars who are the butt of the game's stupid jokes as well as anybody unfortunate enough to buy the CD-ROM. The host of *Sportz Freakz*, the eternally annoying comedian Gilbert Gottfried, even calls you "a pathetic loser" at the end of the game.

The lame idea behind *Sportz Freakz* is a trivia contest between two cartoon characters, "Rainbow Head" and "Cuckoo Fan," who take turns punching and kicking each other on screen. The first with four correct answers in a row gets to knock out his opponent, while Gottfried—appearing in video clips—yells in the background. The CD-ROM contains only 140 questions, presented randomly, so players will go through the whole list in just an hour or two. Most of the questions involve sports bloopers, shown in ten-second video clips, that don't have real answers, and many of the questions are inexcusably sexist. One blooper shows a tiger mascot at a basketball game rubbing his paws all over an unhappy cheerleader. The game then asks if the tiger's cheer is (a) "Go, Louisiana, Go!," (b) "We're great!," or (c) "Let me put a tiger in your tank." The "correct" answer is (b). Another question, which mercifully doesn't include a video clip, asks if Wilt Chamberlain's "chicks scored" to "points scored" ratio is three to two or two to one. The answer to this tacky question, which shouldn't have been asked in the first place, is three to two. It's too bad the CD-ROM business doesn't have referees; they would certainly throw *Sportz Freakz* off the market for unsportsmanlike conduct.

d. Health and Fitness

COMPLETE GUIDE TO PRESCRIPTION AND NON-PRESCRIPTION DRUGS
★
Developer: Great Bear Technology Inc.; 800-795-4325
Format: Windows
Price: $39

A skeleton in the pharmacy closet, *Complete Guide to Prescription and Non-Prescription Drugs* doesn't live up to its name. The information is presented in outline form and doesn't appear to go beyond a book of the same name written by Dr. H. Winter Griffith. Here is the entire description of the drug Zantac, one of the most widely prescribed antiulcer medications: "Treatment for duodenal ulcer, decreases acid in the stomach." There are a few additional bits of information on dosage and side effects, as well as audio pronunciation of drug names, but none of these extras justifies spending time with this thinly developed CD-ROM.

RICHARD SIMMONS DEAL-A-MEAL
★★★
Developer: GT Interactive Software Corp.; 800-362-9400
Format: Windows
Price: $45

If instilling an upbeat attitude were the only necessary step for losing weight, then Richard Simmons could track down and eliminate every ounce of excess flab on the planet. The endlessly bouncy exercise guru has been selling his "Deal-A-Meal" weight-loss program for a decade; now he's gone beyond books and television into CD-ROM. If Simmons's continual drumbeat of "you can do it" encouragement doesn't grate on your nerves, then you might like *Richard Simmons Deal-A-Meal*.

The CD-ROM delivers a personalized version of the Simmons program. You start by watching a half-hour presentation by Simmons in a series of video clips, explaining his philosophy and asking you to enter information about your current health and weight loss goals. He even asks you to select a password to keep your weight records private. Simmons finishes the introduction by asking you to come back on a regular basis to update your weight and get more video pep talks. "You have me right at your fingertips whenever you need me," he declares. Those pep talks are long on self-esteem and short on diet specifics. A sample: "Approach each and every day with confidence. Remember, if you have faith in yourself, you will succeed."

Unfortunately, Simmons can't offer a magic formula—the Deal-A-Meal program stresses gradual weight loss by eating less and exercising regularly. Included in the box with the CD-ROM are the program's thirty-five Deal-A-Meal cards, which specify how much of certain foods you can eat each day. If you're allowed two Dairy cards daily, for example, you can eat one cup of frozen yogurt or two cups of whole milk.

To help you follow the program, the CD-ROM has an extensive list of recipes based on the Deal-A-Meal cards with silly names such as "Happy Coat Fish Fillets with Gingered Cucumbers" and "Man-O-Manicotti." There's also a table for converting regular food into Deal-A-Meal equivalents—a single Big Mac, for instance, requires trading away two days' worth of Fat cards.

DR. RUTH'S ENCYCLOPEDIA OF SEX
★★★½
Developer: Creative Multimedia Corp.; 800-262-7668
Format: Windows
Price: $29

Dr. Ruth Westheimer is the Stealth fighter of sex education. This tiny woman with the German accent, who turns 67 in 1995, knows how to talk about important sexual issues without triggering fear or embarrassment among the readers of her books, listeners to her radio talk show, and viewers of her frequent television appearances. *Dr. Ruth's Encyclopedia of Sex*, a CD-ROM based on her book of the same name, launches a very effective attack on sexual ignorance by combining text, illustrations, animations, audio, and video—all with the unmistakable Dr. Ruth touch.

I'd particularly recommend *Dr. Ruth* to parents who want assistance in explaining delicate sexual subjects to their children. Dr. Ruth talks in simple sentences that even preadolescents will understand and delves into the most intimate subjects without ever becoming suggestive. In the text, for example, she dispels some common birth control myths: "The most dangerous sexual myth says that a woman cannot get pregnant if the man withdraws before he ejaculates. This myth continues to be propagated by many men, who are desperate to have sex with a woman even when methods of birth control are not available. Since some men will say almost anything in that situation, it is left to the woman to be sensible."

The CD-ROM opens with a computer-generated replica of Dr. Ruth's office. In a video image superimposed on the scene, Dr. Ruth herself invites you to explore the office. Clicking the encyclopedia on her desk summons the book's text. Clicking a radio produces audio excerpts from her radio show. Clicking a television set gives an index to the fourteen animations and 27 videos spread through the encyclopedia, which appear in a four-inch diagonal window on a standard fourteen-inch monitor. "Click around. That you can do without a condom," Dr. Ruth slyly remarks at one point during your wanderings. There is also a multiple-choice "Sex Quiz" and an "Ask Dr. Ruth" section in which she answers questions from readers.

Most of the video clips show Dr. Ruth delivering a few sentences on her favorite subjects, such as the need for men to become more involved in foreplay and accepting masturbation as a natural part of sexuality. But there are several segments of literally life-and-death importance: an animation showing how to apply a condom and video clips demonstrating breast cancer self-examination for women and testicular cancer self-examination for men. Parents will appreciate a password protection feature, which allows them to block children from selected areas of the CD-ROM or from the entire program. But there's almost nothing in *Dr. Ruth* that shouldn't be experienced by everyone except the smallest child. Best of all, this vital information is delivered at a surprisingly affordable price, making *Dr. Ruth* on CD-ROM a great value as well as an excellent educational tool.

THE FAMILY DOCTOR, 3RD EDITION
★★

Developer: Creative Multimedia Corp.; 800-262-7668
Format: Windows, Macintosh
Price: $39

Dr. Allan Bruckheim is a busy man. A practicing family physician, he also finds the time to write a syndicated question-and-answer newspaper column called "The Family Doctor." He's too busy, apparently, to have updated his many columns before they were dumped onto this CD-ROM. During a three-minute video introduction, Dr. Bruckheim concedes that advances in medical science mean "some of the older answers are incomplete by today's standards." But the dates when each of the 2,300 columns first appeared in print isn't given, so we have no way of figuring out whether the information is reasonably current.

It's too bad we're left in the dark. Dr. Bruckheim has a good bedside manner and explains common health problems and their treatment clearly, without a lot of medical jargon. Here's his description of kidney stones: "Stones are formed from the minerals that occur in our urine. Normally, they may form minute crystals that are passed out of our bodies along with the urine flow, but sometimes they clump together and cling to the tissue lining the inside of the kidney. There they continue to grow as new crystals are added, and they harden as time passes . . . Despite the knowledge of [some] factors as possibly contributing to the manufacture of these nasty pebbles, no one is really sure why they occur or why some people develop them while others do not."

Dr. Bruckheim's columns, each running two to four paragraphs, are arranged alphabetically by subject on the CD-ROM and are also accessible through a word-search feature. The developers have thrown in a bunch of extra material, mostly lifted from medical reference books, that would be easier to use in print than on a CD-ROM. There is a guide to prescription drugs that gives information only in outline form, a fairly technical directory of diseases that may be difficult for nonprofessionals to follow, a first-aid section with limited instructions on dealing with everyday catastrophes such as burns and cuts; and a selection of fuzzy anatomy illustrations poorly copied from physician wall charts.

FITNESS PARTNER
★★
Developer: Computer Directions Inc.; 800-600-2348
Format: Windows
Price: $39

Fitness Partner is a breakthrough concept that came to market about five years too soon. Computer Directions, a small software developer in Fresno, California, had the bright idea in 1993 of putting a personal fitness trainer on CD-ROM, allowing the user to design a custom workout program and perform exercises along with the video image of a professional aerobics instructor. These workouts can be varied from day to day, avoiding the inevitable monotony of repeatedly working out with the same Jane Fonda videotape.

But CD-ROM technology can't stretch this far. The video images play in a window filling only a quarter of the screen, so the aerobics instructor you're trying to follow is only about four inches high on a standard fourteen-inch monitor. That's too small to watch when you're on the floor doing leg lifts. The images also appear to be playing at about half the thirty frames a second of normal television, so the instructor's movements are jerky and unrealistic. These problems should be resolved in two or three years, with the introduction of more powerful personal computers that display full-motion, full-screen video and declining prices for larger seventeen- and twenty-inch monitors.

When that happens, a product like *Fitness Partner* could be a big seller, at least for people who have their computer located in a room with sufficient space for exercise. The CD-ROM offers seventy-five exercises with such descriptive names as elbow rolls, bicep curls, and doggie lifts. Each is demonstrated by Roni Smaldino, a relentlessly cheerful Fresno aerobics instructor. Her exertions can be combined into workouts at any one of three levels—beginner, intermediate, or advanced—depending on the user's physical condition. Workouts are divided into three phases: warm-up, workout, and cool-down. The disk will manage exercise programs for as many as ten people, with each person able to set up nine exercise routines.

To compete in this future market, *Fitness Partner* will need a few minor improvements. The CD-ROM offers only three choices of music—country, jazz, or pop/rock—that are cheesy-sounding synthesized organ chords resembling the annoying soundtracks on video games. Also, the program is inflexible once a workout begins. You can stop the action to reprogram your activity, but there is no easy way to skip past a single exercise you want to ignore for the day.

THE DOCTORS BOOK OF HOME REMEDIES
★★

Developer: Compton's NewMedia Inc.; 800-284-2045
Format: DOS, Windows, Macintosh
Price: $25

The Doctors Book of Home Remedies on CD-ROM is a disappointing rehash of a popular book carrying the same name. According to Rodale Press, the book's publisher, the print version has sold 12 million copies. The CD-ROM delivers the full text of the book, written by the editors of *Prevention* magazine in consultation with physicians but doesn't offer much more.

The CD-ROM has three features not found in the book. There is a collection of fifteen video clips, each running only a minute or two, that give superficial explanations for such conditions as snoring, knee injuries, and back pain. An abbreviated version of *Webster's New World Dictionary and Thesaurus* provides definitions of medical terms. And there is a "personal health checkup" in which you enter your age, height, weight, and whether you smoke, drink, and exercise regularly; then you get a few paragraphs of canned text on possible health risks, as well as recommendations for daily caloric intake and target levels for your heart rate, blood pressure, and cholesterol.

I like what's in the book: jargon-free descriptions of how to deal with common complaints in articles such as "Motion Sickness: 25 Quick-Action Cures" and "Tendinitis: 14 Soothing Remedies." There's even a selection of "alternate routes" describing folk treatments that, while harmless, clearly aren't mainstream medicine. Under the heading of folk cures for warts, the suggestions include "rub with a piece of chalk or a raw potato" and "tape the inner side of a banana skin to a plantar wart." Personally, I'd rather keep suffering from a wart than walk around with a banana skin taped to my body.

Anyway, if you want *The Doctors Book of Home Remedies*, I'd recommend buying the print version. You'll save money and avoid tying up eleven megabytes of space on your hard disk, which is required for a full installation of the CD-ROM. If you insist on getting the CD-ROM, make sure you get the newest version, released in November 1994, that says "revised multimedia edition" on the box; some stores and mail-order catalogs may still be selling an older version that contains only text.

KATHY SMITH'S FAT BURNING SYSTEM
★★★
Developer: Xiphias; 800-421-9194
Format: Windows, Macintosh
Price: $29

Like most people, I'm willing to do anything to lose weight except diet and exercise. Fitness trainer Kathy Smith, well known on the workout circuit for her books and videotapes, understands our desire for quick-fix programs that shed extra pounds without effort. But she won't let us accept easy answers. Instead, her programs wisely stress "slow, permanent lifestyle change" that gradually alters unhealthy habits.

Kathy Smith's Fat Burning System combines on one CD-ROM elements from her books, audiotapes, and videotapes. There's no promise of overnight results in this ten-week program, but the disk is full of good advice—if you can stick with it—and helps you with features such as a diary you print out to track all the food you eat. "The purpose of the Daily Diary is to make you aware of why, what, when and how much you eat," the text explains. "Once you understand your habits, you'll be able to identify the thoughts, feelings, situations and behavior patterns that lead to poor food choices or overeating."

Smith appears in audio clips and video clips, displayed in a four-inch diagonal window on a standard fourteen-inch monitor, to offer encouragement. She also provides advice on meal planning, developing an exercise program, and maintaining self-confidence, all divided into 70 "cells" using the *Matrix Interface*, described below. Smith even answers a series of questions posed by her clients, such as whether it's all right to eat cheese. "Cheese is not a food you should plan to snack on every day," she responds, noting that cheese contains up to 98 percent fat. Low-fat cheese, Smith points out, is still 50 percent fat, although she concedes an occasional dish containing low-fat cheese is acceptable.

The CD-ROM, by the way, does not contain a workout video. You'll have to buy a videotape if you want to exercise along with Smith in your living room. But the CD-ROM is still a great deal at $29 in most stores; you're getting a complete fitness program for not much more than the cost of a single Kathy Smith book or videotape.

About the *Matrix Interface*: Xiphias, a small CD-ROM developer based in Los Angeles, took a big gamble in 1993 by adopting a common format for many of its products. Called the *Matrix Interface*, the format chops the contents of a CD-ROM into "cells" that are arrayed in rows and columns on the main screen you encounter when you start the program. Each row has a specific theme, so the CD-ROM can be played in a linear fashion like a book, starting with the leftmost cell in the top column and proceeding to the right and down to the next row. Users can also pick individual cells, which typically contain video clips and text, or select "author mode" for a predesigned tour.

There are advantages to the *Matrix Interface*. Once you've learned how to navigate one Xiphias title, you can instantly switch to another without reading the manual. Also, the *Matrix Interface* is a good way to present certain types of information, such as reference material. But the *Matrix Interface* is too rigid a structure for all the titles put out by Xiphias. In some cases, dividing the material into cells gets in the way of moving naturally from one piece of content to another.

MAYO CLINIC FAMILY HEALTH BOOK
★★★
Developer: IVI Publishing Inc.; 800-432-1332
Format: Windows, Macintosh
Price: $45

If you want to tap the world-famous Mayo Clinic's vast knowledge of medicine without traveling to one of its hospitals, you have two choices. You can buy the *Mayo Clinic Family Health Book* in print. Expect to pay about $30 to $40 for a 1,400-page tome published by William Morrow & Co., that tips the scales at eight pounds. Or you can buy the *Mayo Clinic Family Health Book* on CD-ROM, paying $40 to $50 for the full contents of the printed book, along with about ninety minutes of sound and narration and forty-five short animations.

In print or on CD-ROM, you'll get comprehensive and practical advice on everything from diaper rash to prostate cancer. Suffering from a backache? There are three relevant articles: "Taking Care of Your Back," "How to Protect Your Back," and "Treatment for Your Backache." "Always sleep on a firm surface or mattress or insert a board beneath your mattress," the book declares. "During an episode of back pain, try to remain flat on your back with your legs drawn up for long periods. For a strain or sprain, three or four days of such rest should bring relief. If not, consult your physician."

The additional audio and video on the CD-ROM are only marginally beneficial. All the photo captions from the book, for instance, are narrated in the CD-ROM version. It's a nice touch, but it doesn't convey any extra information. The animations are very brief, and many of them aren't especially useful. In the book, for example, there is an illustration of a man receiving an electrocardiogram, or EKG, showing the wires glued to his chest with an inset image of the squiggly line produced by the EKG machine. On the CD-ROM, you see the same image, only the squiqqly line scrolls across the screen for twenty seconds. A few of the animations are very valuable, although extremely brief, such as a five-second demonstration of the Heimlich maneuver for helping someone who is choking and a twenty-second demonstration of mouth-to-mouth resuscitation.

So, should you buy the book or the CD-ROM? Books are easier to use than computers, making print the better choice for immediate access. I've got both the CD-ROM and the book, and I'll admit to using the book more frequently. On the other hand, there are more ways to search through a CD-ROM. Typing in the word "backache," for example, instantly produces a list of all 11 articles mentioning the word. In contrast, the print book's index entry on backache refers to only six articles. Either way, *Mayo Clinic Family Health Book* is a worthwhile investment in taking care of yourself.

MAYO CLINIC FAMILY PHARMACIST
★★★
Developer: IVI Publishing Inc.; 800-432-1332
Format: Windows
Price: $45

Doctors at the Mayo Clinic seem to have ignored that part of the Hippocratic oath that says physicians always know more than their patients. This refreshing attitude—that we should all participate in our own health-care decisions—runs throughout *Mayo Clinic Family Pharmacist*, a powerful tool for self-education. The CD-ROM contains detailed information on 7,600 prescription and over-the-counter medications and gives you new ways to use the information.

You can, for example, create personal medical histories for

everyone in your family and print them out when visiting doctors. The program will even check for possible drug interactions among each individual's list of medications. Another useful feature is a "search by characteristic" to identify medications. You select from a menu the color, size, and shape (pill, tablet, or capsule) of a particular drug, then the program searches for matching drugs and displays color pictures of what it finds. The drug information in *Family Pharmacist* is comprehensive and only occasionally lapses into impenetrable medical jargon. Most of the data, by the way, comes from a medical reference book called *USP DI Advice for the Patient* from the U.S. Pharmacopeial Convention.

"To get the most out of your medicines, you must make an informed decision as to whether to take the medicine at all, to know about the medicine and its effects, and follow precise directions for use," the introduction to *Family Pharmacist* explains, challenging the all-too-frequent attitude among physicians that their prescriptions are beyond questioning. "As the purchaser from your health-care provider of his or her knowledge, skills and office services, you must weigh the advice given and determine whether you accept it and are willing to follow it. To make that decision, you need to have information from your health-care provider about the therapy being recommended. How are you going to get that information? The same way you get information about any other service or thing you buy. You will have to ask questions—and answer some, too. Communication is a two-way street."

In this spirit of self-reliance, *Family Pharmacist* helps you become your own doctor for treating minor aches and pains. In the over-the-counter medicine section, you can pick an ailment and click a button labeled "Pharmacist Help." You answer a series of questions about your symptoms and overall health, then the program suggests possible medications. The CD-ROM also includes helpful sections on first aid and early disease detection. Both sections include animations demonstrating key procedures, such as breast self-examination for women and testicle self-examination for men. The animations, however, are one of the few disappointments in *Family Pharmacist*, amounting to little more than simple line drawings showing little movement.

One other flaw is excessively greedy hardware requirements. *Family Pharmacist* for Windows demands nine megabytes of precious hard-disk space and insists on reconfiguring your computer's AUTOEXEC.BAT file. Unless you're a major hypochondriac, you're only going to use *Family Pharmacist* occasionally, hardly justifying the permanent loss of nine megabytes on your hard disk.

MAYO CLINIC SPORTS HEALTH & FITNESS
★★
Developer: IVI Publishing Inc.; 800-432-1332
Format: Windows-2
Price: $45

Trying to deliver a personal fitness trainer on CD-ROM, *Mayo Clinic Sports Health & Fitness* instead comes across as impersonal and ineffective. The supposedly customized exercise programs have a one-size-fits-all appearance and a reference section, although full of valuable information, provides nothing you couldn't get in a book for much less money.

Mayo Sports certainly looks slick—the CD-ROM is packed with video clips taken from the ESPN cable television sports network. But the clips, playing in a window filling a quarter of the screen, don't really contribute anything other than visual distraction. In the section on sports injuries, for example, there is a button on screen labeled "Try to avoid doing this!" When you push the button, you see sixty seconds of downhill skiers and surfers tumbling head over heels. Another video clip on the importance of wearing sunglasses and sunscreen when exercising outdoors merely shows scenes of beach volleyball.

The CD-ROM is divided into three parts. "Survey" prompts you to enter basic information about your health, much like the forms you fill out in a doctor's office. ESPN reporter Jimmy Roberts is superimposed on the screen, explaining each step of the questionnaire. After completing the survey, you get canned suggestions for an exercise program listing the number of minutes per day you should spend on each activity. The "Journal" section lets you keep track of the survey results and type notes into an on-screen diary. But the program does nothing to support your exercise program; for example, *Mayo Sports* offers no easy way to reexamine your health status and determine when you should increase or decrease the amount of exercise. Finally, the "Reference" section provides 235 on-screen pages covering eight sports fitness topics: general fitness, anatomy, nutrition, exercise, injury prevention and management, equipment, sports psychology, and parents, coaches, and children. The information is useful, although predictable, such as this entry on parents pushing their children into organized athletics: "Forcing children to play sports may rob them of the benefits of participation and negatively affect the relationship between the child and parent. Respect the decision your child makes, and explore other ways to encourage him or her to participate in fitness and exercise."

MAYO CLINIC—THE TOTAL HEART
★★
Developer: IVI Publishing Inc.; 800-432-1332
Format: Windows, Macintosh
Price: $29

Unless you're one of those rare people who prefer reading page after page of text on a computer screen rather than holding a book, don't bother with *Mayo Clinic—The Total Heart*. The CD-ROM is just a retread of the *Mayo Clinic Heart Book*, a 400-page volume published by William Morrow.

The book, available for about $20, is an excellent choice for anyone interested in the heart and its ailments. That's a big audience—70 million Americans suffer some form of cardiovascular disease. Written with the support of more than one hundred cardiologists and health-care professionals at the world-famous Mayo Clinic, the book provides a clearly written and detailed look at how the heart works, along with the diagnosis, treatment, and prevention of heart disease.

The text never talks down to its audience, and the authors aren't afraid to admit that doctors don't have all the answers. Consider this entry on the subject of coffee: "Medical research isn't unanimous on the question of coffee's effect on coronary artery disease . . . Even if coffee drinking were to be conclusively linked with a higher risk of coronary artery disease, the way in which it might cause it remains elusive. Some researchers suggest that coffee drinking is simply more common in people who have other risk factors, such as smoking, fat consumption (for example, coffee drinkers may eat more cream cheese Danish than those who do not drink coffee) or inactivity . . . Although the final word is still out, a prudent recommendation is to limit coffee intake to no more than three or four cups a day. The benefit may be limited, but because it is an easily accomplished goal for most people, it is worth aiming for."

The CD-ROM delivers all this text but not much more. There

are thirty-four very brief, very simple animations. Watching an animated drawing of a catheter moving through a vein isn't much of an improvement from the book's illustration of a catheter already in place. Five separate animations showing how to perform CPR run just over thirty seconds and lose much of their impact by showing illustrations rather than real people. The disk also contains sixty minutes of audio, mostly narration of captions. Although *Mayo Clinic—The Total Heart* is easy to operate and has powerful word-search features, the *Mayo Clinic Heart Book* stands out as the superior learning tool.

PHARMASSIST
★★
Developer: SoftKey International Inc.; 800-227-5609
Format: Windows
Price: $49

PharmAssist comes in a bright and shiny bottle, but there isn't much inside. A guide to both prescription and illegal street drugs, *PharmAssist* has a well-designed on-screen interface. After selecting a drug, you push various buttons to learn about its function, dosage, and side effects. These buttons are decorated with clever little pictures; a pacifier, for example, to find out about possible health risks for infants or a cracked heart to get cautionary information for heart patients. Too often, however, the text you get in response to pushing one of these buttons is just one sentence. Here's the entire description for Nicorette, prescribed to block nicotine cravings in ex-smokers: "This drug is an anti-smoking agent used to treat addictive smoking habits."

One useful feature is a pronunciation guide. Clicking on the picture of any prescription drug summons a female voice clearly stating the name. You'll learn, for example, that the antidepressant drug Tofranil is pronounced "toff-ran-ill," not "toe-fran-ill." A more unusual feature is a guide to illegal drugs, describing their effects and how to recognize drug abusers. There's even a long list of slang terms for each drug; I was surprised to learn that LSD has been called Blue Cheers, Brown Dots, California Triple Dip, Mind Detergent, and Uncle Sid, among other strange names. *PharmAssist* also includes a brief first aid guide and a directory of health warnings and vaccination requirements for international travel. These few distractions, however, don't compensate for the skimpy text.

Chapter Eight:
Business, Career, Education, and Personal Finance

This is the money chapter, covering CD-ROMs for business, career planning, and personal finance. I've also included language instruction, a field often related to career advancement and higher education.

a. Business

BUSINESS LIBRARY VOLUME 1
★★½
Developer: Allegro New Media Inc.; 800-424-1992
Format: Windows
Price: $45

If you walked into a bookstore, went to the "business" shelf, and started pulling out titles at random, you'd get something like *Business Library Volume 1*. This collection of twelve books and three videotapes on a single CD-ROM unquestionably offers a huge amount of information, but the material wanders all over the business landscape. It's unlikely most businesspeople would want more than one or two of these titles, so buyers might be better off back at the bookstore than investing in this CD-ROM. And, although *Business Library* is easy to install and operate, you're still forced to read large amounts of text on a computer screen—not the best way to absorb big chunks of information. The three videotapes are also difficult to follow because the images are displayed in a tiny window measuring three inches diagonally on a standard fourteen-inch monitor.

The twelve books in *Business Library* are *Business to Business Communications Handbook* by Fred R. Messner, *The Feel of Success in Selling* by Jim Schneider, *Finance & Accounting for Nonfinancial Managers* by Steven A. Finkler, *How to Get People to Do Things Your Way* by J. Robert Parkinson, *How to Make Big Money in Real Estate in the Tighter, Tougher '90s Market* by Tyler G. Hicks, *International Herald Tribune Guide to Business Travel Europe* by Alan Tiller and Roger Beardwood, *Joyce Lain Kennedy's Career Book* by Kennedy and coauthor Darryl Laramore, *Meetings Rules & Procedures* by Alice N. Pohl, *State of the Art Marketing Research* by A. B. Blankenship and George Edward Breen, *Successful Direct Marketing Methods* by Bob Stone, *Successful Telemarketing* by Bob Stone and John Wyman, and *Total Global Strategy: Managing for Worldwide Competitive Advantage* by George S. Yip. The three videotapes are *30 Timeless Direct Marketing Principles* by Bob Stone, *From Advertising to Integrated Marketing Communications* by Don E. Schulz, and *New Product Development* by George Gruenwald.

HOW TO REALLY START YOUR OWN BUSINESS
★★
Developer: Zelos Digital Publishing; 800-345-6777
Format: Windows, Macintosh
Price: $49

How to Really Start Your Own Business is a good book that has become a bad CD-ROM. Published by *Inc. Magazine* and written by former *Inc.* editor David Gumpert, the book is full of hard-headed advice for the would-be entrepreneur. The CD-ROM, however, contains little more than a narrated outline of the text with a selection of very brief and trite video clips from a "mentor panel" of nine business owners who've been through the process themselves.

Gumpert goes to great lengths to lay out all the many hurdles to starting a business. In the book's text, which is included on the CD-ROM, he compares the start-up process to marriage—it quickly becomes the most important relationship in the entrepreneur's life and is easier to start than to sustain. Indeed, he notes that 60 to 80 percent of new businesses fail within five years. Such an overwhelming project also has personal risks, Gumpert explains: "Adding pain to much of the suffering endured by the entrepreneurs along the road to success is that for some, their financial accomplishments come at significant personal cost . . . Most troubling are the family problems that grow out of the start-up process . . . Starting a business is all-consuming personally, and family members often have trouble dealing with that fact."

The CD-ROM presents Gumpert's work in ten chapters, such as "Finding the Right People," "Your Cash Flow," and "The Best Business Plan." When you start the program, you're asked a few questions about the type of business you're interested in launching and are assigned three of the nine entrepreneurs who deliver video commentary appropriate to your goal. The group is a mixture of entrepreneurial types, from a self-employed financial writer to the founder of the Pizza Hut restaurant chain. But their statements, delivered in video clips running just ten to thirty seconds, are full of platitudes and short on specific information. For example, Cleveland home builder Jim Buck has this to say on the subject of controlling expenses: "If you don't need it until next week, don't get it until next week. Get it an hour before."

How to Really Start Your Own Business on CD-ROM is also awkward to operate. Every time you start the program, you have to listen to a long narrated introduction. There is no index, glossary, or listing of the video clips. A "Resource Guide" gives a brief bibliography and list of small-business associations but seems to lean heavily toward recommending other books published by *Inc. Magazine*. If you're considering the bold step of starting a business, your first step toward controlling unnecessary expenses should be buying Gumpert's book instead of this CD-ROM.

THE 1994 INFORMATION PLEASE BUSINESS ALMANAC & DESK REFERENCE
★★
Developer: Parsons Technology Inc.; 800-223-6925
Format: DOS, Windows
Price: $29

Here's a business tip you won't find on the CD-ROM version of *The 1994 Information Please Business Almanac & Desk Reference*: You can save a lot of money by purchasing the *Almanac* in print, and you won't miss a thing. The CD-ROM simply delivers the text and charts found in the paperback book, published by Houghton Mifflin, for more than double the price. What's more, the CD-ROM is out of date—it came on the market in late 1994, just as the 1995 print edition was reaching store shelves.

The book is an overstocked warehouse full of valuable information. Among the material I found was the *Forbes* magazine 1992 list of the four hundred wealthiest Americans, an explanation of the ISO 9000 quality-control standard, a list of American Chambers of Commerce abroad, a schedule for major conventions and trade shows in the United States, and a list of the fifty largest banks involved in real estate lending.

The CD-ROM's main screen presents a table of contents dividing the book into twelve main topics: maps and mileage tables, business law and government, communications, corporate administration, finance, human resources, international, manufacturing, marketing, office management, personal computing, and reference. Clicking on a topic displays a submenu of specific articles and tables. There's also an alphabetical index and a word-search feature that allows you to quickly create a list of every entry mentioning a specific word. Still, I don't think the word-search feature and the ability to copy text into a document you're writing with a word processor—the only benefits of the *Almanac* on CD-ROM not matched by the print version—add enough value to justify the CD-ROM's higher cost.

IT'S LEGAL 5.0 DELUXE CD-ROM EDITION
★★★½
Developer: Parsons Technology Inc.; 800-223-6925
Format: Windows
Price: $29

We've all heard the old saying that anyone representing themselves in legal matters has a fool for an attorney. But I'd go a step further and suggest that anyone who seeks legal services unnecessarily is hiring an attorney with a fool for a client. *It's Legal 5.0 Deluxe CD-ROM Edition* is an easy, inexpensive way for small-business people to avoid both forms of foolishness.

The CD-ROM will quickly preprare fifty-four legal documents—which can be customized to meet the legal needs of each state—such as a bill of sale, employee confidentiality agreement, bad check notice, minutes for a board of directors meeting, commerical real estate lease, and promissory note. You select one of two ways to complete a document. "Interview" mode asks you a series of simple questions about what you want from the document, then puts all the relevant data in the right places. "Template" mode shows the document on screen with blank spaces in which you insert the details. If you're unsure what to do at any point, an on-screen "Legal Guide" explains the concept in question.

It's Legal isn't just for business; about half the documents are related to individual and family affairs. To find the document you want, you look in one of nine categories: Estate/Personal, Powers of Attorney, Heath and Medical, Consumer/Credit, Real Estate, Financial, Corporate, Employment, and Other. Using the "Interview" mode, I was able to complete and print a simple will in less than fifteen minutes.

The CD-ROM also includes two helpful bonus programs: a guide to legal terms called *The Plain-Law Language Dictionary* and *Interest Vision* for calculating loan payment schedules and the future value of investments. I'm not going to recommend *It's Legal* as a complete substitute for hiring a lawyer—that might get me in trouble with the American Bar Association. But I have no doubt this program can help reduce legal fees by allowing you to create some documents without a lawyer's help and by better preparing you for those occasions when visiting a lawyer is unavoidable.

MULTIMEDIA MBA SMALL BUSINESS EDITION
★★½
Developer: SoftKey International Inc./Compact Publishing; 800-227-5609
Format: Windows
Price: $79

Starting your own business requires tremendous powers of organization, powers that aren't demonstrated in *Multimedia MBA Small Business Edition*. Presenting itself as the complete guide to starting a business, the CD-ROM instead comes across as a seemingly random collection of material—some of which is quite useful—thrown together with little regard for creating an overall structure that ties everything together.

Most of the text in *Multimedia MBA* comes from Richard D. Irwin, a publisher of business books, and is split into three major sections: the library, tutorials, and tools. The library presents hundreds of articles in seven categories: understanding business, entrepreneurship, business law, accounting, human resources, advertising, and retailing. The tutorials provide more articles in eight categories: starting your own business, Total Quality Management, general ledger accounting, contracts, human resources, advertising, retailing, and international business. "Tools" offers a long menu of model business forms such as partnership agreements, employee evaluations, and warehouse receipts. There's also a small-business accounting program called GLAS that's too complicated for those who aren't already intimately familiar with general-ledger accounting principles. These three main sections are supplemented with a dictionary of business terms, video clips of entrepreneurs talking about business issues, and examples of TV commercials and print ads.

This isn't exciting stuff. The articles are written in a plodding textbook style. Consider this explanation of a business plan: "If we think of the business plan as a road map, we might better understand its significance. Let's suppose you were trying to decide whether to drive from Boston to Los Angeles in a motor home. There are a number of possible routes, each requiring different time frames and costs. Like the entrepreneur, the traveler must make some important decisions and gather information before preparing the plan." *Multimedia MBA* won't work as a primary reference for launching a business. But budding entrepreneurs might pull out useful bits and pieces of information if they're willing to dedicate enough time to wandering through the CD-ROM's many overlapping sections in search of what they need.

PEACHTREE ACCOUNTING FOR WINDOWS RELEASE 3.0
★★★
Developer: Peachtree Software Inc.; 800-228-0068
Format: Windows
Price: $119

Small-business owners are always looking for ways to manage their finances without learning the intricacies of accounting. *Peachtree Accounting for Windows Release 3.0* almost meets that elusive goal—you don't need any accounting knowledge to start using the program. But you'll need to learn at least a little bit as you go along to master all the features, which include handling customer records, payroll, and inventory. Built around the general ledger system of debits and credits, the program is largely successful in avoiding accounting jargon, although users will still have to cope with terms such as "accounts payable" and "accounts receivable." The CD-ROM also throws in a half-dozen pieces of business software that aren't directly related to *Peachtree Accounting*: *Avery LabelPro for Windows*, a program for creating and printing labels; *Multimedia Business Library*, a collection of twelve business books; *FaxWorks 3.0*, a utility for sending and receiving faxes by modem; *Financial Competence*, a series of interactive lessons on accounting principles; *Professor Windows*, a tutorial on Microsoft Windows; and CompuServe's *Information Manager for Windows*, software for accessing the CompuServe on-line service.

QUICKBOOKS DELUXE FOR WINDOWS
★★★½
Developer: Intuit Inc.; 800-624-8742
Format: Windows
Price: $129

Accounting is never fun for nonaccountants. For that matter, I doubt many accountants get excited about their work. Most small-business owners, however, don't have the luxury of avoiding at least some bookkeeping duties. *QuickBooks Deluxe for Windows* is a nearly painless way for nonaccountants to tackle business accounting. The CD-ROM is built around *QuickBooks 3.0 for Windows*, a program also available on floppy disks that hides the complexities of general-ledger accounting behind familiar on-screen forms such as checks, bills, invoices, and customer lists.

But *QuickBooks Deluxe*, which costs only about $30 more than the floppy version, takes two important steps beyond the floppy version. First, the CD-ROM includes a companion program called *QuickPay 3.0* for managing payroll. That fills an important gap; most competing small-business accounting programs already include a payroll module. Second, the CD-ROM provides a "business center" full of helpful reference material. There are seven workbooks on subjects such as "borrowing money for your business" and "managing accounts receivable and collections." The on-screen pages of these workbooks include buttons to push for short audio clips of small-business owners describing how they've solved various problems, while the text offers hard-headed advice: "Bill your customers promptly to encourage timely payment. When that does not work, however, you'll need to have systems in place to collect more efficiently from some customers . . . Consider, for example, billing more often rather than sending the conventional monthly invoice. A weekly reminder will likely bring in payment sooner." The business center also includes the complete text of four Internal Revenue Service publications covering tax issues relevant to small businesses and a ZIP code directory. The full set of manuals for *QuickBooks* and *QuickPay* is available on the CD-ROM, and you get a coupon to order the print set from Intuit for $25.

b. College and Career Planning

BARRON'S PROFILES OF AMERICAN COLLEGES ON CD-ROM
★★★
Developer: Laser Resources Inc.; 800-535-2737
Format: Windows, Macintosh
Price: $49

For many adolescents, the first major life-shaping decision they make on their own is deciding where to go to college. It's a scary process requiring standardized tests, filling out long application forms, and agonizing over finances. *Barron's Profiles of American Colleges on CD-ROM* can help make this rite of passage a little easier.

The disk contains the full text from the twentieth edition of Barron's college guide, with information on 1,650 colleges and universities in the United States current through the 1992-93 academic year. A powerful and easy-to-use search feature lets future college students sort through the many entries using any criteria they wish, far exceeding the performance of the print version's index. Students could search for every college in California, for example, that offers a major in modern dance and has tuition under $6,000 a year.

The CD-ROM also offers a relatively small amount of additional material. There are one- to three-minute promotional video clips from eighteen schools, ranging from the Montana College of Mineral Science and Technology to the University of Connecticut. Some 48 schools have supplied their complete curriculum catalog, including Bryn Mawr College in Pennsylvania and Drake University in Des Moines, Iowa; sixty-six schools have supplied a copy of their admission application, including Boston University and Southern Methodist University in Dallas. These supplements are wonderful if you're interested in one of these schools; perhaps in future years CD-ROMs of this type will include video clips, catalogs, and applications for virtually all colleges.

Barron's college profiles, by the way, stick to a strict formula covering the number of students, ratio of applications to acceptances, financial aid programs, and listings of academic programs. Students won't get much sense of what the school is really like—for that, they have to turn to "underground" college guides that stress subjective impressions over statistics.

JOB-POWER SOURCE
★½
Developer: InfoBusiness Inc.; 800-657-5300
Format: Windows
Price: $39

Confusing quantity with quality, *Job-Power Source* provides more than you'd ever want to know about finding a job—then neglects to give you any effective way to use the information. The CD-ROM contains the full text of twelve job-hunting books and a two-hour video presentation. All this material stresses the importance of carefully planning your job search, but *Job-Power Source* ignores its own advice by dumping redundant and out-of-date text onto the disk without an explanation for how the various pieces could be used to mount an effective job-hunting campaign.

At the core of *Job-Power Source* are eleven books by "renowned career experts" Ron and Caryl Krannich. The source of this renown is left to the user's imagination, however, because the CD-ROM provides no biography or background sketch. The books are filled with peppy you-can-do-it advice and have equally peppy titles: *Discover the Best Jobs for You, Careering and Re-Careering for the '90s, The Best Jobs for the 1990s and Into the 21st Century, Job Search Letters That Get Results, Dynamite Résumés, Dynamite Cover Letters, High Impact Résumés & Letters, Network Your Way to Career Success, Salary Success, Interview for Success,* and *Dynamite Answers to Interview Questions.* Some publisher must be paying these folks by the word, however, because the books are highly repetitive. The twelfth book comes from the U.S. Bureau of Labor Statistics. Released in 1991, *Occupational Outlook Handbook* provides detailed information on just about every job category in the country. But the developers did a poor job of scanning the book's pages on the CD-ROM; the pages look like fuzzy photocopies.

Job-Power Source also claims to offer "interactive work sheets," but these turn out to be nothing more than on-screen fill-in-the-blank checklists on such subjects as "ten things I enjoy about work" and "my most significant achievements." The only halfway worthwhile part of *Job-Power Source* is the video presentation by "award-winning communications specialist and trainer" Pat Sladey, who also has no biography. The developers appear to have taken the videotape of a two-hour Sladey seminar and chopped it into forty-six clips, each running one to four minutes.

Sladey is full of practical advice. Watching her pretend to be an ineffective job candidate—chewing gum, squirming in her chair, and refusing to make eye contact—is a useful warning for anyone embarking on the interview process. But job seekers eager to conserve cash and use their time effectively would be better off just buying a videotape and a few good books rather than trying to make sense of the poorly structured *Job-Power Source.*

LOVEJOY'S COLLEGE COUNSELOR
★★★
Developer: InterMedia Interactive Software Inc.; 215-387-0448
Format: Windows
Price: $49

A college directory similar in structure and content to *Barron's Profiles of American Colleges on CD-ROM,* reviewed in this section, *Lovejoy's College Counselor* is adapted from the print *Lovejoy's College Guide,* 22nd edition; the CD-ROM's information was compiled in 1993 and covers the 1993-94 academic year.

Both the book and the CD-ROM version of *Lovejoy's* provide cookie-cutter profiles of 1,600 colleges; each profile follows the same format and recites dry statistics on student-teacher ratios and admissions criteria. The CD-ROM, however, offers two features the book can't match—one that's of marginal value and another that's extremely useful. The marginal feature is a selection of ninety-six video clips, most running just thirty seconds, describing various colleges. The useful feature is the "college search application," which will sift through the 1,600 listings to find colleges that match specific criteria. You can organize a search using one or more of seven categories: Difficulty of Admission, Size, Tuition Cost, Major, Location, Athletic Programs, and Availability of Special Services such as study-abroad programs.

THE PERFECT RÉSUMÉ
★★★½
Developer: Davidson & Associates Inc.; 800-545-7677
Format: Windows
Price: $39

The Perfect Résumé won't pick up the phone and start calling potential employers on your behalf, but this neatly designed CD-

ROM will do just about everything else required for a typical job search. The name is misleading because the program does more than help you produce a résumé; it also walks you through writing cover letters, provides a simple database for tracking the companies you've contacted, and provides lots of friendly advice.

The advice comes from a career consultant named Tom Jackson, author of two books on finding a job—*The Perfect Résumé* and *Guerrilla Tactics in the New Job Market*—and a regular speaker on the lecture circuit. Jackson's guidance is delivered in the sixty-page instruction manual, through an extensive on-screen help file and in fifty video clips, each running about thirty seconds. What is a perfect résumé? Jackson calls it "a concise written communication that clearly demonstrates your ability to produce results in a particular job in a way that motivates employers to interview you." He gives concrete examples of how to make your career history compelling by using an active writing style. Don't say, "My duties included the preparation and organization of sales information for use by management," Jackson explains, when what you really did was "reorganized and operated a new sales system that provided increased information in half the time."

The Perfect Résumé offers three applications. "Résumé Builder" helps you put together a résumé. You select the type of résumé—chronological, functional, or targeted—and the program presents fill-in-the-blank templates that can be easily edited and printed. For further inspiration, the CD-ROM includes 141 sample resumes from a wide range of occupations. "Power Letters" walks you through the process of preparing five job-search letters: a résumé cover letter, an interview follow-up letter, a letter accepting a job offer, a letter rejecting a job offer, and a letter asking for reconsideration after an initial rejection. In the follow-up letter, for example, you pick one of eleven possible first paragraphs depending on the type of interview and then modify it to suit your needs. "Job Search Manager" lets you keep an individual record for each company you contact, with a notebook to log your mailings, phone calls, and interviews.

YOUR PERSONAL TRAINER FOR THE SAT VERSION 2.0
★★★½
Developer: Davidson & Associates Inc.; 800-545-7677
Format: Windows, Macintosh
Price: $39

Avarice is to wealth as: (a) gluttony is to food, (b) frenzy is to activity, (c) steadfastness is to purpose, (d) foresight is to future, or (e) pushover is to revolution. Ah, the gut-wrenching anxiety of the SAT. Hardly anyone gets through high school without sitting for several hours in a room full of nervous juniors and seniors, clutching their No. 2 pencils and hoping their math and verbal scores are closer to 800 than 200. The Scholastic Aptitude Test is so important in college admissions that it supports a sizable test-preparation industry that offers classroom training intended to raise scores. *Your Personal Trainer for the SAT Version 2.0* is an excellent alternative to those classes, for considerably less money.

Personal Trainer is a complete SAT preparation course on CD-ROM, offering 750 practice questions in all the math and verbal categories. Students began by taking a printed pretest, supplied with the CD-ROM, that looks virtually identical to the real thing. By entering their answers into *Personal Trainer*, the students get a score and a recommended training schedule for working through the numerous test questions. There's also a separate SAT strategy guide. Whenever students get stuck on a question, they can push an on-screen personal trainer button to get a pop-up text window explaining the answer. The answer to the question above, for example, is (a). "Gluttony is an excessive desire for food just as avarice is an excessive desire for wealth," the trainer says.

There are several ways to study for the SAT with *Personal Trainer*. In addition to the practice questions and strategy guides, there is a dictionary for studying vocabulary and a quiz game. The advice is practical and direct. Don't make random guesses, *Personal Trainer* states, because it won't help your score. But do try to eliminate clearly wrong answers to multiple-choice questions as a way of improving your chances. *Personal Trainer* also raises a caution flag regarding the use of electronic calculators, allowed for the first time in 1994: "The biggest mistake students can make in using a calculator is turning their brains off as soon as they turn their calculator on. The calculator is best used as a tool to keep your brain focused on the problem rather than on number-crunching.

Don't try to solve the entire problem using a calculator, but instead, turn to it for help in specific parts of the problem."

In a five-minute introductory video clip, the developers of *Personal Trainer* claim their method increases test scores by an average of 150 to 170 points. That sounds like an awfully big increase, and the developers don't offer any hard evidence to support their statement. But there's no doubt practicing for a big test like the SAT is better than going in cold, and *Personal Trainer* is a powerful way for students to strengthen their mental muscles.

c. Language Guides and Instruction

THE AMERICAN SIGN LANGUAGE DICTIONARY ON CD-ROM
★★★¹/₂
Developer: HarperCollins Interactive; 800-424-6234
Format: Windows, Macintosh
Price: $49

American Sign Language, the primary form of communication for nearly 1 million deaf people in the United States, isn't just English converted to hand gestures. It is a unique and expressive language with a vocabulary of more than five thousand signs and a history stretching back three hundred years. Consider this statement in English: "I want to go tomorrow. You know why? I've been hoping to go for a long time. Now I finally will!" In American Sign Language, or ASL, the same thought is translated to this series of signs: "Tomorrow go want. Why? Hope, hope. Now succeed!"

Learning ASL has always been a challenge for the hearing because of the different linguistic structure and because the many ASL gestures couldn't be effectively taught without a live instructor. The latter obstacle has now been pushed aside with *The American Sign Language Dictionary on CD-ROM*, a remarkable product presenting video clips showing precisely how to make 2,181 signs.

Although it's not a complete instruction course, *The ASL Dictionary* will be an invaluable study tool for anyone learning ASL and a convenient reference for proficient ASL speakers who need to double-check a specific sign. The CD-ROM is based on the print *American Sign Language Concise Dictionary*, published in 1990 by HarperCollins and written by Martin L. A. Sternberg, a professor of education for the deaf at Hofstra and Adelphi universities in New York. Books such as Sternberg's dictionary aren't really an effective method for teaching ASL, however. *The ASL Dictionary* in print can portray hand and facial gestures only through crude line drawings with arrows to show movement. In contrast, the signs come to life on the CD-ROM, as you see a skilled ASL speaker making the correct gestures. Sternberg, himself deaf, serves as one of four models in the many video clips.

After you enter the dictionary, the word you select is displayed in the upper left of the screen, with a text description of its ASL sign directly beneath. Many of the words also have a "hint" describing what the sign is intended to resemble. One of three ASL signs for "computer," for example, is "both index fingers [making] clockwise circles." The hint tells you this is meant to convey "the tape in a mainframe drive." On the right side of the screen is a window that displays video clips of the ASL signers. Each clip runs a few seconds and then automatically repeats; users can adjust the tempo, allowing novices to watch the signs at speeds much slower than normal conversation. For closer review, the window can be expanded from an eighth of the screen to fill half the screen.

Users can search through *The ASL Dictionary* by simply typing in a word they want to see or by selecting one of twenty-one subject categories—such as "animals," "expressions," and "people"—to study groups of signs. The CD-ROM also includes an overview of American Sign Language history and usage, presented entirely in text; a guide for finger spelling of the alphabet's twenty-six letters; and a "Skills" section with practice games using the dictionary's video clips.

BERLITZ LIVE! JAPANESE
★★★
Developer: Sierra On-Line Inc.; 800-757-7707
Format: Windows, Macintosh
Price: $149

For travelers to Japan looking for a quick route to picking up key words and phrases, as well as cultural tips, *Berlitz Live! Japanese* is a suitable tour guide. While it doesn't offer as much depth as *Power Japanese Version 2.0*, reviewed in this section, *Berlitz Japanese* isn't as time-consuming and intellectually demanding.

The instruction in *Berlitz Japanese* is divided into twelve sections: "Language Essentials," "Basic Expressions," "Arrival," "Hotels," "Business," "Using the Phone for Business," "Eating Out," "Traveling Around," "Shopping," "Entertainment and Leisure," "Getting to Know Japan" and "Reference." Each section presents dialogues and interactive instruction with large cartoonlike color illustrations. A male character in medieval Japanese garb named "Sensei," or teacher, appears on every screen to provide narration. Sensei's lip movements are synchronized with his speech to help you follow the intricacies of Japanese pronunciation. In the dialogue scenes, the spoken Japanese is accompanied by the text in romaji, a transliteration of Japanese into the familiar roman letters.

You can block out the voice of any character in the dialogue and read the words yourself; you can also record yourself and play back the results if you have a microphone plugged into your computer.

Going beyond vocabulary and grammar, *Berlitz Japanese* provides a considerable education in Japanese culture and customs. When you move from one lesson to another, a small window pops onto the screen with a one-sentence tidbit, such as "It is not considered unusual to get an ancient Shinto blessing on a new car." The "Reference" section is particularly essential for travelers, covering topics such as currency, street signs, telling time, and phrases to use in emergencies.

If you get bored with the lessons, there is a "Tokyo Subway" game in which you answer quiz questions to move around a map of the Tokyo subway system. The CD-ROM also provides a 15,000-word Japanese-English English-Japanese dictionary, but it is separate—you have to exit *Berlitz Japanese* to use the dictionary.

BERLITZ LIVE! SPANISH
★★★
Developer: Sierra On-Line Inc.; 800-757-7707
Format: Windows, Macintosh
Price: $135

The Spanish-language companion to *Berlitz Live! Japanese*, reviewed in this section, with an identical structure. The instruction in *Berlitz Live! Spanish* is divided into ten sections: "Language Essentials," "Basic Expressions," "Spanish Grammar," "Arrival," "Hotels," "Business," "Phoning," "Eating Out," "Shopping" and "Country Information." There is also a quiz called "Mexico City Adventure Game" and a separate 15,000-word Spanish-English English-Spanish dictionary. The animated on-screen teacher is Rosalinda, "a knowledgeable and mysterious Aztec princess." As with *Berlitz Live! Japanese*, there is generous coverage of culture and customs. A pop-up window, for instance, advises: "In Mexico, when approaching a narrow bridge, the first car to flash its lights has the right-of-way"; while the "Country Information" section gives a few paragraphs of travel information on every country in Latin America.

BERLITZ THINK & TALK FRENCH
★★

Developer: HyperGlot Software Co.; 800-726-5087
Format: Windows, Macintosh
Price: $125

The French-language entry in the *Berlitz Think & Talk* series, described below. The fifty scenes on seven audio disks include "L'Arithméthique," "Repetons l'alphabet!," and "Une invitation à diner."

About the *Berlitz Think & Talk* series: In 1878 a German-born language teacher named Maximilian Berlitz opened his own school in Providence, Rhode Island, and hired an assistant to teach French. The assistant, a French immigrant who spoke little English, had to carry on alone for several weeks when Berlitz took ill. Returning to his classroom, Berlitz found his pupils had made unexpected strides by simply listening to the assistant speak and repeating his words. Thus was born the Berlitz method of language instruction through total immersion. "We learn to do things by doing them," the *Berlitz Think & Talk* manual explains. "At Berlitz, a student learns French by speaking French, not by speaking about French in English."

This immersion method may work miracles in the classroom, where there is real-life give-and-take between teachers and students, but I'm not sure it's effective on CD-ROM. The computer can't sense when you're having trouble understanding a word, then quickly change intonation or add a few pantomime gestures to help you grasp the meaning. What's more, the Berlitz method doesn't provide a full understanding of another language—you absorb vocabulary and phrases but not the rules of grammar or an understanding of cultural context.

Each title in the *Think & Talk* series contains one CD-ROM, with just eleven to fourteen megabytes of program information, and six to eight audio CDs containing fifty "scenes," discussions among two or three people running five to seven minutes. Through confusing on-screen controls that aren't clearly labeled or fully explained in the instruction manual, you listen to the scenes and try to deduce the meaning of one thousand vocabulary words. There is no translation of the dialogue, although you can summon a ten-thousand-word dictionary at the push of an on-screen button when the immersion method fails to communicate a clear understanding.

The scenes are designed to be studied in a four-step process. First, you listen to the dialogue while looking at still pictures that illustrate the scene and are intended to aid in comprehension. Then you listen again while the scene's text scrolls along the screen. "Do not translate from the text," the manual urges, "but simply enjoy this rather painless introduction to reading a foreign language." In the third step, you hear the dialogue again and type the words, checking occasionally to see if you've got the right spelling and accent marks. Finally, there is an open-ended "Think & Talk" feature in which you're supposed to talk in your new language for five to fifteen minutes, recording your words through a microphone hooked to the computer. There is no script to follow; you just free-associate with the vocabulary words.

Think & Talk requires considerable self-motivation and patience from users, especially in following the manual's urgings to listen over and over. "Repeat quite systematically everything you hear—a number, a couple of words, a question, the answer, a command—one such unit at a time," the manual says. "Your purpose right now is mainly this: to imitate, to echo what you hear." To me, endless lonely echoing while confined in front of a computer seems more like a technique for language aversion than language immersion.

BERLITZ THINK & TALK GERMAN
★★
Developer: HyperGlot Software Co.; 800-726-5087
Format: Windows, Macintosh
Price: $125

The German-language entry in the *Berlitz Think & Talk* series, described in the review of *Berlitz Think & Talk French* in this section. The fifty scenes on eight audio disks include "Ist das ein Volkswagen?," "Musik," and "Reservieren Sie, bitte, ein Zimmer!"

BERLITZ THINK & TALK ITALIAN
★★
Developer: HyperGlot Software Co.; 800-726-5087
Format: Windows, Macintosh
Price: $125

The Italian-language entry in the *Berlitz Think & Talk* series, described in the review of *Berlitz Think & Talk French* in this section. The fifty scenes on six audio disks include "Sandra, la segreteria," "Buon week-end a tutti!," and "Una telefonata dalla Sicilia."

BERLITZ THINK & TALK SPANISH
★★
Developer: HyperGlot Software Co.; 800-726-5087
Format: Windows, Macintosh
Price: $125

The Spanish-language entry in the *Berlitz Think & Talk* series, described in the review of *Berlitz Think & Talk French* in this section. The fifty scenes on seven audio disks include "Vocabulario básico," "Una lección de geografía," and "Conversaciónes en la oficina."

AUDIO-VISUAL CHINESE-ENGLISH DICTIONARY
★★★
Developer: SunMedia Inc.; 800-862-3766
Format: Windows
Price: $45

For native English speakers, Chinese is possibly the most difficult language to learn, especially the pronunciation. Consider the simple word "ma." Depending on intonation and context, the word "ma" in Chinese can mean mother, horse, pier, or to scold or to signal that a statement should be considered a question, making it awfully easy to accidentally call your mother a horse.

Audio-Visual Chinese-English Dictionary is a useful tool for language students, with definitions and pronunciations for 2,270 words in Mandarin Chinese. On screen, you see the word's Chinese character and English transliteration, called Pinyin, in the upper left. A cartoon illustration of the word appears in the lower left. A definition in both English and Chinese appears on the right side of the screen. Users can switch between viewing the text in classical or simplified Chinese. To help with writing, users can display a row of cells along the bottom of the screen showing the progression of strokes necessary to create the word. There are three ways to search for words: an index in English, an index in pinyin, and a Chinese index based on the order of strokes.

The dictionary also includes a "fun learning" feature that adds snippets of multimedia material to 141 words scattered throughout the CD-ROM. There are thirty-seven animations or videos, such as a cartoon of swimming fish to illustrate the word "fish" and a video clip of a child being pushed in a park swing for the word "swing"; forty-six word puzzles, which are ten-second audio clips of dialogue; eleven stories, audio narrations running two or three minutes each; seventeen children's songs, presenting audio with the lyrics displayed in Chinese characters; and thirty riddles, each a fifteen-second sound bite. Beginners may be frustrated, however, that no English translations are included for the "fun learning" material, making the items difficult to follow if you aren't already comfortable with spoken Chinese.

Because the dictionary includes no formal instruction in either written or spoken Chinese, I'd recommend the program only as a supplement for students already studying the language. Also, the dictionary appears to have been put together by native Chinese speakers without comprehensive editing by native English speakers, so there are occasional errors in English spelling and grammar.

KEY TRANSLATOR PRO ENGLISH-SPANISH
★★★
Developer: SoftKey International Inc.; 800-227-5609
Format: Windows
Price: $29

One of the most elusive goals in computer science is developing software to translate from one language to another. We're now thirty years past the first breathless predictions of flawless language translation by machine, and human translators still don't need to worry about losing their jobs anytime soon. A number of useful programs, however, have been developed to perform crude translation by simply matching words and applying a few simple grammar rules. *Key Translator Pro English-Spanish* fits into this category—the program, according to the manual, "is not meant to replace a human translator, it is designed to aid translation."

The CD-ROM contains four programs: an English-Spanish/Spanish-English translator, a Spanish grammar checker, a bilingual dictionary, and an accent maker that provides the accent marks required in written Spanish. The translator works within your word processor; it is compatible with the major names—*Microsoft Word*, *WordPerfect*, *Ami Pro*, and *Microsoft Works*—or can be used with *Notepad* or *Microsoft Write*, which are included in Windows. The four programs must be downloaded from the CD-ROM onto the hard drive to operate, requiring a total of eleven megabytes. All the manual's operating instructions are helpfully provided in both English and Spanish.

I decided to test *Key Translator Pro* with a hypothetical four-sentence request a tourist might have for a travel agent: "I am flying to Madrid on Thursday. Can you reserve a hotel room in my name? I will also need a list of car-rental companies. Thank you." Here is what *Key Translator Pro* produced, minus the accent marks: "Yo soy volador a Madrid en Jueves. Usted puede reservaar un cuarto de hotel en mi nombre? Yo tambien necesitare una lista de alquiler do automovil companias. Agradezcausted." I then asked *Key Translator Pro* to put the statement back into English and got: "I am flying to Madrid in Thursday. You can reserve a quarter of hotel in my name? I also will need a rental list of automobile companies. Agradezcausted." Obviously, the results are far from perfect. But it's close enough to provide at least some assistance in the translation process.

LEARN TO SPEAK ENGLISH 3.11
★★★½
Developer: HyperGlot Software Co.; 800-726-5087
Format: Windows, Macintosh
Price: $79

Similar in structure to the outstanding *Learn to Speak French 4.0*, reviewed in this section, but without the video clips showing native speakers. *Learn to Speak English* offers thirty chapters describing a visit to the United States by "Mr. Thomas." Each chapter is divided into a series of lessons, as described in *Learn to Speak French*, with helpful "cultural notes," such as this entry on seeing a movie: "Food and drinks are sold at concession stands in American movie theaters. You will probably pay a good bit more for these items than you would in a grocery store. Many theaters in the U.S. have as many as six different mini-theaters under one roof. Thus, when you buy a ticket, you will need to tell the ticket seller what film you wish to see."

Learn to Speak English is primarily sold with instruction manuals and on-screen notes in English. But the developer also has versions available with the manuals and notes translated into French, German, Italian, Spanish, and Portuguese. Contact Hyper-Glot Software Company at the telephone number listed above for further information.

LEARN TO SPEAK FRENCH 4.0
★★★★
Developer: HyperGlot Software Co.; 800-726-5087
Format: Windows, Macintosh
Price: $119

Learn to Speak French 4.0 and its sister title, *Learn to Speak Spanish 4.0*, are the best examples I've seen of tapping CD-ROM technology for adult education. These disks present a complete language-instruction course for beginners, taking full advantage of the multimedia computer's ability to shift effortlessly between text, sound, and video, liberating students to learn at their own pace.

Moving far beyond the "drill and kill" approach of early language software, which often offered little more than automated flash cards, *Learn to Speak French* combines stories, dialogue, and inventive exercises to offer a variety of learning experiences that nearly match a French course taught in a real classroom. The CD-ROM is built around thirty chapters telling the deliberately innocuous story of Mr. Thomas, an American with no first name, on a business trip to Paris. You follow Thomas as he travels around town for work and pleasure, even listening to his conversation with a policeman after a fender-bender traffic accident.

Each chapter begins with a thirty-second video clip shot in Paris, accompanied by French music. You then move into a series of exercises, starting with the "Vocabulary" screen. On the left side of the screen is a list of vocabulary words, on the right is a small video window in which a native French speaker pronounces the word, and in the center are text windows explaining how the word is used and showing sample sentences. At the bottom of the screen is the program's most powerful feature—a voice recorder. Speaking into a microphone plugged into the computer, you recite the vocabulary words and then hear an instant playback with the native speaker pronouncing the word first and then your imitation. You can instantly tell if your pronunciation is on track and can practice as many times as you like.

After the "Vocabulary" learning screen comes "Vocabulary Drill," quizzing you on the words you've just learned; the "Story," with a narrative of Mr. Thomas's adventures; "The Action," in which you listen and then repeat dialogue from the story; "Listening Skills," in which you spell words after hearing them; "Fill in the Blanks," a basic vocabulary quiz; "Drag and Match," moving words on the screen to match up pairs such as articles and nouns; "Word Jumble," rearranging mixed-up sentences into proper order; and "Communication Skills," in which you type complete sentences to answer questions posed in French.

To help put the language into context, the Action screen includes a "Cultural Notes" text box explaining various nuances of French, such as: "'Salle de bain' means strictly a room for a bath. The toilet is usually in a separate room. When visiting friends, ask 'Ou sont les toilettes?' Otherwise, they will think you want to take a bath." Supplementing the contents of the CD-ROM is a 420-page text and workbook that reproduces much of the lesson material and presents additional vocabulary lists.

One important note: HyperGlot Software has done a poor job of labeling *Learn to Speak French*; there's no clear indication on the box that you're getting the most current version rather than the earlier version 3.0, which does not include the video clips. Make sure the box shows a group sipping coffee under a red-and-white-striped café awning and has the words "See and Hear Native Speakers."

LEARN TO SPEAK SPANISH 4.0
★★★★
Developer: HyperGlot Software Co.; 800-726-5087
Format: Windows, Macintosh
Price: $119

The Spanish companion to the excellent *Learn to Speak French 4.0*, reviewed in this section. In *Learn to Speak Spanish*, the thirty chapters revolve around the story of Thomas Smith, a businessman from Chicago visiting Mexico City. Using the same structure for vocabulary and grammar study as *Learn to Speak French*, accompanied by a 360-page print text and workbook, the program also includes useful "Cultural Notes." An example: "Although we have included a dialogue in which two people bargain, such a scene will not be as commonplace as you might think. You should not expect to bargain for a price when riding public transportation, such as a bus or the subway, or when shopping in department stores, drugstores or shops when fixed prices exist. Bargaining will be limited, for the most part, to some marketplaces and perhaps to dealing with individual merchants, such as street vendors." Note that HyperGlot Software does a poor job of labeling its products—make sure the box shows a group of five people sitting inside an open wrought-iron gate and has the words "See and Hear Native Speakers." Otherwise, you might inadvertently get an older version that doesn't include video clips.

POWER JAPANESE VERSION 2.0
★★★½
Developer: BayWare Inc.; 800-538-8867
Format: Windows
Price: $189

A comprehensive yet friendly program for learning both written and spoken Japanese, *Power Japanese* claims you can master the basics in just twelve weeks if you'll spend an hour a day with the program for five days each week. I can't vouch for that claim, but I did find *Power Japanese* easy to follow and full of useful features. Learning Japanese is a huge challenge for Westerners, but with *Power Japanese* it isn't impossible.

The instructional material is divided into four sections. "The Basic Foundation: Hiragana" teaches the Japanese syllables and their representations in the phonetic Hiragana alphabet. "Dialogues and Basic Grammar" covers the fundamentals of putting together phrases. "The Homestretch" goes into advanced grammar and presents dialogues covering everyday situations. "Katakana" teaches the Katakana phonetic alphabet used to transcribe foreign words and phrases.

Each section unfolds through a series of on-screen pages filled with text and colorful symbols that look something like overhead transparencies from a fancy corporate presentation. Almost every page presents an interactive exercise, such as repeating phrases or trying to follow a handwriting animation. You start learning on the very first page, listening to several handy expressions in Japanese such as "good morning," "thank you," and "you're welcome." You also get a friendly warning: "Toss these phrases about at your own risk! They may make others think that you actually know Japanese, thereby possibly inviting enthusiastic outpourings of Japanese which you are not—yet—ready to receive." *Power Japanese* is constantly delivering such informal encouragement, as in this morale booster: "It takes a Japanese child a year or more, on average, to master all the Hiragana symbols. You will, however, handily accomplish this feat in about ten hours spread over two weeks! Thus you will debunk—yet again—the popular misconception that children pick up languages faster than adults."

Two other modules, separate from the four instructional sections, are included: a text editor that lets you compose and print Hiragana and Katakana characters, as well as a feature called "Voicetracks" that lets you create personalized practice sessions by putting together a list of phrases from the program to hear and repeat. In the box with the CD-ROM are a set of flash cards and a pocket-size 190-page "Learner's Dictionary." Also, if you send in the registration card for *Power Japanese*, Bayware Inc. promises to send a ten-thousand-word Japanese-English dictionary on floppy disk. Students who successfully complete *Power Japanese* can move up to another Bayware Inc. program on floppy disk called *Kanji Moments for Windows* that teaches one thousand Kanji ideographic symbols.

POWER SPANISH
★★½
Developer: BayWare Inc.; 800-538-8867
Format: Windows
Price: $149

Power Spanish tries to offer a quick, comprehensive introductory course in Spanish but gets bogged down with overactive animations and inanely cheerful slogans. The format isn't all that different from BayWare's other and much better title, *Power Japanese*, but Japanese is a more difficult language to learn, so the animations and encouragement don't seem quite so gimmicky.

The instructional material in *Power Spanish* is divided into two sections called "The Foundation," covering basic vocabulary and grammar, and "The Payoff," delving into more advanced concepts. BayWare says you can complete the program in ten weeks if you'll give it an hour a day for five days each week. Both sections present a succession of on-screen pages offering instruction and exercises. The pages are full of confusing activity, with words swooping around the screen, text automatically scrolling like movie credits and buttons to push for pop-up windows with extra information. Upbeat messages are repeated over and over, such as a screen full of road signs declaring, "You do not need to have a perfect command of Spanish to start using it" and "It's OK to have an English accent when speaking Spanish!" *Power Spanish* includes a "record/playback" feature that lets you record your voice pronouncing a Spanish phrase—if you've got a microphone plugged into your computer—and hear it played back immediately after a native Spanish speaker. There's also a "VoiceStretch" feature that slows down the pronunciation of phrases, but it requires ten seconds or more to alter a single audio clip.

BayWare's marketing department appears to have insisted the CD-ROM contain video clips to compete with other language-instruction disks that do the same. But the authors of *Power Spanish* evidently weren't thrilled with the task: A section called "Video Potpourri" offers only twenty very brief head shots of Spanish speakers reciting a single sentence. And the section opens with a "warning" that disavows the contents: "While the usefulness of being able to view tiny video clips on a computer monitor is at best questionable from a learning standpoint, we feel compelled to include some clips in *Power Spanish* if only so that you can judge for yourself." We can't really judge for ourselves, though, if BayWare doesn't conduct a fair trial.

The CD-ROM does offer one useful bonus, a Spanish-English and English-Spanish translation program called *Spanish Assistant* from Microtac Software Inc. But I'd still recommend the excellent *Learn to Speak Spanish 4.0*, reviewed in this section, as a better and significantly less expensive alternative.

TRIPLEPLAY PLUS! ENGLISH
★★★
Developer: Syracuse Language Systems; 800-688-1937
Format: Windows
Price: $35

The English-language entry in the *Playing with Language* series, described in the review of *TriplePlay Plus! Spanish* in this section. Intended for non-English speakers, the CD-ROM nevertheless comes with instruction manuals and on-screen help windows in English. Students with little or no knowledge of English will probably need assistance to install and learn how to operate the program.

TRIPLEPLAY PLUS! FRENCH
★★★
Developer: Syracuse Language Systems; 800-688-1937
Format: Windows
Price: $35

The French-language entry in the *Playing with Language* series, described in the review of *TriplePlay Plus! Spanish* in this section.

TRIPLEPLAY PLUS! SPANISH
★★★
Developer: Syracuse Language Systems; 800-688-1937
Format: Windows
Price: $35

The Spanish language entry in the *Playing with Language* series, described below.

About the *Playing with Language* series: Departing from the typical academic approach to language instruction, which focuses on grammar and memorizing vocabulary, the *Playing with Language* series from Syracuse Language Systems Inc. seeks to teach through a series of games that grow progressively more intricate as the student gains skill. These games use the immersion method to teach one thousand words and phrases—you only hear and see the language being taught, with no help in English unless you turn to the instruction manual.

Syracuse Language Systems has also gambled on the cutting edge of computer technology by including speech recognition—you speak into a microphone, and the computer decides if you've given the right answer. Speech recognition, however, is still in its infancy, and I often had to pronounce words several times before the program recognized what I was saying. To help you get started, by the way, each *Playing with Language* title comes with a microphone to plug into your computer's soundboard.

When you start one of the programs, you encounter a main screen, where you select a game. First, you pick one of three modes—games that teach aural comprehension, requiring that you listen to audio cues and enter answers on the keyboard; games that teach reading, again using the keyboard for answers; or games that teach speaking, using the microphone for speech recognition. Then you pick a subject for your game from six choices—"Food," "Numbers," "Home & Office," "Places & Transportation," "People & Clothing," and "Activities." Finally, you pick one of thirty-three games divided into three difficulty levels. Syracuse Language Systems says playing all the game combinations just once would require more than one hundred hours.

If, for example, you select the "Bingo" game in Level I of *TriplePlay Plus! Spanish* using speech recognition and the "Places & Transportation" category, you are presented with a grid showing twenty-five small color illustrations. A picture of the beach could be highlighted, and a voice will ask if the scene is "una playa" or "una escuela." You're supposed to reply "una playa," the Spanish word for beach, rather than "una escuela," for school. If the program succeeds in recognizing your pronunciation of "una playa," the voice says "correcto," and you move on to the next question.

Level II games require answering open-ended questions. In the "Where Is It?" game, for example, you see a map of South America and hear a voice describing the location of a country in Spanish without giving the country's name. You then have to click the right spot on the map. Level III games present comic strips showing simple scenes, such as a woman departing on an out-of-town trip, and require you to fill in parts of the dialogue.

In keeping with the immersion philosophy, there is no organizational structure in the *Playing with Language* series. You're on your own, wandering through the various games as you try to soak up a new language. While this approach might work in a classroom, where a real teacher can help you through rough spots, I'm not sure this is an effective way to learn on a computer, although the *Playing with Language* titles could be a worthwhile supplement to classroom instruction, especially for children who might find the games more appealing than conventional textbooks.

VIDEO LINGUIST FRENCH
★★½
Developer: Cubic Media Inc.; 800-232-8242
Format: Windows, Macintosh
Price: $79

Video Linguist French is a handy refresher course for those already fluent in the language, but it isn't suitable for beginners—a fact that isn't made clear on the box or in the promotional literature. The CD-ROM contains thirty-eight video clips, each running about two minutes, taken from French television. The grainy clips are displayed in a tiny window, measuring just three inches diagonally on a standard fourteen-inch monitor. While watching the clips, users have the option of displaying the transcribed text in French as well as English. If you're unsure of a French word, you can click on it with the mouse and a definition pops onto the screen. You can also slow down the speech to make comprehension easier, although you're limited to hearing one phrase at a time. And if you have a microphone plugged into your computer, you can record and play back your own voice to practice pronunciation.

But that's all you get—*Video Linguist French* offers no language instruction, games, or other activities. Because the video clips show native French speakers talking to a native audience, students who aren't fluent will quickly get lost. Those with minimal fluency, however, might enjoy *Video Linguist French* as a painless way to strengthen their skills. Among the subjects covered in the thirty-eight clips, all of which appear to have come from TV news reports, are "Mozart at Versailles," "Tourism in Paris," "Tour de France," "Wine Harvest," and "Modern Cheesemaking."

VIDEO LINGUIST SPANISH
★★½
Developer: Cubic Media Inc.; 800-232-8242
Format: Windows, Macintosh
Price: $79

The Spanish-language twin of *Video Linguist French*, reviewed in this section. *Video Linguist Spanish* contains forty-four video clips taken from television news reports in Spain on subjects such as "bullfighting," "Flamenco dancing," "women in the workplace," and "carnival in Canarias." Unlike the other Spanish-language CD-ROMs in this section, which teach the pronunciation and usage common in Latin America, *Video Linguist Spanish* presents the language as spoken in Spain. That could be confusing to beginners who aren't already familiar with the differences.

d. Personal Finance

CHARLES J. GIVENS MONEY GUIDE
★★★
Developer: Friendly Software Corp.; 800-968-4654
Format: Windows
Price: $29

Charles J. Givens, a self-made success story who claims he's worth $200 million, writes popular financial self-help books that remind me of fad diet programs. Often, these "miracle" weight-loss systems turn out to be nothing more than predictable—and difficult to follow—advice on eating less and exercising more. Givens's books such as *Wealth Without Risk, Financial Self-Defense,* and *More Wealth Without Risk* appear on the surface to offer surefire get-rich-quick schemes. But most of Givens's suggestions are hardheaded, mainstream strategies for doing a better job of managing your money. Following Givens's path won't make you wealthy overnight, but it will prevent you from making stupid mistakes and help you plan for the future—if you stick with it.

Charles J. Givens Money Guide on CD-ROM combines text and video clips of Givens to explain his complete system for taking control of your finances. This shouldn't be confused with a personal finance management program, such as *Quicken*, reviewed in this section. The *Money Guide* helps you decide on financial strategies and goals but doesn't keep track of your checking account or investment portfolio.

The program is divided into three sections. "Wealth Management" reviews Givens's philosophy: keep careful records, set clear financial goals, and then work to achieve them. Also, don't rely on the usual sources of investment advice. "The only money pros in this country are those with self-made wealth, not those who talk about it for a living like many stockbrokers, financial planners, insurance agents, college finance professors and financial writers for magazines and newspapers," Givens declares in one of the video clips. "Most financial people, whether well meaning or not, usually have one thing in common: They're living paycheck to paycheck, struggling to pay bills, struggling to get out of debt, and are hoping for a financial miracle just like you. In other words, they're basically broke, and broke people obviously are not qualified to give financial advice."

In the "Ten Biggest Money Management Mistakes" section, Givens explains how to avoid such common pitfalls as buying too much auto or life insurance and includes worksheets on which you enter numbers to see how much you'd save by switching to a low-interest-rate credit card or getting a fifteen-year home mortgage instead of a thirty-year loan. He also asks you to sign an agreement with yourself to save at least 10 percent of your income. "Ask Charles J. Givens," the final section, gives more advice on everyday financial matters. His very conventional recommendations on best investments include mutual funds and buying a home; his list of worst investments include vacant land, precious metals, and "anything sold over the phone and anything sold by a commissioned financial salesperson."

The video clips in *Money Guide* play in a tiny window, measuring three inches diagonally on a standard fourteen-inch monitor, but that's not a huge liability, since most of the time you're just looking at Givens's head. And I found that hearing Givens personally deliver his message helped drive home details in the text.

KIPLINGER TAXCUT MULTIMEDIA
★★★
Developer: The Kiplinger Washington Editors Inc.; 800-235-4060
Format: Windows
Price: $39

Taxpayers, I've found, are split into three groups: those brave souls who complete their own Internal Revenue Service forms without any assistance other than a 1040 instruction manual, a slightly more cautious bunch who rely on tax-preparation guides, and total chickens who dump the whole chore into the lap of an accountant. I'm firmly in the third group, but do-it-yourselfers can benefit tremendously from tax-preparation software. Programs such as *Kiplinger TaxCut Multimedia* and *TurboTax Multimedia*, reviewed in this section, will walk you through all the steps in preparing IRS and state income tax forms while offering lots of advice and making sure your returns are free of arithmetic errors. Selling for under $50, these programs are considerably cheaper than visiting a professional tax preparer.

Tax-preparation software, by the way, is an annual investment—you have to buy the entire program each year to get the latest IRS forms. *Kiplinger* and *TurboTax* both release a "head-start" edition in October or November, before final IRS forms are available, for those who want to get their taxes organized in advance. A final version is released in January and is generally shipped free to registered buyers of the "head-start" edition. If you live in a state with income tax, you also have to pay an extra fee—typically about $20 to $25—for a diskette with that state's tax forms.

Kiplinger combines an easy-to-use tax-preparation program with extensive advice prepared by Kiplinger Washington Editors Inc., publishers of tax-related newsletters and *Kiplinger's Personal Finance Magazine*. The CD-ROM also provides twenty-eight video clips, each running from thirty seconds to two minutes, with various Kiplinger tax experts commenting on key issues.

The program walks you through eight steps to complete your taxes: "Start," in which the program is explained and you can download data from personal finance programs such as *Quicken* and *Managing Your Money*; "Q&A," in which you enter answers to the kind of questions an accountant would ask, such as the sources of your income during the last year; "Forms," in which you scan IRS forms on screen to double-check entries made by the program; "Review," in which you get the bottom-line total of the taxes you owe and discover whether you get a refund; "Audit," in which the program combs through your return looking for tax savings you might have missed; "State," in which you complete a state return, if necessary; "Print," in which you print the results; and "Wrap-up," in which you can make a backup copy of your return on diskette.

The tax advice from Kiplinger editors is a model of clarity, free from accounting jargon, even when the information isn't exactly comforting, as in this description of an IRS audit: "There's a 20 percent chance that you won't have to pay more tax. You may even get a refund. But most folks called in for an audit come out poorer. The latest IRS statistics show that the average office audit results in the payment of almost $2,300 in extra tax and penalties. And even if you escape without owing an extra dime in tax, the time, hassle and stress involved are indisputably costly."

Kiplinger TaxCut Multimedia is not sold through stores or mail-order catalogs; it is only available by calling the toll-free number listed above. The tax-preparation software, by the way, comes from Block Financial Software, a subsidiary of H & R Block Inc. Block Financial Software sells its own version, called simply *TaxCut*, reviewed in this section. I found the supplementary material in *Kiplinger TaxCut Multimedia* superior, however, and would recommend it over the *TaxCut* CD-ROM.

MONEY IN THE 90s
★★½
Developer: Laser Resources Inc.; 800-535-2737
Format: Windows, Macintosh
Price: $49

Money In The 90s is the CD-ROM equivalent of a shelf stacked with back issues of *Money* magazine, the most popular monthly publication dedicated to personal finance. The disk contains full text for each issue from January 1990 through the end of 1993. You can browse through this wealth of material in three ways: using a subject index, looking at the table of contents for each issue, or searching for specific words, such as "mutual fund" and "Japan" to find articles discussing mutual funds that invest in Japanese stocks.

Although the magazine aims for as wide an audience as possible, I find most of the advice in *Money* focused on middle-class and upper-middle-class home owners over age thirty. If you're in that category, you might find *Money In The 90s* to be a useful reference tool. But the CD-ROM isn't a comprehensive personal finance guide; you have to find your own way through the many articles.

The developers of *Money In The 90s* have added three brief video segments that aren't particularly useful—a four-minute introduction by a *Money* magazine editor and monologues by two other editors discussing stories from the 1993 issues. Software for a free trial of an on-line service called the Reuters Money Network is also included, although it works only with PCs, not the Macintosh. *Money* magazine promises to issue an updated CD-ROM every year, so a new edition should be out in mid-1995 adding the 1994 issues.

YOUR MUTUAL FUND SELECTOR
★★★½
Developer: Intuit Inc.; 800-624-5710
Format: Windows
Price: $39

Mutual funds are one of the best investment options for the typical middle-class family—that's why they're so popular. This popularity is both a blessing and a curse; there are several thousand mutual funds to choose from, making the investment process incredibly confusing. *Your Mutual Fund Selector* is an excellent way to sort through this profusion. An interactive book with 145 on-screen pages, the *Selector* both explains how mutual funds operate and gathers information about your financial goals. The program then combs through a database with information on one thousand mutual funds, compiled by the research firm Morningstar Inc., for funds that best match your criteria for performance and risk.

The text, supplemented by video clips of a fictional suburban couple explaining the process, delivers clear and simple advice. "Every few years, you'll think you were a total lunatic for investing in stocks, bonds, even money funds," the *Selector* cautions. "That's because, for some reason, your fund will have disappointed you. But don't panic and sell . . . If you follow your investment goals and invest prudently, you'll come out all right in the long run."

Most investors will be able to read the CD-ROM's eight chapters and complete the financial questionnaire in a few hours. Data in the questionnaires can be adjusted later if your investment criteria change or you want to look for different funds. You can also look at Morningstar's report on each fund, resembling a baseball card, with up to fifteen years of performance statistics as well as details on the fund's minimum investment, load, and fees.

The Morningstar database is updated quarterly; the CD-ROM comes with a coupon for one free update delivered on a floppy disk. Additional updates are available for $14 each or $45 per year. Buying the *Selector* by itself may not be the best investment, however. For just $20 more, you can get the excellent *Quicken Deluxe 4 for Windows CD-ROM*, reviewed in this section, which includes *Your Mutual Fund Selector* among its many bonus features. You won't get the free-update coupon, but you'll have a copy of the *Quicken* financial management program and lots of other useful financial advice.

PLAN AHEAD FOR YOUR FINANCIAL FUTURE
★★★½
Developer: Dow Jones & Co. Inc.; 800-522-3567 x319
Format: Windows
Price: $39

Along with visiting the dentist and cleaning out closets, one of the tasks most of us avoid far too long is preparing for retirement. *Plan Ahead for Your Financial Future*, a CD-ROM assembled by writers and editors from *The Wall Street Journal*, is an excellent tool for learning about long-term financial planing and for devising your own retirement strategy. I just wish the subject matter weren't quite so depressing—the typical middle-class wage earner is stashing away far too little to live comfortably in his or her golden years.

Plan Ahead is an interactive workbook with 122 on-screen pages. Most of the pages offer one or two paragraphs of text along with one of two multimedia features—video clips of advice from eight investment experts and fill-in-the-blank forms for entering information about your current financial status and retirement goals. Working through *Plan Ahead* takes no more than a few hours. At the end of the process, you get the bottom line: a chart showing whether you're saving enough to live comfortably in retirement, with explanatory text on how to close any gaps. If the numbers don't add up, you can go back to previous pages and adjust the information you've entered, such as increasing your 401(k) contributions or decreasing the number of postretirement tropical cruises. The on-screen pages, which include a glossary and index, are divided into seven chapters: "Your Retirement Goals," "Where Are You Now?," "Investing for Retirement," "Tax-Deferred Savings," "Retirement Income," "Other Life Goals," and "Your Retirement Plan."

An anonymous woman in a flowery dress appears in video clips to explain how *Plan Ahead* works. The eight investment experts are presented through thirty-three video clips, each running from thirty seconds to one minute in a tiny window, offering practical advice on subjects such as balancing safety against risk and how to get started with a savings plan. "Three key points: Start now, save more and save better," declares Jon S. Fossel, head of the Oppenheimer group of mutual funds, in one video clip. "What I mean by saving better is investing in long-term high-return kind of investments [such as] stock mutual funds and corporate bonds."

Plan Ahead keeps hammering on the idea of starting to save for retirement as soon as possible. For example, the CD-ROM points out that a thirty-five-year-old who puts away $100 a month in a tax-deferred account paying 6 percent annually will have $100,452 at age sixty-five. A forty-five-year-old seeking to build the same nest egg by age sixty-five must save $217 a month.

Some of the features in *Plan Ahead* are almost fun; I enjoyed an interactive pie chart in which you can adjust the balance of stocks, cash, and bonds in your portfolio and see how it affects the blended return. But there are also parts of the planning process that, while necessary, are distinctly distasteful. At one point, *Plan Ahead* asks you to complete the sentence, "I expect to live until age ___." No one likes thinking about the downside of growing old, such as increased medical expenses, relying on a fixed income that can be undermined by inflation, and the possible collapse of Social Security. But it's something every adult should do, and *Plan Ahead* makes it as painless as possible.

One very important footnote: *Plan Ahead* is not sold in stores or mail-order catalogs. It is available only by direct order from Dow Jones & Company, the corporate parent of *The Wall Street Journal*, at the number listed above.

QUICKEN DELUXE 4 FOR WINDOWS CD-ROM
★★★★
Developer: Intuit Inc.; 800-964-1040
Format: Windows
Price: $59

Forget those hot tips from Uncle Herman the stockbroker. Stop pestering your Aunt Betty the accountant for retirement advice. *Quicken for Windows Deluxe* puts you in total control of your money—tracking expenses, preparing financial projections, and studying investment strategy.

Quicken—available on floppy disk for DOS, Windows, and the Macintosh—has a well-earned reputation as the best and easiest-to-use personal finance program. Copying the look of a paper checkbook, the program monitors your financial picture as you enter income and expenses. *Quicken for Windows Deluxe* contains the latest version—*Quicken 4.0 for Windows*—but that's only the beginning of what the CD-ROM offers.

You also get a comprehensive library of personal finance

guides and Quicken tips. The best of these extras are "Ask the Experts" and "Your Mutual Fund Selector." "Ask the Experts" presents video clips of financial commentators Jane Bryant Quinn and Marshall Loeb answering fifteen fundamental questions such as "Is buying a home better than renting?" and "How can I put my kids through college without borrowing a small fortune?" The one-minute answers are simple and direct, even when the two disagree. Loeb, for example, suggests starting a college nest egg by purchasing U.S. Savings Bonds for young children. Quinn prefers mutual funds. "Your Mutual Fund Selector" is an interactive book explaining how to choose a mutual fund, one of the best investments for middle-class families. With prompting from the text and a series of video clips, you enter a personal financial profile that identifies how much you can afford to invest, what degree of risk you can accept, and which specific funds meet your needs.

The library also includes a text-only tax guide covering both the United States and Canada, as well as several Quicken manuals. These manuals explain how Quicken can be harnessed to produce all kinds of financial information, everything from preparing an inventory of your household possessions to tracking frequent-flyer mileage. For modem owners, the manuals also explain how to get up-to-the-minute stock quotes, pay bills on-line, and download monthly credit-card statements.

I found just one weakness in *Quicken for Windows Deluxe*, a reference called "Tradeline Electronic Stock Guide" that provides stock-price data for six thousand companies. The stock charts cover only twelve months, ending on August 31, 1994, so the information is significantly out of date. But otherwise, *Quicken for Windows Deluxe* gives you an awesome set of tools for effective financial management—all you need is the self-discipline to enter your income and spending into your computer regularly.

TAXCUT
★★½
Developer: Block Financial Software; 800-288-6322
Format: Windows
Price: $39

Block Financial Software, a subsidiary of the tax-preparation firm H & R Block Inc., has licensed the rights to its *TaxCut* software to the editors of *Kiplinger's Personal Finance Magazine*. The

Kiplinger editors took the program, added their own well-written advice on tax issues, and created the credible *Kiplinger TaxCut Multimedia*, reviewed in this section. Ironically, it's a better CD-ROM than Block's own *TaxCut*.

TaxCut presents advice from Daniel Caine, the tax attorney who supervised development of the software package. Caine may be a good tax attorney, but he's not much of a performer—his presentation in thirty-one video clips and nine hundred audio clips comes across as wooden and dull. What's more, Caine's written and oral advice contains a much higher level of jargon than *Kiplinger* or *TurboTax Multimedia*, also reviewed in this section. Discussing how to account for the sale of a mutual fund, for instance, Caine writes: "If you paid tax on distributions—e.g., 'capital gains' distributions—from mutual funds in prior years, and these distributions were undistributed or reinvested, then increase your basis in your stock by the amount of these distributions." Arggh! That's the kind of language that sends most of us scurrying to see accountants every year.

For no good reason related to tax preparation, *TaxCut* also throws in two programs from Block Financial: *Personal Attorney*, which helps prepare sixteen legal documents such as wills and powers of attorney, and *Mortgages, Insurance and More*, a financial calculator for tasks such as figuring out home-loan payments and the value of life-insurance policies.

TURBOTAX MULTIMEDIA
★★★½
Developer: Intuit Inc.; 800-964-1040
Format: Windows
Price: $39

TurboTax Multimedia makes tax preparation as simple as it's ever going to get on a computer, providing step-by-step guidance through the process of completing Internal Revenue Service forms, with easy access to extensive commentaries on IRS regulations. The CD-ROM even offers two hosts, financial commentator Marshall Loeb and tax attorney Mary L. Sprouse, in ninety-two video clips, giving the inhuman process of paying taxes a nice human touch.

I'd especially recommend *TurboTax* for users of the popular personal finance management program *Quicken*, reviewed in this section. Both are published by Intuit Inc., and Intuit has designed links that allow *TurboTax* to work effortlessly with financial information stored in *Quicken*.

TurboTax walks you through a seven-stage process for completing tax returns: "Start" explains how the program works; "Import" lets you bring in data from other personal-finance software; "Interview" prompts you to enter information with a series of questions similar to those an accountant might ask; "Review" automatically examines your return for errors, omissions, possible tax savings, and entries that might attract an IRS audit; "Filing" prints the return; "State" uses the data from your IRS filing to prepare state income tax returns, if necessary; and "Finish" provides suggestions for tax planning and plugs for several other Intuit products.

Loeb and Sprouse pop up in video clips throughout *TurboTax* to offer friendly advice. With the click of a mouse button, you can also summon the full text of *The Money Income Tax Book*, written by Sprouse, or a library of sixty IRS publications on tax-related subjects such as "Business Use of a Car" and "Reporting Income from Tips." If you're trying to decide whether you qualify for a home-office deduction, for example, Sprouse's book has this to say: "You can't just point to a desk in the corner and christen it your office. It must be broken in by regular use. This use does not have to occur every day, but it must happen frequently enough to show that you are actively engaged in business . . . You cannot sit at your desk and write personal letters, prepare your income tax returns, pay personal bills or even do work you brought home from the office if you have another job."

As with *Kiplinger TaxCut Multimedia*, reviewed in this section, you have to buy *TurboTax* each year in order to get the latest IRS forms. A "Head Start" version of both programs is released in October or November, before final IRS forms are available, for those who want to get an early start. A final version is released in January and is generally shipped free to registered buyers of the "Head Start" edition. If you live in a state with income tax, you also have to pay an extra fee—typically $20 to $25—for a diskette with that state's tax forms.

Chapter Nine:
Computer Applications

Increasingly, CD-ROMs are replacing floppy disks as the preferred way to deliver basic applications and utilities such as word processors, spreadsheets, and screen savers. These programs are covered in Section a. Other computer-related CD-ROMs are reviewed in Sections b, c, and d.

a. Applications and Utilities

THE COMPLETE AFTER DARK SCREEN SAVER COLLECTION
★★★½
Developer: Berkeley Systems Inc.; 800-344-5541
Format: Windows, Macintosh
Price: $39

After Dark, a popular line of screen savers from Berkeley Systems Inc., is irresistibly cute and even a little bit useful. Every computer owner should know that a monitor left running for a long period of time with a fixed image on the screen, such as the Program Manager in Windows or the Macintosh desktop, can suffer "burn-in," a permanent ghostly image that can't be erased. Preventing such damage is simple; you only need a simple utility program to turn your screen blank automatically after a minute or two without any keyboard or mouse activity. Indeed, Windows comes with a perfectly adequate screen saver program.

But why just let your screen go blank when your computer could instead stage a little show every time it's left unattended? That's where *After Dark* comes into the picture. The many screen saver choices send bouncing balls careening around your monitor, unleash mischievous dogs who eat your files, and turn your computer into a tropical fish tank—all with images that disappear as soon as you touch the keyboard or move the mouse. The trademark *After Dark* screen saver module is flying toasters—literally, toasters with flapping wings that move across the screen next to slices of nicely browned toast. It's silly, but it's sold zillions of copies.

The Complete After Dark Screen Saver Collection contains eighty screen saver modules from four releases in the *After Dark* line: *More After Dark, After Dark 2.0, After Dark 3.0* and *Art of Darkness*. The strangest is a quiz game called "You Bet Your Head," in which two floating cartoon heads compete in answering trivia questions and a giant floating hammer delivers severe penalties for wrong answers. You can set the game to play automatically or participate yourself in answering questions such as "What's a dowser do? 1. Dig ditches. 2. Put together package tours of minor league spring training camps. 3. Find water with a divining rod." (Before you hit yourself in the head with a hammer, the answer is 3.)

Aside from all this amusement, the *After Dark* CD-ROM offers several genuinely useful features. A utility called "EcoLogic" will switch off your monitor or even your entire computer after a specified period of inactivity. You won't see any flying toasters, but you'll save lots of electricity. There's also a password protection feature, so you can prevent coworkers or family members from poking into the computer when you're not around.

CALENDAR CREATOR PLUS
★★
Developer: SoftKey International Inc.; 800-227-5609
Format: Windows
Price: $49

Calendar Creator Plus should be a snap to learn. After all, the program's sole purpose is making and printing calendars. Not so. This inordinately complex piece of software comes with a 388-page manual, and the on-screen controls are so convoluted that you need the "quick reference card" included in the box to keep track of all the different buttons and icons.

In addition to *Calendar Creator Plus*, the CD-ROM provides a clip-art management tool called "PowerAlbum" and two thousand unimpressive clip-art images for insertion onto calendar pages. The program is capable of making a range of calendars, from conventional month-to-month wall calendars to weekly calendars and daily agendas. You can enter a list of events, such as birthdays and anniversaries, that will be automatically inserted in these calendars. But unless you've got an urgent need to produce a lot of calendars, it isn't worth the time and effort required to master *Calendar Creator Plus*.

KEY CAD COMPLETE
★★
Developer: SoftKey International Inc.; 800-227-5609
Format: Windows, Macintosh
Price: $29

"Until now, the power of CAD was for the technical elite ... It took an engineer to master the complex commands and concepts required to use Computer Aided Design," declares the box for *Key CAD Complete*. "No longer. Now there is *Key CAD Complete* CD-ROM, the next generation that puts high-performance CAD at your fingertips." That's half right. True, CAD software is very difficult to master and also very expensive, with professional CAD packages typically costing $1,000 or more. But *Key CAD*, though inexpensive, doesn't offer high performance and isn't all that easy to grasp.

CAD is the high-tech equivalent of drawing blueprints at a drafting table. By selecting from a variety of drawing tools, you can create different shapes on the screen, specifying exact lengths and precise angles. CAD software is typically used to draw architectural plans, design circuit boards, and make flow charts. *Key CAD* provides enough tools to create simple two-dimensional layouts and adds a library of common symbols used in drafting, such as overhead outline views of tables and chairs for interior design. To work in three dimensions, however, you have to buy one of the professional CAD packages.

Experienced CAD users will be able to adapt quickly to *Key CAD*, although they might chafe at its limitations. But beginners will be swamped by the numerous on-screen control buttons. The two-hundred-page manual isn't much help; it presumes you already understand the basics of drafting. A fourteen-page tutorial in the manual walks you through a few simple steps, but doesn't give an overview of how to use *Key CAD*. I'm also not sure why this program comes on a CD-ROM. The contents total less than two megabytes, so *Key CAD* could have been shipped on two floppy disks.

LAUNCH PAD
★★★
Developer: Berkeley Systems Inc.; 800-344-5541
Format: Windows, Macintosh
Price: $29

Most parents want their children to explore the family computer freely. But many parents also worry, with good reason, that little Johnny or Suzy might accidentally erase Mom and Dad's tax records. *Launch Pad* is the perfect solution—an ever-vigilant electronic baby-sitter that sets up an easily customizable security system. Whenever the computer is turned on, children are confined to the world of *Launch Pad* and can use only software preapproved by parents. Getting out of *Launch Pad* to work with grown-up programs and data files requires Mom or Dad to enter a secret password. *Launch Pad* also includes a few small diversions that children will enjoy—an on-screen tape recorder, which requires a microphone plugged into the computer; a talking calculator; and a talking clock. Now if only the developers of *Launch Pad* could come up with a foolproof method for preventing juice from getting spilled onto the keyboard or peanut butter from getting smeared inside the disk drive slot.

LOTUS 1-2-3 RELEASE 5 MULTIMEDIA EDITION
★★★
Developer: Lotus Development Corp.; 800-343-5414
Format: Windows
Price: $329

Lotus 1-2-3 once had a near monopoly on the market for computer spread sheets, the ubiquitous programs that manage rows and columns of numbers. Although *1-2-3* is still one of the most popular spread sheets, it is now in a neck-and-neck battle for first place with *Microsoft Excel*, part of the *Microsoft Office* software suite reviewed in this section. Both are excellent products and surprisingly easy to use, considering their powerful features for tackling all kinds of financial analysis and record keeping.

Lotus 1-2-3 Release 5 Multimedia Edition on CD-ROM offers several extras that aren't included with *1-2-3* on floppy disk. The biggest bonus is the "Guided Tour," a forty-minute tutorial featuring the small outline figure of a magician in top hat and tails who bounds around the screen pointing out various program features while you listen to narration. The help function is expanded with thirty-one "QuickMovie" animations, narrated slide shows on subjects such as "how to create a query table" and "how to let *1-2-3* write your macros." Other features exclusive to the CD-ROM include "The Reader," a tool to help with proofing spread sheets by having the computer read words and numbers out loud.

The Guided Tour and QuickMovies are best suited to users already familiar with the basics of operating a spread sheet; if you're not comfortable with terms such as "cell" and "range," you'll probably want to buy a beginner's book rather than relying solely on the CD-ROM. Also, you get the extensive user's guide on disk instead of in print—a big drawback if you prefer reading instruction manuals on paper.

LOTUS SMARTSUITE 3.0 CD-ROM EDITION
★★★
Developer: Lotus Development Corp.; 800-343-5414
Format: Windows
Price: $499

When it comes to installing really big programs, CD-ROM is a blessing. *Lotus SmartSuite*, for instance, is a "suite" of office applications normally delivered on 45 floppy diskettes. Shuffling all those disks into and out of the drive slot can drag out the installation process for more than an hour. The same data can be downloaded from a CD-ROM in about ten minutes. The CD-ROM also takes up less shelf space and isn't at risk of being erased if stored in the vicinity of a magnet.

Lotus SmartSuite 3.0 CD-ROM Edition provides the full Lotus suite of five applications: the *Ami Pro 3.1* word processor, the *1-2-3 Release 5* spread sheet, the *Approach 3.0* database, the *Freelance Graphics 2.1* presentation package, and the *Organizer 1.1* personal information manager. As a bonus, the CD-ROM includes a Lotus program called *ScreenCam 1.1*, a tool for quickly preparing multimedia presentations. All the programs in *SmartSuite* get high marks for power and ease of use, although Lotus is a distant second in the suite market to the popular *Microsoft Office*, reviewed in this section.

The CD-ROM version of *SmartSuite* also offers an animated "Guided Tour" with narration, giving an overview of the individual programs and how they work together. as well as ten "ScreenCam Movies," one-minute narrated slide shows on specific subjects such as "copying a *1-2-3* range to *Ami Pro*" and "creating *Approach* mail labels in *1-2-3*." There's a trade-off, though, for all this computer-based assistance—you don't get the print instruction manuals. Instead, the hundreds of pages of information are included on the disk.

MPC WIZARD 3.0
★★
Developer: SoftKey International Inc.; 800-227-5609
Format: Windows
Price: $15

If CD-ROM technology were truly reliable and easy to use, *MPC Wizard 3.0* wouldn't exist. This CD-ROM is a diagnostic tool for measuring the peformance of CD-ROM drives, soundboards, and monitors in Windows-based personal computers. You can check, for example, whether your double-speed CD-ROM drive really transfers data at three hundred kilobytes per second or whether your monitor is capable of displaying 256 colors. *MPC Wizard 3.0* also contains a large selection of "drivers," software for controlling peripherals such as video cards, soundboards and CD-ROM drives. Released in October 1994, *MPC Wizard 3.0* is the third in a line of perennial best-sellers because of its low price—generally $10 to $15—and the pervasive sense of insecurity among many computer owners, who believe their complicated systems contain hidden flaws.

But unless you're unusually nervous about the health of your PC, there probably isn't any reason to buy *MPC Wizard*. It's very rare for CD-ROM drives, soundboards, or monitors not to match the performance specifications set by the manufacturers. The most common problems home users encounter—incorrect hardware installation and errors in software setup—won't be identified by *MPC Wizard*. If you need updated drivers for any part of your system, you should get them directly from the manufacturer. Drivers are usually available for free or at very low cost, and you'll be assured of getting the most current version.

MICROSOFT OFFICE STANDARD
★★★½
Developer: Microsoft Corp.; 800-426-9400
Format: Windows
Price: $499

Corporate computer buyers are increasingly turning to "suites" of software that offer all the major applications—word processing, spread sheet, and presentation graphics—in a single package. Microsoft Corporation dominates this rapidly growing market with its *Microsoft Office* line. Partly that's because Microsoft is so big it can muscle aside competitors such as Lotus Development Corporation and Novell Inc. But even Microsoft's critics concede the programs in *Microsoft Office* are leaders in the field, combining power with ease of use.

Microsoft Office Standard on CD-ROM offers four applications: *Microsoft Word 6.0* for word processing, *Microsoft Excel 5.0* for spread sheets, *Microsoft PowerPoint 4.0* for presentations, and *Microsoft Mail 3.2* for receiving electronic mail on a computer network. The disk also includes *Microsoft Office Manager*, a utility program for controlling the suite and moving data between the programs. If you need two or more of these programs, *Microsoft Office* is a bargain, typically selling for less than the cost of buying *Word* and *Excel* separately.

Acquiring *Microsoft Office* on CD-ROM instead of floppy disks offers several big advantages and one potential disadvantage. On the plus side, you get all the software on a single disk instead of thirty-six or more floppies, greatly reducing installation time and eliminating the risk of damaged or lost diskettes. There's also an option that lets you run *Microsoft Office* from the CD-ROM. The programs will run more slowly, but you'll save lots of hard-disk space—a full installation of *Microsoft Office Standard* requires seventy-six megabytes. Finally, you get all the program manuals on screen instead of in print, replacing a two-foot cardboard box stuffed with several thousand pages of documentation. For users who prefer getting help from the computer, it's a tree-saving way to keep lots of information on hand. But it's a big disadvantage for users like me who'd rather learn about new software from print manuals; ordering the print manuals will set you back $129. It's your call—if you don't mind sacrificing the print manuals, *Microsoft Office* on CD-ROM is clearly superior to a huge stack of floppy disks.

MICROSOFT OFFICE PROFESSIONAL
★★★½
Developer: Microsoft Corp.; 800-426-9400
Format: Windows
Price: $599

An expanded version of *Microsoft Office Standard*, reviewed in this section, that includes *Microsoft Access 2.0*, a database program. *Microsoft Office Professional*, like the *Standard* version, puts all the instruction manuals on CD-ROM. Ordering the full set of print manuals, including those for *Access*, costs $179.

MICROSOFT WORD & BOOKSHELF
★★
Developer: Microsoft Corp.; 800-426-9400
Format: Windows
Price: $399

Microsoft Word 6.0 and *Microsoft Bookshelf '94* are both excellent products, but I'm not sure they belong on the same CD-ROM. *Bookshelf*, a powerful reference tool reviewed in Chapter Four, Section b, is updated every year in the spring—so this CD-ROM will be obsolete with the introduction of *Bookshelf '95* in April or May. Nor do you gain anything by getting *Bookshelf* on the same disk as *Word*, the most popular Windows word-processing software; the two programs operate together through the "Quickshelf" feature in just the same way they would if purchased separately. What's more, you don't get the print manuals for *Word* with the CD-ROM; you have to pay $49 to order them separately from Microsoft Corporation. The only reason to buy *Microsoft Word & Bookshelf*, then, is if you don't already own either product and can get a deal to buy the disk for significantly less than purchasing the two programs separately.

MICROSOFT WORKS 3.0
★★★½
Developer: Microsoft Corp.; 800-426-9400
Format: Windows
Price: $99

Microsoft Works is so good that I'm convinced the executives of Microsoft Corporation are deliberately undermarketing the product. This integrated package, which I've used to do much of the writing and organization for the book you're reading now, combines a word processor, spread sheet, database, and drawing program for under $100. Most home and small-business users will find *Works* does everything they'll need for less than a third the cost of the company's heavily promoted *Microsoft Office* suite of applications—*Word* for word processing, the *Excel* spread sheet, and the *Access* database. *Works* is also perfect for laptop computers and anyone with limited hard-drive space, as it requires only six megabytes for full installation. *Microsoft Office*, in contrast, is a hard-disk hog, requiring up to seventy-six megabytes.

Works on CD-ROM is a trade-off. You get the full program

for the same price as the floppy-disk version. What you don't get is the 634-page print manual. Instead, all the manual's text is available on screen. Microsoft, however, has added a package of animated tutorials on the CD-ROM as compensation for leaving out the manual. The tutorials, essentially slide shows with narration and occasional bits of music, begin with the absolute basics, explaining such terms as "hardware" and "software." All the instruction is built around simple, real-world examples. For example, you learn how to create a database by watching the computer prepare an inventory for the fictional Hank's Novelty Toy Store. My *Works* manual is creased, smudged, and dog-eared from countless consultations. I'd never want to be without it. But if you're willing to learn *Works* from the program itself, the CD-ROM version is a winner.

MICROSOFT MULTIMEDIA WORKS 4.0 & MICROSOFT BOOKSHELF '94
★★★½
Developer: Microsoft Corp.; 800-426-9400
Format: Macintosh
Price: $99

If you're willing to live without the 680-page instruction manual for the Macintosh version of *Microsoft Works*, Microsoft Corporation will give you a free copy of *Microsoft Bookshelf '94*. That, in a nutshell, is the deal behind this single CD-ROM with a very long name: *Microsoft Multimedia Works 4.0 & Microsoft Bookshelf '94*.

Works for the Macintosh is similar, but not identical, to the Windows version, also available on CD-ROM and reviewed in this section. Both versions offer an integrated package of applications that—for most home users—is a perfectly adequate replacement for the much more expensive *Microsoft Office*. *Works* gives you a word processor, spreadsheet, database, communications utility, and painting program, all linked.

The CD-ROM version of *Works* for the Macintosh offers a few extras—a multimedia tutorial section that has short narrated animations explaining key operations as well as a clip-art library with 1,100 drawings, 20 sound clips, and 10 very short video clips. The instruction manual's text is available on-screen instead of in print. Because the CD-ROM sells for the same price as *Works* on floppy disk, you're essentially getting *Bookshelf*, reviewed in Chapter Four, Section b, for free. If you don't mind living without the print manual, it's a bargain—the control buttons for *Bookshelf* can be displayed in a corner of the screen while you're using *Works*, making it easy to quickly look up a word or check a statistic.

b. Shareware

Not all personal computer software is sold through stores and mail-order catalogs. There is a flourishing market for "shareware" programs that are distributed free through on-line services and computer bulletin boards on the honor system—you're welcome to try the program, and you're expected to send a small payment to the developer if you like it. Shareware is often the only source for special-interest programs that don't have enough demand for commercial distribution. Do you want to keep lists and schedules for a Girl Scout troop? Organize your model railroad? Test your abilities at extrasensory perception? You can find what you're looking for in shareware. Several popular mainstream software programs started as shareware, by the way, before getting snatched up by commercial publishers, including the *Kid Pix* drawing program for children, the action game *Doom*, and the *Procomm* modem manager.

But searching through the thousands of available shareware programs using your modem is both time-consuming and expensive. Several companies are now providing shareware collections on CD-ROM, letting you quickly access hundreds of programs and download the ones you want to your hard disk. Most of these CD-ROMs are updated quarterly, adding new shareware programs and deleting those no longer available. Be prepared for surprises, both good and bad—the quality of shareware programs varies widely. But you won't give up anything more than your time checking out these programs since you don't pay for what you don't like. Even if you like a program, you can violate the honor system and use it without paying, although developers usually give several strong incentives for sending in the registration fee, including access to technical support, full instruction manuals, and discounts for upgrades.

THE ASP ADVANTAGE
★★★
Developer: Association of Shareware Professionals; 616-788-5131
Format: DOS
Price: $25

The ASP Advantage is assembled quarterly by the Association of Shareware Professionals, which screens all the one thousand or more DOS and Windows programs to make sure they meet the association's standards. Those standards include closely checking for any computer viruses and making sure the programs come with adequate instructions.

I looked at *The ASP Advantage* for the first quarter of 1994. The disk provides a helpful DOS viewer program that displays a catalog for the many offerings, divided into thirty-seven categories such as "Business," "Education," "Engineering," "Games," "Music," "Religion & Philosophy," "Sports," and "Utilities." Within each category, there is a long list of programs, with each entry including a one- or two-sentence description of what the program does. Among the programs that caught my eye were *PC Music Maker, Lotto Prophet, Employee Scheduling Assistant, Treasure Hunt Math, Interactive Physics Manual, Hoosier City: Attack of the Orcs* and *Cliche Finder.*

CICA SHAREWARE FOR WINDOWS
★★½
Developer: Walnut Creek CDROM; 800-786-9907
Format: Windows
Price: $19

According to Walnut Creek CD-ROM, the developer of this disk, the Center for Innovative Computer Applications—or CICA—maintains the largest site on the Internet for Windows shareware. *CICA Shareware for Windows* contains the entire CICA database, some three thousand programs. These programs, by the way, are stored on the CD-ROM in compressed form; you have to use an "unzipping" utility included on the disk before running any of the software.

Most of these programs in *CICA Shareware* are intended for computer professionals and for business applications, with limited appeal for home computer enthusiasts. I examined the September 1994 edition and found a large number of utilities for working with the *C++, Turbo Pascal* and *Visual Basic* programming languages; add-on programs that work with popular office applications including *Microsoft Word, Microsoft Excel, Microsoft Access,* and *WordPerfect for Windows*; and a big selection of printer and video-card drivers. The CD-ROM comes with a viewer program that displays a listing of all the contents, but there are no descriptions other than names, making it difficult to tell much about a program before loading it on your computer. Probably the only reason to buy *CICA Shareware* for home use is the CD-ROM's library of two hundred games, with fascinating names such as *Alien TicTacToe, Destroy the Evil Fruit Empire,* and *Rubik's Cube for Windows.*

THE PC-SIG WORLD OF GAMES CD-ROM
★★★
Developer: PC-SIG; 408-730-9291
Format: DOS
Price: $19

A collection of 550 shareware games; most are for DOS, with about sixty titles for Windows. The CD-ROM includes a well-designed viewer program that divides the games into ten categories: "Adventure and Text," "Arcade," "Board and Dice," "Cards," "Educational Games for Children," "General Entertainment," "Practical Jokes," "Sports," "Trivia" and "Windows." By clicking on the name of an individual game, you summon several paragraphs of information describing the game and specifying the registration fee. Most of the programs can be run directly from the CD-ROM without downloading, a great time-saver when you're just browsing. Among the game titles are *Backgammon, Baseball Trivia, Blackjack for Windows, Dracula in London, Googol Math Games,* and *Warheads for Windows.*

THE PC-SIG WORLD OF WINDOWS CD-ROM
★★★
Developer: PC-SIG; 408-730-9291
Format: Windows
Price: $19

A collection of 375 Windows shareware programs of all types, identical in structure to *The PC-SIG World of Games CD-ROM* reviewed in this section. As with the *Games* disk, *The PC-SIG World of Windows CD-ROM* includes a well-designed viewer program that provides several paragraphs of information on each program. About two hundred of the programs can be run directly from the CD-ROM without downloading, a great time-saver when you're just browsing. The programs in *World of Windows* are divided into twelve categories: "Education," "File/Program Managers,"

"Finance," "Fonts / Screen Drivers," "Games," "Graphics," "Icons," "Miscellaneous," "Personal Information Managers," "Sound," "Utilities," and "Word Processors/Printers." Among the titles are *Banking Buddy*, *Graphic Workshop*, *Look and Listen Dinosaurs*, *Magic Screen Saver*, *Mah Jongg*, and *The Palace of Deceit*.

SIMTEL
★★½
Developer: Walnut Creek CDROM; 800-786-9907
Format: DOS
Price: $25

A truly massive collection of ten thousand DOS shareware programs—the September 1994 edition of *Simtel* that I reviewed fills two disks. The material is divided into two hundred categories covering everything from anti-virus software to hurricane tracking programs. Most of the entries, however, are utilities, drivers and programming tools intended for experienced computer users who want to improve the performance of their hardware. Still, there are some categories that aren't just for power users, including a large selection of educational games for children, utilities to help the handicapped use computers, and a library of software for ham radio operators. The programs are stored on the CD-ROM in compressed form; you have to use an "unzipping" utility included on the disk before running any of the software. Also, although *Simtel* comes with a viewer program that displays a listing of all the contents, there are no descriptions other than the names, making it difficult to tell much about a program before loading it on your computer.

c. Desktop Publishing

Personal computers have revolutionized the field of graphic design. With the low-cost programs reviewed in this section, almost anyone can produce sophisticated-looking documents ranging from greeting cards to multipage newsletters.

AMERICANA
★★½
Developer: SoftKey International Inc.; 800-227-5609
Format: Windows, Macintosh
Price: $19

Part of the *MediaClips* series, described below. The one hundred photographs in *Americana* are a cross section of familiar visual images depicting the United States. There are famous sights such as the White House, the Grand Canyon, and San Francisco cable cars, as well as generic scenes such as a buffalo, a red barn, and a steamboat. With one hundred music clips and twenty-five video clips.

About the *MediaClips* series: SoftKey International Inc. has produced fifteen clip-art CD-ROM titles that provide an affordable, easy-to-access gallery of color photographs. The disks also contain brief snippets of music and, in some cases, video clips, but these aren't as useful.

Each CD-ROM presents one hundred photos, along with captions describing the pictures and where they were taken, stored as both low-resolution eight-bit images and high-resolution twenty-four-bit images for either a Macintosh or a PC running Windows. Photos are available in the BMP and TIFF formats for Windows and in the PICT format for the Macintosh. Windows users also get a shareware conversion program called *Image Alchemy* for translating BMP and TIFF files into formats used by other graphics programs.

In addition, each title contains either fifty or one hundred music clips. The individual music clips run anywhere from one second to eighty seconds, with most around twenty seconds, and are performed with actual instruments rather than a synthesizer. Unfortunately, the music isn't clearly labeled and doesn't follow any recognizable pattern—it isn't clear, for example, why the *Wild Places* disk with pictures of beaches and deserts has only New Age music, while the *Jets & Props* disk on jet aircraft has only rock music. Some of the titles also include twenty-five video clips, again averaging about twenty seconds each, that are almost worthless because of their grainy images and faded colors.

The *MediaClips* CD-ROMs are acceptable, however, on the strength of the photographs alone, which are clear, sharp, and well composed. All the contents are royalty-free; the developer asks only that an appropriate copyright notice be attached to your publication. Although each of the *MediaClips* titles can be purchased separately, the best deal is to buy a bundle combining several of the CD-ROMs. To find out what's available, call SoftKey.

Other titles in the *MediaClips* series: *Animal Kingdom*; *Batik Designs*; *Business Backgrounds*; *Deep Voyage*; *Full Bloom*; *Jets & Props*; *Majestic Places*; *Money, Money, Money!*; *New York, NY*; *Space Odyssey*; *Tropical Rainforest*; *Vintage Aloha*; *Wild Places*, and *World View*. All are reviewed briefly in this section.

ANIMAL KINGDOM
★★½
Developer: SoftKey International Inc.; 800-227-5609
Format: Windows, Macintosh
Price: $19

Part of the *MediaClips* series, described in the review of *Americana* in this section. The one hundred photographs in *Animal Kingdom* show familiar African wildlife such as elephants, lions, and giraffes as well as North American creatures including sea lions, rabbits, and bald eagles. With one hundred music clips and twenty-five video clips.

BATIK DESIGNS
★★½
Developer: SoftKey International Inc.; 800-227-5609
Format: Windows, Macintosh
Price: $4

Part of the *MediaClips* series, described in the review of *Americana* in this section. The one hundred photographs in *Batik Designs* show Batik fabrics from Indonesia, which resemble tie-dyed clothing. With fifty clips of Indonesian music.

BUSINESS BACKGROUNDS
★★1/2
Developer: SoftKey International Inc.; 800-227-5609
Format: Windows, Macintosh
Price: $4

Part of the *MediaClips* series, described in the review of *Americana* in this section. The one hundred photographs in *Business Backgrounds* are typical images from the workplace, such as a handshake, a computer keyboard, and a "no smoking" sign. With fifty music clips.

CLIPART LIBRARY
★★★
Developer: SoftKey International Inc.; 800-227-5609
Format: Windows, Macintosh
Price: $39

Desktop publishing professionals, as well as serious amateurs, are always running around in search of drawings to dress up their newsletters or brochures. *ClipArt Library* is a good place to start looking. The CD-ROM is jammed with 3,003 color line drawings covering a wide range of topics. You'll find everything from playing cards to gingerbread men, from computer disks to famous places. The content is divided into twenty-six categories such as "Communications," "Health" and "People." Each category provides a comprehensive selection; "Transportation," for example, contains fifty-two images of airplanes, trucks, trains, cars, ships, street signs, and traffic lights. For Windows, the files are in CGM, PCX, and WMF formats. For Macintosh, the files are in EPS and TIFF formats.

   No one will mistake these clip-art images for the work of Picasso or Rembrandt, but—for the price—you can't complain about the bland and utilitarian style. One cautionary note for beginners: While experienced users of graphics software will have no trouble figuring out how to operate *ClipArt Library*, the manual and the program itself presume at least a limited knowledge of desktop publishing.

CORELDRAW 3
★★★
Developer: Corel Corp.; 800-772-6735
Format: Windows
Price: $125

Corel Corporation takes a unique "hand-me-down" approach to selling desktop publishing software. Every year, the company brings out a new version of its flagship *CorelDraw* graphics package priced for the professional market, then lowers the cost of earlier versions for sale to home and small-business users. *CorelDraw 5* came out in May 1994 for about $500, the previous year's *CorelDraw 4* was then marked down to about $275, and the older *CorelDraw3* from 1992 sank down to between $100 and $150. Although Corel hasn't made any firm announcements, *CorelDraw 6* is likely in mid-1995, and *CorelDraw 4* could then move into the bargain-basement category.

This approach differs markedly from the strategy of other software publishers who develop "light" versions of professional software to sell in the home market, stripping out some of the more complicated features. For nonprofessional users, there are both benefits and drawbacks to Corel's strategy. On the plus side, *CorelDraw 3* is a very powerful tool for producing newsletters, advertising, presentations, and business logos. On the down side, it is also much more difficult to master than desktop publishing software created specifically for the home/small-business market, such as *The Print Shop Deluxe CD Ensemble* and *Microsoft Publisher*, both reviewed in this section.

CorelDraw 3 packs a massive package onto a single CD-ROM. In addition to the namesake *CorelDraw* program for creating graphics, there is *CorelChart* for making charts, *CorelPhoto-Paint* for editing and retouching photographs, and *CorelShow* for organizing slide-show presentations. The disk also includes a whopping 250 fonts and 14,000 clip-art images and symbols. To help you sort through this abundance, Corel includes a fifty-four-minute videotape in the box as well as a hefty six-hundred-page manual and a three-hundred-page clip-art guide.

If you want to move up from amateur to semiprofessional status in desktop publishing, *CorelDraw3* is a good way to start at a reasonable price, although you should probably shift to Corel's current release if you become a heavy user of the software. The real expense isn't the software itself but the hours and hours of study required to become proficient with these complicated tools.

CORELFLOW
★★★
Developer: Corel Corp.; 800-772-6735
Format: Windows
Price: $85

CorelFlow is a specialized desktop publishing program dedicated to the production of flow charts, diagrams, organizational charts, schematics, and floor plans. Though it borrows heavily from Corel Corporation's flagship *CorelDraw*, reviewed in this section, *CorelFlow* is easier to use than *CorelDraw* because it offers fewer functions. Included along with the program are one hundred fonts, one thousand clip-art images, one thousand photographs, and two thousand symbols. The symbols are especially useful for charting—there are electrical symbols to draw circuit diagrams, for example, and architectural symbols for preparing office layouts. A three-hundred-page combination user's manual and clip-art guide presents a clear explanation of how to use *CorelFlow*, although it's written at a level that assumes some previous experience with desktop publishing software.

COREL GALLERY
★★★½
Developer: Corel Corp.; 800-772-6735
Format: Windows, Macintosh
Price: $35

A huge collection of quality clip art at a reasonable price, *Corel Gallery* offers an awesome ten thousand color images that are compatible with most Windows word-processing, presentation, and desktop publishing applications. The drawings, symbols, cartoons, maps, and flags are divided into fifty categories such as animals, electronics, money, ships, and weather. You can find almost anything in *Corel Gallery*, from a cameo sketch of Paula Abdul to a drawing of a hammerhead shark to the flag of the Falkland Islands. Corel has made the CD-ROM simple to use through two key features: a browser program that requires only two megabytes of hard-disk space and a 344-page guidebook with a color reproduction of every image.

COREL PROFESSIONAL PHOTOS CD-ROM SAMPLER
★★★
Developer: Corel Corp.; 800-772-6735
Format: Windows, Macintosh
Price: $19

Corel Corporation is one of the most ambitious producers of clip-art photography through its *Corel Professional Photos* series, which includes more than one hundred titles, with more being added all the time. Each disk contains one hundred well-made, royalty-free color photographs stored in the Kodak Photo CD format, along with programs to view the images, use the photographs as a screen saver, and—for Windows users only—an editing program to adjust color, size, and resolution. *Corel Professional Photos CD-ROM Sampler* offers one hundred images plucked from the collection, a good way to learn about the series while acquiring a smattering of clip-art photos. Among the many titles in the series are *Autumn, Birds, California Coasts, English Country Gardens, Grapes & Wine, Mayan & Aztec Ruins, Orchids of the World, Southeast Asia,* and *Windsurfing.* For a full up-to-date catalog, contact Corel.

DEEP VOYAGE
★★$^{1}/_{2}$
Developer: SoftKey International Inc.; 800-227-5609
Format: Windows, Macintosh
Price: $19

Part of the *MediaClips* series, described in the review of *Americana* in this section. The one hundred photographs in *Deep Voyage* are all underwater shots, mostly of coral reefs and sea sponges. With one hundred music clips and twenty-five video clips.

2000 FANTASTIC FONTS
★★½
Developer: Expert Software Inc.; 800-759-2562
Format: Windows
Price: $15

What does a font cost? Something less than one cent, if you buy *2000 Fantastic Fonts*, which sells for under $20. The CD-ROM provides five "families" of type fonts in the TrueType format used by Windows and the Postscript format used by Adobe Type Manager. In the offbeat tradition of font designers, many of these fonts have weird names such as Alien Tongue, Blippo, Kudzu, Narcosis, Red Dwarf, and Zebu Caps.

Fantastic Fonts includes a simple installer program to preview and load the many selections. The five font families are: "dingbats," special characters for making checkmarks and other symbols; "display," artistic fonts for special designs such as advertising flyers; "fixed," where each letter has the same spacing for use in columnar reports; "sans serif," the "serious" fonts for use in business documents; "script," with cursive letters for invitations and thank-you notes; and "serif," the most readable fonts intended for long documents.

You'll have a hard time looking at all these choices, however. The installer shows just one font at a time and displays only twelve characters rather than the full range of letters, numbers, and symbols. The CD-ROM should—but doesn't—come with a print directory listing all the fonts and showing their appearance.

FULL BLOOM
★★½
Developer: SoftKey International Inc.; 800-227-5609
Format: Windows, Macintosh
Price: $4

Part of the *MediaClips* series, described in the review of *Americana* in this section. The one hundred photographs in *Full Bloom* show close-ups of flowers, including roses, daisies, sunflowers, and daffodils. With one hundred music clips, all classical, and twenty-five video clips showing time-lapse photography of buds opening up into flowers.

JETS & PROPS
★★½
Developer: SoftKey International Inc.; 800-227-5609
Format: Windows, Macintosh
Price: $13

A two-disk set that is part of the *MediaClips* series, described in the review of *Americana* in this section. The one hundred photographs in *Jets* mostly show modern jet fighters and bombers, although there are a few shots of the Boeing 747 and the Concorde. The one hundred photographs in *Props* show World War I and World War II combat aircraft, as well as a few helicopters. Each disk includes one hundred music clips and twenty-five video clips.

KEY COLOR CLIPART
★★½
Developer: SoftKey International Inc.; 800-227-5609
Format: Windows, Macintosh
Price: $29

A scaled-down version of *ClipArt Library*, reviewed in this section, at a scaled-down price. The two CD-ROMs are identical, except that *Key Color ClipArt* has only 2,550 images, while *ClipArt Library* has 3,003.

KEY FONTS PRO
★★½
Developer: SoftKey International Inc.; 800-227-5609
Format: Windows, Macintosh
Price: $29

Nothing marks the dividing line between professional graphic artists and amateurs more precisely than the use of fonts. When computer novices discover how easy it is to select different typefaces, they often go off the deep end by designing documents that look like an explosion in a type factory. *Key Fonts Pro* is a powder keg for fledgling desktop publishers with more enthusiasm than common sense. The CD-ROM contains 1,550 typefaces for the Macintosh and PCs running Windows, in both the TrueType and PostScript formats. Some 1,200 of the fonts include international characters such as letters with accents and umlauts.

Any one of these fonts can be copied from the disk with just a few mouse clicks. Type designers are always competing with each other to come up with humorous or bizarre names for their latest creations, such as these from *Key Fonts Pro*: Bauget, Boozle, Cheap Shot, Eyechart, Jargon, Leakin, Loblolly, Perkle, Petticoat, Slim Pickens, Twinkie, Vice Prez, Wahoo, and Wowser. The biggest problem with *Key Fonts Pro* is sorting through all these choices. A very small sample of each font is printed on the *Key Fonts Pro* box; the only other way to judge their appearance is previewing them one at a time on your computer screen. To help in the selection process, the developer should have thrown a pamphlet into the box displaying the full alphabet for each font.

KEY PHOTO CLIPS
★½
Developer: SoftKey International Inc.; 800-227-5609
Format: Windows, Macintosh
Price: $29

A somewhat reduced version of *Photo Library*, reviewed in this section, at a somewhat lower price. The two CD-ROMs are identical, except that *Key Photo Clips* contains only 2,100 color photographs, while *Photo Library* has 2,500.

MAJESTIC PLACES
★★½
Developer: SoftKey International Inc.; 800-227-5609
Format: Windows, Macintosh
Price: $4

Part of the *MediaClips* series, described in the review of *Americana* in this section. The one hundred photographs in *Majestic Places* depict outdoor scenery, such as the Himalayas, South Pacific sunsets, and the Half Dome rock formation in Yosemite National Park. With one hundred music clips.

MONEY, MONEY, MONEY!
★★½

Developer: SoftKey International Inc.; 800-227-5609
Format: Windows, Macintosh
Price: $4

Part of the *MediaClips* series, described in the review of *Americana* in this section. The one hundred photographs in *Money, Money, Money!* show coins, coins, coins and bills, bills, bills—both U.S. currency and foreign currencies from Europe and Asia. With one hundred music clips, including sound effects of coins dropping on tables, and twenty-five video clips showing the production of dollar bills.

NEW YORK, NY
★★½

Developer: SoftKey International Inc.; 800-227-5609
Format: Windows, Macintosh
Price: $19

Part of the *MediaClips* series, described in the review of *Americana* in this section. The one hundred photographs in *New York, NY* present the glamorous side of the nation's biggest, most exciting, and scariest city. All the familiar sights are here—the Statue of Liberty, the Manhattan skyline at night, and the Empire State Building. We are spared any photos of cabdrivers making rude gestures at each other or homeless people in the streets. With one hundred music clips and twenty-five video clips.

PC PAINTBRUSH PHOTO LIBRARY
★★

Developer: SoftKey International Inc.; 800-227-5609
Format: Windows, Macintosh
Price: $49

Quantity, in this case, does not make up for lack of quality. *Photo Library* is stuffed with 2,500 royalty-free color photographs in 88 categories such as "Agriculture," "Planes," and "Sunsets," with particular emphasis on animals and scenes from around the United States. The images are stored in the TIFF format for either the Macintosh or PCs running Windows as well as the BMP format for Windows only.

The biggest weakness in this CD-ROM is the photographs themselves, clearly not the work of topnotch professionals. Many of the images suffer from poor lighting and faded colors. Caption information is also woefully inadequate; you don't know where on the California coast that shot of pounding surf was taken or whether that grazing animal with antlers is a deer or an elk.

PRINT ARTIST CD EDITION
★★★
Developer: Maxis; 800-336-2947
Format: Windows
Price: $59

An easy-to-use desktop publishing program backed up with a huge library of clip-art and extra fonts, *Print Artist CD Edition* provides the tools to quickly churn out all kinds of graphics. In addition to the *Print Artist* program, the CD-ROM provides 2,300 high-quality clip-art images and 112 fonts. Included in the box is a bonus CD-ROM with an additional four thousand pieces of clip-art and another three hundred fonts.

Print Artist begins by giving you a choice of 10 types of document to create: a sign, letterhead, greeting card, post card, calendar, business card, certificate, banner, envelope, or "craft." Within each document type are hundreds of canned layouts that can be easily modified—a "for rent" sign, for instance, in which you insert your phone number or a Mother's Day card with an open inside page for adding a personal message. These layouts are about evenly divided between typical small-business applications, such as creating restaurant menus and clearance-sale banners, and home "craft" projects, such as Christmas cards and making party hats.

You can get started in *Print Artist* without bothering to read the 176-page instruction manual, but becoming truly proficient with the program's many features takes effort. Also, a full installation of *Print Artist* requires twenty megabytes of hard-disk space, although the program works almost as well with an abbreviated installation requiring only 6.5 megabytes.

PRINTMASTER GOLD CD BONUS PACK
★★★
Developer: MicroLogic Software; 800-888-9078
Format: Windows
Price: $55

PrintMaster Gold CD Bonus Pack is perhaps the easiest home desktop publishing software to learn, although it offers fewer features than its two main competitors, *The Print Shop Deluxe CD Ensemble* and *Print Artist CD Edition*, both reviewed in this section. All three CD-ROMs include a huge library of material for your creations; *PrintMaster Gold* provides 145 fonts and 1,800 clip-art images. There are four types of projects in *PrintMaster Gold*: posters, greeting cards, banners, and calendars. You can make any one of these from scratch or call up numerous templates to customize—there are, for example, thirty-two designs for birthday cards. *PrintMaster Gold* comes with a 250-page book that serves as both a manual and a clip-art guide, with about one hundred pages devoted to explaining how the program works. Most users won't need to look at the manual, though, because every step of the creative process is clearly explained by text on the screen. The CD-ROM even provides audio help; a voice automatically begins giving suggestions on what to do whenever you enter a new screen. The narration quickly gets tiresome, however, and I turned it off as soon as I got comfortable navigating on my own.

THE PRINT SHOP DELUXE CD ENSEMBLE
★★★
Developer: Broderbund Software Inc.; 800-521-6263
Format: Windows, Macintosh
Price: $79

In the crowded field of desktop publishing software, *The Print Shop* product line from Broderbund Software Inc. stands out as the best choice for home users. With barely a glance at the instruction manual, you can use the programs and clip-art collections on *The Print Shop Deluxe CD Ensemble* to crank out greeting cards, banners, calendars, office stationery, and mailing labels. Broderbund claims to have sold 7 million copies of *The Print Shop* line, mostly on floppy disk, since introducing the first version in 1984. Although the CD-ROM is available only for Windows, the individual programs on the disk can be purchased separately on floppies for personal computers running DOS or for the Macintosh.

The CD-ROM provides *The Print Shop Deluxe*; *Print Shop Deluxe Companion*, an accessory program for creating business-oriented documents such as certificates and envelopes; and three clip-art collections: *Business Graphics*, *Graphics Folio*, and *Sampler Graphics*. In total, you get one thousand clip-art images, seventy-three fonts, and twenty royalty-free photographs in the Kodak Photo CD format. If your hard disk is running out of space, you'll appreciate the minimum installation option, which requires only 1.5 megabytes. That leaves most of the program files and graphics on the CD-ROM, causing the program to run slightly slower. But that's only a minor inconvenience for occasional *Print Shop* users.

MICROSOFT PUBLISHER
★★½
Developer: Microsoft Corp.; 800-426-9400
Format: Windows
Price: $99

Microsoft Publisher is a powerful and somewhat complicated desktop publishing program. For business applications such as producing flyers and brochures, though, *Publisher* outperforms the more popular *The Print Shop Deluxe CD Ensemble* reviewed in this section. In offering *Publisher* on CD-ROM, Microsoft has both added and subtracted from the floppy-disk version without changing the price. The additions are a *Special Occasions Design Pack*, worth about $39, with extra clip art, borders, fonts, and templates. Microsoft also throws in a selection of prewritten human interest stories intended to fill that annoying empty half column on the back page of your association's monthly newsletter. It's innocuous stuff, such as a two-paragraph item noting that while dogs say "bow-wow" in English, they say "bau-bau" in Italian and "ham-ham" in Romanian.

What Microsoft has taken away is potentially much more important: the print manual. The floppy version of *Publisher* comes with a 430-page book describing all of the program's many features. On the CD-ROM, you only get the manual on screen. If you're like me—the type of person who likes to flip through the pages of a manual in search of answers to software headaches—you might want to get *Publisher* on floppy disk.

SPACE ODYSSEY
★★½

Developer: SoftKey International Inc.; 800-227-5609
Format: Windows, Macintosh
Price: $19

Part of the *MediaClips* series, described in the review of *Americana* in this section. The one hundred photographs in *Space Odyssey* show planets in our solar system and stars in distant galaxies; there's even a shot by the Hubble space telescope of the Shoemaker-Levy 9 comet that hit Jupiter in July 1994. With one hundred audio clips, all New Age electronic "space" music, and twenty-five video clips.

TROPICAL RAINFOREST
★★½

Developer: SoftKey International Inc.; 800-227-5609
Format: Windows, Macintosh
Price: $19

Part of the *MediaClips* series, described in the review of *Americana* in this section. The one hundred photographs in *Tropical Rainforest* depict animals and plants from the South American jungle. With one hundred music clips, mostly Latin American flute and guitar, and twenty-five video clips.

VINTAGE ALOHA
★★½

Developer: SoftKey International Inc.; 800-227-5609
Format: Windows, Macintosh
Price: $4

Part of the *MediaClips* series, described in the review of *Americana* in this section. The one hundred photographs in *Vintage Aloha* show close-ups of designs from classic Hawaiian shirts. With fifty clips of Hawaiian music.

WILD PLACES
★★½
Developer: SoftKey International Inc.; 800-227-5609
Format: Windows, Macintosh
Price: $15

Part of the *MediaClips* series, described in the review of *Americana* in this section. The one hundred photographs in *Wild Places* show wilderness landscapes, mostly beaches and deserts. With one hundred clips of New Age music.

WORLD VIEW
★★½
Developer: SoftKey International Inc.; 800-227-5609
Format: Windows, Macintosh
Price: $15

Part of the *MediaClips* series, described in the review of *Americana* in this section. The one hundred photographs in *World View* are related to space exploration, showing the Earth from orbit, *Apollo* astronauts on the moon, and close-ups of other planets taken by NASA spacecraft. With one hundred clips of New Age music and twenty-five video clips of rocket launches and moon landings.

d. About Computers

COMPUTER WORKS
★
Developer: SoftKey International Inc.; 800-227-5609
Format: DOS
Price: $29

Computer Works is an embarrassment that doesn't take advantage of the very technology it attempts to describe. Intended as a guide to personal computers, the CD-ROM's content is shallow, boring, and full of inaccuracies. The box promises "colorful animated graphics," but the program delivers only tiny and insignificant animations such as a blinking green light in a drawing of a computer monitor.

The subject matter is divided into ten sections: "Computer Systems," "Displays," "Disk Drives," "Printers," "Keyboards," "Circuit Boards," "Software," "Peripherals," "History of Computers," and "Related Topics." Each section has from five to twenty-two articles on the subject. Most of these articles, however, are no more than three paragraphs. Here, for example, is the entire description of the computer industry's history from 1972 to 1989: "Once the personal computer (PC) started making its way into homes, the PC revolution had begun. Market competition between manufacturers such as IBM and Apple Computer led to rapid advances in the field. For the first time, high-level computing ability was in the households of hundreds of thousands of people, rather than a privileged few. Computers had finally become tools of the common people." That's it. Nothing about the invention of the microprocessor, one of the great technology breakthroughs of human history. Nothing about how the PC is changing the way the world does business. Nothing about the human drama swirling around such figures as Steve Jobs and Bill Gates.

The articles are illustrated with second-rate line drawings rather than photographs. What's more, *Computer Works* contains no true animations and no sound. There are also significant errors. The three-sentence article on CD-ROM drives says CD-ROM disks "typically [hold] around 500 megabytes." But CD-ROMs actually hold 660 megabytes. *Computer Works*, in short, doesn't work and should be deleted from your shopping list.

HOW COMPUTERS WORK
★★★

Developer: Time Warner Interactive; 800-482-3766
Format: Macintosh
Price: $59

Computers, among their many talents, are capable of explaining themselves to humans. *How Computers Work* is a useful tutorial for beginners, covering computer technology and history through well-written text and colorful illustrations. Based on two Time-Life books, *Understanding Computers* and *How Things Work*, the CD-ROM is divided into seven categories: input, processing, memory and storage, output, programming, applications, and time line. Within each category, you select from six to ten subjects, such as an explanation of how laser printers work or a definition of random-access memory. The information is presented in slide shows, with illustrations from the Time-Life books accompanied by audio narration.

The text is aimed at computer neophytes, as shown in this passage from the introduction: "UNIVAC, the first commercial computer, was used to predict the outcome of the 1952 United States presidential election. A modern desktop computer is only a fraction the size of this illustrious predecessor, but its essential elements are virtually identical. It uses input devices to accept data and programs and output devices to present information to the user. Inside the cabinet, a CPU, or central processing unit, manipulates data and controls the computer. An electronic memory stores data, instructions, intermediate calculations and final results."

Beyond the slide shows, *How Computers Work* offers several interesting side features. There is a comprehensive index and glossary, as well as supplementary text from the Time-Life books. The best of these extras is a package of demo software. You can operate trial versions of several popular Macintosh applications, including Microsoft Word, Microsoft Excel, Claris FileMaker Pro, and Quark Xpress. The only drawback to *How Computers Work* is the rapid pace of change in the computer industry. Some of the content on the CD-ROM, which was released in April 1993, is already dated. Time Warner Interactive promises to release a revised version, however, sometime in the first half of 1995.

PC/COMPUTING: HOW MULTIMEDIA COMPUTERS WORK
★★★
Developer: Mindscape Inc.; 800-234-3088
Format: Windows
Price: $29

Even experienced computer users often know little about what really goes on inside the case housing their machines. *PC/Computing: How Multimedia Computers Work* presents narrated animations—using beautifully drawn, photorealistic three-dimensional images—to explain fifty-three parts of a typical IBM-compatible personal computer. This isn't a technical reference—many of the explanations are only a few sentences—but the animations are a fun and easy way to learn.

The CD-ROM draws much of its material from a book called *How Computers Work* from Ziff-Davis Press; the book in turn was assembled from a popular monthly feature in Ziff's *PC/Computing* magazine called "How It Works." I particularly like the book, which stands above the CD-ROM in offering more detailed descriptions of the various components.

Both the book and CD-ROM fill me with a sense of wonder at the complexity of personal computers, perhaps the most complicated device ever sold on the mass market. An animation describing the 486 central processing unit, for example, shows the flow of information through eight subunits named prefetch, segment, paging, decode, bus interface, cache, numeric processor, and execution. You'll also find a few surprises. I suspect, for example, that most computer owners don't realize every PC contains a small battery. The battery keeps an essential trickle of electricity running through a special memory chip that retains important system configuration information even when the computer is turned off. Among the many components covered in *How Multimedia Computers Work* are the monitor, mouse, keyboard, CD-ROM drive, fax-modem, hard drive, and random-access memory.

In addition to the animations, the CD-ROM includes eight fascinating narrated tours explaining computer functions such as formatting a floppy disk and running a program. Two other features are less successful. Excerpts from several Ziff-Davis computer books have been dumped on the CD-ROM, but the text is displayed without adequate navigation controls—in a five-hundred-word computer glossary, for example, there's no way to jump to a specific word you want to look up. Another section presents four "experts," all Ziff-Davis editors, in one-minute video clips answering four dull questions about multimedia computers. I could also do without a little animated character named "Zip Data," resembling a yellow raindrop, who bounces around the edges of some scenes in an unnecessary attempt at providing comic relief.

Chapter Ten:
In a Class by Themselves

CD-ROM software is constantly pushing into new categories, moving far beyond the well-worn paths of interactive games and children's learning programs. In this final chapter, you'll find titles on everything from astrology to videography.

a. Special Interest

ASTROLOGY SOURCE
★★½
Developer: Multicom Publishing Inc.; 800-850-7272
Format: Windows, Macintosh
Price: $39

There's more than a little irony surrounding *Astrology Source*. Here's a product that harnesses one of the most powerful human creations of this century—affordable multimedia personal computers—and uses that technology to explore the totally untechnological pseudoscience of astrology. *Astrology Source* attempts to fill two functions: preparing personal horoscopes and presenting information on the history and practice of divining the future by studying the movements of stars and planets. Much of the text, by the way, is drawn from *The Only Astrology Book You'll Ever Need* by Joanna Martine Woolfolk. In commenting on the status of astrology today, *Astrology Source* makes some rather bold and unsupportable assertions: "More and more, astrology has entered the mainstream of our culture. It is no longer considered out of the ordinary for people in business, commerce, banking, the law, the arts, politics—in fact, almost every major profession—to consult a personal astrologer."

To prepare a personal horoscope, you enter your name, birth date, time of birth, and birthplace by city and state. You can view or print a personal star chart or summon a horoscope for any date you want. There's also a gallery of fifty famous people and their star charts. I learned that George Washington and Albert Einstein are both Pisces, while Madonna and Bill Clinton are Leos. *Astrology Source* will also analyze compatibility among any of these celebrities or among any personal profiles you enter, so you can gauge your future happiness sticking with your current significant other against switching to Cher or Paul Newman.

Astrology enthusiasts will require only a few hours to soak up all the instructional information in *Astrology Source*. The only reason to continue using the CD-ROM would be casting daily horoscopes. But then again you can get the same thing—with the same degree of scientific accuracy—from a daily newspaper or even a fortune cookie.

DARING TO FLY! FROM ICARUS TO THE RED BARON
★★½
Developer: Arnowitz Studios; 800-336-2947
Format: Windows, Macintosh
Price: $45

In the early days of flight, aircraft designers and pilots often didn't understand enough about aeronautics to get their new designs off the ground. It's the same today for CD-ROM developers, who often don't know enough about this new medium to prevent well-meaning efforts from sinking into confusion and disorganization. *Daring to Fly! From Icarus to the Red Baron* is one such pioneering effort that doesn't quite take wing.

Intended to span the history of aviation from prehistory through World War I, *Daring to Fly!* offers a jumble of photographs, video clips from old newsreels, excerpts from historical documents, and modern essays. There's no consistency—some subjects are explored in depth, others are just skimmed. The content is divided into eight fuzzily defined topics: "science of flight," "sprouting wings," "coming of age," "wings of war," "taking off," "lighter than air," "dreaming of flight," and "women aloft." Each topic is subdivided into three to five "exhibits" that explore a single subject such as the Wright Brothers' first powered flight at Kitty Hawk in 1903. "With no publicity and against all odds, they fly their plane 120 feet in 12 seconds. They get only 10 feet off the ground in their attempt, but they accomplish their goal," declares a text essay accompanied by eight photographs. There is also a library of twelve "stories," narrated slide shows drawn from the disk's many photos and drawings. You'll learn about the brief and glamorous career of Harriet Quimby, the first licensed female pilot in the United States, who started flying in 1911, became the first woman to fly the English Channel in 1912, and died three months later when she fell out of her plane into Boston harbor.

Beyond the lack of a unifying structure, *Daring to Fly!* is also hobbled by several technical and editorial flaws. To dig up forty-five minutes of video clips, the developers resort to throwing in footage from the 1920s and 1930s, even though World War I ended in 1918. On the technical side, the program offers no way to print the text of articles; instead, the material must be copied to a word processor. Finally, the Windows version of *Daring to Fly!* greedily demands fifteen megabytes of hard disk space but still moves sluggishly between topics.

FAMILY TREE MAKER DELUXE CD-ROM VERSION 2.0
★★★
Developer: Banner Blue Software Inc.; 510-794-6850
Format: Windows
Price: $59

Researching your ancestry requires the combined skills of a detective, a historian, and a reference librarian. *Family Tree Maker Deluxe CD-ROM Version 2.0* won't make you an instant expert in this complex endeavor, but it's a good starting point. The easy-to-use program completely automates the process of compiling a database of family members—recording date of birth, date of death, marriages, and children—as well as printing out a variety of family trees. Although you can start using *Family Tree Maker* without any instruction, all the program's many features are clearly explained in a hefty 413-page manual.

A feature called "Scrapbook" allows you to include photographs in printed family trees, as well as audio or video clips in multimedia presentations. How do you get family snapshots into a computer? The easiest method is Kodak Photo CD. You take a roll of film, a negative, a slide, or a photograph to a photo finisher who works with Photo CD and get back a digitized version of your image on a CD-ROM. Almost all newer CD-ROM drives will handle Photo CDs; the only drawback is that most home PC printers don't do a very good job of reproducing photographs.

The CD-ROM also provides two valuable reference tools. The "How-To Guide" is an on-screen book giving detailed advice on organizing a family research project. There's also a long list of sources, including the names of local genealogical societies and the address of every county courthouse across the country. "FamilyFinder" is a staggeringly huge index of 100 million names, mostly deceased residents of the United States, with instructions on how to learn more about each individual. If you find an ancestor's name on the list, you then have to buy another CD-ROM from Banner Blue Software Inc., the developer of *Family Tree Maker*, to get the available information; an order form for fifty-two different archival CD-ROMs is included in the box. Even the archival information is limited, however. Social Security records, for example, give only date of birth and date of death, Social Security number, and ZIP code of the last known residence. That's where the role of detective becomes important— *Family Tree Maker* shows where you're likely to find information, but you still have to do a lot of sleuthing on your own.

Using *Family Tree Maker* to enter and maintain a family tree doesn't require a fancy computer—four megabytes of random-access memory and five megabytes of space on your hard disk are all that's needed. But be warned the "Scrapbook" feature demands eight megabytes of RAM in order to manipulate and display pictures; storing a large number of digitized photographs also calls for lots of hard-disk space.

5-FT. 10-PAK VOLUME II
★★½
Developer: Sirius Publishing Inc.; 800-247-0307
Format: Windows
Price: $29

5-Ft. 10-Pak is CD-ROM's bargain basement. This collection of ten disks, mostly discontinued and slow-selling merchandise, has been a huge seller because of its low price—typically $25 to $29. More than a million copies of the first volume of *5-Ft. 10-Pak*, given its name because the disks are shipped in an accordion-folded plastic sleeve that stretches five feet when extended, were sold from its introduction in March 1994 until the second volume came out in October. A third volume is due in early 1995, with other volumes likely to follow.

But you get what you pay for; most of the CD-ROMs in *5-Ft. 10-Pak* are schlock. Indeed, many CD-ROM developers are worried that *5-Ft. 10-Pak* is damaging the whole industry's image with consumers who'll falsely conclude that the ten disks represent the best of what's available. So should you consider buying *5-Ft. 10-Pak*? If you enjoy browsing through CD-ROMs and aren't looking for anything that's particularly compelling, you'll probably find at least one or two of the disks amusing. But you'll be disappointed if you expect *5-Ft. 10-Pak* to deliver a great value.

In the second volume of *5-Ft. 10-Pak*, the ten CD-ROMs are *Microsoft Multimedia Jumpstart* from Microsoft Corporation, a technical guide to developing multimedia software, intended for software professionals; *Mega Rock Rap 'N Roll* from Paramount Interactive, a do-it-yourself recording studio reviewed in Chapter Six, Section e; *Movie Select* from Paramount Interactive, a discontinued and out-of-date movie guide; *Sherlock Holmes Consulting Detective, Volume I* from Viacom New Media, a mystery game reviewed in Chapter Three, Section a; *Space Quest IV* from Sierra

On-Line Inc., a humorous science-fiction adventure game; *PC Karaoke Family Fun* from Sirius Publishing Inc., a sing-along program featuring ten classic songs such as "Camptown Races" and "On Top of Old Smoky"; *The Home Medical Advisor* from Pixel Perfect, a guide to common medical problems; *Arts & Letters War Birds* from Computer Support Corporation, a compilation of aircraft pictures; *Fantasia's 2000 Fonts* from Fantasia Concepts Inc., a collection of Windows fonts; and *Battle Chess* from Interplay Productions Inc., an animated chess game where knights in armor appear as the pieces reviewed in Chapter Three, Section c. The *PC Karaoke Family Fun* disk also includes software to sign up for a free test of the Prodigy on-line service.

JETS!
★★½
Developer: Medio Multimedia Inc.; 800-788-3866
Format: Windows
Price: $39

Jets! moves through the recent history of aviation faster than the speed of sound, never slowing down long enough to provide a comprehensive history of modern aircraft. Indeed, the CD-ROM limits itself to military aircraft, mostly from the United States, totally ignoring the immense impact of commercial jet transportation.

The contents of *Jets!* is divided into five sections: "Aircraft," "Test Pilots," "Interactive Documentaries," "Books," and "Time Line." "Aircraft" presents abbreviated profiles of 144 military jets, including a handful from Europe and the Soviet Union, with a paragraph or two of text, several photos, occasional video clips, and a few design statistics. "Test Pilots" profiles thirty-four test pilots and aircraft designers, again with a small amount of text, photos, and video. Chuck Yeager, the first pilot to fly faster than sound in level flight, gets only two paragraphs, along with a one-minute video clip taken from a newsreel. There are five "Interactive Documentaries," narrated slide shows based on the aircraft and test-pilot profiles, that each run between ninety seconds and three minutes. "Books" contains the complete text of two dry-as-dust technical histories: *The X-Planes* by Jay Miller and *Test Pilots, The Frontiersmen of the Flight* by Richard Hallion. Finally, "Time Line" shows a video clip of morphing aircraft, so you see the first

German fighter from 1942 melt and change into a succession of designs concluding with test models that won't be flying until the late 1990s.

Except for the two books, there isn't enough material in *Jets!* to support more than an hour or two of browsing. And the books offer only dull recitations of aircraft performance reports that are confined to a text window filling just half the screen, making them difficult to read. There are a few exciting moments scattered through the disk; I was captivated by a short video clip of a test pilot spinning out of control and saving himself just a few thousand feet from the ground. But serious aviation buffs will want more depth than *Jets!* provides, while casual viewers will want more thrills along with the many aircraft statistics.

MAVIS BEACON TEACHES TYPING! VERSION 3
★★★½
Developer: Mindscape Inc.; 800-234-3088
Format: Windows
Price: $39

As computers become a bigger part of everyday life, touch typing is an increasingly important skill for everyone from elementary school students to high-powered executives who once delegated all their memos and letters to secretaries. Personal computers, equipped with the right software, can serve as very effective and infinitely patient teachers for touch-typing students. *Mavis Beacon Teaches Typing!* is by far the most popular touch-typing instruction software, with a well-deserved reputation for ease of use and flexibility. Introduced on floppy disk in 1986, *Mavis Beacon* has sold more than 3 million copies according to the developers at Mindscape Inc. The CD-ROM version, released in September 1994, is virtually identical to the floppy software, with the addition of extensive audio narration.

Mavis Beacon is a complete course for learning to type. The program asks you to set your own goals—in words per minute and accuracy—then tracks your progress through a series of lessons and games until you reach your desired level of proficiency. The lessons are simple: You see a computer monitor and keyboard on the screen, with a pair of transparent blue hands poised over the keyboard. When Mavis tells you to push a certain key, you see the appropriate finger of the blue hands pushing the correct key. You then match that movement. To break up the monotony, Mavis will occasionally send you off to play one of four "Circus Games," in which correct keystrokes let you throw darts at balloons or participate in a clown race.

Almost every feature of *Mavis Beacon* can be altered to suit your whims. Each user of the program, for example, selects an age bracket from three choices: five to eight, nine to thirteen, and fourteen to adult. Users also select their skill level, choosing from beginner, intermediate, and advanced. Once you've started a lesson, you can turn the voice of Mavis on or off, adjust the pace at which Mavis moves you through the lessons, and control whether Mavis takes your previous performance into account when deciding on your next lesson.

I'm convinced almost anyone can learn to type with *Mavis Beacon*, although the software can't provide the most important ingredient for success: the determination to stick with it. The developers don't say how long it takes to complete the course, but I suspect most beginners will need at least several months to become flawless touch typists. In the manual, however, the developers make it clear that you can't rush the process: "Studies have shown that typing is learned more efficiently if you practice for about one hour a day; not more, not less. Learning to type is more like learning a sport than learning an academic subject such as math or economics. Typing has more to do with your muscles than your mind . . . Don't over practice. You won't learn any faster if you spend eight hours in front of your keyboard and video screen."

Although *Mavis Beacon* designates an age bracket for children five to eight, I don't think the program is suited for that age level. The developers apparently agree and have created *Mavis Beacon Teaches Typing! for Kids*, reviewed in Chapter Two, Section a. One interesting footnote: Although the lessons in *Mavis Beacon* are hosted by a smiling young woman dressed in a business suit with her hair pulled back in a tight bun, there is no Mavis Beacon in real life. The developers created Mavis to personalize the program, then hired a model to pose for the picture on the box and for the on-screen images.

SHOOT VIDEO LIKE A PRO
★★½
Developer: Zelos Digital Publishing; 800-345-6777
Format: Windows-2, Macintosh-2
Price: $49

Shoot Video Like a Pro won't really transform amateur camcorder buffs into Steven Spielberg, although beginners might pick up a few useful tips from this lightweight CD-ROM. Even the greenest of novices, however, won't need more than about an hour to absorb all the lessons. Also, true to its name, *Shoot Video Like a Pro* covers only shooting—there's nothing on editing, titling, or special effects.

The contents are divided into four sections: "Camera," "Composing," "Lighting," and "Sound." Within each section are two to five articles such as "Camera Basics," "Virtual Light," and "Virtual Microphone." Each article runs only two or three paragraphs; most are illustrated with video clips demonstrating everything from the difference between hard light and soft light to simultaneous panning and zooming. In a kind of video sidebar, unnamed experts appear in each article to deliver "trade secrets." Some trade secrets are practical hints, while others are annoyingly obvious, such as this tip on composing a scene: "Think about your audience. What are you trying to say to them? What's the main point? Thinking about these things before you shoot will make your videos much better."

Shoot Video Like a Pro also has a glossary with a mere twenty-seven definitions. A "jump cut," for example, is defined as "an edit in which an object or person moves too abruptly or in an unnatural motion." Anyone genuinely committed to making better home videos will certainly want more than these slender articles and quick definitions.

SOFT KILL
★½
Developer: Xiphias; 800-421-9194
Format: Windows, Macintosh
Price: $29

Soft Kill is an ambitious attempt to create a techno-thriller on CD-ROM that falls drastically short of its target. Created by Peter Black, an aspiring novelist and head of the software company

Xiphias, *Soft Kill* collapses under the weight of a hackneyed plot and laughably bad graphics. The disk ruins what could have been a good story exploring the concept of "nonlethal" warfare where computer viruses and radio jamming, not guns and bombs, are the weapons of choice for World War III.

Using the *Matrix Interface* described in the review of *Kathy Smith's Fat Burning System* in Section d of Chapter 7, *Soft Kill* appears to be the result of extensive research by Black into a wide range of subjects from secret government satellites to operation of the Alaska pipeline. The story opens at a U.S. satellite tracking center, where a technician scanning the pipeline is stunned by an explosion that simultaneously destroys a pumping station and blinds a crucial intelligence satellite. An urgent call goes out to Jeremy Schmidt, an aging operative for the Defense Intelligence Agency, who quickly becomes embroiled in a save-the-world race against the clock, assisted by a wisecracking computer programmer named Whitfield Draper. Without giving away any surprises, Schmidt and Draper's enemy turns out to be a right-wing faction of the Japanese government out for nothing less than world domination.

The *Matrix Interface* slices and dices the story into ten columns and seven rows. The columns, moving from left to right, mark the progress of time throughout the two-day span of the story. The rows present a different part of the plot—the White House, for example, where a Bill Clinton sound-a-like presides over tense top-level meetings, or the bridge of a U.S. Navy cruiser near Singapore, where the crew is anxiously watching a buildup of Japanese warships. Each of the seventy "cells" contains a snippet of action, typically running two to three minutes. There's an "Author Mode" that guides you through twenty-three of the seventy cells in fifty-five minutes, hitting all the plot's high points. Exploring all the cells takes about three hours. Each cell is also linked to an information screen providing a few paragraphs of text about the subject at hand, such as describing the navy's "Empress" device for generating an electromagnetic pulse, or EMP, to disable the electronic systems of our enemies.

But aside from these interesting tidbits, the individual cells are a huge disappointment. Xiphias has taken still photographs and painted poorly drawn artwork on top of the images to portray the various characters. These frozen images, which change only once or twice in each cell, are accompanied by dialogue, sound effects, and music. The combination is something like listening to a radio drama while looking at pictures in a book. *Soft Kill* could have been saved by creating genuine suspense and sharp dialogue. Instead, we get unconvincing plot twists putting the fate of the world on one man's shoulders. That man, by the way, appears to be very closely modeled on best-selling author Tom Clancy's fictional hero Jack Ryan, even to the point of sharing Ryan's fear of helicopters.

TAKE FIVE
★★
Developer: Voyager Co.; 800-446-2001
Format: Windows, Macintosh
Price: $19

Shortly after releasing *Take Five* in mid-1993, Voyager Company moved its headquarters from a beachfront property in Santa Monica, California, to Manhattan. Voyager escaped the West Coast none too soon—*Take Five* is overflowing with shallow New Age thinking that's all too common in California. What's worse, the concept behind the creation of *Take Five* is more than a little off base.

Many of us are spending too much time with our computers. How do the creators of *Take Five* suggest we relax for a few minutes in the middle of a busy day? By slipping a relaxation disk into the CD-ROM drive. *Take Five* offers four separate sections with different approaches to stress relief.

"Visual Vacation" lets you pick among forty-two photographs of tranquil country scenes, with optional accompaniment from any one of eight sound loops. You can stare at a lighthouse while listening to the sea and a foghorn. Or gaze at fall foliage as songbirds chirp on your computer's speakers.

"Music of the Spheres" provides ten musical interludes, most of them wallowing in New Age chimes and flutes. The most bizarre selection is "Miranda," which consists of "recordings taken directly from the NASA *Voyager II* Space Probe as it passed near Miranda, the innermost moon of Uranus, on January 24, 1986." To me it sounds like someone left a microphone outdoors on a windy day.

"The Mind's Eye" gives nineteen "guided imagery" exercises, with a soothing female voice encouraging you to relax and get in touch with your feelings. One selection called "Bubbles" tells you to breathe deeply in and out as you put all your problems into "imaginary bubbles just outside your head" that drift away on an equally imaginary breeze.

"Stretch Yourself" is the only useful part of the disk, a menu of forty-seven relaxation exercises. Each exercise is accompanied by a brief demonstration video clip featuring Lisa Sloan, a former Broadway actress described as "running a private healing and shamanistic counseling service" in the ultra-self-aware Los Angeles suburb of Topanga. While the exercises might prevent muscle cramps, you'll probably need complete privacy to perform "the chipmunk," which calls for blowing your cheeks out as far as possible, or "the face scrunch."

What's missing from *Take Five* is a dose of common sense. If you're spending too much time at your computer, make yourself get up. Go for a short stroll. Talk to a coworker. Lounge around the water cooler. Give the computer—and yourself—a break.

MULTIMEDIA TYPING INSTRUCTOR
★★½
Developer: Individual Software Inc.; 800-822-3522
Format: Windows
Price: $29

A well-designed program for learning to touch-type, *Multimedia Typing Instructor* nonetheless lacks some of the best features of the superior *Mavis Beacon Teaches Typing!*, reviewed in this section. The original *Typing Instructor* on floppy disk dates back to 1983; the CD-ROM version, released in December 1994, adds extensive audio and video.

To lessen the monotony of repetitive drills, *Multimedia Typing Instructor* uses the metaphor of air travel to provide a small amount of distraction. The program begins in an airport terminal, where you go to a gate to board a flight for your first lesson. On the screen, you see a laptop computer sitting on a seat-back tray table. The words and letters of the lesson appear on the laptop's screen, while the key you must press next lights up on the laptop's keyboard. When you need a break, you can play two games—"Flotsam Fighter" and "Sea Adventure"—although both operate at an annoyingly slow pace. There's also a "Magazine Rack" that lets you select reprints of magazine articles for advanced typing exercises, everything from "Joan Collins—Her Climb to Fame" to "The Health of Vegetarian Diets."

Intended for ages twelve and above, *Multimedia Typing Instructor* offers instruction at four levels: "Just Starting," "Look and Type Typist," "Touch Typist," and "Expert Touch Typist." The program will keep track of multiple students, produces regular progress reports, and can be customized in several ways, such as picking the type of background music. But the CD-ROM doesn't come with a print instruction manual; instead, there is a help file included with the program and a narrated overview. None of this material, however, explains such crucial issues as how often to practice or when to move from one level to the next. The lessons also fail to show where the hands should be placed on the keyboard. *Mavis Beacon*, in contrast, shows a pair of transparent blue hands hovering over its on-screen keyboard. Watching those hands press the proper keys is a much more powerful instructional technique than the lighted keys of *Multimedia Typing Instructor*.

UFO—THIS PLANET'S MOST COMPLETE GUIDE TO CLOSE ENCOUNTERS
★½
Developer: SoftKey International Inc.; 800-227-5609
Format: DOS
Price: $39

I grew up just a few miles from Grovers Mill, a real town in New Jersey where Orson Welles set his fictitious invasion of marauding Martians in the famous 1938 radio broadcast "War of the Worlds." Welles created genuine panic with his story, which is more than I can say for *UFO—This Planet's Most Complete Guide to Close Encounters*. This poorly designed CD-ROM presents skimpy text, blurry photographs, and muddy video clips of supposed encounters with unidentified flying objects, evidence so unconvincing it will test the faith of the most devout UFO fanatics.

UFO contains 1,200 "sighting reports" from around the world, stretching from 1000 B.C. to 1993. Most of these reports offer only a few sentences of inconclusive text; two hundred entries include photographs, and twenty-five have video clips. Here's a typical entry, from Bernalillo, New Mexico, on April 18, 1965: "On Easter Sunday, Apolinar Vila was guided telepathically to this spot, where he spotted this craft hovering silently in the air and photographed it." The text is accompanied by an out-of-focus black-and-white picture of the desert. Something is hovering in the sky, a round object that could be a hubcap or could be visitors from the Andromeda Galaxy. We aren't told anything more and are left with lots of obvious questions: Who is Vila? What kind of "telepathic" guidance did he receive? Did any authorities investigate this incident? If so, what did they conclude?

Navigating through *UFO* is awkward, almost like taking the controls of a flying saucer designed to be operated by another species. There is no master index of the UFO sightings; to search through the material, you have to use a "sightings parameters" feature that sorts by date and type of encounter. You then have to move to a locater map to narrow the search geographically. But it's not worth the effort. I'm sure we're not the only intelligent creatures in the universe, but I don't think *UFO* presents a single shred of credible proof that we've entertained visitors from other worlds.

UNDERSTANDING EXPOSURE: HOW TO SHOOT GREAT PHOTOGRAPHS
★½
Developer: Diamar Interactive Corp.; 800-234-2627
Format: Windows, Macintosh
Price: $55

Did you ever get a roll of film back from the one-hour photo shop only to discover your camera was broken and you didn't get a single picture? That same feeling of disappointment will hit anyone who buys *Understanding Exposure: How to Shoot Great Photographs*. In an excessively honest bit of marketing, the CD-ROM is sold along with the book of the same name, making it painfully clear you're getting almost nothing extra for more than double the price.

Freelance photographer and instructor Bryan Peterson wrote the book *Understanding Exposure* in 1990. Published by Amphoto, the 144-page paperback has a cover price of $22.50 and is filled with useful tips illustrated with plenty of color photographs. Peterson clearly and simply explains what he calls the "photographic triangle" of aperture, shutter speed, and film speed that can be manipulated to create different visual effects.

But I could detect only a few very small enhancements on the CD-ROM, which contains all the book's text and photographs. There appear to be some additional photos, and some of them are accompanied by a sentence or two of audio commentary from Peterson. There's also a feature called "Photolab" that lets you change the aperture, film speed, or shutter speed of a photograph and see the results. By shifting the aperture from $f/2.8$ to $f/32$, for example, you can observe a dramatic change in depth of field. Of course, the book could be revised to offer the same thing just by printing a series of photos shot at the different settings.

In a brief introductory video clip, Peterson says he's planning more photography CD-ROMs in the next few years. I just hope someone puts out a disk called *Understanding CD-ROM: How to Add Great Content* and sends a copy to Peterson so he'll know how to do better the next time around.

VIRTUAL TAROT
★★★
Developer: Virtual Media Works; 800-292-3157
Format: Windows, Macintosh
Price: $45

For computer-literate believers in the occult, *Virtual Tarot* is an amusing and possibly insightful guide to fortune-telling through the colorful cards of the Tarot deck. The exact origins of Tarot are lost in the mists of the Middle Ages but may be related to a sect of Jewish mystics called the Qabbalah. Modern Tarot dates to the turn of the century, when an English occultist named Arthur Edward Waite created the popular seventy-eight-card Rider-Waite deck with elegant illustrations of such characters as The Magician, The Fool, and The Lovers. In a Tarot "divination," you deal out cards and attempt to see the future based on what cards appear and whether they are "dignified," meaning right-side-up, or "ill-dignified," meaning upside-down.

Virtual Tarot displays detailed reproductions of a Rider-Waite deck, along with soothing New Age music and photorealistic background images of sunsets, galaxies, and other suitably ethereal scenes. The user clicks on a stack of cards to make selections or can use a real Tarot deck and manually enter card selections into *Virtual Tarot*. The CD-ROM then delivers a brief audio description of each card's meaning in the context of the specific divination; users can choose between a classical interpretation by Waite or a modern interpretation. The dignified Hanged Man card, for example, indicates "wisdom, trials, sacrifice" in the Waite intereperetation or "surrender, transition, sacrifice" in the modern interpretation, while the ill-dignified Hanged Man means "selfishness" to Waite or "content [as in contentment], stagnant, recognize priorities" in the modern interpretation.

The developers of *Virtual Tarot* appear in a series of brief video clips to explain the history and meaning of the Tarot deck as well as their personal philosophy in developing the program. They seem reluctant to fully commit to the Tarot as a reliable tool, noting that "meaning is refined by your life's perspective" and "outcomes are not immutable, you can control your future." In other words, the results of a Tarot reading can mean anything you want them to mean. Still, if nothing else, the CD-ROM is cheaper than visiting a professional Tarot card reader.

WARPLANES — MODERN FIGHTING AIRCRAFT
★★★
Developer: Maris Multimedia Ltd.; 800-336-0185
Format: Windows, Macintosh
Price: $49

Fighter-pilot wanna-bes will soar into aviation heaven with *Warplanes—Modern Fighting Aircraft*, an intensely detailed almanac of military aircraft from 1976 through 1994. The CD-ROM is packed with eye-popping photorealistic illustrations of fighters, helicopters, and transports, along with seventy minutes of video clips showing the aircraft in action, scads of performance statistics, and three flight simulators.

The audience for *Warplanes*, though, isn't likely to extend much beyond hard-core aviation fanatics. The extensive descriptions of 530 aircraft—covering their history, armaments, engines, performance, and dimensions—are thick with aviation jargon, such as this entry on the MiG-31M, Russia's newest fighter: "A much improved version of the MiG-31, from which it is obviously distinguished by the rear seater's smaller windows, wider dorsal spine, more rounded wing tips with dielectric areas flush-set at front and back, curved and larger air fillets, enlarged and modified leading-edge root extensions, the port-side semi-retractable inflight-refueling probe replaced by a starboard-side fully retractable inflight refueling probe, and four underwing hardpoints for a new AAM (anti-aircraft missile)."

The flight simulators let you take the controls of a U.S. Air

Force A-10 tank killer during the Persian Gulf War, an Israeli C-130 transport heading out for a combat supply mission, and a Soviet SU-27 fighter on a test flight. These aren't full-featured flight simulators with all the bells and whistles found in specialized simulation games, but they're still fun. *Warplanes* also has slide-show narrations describing important air battles and a time line covering recent aviation history.

b. Religion

THE FIRST ELECTRONIC JEWISH BOOKSHELF
★★½
Developer: Scanrom Publications Inc.; 800-269-2237
Format: Windows
Price: $79

Judaism is more than a religion—it's also a way of life with a long and rich historical tradition. *The First Electronic Jewish Bookshelf* covers both, with a particular emphasis on Judaism's many cultural facets. Combining the text and photographs from twelve books, along with an hour of Jewish music, the CD-ROM sells for less than the cost of buying all the material in print.

The twelve books are *The Jewish Book of Why, The Second Jewish Book of Why, The Jewish Book of Knowledge, This Is the Torah, A Treasury of Jewish Folklore, Joys of Jewish Folklore, The Name Dictionary, Kosher Cookery: Classic and Contemporary, Great Jews in Stage and Screen, The Jews in Comedy Catalog, Great Jews in Sports,* and *Great Jews in Music.* My favorite is *The Jewish Book of Why,* which offers simple answers to all kinds of questions, such as "Why are the words *shaygetz* and *shiksa* used? *Shaygetz* and its feminine counterpart, *shiksa*, are derogatory words for 'non-Jew.' They are distorted forms of the Hebrew root word *sheketz*, which appears in the Bible four times and refers to the flesh of a tabooed animal. Hence, anything taboo or abominable becomes known as *sheketz*. Since intermarriage with non-Jews is taboo, this term was applied to them. *Sheketz*, the masculine form, is pronounced *shaygetz* in the vernacular, and a *shiktza*, the feminine form, is pronounced *shiksa* in the vernacular."

To get to this wealth of information, however, you'll have to tolerate a string of minor technical annoyances. The installation program, for example, is unnecessarily complicated, asking difficult questions such as what brand of chip set is used in your video board. Although *Jewish Bookshelf* runs under DOS or Windows, the packaging doesn't make it clear you'll need Windows and eight megabytes of random-access memory to hear the music. And once you're listening to the music, performed by a klezmer group called the Neshoma Orchestra, there's no way to stop a song other than shutting down the program. Finally, although you can print the text simply by pushing an on-screen button, the procedure for copying text to a word processor requires going through several awkward steps to create a separate file.

THE COMPLETE MULTIMEDIA BIBLE
★★½
Developer: Compton's NewMedia Inc.; 800-284-2045
Format: Windows
Price: $25

Who can speak the word of God with the most majesty and eloquence? Actors Charlton Heston and James Earl Jones are certainly top contenders, and both have been recruited to lend their rich speaking voices to CD-ROM versions of the Bible. Heston's effort—*Charlton Heston's Voyage Through the Bible* from Jones Interactive Inc.—won't be out until late 1995, but Jones's deep bass can be heard on *The Complete Multimedia Bible*. Unfortunately, the CD-ROM provides only about fifteen minutes of Jones reading from the King James Bible and doesn't deliver much else that's unique.

The Complete Multimedia Bible contains the full text of the King James Version, which can easily be searched by word or topic and then copied to a word processor or printed. Supplementing the text are photographs, drawings, tables, and maps. The multimedia content is fourteen video clips, each running about two minutes, showing scenes from the modern-day Middle East, and thirty-one audio clips, about half featuring Jones reading passages such as the Lord's Prayer and the Ten Commandments, while the other half are excerpts of holy music. A section called "Guidance & Inspiration" delivers biblical quotes on 101 subjects such as anger, forgiveness, humility, and sin. A sample, from Proverbs 16:32, on the subject of patience: "He that is slow to anger is better than the mighty; and he that ruleth his spirit than he that taketh a city."

The CD-ROM also includes a long essay—almost a short book—called "Introduction & Information," which gives a history of the Bible and recommendations for Bible study. Although the essay is well written, the developers give no clue as to who contributed this material. That's troubling because the essay makes definitive statements on theological issues that might not be universally accepted, such as this comment on the dual nature of Christ:

"Jesus never tried to explain how his human and divine nature were combined in himself, he simply lived out the reality. The church has not tried to explain it rationally, either. It has been content to say that Jesus was 'fully God' and 'fully man.'"

THE NEW FAMILY BIBLE
★★½
Developer: Time Warner Interactive; 800-482-3766
Format: Windows, Macintosh
Price: $39

The New Family Bible is a respectful and artistic presentation of the Old Testament, but the CD-ROM is hurt by several design flaws. All thirty-nine books of the Old Testament are here, from Genesis to Malachi, divided into the familiar chapter and verse and displayed in a suitably stately typeface. In addition, the disk presents a selection of forty Bible stories, such as Adam and Eve and the trials of Job. Half of these stories are slide shows, with narration and a series of still pictures, each running several minutes; the others are text only. The disk also includes a helpful pronunciation guide, giving both the Hebrew and English pronunciation of Old Testament names. The thirty-nine books, taken from the New Revised Standard Version of the Bible, are divided into eight sections—The Beginning, The Patriarchs, In Egypt, The Exodus, The Promised Land, The Monarchy, The Monarchy Divided, and Exile and Resoration. Each section is anchored by a contents page showing stories related to those chapters and a map covering the relevant region of the Middle East.

The overall presentation is weakened, however, by several lapses. The biggest drawback is the lack of an option to print or copy text from *The New Family Bible*. The only way to save a passage is to write down the words by hand. Also, the text is annotated with overly technical footnotes. Rather than explain what's behind some of the more complicated passages, the footnotes merely flag esoteric points in translating from the original Hebrew. Finally, many of the story pictures come from *The Children's Book of Bible Stories*, first published by Sears Roebuck in 1942. These pictures show their age and might trouble some buyers of *The New Family Bible* because all the figures—Israelites, Egyptians, Philistines, and more—are depicted as white Europeans.

THE QUICKVERSE BIBLE REFERENCE LIBRARY
★★★
Developer: Parsons Technology Inc.; 800-223-6925
Format: Windows
Price: $129

For those devoted to Bible study, *The QuickVerse Bible Reference Library* offers an extensive set of tools for searching through the Scriptures. Parsons Technology Inc., which has a "church software division" specializing in Christian religious study, has put six of its interrelated Bible programs on this CD-ROM.

The primary program is *QuickVerse for Windows Version 3.0*, which performs topic and keyword searches of the New International Version of the Bible. The five other programs are all accessed through *QuickVerse*: the King James Version of the Bible; *Strong's Hebrew and Greek Transliterated Bible*, presenting the original biblical text in the English-language alphabet; the *Holman Bible Dictionary for Windows*, with definitions and background information on Bible terms; *Nave's Topical Bible*, a subject index to the Bible; and *PC Bible Atlas for Windows*, which displays color maps of biblical and modern sites throughout the Middle East.

With all the programs linked, you can quickly complete many kinds of analysis, such as comparing the first three verses of Genesis in the King James and New International versions. The familiar King James verses are "In the beginning God created the heaven and the earth. And the earth was without form, and void; and darkness was upon the face of the deep. And the Spirit of God moved upon the face of the waters. And God said, 'Let there be light': and there was light." In the New International, these verses have become "In the beginning God created the heavens and the earth. Now the earth was formless and empty, darkness was over the surface of the deep, and the Spirit of God was hovering over the waters. And God said, 'Let there be light,' and there was light." With *PC Bible Atlas*, you can see the path Moses took through the desert and pinpoint the location of Mount Sinai. *Nave's*, for example, can instantly produce a list of 147 Bible verses on the subject of "jealousy."

Although the *QuickVerse* CD-ROM programs are easy to learn and operate, the programs are designed for serious research. With the exception of the maps in *PC Bible Atlas*, the CD-ROM offers only text—there is no sound, animation, video, or graphics to entertain those who need some encouragement to embark on Bible study. So I wouldn't recommend the disk to casual Christians or for children under age twelve.

c. Catalog Shopping

CD-ROM technology is about to reshape mail-order catalogs. With a CD-ROM, you can show video clips of products, provide audio narration along with text, and dream up all kinds of special features, such as changing the color of a model's clothing with a click of the mouse button. And, of course, CD-ROM catalogs are a great way to sell software—including CD-ROMs—by offering product demonstrations. But this promising concept has gotten off to a slow start, partly because mail-order retailers are reluctant to invest in developing multimedia material and partly because customers haven't yet gotten into the habit of ordering merchandise from CD-ROM catalogs. But this category is sure to grow. And, as the audience gets bigger, CD-ROM catalogs are likely to add more and more multimedia features that can't be matched by old-fashioned print catalogs.

CLUB KIDSOFT
★★★★
Developer: KidSoft Inc.; 800-354-6150
Format: Windows, Macintosh
Price: $7.95 per issue

Club KidSoft solves one of the biggest problems for parents who want the best software for their children: figuring out which programs will appeal to their finicky offspring. Published bimonthly for just $45 a year, *Club KidSoft* combines a print magazine with a CD-ROM sampler disk that lets children try out demonstration versions of dozens of software titles. Even if Mom and Dad don't want to spend heavily on new software, children will have lots of fun just exploring the *Club KidSoft* magazine and CD-ROM.

Designed for children ages four through twelve, with particular focus on ages eight to ten, the magazine is full of pictures and stories written by children, as well as games, news items, and how-to articles on topics such as making greeting cards with a computer. The CD-ROM is primarily a catalog but also offers the "Club Room," which displays animated computer artwork created by club members, details of contests, and silly songs such as "The Turkey from Albuquerque."

In the Windows version of the last issue of 1994 CD-ROM,

the catalog section offered sixty-nine titles. Demonstration versions were available with thirty-six of these titles. And forty-six of the titles were stored in "locked" form directly on the disk. By calling the company's toll-free number and giving a credit-card number, parents can get a special code to unlock the programs and install them to their computer's hard disk. The Macintosh version of the fourth-quarter CD-ROM offered eighty-three titles, with fifty demonstrations and sixty-two programs available by unlocking. *Club KidSoft* doesn't offer the absolute lowest prices on software, by the way, but appears to be within range of what's charged by high-volume discount stores and big mail-order catalogs.

Even if you don't buy software directly from *Club KidSoft*, the magazine and CD-ROM are a bargain for all the information they deliver on new products. Indeed, that may be the only drawback to *Club KidSoft*—parents are likely to face incessant demands to buy some fascinating new piece of software their children have just discovered on the CD-ROM.

THE MERCHANT
★★★
Developer: Magellan Systems; 800-561-3114
Format: Windows, Macintosh
Price: $4.50 per issue

The Holiday 1994 issue of *The Merchant*, released in November, is an impressive and eclectic collection of five thousand items from twenty-three mail-order catalogs—everything from fly-fishing lures offered by Bass Pro Shops to Lenox fine china. Shopaholics will enjoy wandering through the many offerings and won't be overly taxed by the $4.50 price for a single issue; three new CD-ROMs are promised in 1995.

Most of the *The Merchant* looks like a conventional catalog, displaying color photographs and a few sentences of text on the screen. But interesting multimedia content is scattered irregularly throughout. Among the enticements: a video clip in Chef's Catalog showing in great detail how to carve a turkey; the ability to change the picture of a scoop neck sweater in the Spiegel catalog to any of seven colors; a brief audio clip demonstrating the howl of a "squeeze-powered" stuffed wolf cub doll in the National Wildlife Federation catalog; a video demonstration of an apple peeler sold by L. L. Bean; a video clip of a Tyrannosaurus rex attack from

Jurassic Park in the Critics' Choice Video catalog; and audio narration of greeting-card messages in the Greet Street catalog.

Magellan Systems, developer of *The Merchant*, says it will link up with a major on-line service so that orders can be placed directly through your computer, although the company hadn't given any specifics by the end of 1994. *The Traveler*, a companion CD-ROM from Magellan, is also reviewed in this section.

SHOPPING 2000
★★½
Developer: Contentware Inc.; 800-273-5757
Format: Windows, Macintosh
Price: $4.95 per issue

Shopping 2000 is the biggest of the CD-ROM catalogs in sheer volume of information, as it contains catalogs or advertising from fifty-four vendors. But it also delivers the least multimedia; there's very little beyond photos and text in the debut disk released in December 1994. Contentware Inc., the developer of *Shopping 2000*, promises to release five more disks in 1995—perhaps it will add more audio and video in these subsequent issues.

Among the retailers on the first disk are Barnes and Noble, the Boston Museum of Fine Arts, FTD Direct, Harry and David, Lens Express, Plymouth, Sears, Spiegel, and Tower Records. There are also several computer-related vendors, including PC Connection and Dell Computers. The presentation is predictable: You see a catalog page on the screen, with an occasional button to push for more information or an additional photo. Among the few bits of multimedia I found were a narrated introduction to the Chef's Catalog, which sells cookware, and a commercial for the Plymouth Neon that played in tiny on-screen windows.

I was disappointed to find that *Shopping 2000* doesn't have a true index—there's no easy way to find every woman's sweater, for example, offered by the various retailers. All of the vendors participating on the CD-ROM, by the way, are also part of an Internet on-line shopping service established by Contentware, also called *Shopping 2000*. The address for *Shopping 2000* on the Internet's World Wide Web is "http://shopping2000.com".

SOFTBANK ON HAND
★★½
Developer: Softbank Inc.; 800-763-8226
Format: Windows
Price: $13 per issue

Softbank On Hand is a powerful, well-designed quarterly software catalog on CD-ROM with one huge problem: Many of the programs advertised on the disk are already out of date. I looked at "Release 5" of *Softbank On Hand*, issued in October 1994, and found more than a few examples of obsolete products. There was, for example, an opportunity to test Release 4 of the *Lotus 1-2-3* spreadsheet, even though Release 5 was already on the market in late 1994. Similarly, *Softbank On Hand* pitched the *Microsoft Cinemania '94* movie guide and *Microsoft Encarta '94* encyclopedia when both CD-ROMs had been superseded by 1995 editions.

If the developers of *Softbank On Hand* find a way to get more current products on the CD-ROM, they could have a winner. Release 5 contained information on 115 software products; some contained just a few paragraphs describing the program, but others had animated slide-show presentations and even let you temporarily try out the program. Many of the programs were encrypted on the disk; by calling a toll-free number and giving credit-card information, you get a code to unscramble the software and install it on your hard disk. Other products, including all the CD-ROMs, have to be ordered by phone for delivery by mail.

The 115 titles were in a wide range of categories, including word processing, spreadsheets, graphics, games, and education. Among the better-known names: sign-up software for the America Online and CompuServe on-line services, the *WordPerfect 6.0* word processor, *The Print Shop Deluxe* home desktop publishing program, the *Mayo Clinic Family Pharmacist* health guide, and *Kid CAD* children's design program.

TESTDRIVE SUPER STORE
★★
Developer: TestDrive Corp.; 800-788-8055
Format: Windows
Price: $9.95 per issue

TestDrive Corporation calls its *TestDrive Super Store* a "quarterly" CD-ROM software catalog. But after a year of trying, *Test-*

Drive in early 1995 was nowhere near coming out every three months, even though the company continues urging users to buy an annual subscription for $20. The first issue of *TestDrive* came out several months behind schedule in December 1993, the second issue arrived in August 1994 and the third in December 1994. *TestDrive* pressures you to become a subscriber by offering a selection of free software—including a money-management program, a screen saver, and a children's word game—if you fork over $20. But I wouldn't suggest signing up anytime in 1995; wait until 1996 and see if *TestDrive* manages to put out new editions consistently every three months.

Putting aside the erratic production schedule, however, *TestDrive* isn't a bad way to preview software. The third issue contained information on 195 products from 78 publishers, including such big names as Microsoft Corporation, Novell Inc., and Lotus Development Corporation. Each product is depicted by a color photograph of its box, along with descriptive text and, in some cases, the ability to take several "test drives" of the program. You can, for example, run Intuit's excellent *Quicken* personal finance software three times before deciding whether to buy. Many of the products, including *Quicken*, are encrypted on the *TestDrive* CD-ROM—by calling a toll-free line and giving a credit-card number, you get a code allowing you to download the program to your hard disk.

As with *Softbank On Hand*, a similar CD-ROM catalog reviewed in this section, some of the software on *TestDrive* is out of date. I found entries for the movie guide *Microsoft Cinemania '94* and the encyclopedia *Microsoft Encarta '94*, even though both had already been replaced by 1995 editions more than a month before the release of *TestDrive*.

2MARKET
★★★
Developer: 2Market Inc.; 800-622-6600
Format: Windows, Macintosh
Price: $4.95 per issue

2Market stands out as the most feature-laden CD-ROM shopping catalog, with extras that include an interesting "find a gift" function that will make gift suggestions tailored to specific individuals. The Holiday 1994 edition, released in November, offers products from twenty-six retailers, including Hammacher Schlemmer, Land's End, The Nature Company, The Sharper Image, and Spiegel.

The multimedia content in *2Market* is similar to the *The Merchant*, reviewed in this section—both carry the Chef's Catalog of professional cookware, for example, with the same video on how to carve a turkey. *2Market*, however, is stronger on entertainment, with catalogs from Sony Music, Time-Life Music, and Windham Hill Records as well as a selection of sixty-eight software titles for both children and adults. But a number of retailers in *2Market*, including Land's End, don't offer anything more than photographs and text from their print catalog.

What's unique in *2Market* is the "gift shopping" section that helps you sort through the hundreds of on-screen pages. You can look at offerings from all the retailers in categories such as "for holiday hosts" or "great gifts for guys." The "find a gift" prompts you to enter information about an individual—such as the person's age, gender, and interests—then produces a list of items that might be appropriate. *2Market* thought my wife, Debbie, would enjoy a personal shiatsu massager or a set of matching luggage, among other suggestions. The CD-ROM will even provide reminders of upcoming birthdays, anniversaries, and holidays, after you enter the relevant information.

If you decide to purchase an item in *2Market*, you can order directly through your computer, if it's equipped with a modem, or by dialing a toll-free number at 2Market Inc. and having your call routed to the appropriate retailer. To urge you on, the CD-ROM is programmed to automatically announce special discounts on certain dates. The backers of *2Market*—a partnership of Apple Computer Inc., America Online Inc., and a small software company called Medior Inc.—are promising four new issues in 1995. The same information on the *2Market* CD-ROM, by the way, is available in the America Online service by entering the keyword "2Market." But you get only text and low-resolution photographs, without the audio and video, and browsing is much slower than with the disk.

THE TRAVELER
★★½

Developer: Magellan Systems; 800-561-3114
Format: Windows, Macintosh
Price: $4.50 per issue

If nothing else, *The Traveler* is a boon to the environment—instead of collecting piles and piles of travel brochures on glossy paper that's difficult to recycle, you can get them crammed onto this CD-ROM. The catalog, scheduled to be updated with two new issues in 1995, offers slick advertising from airlines, tour operators, and national tourism boards but rarely goes beyond superficial photos of beautiful sunsets and gushy text describing the friendly natives.

I looked at the October 1994 issue, which contains material from about sixty participants. The opening screen displays a map of the world, divided into eight regions you can explore: the United States, Canada, Central America, South America, Europe/Middle East, Africa, Asia, and Pacific. Each region presents a more detailed map with further choices, such as individual U.S. states or South Pacific islands. You can also look at the contents through an "activities" menu, listing leisure pursuits from golf to jungle exploration; or by travel category, such as an index of hotels.

Most of *The Traveler* is nothing more than reproductions of print brochures, but some multimedia content is added—a promotional video clip for the *Back to the Future* ride at Universal Studios in Hollywood, for example, and another video clip of a tour guide inviting you to join him on an expedition to Antarctica. But these distractions don't make up for the lack of more useful content; for example, I'd like to see extensive listings of hotels and restaurants for each destination. The contents are also incomplete. You can get information on Kentucky and Georgia, but there's nothing on Tennessee, making it difficult to plan a road trip through all three states. Perhaps future issues of *The Traveler* will venture into uncharted territory, mixing advertising with comprehensive factual information. *The Merchant*, a companion product from the same developer, is also reviewed in this section.

d. Adults Only

Beginning with the first prehistoric scribbling on cave walls, humans—specifically, male humans—have taken advantage of every new form of communication to portray sex and violence graphically. CD-ROM software is no exception; there's a flourishing market for pornography that I'm not going to cover in this book. But there is also a growing selection of nonpornographic CD-ROMs that involve violence and sex, much as there are large numbers of R-rated movies that aren't appropriate for children yet are enjoyed by adults. That's my yardstick for what's in this section: I've included CD-ROMs that would carry an R rating if they were movies and left out those that would rate NC-17.

NATIONAL LAMPOON'S BLIND DATE
★★
Developer: Trimark Interactive; 310-314-3046
Format: Windows-2, Macintosh-2
Price: $39

Never rising above sniggering adolescent humor, *National Lampoon's Blind Date* is the CD-ROM equivalent of a bad blind date—it doesn't deliver satisfaction, and you know it's a waste of time almost as soon as you start. The teasing starts with the box, which urges you to buy *Blind Date* because the game offers "hot babes" and is "designed by guys who really have sex." But once you start playing, you mostly get insulted and punched.

Blind Date puts you in the position of a horny guy sent out by a dating agency called D.U.D.S., short for Dates Unlimited for Desperate Schmucks, to meet the beautiful Sandi. You watch the action unfold through video clips filling a quarter of the screen, showing the date from the guy's perspective. Sandi, popping out of a tiny black dress, takes you to a pool hall and invites you to join her in a game. The video stops every fifteen seconds or so when Sandi asks you a question or makes a statement, and you have to think of the appropriately tasteless answer. Sandi, for example, says, "You don't hit my balls, I won't hit your balls." You then have to pick one of two possible responses: "We *are* talking about pool, right?" or "I think I heard a cross-dresser say the same thing to his boyfriend last week on 'Geraldo.'" If you pick the right answer, you keep moving through the game. If you pick the wrong answer, something bad happens—Sandi's jealous ex-boyfriend punches you or she jabs your private parts with her pool cue—and you have to start over. To help you through the game, there is a "mood ring" on the screen that changes color to show whether Sandi likes your responses. There's also a "hint" button and a "save game" button so you don't have to go back to the beginning every time you're booted out.

Real-life horny guys will enjoy watching Sandi and several other women who cavort through *Blind Date*, three of whom are former *Playboy* Playmates. But they shouldn't expect too much; the girls never wear anything less than a bikini. What's more, experienced computer game players are likely to be disappointed with the lack of challenge. Even gaming novices should be able to work through *Blind Date* in just an hour or two.

DOOM II: HELL ON EARTH
★★★½
Developer: GT Interactive Software Corp.; 800-362-9400
Format: DOS
Price: $49

Id Software's crew of twenty-something game developers isn't lacking in ego. Whenever you stop playing Id's incredibly violent *Doom II* and briefly return to the real world, a farewell message pops onto the screen: "Thanks for purchasing *Doom II*. We hope you have as much fun playing it as we had making it. If you don't, then something is really wrong with you and you're different and strange. All your friends think *Doom II* is great."

This outburst of self-congratulation is forgivable because *Doom II* is an incredible nonstop adrenaline rush. A sequel to the overwhelmingly popular floppy-disk game *Doom*, released in 1993, *Doom II* was a guaranteed best-seller even before its official launch in October 1994—retailers preordered a staggering 500,000 copies from GT Interactive Software of New York, which distributes the game for Id.

Doom II is really nothing more than a continuation of *Doom*, with a few added features. Both games are shoot-'em-ups. You are placed in the role of a United States marine, stationed sometime in the near future on the planet Mars. In *Doom*, you go to the Martian moon Phobos to fight hordes of mutant humans and evil creatures from another dimension. In *Doom II*, you're back on Earth fighting the same collection of monsters and mutants, culminating in a trip to the center of Hell to face off against the Devil himself.

Doom and *Doom II* are played from a first-person perspective. You look through the eyes of the nameless marine, controlling his movements with either the keyboard or a mouse, and you see the weapon he's holding near the bottom of the screen. When enemies come into view, you press the "fire" button and watch them crumple into bloody piles of twitching flesh and bone. A status bar at the very bottom of the screen shows a Dorian Gray picture of the marine's face—as you suffer injuries from enemy fire or wading through pits of radioactive waste, you see the marine become increasingly bloody and battered.

What makes *Doom* and *Doom II* so compelling is the incredible speed of play. You move through the corridors of mysterious buildings at a brisk jogging pace, and the computer responds instantly whenever you turn around. The action is so fast that some *Doom* players report bouts of nausea from the sudden shifts in perspective. *Doom* is particularly popular in offices because up to four players can face each other through a computer network. Two players can also blast away at each other through a modem.

But it takes more than just an itchy trigger finger to survive. You have to pay close attention to your surroundings, searching for helpful objects such as first-aid kits, armor, ammunition, and extra weapons. Mastering all thirty levels of *Doom II* will take even expert computer gamers many hours of blood-spattering adventure.

And what about the outrageous violence? I don't think *Doom* and *Doom II* will do any harm to adults. Partly that's because the developers have sacrificed graphic detail for speed—the bad guys are small, crude images that bear no resemblance to real people or even real outer-space aliens. I'm much more troubled by CD-ROM games that use video clips of live actors to portray torture and death. Obviously, *Doom* and *Doom II* are absolutely not for children and aren't even appropriate for most adults. But there's no reason those adults who want to play the two games should be deprived of the opportunity. Parents will have to shoulder the responsibility for keeping their children away from *Doom II*, much as they're responsible for preventing kids from getting to cigarettes, alcohol, or X-rated movies.

Doom, by the way, was released as shareware: The first of

the game's three episodes was available free and could be downloaded by modem from many game bulletin boards. To play the next two episodes, you had to buy the complete game from Id for about $40. *Doom II*, in contrast, is being sold only through conventional retail channels—you have to buy the whole game for about $49 in most stores or mail-order catalogs.

LEISURE SUIT LARRY 6: SHAPE UP OR SLIP OUT
★★½
Developer: Sierra On-Line Inc.; 800-757-7707
Format: DOS, Macintosh
Price: $59

All talk and no action, the *Leisure Suit Larry* series from Sierra On-Line Inc. is full of juvenile double entendres and on-screen illustrations of pouty young women about to burst out of tiny bikini tops. *Leisure Suit Larry 6: Shape Up or Slip Out* is the first installment upgraded for CD-ROM, adding voices for the principal characters. What you see on the screen, though, hasn't been changed from the floppy-disk version: cartoonlike computer graphics with jagged edges and limited animation.

Larry Laffer, hero of the *Leisure Suit Larry* series, is a perennial loser who keeps getting himself into situations in which he can't quite get lucky. In the opening of *Leisure Suit Larry 6*, he's recruited for the TV dating show "Stallions," described by the announcer as "the latest and greatest in embarrassment television," and wins two weeks at La Costa Lotta Spa. Larry's goal is hitting on a succession of women and getting a valuable object from each, allowing him to go on the ultimate date with a character named Shamara Payne. In the High Colonic Treatment Suite, for example, Rose Eleeta promises, "I will make you experience feelings you've never experienced before." Larry, who doesn't know the meaning of high colonic, thinks he's about to get something other than an enema. That's the level of humor throughout *Leisure Suit Larry 6*. Indeed, the box carries a humorous but completely accurate advisory for buyers: "Warning: This game portrays adult themes in a completely non-explicit fashion which may offend those looking for real R-rated stuff."

If you haven't played Sierra games before, you may be surprised to discover *Leisure Suit Larry 6* is a fairly complicated problem-solving adventure. You move Larry from scene to scene inside

La Costa Lotta by clicking on different icons to walk, look at objects, pick up objects, and talk to other people. To advance through the game, you need to grab everything that isn't nailed down. Rose Eleeta, for instance, wants a bouquet of flowers. That sends you back to your hotel room to get flowers off the coffee table that you take to her suite. For nongamers, this constant marching around grows tedious, and Larry's repeated failures to find romance are scant incentive to stick with the game until his one moment of fulfillment in the final scene.

MAN ENOUGH
★★
Developer: Time Warner Interactive/Tsunami Media Inc.; 800-482-3766
Format: DOS
Price: $29

You're a single guy cruising the gym when you meet an attractive young woman pumping iron. Do you say:

1. "Ah, if I've died and gone to heaven, are you a naughty angel?"

2. "Pardon me, but could I lift those barbells of yours sometime?"

3. "Excuse me, but are you filming a Playmate workout video here?"

If you chose number two, you're ready for *Man Enough*. But you're probably not ready for the real world. Advertised as the first "virtual dating" game on CD-ROM and "an interactive social guide for the '90s male," *Man Enough* instead reduces male-female relationships to leering adolescent double entendres and delivers nothing more than a long electronic tease.

The game puts you in the position of a dateless wonder on the prowl at a gym where five women are working out. You are presented with a series of questions, such as the one above, and must select one of three responses to win the women's attention. After figuring out the "right" answers to these questions, players go on dates with the women: Blair, a wealthy pilot; Erin, a lawyer; Fawn, a sales representative; Quinn, a television news anchor; and Kellie, a psychologist. The action proceeds through a montage of full-screen still photographs, some of which feature Victoria's Secret-style lingerie poses and suggestive audio comments from the five women. You're encouraged or scolded, depending on your progress, in brief video appearances by Jeri, head of the Man Enough dating service, played by Tonia Keyser, a former Miss California/World.

If you succeed in answering more questions on your date, you get a brief video clip with a kiss. But something always intervenes before the action escalates much beyond the PG-13 level. The final date, which fills the second of the two *Man Enough* disks, is a skydiving adventure with Jeri herself. Unlike the earlier date, most of the action is portrayed through video clips, although the image quality is so poor that the developers should have stuck with stills.

MIDNIGHT STRANGER
★
Developer: Gazelle Technologies Inc.; 800-843-9497
Format: Windows, Macintosh
Price: $59

Midnight Stranger is a sleazy and unsuccessful attempt at interactive soft-core pornography. Carrying a well-deserved label on the box stating "18+ Adults Only," the CD-ROM features lots of obscene language, drug references, and a few embarrassingly voyeuristic sex scenes. The box also boasts of offering something called "virtual intimacy" and includes a cheap pair of stereo headphones to help you achieve a sense of being inside the story. But the small, grainy video images eliminate any possible sense of intimacy, virtual or otherwise.

The rambling and confused story of *Midnight Stranger* unfolds from a first-person perspective. You are a nameless libidinous male wandering the dark streets of a big city, shown through a succession of still photographs. Entering a disco, diner, comedy club, or singles bar exposes you to one or more of the story's eighteen characters, a menagerie that includes a psychopathic criminal, an exotic barfly who may or may not be a woman, a stand-up comic involved in a mysterious smuggling case, and a woman suffering multiple-personality disorder. You interact with these characters through a bizarre device at the bottom of the screen called the "mood bar." Clicking on the right end of the mood bar indicates a positive or happy response to what the person is saying to you, while clicking on the left indicates a negative response. The center is neutral. You don't hear actual dialogue after pressing the mood bar, but the person reacts as if you've said something specific. Apparently, though, you have limited social skills—while chatting up a waitress in the diner, she points out a zit on your chin and you proceed to pop it in front of her.

Midnight Stranger contains sixty minutes of video clips, most of which are shots of the characters' head and shoulders superimposed over still photographs, creating an unpleasant scarecrow effect with talking heads stuck on lifeless bodies. There are numerous outcomes to these encounters, anything from being shot by the criminal to a sexual encounter with a topless party girl and a truly tasteless rape scene, although there is no clear ending or specific goal to achieve. The game's obtuse structure and aimless detours will turn off even the most dedicated fans of tacky sex trash.

NIGHT TRAP
★½
Developer: Digital Pictures Inc.; 800-262-5020
Format: Macintosh
Price: $45

Of all the blood and gore dished out by Hollywood, nothing disturbs me more than "teen slasher" films with their unrelenting images of nubile teenage girls being stalked and brutally murdered by deformed deviants. The message in these movies seems to be that young women can't take care of themselves and, because the attacks often take place when a girl is making out with her boyfriend, that any expression of sexuality must be punished. *Night Trap* is a teen slasher story on CD-ROM, displaying the same repulsive social values.

There's quite a history to this game. First released for the Sega CD video game system in late 1992, *Night Trap* raised loud protests from concerned parents. The game was banned outright in the United Kingdom, was pulled off store shelves by some retailers in the United States, and helped trigger Senate hearings on video game violence. Of course, the developer—Digital Pictures Inc.—relished all the publicity, which only heightened demand for *Night Trap* among the intended audience of teenage boys. *Night Trap* became one of the best-selling games for the Sega CD system and was released for the Macintosh in November 1994 with a "mature" rating that supposedly limits sale to ages seventeen and above.

The premise of *Night Trap* is familiar: Five teenage girls, who seem to spend most of their time lounging around in revealing clothes, visit a mysterious house for the weekend. A paramilitary security team has the house under observation, and you're recruited by a tough-talking commander to protect the girls. "If you don't have the brains or the guts for this assignment, give the controls to someone who does," the commander declares in the introductory video sequence, the first of many insults he hurls at players.

For reasons that are never fully explained, the house is being invaded by terrorists dressed entirely in black. The house is also equipped with a series of trapdoors, which you control. Looking through one of eight surveillance cameras located throughout the house, you watch the story unfold and try to eliminate the terrorists by pushing a button whenever they wander near a trap. The consequences of failure are ugly—at one point, the terrorists grab a girl in lingerie, clamp a large metal arm around her neck, and suck out her blood. If you don't dispatch the terrorists fast enough, you're thrown out of the game with another insult from the commander: "Until you figure out how to do your job, and do it right, you're dismissed."

The video plays in a movie-screen-like rectangular window that is four inches high and seven and a half inches wide on a standard fourteen-inch monitor; *Night Trap* contains a total ninety minutes of footage on two disks. Learning to play the game is easy—all you have to do is check the different surveillance cameras, keep track of various codes to activate the traps, and push the trap door buttons at the right moment. But staying ahead of the ever-increasing influx of terrorists makes the game a tough challenge.

Of course, I don't think this is a challenge anyone should consider. But my disapproval isn't likely to accomplish much. Slasher-movie fans are going to flock to *Night Trap* no matter what I say, and they'll probably enjoy the game—taking a sad step away from CD-ROM's potential to provide worthwhile entertainment.

THE WOMEN OF PLAYBOY MULTIMEDIA SCREEN SAVER
★★½
Developer: Sony Imagesoft; 800-922-7669
Format: Windows
Price: $39

Yes, guys, it's all here: four hundred photographs and illustrations from *Playboy* magazine including the famous Playmate centerfolds and pictorials. You can even claim you bought the CD-ROM for a useful purpose—after all, it is a screen saver, and you wouldn't want your monitor to get damaged.

When you're not using your computer, *The Women of Playboy Multimedia Screen Saver* can be programmed to display images you select in advance or show pictures randomly. The developers are selling two versions—one for "Mature Audiences," which presumably leaves out full nudity, and one for "Adults Only," with everything you see in the magazine. I looked at the "Adults Only" version, which also includes twelve video clips of cavorting *Playboy* bunnies. Each clip runs one to three minutes, filling a quarter of the screen, and can be included in the screen saver lineup along with the pictures and illustrations.

The photographs include *Playboy* covers from May 1956 to April 1993; centerfolds from Jayne Mansfield in February 1955 to Jenny McCarthy in October 1993; and Playmate pictorials from December 1973 to October 1994. There's also a selection of cartoons and artwork from the magazine, as well as several images of the famous *Playboy* rabbit-head logo and a collection of twenty-five sound effects. Gawking males will be pleased to see the images displayed in sharp, full-screen color.

Putting aside any moral issues, however, I question whether this CD-ROM is practical. To run the screen saver, you have to leave the disk in your computer—something you're not likely to remember if you're regularly using other CD-ROMs. What's more, screen savers keep running even if you walk away from the computer. That makes the *Playboy* screen saver particularly inappropriate for any work setting, where co-workers may not be eager to stumble on Miss September in her birthday suit.

SPORTS ILLUSTRATED SWIMSUIT CALENDAR
★★
Developer: SoftKey International Inc.; 800-227-5609
Format: Windows
Price: $29

Once a year, the collective male hormones of America go into overdrive when the *Sports Illustrated* swimsuit edition hits the newsstands. It's a slender excuse for the magazine to pump up its circulation and for its jock audience to ogle tall, skinny women in teeny-weeny bikinis. But even the most devoted fans of this somewhat tacky display will be disappointed with *Sports Illustrated Swimsuit Calendar* on CD-ROM.

The disk contains seventy photographs of eighteen models, including supermodels Kathy Ireland, Elle MacPherson, Rachel Hunter, and Vendela. To give the product a tenuous claim of socially redeeming value, there are also two excessively complicated programs for creating calendars and screen savers. The calendar program is lifted from SoftKey's poorly designed *Calendar Creator Plus*, reviewed in Chapter Nine, Section a—that's why *Swimsuit Calendar* comes with a two-hundred-page manual. Novice computer users, in particular, will be frustrated at the many steps required to view the photographs. If you want a cheap thrill, just buy the magazine.

Index of Four-Star Reviews

Amnesty Interactive, 267
Antonin Dvořák's Symphony No. 9, "From the New World", 333
Arthur's Teacher Trouble, 23
Club KidSoft, 502
The Complete Maus, 321
Compton's Interactive Encyclopedia, 1995 Edition, 192
Franz Schubert: The "Trout" Quintet, 342
I Photograph to Remember, 233
Igor Stravinsky: The Rite of Spring, 344
Just Grandma and Me, 28
Kid Pix Studio, 48
Learn to Speak French 4.0, 427
Learn to Speak Spanish 4.0, 428
Little Monster at School, 31
Ludwig van Beethoven: Symphony No. 9, 329
Microsoft Encarta '95, 193
Microsoft Multimedia Beethoven: The Ninth Symphony, 337
Microsoft Multimedia Mozart: The "Dissonant" Quartet, 338
Microsoft Multimedia Schubert: The "Trout" Quintet, 338
Microsoft Multimedia Strauss: Three Tone Poems, 339
Microsoft Multimedia Stravinsky: The Rite of Spring, 339
The 1995 Grolier Multimedia Encyclopedia, 194
Quicken Deluxe 4 for Windows CD-ROM, 442
The Residents' Freak Show, 347
Richard Strauss: Three Tone Poems, 343
Storybook Weaver Deluxe, 86
Street Atlas USA, Version 2.0, 217
The Tortoise and the Hare, 36
The Way Things Work, 109
Wolfgang Amadeus Mozart: The "Dissonant" Quartet, 337

Index By Platform

DOS
The ASP Advantage, 457
Aegis: Guardian of the Fleet, 171
America Adventure, 62
American Heritage Illustrated Encyclopedic Dictionary, 197
Backroad Racers, 120
Bailey's Book House, 5
Barron's Complete Book Notes, 313
The Berenstain Bears Learning at Home Volume One, 38
The Berenstain Bears Learning at Home Volume Two, 39
Betrayal at Krondor, 171
Bug Adventure, 94
Canada Phone, 207
Castles II: Siege & Conquest Enhanced CD-ROM, 172
Clinton: Portrait of Victory, 268
Comanche CD, 173
Computer Works, 476
Direct Phone, 207
The Doctors Book of Home Remedies, 397
Doom II: Hell on Earth, 510
Dracula Unleashed, 132
Dragon's Lair, 153
Europages, 208
FIFA International Soccer, 154
Falcon Gold, 174
Free Phone, 209
Home Phone, 209
Hometime Weekend Home Projects, 369
The Horde, 156
Isaac Asimov Science Adventure II, 103
JumpStart Kindergarten, 46

Kid's Zoo, 50
Kids On Site, 49
Leisure Suit Larry 6: Shape Up or Slip Out, 512
Library of the Future Third Edition, 319
Mammals: A Multimedia Encyclopedia, 246
Man Enough, 513
Mario Teaches Typing Enhanced CD-ROM, 76
Mars Explorer, 247
Mega Race, 158
Murmurs of Earth, 247
NHL Hockey '95, 159
The New Basics Electronic Cookbook, 376
9-Digit ZIP Code Directory, 212
The 1994 Information Please Almanac, 202
The 1994 Information Please Business Almanac & Desk Reference, 408
Operation AirStorm, 128
Operation Neptune, 83
The PC-SIG World of Games CD-ROM, 459
PGA Tour Golf 486, 160
PhoneDisc Business & Residential, 209
PhoneDisc PowerFinder, 210
Picture Atlas of the World, 217
The Presidents: A Picture History of Our Nation, 263
Project Gutenberg, 324
Putt-Putt Joins the Parade, 53
Putt-Putt's Fun Pack, 54
Rebel Assault, 161
Return to Ringworld, 178

Return to Zork, 141
SSN-21 Seawolf, 179
Sammy's Science House, 55
Select Phone, 211
Sesame Street: Numbers, 18
Seven Days in August, 264
The 7th Guest, 142
70 Million Households Phone Book, 211
Sherlock Holmes, Consulting Detective, 144
Sherlock Holmes, Consulting Detective, Volume II, 145
Sherlock Holmes, Consulting Detective, Volume III, 145
SimCity 2000 CD Collection, 180
Simtel, 460
Space Adventure II, 104
Speed, 106
Star Trek: 25th Anniversary Enhanced CD-ROM, 182
Super Solvers Spellbound!, 19
Tetris Gold, 168
Thinkin' Things Collection 1, 57
3-D Body Adventure, 93
3-D Dinosaur Adventure, 95
Time Table of History: Arts & Entertainment, 204
Time Table of History: Business, Politics & Media, 205
Time Table of History: Science & Innovation, 205
Trivial Pursuit, 169
U.S. Atlas, 219
UFO—This Planet's Most Complete Guide to Close Encounters, 492
Under a Killing Moon, 147
Undersea Adventure, 108
Voyeur, 149
Wing Commander III: Heart of the Tiger, 183
WolfPack, 184
World Atlas, 220

Windows

AAA Trip Planner, 213
A.D.A.M. The Inside Story, 236
The Aladdin Activity Center, 37
Amanda Stories, 22
America's Civil War—A Nation Divided, 255
The American Golf Guide Presented by Arnold Palmer, 379
The American Heritage Talking Dictionary, 197
The American Sign Language Dictionary on CD-ROM, 419
American Visions Journeys through Art: Act One, 228
Americana, 461
Americans in Space, 89
Animal Kingdom, 462
AnnaTommy, 91
Anno's Learning Games, 64
The Art of Making Great Pastries, 375
Arthur's Birthday, 22
Arthur's Teacher Trouble, 23
Astrology Source, 481
Audio-Visual Chinese-English Dictionary, 424
Automap Road Atlas, 214
Automap Streets, 215
Aviation Adventure, 92
The Awesome Adventures of Victor Vector and Yondo: The Cyberplasm Formula, 116
The Awesome Adventures of Victor Vector and Yondo: The Hypnotic Harp, 117
The Awesome Adventures of Victor Vector and Yondo: The Last Dinosaur Egg, 117
The Awesome Adventures of Victor Vector and Yondo: The Vampire's Coffin, 117
Barron's Complete Book Notes, 313
Barron's Profiles of American Colleges on CD-ROM, 413
Baseball's Greatest Hits, 380
Batik Designs, 462
Battle Chess Enhanced CD-ROM, 163
Beethoven's 5th, 329
Berlitz Live! Japanese, 420
Berlitz Live! Spanish, 421
Berlitz Think & Talk French, 422
Berlitz Think & Talk German, 423
Berlitz Think & Talk Italian, 424

Berlitz Think & Talk Spanish, 424
Better Homes and Gardens Complete Guide to Gardening, 361
Better Homes and Gardens Healthy Cooking CD Cookbook, 371
Beyond Planet Earth, 237
Bicycle Limited Edition CD-ROM, 164
Big Anthony's Mixed-Up Magic, 24
Blown Away, 131
Bodyworks 3.0, 238
A Brief History of Time, 239
Britannica CD, 191
Business Backgrounds, 463
Business Library Volume 1, 406
CICA Shareware for Windows, 458
CNN Newsroom Global View, 269
CNN Time Capsule 1994, 270
Calendar Creator Plus, 448
Canada Phone, 207
Capitol Hill, 65
The Cartoon History of the Universe, Volumes 1–7, 68
The Cat Came Back, 26
Charles J. Givens Money Guide, 436
The Chessmaster 3000, 164
Chinese Family Cooking, 372
Chuck Jones' Peter and the Wolf, 115
ClipArt Library, 463
Club KidSoft, 502
Comedy Central's Sports Shorts, 309
The Complete After Dark Screen Saver Collection, 447
Complete Guide to Prescription and Non-Prescription Drugs, 392
Complete House, 362
The Complete Multimedia Bible, 498
Composer Quest, 332
Compton's Interactive Encyclopedia, 1995 Edition, 192
CompuServeCD, 281
Corel Gallery, 465
Corel Professional Photos CD-ROM Sampler, 466
CorelDraw 3, 464
CorelFlow, 465
CountDown, 6
Cowboy Casino, 166
Crayola Amazing Art Adventure, 41
Crayola Art Studio, 121

Creation Stories, 313
Creative Writer, 69
Criterion Goes to the Movies, 291
The D-Day Encyclopedia, 256
Dandy Dinosaurs, 42
Daring to Fly! From Icarus to the Red Baron, 482
Dating & Mating, 303
Deep Voyage, 466
Deluxe Reader Rabbit 1, 14
Dennis Miller That's Geek to Me, 303
Dennis Miller That's News to Me, 304
Desert Storm: The War in the Persian Gulf, 271
Direct Phone, 207
Disney's Animated StoryBook: The Lion King, 30
Distant Suns 2.0, 242
The Doctors Book of Home Remedies, 397
Dr. Ruth's Encyclopedia of Sex, 393
ESPN Baseball: Hitting, 383
ESPN Golf: Lower Your Score with Tom Kite—Shot Making, 384
ESPN Let's Play Soccer, 385
ESPN Sports Shorts, 386
Earthquake, 243
11 Million Businesses Phone Book, 208
Ephemeral Films 1931–1960, 292
Europages, 208
Everywhere USA Travel Guide, 221
The Exotic Garden, 363
Expert CD-ROM Home Design Gold Edition for Windows, 364
Eyewitness Encyclopedia of Science, 99
The Family Doctor, 3rd Edition, 394
Family Tree Maker Deluxe CD-ROM Version 2.0, 483
Fatty Bear's Birthday Surprise, 43
Fatty Bear's Fun Pack, 44
Firefighter!, 123
The First Electronic Jewish Bookshelf, 497
The First Emperor of China, 257
Fitness Partner, 395
5-Ft. 10-Pak Volume II, 484
4 Paws of Crab, 372

The Four Seasons of Gourmet French Cuisine, 374
Freddi Fish And The Case of The Missing Kelp Seeds, 45
Free Phone, 209
From Alice to Ocean, 317
Full Bloom, 467
Funny, 293
Gettysburg, 176
Global Explorer, 215
Great Restaurants, Wineries & Breweries, 222
The Haldeman Diaries: Inside the Nixon White House, The Complete Multimedia Edition, 258
A Hard Day's Night, 294
Harry and the Haunted House, 27
Hawaii High: The Mystery of the Tiki, 112
The Heinemann Children's Multimedia Encyclopedia, 71
Home Phone, 209
Home Repair Encyclopedia, 364
How to Really Start Your Own Business, 407
I Photograph to Remember, 233
Illustrated Facts: How Things Work, 200
Illustrated Facts: How the World Works, 201
Imagination Express, 124
In the Company of Whales, 240
Interactive Entertainment, 282
Iron Helix, 134
Isaac Asimov's The Ultimate Robot, 318
It's All Relative, 304
It's Legal 5.0 Deluxe CD-ROM Edition, 409
J.F.K. Assassination: A Visual Investigation, 260
Jazz: A Multimedia History, 349
Jets & Props, 468
Jets!, 485
Job-Power Source, 414
Journey to the Planets, 244
The Journeyman Project Turbo, 135
Jump Raven, 157

Jump: The David Bowie Interactive CD-ROM, 350
Just Grandma and Me, 28
Kathy Smith's Fat Burning System, 398
Key CAD Complete, 448
Key Color ClipArt, 468
Key Fonts Pro, 468
Key Photo Clips, 469
Key Translator Pro English-Spanish, 425
Kid CAD, 125
Kid Pix Studio, 48
Kid Works 2, 126
King's Quest VII, 136
Kiplinger TaxCut Multimedia, 437
LandDesigner Multi-Media for Gardens, 366
Last Chance to See, 245
Launch Pad, 449
Learn to Play Guitar, 336
Learn to Speak English 3.11, 426
Learn to Speak French 4.0, 427
Learn to Speak Spanish 4.0, 428
Legends and Superstars Baseball, 386
The Legends of Oz, 113
Lenny's MusicToons, 74
Leonardo, The Inventor, 261
Let's Go: The Budget Guide to Europe 1994, 223
Library of the Future Third Edition, 319
The Lifestyles of the Rich and Famous Cookbook, 375
Little Monster at School, 31
Lotus 1-2-3 Release 5 Multimedia Edition, 450
Lotus SmartSuite 3.0 CD-ROM Edition, 451
Lovejoy's College Counselor, 415
MPC Wizard 3.0, 451
MTV's Beavis and Butt-head Multimedia Screen Saver, 302
The Madness of Roland, 320
Magic Theatre, 127
Majestic Places, 469
Map'n'Go, 216
Math Blaster: Episode 2—Secret of The Lost City, 78
Math Blaster: In Search of Spot, 77

Platform Index

Math Rabbit, 7
Math Workshop, 78
Mavis Beacon Teaches Typing! Version 3, 486
Mavis Beacon Teaches Typing! for Kids, 79
Mayo Clinic Family Health Book, 399
Mayo Clinic Family Pharmacist, 400
Mayo Clinic Sports Health & Fitness, 402
Mayo Clinic—The Total Heart, 403
Medio Magazine, 283
Mega Movie Guide Version 3.0, 295
Mega Rock Rap 'N Roll, 354
The Merchant, 503
Microsoft Ancient Lands, 63
Microsoft Art Gallery, 229
Microsoft Bookshelf '94, 198
Microsoft Cinemania '95, 289
Microsoft Complete Baseball, 1994 Edition, 381
Microsoft Complete NBA Basketball, 382
Microsoft Dangerous Creatures, 241
Microsoft Dinosaurs, 98
Microsoft Encarta '95, 193
Microsoft Explorapedia: The World of Nature, 70
Microsoft Golf, 155
Microsoft Golf Championship Course Pinehurst, 156
Microsoft Multimedia Beethoven: The Ninth Symphony, 337
Microsoft Multimedia Mozart: The "Dissonant" Quartet, 338
Microsoft Multimedia Schubert: The "Trout" Quintet, 338
Microsoft Multimedia Strauss: Three Tone Poems, 339
Microsoft Multimedia Stravinsky: The Rite of Spring, 339
Microsoft Musical Instruments, 339
Microsoft Office Professional, 453
Microsoft Office Standard, 452
Microsoft Publisher, 473
Microsoft Word & Bookshelf, 454
Microsoft Works 3.0, 454
Midnight Movie Madness, 296
Midnight Stranger, 514

Mighty Morphin Power Rangers, 114
Millennium Auction, 137
Millie's Math House, 8
Monarch Notes For Windows, 322
Money In The 90s, 439
Money, Money, Money!, 470
Monty Python's Complete Waste of Time, 305
Multimedia MBA Small Business Edition, 410
Multimedia Songbook, 338
Multimedia Typing Instructor, 491
The Multimedia Workshop, 80
MusicMentor Maestro Edition, 340
The Musical World of Professor Piccolo, 81
My First Encyclopedia, 10
My First Incredible, Amazing Dictionary, 9
Myst, 138
National Lampoon's Blind Date, 509
NautilusCD, 284
The New Family Bible, 499
The New Kid on the Block, 32
New York, NY, 470
1994 Guinness Multimedia Disc of Records, 199
The 1994 Information Please Almanac, 202
The 1995 Grolier Multimedia Encyclopedia, 194
The 1994 Information Please Business Almanac & Desk Reference, 408
Normandy: The Great Crusade, 262
Oceans Below, 101
The Official NFL Interactive Yearbook '94-'95, 387
Open Roads: Driving the Data Highway, 272
The Oregon Trail, 84
Our Earth, 12
Outpost, 177
PC Paintbrush Photo Library, 470
The PC-SIG World of Windows CD-ROM, 459
PC/Computing: How Multimedia Computers Work, 478
Peachtree Accounting for Windows Release 3.0, 411

People Behind the Holidays, 12
People: 20 Years of Pop Culture, 273
The Perfect Résumé, 415
PharmAssist, 404
PhoneDisc Business & Residential, 209
PhoneDisc PowerFinder, 210
Plan Ahead for Your Financial Future, 441
The Playboy Interview, 274
The Playroom CD-ROM, 13
Poetry in Motion, 296
Power Japanese Version 2.0, 429
Power Spanish, 430
Prehistoria, 248
"Prince" Interactive, 353
Print Artist CD Edition, 471
The Print Shop Deluxe CD Ensemble, 472
PrintMaster Gold CD Bonus Pack, 472
Project Gutenberg, 324
Putt-Putt Goes to the Moon, 52
Quantum Gate: The Saga Begins, 140
QuickBooks Deluxe for Windows, 411
The QuickVerse Bible Reference Library, 500
Quicken Deluxe 4 for Windows CD-ROM, 442
Random House Kid's Encyclopedia, 73
Random House Unabridged Electronic Dictionary, 203
Reader Rabbit 2, 15
Reader Rabbit 3, 16
Reader Rabbit's Interactive Reading Journey, 17
Reading Blaster: Invasion of the Word Snatchers, 85
RedShift Multimedia Astronomy, 250
The Residents' Gingerbread Man, 348
Richard Simmons Deal-A-Meal, 392
Rodney's Wonder Window, 54
Ruff's Bone, 33
Sammy's Science House, 55
The San Diego Zoo Presents . . . The Animals!, 90
Saturday Night Live! The First Twenty Years, 307
Scholastic's The Magic School Bus Explores the Human Body, 100

Secrets of Stargate, 298
Seinfeld CD-ROM Screensaver & Planner, 307
Select Phone, 211
70 Million Households Phone Book, 211
Sharks!, 251
Shelley Duvall's It's a Bird's Life, 25
Shoot Video Like a Pro, 488
Shopping 2000, 504
A Silly Noisy House, 56
SimCity 2000 CD Collection, 180
Sitting on the Farm, 33
Soft Kill, 488
Softbank On Hand, 505
Space Odyssey, 474
Space Shuttle, 105
Spaceship Warlock, 146
The Sporting News 1994 Multimedia Pro Football Guide, 388
Sports Illustrated Multimedia Sports Almanac, 1995 Edition, 389
Sports Illustrated Swimsuit Calendar, 518
Sportz Freakz, 390
Star Trek: The Next Generation Interactive Technical Manual, 309
Star Wars Chess, 167
Stephen Biesty's Incredible Cross-Sections Stowaway!, 128
Storybook Weaver Deluxe, 86
Street Atlas USA, Version 2.0, 217
Student Writing Center, 87
Substance Digizine, 286
Take Five, 490
Tate Gallery—Exploring Modern Art, 232
TaxCut, 443
Taxi for New Orleans, Denver, Seattle, Phoenix & Orange County, 225
Taxi for New York, Chicago, Los Angeles, San Francisco & Washington, D.C., 224
Taxi for Philadelphia, Boston, Atlanta, Miami & Orlando, 226
TestDrive Super Store, 505
Tetris Gold, 168
The Tortoise and the Hare, 36
Thinkin' Things Collection 1, 57

3D Home Architect, 367
3D Landscape, 368
Thumbelina: An Interactive Adventure, 35
Time Almanac 1990s, 276
Time Almanac Reference Edition, 277
Time Almanac of the 20th Century, 278
2Market, 506
The Traveler, 508
TripMaker, 218
TriplePlay Plus! English, 432
TriplePlay Plus! French, 432
TriplePlay Plus! Spanish, 432
Tropical Rainforest, 474
TuneLand, 58
TurboTax Multimedia, 444
Twain's World, 327
The Twilight Zone Screen Saver, 311
2000 Fantastic Fonts, 467
USA Today: The '90s, Volume I, 278
USA Today: The '90s, Volume II, 280
The Ultimate Human Body, 252
Understanding Exposure: How to Shoot Great Photographs, 493
Vid Grid, 355
Video Cube: Space, 170
Video Linguist French, 434
Video Linguist Spanish, 435
Video Movie Guide, 301
VideoHound Multimedia, 300
The View from Earth, 253
The Viking Opera Guide, 346
Vintage Aloha, 474
Virtual Tarot, 494
The Vortex: Quantum Gate II, 148
Warplanes—Modern Fighting Aircraft, 495
The Way Things Work, 109
What's the Secret?, 110
Where in the USA is Carmen Sandiego? CD-ROM, 66
Where in the World is Carmen Sandiego? CD-ROM, 68
Where in the World is Carmen Sandiego? Junior Detective Edition, 39
Who Killed Brett Penance?, 150
Who Killed Elspeth Haskard?, 151

Who Killed Sam Rupert?, 151
Who Killed Taylor French?, 152
Wild Places, 475
Wines of the World, 377
The Women of Playboy Multimedia Screen Saver, 517
Woodstock: The 25th Anniversary CD-ROM, 356
Word Tales, 20
A World Alive, 254
World Beat, 357
The World Book New Illustrated Information Finder, 195
World View, 475
A World of Animals, 21
A World of Plants, 21
Xplora 1: Peter Gabriel's Secret World, 358
Your Mutual Fund Selector, 440
Your Personal Trainer for the SAT Version 2.0, 417
Zurk's Rainforest Lab, 59

Macintosh
A.D.A.M. The Inside Story, 236
The Aladdin Activity Center, 37
All My Hummingbirds Have Alibis, 335
Amanda Stories, 22
Amazing Animation, 119
The American Heritage Talking Dictionary, 197
American Poetry: The Nineteenth Century, 312
The American Sign Language Dictionary on CD-ROM, 419
American Visions Journeys through Art: Act One, 228
Americana, 461
Americans in Space, 89
Amnesty Interactive, 267
Animal Kingdom, 462
Animals and How They Grow, 4
Anno's Learning Games, 64
Antonin Dvořák's Symphony No. 9, "From the New World", 333
The Art of Making Great Pastries, 375
Arthur's Birthday, 22

Platform Index

Arthur's Teacher Trouble, 23
Astrology Source, 481
The Awesome Adventures of Victor Vector and Yondo: The Cyberplasm Formula, 116
The Awesome Adventures of Victor Vector and Yondo: The Hypnotic Harp, 117
The Awesome Adventures of Victor Vector and Yondo: The Last Dinosaur Egg, 117
The Awesome Adventures of Victor Vector and Yondo: The Vampire's Coffin, 117
Bailey's Book House, 5
Barron's Profiles of American Colleges on CD-ROM, 413
Baseball's Greatest Hits, 380
Batik Designs, 462
Battle Chess Enhanced CD-ROM, 163
Berlitz Live! Japanese, 420
Berlitz Live! Spanish, 421
Berlitz Think & Talk French, 422
Berlitz Think & Talk German, 423
Berlitz Think & Talk Italian, 424
Berlitz Think & Talk Spanish, 424
Better Homes and Gardens Complete Guide to Gardening, 361
Better Homes and Gardens Healthy Cooking CD Cookbook, 371
Big Anthony's Mixed-Up Magic, 24
A Brief History of Time, 239
Business Backgrounds, 463
CNN Time Capsule 1994, 270
Canada Phone, 207
Capitol Hill, 65
The Cartoon History of the Universe, Volumes 1–7, 68
Chuck Jones' Peter and the Wolf, 115
Cinema Volta, 230
Clinton: Portrait of Victory, 268
ClipArt Library, 463
Club KidSoft, 502
Comedy Central's Sports Shorts, 309
Comic Book Confidential, 290
The Complete After Dark Screen Saver Collection, 447
The Complete Maus, 321
Compton's Interactive Encyclopedia, 1995 Edition, 192
Corel Gallery, 465
Corel Professional Photos CD-ROM Sampler, 466
Cosmic Osmo and the Worlds Beyond the Mackerel, 40
CountDown, 6
Cowboy Casino, 166
Creative Writer, 69
Criterion Goes to the Movies, 291
The Crucible CD-ROM, 231
Dandy Dinosaurs, 42
Daring to Fly! From Icarus to the Red Baron, 482
Deep Voyage, 466
Deluxe Reader Rabbit 1, 14
Dennis Miller That's Geek to Me, 303
Dennis Miller That's News to Me, 304
Desert Storm: The War in the Persian Gulf, 271
Direct Phone, 207
Disney's Animated StoryBook: The Lion King, 30
Distant Suns 2.0, 242
The Doctors Book of Home Remedies, 397
Dracula Unleashed, 132
Dragon's Lair, 153
ESPN Baseball: Hitting, 383
ESPN Golf: Lower Your Score with Tom Kite—Shot Making, 384
ESPN Let's Play Soccer, 385
Ephemeral Films 1931–1960, 292
Europages, 208
Eyewitness Encyclopedia of Science, 99
The Family Doctor, 3rd Edition, 394
Fatty Bear's Birthday Surprise, 43
Fatty Bear's Fun Pack, 44
Firefighter!, 123
The First Emperor of China, 257
First Person: Donald A. Norman—Defending Human Attributes in the Age of the Machine, 314
First Person: Marvin Minsky—The Society of Mind, 326
First Person: Stephen Jay Gould—On Evolution, 315

Platform Index

4 Paws of Crab, 372
The Four Seasons of Gourmet French Cuisine, 374
Franz Schubert: The "Trout" Quintet, 342
Free Phone, 209
From Alice to Ocean, 317
Full Bloom, 467
A German Requiem, 334
A Hard Day's Night, 294
Harry and the Haunted House, 27
Hawaii High: The Mystery of the Tiki, 112
The Heinemann Children's Multimedia Encyclopedia, 71
Hell Cab, 133
Home Phone, 209
Hometime Weekend Home Projects, 369
How Computers Work, 477
How to Really Start Your Own Business, 407
The Human Body, 7
I Photograph to Remember, 233
Igor Stravinsky: The Rite of Spring, 344
Illustrated Facts: How Things Work, 200
Illustrated Facts: How the World Works, 201
Imagination Express, 124
Iron Helix, 134
Isaac Asimov's The Ultimate Robot, 318
It's All Relative, 304
Jazz: A Multimedia History, 349
Jets & Props, 468
Journey to the Planets, 244
The Journeyman Project Turbo, 135
Jump Raven, 157
Jump: The David Bowie Interactive CD-ROM, 350
Just Grandma and Me, 28
Kathy Smith's Fat Burning System, 398
Key CAD Complete, 448
Key Color ClipArt, 468
Key Fonts Pro, 468
Key Photo Clips, 469
Kid Pix Studio, 48

Kid Works 2, 126
Kids On Site, 49
King's Quest VII, 136
Last Chance to See, 245
Launch Pad, 449
Learn to Speak English 3.11, 426
Learn to Speak French 4.0, 427
Learn to Speak Spanish 4.0, 428
The Legends of Oz, 113
Leisure Suit Larry 6: Shape Up or Slip Out, 512
Lenny's MusicToons, 74
Leonardo, The Inventor, 261
Little Monster at School, 31
Ludwig van Beethoven: Symphony No. 9, 329
Macbeth, 234
The Madness of Roland, 320
Majestic Places, 469
Mammals: A Multimedia Encyclopedia, 246
The Manhole CD-ROM Masterpiece Edition, 51
Mario Teaches Typing Enhanced CD-ROM, 76
Mars Explorer, 247
Math Blaster: In Search of Spot, 77
Math Rabbit, 7
Math Workshop, 78
Mayo Clinic Family Health Book, 399
Mayo Clinic—The Total Heart, 403
Mega Rock Rap 'N Roll, 354
The Merchant, 503
Microsoft Art Gallery, 229
Microsoft Bookshelf '94, 198
Microsoft Cinemania '95, 289
Microsoft Dangerous Creatures, 241
Microsoft Dinosaurs, 98
Microsoft Encarta '95, 193
Microsoft Multimedia Works 4.0 & Microsoft Bookshelf '94, 455
Microsoft Musical Instruments, 339
Midnight Stranger, 514
Mighty Morphin Power Rangers, 114
Millie's Math House, 8
Money In The 90s, 439
Money, Money, Money!, 470
The Multimedia Workshop, 80
Murmurs of Earth, 247

The Musical World of Professor Piccolo, 81
My First Incredible, Amazing Dictionary, 9
Myst, 138
National Lampoon's Blind Date, 509
NautilusCD, 284
The New Family Bible, 499
The New Kid on the Block, 32
New York, NY, 470
Night Trap, 515
1994 Guinness Multimedia Disc of Records, 199
The 1995 Grolier Multimedia Encyclopedia, 194
No World Order, 352
Oceans Below, 101
The Official NFL Interactive Yearbook '94-'95, 387
Open Roads: Driving the Data Highway, 272
The Orchestra, 341
The Oregon Trail, 84
Our Earth, 12
PC Paintbrush Photo Library, 470
People Behind the Holidays, 12
People: 20 Years of Pop Culture, 273
PhoneDisc Business & Residential, 209
PhoneDisc PowerFinder, 210
Picture Atlas of the World, 217
Planetary Taxi, 102
The Playroom CD-ROM, 13
Poetry in Motion, 296
Prehistoria, 248
"Prince" Interactive, 353
The Print Shop Deluxe CD Ensemble, 472
Project Gutenberg, 324
Putt-Putt Goes to the Moon, 52
Putt-Putt Joins the Parade, 53
Putt-Putt's Fun Pack, 54
Quantum Gate: The Saga Begins, 140
Reader Rabbit 2, 15
Reader Rabbit 3, 16
Reader Rabbit's Interactive Reading Journey, 17
Rebel Assault, 161
RedShift Multimedia Astronomy, 250
The Residents' Freak Show, 347

The Residents' Gingerbread Man, 348
Return to Zork, 141
Richard Strauss: Three Tone Poems, 343
Rodney's Wonder Window, 54
Ruff's Bone, 33
Salt of the Earth, 297
Sammy's Science House, 55
The San Diego Zoo Presents . . . The Animals!, 90
Saturday Night Live! The First Twenty Years, 307
Secrets of Stargate, 298
Select Phone, 211
Sesame Street: Numbers, 18
Seven Days in August, 264
The 7th Guest, 142
Sharks!, 251
Shelley Duvall's It's a Bird's Life, 25
Sherlock Holmes, Consulting Detective, 144
Sherlock Holmes, Consulting Detective, Volume II, 145
Sherlock Holmes, Consulting Detective, Volume III, 145
Shining Flower, 325
Shoot Video Like a Pro, 488
Shopping 2000, 504
A Silly Noisy House, 56
SimCity 2000 CD Collection, 180
Sitting on the Farm, 33
So I've Heard, Volume 1: Bach and Before, 328
So I've Heard, Volume 2: The Classical Ideal, 332
Soft Kill, 488
Space Odyssey, 474
Space Shuttle, 105
Spaceship Warlock, 146
Sports Illustrated Multimedia Sports Almanac, 1995 Edition, 389
Star Trek: The Next Generation Interactive Technical Manual, 309
Stephen Biesty's Incredible Cross-Sections Stowaway!, 128
Storybook Weaver Deluxe, 86
Street Atlas USA, Version 2.0, 217
The String Quartet, 345
Take Five, 490

Platform Index

Tetris Gold, 168
The Tortoise and the Hare, 36
Thinkin' Things Collection 1, 57
Time Almanac Reference Edition, 277
2Market, 506
The Traveler, 508
Trivial Pursuit, 169
Tropical Rainforest, 474
The Ultimate Human Body, 252
Understanding Exposure: How to Shoot Great Photographs, 493
Video Linguist French, 434
Video Linguist Spanish, 435
The View from Earth, 253
Vintage Aloha, 474
Virtual Tarot, 494
Warplanes—Modern Fighting Aircraft, 495
The Way Things Work, 109
What's the Secret?, 110
Where in the USA is Carmen Sandiego? CD-ROM, 66
Where in the World is Carmen Sandiego? CD-ROM, 68
Who Built America?, 265
Who Killed Elspeth Haskard?, 151
Who Killed Sam Rupert?, 151
Wild Places, 475
Wines of the World, 377
WolfPack, 184
Wolfgang Amadeus Mozart: The "Dissonant" Quartet, 337
Woodstock: The 25th Anniversary CD-ROM, 356
Word Tales, 20
A World Alive, 254
World Atlas, 220
The World Book New Illustrated Information Finder, 195
World View, 475
A World of Animals, 21
A World of Plants, 21
Xplora 1: Peter Gabriel's Secret World, 358
Your Personal Trainer for the SAT Version 2.0, 417
Zurk's Rainforest Lab, 59

Index By Developer

A.D.A.M. Software Inc.
A.D.A.M. The Inside Story, 236

Access Software Inc.
Under a Killing Moon, 147

Activision
Return to Zork, 141

Advanced Multimedia Solutions Inc.
Video Movie Guide, 301

Allegro New Media Inc.
Business Library Volume 1, 406

American Business Information Inc.
11 Million Businesses Phone Book, 208
9-Digit ZIP Code Directory, 212
70 Million Households Phone Book, 211

Arnowitz Studios
Daring to Fly! From Icarus to the Red Baron, 482

Association of Shareware Professionals
The ASP Advantage, 457

Attica Cybernetics Ltd.
Tate Gallery—Exploring Modern Art, 232

Automap Inc.
Automap Road Atlas, 214
Automap Streets, 215

Banner Blue Software Inc.
Family Tree Maker Deluxe CD-ROM Version 2.0, 483

BayWare Inc.
Power Japanese Version 2.0, 429
Power Spanish, 430

Berkeley Systems Inc.
The Complete After Dark Screen Saver Collection, 447
Launch Pad, 449

Block Financial Software
TaxCut, 443

Books That Work Inc.
Home Repair Encyclopedia, 364
3D Landscape, 368

Broderbund Software Inc.
Kid Pix Studio, 48

Developer Index

Math Workshop, 78
Myst, 138
The Playroom CD-ROM, 13
The Print Shop Deluxe CD Ensemble, 472
3D Home Architect, 367
Where in the USA is Carmen Sandiego? CD-ROM, 66
Where in the World is Carmen Sandiego? CD-ROM, 68
Where in the World is Carmen Sandiego? Junior Detective Edition, 39

Broderbund Software Inc./Cyan Inc.
Cosmic Osmo and the Worlds Beyond the Mackerel, 40
The Manhole CD-ROM Masterpiece Edition, 51

Bureau of Electronic Publishing Inc.
Monarch Notes For Windows, 322
Twain's World, 327

Cambrix Publishing Inc.
The Art of Making Great Pastries, 375
The Four Seasons of Gourmet French Cuisine, 374
Learn to Play Guitar, 336

Claris Corp.
Amazing Animation, 119

Claris Corp./Against All Odds Productions
From Alice to Ocean, 317

Compton's NewMedia Inc.
AAA Trip Planner, 213
The Berenstain Bears Learning at Home Volume One, 38
The Berenstain Bears Learning at Home Volume Two, 39
The Complete Multimedia Bible, 498
Compton's Interactive Encyclopedia, 1995 Edition, 192
The Doctors Book of Home Remedies, 397
Jazz: A Multimedia History, 349
Let's Go: The Budget Guide to Europe 1994, 223
The Lifestyles of the Rich and Famous Cookbook, 375
Secrets of Stargate, 298
The Sporting News 1994 Multimedia Pro Football Guide, 388

CompuServe Inc.
CompuServeCD, 281

Computer Directions Inc.
Fitness Partner, 395

Contentware Inc.
Shopping 2000, 504

Context Systems Inc.
The D-Day Encyclopedia, 256
USA Today: The '90s, Volume I, 278
USA Today: The '90s, Volume II, 280

Corel Corp.
Corel Gallery, 465
Corel Professional Photos CD-ROM Sampler, 466
CorelDraw 3, 464
CorelFlow, 465

Creative Labs Inc.
American Visions Journeys through Art: Act One, 228
A Brief History of Time, 239

Creative Multimedia Corp.
Dr. Ruth's Encyclopedia of Sex, 393

Developer Index

The Family Doctor, 3rd Edition, 394
Who Killed Brett Penance?, 150
Who Killed Elspeth Haskard?, 151
Who Killed Sam Rupert?, 151
Who Killed Taylor French?, 152

Crystal Dynamics Inc.
The Horde, 156

Cubic Media Inc.
Video Linguist French, 434
Video Linguist Spanish, 435

DataTech Software Inc.
The American Golf Guide Presented by Arnold Palmer, 379

Davidson & Associates Inc.
Kid CAD, 125
Kid Works 2, 126
Math Blaster: Episode 2—Secret of The Lost City, 78
Math Blaster: In Search of Spot, 77
The Multimedia Workshop, 80
The Perfect Résumé, 415
Reading Blaster: Invasion of the Word Snatchers, 85
Your Personal Trainer for the SAT Version 2.0, 417

DeLorme Mapping
Global Explorer, 215
Map'n'Go, 216
Street Atlas USA, Version 2.0, 217

Deep River Publishing Inc.
Complete House, 362
Everywhere USA Travel Guide, 221
Great Restaurants, Wineries & Breweries, 222

Diamar Interactive Corp.
Understanding Exposure: How to Shoot Great Photographs, 493

Digital Directory Assistance Inc.
PhoneDisc Business & Residential, 209
PhoneDisc PowerFinder, 210

Digital Pictures Inc.
Kids On Site, 49
Night Trap, 515

Discovery Communications Inc.
Beyond Planet Earth, 237
In the Company of Whales, 240
Normandy: The Great Crusade, 262
Sharks!, 251

Dorling Kindersley Publishing Inc.
Eyewitness Encyclopedia of Science, 99
My First Incredible, Amazing Dictionary, 9
Stephen Biesty's Incredible Cross-Sections Stowaway!, 128
The Ultimate Human Body, 252
The Way Things Work, 109

Dow Jones & Co. Inc.
Plan Ahead for Your Financial Future, 441

Edmark Corp.
Bailey's Book House, 5
Imagination Express, 124
Millie's Math House, 8
Sammy's Science House, 55
Thinkin' Things Collection 1, 57

Eidolon Inc.
Millennium Auction, 137

Developer Index

Electronic Arts Inc.
No World Order, 352
SSN-21 Seawolf, 179

Electronic Arts Inc./EA Kids
Sesame Street: Numbers, 18

Electronic Arts Inc./EA Sports
FIFA International Soccer, 154
NHL Hockey '95, 159
PGA Tour Golf 486, 160

Electronic Arts Inc./Origin Systems Inc.
Wing Commander III: Heart of the Tiger, 183

Encyclopaedia Britannica Inc.
Britannica CD, 191

Expert Software Inc.
Backroad Racers, 120
Expert CD-ROM Home Design Gold Edition for Windows, 364
Operation AirStorm, 128
2467 Fantastic Fonts, 467

Friendly Software Corp.
Charles J. Givens Money Guide, 436

Future Vision Multimedia Inc.
Beethoven's 5th, 329
Leonardo, The Inventor, 261

GT Interactive Software Corp.
Doom II: Hell on Earth, 510
Richard Simmons Deal-A-Meal, 392

GameTek Inc.
Saturday Night Live! The First Twenty Years, 307

Gazelle Technologies Inc.
Midnight Stranger, 514

Graphix Zone
"Prince" Interactive, 353

Great Bear Technology Inc.
Complete Guide to Prescription and Non-Prescription Drugs, 392
Sportz Freakz, 390

Green Thumb Software Inc.
LandDesigner Multi-Media for Gardens, 366

Grolier Electronic Publishing Inc.
1994 Guinness Multimedia Disc of Records, 199
The 1995 Grolier Multimedia Encyclopedia, 194
Prehistoria, 248

HarperCollins Interactive
The American Sign Language Dictionary on CD-ROM, 419

Humongous Entertainment Inc.
Fatty Bear's Birthday Surprise, 43
Fatty Bear's Fun Pack, 44
Freddi Fish And The Case of The Missing Kelp Seeds, 45
Putt-Putt Goes to the Moon, 52
Putt-Putt Joins the Parade, 53
Putt-Putt's Fun Pack, 54

HyperBole Studios
The Madness of Roland, 320
Quantum Gate: The Saga Begins, 140
The Vortex: Quantum Gate II, 148

Developer Index

HyperGlot Software Co.
Berlitz Think & Talk French, 422
Berlitz Think & Talk German, 423
Berlitz Think & Talk Italian, 424
Berlitz Think & Talk Spanish, 424
Learn to Speak English 3.11, 426
Learn to Speak French 4.0, 427
Learn to Speak Spanish 4.0, 428

IBM Multimedia Publishing Studio
The Playboy Interview, 274

IVI Publishing Inc.
AnnaTommy, 91
Blown Away, 131
Hometime Weekend Home Projects, 369
Mayo Clinic Family Health Book, 399
Mayo Clinic Family Pharmacist, 400
Mayo Clinic Sports Health & Fitness, 402
Mayo Clinic—The Total Heart, 403

Individual Software Inc.
Multimedia Typing Instructor, 491

InfoBusiness Inc.
Job-Power Source, 414
Mega Movie Guide Version 3.0, 295

Intellimedia Sports Inc.
Cowboy Casino, 166
ESPN Baseball: Hitting, 383
ESPN Golf: Lower Your Score with Tom Kite—Shot Making, 384
ESPN Let's Play Soccer, 385

InterMedia Interactive Software Inc.
Lovejoy's College Counselor, 415

Interactive Entertainment
Interactive Entertainment, 282

Interplay Productions Inc.
Battle Chess Enhanced CD-ROM, 163
Castles II: Siege & Conquest Enhanced CD-ROM, 172
Mario Teaches Typing Enhanced CD-ROM, 76
Star Trek: 25th Anniversary Enhanced CD-ROM, 182
Voyeur, 149

Interplay Productions Inc./MacPlay
Xplora 1: Peter Gabriel's Secret World, 358

Intuit Inc.
QuickBooks Deluxe for Windows, 411
Quicken Deluxe 4 for Windows CD-ROM, 442
TurboTax Multimedia, 444
Your Mutual Fund Selector, 440

Ion
Jump: The David Bowie Interactive CD-ROM, 350
The Residents' Gingerbread Man, 348

Jasmine Multimedia Publishing Inc.
Vid Grid, 355

Kelly Russell Studios Inc.
Legends and Superstars Baseball, 386

KidSoft Inc.
Club KidSoft, 502

Knowledge Adventure Inc.
America Adventure, 62
Aviation Adventure, 92
Bug Adventure, 94
Isaac Asimov Science Adventure II, 103
JumpStart Kindergarten, 46
Kid's Zoo, 50

Magic Theatre, 127
My First Encyclopedia, 10
Random House Kid's Encyclopedia, 73
Space Adventure II, 104
Speed, 106
3-D Body Adventure, 93
3-D Dinosaur Adventure, 95
Undersea Adventure, 108

Laser Resources Inc.
Barron's Profiles of American Colleges on CD-ROM, 413
Money In The 90s, 439

The Learning Company
Deluxe Reader Rabbit 1, 14
Math Rabbit, 7
Operation Neptune, 83
Reader Rabbit 2, 15
Reader Rabbit 3, 16
Reader Rabbit's Interactive Reading Journey, 17
Student Writing Center, 87
Super Solvers Spellbound!, 19

Live Oak Multimedia Inc.
4 Paws of Crab, 372

Living Books
Arthur's Birthday, 22
Arthur's Teacher Trouble, 23
Harry and the Haunted House, 27
Just Grandma and Me, 28
Little Monster at School, 31
The New Kid on the Block, 32
Ruff's Bone, 33
The Tortoise and the Hare, 36

Lotus Development Corp.
Lotus 1-2-3 Release 5 Multimedia Edition, 450
Lotus SmartSuite 3.0 CD-ROM Edition, 451

LucasArts Entertainment Co.
Rebel Assault, 161

MECC
The Oregon Trail, 84
Storybook Weaver Deluxe, 86

Magellan Systems
The Merchant, 503
The Traveler, 508

Maris Multimedia Ltd.
RedShift Multimedia Astronomy, 250
Warplanes—Modern Fighting Aircraft, 495

Maxis
Print Artist CD Edition, 471
SimCity 2000 CD Collection, 180

Medio Multimedia Inc.
J.F.K. Assassination: A Visual Investigation, 260
Jets!, 485
Medio Magazine, 283
Midnight Movie Madness, 296
World Beat, 357

Metatec Corp.
NautilusCD, 284

MicroLogic Software
PrintMaster Gold CD Bonus Pack, 472

Micrografx Inc.
Crayola Amazing Art Adventure, 41
Crayola Art Studio, 121

Microsoft Corp.
Creative Writer, 69

Isaac Asimov's The Ultimate Robot, 318
Microsoft Ancient Lands, 63
Microsoft Art Gallery, 229
Microsoft Bookshelf '94, 198
Microsoft Cinemania '95, 289
Microsoft Complete Baseball, 1994 Edition, 381
Microsoft Complete NBA Basketball, 382
Microsoft Dangerous Creatures, 241
Microsoft Dinosaurs, 98
Microsoft Encarta '95, 193
Microsoft Explorapedia: The World of Nature, 70
Microsoft Golf, 155
Microsoft Golf Championship Course Pinehurst, 156
Microsoft Multimedia Beethoven: The Ninth Symphony, 337
Microsoft Multimedia Mozart: The "Dissonant" Quartet, 338
Microsoft Multimedia Schubert: The "Trout" Quintet, 338
Microsoft Multimedia Strauss: Three Tone Poems, 339
Microsoft Multimedia Stravinsky: The Rite of Spring, 339
Microsoft Multimedia Works 4.0 & Microsoft Bookshelf '94, 455
Microsoft Musical Instruments, 339
Microsoft Office Professional, 453
Microsoft Office Standard, 452
Microsoft Publisher, 473
Microsoft Word & Bookshelf, 454
Microsoft Works 3.0, 454
Scholastic's The Magic School Bus Explores the Human Body, 100

Midisoft Corp.
Multimedia Songbook, 338
MusicMentor Maestro Edition, 340

Mindscape Inc.
Capitol Hill, 65
The Chessmaster 3000, 164
Mavis Beacon Teaches Typing! Version 3, 486
Mavis Beacon Teaches Typing! for Kids, 79
Mega Race, 158
Oceans Below, 101
PC/Computing: How Multimedia Computers Work, 478
The San Diego Zoo Presents . . . The Animals!, 90
Space Shuttle, 105
Star Wars Chess, 167
U.S. Atlas, 219
World Atlas, 220

Moon Valley Software
ESPN Sports Shorts, 386

Multicom Publishing Inc.
Americans in Space, 89
Astrology Source, 481
Better Homes and Gardens Complete Guide to Gardening, 361
Better Homes and Gardens Healthy Cooking CD Cookbook, 371
Dandy Dinosaurs, 42
Journey to the Planets, 244
The Legends of Oz, 113
Wines of the World, 377

National Geographic Society
Animals and How They Grow, 4
The Human Body, 7
Mammals: A Multimedia Encyclopedia, 246
Our Earth, 12
People Behind the Holidays, 12
Picture Atlas of the World, 217
The Presidents: A Picture History of Our Nation, 263
A World of Animals, 21
A World of Plants, 21

News Electronic Data Inc.
Taxi for New Orleans, Denver, Seattle, Phoenix & Orange County, 225
Taxi for New York, Chicago, Los Angeles, San Francisco & Washington, D.C., 224
Taxi for Philadelphia, Boston, Atlanta, Miami & Orlando, 226

Newsweek Inc.
Open Roads: Driving the Data Highway, 272

NovaLogic Inc.
Comanche CD, 173
WolfPack, 184

Opcode Interactive
Composer Quest, 332
The Musical World of Professor Piccolo, 81

PC-SIG
The PC-SIG World of Games CD-ROM, 459
The PC-SIG World of Windows CD-ROM, 459

Parsons Technology Inc.
It's Legal 5.0 Deluxe CD-ROM Edition, 409
The 1994 Information Please Almanac, 202
The 1994 Information Please Business Almanac & Desk Reference, 408
The QuickVerse Bible Reference Library, 500

Peachtree Software Inc.
Peachtree Accounting for Windows Release 3.0, 411

Penguin USA
The Crucible CD-ROM, 231
The Viking Opera Guide, 346

Pro CD Inc.
Canada Phone, 207
Direct Phone, 207
Europages, 208
Free Phone, 209
Home Phone, 209
Select Phone, 211

Putnam New Media
Anno's Learning Games, 64
Big Anthony's Mixed-Up Magic, 24
The Cartoon History of the Universe, Volumes 1–7, 68

Rand McNally & Company
TripMaker, 218

Random House Inc.
Random House Unabridged Electronic Dictionary, 203

Reactor Inc.
Spaceship Warlock, 146

ReadySoft Inc.
Dragon's Lair, 153

RealTime Sports Inc.
The Official NFL Interactive Yearbook '94 '95, 387

Reed Interactive
The Heinemann Children's Multimedia Encyclopedia, 71

Developer Index

Sanctuary Woods Multimedia Corp.
The Awesome Adventures of Victor Vector and Yondo: The Cyberplasm Formula, 116
The Awesome Adventures of Victor Vector and Yondo: The Hypnotic Harp, 117
The Awesome Adventures of Victor Vector and Yondo: The Last Dinosaur Egg, 117
The Awesome Adventures of Victor Vector and Yondo: The Vampire's Coffin, 117
The Cat Came Back, 26
Dennis Miller That's Geek to Me, 303
Dennis Miller That's News to Me, 304
Hawaii High: The Mystery of the Tiki, 112
The Journeyman Project Turbo, 135
Shelley Duvall's It's a Bird's Life, 25
Sitting on the Farm, 33

Scanrom Publications Inc.
The First Electronic Jewish Bookshelf, 497

7th Level Inc.
Monty Python's Complete Waste of Time, 305
TuneLand, 58

Sierra On-Line Inc.
Berlitz Live! Japanese, 420
Berlitz Live! Spanish, 421
King's Quest VII, 136
Leisure Suit Larry 6: Shape Up or Slip Out, 512
Outpost, 177

Sierra On-Line Inc./Dynamix Inc.
Betrayal at Krondor, 171

Simon & Schuster Interactive
Firefighter!, 123

Star Trek: The Next Generation Interactive Technical Manual, 309

Sirius Publishing Inc.
5-Ft. 10-Pak Volume II, 484

SoftKey International Inc.
America's Civil War—A Nation Divided, 255
The American Heritage Talking Dictionary, 197
Americana, 461
Animal Kingdom, 462
Batik Designs, 462
Bodyworks 3.0, 238
Business Backgrounds, 463
Calendar Creator Plus, 448
ClipArt Library, 463
Computer Works, 476
Deep Voyage, 466
Full Bloom, 467
Jets & Props, 468
Key CAD Complete, 448
Key Color ClipArt, 468
Key Fonts Pro, 468
Key Photo Clips, 469
Key Translator Pro English-Spanish, 425
MPC Wizard 3.0, 451
Majestic Places, 469
Money, Money, Money!, 470
New York, NY, 470
PC Paintbrush Photo Library, 470
PharmAssist, 404
Space Odyssey, 474
Sports Illustrated Swimsuit Calendar, 518
Time Almanac of the 20th Century, 278
Tropical Rainforest, 474
UFO—This Planet's Most Complete Guide to Close Encounters, 492
Video Cube: Space, 170
Vintage Aloha, 474
Wild Places, 475
World View, 475

SoftKey International Inc./Compact Publishing
CNN Newsroom Global View, 269
Multimedia MBA Small Business Edition, 410
Time Almanac 1990s, 276
Time Almanac Reference Edition, 277

Softbank Inc.
Softbank On Hand, 505

Soleil Software Inc.
Zurk's Rainforest Lab, 59

Sony Imagesoft
Earthquake, 243
The Haldeman Diaries: Inside the Nixon White House, The Complete Multimedia Edition, 258
MTV's Beavis and Butt-head Multimedia Screen Saver, 302
The Women of Playboy Multimedia Screen Saver, 517

Sound Source Interactive
The Twilight Zone Screen Saver, 311

Spectrum HoloByte Inc.
Falcon Gold, 174
Iron Helix, 134
Tetris Gold, 168

StarPress Multimedia Inc.
Sports Illustrated Multimedia Sports Almanac, 1995 Edition, 389

Substance Interactive Media Inc.
Substance Digizine, 286

SunMedia Inc.
Audio-Visual Chinese-English Dictionary, 424
Chinese Family Cooking, 372

Swfte International Ltd.
Bicycle Limited Edition CD-ROM, 164

Syracuse Language Systems
TriplePlay Plus! English, 432
TriplePlay Plus! French, 432
TriplePlay Plus! Spanish, 432

TestDrive Corp.
TestDrive Super Store, 505

The Kiplinger Washington Editors Inc.
Kiplinger TaxCut Multimedia, 437

3M Corp.
What's the Secret?, 110

Time Warner Interactive
Aegis: Guardian of the Fleet, 171
Chuck Jones' Peter and the Wolf, 115
Clinton: Portrait of Victory, 268
Comedy Central's Sports Shorts, 309
Creation Stories, 313
Dating & Mating, 303
Desert Storm: The War in the Persian Gulf, 271
Funny, 293
A German Requiem, 334
Hell Cab, 133
How Computers Work, 477
It's All Relative, 304
Murmurs of Earth, 247
The New Family Bible, 499
The Orchestra, 341
Seinfeld CD-ROM Screensaver & Planner, 307
Seven Days in August, 264
The String Quartet, 345

Developer Index

Thumbelina: An Interactive Adventure, 35
The View from Earth, 253
Woodstock: The 25th Anniversary CD-ROM, 356
Word Tales, 20

Time Warner Interactive/Tsunami Media Inc.
Man Enough, 513
Return to Ringworld, 178

2Market Inc.
2Market, 506

Trimark Interactive
National Lampoon's Blind Date, 509

Turner Home Entertainment
Gettysburg, 176

VT Productions Inc.
The Exotic Garden, 363

Viacom New Media
Dracula Unleashed, 132
Lenny's MusicToons, 74
Mega Rock Rap 'N Roll, 354
Sherlock Holmes, Consulting Detective, 144
Sherlock Holmes, Consulting Detective, Volume II, 145
Sherlock Holmes, Consulting Detective, Volume III, 145

Viacom New Media/Cyberflix Inc.
Jump Raven, 157

Vicarious Entertainment
CNN Time Capsule 1994, 270

Virgin Interactive Entertainment
The 7th Guest, 142
Trivial Pursuit, 169

Virtual Media Works
Virtual Tarot, 494

Virtual Reality Laboratories Inc.
Distant Suns 2.0, 242
Mars Explorer, 247

Visible Ink Software
VideoHound Multimedia, 300

Voyager Co.
All My Hummingbirds Have Alibis, 335
Amanda Stories, 22
American Poetry: The Nineteenth Century, 312
Amnesty Interactive, 267
Antonin Dvořák's Symphony No. 9, "From the New World", 333
Baseball's Greatest Hits, 380
Cinema Volta, 230
Comic Book Confidential, 290
The Complete Maus, 321
CountDown, 6
Criterion Goes to the Movies, 291
Ephemeral Films 1931–1960, 292
The First Emperor of China, 257
First Person: Donald A. Norman—Defending Human Attributes in the Age of the Machine, 314
First Person: Marvin Minsky—The Society of Mind, 326
First Person: Stephen Jay Gould—On Evolution, 315
Franz Schubert: The "Trout" Quintet, 342
A Hard Day's Night, 294
I Photograph to Remember, 233
Igor Stravinsky: The Rite of Spring, 344
Last Chance to See, 245

Ludwig van Beethoven: Symphony No. 9, 329
Macbeth, 234
People: 20 Years of Pop Culture, 273
Planetary Taxi, 102
Poetry in Motion, 296
The Residents' Freak Show, 347
Richard Strauss: Three Tone Poems, 343
Rodney's Wonder Window, 54
Salt of the Earth, 297
Shining Flower, 325
A Silly Noisy House, 56
So I've Heard, Volume 1: Bach and Before, 328
So I've Heard, Volume 2: The Classical Ideal, 332
Take Five, 490
Who Built America?, 265
Wolfgang Amadeus Mozart: The "Dissonant" Quartet, 337
A World Alive, 254

Walnut Creek CDROM
CICA Shareware for Windows, 458
Project Gutenberg, 324
Simtel, 460

Walt Disney Computer Software Inc.
The Aladdin Activity Center, 37
Disney's Animated StoryBook: The Lion King, 30

World Book Inc.
The World Book New Illustrated Information Finder, 195

World Library Inc.
Barron's Complete Book Notes, 313
Library of the Future Third Edition, 319

Xiphias
American Heritage Illustrated Encyclopedic Dictionary, 197
Illustrated Facts: How Things Work, 200
Illustrated Facts: How the World Works, 201
Kathy Smith's Fat Burning System, 398
Mighty Morphin Power Rangers, 114
The New Basics Electronic Cookbook, 376
Soft Kill, 488
Time Table of History: Arts & Entertainment, 204
Time Table of History: Business, Politics & Media, 205
Time Table of History: Science & Innovation, 205

Zelos Digital Publishing
How to Really Start Your Own Business, 407
Shoot Video Like a Pro, 488

Index By Title

A Hard Day's Night ★★★½, 294
AAA Trip Planner ★★★, 213
A.D.A.M. The Inside Story ★★★, 236
The ASP Advantage ★★★, 457
Aegis: Guardian of the Fleet ★★★, 171
The Complete After Dark Screen Saver Collection ★★★½, 447
The Aladdin Activity Center ★★★, 37
All My Hummingbirds Have Alibis ★★, 335
Amanda Stories ★★, 22
Amazing Animation ★★½, 119
Crayola Amazing Art Adventure ★★★, 41
America Adventure ★★★½, 62
America's Civil War—A Nation Divided ★, 255
The American Golf Guide Presented by Arnold Palmer ★½, 379
American Heritage Illustrated Encyclopedic Dictionary ★½, 197
The American Heritage Talking Dictionary ★★½, 197
American Poetry: The Nineteenth Century ★★★, 312
The American Sign Language Dictionary on CD-ROM ★★★½, 419
American Visions Journeys through Art: Act One ★★½, 228
Americana ★★½, 461
Americans in Space ★★★, 89
Amnesty Interactive ★★★★, 267
Microsoft Ancient Lands ★★★, 63
Animal Kingdom ★★½, 462
Animals and How They Grow ★★★, 4

The San Diego Zoo Presents... The Animals! ★★★½, 90
AnnaTommy ★½, 91
Anno's Learning Games ★★★, 64
Antonin Dvořák's Symphony No. 9, "From the New World" ★★★★, 333
Microsoft Art Gallery ★★★½, 229
Crayola Art Studio ★★★, 121
The Art of Making Great Pastries ★★, 375
Arthur's Birthday ★★★½, 22
Arthur's Teacher Trouble ★★★★, 23
Astrology Source ★★½, 481
Audio-Visual Chinese-English Dictionary ★★★, 424
Automap Road Atlas ★★½, 214
Automap Streets ★½, 215
Aviation Adventure ★★★½, 92
The Awesome Adventures of Victor Vector and Yondo: The Cyberplasm Formula ★★, 116
The Awesome Adventures of Victor Vector and Yondo: The Hypnotic Harp ★★, 117
The Awesome Adventures of Victor Vector and Yondo: The Last Dinosaur Egg ★★, 117
The Awesome Adventures of Victor Vector and Yondo: The Vampire's Coffin ★★, 117

So I've Heard, Volume 1: Bach and Before ★★½, 328
Backroad Racers ★★½, 120

545

Title Index

Bailey's Book House ★★★½, 5
Barron's Complete Book Notes ★★★, 313
Barron's Profiles of American Colleges on CD-ROM ★★★, 413
Baseball's Greatest Hits ★★★½, 380
Batik Designs ★★½, 462
Battle Chess Enhanced CD-ROM ★★, 163
MTV's Beavis and Butt-head Multimedia Screen Saver ★★★, 302
Beethoven's 5th ★★★, 329
Ludwig van Beethoven: Symphony No. 9 ★★★★, 329
Microsoft Multimedia Beethoven: The Ninth Symphony ★★★★, 337
The Berenstain Bears Learning at Home Volume One ★★, 38
The Berenstain Bears Learning at Home Volume Two ★★, 39
Berlitz Live! Japanese ★★★, 420
Berlitz Live! Spanish ★★★, 421
Berlitz Think & Talk French ★★, 422
Berlitz Think & Talk German ★★, 423
Berlitz Think & Talk Italian ★★, 424
Berlitz Think & Talk Spanish ★★, 424
Betrayal at Krondor ★★½, 171
Better Homes and Gardens Complete Guide to Gardening ★½, 361
Better Homes and Gardens Healthy Cooking CD Cookbook ★★★, 371
Beyond Planet Earth ★★½, 237
Bicycle Limited Edition CD-ROM ★★★, 164
Big Anthony's Mixed-Up Magic ★★★½, 24
Shelley Duvall's It's a Bird's Life ★★, 25
National Lampoon's Blind Date ★★, 509
Blown Away ★★★, 131
3-D Body Adventure ★★½, 93
Bodyworks 3.0 ★★½, 238
Microsoft Bookshelf '94 ★★★½, 198
A Brief History of Time ★★, 239
Britannica CD ★★, 191
Bug Adventure ★★★½, 94

Business Backgrounds ★★½, 463
Business Library Volume 1 ★★½, 406

CICA Shareware for Windows ★★½, 458
CNN Newsroom Global View ★½, 269
CNN Time Capsule 1994 ★★½, 270
Calendar Creator Plus ★★, 448
Canada Phone ★★, 207
Capitol Hill ★★½, 65
Where in the USA is Carmen Sandiego? CD-ROM ★★★½, 66
Where in the World is Carmen Sandiego? CD-ROM ★★★½, 68
Where in the World is Carmen Sandiego? Junior Detective Edition ★★★, 39
The Cartoon History of the Universe, Volumes 1-7 ★★★, 68
Castles II: Siege & Conquest Enhanced CD-ROM ★★★, 172
The Cat Came Back ★★★, 26
Charles J. Givens Money Guide ★★★, 436
The Chessmaster 3000 ★★★½, 164
Chinese Family Cooking ★★, 372
Audio-Visual Chinese-English Dictionary ★★★, 424
Chuck Jones' Peter and the Wolf ★★½, 115
Cinema Volta ★½, 230
Microsoft Cinemania '95 ★★★½, 289
So I've Heard, Volume 2: The Classical Ideal ★★½, 332
Clinton: Portrait of Victory ★★★, 268
ClipArt Library ★★★, 463
Club KidSoft ★★★★, 502
Comanche CD ★★½, 173
Comedy Central's Sports Shorts ★★, 309
Comic Book Confidential ★★★½, 290
The Complete After Dark Screen Saver Collection ★★★½, 447
Microsoft Complete Baseball, 1994 Edition ★★★½, 381
Complete Guide to Prescription and Non-Prescription Drugs ★, 392

Title Index

Complete House ★★, 362
The Complete Maus ★★★★, 321
The Complete Multimedia Bible ★★½, 498
Microsoft Complete NBA Basketball ★★★½, 382
Composer Quest ★★, 332
Compton's Interactive Encyclopedia, 1995 Edition ★★★★, 192
CompuServeCD ★★, 281
Computer Works ★, 476
Corel Gallery ★★★½, 465
Corel Professional Photos CD-ROM Sampler ★★★, 466
CorelDraw 3 ★★★, 464
CorelFlow ★★★, 465
Cosmic Osmo and the Worlds Beyond the Mackerel ★★★, 40
CountDown ★★, 6
Cowboy Casino ★★, 166
Crayola Amazing Art Adventure ★★★, 41
Crayola Art Studio ★★★, 121
Creation Stories ★½, 313
Creative Writer ★½, 69
Criterion Goes to the Movies ★★★, 291
The Crucible CD-ROM ★★★½, 231

The D-Day Encyclopedia ★★, 256
Dandy Dinosaurs ★, 42
Microsoft Dangerous Creatures ★★½, 241
Daring to Fly! From Icarus to the Red Baron ★★½, 482
Dating & Mating ★★, 303
Richard Simmons Deal-A-Meal ★★★, 392
Deep Voyage ★★½, 466
Deluxe Reader Rabbit 1 ★★★½, 14
Dennis Miller That's Geek to Me ★★, 303
Dennis Miller That's News to Me ★★, 304
Desert Storm: The War in the Persian Gulf ★★, 271
3-D Dinosaur Adventure ★★½, 95
Microsoft Dinosaurs ★★★½, 98
Direct Phone ★★, 207

Disney's Animated StoryBook: The Lion King ★★★½, 30
Distant Suns 2.0 ★★★½, 242
The Doctors Book of Home Remedies ★★, 397
Doom II: Hell on Earth ★★★½, 510
Dr. Ruth's Encyclopedia of Sex ★★★½, 393
Dracula Unleashed ★★★, 132
Dragon's Lair ★★, 153
Antonín Dvořák's Symphony No. 9, "From the New World" ★★★★, 333

ESPN Baseball: Hitting ★★½, 383
ESPN Golf: Lower Your Score with Tom Kite—Shot Making ★★, 384
ESPN Let's Play Soccer ★½, 385
ESPN Sports Shorts ★★½, 386
Earthquake ★★½, 243
11 Million Businesses Phone Book ★★, 208
Microsoft Encarta '95 ★★★★, 193
Ephemeral Films 1931-1960 ★★½, 292
Europages ★★½, 208
Everywhere USA Travel Guide ★★, 221
The Exotic Garden ★★, 363
Expert CD-ROM Home Design Gold Edition for Windows ★★, 364
Microsoft Explorapedia: The World of Nature ★★★, 70
Eyewitness Encyclopedia of Science ★★½, 99

FIFA International Soccer ★★★, 154
Falcon Gold ★★★, 174
The Family Doctor, 3rd Edition ★★, 394
Family Tree Maker Deluxe CD-ROM Version 2.0 ★★★, 483
2000 Fantastic Fonts ★★½, 467
Fatty Bear's Birthday Surprise ★★★, 43
Fatty Bear's Fun Pack ★★★, 44
Firefighter! ★★★, 123

Title Index

The First Electronic Jewish Bookshelf ★★½, 497
The First Emperor of China ★★½, 257
First Person: Donald A. Norman—Defending Human Attributes in the Age of the Machine ★★★, 314
First Person: Marvin Minsky—The Society of Mind ★★½, 326
First Person: Stephen Jay Gould—On Evolution ★★½, 315
Fitness Partner ★★, 395
5-Ft. 10-Pak Volume II ★★½, 484
4 Paws of Crab ★★★, 372
The Four Seasons of Gourmet French Cuisine ★★, 374
Franz Schubert: The "Trout" Quintet ★★★★, 342
The Residents' Freak Show ★★★★, 347
Freddi Fish And The Case of The Missing Kelp Seeds ★★★½, 45
Free Phone ★★½, 209
From Alice to Ocean ★★★½, 317
Full Bloom ★★½, 467
Funny ★★, 293

A German Requiem ★★★½, 334
Gettysburg ★★½, 176
The Residents' Gingerbread Man ★★★, 348
Charles J. Givens Money Guide ★★★, 436
Global Explorer ★★½, 215
Microsoft Golf Championship Course Pinehurst ★★★½, 156
The American Golf Guide Presented by Arnold Palmer ★½, 379
Microsoft Golf ★★★½, 155
First Person: Stephen Jay Gould—On Evolution ★★½, 315
Great Restaurants, Wineries & Breweries ★★, 222
The 1995 Grolier Multimedia Encyclopedia ★★★★, 194
1994 Guinness Multimedia Disc of Records ★★, 199

The Haldeman Diaries: Inside the Nixon White House, The Complete Multimedia Edition ★★★, 258
A Hard Day's Night ★★★½, 294
Harry and the Haunted House ★★★½, 27
Hawaii High: The Mystery of the Tiki ★★½, 112
The Heinemann Children's Multimedia Encyclopedia ★★, 71
Hell Cab ★★, 133
3D Home Architect ★★★½, 367
Expert CD-ROM Home Design Gold Edition for Windows ★★, 364
Home Phone ★★, 209
The Doctors Book of Home Remedies ★★, 397
Home Repair Encyclopedia ★★★, 364
Hometime Weekend Home Projects ★★½, 369
The Horde ★★, 156
How Computers Work ★★★, 477
PC/Computing: How Multimedia Computers Work ★★★, 478
How to Really Start Your Own Business ★★, 407
The Human Body ★★★, 7

I Photograph to Remember ★★★★, 233
Igor Stravinsky: The Rite of Spring ★★★★, 344
Illustrated Facts: How Things Work ★★, 200
Illustrated Facts: How the World Works ★★, 201
Imagination Express ★★½, 124
In the Company of Whales ★★, 240
The 1994 Information Please Almanac ★★, 202
The 1994 Information Please Business Almanac & Desk Reference ★★, 408
Interactive Entertainment ★★★, 282
Iron Helix ★★★, 134
Isaac Asimov Science Adventure II ★½, 103

Isaac Asimov's The Ultimate Robot ★★, 318
It's All Relative ★★, 304
It's Legal 5.0 Deluxe CD-ROM Edition ★★★½, 409
Shelley Duvall's It's a Bird's Life ★★, 25

J.F.K. Assassination: A Visual Investigation ★★★, 260
Jazz: A Multimedia History ★★½, 349
Jets & Props ★★½, 468
Jets! ★★½, 485
The First Electronic Jewish Bookshelf ★★½, 497
Job-Power Source ★½, 414
Journey to the Planets ★★, 244
The Journeyman Project Turbo ★★½, 135
Jump Raven ★★★, 157
Jump: The David Bowie Interactive CD-ROM ★★½, 350
JumpStart Kindergarten ★★, 46
Just Grandma and Me ★★★★, 28

Kathy Smith's Fat Burning System ★★★, 398
Key CAD Complete ★★, 448
Key Color ClipArt ★★½, 468
Key Fonts Pro ★★½, 468
Key Photo Clips ★½, 469
Key Translator Pro English-Spanish ★★★, 425
Kid CAD ★★½, 125
Kid Pix Studio ★★★★, 48
Kid Works 2 ★★★½, 126
Kid's Zoo ★½, 50
Club KidSoft ★★★★, 502
Kids On Site ★★½, 49
King's Quest VII ★★★½, 136
Kiplinger TaxCut Multimedia ★★★, 437

LandDesigner Multi-Media for Gardens ★★, 366
3D Landscape ★★★, 368
Last Chance to See ★★½, 245

Launch Pad ★★★, 449
Learn to Play Guitar ★★, 336
Learn to Speak English 3.11 ★★★½, 426
Learn to Speak French 4.0 ★★★★, 427
Learn to Speak Spanish 4.0 ★★★★, 428
Legends and Superstars Baseball ★½, 386
The Legends of Oz ★★, 113
Leisure Suit Larry 6: Shape Up or Slip Out ★★½, 512
Lenny's MusicToons ★★½, 74
Leonardo, The Inventor ★★½, 261
Let's Go: The Budget Guide to Europe 1994 ★★½, 223
Library of the Future Third Edition ★★½, 319
The Lifestyles of the Rich and Famous Cookbook ★★★, 375
Disney's Animated StoryBook: The Lion King ★★★½, 30
Little Monster at School ★★★★, 31
Lotus 1-2-3 Release 5 Multimedia Edition ★★★, 450
Lotus SmartSuite 3.0 CD-ROM Edition ★★★, 451
Lovejoy's College Counselor ★★★, 415
Ludwig van Beethoven: Symphony No. 9 ★★★★, 329

MPC Wizard 3.0 ★★, 451
MTV's Beavis and Butt-head Multimedia Screen Saver ★★★, 302
Macbeth ★★★, 234
The Madness of Roland ★★½, 320
Scholastic's The Magic School Bus Explores the Human Body ★★★½, 100
Magic Theatre ★★½, 127
Majestic Places ★★½, 469
Mammals: A Multimedia Encyclopedia ★★, 246
Man Enough ★★, 513

Title Index

The Manhole CD-ROM Masterpiece Edition ★★½, 51
Map'n'Go ★★★, 216
Mario Teaches Typing Enhanced CD-ROM ★★½, 76
Mars Explorer ★★½, 247
Math Blaster: Episode 2—Secret of The Lost City ★★★, 78
Math Blaster: In Search of Spot ★★★, 77
Math Rabbit ★★★, 7
Math Workshop ★★½, 78
The Complete Maus ★★★★, 321
Mavis Beacon Teaches Typing! Version 3 ★★★½, 486
Mavis Beacon Teaches Typing! for Kids ★★, 79
Mayo Clinic Family Health Book ★★★, 399
Mayo Clinic Family Pharmacist ★★★, 400
Mayo Clinic Sports Health & Fitness ★★, 402
Mayo Clinic—The Total Heart ★★, 403
Medio Magazine ★★, 283
Mega Movie Guide Version 3.0 ★★, 295
Mega Race ★★½, 158
Mega Rock Rap 'N Roll ★★½, 354
The Merchant ★★★, 503
Microsoft Ancient Lands ★★★, 63
Microsoft Art Gallery ★★★½, 229
Microsoft Bookshelf '94 ★★★½, 198
Microsoft Cinemania '95 ★★★½, 289
Microsoft Complete Baseball, 1994 Edition ★★★½, 381
Microsoft Complete NBA Basketball ★★★½, 382
Microsoft Dangerous Creatures ★★½, 241
Microsoft Dinosaurs ★★★½, 98
Microsoft Encarta '95 ★★★★, 193
Microsoft Explorapedia: The World of Nature ★★★, 70
Microsoft Golf ★★★½, 155
Microsoft Golf Championship Course Pinehurst ★★★½, 156

Microsoft Multimedia Beethoven: The Ninth Symphony ★★★★, 337
Microsoft Multimedia Mozart: The "Dissonant" Quartet ★★★★, 338
Microsoft Multimedia Schubert: The "Trout" Quintet ★★★★, 338
Microsoft Multimedia Strauss: Three Tone Poems ★★★★, 339
Microsoft Multimedia Stravinsky: The Rite of Spring ★★★★, 339
Microsoft Multimedia Works 4.0 & Microsoft Bookshelf '94 ★★★½, 455
Microsoft Musical Instruments ★★½, 339
Microsoft Office Professional ★★★½, 453
Microsoft Office Standard ★★★½, 452
Microsoft Publisher ★★½, 473
Microsoft Word & Bookshelf ★★, 454
Microsoft Works 3.0 ★★★½, 454
Midnight Movie Madness ★½, 296
Midnight Stranger ★, 514
Mighty Morphin Power Rangers ★★★, 114
Millennium Auction ★★, 137
Millie's Math House ★★★½, 8
First Person: Marvin Minsky—The Society of Mind ★★½, 326
Monarch Notes For Windows ★★★, 322
Money In The 90s ★★½, 439
Money, Money, Money! ★★½, 470
Monty Python's Complete Waste of Time ★★★, 305
Microsoft Multimedia Mozart: The "Dissonant" Quartet ★★★★, 338
Wolfgang Amadeus Mozart: The "Dissonant" Quartet ★★★★, 337
Multimedia MBA Small Business Edition ★★½, 410
Multimedia Songbook ★½, 338
Multimedia Typing Instructor ★★½, 491
The Multimedia Workshop ★★½, 80
Murmurs of Earth ★★, 247
MusicMentor Maestro Edition ★½, 340

Microsoft Musical Instruments ★★½, 339
The Musical World of Professor Piccolo ★★★, 81
Your Mutual Fund Selector ★★★½, 440
My First Encyclopedia ★★★½, 10
My First Incredible, Amazing Dictionary ★★½, 9
Myst ★★½, 138

The Official NFL Interactive Yearbook '94–'95 ★★★, 387
NHL Hockey '95 ★★★, 159
National Lampoon's Blind Date ★★, 509
NautilusCD ★★★, 284
The New Basics Electronic Cookbook ★★★, 376
The New Family Bible ★★½, 499
The New Kid on the Block ★★★½, 32
New York, NY ★★½, 470
Night Trap ★½, 515
9-Digit ZIP Code Directory ★★★, 212
1994 Guinness Multimedia Disc of Records ★★, 199
The 1994 Information Please Almanac ★★, 202
The 1995 Grolier Multimedia Encyclopedia ★★★★, 194
The 1994 Information Please Business Almanac & Desk Reference ★★, 408
No World Order ★★, 352
First Person: Donald A. Norman—Defending Human Attributes in the Age of the Machine ★★★, 314
Normandy: The Great Crusade ★★★, 262

Oceans Below ★★, 101
Microsoft Office Professional ★★★½, 453
Microsoft Office Standard ★★★½, 452
The Official NFL Interactive Yearbook '94–'95 ★★★, 387

Open Roads: Driving the Data Highway ★★★, 272
The Viking Opera Guide ★★★, 346
Operation AirStorm ★★½, 128
Operation Neptune ★★½, 83
The Orchestra ★★★½, 341
The Oregon Trail ★★★½, 84
Our Earth ★★★, 12
Outpost ★★★½, 177

PC Paintbrush Photo Library ★★, 470
The PC-SIG World of Games CD-ROM ★★★, 459
The PC-SIG World of Windows CD-ROM ★★★, 459
PC/Computing: How Multimedia Computers Work ★★★, 478
PGA Tour Golf 486 ★★★½, 160
Peachtree Accounting for Windows Release 3.0 ★★★, 411
People Behind the Holidays ★★★, 12
People: 20 Years of Pop Culture ★★½, 273
The Perfect Résumé ★★★½, 415
Chuck Jones' Peter and the Wolf ★★½, 115
PharmAssist ★★, 404
PhoneDisc Business & Residential ★★★, 209
PhoneDisc PowerFinder ★★★, 210
Picture Atlas of the World ★★½, 217
Plan Ahead for Your Financial Future ★★★½, 441
Planetary Taxi ★★½, 102
The Playboy Interview ★★, 274
The Women of Playboy Multimedia Screen Saver ★★½, 517
The Playroom CD-ROM ★★★½, 13
Poetry in Motion ★★, 296
Power Japanese Version 2.0 ★★★½, 429
Power Spanish ★★½, 430
Prehistoria ★★½, 248
The Presidents: A Picture History of Our Nation ★★, 263
"Prince" Interactive ★★½, 353
Print Artist CD Edition ★★★, 471

Title Index

The Print Shop Deluxe CD Ensemble ★★★, 472
PrintMaster Gold CD Bonus Pack ★★★, 472
Project Gutenberg ★★½, 324
Microsoft Publisher ★★½, 473
Putt-Putt Goes to the Moon ★★★, 52
Putt-Putt Joins the Parade ★★★, 53
Putt-Putt's Fun Pack ★★★½, 54

The Vortex: Quantum Gate II ★★★, 148
Quantum Gate: The Saga Begins ★★½, 140
QuickBooks Deluxe for Windows ★★★½, 411
The QuickVerse Bible Reference Library ★★★, 500
Quicken Deluxe 4 for Windows CD-ROM ★★★★, 442

Random House Kid's Encyclopedia ★★, 73
Random House Unabridged Electronic Dictionary ★★½, 203
Deluxe Reader Rabbit 1 ★★★½, 14
Reader Rabbit 2 ★★★½, 15
Reader Rabbit 3 ★★★½, 16
Reader Rabbit's Interactive Reading Journey ★★★½, 17
Reading Blaster: Invasion of the Word Snatchers ★★★, 85
Rebel Assault ★★★½, 161
RedShift Multimedia Astronomy ★★, 250
The Residents' Freak Show ★★★★, 347
The Residents' Gingerbread Man ★★★, 348
Return to Ringworld ★★½, 178
Return to Zork ★★★, 141
Richard Simmons Deal-A-Meal ★★★, 392
Richard Strauss: Three Tone Poems ★★★★, 343
Mega Rock Rap 'N Roll ★★½, 354
Rodney's Wonder Window ★★, 54
Ruff's Bone ★★★, 33

SSN-21 Seawolf ★★, 179
Salt of the Earth ★★★½, 297
Sammy's Science House ★★★½, 55
The San Diego Zoo Presents... The Animals! ★★★½, 90
Saturday Night Live! The First Twenty Years ★½, 307
Scholastic's The Magic School Bus Explores the Human Body ★★★½, 100
Franz Schubert: The "Trout" Quintet ★★★★, 342
Microsoft Multimedia Schubert: The "Trout" Quintet ★★★★, 338
Isaac Asimov Science Adventure II ★½, 103
Secrets of Stargate ★★½, 298
Seinfeld CD-ROM Screensaver & Planner ★½, 307
Select Phone ★★, 211
Sesame Street: Numbers ★★, 18
Seven Days in August ★★★½, 264
The 7th Guest ★★★½, 142
70 Million Households Phone Book ★★½, 211
Sharks! ★★★, 251
Shelley Duvall's It's a Bird's Life ★★, 25
Sherlock Holmes, Consulting Detective ★★★, 144
Sherlock Holmes, Consulting Detective, Volume II ★★★, 145
Sherlock Holmes, Consulting Detective, Volume III ★★★, 145
Shining Flower ★★, 325
Shoot Video Like a Pro ★★½, 488
Shopping 2000 ★★½, 504
A Silly Noisy House ★★★½, 56
SimCity 2000 CD Collection ★★★½, 180
Simtel ★★½, 460
Sitting on the Farm ★★½, 33
So I've Heard, Volume 1: Bach and Before ★★½, 328
So I've Heard, Volume 2: The Classical Ideal ★★½, 332
Soft Kill ★½, 488
Softbank On Hand ★★½, 505
Space Adventure II ★★, 104

Title Index

Space Odyssey ★★½, 474
Space Shuttle ★★, 105
Spaceship Warlock ★★★½, 146
Speed ★★, 106
The Sporting News 1994 Multimedia Pro Football Guide ★★½, 388
Sports Illustrated Multimedia Sports Almanac, 1995 Edition ★★½, 389
Sports Illustrated Swimsuit Calendar ★★, 518
Comedy Central's Sports Shorts ★★, 309
Sportz Freakz ★, 390
Star Trek: 25th Anniversary Enhanced CD-ROM ★★★, 182
Star Trek: The Next Generation Interactive Technical Manual ★★½, 309
Star Wars Chess ★½, 167
Stephen Biesty's Incredible Cross-Sections Stowaway! ★★★½, 128
Storybook Weaver Deluxe ★★★★, 86
Microsoft Multimedia Strauss: Three Tone Poems ★★★★, 339
Richard Strauss: Three Tone Poems ★★★★, 343
Igor Stravinsky: The Rite of Spring ★★★★, 344
Microsoft Multimedia Stravinsky: The Rite of Spring ★★★★, 339
Street Atlas USA, Version 2.0 ★★★★, 217
The String Quartet ★★★½, 345
Student Writing Center ★★★½, 87
Substance Digizine ★★, 286
Super Solvers Spellbound! ★★★, 19

Take Five ★★, 490
Tate Gallery—Exploring Modern Art ★★, 232
TaxCut ★★½, 443
Taxi for New Orleans, Denver, Seattle, Phoenix & Orange County ★★★, 225
Taxi for New York, Chicago, Los Angeles, San Francisco & Washington, D.C. ★★★, 224

Taxi for Philadelphia, Boston, Atlanta, Miami & Orlando ★★★, 226
TestDrive Super Store ★★, 505
Tetris Gold ★★★, 168
The Tortoise and the Hare ★★★★, 36
Thinkin' Things Collection 1 ★★★, 57
3-D Body Adventure ★★½, 93
3-D Dinosaur Adventure ★★½, 95
3D Home Architect ★★★½, 367
3D Landscape ★★★, 368
Thumbelina: An Interactive Adventure ★★★, 35
Time Almanac 1990s ★★½, 276
Time Almanac Reference Edition ★★, 277
Time Almanac of the 20th Century ★★½, 278
Time Table of History: Arts & Entertainment ★½, 204
Time Table of History: Business, Politics & Media ★½, 205
Time Table of History: Science & Innovation ★½, 205
2Market ★★★, 506
The Traveler ★★½, 508
TripMaker ★★½, 218
TriplePlay Plus! English ★★★, 432
TriplePlay Plus! French ★★★, 432
TriplePlay Plus! Spanish ★★★, 432
Trivial Pursuit ★★, 169
Tropical Rainforest ★★½, 474
TuneLand ★★★, 58
TurboTax Multimedia ★★★½, 444
Twain's World ★★½, 327
The Twilight Zone Screen Saver ★★½, 311
2000 Fantastic Fonts ★★½, 467
Multimedia Typing Instructor ★★½, 491

U.S. Atlas ★★½, 219
UFO—This Planet's Most Complete Guide to Close Encounters ★½, 492
USA Today: The '90s, Volume I ★★★, 278
USA Today: The '90s, Volume II ★★★, 280
The Ultimate Human Body ★★★, 252

Title Index

Isaac Asimov's The Ultimate Robot ★★, 318
Under a Killing Moon ★★★, 147
Undersea Adventure ★★★, 108
Understanding Exposure: How to Shoot Great Photographs ★½, 493

Vid Grid ★★½, 355
Video Cube: Space ★½, 170
Video Linguist French ★★½, 434
Video Linguist Spanish ★★½, 435
Video Movie Guide ★★★, 301
VideoHound Multimedia ★★, 300
The View from Earth ★★½, 253
The Viking Opera Guide ★★★, 346
Vintage Aloha ★★½, 474
Virtual Tarot ★★★, 494
The Vortex: Quantum Gate II ★★★, 148
Voyeur ★★★, 149

Warplanes—Modern Fighting Aircraft ★★★, 495
The Way Things Work ★★★★, 109
In the Company of Whales ★★, 240
What's the Secret? ★★, 110
Where in the USA is Carmen Sandiego? CD-ROM ★★★½, 66
Where in the World is Carmen Sandiego? CD-ROM ★★★½, 68
Where in the World is Carmen Sandiego? Junior Detective Edition ★★★, 39
Who Built America? ★★★, 265
Who Killed Brett Penance? ★★★, 150
Who Killed Elspeth Haskard? ★★★, 151
Who Killed Sam Rupert? ★★½, 151

Who Killed Taylor French? ★★★, 152
Wild Places ★★½, 475
Wines of the World ★★★, 377
Wing Commander III: Heart of the Tiger ★★½, 183
WolfPack ★★★, 184
Wolfgang Amadeus Mozart: The "Dissonant" Quartet ★★★★, 337
The Women of Playboy Multimedia Screen Saver ★★½, 517
Woodstock: The 25th Anniversary CD-ROM ★★★½, 356
Microsoft Word & Bookshelf ★★, 454
Word Tales ★★, 20
Microsoft Works 3.0 ★★★½, 454
Microsoft Multimedia Works 4.0 & Microsoft Bookshelf '94 ★★★½, 455
A World Alive ★★, 254
World Atlas ★★½, 220
World Beat ★★½, 357
The World Book New Illustrated Information Finder ★★½, 195
World View ★★½, 475
A World of Animals ★★★, 21
A World of Plants ★★½, 21

Xplora 1: Peter Gabriel's Secret World ★★★½, 358

Your Mutual Fund Selector ★★★½, 440
Your Personal Trainer for the SAT Version 2.0 ★★★½, 417

9-Digit ZIP Code Directory ★★★, 212
Zurk's Rainforest Lab ★★★, 59